ARCHETYPE

OF THE

ABSOLUTE

ARCHETYPE OF THE ABSOLUTE

THE UNITY OF OPPOSITES IN
MYSTICISM, PHILOSOPHY, AND PSYCHOLOGY

Sanford L. Drob

Fielding University Press is an imprint of Fielding Graduate University.
Its objective is to advance the research and scholarship of Fielding faculty, students and alumni around the world, using a variety of publishing platforms. For more information, please contact Fielding University Press, attn. Greta Walters, 2020 De la Vina Street, Santa Barbara, CA 93105. Phone: (805) 898-2924. Fax: (805) 690-4310. On the web: www.fielding.edu/UniversityPress

Library of Congress Cataloging-in-Publication data

Archetypes of the Absolute by Sanford L. Drob

1. History - Philosophy

TABLE OF CONTENTS

PREFACE   9

FOREWORD by Paul Bishop   11

INTRODUCTION: Mapping the Unity of Opposites   23
A Single, Unified Self and World? • Forms of Interdependence • The Car-
tographic Model • Dialectics: Pushing the Limits of Reason • A Note on
Terminology

CHAPTER ONE: The Opposites in Historical Context   43
The Coincidence of Opposites • Chinese Philosophy: "Yin" and "Yang" •
The Opposites in Hindu and Buddhist Thought • Heraclitus: The Conflict and
Harmony of Opposites • Plato: The Being of Not Being • Gnosticism: "God
Created Man and Man Created God" • Plotinus: The One is Everywhere and
Nowhere • Nicholas of Cusa: Transcending the Principle of Non-Contra-
diction • The Opposites in Modern Thought • Immanuel Kant's Dual-World
Solution • Friedrich Schelling: The "Vanishing Point" of All Distinctions •
Georg Wilhelm Friedrich: Hegel's Dialectical Idealism • Heinrich Rickert's
"Heterological Principle" • John Dewey and the Metaphysics of Art and
Experience • Alfred North Whitehead: Process, God, and the World • J. N.
Findlay's Unitive Logic • Paradox and Contradiction as the Hallmark of
Philosophy • Graham Priest and Dialetheism • Niels Bohr: Complementarity
in Modern Physics • Jacques Derrida: The Deconstruction of Polar Opposi-
tions • C. G. Jung: The Non-rational Union of Opposites • Hector Sabelli: The
Universality of Opposition

CHAPTER TWO: The Union of Opposites in Mysticism—Kabbalah and
Chasidism   96
The Opposites in World Mysticism • Opposition as a Function of Thought and
Language • The Opposites in Jewish Mysticism • The Early Kabbalah: The
Synthesis of Everything and Its Opposite • The Lurianic Kabbalah: A System
Rife with Paradox • *Tzimtzum*: Creation as Concealment and Contraction •
Shevirah: Creation as Destruction

CHAPTER TWO (Continued)

The Opposites in Other Lurianic Symbols • Chabad Hasidism: The Unification of the Opposites and the Meaning of the World • Schneur Zalman of Lyadi: The Interdependence of Divine and Human Points of View • Dov Baer of Lubavitch: The Coincidence of Joy and Sadness • Rabbi Yosef Yitzhak Schneerson: The Opposites as a Function of Divine Speech • Dialectics in Chabad Hasidic Thought

CHAPTER THREE: The Dialectic of Georg Wilhelm Friedrich Hegel   124

Hegel and the Coincidence of Opposites • "Understanding," Dialectic," and "Speculation" • The Dialectic of Perspectives and Interpretations • The Dialectics of Knowledge and Being, Being and Nothing •
Dialectic in Hegel's *Phenomenology of Spirit* • Hegel's Demurrer • The Hegelian System • The Opposites in Hegel's Understanding of the Absolute • Is There a Dialectical Method? • Hegel on Contradiction • Kinds of Opposition • More on the "World" as Contradictory • First- Versus Third-Person Descriptions • Dialectics in the *Interpretation of Hegel* • The Dialectic of Desire • Hegel and Psychology • Dialectics, Irony, and Dynamic Psychology

CHAPTER FOUR: C. G. Jung and "Coincidentia Oppositorum"   182

The Non-Rational Integration of Opposites • Friedrich Nietzsche: The Apollonian and the Dionysian • Imagination as the Principle of Reconciliation • Compensation and Enantiodromia • The Tension and Conflict of the Opposites • The Discipline of Psychology and the Union of Thinking and Feeling • Jung's Attitude and Function Types • Jung on the Previous and Partial Solutions to the Problem of the Opposites • The Opposites: Self and God • Alchemy and the Play of Opposites • Stages in the Alchemical Process • Sol and Luna: The Union of Masculine and Feminine • Incest, Transgression, and the Shadow • Christ and Christianity • Life/Death, Matter, and Spirit • The Origin of Opposition • The Opposites in Psychotherapy • An Impossible and Unknowable Union • Limitations and Dangers of the *Coincidentia* Idea • Nietzsche: There Are No Opposites • The Opposites in Jung and Hegel Revisited: Hegel on the Imagination • Wolfgang Giegerich on Jung and Hegel • Modes of the Psyche/Soul

CHAPTER FIVE: The Coincidence of Opposites in Contemporary Psychology 259

William James and the "Opposites of the World" • Fragmentation in Psychology • Six Psychological Paradigms • Six Potential Solutions • Complementarity in Psychology • A Matter of "Perspective" • Seeing the World in "2-D" • A Synoptic View of the Mind? • Antinomies of the Mind • "Possible" and "Actual" Psychological Schools • The Dialectical Integration of Perspectives in Psychology • The Opposite is the Completion

CHAPTER SIX: Understanding the Mystical Paradox 302

The Idea of an Absolute • Can the Coincidence of Opposites Be Understood in Rational Terms? • Model 1: A Two-Dimensional World • From Analogy to Analysis: Three Fundamental Distinctions • An "Undecidable" Philosophical Vocabulary • Subject and Object • The Idealist Challenge to Objectivism • The Argument from the Simulated Universe • Sign and Signified: Overcoming the Distinction between Language and the World • The Interdependence of Words and Things • Linguistic Constructivism/Idealism • Excursus: Linguistic Constructivism in Jewish Mysticism • Sign and Signified: Reclaiming the Distinction • The Dissolution of the Distinction between Identity and Difference • The Dissolution of Philosophical Problems and the Unified World • Theism and Atheism • On Thinking the World Whole: The Application of the Principle of *Coincidentia Oppositorum* to Itself • Truth and Reality • Dialectical Ontology • Return to Mysticism: "Formal Indicators," Unity, and Difference in Relation to the Absolute

CHAPTER SEVEN: Intimations or Fabrications of an Absolute 360

Challenges to the Doctrine of *Coincidentia Oppositorum* • A Linguistic Illusion? • "Hard Reality" and the Undifferentiated "One" • Negative and Positive Philosophy • Process or Content? • The Historicist Critique • Beyond Reason, Language, and Representation • Contradiction Revisited • The Nature of God • The Role of the Imagination in the Dialectic and the Open Economy of Thought • The Problem of Evil • Archetype of the Absolute? "Strong" versus "Weak" *Coincidentia Oppositorum* • A Philosophical Pyramid

NOTES 405

BIBLIOGRAPHY 474

INDEX 491

BIOGRAPHY 509

PREFACE

This work provides an account of "the Absolute" that is rooted in Neo-platonic, Hegelian, Jewish mystical, and Jungian thought. In it, I appeal to the principles of the coincidence of opposites and the open economy of thought and experience to provide psychology, philosophy, and theology with a vehicle for understanding the mind and world as a whole. I introduce a cartographic analogy based on the notion that multiple two dimensional maps of a three dimensional world complement one another and serve as a means for approximating a three-dimensional globe. My main "hypothesis" is that like the people in Edwin Abbott's novel "Flatland," who cannot perceive the world as a three-dimensional whole, we have no direct access to the mind and world as a whole and must in effect "piece it together" based upon our limited and distorted (but mutually corrective) models. I argue that while language, and representation in general, sunders an original unity, we can metaphorically "listen to the echo" of that unity by grasping the interdependence of apparently contrary philosophical, theological and meta-psychological ideas. Further, I show how there is a complementarity between rational (Hegelian) and imaginative (Jungian) approaches to the problem of the opposites.

As with virtually all of my theoretical work, I am indebted to J. N. Findlay, who not only provided me with a vital and contemporary reading of Neoplatonism and Hegel, but also introduced me to the notion that fundamental controversies in philosophy involve inter-dependent as opposed to contradictory ideas.

I would also like to express my continuing thanks to Thomas J. J. Altizer, the "death of God" theologian, who at Stony Brook in the early 1970s introduced me to Jung and Nietzsche and to the idea that if God was not dead he or she needed to be re-experienced and re-conceptualized in mystical and/or dialectical terms.

I am grateful also to the assistance of Rabbis Joel Kenny, Shimon Hecht and Zalman Abramowitz who over the years guided me in the study of various Jewish mystical texts. However, they should not be held responsible for the interpretations I have placed upon these texts and on Jewish mysticism in general, as these are completely my own.

I want to thank Barbie Carpenter for her review of an earlier version of the manuscript and for her assistance with the formatting of the voluminous footnotes. I would like to thank Jean-Pierre Isbouts, Editor at Fielding Graduate University Press for his interest in and support of this project, and Casandra Lindell, Associate Editor at Fielding for her tireless efforts in *twice* providing a word by word review and commentary on my use of language, sentence structure, and style. I would also like to thank Cathie Labrador of Fielding University Press for her efforts in seeing this manuscript through to publication. My thanks also to Stanton Marlan for his helpful review of an early manuscript of this work. Finally, a special thanks to Professor Paul Bishop for graciously agreeing to write the illuminating Foreword!

Sanford L. Drob

FOREWORD

By Paul Bishop

William Jacks Chair of Modern Languages
University of Glasgow

What is the problem of the opposites? And how can they be united? If any questions can be regarded as leading into the core of the thought of C. G. Jung, then surely these are. After all, Jung is known as a thinker who urges us to "unite the opposites." At the same time, they are questions that one encounters on an almost daily basis. One does not have to go far in the average home, office, or other institutional environment to run up against the opposites. Some days it can even seem that everywhere one turns, opposition is at hand. Or, to use Jung's language, we encounter on a regular basis the problem of the relationship between different *psychological types*.

Ultimately, as Sanford Drob emphasizes in this work, the problem of the opposites is a logical, or even a metaphysical, one. In the literature, it is known as the principle of non-contradiction, stated in the following form by Socrates in book 4 of the *Republic*: "The same thing won't be willing at the same time to do or suffer the opposites with respect to the same part and in relation to the same thing" (439b).[1] As immediately becomes clear, however, this principle of the opposites is bound up with another central problem in Plato, the problem of the one and the many: "So if we should ever find that happening in these things, we'll know they weren't the same but many" (439b-c).

In this form, the problem lies at the heart of one of Plato's most challenging dialogues, the *Parmenides*; inspiring the equally, if not even more, challenging commentary by Proclus.[2] Yet the analysis of the problem in the *Republic* is arguably a more appropriate text to discuss in the context of Jung because of this dialogue's basic premise—that there is an analogy between the city and the *soul* of the human being. Time and again in this dialogue, Plato returns to the problem of the one and the many. At the beginning of Book 10, Socrates tells Glaucon, "We are accustomed to set down one particular form for each of the particular 'manys' to which we apply the same name" (586a).[3] In turn, Aristotle picked up and further examined this problem.[4] Couched in this form, we are dealing with what came to be known as the problem of universals, and as such it was hotly debated in medieval scholastic thought.[5] So it is with good reason that Jung, in the opening chapter of *Psychological Types* (1921), moves swiftly from a discussion of the Gnostics, Tertullian, and Origen, through the theological disputes in the early Church and the controversy over transubstantiation, to a long discussion of nominalism and realism.[6]

In fact, throughout his work on psychological typology—both his major monograph on this subject of 1921, as well as a later intervention on the topic in the form of an article published in the *Süddeutsche Monatshefte* in 1936[7]—Jung goes to remarkable lengths to anchor his argument about the opposites in a variety of intellectual-historical contexts. Of course, Jung's determination to present his own ideas against the backdrop of the history of ideas is precisely why we need such book as the present one, in which Sanford Drob examines the historical background of the opposites in Jung's thought at a length and in a depth which has, surprising as it may seem, never been attempted before. If, for Plato, the problem of the opposites takes the form of the one and the many—specifically, the relation of the immaterial one to the material many, of the ideal to the real, or of the mind to the body—then for Jung the problem of the opposites took the form of the relation of the psyche (with its striving for unity) to the body (with its conflicting drives and desires).

Sanford Drob's *Archetype of the Absolute*, while it examines the problem of the opposites from a range of mystical, philosophical, and psychological perspectives, will be of particular interest to Jungian scholars and practitioners of analytical psychology, as it places Jung's understanding of *coincidentia oppositorum* within the wide historical context which is its origin and home. In a curious way, however, the problem of the opposites, although centuries old, defines humankind's modernity. As Jung puts it in his paper on psychological typology, "the ancients could still see body and psyche together, as an undivided unity, because they were closer to that primitive world where no moral rift yet ran through the personality" and, as a consequence, "the pagan could still feel himself indivisibly one, childishly innocent and unburdened by responsibility."[8] Jung points to the Homeric world as a case in point, where heroes "wept, laughed, raged, outwitted, and killed each other in a world where these things were taken as natural and self-evident by men and gods alike."[9] It was, he says, a world in which "the Olympians amused themselves by passing their days in a state of amaranthine irresponsibility."[10]

Jung describes humankind at this time as being "pre-philosophical" and as living and experiencing the world on an "archaic level."[11] On the archaic level, he explains, consciousness is identical to passion, and the experience of oneness is predominant. (The proximity of this account to Lucien Lévy-Bruhl's notions of "primitive mentality" and *participation mystique* or Ludwig Klages's description of the Pelasgians, the indigenous people who were the ancestors of the Greeks, is evident.) So, what we today describe as manifestation of "soul" was experienced at that time (so Jung suggests) in physiological terms: passions made the blood boil or the heart pound, took one's breath away or "turned one's bowels to water"; correspondingly, the ancients located the soul in the diaphragm (in Greek, *phren* means "mind") and the heart. It was only later, and with the philosophers, that the seat of reason shifted upward—from the diaphragm or heart to the head.

And yet: as Jung is well aware, nothing can last forever. Archaic humankind, "serene and tragic at once," *started to think*. Jung traces the initial stages of this development, beginning with the Ionian Greek philosopher Pythagoras of Samos (c. 580–495 BCE). According to Jung, the responsibility for this epochal change in consciousness is to be laid at the door of the Pythagoreans and "their doctrine of moral responsibility and the grave metaphysical consequences of sin."[12] Over the course of the centuries and thanks to the spread of the Orphic and Pythagorean mysteries, this belief "percolated through to all strata of the population."[13] As Jung goes on to mention, in the sixth century BCE Pythagoreanism was to become in Graecia Magna something akin to a "state religion"; whatever the truth of this assertion, it is clear that Pythagorean thought was at the height of its influence at this time. (For an alternative account of the origin of this change in consciousness, Jung turns to Nietzsche, and his assertion in *Ecce Homo* that the discovery of pairs of opposites—the division into "odd and even," into "above and below," and especially into "good and evil"—should be laid at the door of the Iranian prophet, Zoroaster. As Nietzsche himself puts it:

> What constitutes the tremendous uniqueness of that Persian in history is [that] Zarathustra was the first to see in the struggle between good and evil the actual wheel in the working of things: the translation of morality into the realm of metaphysics, as force, cause, end-in-itself, is *his* work.[14]

And Nietzsche explains why he went on to write *Thus Spoke Zarathustra* and to reverse this operation: "Zarathustra *created* this most fateful of errors, morality: consequently he must also be the first to *recognize* it.")[15]

On Jung's account, what was practiced in the Orphic and Pythagorean mysteries came to underpin *all* the mystery cults (the Eleusinian, the Dionysian, the Samothracean, etc.) in the ancient world.[16] What these mysteries proclaimed, he maintains, was "the doctrine of the good rewarded in the Hereafter and of the wicked punished in hell."[17] Although

Jung does not mention it, this doctrine can clearly be found in Plato, in the form of the myth of Er told in Book 10 of the *Republic*. But Jung does point to the parable in the *Phaedo* of the white and black horses:

> Let [the soul] be likened to the union of powers in a team of winged steeds and their winged chari- oteer.... Now of the steeds, so we declare, one is good and the other is not.... He that is on the more honorable side is upright and clean-limbed, carrying his neck high, with something of a hooked nose; in color he is white, with black eyes; a lover of glory, but with temperance and modesty; one that consorts with genuine renown, and needs no whip, being driven by the word of command alone. The other is crooked of frame, a massive jumble of a creature, with thick short neck, snub nose, black skin, and gray eyes; hot-blooded, consorting with wantonness and vainglory; shaggy of ear, deaf, and hard to con- trol with whip and goad.... Hence the task of our charioteer is difficult and troublesome (246a; 253d- e; 246b).[18]

Jung was particularly interested in this parable with its representa- tion of the opposites, and he discussed it on a number of occasions.[19] In his paper on psychological typology, Jung reads the parable as an illustration of "the intractability and polarity of the human psyche."[20] Of course, part of Plato's parable of the two horses involves an account of how, despite their troublesome nature, the horses are eventually tamed by the charioteer—or, to put it another way, how the opposites are unit- ed. Yet this account also involves a notion that constantly causes prob- lems for Jung—the notion of beauty and *the aesthetic*.

For in Plato's parable, the driver beholds the person of the beloved, and the horses begin to struggle (253e-254a). After the driver regains control of them, he draws closer to the beloved, until they "behold the spectacle of the beloved flashing upon them" (254b). What happens then in Plato's account is as sudden as it is dramatic:

At that sight the driver's memory goes back to that form of beauty [cf. *Phaedo*, 249e-250c], and he sees her once again enthroned by the side of temperance upon her holy seat; then in awe and reverence he falls upon his back, and therewith is compelled to pull the reins so violently that he brings both steeds down on their haunches, the good one willing and unresistant, but the wanton horse against his will.... Once again he tries to force them to advance... struggling and neighing and pulling until he compels them a second time to approach the beloved and renew their offer.... And so it happens time and again, until the evil steed casts off his wantonness: humbled in the end, he obeys the counsel of his driver.... Wherefore at long last the soul of the lover follows after the beloved with reverence and awe. (254b-e)[21]

What Plato describes here, in allegorical form (and in a way that attracted the attention of Plotinus),[22] is the union of the opposites *through beauty*. It is worth noting that it is no easy reconciliation. Just as, in the famous allegory of the cave in the *Republic*, the liberated prisoner has to be "dragged out" into the light of the sun, and is "distressed and annoyed at being so dragged" (515e), so the second of the horses is difficult to control: The driver "jerks back the bit in the mouth of the wanton horse with an even stronger pull, bespatters his railing tongue and his jaws with blood, and forcing him down on legs and haunches delivers him over to anguish" (254e). The union of the opposites through beauty is no easy or facile exercise; something which Jung appears to have understood well, to judge by some of the more startling moments in the narrative of his *Red Book*.[23]

Yet redemption (or the unification of the opposites) through beauty is a notion that always exercised Jung, not simply in the form of his emphatic rejection (as recorded in *Memories, Dreams, Reflections*) that the *Red Book* had anything at all to do with art.[24] (And this, despite the sheer fact of the appearance of the *Red Book*: its text, its pictures, its rhetorical style. If something looks like art, sounds like art, and has an aesthetic effect on us, surely it *is* art ...?) For instance, in his earlier monograph study on psychological types Jung devotes an extensive discussion—one of the most extensive to be found in the twentieth century, which is why it is all the more surprising that it is so frequently overlooked—to Schiller and to his two treatises, *On the Aesthetic Education of Man* (1795) and *On the Naïve and the Sentimental in Poetry* (1796).

Now the thought of Schiller, which on the one hand reaches back to the thought of Plato and on the other anticipates the later philosophy of Nietzsche,[25] is rich in antitheses and abounds in opposites, as Wilhelm Dilthey pointed out.[26] This is not the time and place to rehearse in detail the intricacies of Schiller's thinking, but certain common structures of thought are evident. If *On the Naïve and the Sentimental in Poetry* is governed by the opposition between the "naïve" and the "sentimental," then the *Aesthetic Education* is governed by the opposition between the "material drive" and the "formal drive." It is Schiller's contention in the *Aesthetic Education* that the interaction of these drives, in a dialectic of reciprocal subordination, gives rise to a third drive, the "ludic drive," a core impulse behind achieving what Schiller terms the "aesthetic state." Yet at this juncture Jung sounds a decidedly skeptical note.

In his ninth letter, Schiller evokes precisely the ancient Greek world in which Jung was, as we have seen, so interested, and links it to the work of the artist in the present day:

> Let some beneficent deity snatch the suckling be-
> times from his mother's breast, nourish him with
> the milk of a better age, and suffer him to come to
> maturity under a distant Grecian sky. Then, when
> he has become a man, let him return, a stranger, to
> his own century; not, however, to gladden it by his
> appearance, but rather, terrible like Agamemnon's
> son, to cleanse and purify it.[27]

It is worth noting that this is a very curious passage. In it, Schiller envisages some kind of divine abduction, involving travel through space and time back to ancient Greece. Then, once he has matured, the individual is to be returned, as from the dead, to his own time and place; the reference to Agamemnon's son is, of course, to Orestes, the central focal figure of a nexus of myths around the themes of madness and purification. For Jung, what matters is not just Schiller's predilection for ancient Greece, but the idea that the artist is characterized by the adoption of a perspective that transcends time: "His theme he will, indeed, take from the present; but his form he will borrow from a nobler time, nay, from beyond time all together, from the absolute, unchanging, unity of his being."[28]

Not surprisingly, Jung is alert to the archaic-archetypal undertones in this passage—in other words, going back beyond the classical to "some primordial heroic age where human beings were still half divine"[29] and indeed Schiller evokes this expression of an "absolute, unchanging, unity of…being" in terms of a kind of aesthetic effervescence: "Here, from the pure aether of his genius [i.e., daimonic nature], the living source of beauty flows down, untainted by the corruption of the generations and ages wallowing in the dark eddies below."[30]

As Elizbeth M. Wilkinson and L. A. Willoughby note in their commentary, both of the terms "aither" and "daimon" are significant ones in ancient Greek thought.[31] In ancient cosmology, "aither" referred not just to the element that surrounds us but to an element filling the space in the heavens.[32] In one of the surviving fragments of his work, Empedocles identified "aither" in the mythic form of Zeus as one of the four elements of which the world is made,[33] and it was from this rarefied atmosphere that artistic inspiration was held to proceed. And the "daimon" (or, as Wilkinson and Willoughby prefer to translate it, the "genius") relates equally to the theme of creativity, referring to the intermediate being between gods and humans that provides a link between them.[34]

In this passage from Letter 9, Jung appreciates the "beautiful illusion" of a Golden Age "when men were still gods and were ever refreshed by the vision of eternal beauty."[35] Yet it is, he insists, no more than an illusion. Jung diagnoses the cause of this illusion as being that, within Schiller himself, there is a battle or interplay between opposites going on, and "the poet has overtaken the thinker."[36]

Further on, in Letter 10, §4, Jung believes that this polarity has reversed and now the thinker gets the upper hand again. Here Schiller sets up an opposition between *aesthetics* on the one hand and *morality* on the other—"in almost every epoch of history when the arts are flourishing and taste prevails, humanity is in a state of decline"—and he explicitly works a structure of opposition into his argumentational rhetoric: Is there a single instance, he asks, of "a high degree and wide diffusion of culture going hand in hand with political freedom and civic virtue, fine manners with good morals, refinement of conduct with truth of conduct"?[37] And this passage prompts Jung to an assertion of the view that we have already seen he holds, which is that life in ancient Greece must have been amoral—and to one of his most stringent critiques of Schiller:

> In accordance with this familiar and in every way undeniable experience those heroes of olden time must have led a none too scrupulous life, and indeed not a single myth, Greek or otherwise, claims that they ever did anything else. All that beauty could revel in its existence only because there was as yet no penal code and no guardian of public morals.[38]

To Schiller's opposition of the *aesthetic* and the *moral*, Jung adds his own, opposing the *psychological* to the *aesthetic*:

> With the recognition of the psychological fact that living beauty spreads her golden shimmer only when soaring above a reality full of misery, pain, and squalor, Schiller cuts the ground from under his own feet; for he had undertaken to prove that what was divided would be united by the vision, enjoyment, and creation of the beautiful. Beauty was to be the mediator which should restore the primal unity of human nature. *On the contrary, all experience*

> *goes to show that beauty needs her opposite as a*
> *condition of her existence*[39] (my emphasis).

Jung's argumentational rhetoric is just as shot through with oppositionality as Schiller's was; and, leaving aside whether Jung is right to voice this conventional criticism of Schiller,[40] it reveals the core reason behind Jung's distrust of beauty—a distrust which, however, he is keen to impute to Schiller.[41]

For Schiller, beauty is a means of uniting the opposites. To this extent, Jung is in agreement with Schiller about the reconciling effect of the symbol or the "living shape" (*lebende Gestalt*). For Jung, however, beauty can also call forth its own opposite—ugliness. Several times in his monograph on psychological types, Jung returns to this problem. He writes that Schiller's claim (that the mediating function of beauty is encountered in "the enjoyment of genuine beauty" (Letter 22, §2)) is challenged when Schiller runs up against "a barrier common both to himself and his time which it was impossible for him to overstep, for everywhere he encountered the invisible 'ugliest man,' whose discovery was reserved for our age by Nietzsche."[42] For in *Thus Spoke Zarathustra*, Jung claims that Nietzsche "brings to light the contents of the collective unconscious of our time…: iconoclastic revolt against the conventional moral atmosphere, and acceptance of the 'ugliest man,' which leads to the shattering unconscious tragedy presented in *Zarathustra*."[43] Elsewhere, Jung remarks that, in the "Ugliest Man," Zarathustra discovers his *shadow* or his "suppressed antithesis."[44]

In fact, it would be no exaggeration to say that, for Jung, the chief pair of opposites is not so much the one and the many, or art and morality, or good and evil, or the mind and the body, or even aesthetics and psychology; rather, it is *beauty and ugliness*. And if this is right, then the problem of the opposites is not only one of the central issues of Jungian thought, it is *the* key issue involved in understanding the project of analytical psychology in its relations to aesthetics—and much else besides.

For this reason, all readers of Jung will welcome this new study by

Sanford Drob, who extends his previous work on Jung, Kabbalah, and Jewish mysticism and on the *Red Book*, and takes it in a new direction, undertaking in the pages that follow a systematic investigation of the problem of the opposites. This is truly pioneering work, and involves the broadest of all possible scopes—from the Presocratics to contemporary postmodern thought and quantum physics, via the Tao, the Kabbalah, and German Idealism. In taking this approach, Drob evinces not just wide learning but a convincing acuity of thought. No reader will be able to finish his book without feeling exhilarated, challenged, and enlightened.

In the course of his fascinating analysis, Drob argues that "not only the distinction between signifier and signified, but also such fundamental distinctions as identity and difference, and subject and object, and thought and imagination—which lie at the foundation of controversies in philosophy, psychology, and theology—collapse under close scrutiny." Consequently, he presents the case that "one can work through language and reason to intuit the unity that is sundered by language and thought." Without wishing here to anticipate the consequences of these conclusions, we might at this stage pause and ask ourselves if Jung, as read through the prism of Drob's account of analytical psychology, could be said to rearticulate an essentially *Goethean* position? After all, in one of his *Maxims and Reflections*, Goethe remarked: "People say that between two opposed opinions truth lies in the middle. Not at all! A problem lies in-between: invisible, eternally active life, contemplated in peace."[45]

INTRODUCTION:
Mapping the Unity of Opposites

Looking back on my own experiences, they all converge towards a kind of insight to which I cannot help ascribing some metaphysical significance. The keynote of it is invariably a reconciliation. It as if the opposites of the world, whose contradictoriness and conflict make all our difficulties and troubles, were melted into unity.... This is a dark saying, I know, when thus expressed in terms of common logic, but I cannot wholly escape from its authority. I feel as if it must mean something, something like what the Hegelian philosophy means, if one could only lay hold of it more clearly.
–William James[1]

In the Institute in Copenhagen, where through these years a number of young physicists from various countries came together for discussions, we used, when in trouble, often to comfort ourselves with jokes, among them the old saying of the two kinds of truth. To the one kind belonged statements so simple and clear that the opposite assertion obviously could not be defended. The other kind, the so-called "deep truths," are statements in which the opposite also contains deep truth.
–Niels Bohr[2]

The self is made manifest in the opposites and the conflicts between them; it is a "coincidentia oppositorum."
–C. G. Jung.[3]

A SINGLE, UNIFIED SELF AND WORLD?

C. G. Jung held that the self is a *coincidentia oppositorum*, a unity of opposing ideas, attitudes, emotions, and impulses.[4] In making this claim, he was affirming, in psychological language, an idea *about the cosmos* that can be traced to various forms of Eastern and Western mysticism, was a significant undercurrent in ancient, medieval, and renaissance thought, and which, in the nineteenth century, played a central role in the philosophy of Hegel. At its core, this idea suggests that oppositions and even apparent contradictions are neither fatal nor destructive to thought and experience but rather reflect deep truths about the nature of the mind and the world. In this book, I place the doctrine of *coincidentia oppositorum* in historical context and argue that "rational" and "imaginative" interpretations of this doctrine, provided by G. W. F. Hegel and C. G. Jung respectively, are complementary. I argue that dialectical, bi-linear, or multi-linear thinking and living—in which the "truth" of opposing and apparently contradictory notions and experiences is recognized—is essential to progress in philosophy, theology, psychology and the conduct of life. Finally, I suggest that by elucidating the inter-dependencies between seemingly contradictory ideas and experiences, we can approach and perhaps even "arrive" an understanding of the "world" and "self" as a unified whole.

In this work, I develop the view that the coincidence of opposites is both an "echo" of an original unity that has been sundered by thought and language, and an achievement or goal resulting from careful reflection upon our experiences and ideas. In addition, by tracing the interdependencies between a variety of contrasting and apparently conflicting philosophical and psychological notions, I provide the basis for a perspective on language, mind, and the world that I believe can lead to substantial progress in resolving basic theoretical controversies in philosophy theology and psychology, and that will enable us to overcome the fragmentation that is current among various psychological paradigms or schools. These are, of course, ambitious goals, and the extent to which they can be achieved will only be clear at the conclusion of this work.

The idea that a single, unified reality lies behind, and is fragmented by, the oppositions of thought and language is present in at least several mystical traditions, including Vedanta, Taoism, Kabbalah, and Sufism. The notion that "the opposites" are, in an important sense, an "illusion" lies at the heart of various mystical efforts to ascend to a unified "Absolute" or "One." In this work, I will argue that the non-linear, dialectical thinking that produces an awareness of the complementary of apparently opposing philosophical, theological, and psychological ideas leads to a "limit" that approaches the singular "One," which mystics have often held to underlie the world of appearances. Further, I will show how the coincidence of opposites serves as an "archetype of the Absolute," which leads to critical, open-ended, and indefinitely revisable modes of thought and experience. In making these claims, I realize I am at odds with 250 years of Western philosophy that rejects the very possibility of an all-encompassing view of reality, contrasts such a view with the "open economy of thought," and indeed questions the very notions of "world," "reality," and "totality." Nonetheless, it is my intention to utilize the very skepticism toward my project, a skepticism grounded in linguistic and postmodern philosophy, as a vehicle for its realization. I believe the skepticism regarding the distinction between words and things, the view that language is indefinitely interpretable, and the belief that in matters of philosophy we can "say what we like," each of which are characteristic of certain trends in recent philosophy, can themselves be utilized and subsumed by an effort to "think the world whole" via *coincidentia oppositorum*. Minimally, these ideas help us push our efforts at intuiting a "whole world" to a limit prior to any thought of surrendering the project of doing so.

The "oppositions" I will consider in this work have served as the impetus to controversies in philosophy, psychology, and theology. They have engendered an impasse between a host of opposing ideas, including realism and idealism, theism and atheism, free will and determinism, meaning and absurdity, absolute truth and relativism, and reason and the imagination. In addition, these oppositions underlie the fragmented state of contemporary psychology, in which competing biological, cognitive, psychoanalytic, humanistic, and other paradigms each claim to achieve an understanding of the human psyche. Philosophers typically formulate arguments in support of one or the other pole of various binary oppositions, and the idea that *each* side of these oppositions are true (for example, that both realism *and* idealism, theism *and* atheism are *each* true) is now rarely entertained because this presumed reconciliation is thought to violate the fundamental principle of reason: the law of non-contradiction. Nonetheless, in this book I explore a perspective within which the acceptance of the truth and interdependence of apparently contradictory philosophical positions is the key to both resolving the controversies engendered by them and the vehicle for approximating a complete map or description of the "world" and the place of the human psyche within it. It is through both a rational and experiential understanding of these *coincidentia*, the interdependence of seemingly opposing ideas, that we are able to "think the world whole" (or think of a "whole world") and in effect "listen to the echo" of a primal unity that was sundered by thought and language.

It is important to state from the outset that the notion of the coincidence of opposites, if brought to its logical conclusion, requires that we consider even the most general philosophical oppositions to be interdependent ideas. This includes, as Jung noted, oppositions related to the coincidence of opposites itself.[5] Thus the idea that philosophical oppositions are in *coincidentia oppositorum* is complemented by and interdependent with the notion that such oppositions are *in* conflict. While this leads to a contradiction—i.e., that the interdependence of opposites leads to the conclusion that the opposites are distinct and not interdependent—this contradiction (like other philosophical contradictions) is not fatal to the *coincidentia* idea but essential to it.[6] In this connection, we will see that the *coincidentia* archetype enables us to move toward a "limit" of thought and experience, in which all ideas and experiences are subject to critique and transcendence and all oppositions dissolve. It is through this process that we can achieve an "open economy" of thought and experience, and *approach* a comprehensive view of "reality" and a unified "Absolute." While the coincidence of opposites will enable us to gain an extremely wide perspective on mind and world, no such perspective can be thought to be final and complete. The *coincidentia* archetype enables us to approach a "limit of thinking the world whole" and achieve an expanded understanding of "truth" and "reality." However, our understanding can never conclude with a fixed idea or content but must also be identified with the dialectical process itself—and ultimately with an indefinitely open economy of thought and experience.

In the course of this book, I will address several problems raised by the principle of *coincidentia oppositorum*, including the questions of whether the "contradictions" it reconciles are real or only apparent, whether admitting the truth of opposites results in a failure of the capacity to distinguish between truth and error, and whether the coincidence of opposites—when applied to the ethical realm, for example in the psychology of Jung—leads to an inability to differentiate good from evil. These important questions are taken up primarily in the chapters on Hegel (Chapter 3) and Jung (Chapter 4), and the final chapter (Chapter 7) where I specifically consider the objections and challenges to the *coincidentia* idea.

In writing this work, I am operating both within and beyond the borders of philosophy, psychology, and mysticism. I am reaching for a mode of "bilinear" or "multilinear" thinking and experience in which one accepts the truth or validity of two (or more) seemingly contrasting propositions or experiences at once, and in which one thinks and experiences in two or more different directions at the same (logical if not temporal) time. I will consider the notion of "bilinear thinking and experience" from a variety of perspectives, placing it within the context of the ambiguity and multi-valence of the very terms (for example, "truth," "world," "reality," and "contradiction") that must, of necessity, be utilized in its description.

I believe that "bilinear thinking and experience" is relevant in those fields, including philosophy, theology, and psychology, where higher order abstract ideas and subtle experiences come into play and theoretical fragmentation and impasse is inevitable. In the course of this book, I hope to present a *general program* for the resolution of certain conceptual problems in these fields, one that neither insists upon unique (one-sided) solutions to these problems nor abandons these problems as insoluble, or attempts to "dissolve" them (as per Ludwig Wittgenstein) on the grounds that they result from linguistic confusion. While I agree that language/representation is the source of our philosophical conundrums, I do not believe that the end result of this realization is the abandonment of either philosophy or language, but is, rather, the need to utilize language to provide an intuition of a pre-linguisticized reality that lies behind the conceptual oppositions that "bewitch" our understanding. While I cannot pretend to have carried my philosophical program to a full conclusion and I am aware that there are important issues that remain to be clarified, I will offer examples of the program's application to various philosophical controversies, including several in the philosophy of psychology related to mind/brain identity, freedom of the will, and the distinction between first- and third-person epistemological points of view.

This work begins with an examination of the history of the *coincidentia oppositorum* idea. After a general overview of its history in Chapter 1, I will provide a sustained examination in Chapters 2 through 4 of the coincidence of opposites as described in three representative arenas: Jewish mysticism, Hegelian philosophy, and Jungian psychology. In later chapters I will explore the relevance of the coincidence of opposites to specific problems in contemporary psychology, philosophy and theology. Chapter 5 is devoted to problems associated with the fragmentation of psychology, by which I mean the various conflicting paradigms that compete for hegemony within the arenas of psychological research and clinical practice. Chapters 6 and 7 explore the coincidence of opposites as it is relevant to problems in philosophy and theology.

In contrast to previous accounts, which have understood the coincidence of opposites in either rational *or* imaginative terms, the current work seeks to situate *coincidentia oppositorum* within *both* rational and imaginative-symbolic discourse. While one of my main goals is to demonstrate that the *coincidentia* idea is amenable to clear, discursive, and analytic exposition, I believe that reason is itself dialectically conditioned by such non-rational modes of consciousness as desire and imagination, and in this regard, the psychology of Jung provides a critical complement to the rational dialectic of Hegel.

In addition to its mystical and philosophical implications, the *coincidentia* idea has important applications to fundamental problems of living, including problems related to emotions, attitudes, individual identity, and the meaning of life. We will see that for Jung the human subject is divided into such polarities as conscious/unconscious, animus/anima, and persona/shadow, and it is only through recognizing and experiencing the intricate relationships between the poles of these oppositions that the self can be "individuated" and made whole. Jung held that the opposites could not be reconciled through thinking and that the vehicle for this reconciliation must be the imagination.[7] Indeed, for Jung—as for Mercea Eliade[8] and Claude Lévi Strauss[9]—the function of myth, which is the expression of a culture's collective imagination, is to reconcile contradictions that cannot be reconciled in thought. Jung was highly critical of Hegel's efforts to arrive at an intellectual or rational solution to the problem of the opposites, and one goal of the current study is to assess the degree to which this criticism is warranted. We will see that the application of *coincidentia oppositorum* is not limited to the intellect and that in addition to non-linear thinking there is a form of non-linear or dialectical *experiencing*, in which apparently contradictory feelings, images, and attitudes, are understood and experienced *as* mutually supportive and interdependent.

FORMS OF INTERDEPENDENCE

The conceptual interdependence between opposing ideas can be understood on more than one level. On the simplest, most basic level, conceptual oppositions are reciprocally determinative of one another because all things gain significance through a distinction from what they are not, and most pointedly through a contrast with their opposites. Day is *not* night, good is *not* evil, truth is *not* error, life is *not* death, being is *not* nothingness, freedom is *not* determination, etc. Hegel, for example, at times relied upon this "contrast effect" in making the claim that a notion's opposite or contradictory is profoundly written into its essence. Hence, light, is not only *not-darkness*, but requires an element of darkness in order to show itself (by way of contrast) as light. The same can be said of virtually every other category through which we understand and construct the world.

On the other hand, certain oppositions involve what might be characterized as a deeper and more complex interdependence. The relationship between the present and the past, for example, is not simply one of contrast but involves a recognition that any "thing" that is present (or in the present moment) is what it is only by virtue of its "carrying with it" its past, without which it would have no identity in the present. To take another example, *"truth"* which is understood as freedom from error, is itself a species of *"error"* which only approximates an ideal. This is repeatedly demonstrated in the empirical sciences. All so-called scientific "truths" of the past and present have been, or will be, revealed to be *errors* of one form or another. Philosophically speaking, no model can ever be more than an approximate representation of the whole; hence the very notion of modeling, representing, or even speaking the truth involves us in error and can even be said to depend upon error. Conversely, error not only contrasts with truth but in all interesting cases is dependent upon truths that are misinterpreted or mis-contextualized. We would not recognize an error unless it contained a certain truth that permits us to identify it as missing the mark. If I incorrectly believe that Jones killed Graham, it is usually the case that Graham is at least dead, or at least that that there are or were such individuals as Jones and Graham.

An example of an even more complex case (one that I will consider in Chapter 5 where I discuss competing and contrasting paradigms in psychology) is the interdependence between public and private criteria for mental events. One could not label one's experience as an instance of "thinking," "expectation," "knowledge," or "anxiety" (to choose but a few of the "mental" terms that we apply to ourselves and others) unless one learned these terms in an interpersonal, "public" context, within which one's own and others' thinking, expecting, knowing, anxiety, and other mental states are pointed to by others. No one enters our inner experience and points directly to our thoughts, anxieties, or expectations. We learn to label these ourselves on the basis of the "public criteria" for these mental states that are observed and pointed out to us by others. On the other hand, we could not utilize such criteria—that is, we could not label others' behavior and our own behavior unless we had "private" experiences or observations to begin with. What's more, the process through which we learn to label our mental states on the basis of their publicly observable manifestations leads to these labels being directly applied to private experiences, as seen perhaps most graphically in the case of emotions. There is thus a complex interdependence between public and private criteria for mental events that goes well beyond the phenomenon of "contrast." We will see that many of the more interesting *coincidentia oppositorum*, indeed those that have the strongest philosophical implications, involve this type of complex reciprocity.

THE CARTOGRAPHIC MODEL

In order to illustrate the implications of the *coincidentia* idea, I will make use of an analogy from cartography, one that has the advantage of providing a concrete illustration and simplification of one of the major theses of this book. Our cartographic analogy has the advantage of providing insight into the idea that the rupture between polar opposites is grounded in the process of *representation*. I will introduce the cartographic or "map-making" analogy here, with the understanding that its full implications may not be apparent until I have occasion to return to it in Chapters 5 and 7.

It is a well-known cartographic principle that it is impossible to perfectly represent a three-dimensional surface such as the earth on a two-dimensional plane. The very process of representation distorts the earthly sphere in one of a number of ways, depending upon one's map-making strategy. Each cartographic "projection" balances certain distortions with certain accuracies and advantages. A Mercator projection, for example, maintains the parallelism of longitude and latitude at the expense of distorting the size of landmasses near the poles. Certain "equal area" projections maintain the correct relative sizes of land and sea masses at the expense of breaking apart lines of latitude and longitude, creating what appear to be huge gaps in the earth. Dual polar projections have the advantage of maintaining the full continuity of the circles of latitude around each pole, while creating the illusion that the northern and southern hemispheres are distinct spheres. While each projection serves one or more purposes, no single projection is able to adequately represent the earth in the manner of a three-dimensional globe. Were we unable to visualize the world in three-dimensions (that is, if we had no globes or no capacity to understand them), we would be limited to a series of imperfect maps, each purporting to represent the entire earth yet each filled with distortions and each apparently incompatible with all of the others. Under such circumstances, we might want to consider how each of our projections or representations was related to, and potentially complementary with, each of the others. For the moment, let us consider two possible world projections, the Mercator and the Dual Polar.

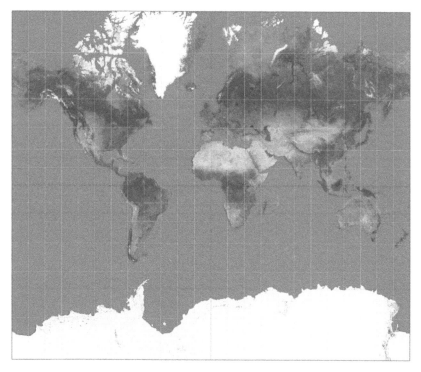

Figure 1. Mercator Projection

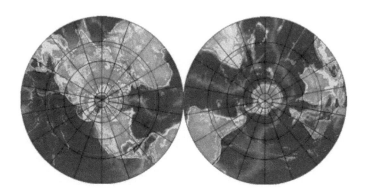

Figure 2. Polar Projection

Taking these projections very concretely, we can conceive of them as respectively standing for the propositions that the world is either singular and rectangular, or dual and circular. These propositions seem incompatible, if not contradictory. However, by mapping points from one

33

of these projections onto the other, we could see that what is a line (for example, the equator) on the Mercator projection is a circle on the Polar projection, and that what is represented as two separate hemispheres on the Polar projections is a single world on the Mercator projection. In short, we would see that these maps, which are superficially incompatible, are actually complementary. Indeed, each can be understood as the other's foundation: The correctly represented spherical equator in each of the polar projections is the foundation for the [distorted] linear representation of the equator on the Mercator map, and the correctly represented "single earth" in the Mercator map is the foundation for the [distorted] doubling of the earth in the polar projections. Here we have a clear and tangible analogy to the philosophical conception of *coincidentia oppositorum*, of seemingly incompatible representations passing over into one another and serving as each other's basis. Our contrasting cartographic projections illustrate how the very process of *representation* sunders the world—in this case the "earthly sphere"—and results in apparent incompatibilities that must be resolved on a "higher level" via complementarity or *coincidentia oppositorum* in order to achieve an adequate conception (though not "representation") of the whole.

Our analogy also suggests that the coincidence of opposites may indeed apply to more than just two seemingly incompatible representations of a single object of knowledge. One can readily see that each of many two-dimensional representations of a three-dimensional globe are complementary to and even "foundational" for each of the others because each is a (relatively distorted) projection of a whole. For example, the "equal area," "orange peel" projection illustrated on page 35, despite its obvious shortcomings, has the decided advantage of accurately representing the sizes of the world's major land masses, and providing a foundation for a representation of the world's spherical nature. It thus provides corrections for (and is corrected by) aspects of both the Mercator and the Polar projections.

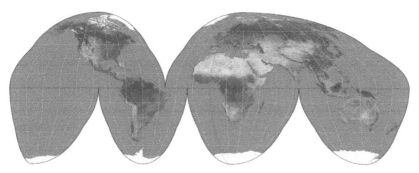

Figure 3. Equal Area ("Orange Peel") Projection

My argument in this book is that while in the case of map-making we are able to see and grasp the three-dimensional globe that serves as the ultimate foundation for our various two-dimensional cartographic images, we are not in an analogous position with respect to our philosophical, theological, and psychological representations. With respect to these, we are like the denizens of "Flatland" depicted in Edwin Abbott's 1884 novel about a people who are only able to perceive and think two-dimensionally.[10] Like people living in three dimensions but only capable of perceiving and thinking in two, we are burdened with having to reconcile divergent philosophical and psychological views (which we are inclined to take literally) without having direct access to a comprehensive perspective. In later chapters, I will describe why I believe we are in such a predicament and provide a more detailed analysis of how contrasting philosophical and psychological points of view can be reconciled through the *coincidentia* idea. Here, I introduce the cartographic example as an imprecise analogy to our general philosophical dilemma and its potential solution.

I am aware that my cartographic analogy and the "perspectival realism" that it suggests fly in the face of the relativism and celebration of multiplicity and difference that has come to be *de rigour* in postmodern philosophy. Slavoj Žižek, for example, in considering this very topic of multiple perspectives on "reality" argues that there is no "neutral reality" that our perspectives are about, and that it is absurd to theorize about the "All." Žižek, whose ideas I will consider in detail in Chapter 7, holds that multiple perspectives simply fill in the gaps of one another, without converging upon a single object. Epistemology, on his view, discerns a continuous play of perspectives that never results in a totality.[11] While I am in many ways sympathetic with a view that seeks to forestall the possibility of epistemological closure, and I wholeheartedly agree that the multiplicity of perspectives does not come to an end, I regard the "All" as an important experiential intuition and regulative idea, without which the notions of "perspectives" and "parallax" make no sense. As we will see, postmodern relativism also exists as a pole of a binary opposition with mystical (and even modernist) totality, and the two are in *coincidentia oppositorum*.

The analogy of the earthly globe has a second advantage, and this is its capacity to represent the problem of the psyche or the self. Jung hints that the globe is an alchemical symbol of the whole self,[12] and we can understand our various cartographic projections as analogous to different perspectives or theories of the psyche, self, or mind. I will argue that various cognitive, neurobiological, psychoanalytic, behavioral, and existential perspectives on the mind are analogous to the varied two-dimensional maps of a three-dimensional world. These contrasting psychological paradigms rest upon theoretical assumptions that are seemingly incompatible but are actually interdependent. However, the coincidence of opposites is also applicable to the psyche in a more intimate, day-to-day sense—in the form of an interdependence between the opposing, often contradictory ideas, attitudes, and emotions that comprise the individual human mind. Jung observed a *coincidentia oppositorum* between persona and shadow, anima and animus, chaos and order, rational and irrational, and various other polarities of the self. In Chapter 4, we will have occasion to explore Jung's psychological perspective on the *coincidentia* idea, a perspective that Jung held to be the foundation and "truth" of its philosophical counterpart.

Our cartographic analogy, as it applies to the psyche and more generally in its application to the "world," is beset with difficulties resulting

36

from the fact that we, as "knowing subjects," are not only the mapmakers, but are, in effect, also the territory being mapped and the map itself. As Hegel well understood, thinker, thought, and subject matter cannot be fully distinguished: We, if not God, are, in Aristotle's famous phrase, "thought thinking itself," and it is a grievous error to believe that we can somehow view either the psyche or the entire cosmos from the same "external" point of view that we can conceivably take upon the earth's sphere. We cannot, therefore, claim that our cartographic, multi-perspective approach to the world and mind can enable us to achieve anything more than a "limit" of intuition and understanding. Further, the very *process* of mapping cosmos and psyche, and of endeavoring to comprehend apparent oppositions as complementary and interdependent, may be closer to our "goal" than any "results" that process attains. Hegel, it is has been said, identified the Absolute with the dialectic—that is to say, with thinking itself, as opposed to any of thought's results[13] (which would by definition be static and incomplete)—and we must be cautious ourselves in accepting any "results" as the "gold" of our quarry. I will return to this important question in the final chapter.

My claim that it is representation that sunders a unified world into a multiplicity of apparently incompatible perspectives and ideas rests upon a distinction that is fundamental to representation itself—the distinction between representation and represented, and in the case of language the distinction between signifier and signified, between the "words" and the "things." I will argue in Chapter 6 that this distinction between words and things—and moreover the second order distinction between the ideas that *there is and is not* a genuine distinction between words and things—are themselves distinctions between complementary ideas and are instances of *coincidentia oppositorum*. Once we recognize that the very language/world distinction that is foundational for language and representation is itself a problematic dichotomy—and further that the idea that the language/world distinction is a false dichotomy is interdependent with the idea that this dichotomy is absolutely necessary for experience and communication—we will be on our way to "thinking the world whole," and to recovering the singular, unitary plenum that for the mystics is the foundation for "All." This recovery will not, strictly speaking, enable us to grasp the mystical Absolute in thought and language, for thought and language can only exist on the basis of distinctions and oppositions. However, by showing *within language* that the very oppositions created by language are themselves completely interdependent, we can understand that a "hidden" unity lies at the foundation of all oppositions, and we can thereby, in effect, "listen to the echo" of the primal unified plenum that stands before and behind all distinctions.

In this book, I will argue that not only the distinction between signifier and signified, but also such fundamental distinctions as identity and difference, subject and object, and thought and imagination—which lie at the foundation of controversies in philosophy, psychology, and theology—collapse under close scrutiny. The view presented in this work is that one can work through language and reason to intuit the unity that is sundered by language and thought. This view stands in contrast to the more dominant mystical understanding that, since it is thought and language that dichotomizes reality, these faculties cannot be utilized to intuit the world's unity.[14]

DIALECTICS: PUSHING THE LIMITS OF REASON

A question that arises in connection with the *coincidentia* idea is its relationship to dialectical thought and philosophy. "Dialectics" has accrued a number of meanings in Western philosophy, among which are (1) the verbal disputation that clarifies philosophical ideas (Socratic dialectic), (2) the emergence of new ideas through the clash and ultimate transcendence and integration of apparent opposites (Fichte, Hegel), and (3) the engine that produces change and especially progress in history (Hegel and Marx). In at least some of his usages, Hegel held that dialectics refers to the tendency of ideas to pass into their contraries or opposites when they are fully explicated and each of their implications are understood. For Hegel, this is a supremely rational process, one that is prefigured in mysticism and mythology but which achieves rational expression in (his own) philosophy. Because my method in writing this book is discursive and rational, it is the rational notion of dialectics that is emphasized in my discussion of *coincidentia oppositorum*, especially in the closing chapters of this work. This should not be interpreted to mean that I view the rational understanding of the coincidence of opposites as the only or superior point of view. Indeed, as will become clear, it is my view that rational and imaginative modes of understanding are themselves each necessary and interdependent. It is thus important to emphasize that while it is part of my goal in this work to return the *coincidentia* idea to the realm of reason and analysis, I recognize that reason has its limitations and exists in *coincidentia oppositorum* with that which is non-rational. While it is my view that a singular, unitary "Absolute" leaves traces in the realm of rational philosophy and psychology, it is ultimately not completely fathomable via rational means. Yet the very unfathomability of the "Absolute" conditions the enterprise of reason in a profound manner.

Since the demise of British Idealism in the early years of the twentieth century, those thinkers who have appealed to the *coincidentia* idea (Jung, Eliade, Corbin, Gershom Scholem, Lévi-Strauss, and Borges all come to mind) have understood it in non-rational terms. While I believe that there is a non-rational, symbolic, mythological aspect to *coincidentia oppositorum*, without its rational aspect the *coincidentia* idea threatens to become meaningless and even pernicious. We will discuss the dangers of the *coincidentia* principle, especially in its imaginative non-rational form, in a later chapter. Such dangers include the possibility of an *irrational* conflation of good and evil under the guise of a symbolic coincidence of opposites. Indeed, we will see that it was this very conflation that was at the heart of Jung's grievous error regarding the positive potential of National Socialism in the 1930s. We will also, in the closing chapters of this book, explore the implications of the coincidence of opposites when it is applied to itself. In the process, we will take up several additional challenges to the *coincidentia* doctrine, including those implied by the philosophies of Wittgenstein, Žižek, and others. These challenges include the views that (1) an appeal to the co-incidence of opposites produces an illusory, purely "verbal" resolution of philosophical disputes, (2) such an appeal is grounded in the ulti-mately incoherent assumptions of a "hard reality" and a unified world, (3) dialectics cannot result in a specifiable "content" view of reality, and (4) *coincidentia oppositorum* violates the laws of reason and logic.

A NOTE ON TERMINOLOGY

In this work, I treat several related ideas that are not always distin-guished by others but that should nonetheless be clarified and separated.

The term *"coincidentia oppositorum"* or the "coincidence of oppo-sites" reflects the view that apparently opposing ideas "coincide" or do not exclude one another. In many instances (including my own), the use of the term "coincidence of opposites" assumes the *interdependence* of the opposing ideas, but this assumption is not always made by previous thinkers. As I use the term in this book, *coincidentia opporitorum* in-volves the recognition that contrary ideas *and* experiences not only co-exist and pass over into their opposite but prove to be grounded in their opposites as well. The image of a Mobius strip or Klein bottle comes to mind as an illustration of the *coincidentia* idea, for in these figures what is inside is not only perceived to pass over into what is outside (and vice versa), but inside and outside are each seen to be grounded in and supported by one another.

As noted above, the terms "dialectic" or "dialectical" have various meanings, but are often used (initially, and especially, by Hegel) to refer to the phenomenon whereby an idea (or historical trend) is shown to depend upon, and "evolve" (logically or historically) into, its presumed opposite.

The "unity of opposites" or "union of opposites" is often used to describe a situation wherein opposing ideas or qualities are united within a single subject (for example, the Absolute or God) without retaining their distinct identity.

"Multi-valued" and "dialetheistic" logic refer to a form of purportedly rational thought that admits logical possibilities other than *true* and *false*: for example, *both true and false* and *neither true nor false*. Advocates of such logic, in holding for example that *P* and *not P* are both true, may or may not hold that the truth of these opposing or "contradictory" ideas are interdependent. Those who make use of the coincidence of opposites may or may not resort to multi-valued logic, depending on whether they regard the opposites they treat to involve logical contradiction.

Finally, it must be pointed out that not all thinkers (or mystics) who utilize *paradoxical language* to express ideas or emotions (or to produce experience or action—as in the case of a Zen Koan) are committed to any of the above logical or metaphysical views. My review of the history of thought about the opposites in the ensuing chapters, will range over thinkers who espouse one or the other or several of the ideas about the opposites I have just outlined, and it will not always be possible to specify their precise positions.

I have, for the most part, used masculine pronouns throughout this work. A decision to do so was made in order to maintain consistency with (and avoid confusion when speaking about) virtually all of the thinkers discussed in this work.

CHAPTER ONE

THE OPPOSITES IN HISTORICAL CONTEXT

THE COINCIDENCE OF OPPOSITES

The doctrine of the coincidence of opposites and the related notion of the unification of opposites[1] has had a long, if often ignored and poorly understood, history in both Eastern and Western thought. Many mystics, and a number of (mainly Eastern) philosophers, have held that spiritual experience, and ultimately the world as a whole, can only be accounted for with language that merges certain opposites and at least appears to violate the "principle of non-contradiction." While philosophers in the West have generally held this logical principle to be inviolable,[2] a handful of them, including Nicholas of Cusa, Meister Eckhart, and G. W. F. Hegel have argued that contrasting philosophical doctrines (including idealism and materialism, determinism and free-will, and even theism and atheism) are equally, and even necessarily, true. In the nineteenth century, Hegel made the movement between and ultimate integration of opposites the foundation of his philosophical system, and his "dialectical logic" was adopted by Karl Marx and a number of other thinkers. In the twentieth century, the physicist Niels Bohr, in an effort to explain the dual wave-particle understanding of quantum entities, famously spoke about two kinds of truths: "superficial truths," whose opposites are false, and "deep truths," whose opposites or apparent contradictories are true.[3] The psychologist Carl Jung (1875–1961) maintained that the human psyche is a mix of opposing ideas, feelings, and attitudes, that the self is a *coincidentia oppositorum*,[4] and that the task of "indi-

43

viduation" (and psychotherapy) involves the integration of these opposing tendencies. Jung and his contemporaries, Mercea Eliade and Claude Lévi-Strauss, explored the integration of the opposites in religion and myth.[5] More recently, Jacques Derrida and other "postmodern" thinkers have appealed to the permeability and interdependence of opposites in order to overcome the "privileging" of particular poles of the binary oppositions in Western thought and thereby "deconstruct" the foundational ideas of Western metaphysics.[6]

In this chapter, I survey a number of ancient, medieval, modern, and postmodern thinkers who have regarded the problem of opposition to be central to philosophy. My survey does not pretend to be anything more than a representative sampling. Several of the thinkers I consider in this chapter, notably G. W. F. Hegel and C. G. Jung, will be treated in greater depth in later chapters.

CHINESE PHILOSOPHY: "YIN" AND "YANG"

Interest in the power of the opposites is as old as philosophy itself. In China, the opposition of "yin" and "yang" (literally dark and light) was posited as an underlying principle that describes how contrary forces give rise to, interact with, and complement each other in producing nature, life, and spirit.[7] Attention to these complementary forces, then, serves as a foundation for various disciplines, including philosophy, medicine, nutrition, and the martial arts. In Taoism, the implicit duality of yin and yang, especially as it manifests in the moral and spiritual realm, is regarded as a perceptual illusion, and reality is conceived of as a unified whole.

Generally speaking, "yin" is regarded in Chinese thought as a negative, feminine, and lunar principle, one that is dark, passive, and cold in its nature. "Yang" is thought of as masculine, positive, solar, light, warm, active, and dry. (As we will see, the association of the feminine with the negative and the masculine with the positive is present in much of Western thought as well.) However, it is only the complementarity of the two principles, each in effect giving rise to and complementing the other, which results in phenomenal reality. According to Chuang Tzu, yin as "cold" derives from heaven, and yang as "warmth" proceeds forth from the earth.[8] However, the two principles are not metaphysically distinct, and neither is axiologically superior to the other. "Yinyang," in fact, is expressed in one breath, a single word, representing the complementarity and unity of opposites that is the foundation of all.

The classic Chinese text, the *Tao Te Ching*, describes a merging, and at times a reversal, of opposites:

> The whole world recognizes the beautiful as the beautiful, yet this is only the ugly; the whole world recognizes the good as the good, yet this is only the bad.

> Thus, Something and Nothing produce each other; the difficult and the easy complement each other;

> The long and the short offset each other;
> the high and the low incline towards each other;
> note and sound harmonize with each other;
> before and after follow each other.[9]

> In the world there is nothing more submissive and weak than water. Yet for attacking that which is hard and strong nothing can surpass it.[10]

The *Tao Te Ching* promotes a practical philosophy of action through non-action ("The way never acts yet nothing is left undone"[11]) and the production of specific ends through doing their opposites:

> If you would have a thing shrink,
> You must first stretch it;
> If you would have a thing weakened,
> You must first strengthen it;
> If you would have a thing laid aside,
> You must first set it up;
> If you would take from the thing,
> You must first give to it

This is called subtle discernment:
The submissive and weak will overcome the hard and
strong.[12]

The reversal of opposites even extends into the ethical sphere:
Through compassion, one will triumph in attack and be im-
pregnable in defense.[13]

A man of the highest virtue does not keep the virtue and that
is why he has virtue. A man of the lowest virtue never strays
from virtue and that is why he is without virtue.[14]

The meaning of this last quoted passage is somewhat obscure, but
the *Tao Te Ching* suggests that a rigid adherence to virtue degenerates,
first from virtue to "benevolence," then to "rectitude," and finally to
ritual "rites."[15]

THE OPPOSITES IN HINDU AND BUDDHIST THOUGHT

The complementarity of opposites, the acceptance of paradox, and a
less than strict adherence to the law of non-contradiction are important
characteristics of traditional Indian religion and philosophy. The San-
skrit term "Brahman-Atman" expresses the notion, accepted by such
non-dualist Hindu schools as the Advata Vedanta, that the infinite and
the finite, the Absolute and the individual human soul are complementary aspects of a single reality, each of which is regarded to be the origin
of the other. The Upanishads identify Brahman, the infinite principle of
the universe, with the self.[16] According to the Aitareya Upanishad, the
self is both "smaller than a grain of rice…and greater than the earth…
sky [and] worlds."[17] The Isa Upanishad speaks of the paradoxical unity
that underlies the diverse phenomena of the universe. Speaking of the
Absolute as Atman, this Upanishad recites, "It moves. It moves not. It is
far, and It is near. It is within all this, and It is outside of All this."[18] Atman is conjointly both "knowledge and non-knowledge, and it is "oth-

er" than both knowledge and non-knowledge as well.[19] The Upanishad famously declares, "It is not understood by those who [say they] understand It. It is understood by those [who say they] understand It not."[20]

In the *Bhagavad Gita* we learn that the "blessed lord" describes himself as father and mother, origin and dissolution, death and deathlessness.[21] This work also provides a pragmatic, psychological perspective on the equivalence of the opposites when it exhorts the reader to treat alike "pleasure and pain, gain and loss, victory and defeat...."[22]

Paradox, contradiction, and the equivalence of contraries are also characteristic of much Buddhist thought. As Graham Priest has pointed out, the early Buddhist logicians routinely held that propositions could be (1) true only, (2) false only, (3) both true and false, or (4) neither true nor false, to which some Buddhists also added "none of these."[23] The Jains went so far as to hold that a proposition could be both true only *and* both true and false.[24] Propositions in which both poles of a contradiction are said to be true are found in the Japanese school of Buddhism (Chan or Zen), which fused the teachings of the Buddha and the Tao, and for which contradictions (in the form of aphorisms or *Koans*) play a significant role in propelling the adherent toward enlightenment.[25] An interesting and difficult question that we will consider in later chapters is whether the coincidence of opposites necessarily (or ever) implies a dialetheistic logic that admits *formal* contradictions.

Among Buddhist thinkers, Nagarjuna (c. 150-220 CE), who founded the Madhyamaka (Middle Path) school of Mahayana Buddhist philosophy, is well-known for advocating such apparently contradictory ideas as "space is not an entity [and] it is not a non-entity" and "the assertion that effect and cause are similar is not acceptable (and) the assertion that they are not similar is also not acceptable." Nagarjuna held that nirvana is equivalent to samsara, the "depths" of things are equivalent to their "surface" and "the ultimate truth is that there is no ultimate truth."[26] While it is arguable that at least some of these contradictions are only apparent (i.e., they can be "corrected" by placing them in their polemical contexts or showing that a single term is used in more than one sense), there is little doubt that Nagarjuna (and Buddhism in general) allows that certain "deep truths" can only be expressed using paradoxical language, and that there is a coincidence and even union between at least some opposing terms and ideas.

According to Dennis McCort, the *coincidentia oppositorum* that is an important element in Buddhist practice is decidedly non-rational.

> The solution to any koan is some realization of a dialectical synthesis that shifts the aspirant to a phase of consciousness deeper and more comprehensive than the logico-rational, one that can effortlessly accommodate both terms of the conflict. This realization must be more than intellectual (in fact, intellect need hardly be involved at all); it must have the immediacy of an insight grounded in experience and must take one well beyond the pairs of opposites that are forever dogging the human mind.[27]

HERACLITUS: THE CONFLICT AND HARMONY OF OPPOSITES

In the West, "opposition" plays an important role in several pre-Socratic philosophers, including Anaximander, Heraclitus, and the Pythagoreans. Aristotle informs us that the pre-Socratic philosopher Anaximander (c. 610–546 BCE) understood creation as the separation of the opposites from an original and indefinite "One,"[28] an idea that we will explore in detail in later chapters.

The fragmentary writings of Heraclitus (c. 535–575 BCE), articulate a doctrine of the unity of the opposites, with each pair of opposites producing both a unity and a plurality. At times, Heraclitus' "unities" appear to simply reflect the effects of contrast ("Disease makes health pleasant and good, hunger satiety, weariness rest"[29]), or temporal succession (such as the unity of "day and night," "waking and sleeping," "young and old"). At other times, they suffer from the "fallacy of the dropped qualifier," as when he declares, "Sea is the most pure and the most polluted water; for fishes it is drinkable and salutary, but for men it is drinkable and deleterious."[30]

However, there are fragments where Heraclitus suggests a simultaneity or integration of opposites that, if enigmatic, is of philosophical moment. While the nature of his doctrine of the unity of opposites, like everything else in Heraclitus, is subject to controversy, many of the critical issues that arise in subsequent discussions of *coincidentia oppositorum* are presaged in the Heraclitean fragments. These include questions regarding whether the coincidence of opposites violates the law of contradiction and results in epistemological uncertainty, whether opposites are ever truly identical or rather stand to each other in a relationship of difference yet inter-dependence, and whether the relationship between the opposites is best understood in logical, linguistic, or imaginative terms.

Several of the fragments can serve to illustrate Heraclitus's handling of the opposites:

> Things taken together are whole and not whole, something which is being brought together and brought apart, which is in tune and out of tune; out of all things there comes a unity, and out of a unity all things.[31]

> God is day night, winter summer, war peace, satiety hunger [all opposites, this is the meaning]: he undergoes alteration in the way that fire, when it is mixed with spices, is named according to the scent of each of them.[32]

> The path up and down is one and the same.[33]

> If one does not expect the unexpected one will not find it out, since it is not to be searched out, and difficult to compass."[34]

> All things are and are not.[35]

> The part is something different from the whole and

is yet the same as the whole; substance is the whole and the part, the whole in the universe and the part in this living being.[36]

They do not apprehend how being at variance it agrees with itself [literally, how being brought apart it is brought together with itself]: there is a back-stretched connexion, as in the bow and the lyre.[37]

As Hegel notes, Plato references this last fragment in his *Symposium* when he says that for Heraclitus, "The one, separated from itself, makes itself one with itself, like the harmony of the bow and the lyre."[38]

According to Daniel W. Graham, Heraclitus understood himself to be accessing a timeless truth, one, however, that required a certain ambiguity and multiplicity of meaning for its proper expression.[39] His *logoi* or propositions were designed to produce both intellectual insight and an experiential transformation in those who understood them.[40] However, because we only possess "fragments" of the one book Heraclitus is said to have written, and many of these fragments appear in several versions (some of which may not be genuine), his philosophical positions, especially on the subject of the opposites, are difficult to pin down with certainty. For example, there are three fragments pertaining to Heraclitus' famous demurrer regarding one's ability to step into the same river:

12. You cannot step twice into the same rivers; for fresh waters are flowing in upon you.[41]

49a. We step and do not step into the same rivers; we are and are not.[42]

91. You cannot step twice into the same rivers.[43]

While Plato, in the Cratylus, suggests that Heraclitus was of the view "that all things are in motion and nothing at rest"[44] (the so-called Heraclitean doctrine of "the flux"), according to Graham a more plausible reading of these fragments is that many things, as illustrated by the flowing river, "stay the same only by changing."[45] On this reading Heraclitus sees change as a necessary condition for constancy, a *coincidentia oppositorum* that is paradoxical *but not logically contradictory.*

According to Graham, Heraclitus' doctrine of the flux is "a special case of the unity of opposites, pointing to the ways things are both the same and not the same over time."[46] For example:

> And it is the same thing in us that is quick (living) and dead, awake and asleep, young and old; the former are shifted and become the latter, and the latter in turn are shifted and become the former.[47]

In Graham's view, Heraclitus does not hold to an identity of opposites but rather articulates a doctrine in which opposing poles of an opposition are interconnected and may succeed one another in time.

Aristotle's view that Heraclitus' doctrine of the "identity" of the opposites led to a violation of the most fundamental law of thought, the law of contradiction,[48] though perhaps plausible with respect to some of the fragments (for example, "All things are and are not"[49]) certainly does not apply to them as a whole. Even Aristotle recognized that under certain circumstances (e.g., as a result of continuity) opposites could be called "one."[50] As Graham and C. J. Emlyn-Jones point out, it is clear and uncontroversial that in certain cases for Heraclitus (frag. 88: "awake and asleep, young and old,"[51]) opposites are related to one another either through contrast or succession.[52] At any rate, according to Kirk and Raven, Aristotle's objection is both anachronistic and largely inapplicable.[53] Heraclitus lived during an era prior to both the advent of formal logic and the clear distinction between perceptible entities and abstract principles. As such, his pronouncements were often multivalent. For example, he seems to have thought that the "Logos," which he conceived of as the unifying measure or arrangement of things in the world, was somehow equivalent to fire, which he understood to be the fundamental element.[54] His view that certain opposites are the "same" was not meant to suggest that they were virtually "identical" but rather interconnected or inseparable.

Nevertheless, Heraclitus' use of multivalent, paradoxical language (in contrast to the Sophists') was non-rhetorical and meant to reflect what the philosopher understood to be the multivalent or paradoxical nature of the world. For example:

> The bow (βιός) is called life (βίος), but its work is death.[55]

According to Emlyn-Jones, for Heraclitus this fragment exemplifies a view in which opposites are related through linguistic similarity, in this case the similarity in Greek between bow (βιός) and life (βίος). However, the question of how the bow simultaneously contains both life and death is not answerable. It is not a rational conclusion but a hermeneutic one "based upon the juxtaposition of words similar in form but, potentially at least, opposite in meaning."[56] On this view, for Heraclitus "the relationship between opposites was displayed as self-evident in language, which he believed reflected the structure of reality."[57] For Emlyn-Jones the combination of opposites "defy logical analysis" and is "associated with a mode of thought whose linguistic origins…may well constitute…the ultimate origin of his belief in the identity of opposites." However, as Heraclitus held that language (the "Logos," which has the connotation of both "orderly relationship" and "account or narration") directs or at least reflects the ordering of the world, we might discern a deeper coincidence of opposites implicit in his thought, one that transcends his particular examples and reflects the interdependence and even the identity of thought, language, and the world.

The understanding of Heraclitus was for centuries conditioned by Plato's reference to (but failure to actually quote) him in the Cratylus and the Thaetetus.[58] Matthew Colvin has argued that Plato misrepresents Heraclitus' theory of the flux in both dialogues by claiming that the earlier philosopher championed a "flux" that precluded the possibility of stability, identity, and knowledge. However, Heraclitus wrote of a "union of stability and flux," where flux—motion in the case of the flowing river—is the *sine qua non* of identity and stability.[59] Heraclitus speaks of flux and stability *together.* They are productive of a unity of opposites that *provides certain objects with their identity.* The "flux" is not meant as a challenge to the possibility of knowledge—rather its integration with its opposite is necessary for knowledge.

Plato, however, considers the flux and the unity of opposites in separation from one another.[60] For Plato, the "compresence" of opposites in the particulars of sense is part of the motivation for his positing ideal forms to guarantee purity and stability. According to Colvin, Plato views the compresence of opposites as a species of the flux—even in cases where there is no temporal dimension to this compresence. In the *Thaetetus*, the problem is stated, "But if nothing is at rest, every answer upon whatever subject is equally right: you may say a thing is or is not…."[61] This results in a situation where objects cannot be univocally named. Things are then constantly "slipping out from under our words."[62] However, in these dialogues Plato does did not perform an exegesis of Heraclitus' words but rather associates him with a radical flux doctrine. This resulted in the popular but mistaken view of subsequent philosophers that to be a Heraclitean is to believe in a radical, material, and epistemologically upsetting flux doctrine,[63] as opposed to the harmonious unity of flux and stability that appears to have been advocated by Heraclitus himself.

Taken as a whole, Heraclitus seems to be pointing to a doctrine in which a primal energy or One is differentiated into opposing ideas, objects, and events, which can then be cognized as working complementarily and in harmony. Hegel points out that Plato references this idea in his *Symposium* when he speaks of Heraclitus' views on the harmony between the bow and the lyre.[64] Indeed, Heraclitus anticipates Hegel in connecting the opposites with God or the Absolute: "God is day and night, winter and summer, war and peace, surfeit and hunger; but he takes various shapes, just as fire, when it is mingled with spices, is named according to the savour of each."[65]

However, as Emlyn-Jones points out, Heraclitus's "God," which he identifies with the pairs of opposites, is "far removed from the traditional anthropomorphic deity"[66] and is better "identified with the controlling power of the universe"—albeit one that according to Emlyn-Jones does not transcend the universe itself; again, ideas that reappear in, and by his own admission, are adopted by Hegel. According to Kirk and Raven, for Heraclitus God is "the common connecting element in all extremes" and is to be identified with the "Logos" or the essential constituent behind both the opposites and the entities of the world.[67] One might even say that Heraclitus is the first to claim that the coincidence of opposites is the "archetype of the Absolute."

Heraclitus not only held that there is a unity of opposites but also that there is a unity in all things: "Couples are things whole and not whole, what is drawn together and what is drawn asunder, the harmonious and discordant. The one is made up of all things, and all things issue from the one."[68]

As we have seen, Heraclitus seems to be of the view that "the One" is a harmony of what, on further analysis, turns out to be conflicting trends: "Men do not know how what is at variance agrees with itself. It is an attunement of opposite tension, like that of the bow and the lyre."[69]

Hegel held that Heraclitus was the first philosopher to develop a truly dialectical philosophy, and the first to understand the Absolute as developing through a conflict between and the ultimate unity of opposites. In his *Lectures on the History of Philosophy*, Hegel declared, "There is no proposition of Heraclitus which I have not adopted in my Logic."[70] Heraclitus anticipated German philosophy and psychology by nearly 2500 years in holding that conflict and strife, in the tension and interaction of opposed substances and ideas, is at the heart of all progress. For Heraclitus, "all things happen by strife and necessity,"[71] and Aristotle tells us that Heraclitus "rebukes the author of the line 'Would that strife might be destroyed from among gods and men': for there would be no musical scale unless high and low existed, nor living creatures without male and female, which are opposites."[72] Fragment 126, attributed to Heraclitus, reads: "Cold things become warm, and what is warm cools; what is wet dries, and the parched is moistened."[73]

Here we have the beginnings of the doctrine of enantiodromia, the idea that things must pass over into and be compensated by their opposites, which Jung attributed to Heraclitus. According to Kirk and Raven, it is Heraclitus' view that, should the strife and balance between opposites cease and one pole come to completely dominate the other (if, for example, cold was not checked by heat, the world would come to an end).[74]

For Heraclitus, there must also be a coincidence of opposites in our approach to experience: "If one does not expect the unexpected one will not find it out, since it is not to be searched out and difficult to compass."[75]

We have seen how, for Heraclitus, individuals typically fail to recognize the hidden connection between opposites: "They do not apprehend how being at variance it agrees with itself."[76] One must adopt an attitude that permits such connections to emerge, and this entails a paradoxical "expectation of the unexpected." While the distinction between knowledge and its objects had not been formally articulated in his time and would have at any rate been alien to his mode of thinking, we might say that for Heraclitus there is both a metaphysical and epistemological aspect to the connection between the opposites.

PLATO: THE BEING OF NOT BEING

Several of the Platonic dialogs reflect the pre-Socratics' preoccupation with the opposites. The interlocutors in these dialogs alternately entertain a deep interpenetration between the opposites and endeavor to maintain their strict separation.

In the *Symposium*, Eryximachus, a physician argues that love induces a reconciliation or harmony between opposites and is therefore a dominant principle in nature. The skilled practitioners of various arts, including medicine, music, and agriculture, seek to induce "loving friendship" among such opposites as hot and cold, bitter and sweet, and moist and dry. Eryximachus turns to music to provide an interpretation of the doctrine of the opposites in Heraclitus, arguing that in music a harmony is created between different notes of higher and lower pitch, which at one time were in discord but are now reconciled through the musical art. The course of the seasons is also produced through the love and harmony of the opposing principles of hot and cold, moist and dry.[77]

In the *Republic*, we find the view that opposites interpenetrate one another, and that in certain instances both poles of an opposition apply to the same concept. We learn, for example, that "opinion...partakes equally of the nature of being and non-being," that from a certain point of view beauty will be found ugly, that the just will be found unjust, and that the holy will be seen to be unholy. All things "great and small" will be denoted both by one characteristic and it's opposite.[78] Plato introduces the idea that with regard to individual objects (as opposed to the ideas which they instantiate), one cannot fix them in the "mind either as being or not being, or both, or neither." Indeed, for Plato, they appear to have a place *between* being and nonbeing.[79] Yet *The Republic* comes up short of arguing for the position that two opposing ideas can be simultaneously predicated of the same object. Plato holds that we should not be inclined to believe "that the same thing at the same time, in the same part or in relation to the same thing, can act or be acted on in contrary ways."[80]

In the *Phaedo*, we find the doctrine that "all things which have opposites [are] generated out of their opposites." This is true for such things as good and evil, just and unjust, and "innumerable other opposites." We read, "There is a passing or process from one [opposite] to the other."[81] This passage back and forth between opposites is the principle of change:

> "If generation were in a straight line only, and there
> were no compensation or circle in nature, no turn
> or return of elements into their opposites, then…all
> things would at last have the same form and pass
> into the same state, and there would be no more gen-
> eration of them."[82]

The Heraclitean principle of the compensation of one opposite by the other effectively prevents the universe from deteriorating into stasis. This is particularly true for the opposites of life and death. Socrates argues that since life is a fusion of body and soul, these two elements must continually be separated and joined. For this reason, we are entitled to believe that the souls in Hades will eventually return to reinvigorate human flesh. J. N. Findlay, in his commentary on the *Phaedo*, infers that for Plato "the presence of life and mind somewhere are as much required by the dead parts of the universe as the latter are required by life and mind."[83]Interestingly, an apparently *opposing* view is expressed by Plato's Socrates later in the *Phaedo*, where he argues that "abso-lute greatness will never be great and also small."[84] One of Socrates' auditors challenges him on the grounds that this contradicts his earlier claim that "opposites were simply generated from opposites." Socrates attempts to explain this apparent contradiction by stating that earlier he was speaking about instances, whereas now he is speaking about ideas and essences. With regard to the former, opposites proceed out of one another; in the case of the latter, they do not. Socrates holds "that essential opposites will never…admit of generation into or out of one another."[85] As we will see, this is a position that will be challenged in later dialogs. It is a challenge that will later be foundational for Hegel, who will hold that opposites coincide and pass into one another both in the world and in thought.

In the *Parmenides*, a complex and enigmatic dialogue where Plato considers the notion of the "One," the interlocutors speak in ways that suggest the adoption of a multivalued logic in which propositions can be both true *and* false, or *neither* true nor false. For example, we hear "the one is and becomes older and younger than itself and others, and neither is nor becomes older or younger than itself or the others."[86] We learn that "the one is both one and many" and "neither one nor many."[87] A little further on we read:

> In the passage from one to many and from many to one, the one is neither one nor many, neither separated nor aggregated; and in the passage from like to unlike, and from unlike to like, it is neither like nor unlike, neither in the state of assimilation nor of dissimilation; and in the passage from small to great and equal and back again, it will be neither small nor great, nor equal, nor in a state of increase or diminution, or equalization.[88]

Here Plato seems to reverse the Socratic position in the *Phaedo* that only instances can pass over into their opposites while essences remain fixed in their nature. By holding that the One participates in a logic far more fluid than the logic that governs its instants, Plato appears to adopt a position that is far more congenial to mysticism and later dialectical thought. In *The Parmenides,* the Platonic *ideas* are conceived of as shading into their opposites, showing a different face in different places and times, and from different points of view.[89] Plato concludes this dialogue with the words,

> "Let this much be said; and further let us affirm
> what seems to be the truth, that, whether one is or
> is not, one and the others in relation to themselves
> and one another, all of them, in every way, are and
> are not, and appear to be and appear not to be."[90]

We can here understand why Hegel called the *Parmenides* the greatest work of ancient dialectic and a true expression of the divine life.[91]

A form of dialectical (or "dialetheistic") logic is also present in the *Sophist*, where it is again applied to the notion of being and non-being. An Eleatic stranger, a follower of Parmenides, initially argues against any conflation between being and non-being. According to the stranger "nonbeing in itself can neither be spoken, uttered, nor thought, but… is unthinkable, unutterable, unspeakable, indescribable…."[92] However, with the introduction of the "image," which is fashioned in the likeness of the real and the true, the stranger is convinced (against his Eleatic principles) that "what we call an image is in reality really unreal" and that at least in this case "non-being" exists. The stranger is also compelled to assert that "falsehood," which on its face has no being whatsoever, exists, at least in opinion and words, and thus exemplifies the "being of not being."[91] The stranger concludes that he "must test the philosophy of his father Parmenides, and try to prove by main force that in a certain sense not being is, and that being, on the other hand, is not."[93] While it is unclear whether Plato regards these conclusions as valid or sophistic, he has presented arguments that imply the simultaneous truth of opposing philosophical principles.

Alfred North Whitehead once noted that all of Western philosophy is a footnote to Plato, and it is indeed true that nearly all of the problems and controversies that have occupied Western philosophy since ancient times have their antecedents in the Platonic dialogues. While it is difficult to ascertain Plato's own views through an analysis of the words of his interlocutors, it appears that the notions of opposites as interdependent, passing into one another and being unified in an all-encompassing "One" are all present in the Platonic corpus.

GNOSTICISM: "GOD CREATED MEN, AND MEN CREATED GOD"

The coincidence of opposites takes on particular significance in the Gnostic religion, which flourished in both Christian and Jewish circles during late Hellenistic times. The Gnostics held, for example, that to know one's *arche* (beginning) is to know one's *telos* (end),[95] that one can become the knowledge that is known (via a reunion with one's divine self), and that both God and reality are androgynous (both "Mother" and "Father"). More radically, certain Gnostics held there to be a radical *coincidentia oppositorum* between God and man, affirming, for example, "God created men, and men created God. So is it also in the world, since men created gods and worship them as their creations it would be fitting that gods should worship men."[96]

In the Gnostic text, *Thunder, The Perfect Mind*, we find an expression of the nature of Sophia (Wisdom) and the human soul in paradoxical terms:[97]

> I am the first and the last...the honored and the scorned...the whore and the holy one...the bride and the bridegroom...the mother of my father...the sister of my husband and he is my offspring...knowledge and ignorance...the one whom they call Life, and you have called Death...a mute who does not speak, and great is my multitude of words.[98]

The Gnostics generally held that there is a coincidence of opposites between perfection and imperfection, good and evil, and law and transgression that characterizes both the biblical God and the world. In contrast to the Kabbalists, who later saw the *coincidentia* between good and evil as an expression of divine perfection, the Gnostics held that *coincidentia oppositorum* provides insight into the *corruption* of the perfect One:

> The world came into being through a transgression. For he who created it wanted to create it imperishable and immortal. He failed and did not attain to this hope. For the incorruption of the world did not exist and the incorruption of him who made the world did not exist.[99]

PLOTINUS: THE ONE IS EVERYWHERE AND NOWHERE

The Neoplatonists developed a philosophical perspective that provided the basis for a great deal of subsequent Christian and Jewish theology. *Coincidentia oppositorum* finds a prominent place in Plotinus' *Enneads*, where we learn that the "All" or "One" is necessarily "made up of contraries."[100] According to Plotinus, the One is both everywhere and nowhere, for

> If it were simply and solely everywhere, all would be this one thing alone: but it is, also, in no place, and this gives, in the final result, that, while all exists by means of it, in virtue of its omnipresence, all is distinct from it in virtue of its being nowhere.[101]

Plotinus further held that "in the Intellectual-Principle Itself there is a complete identity of knower and known,"[102] and, "the Supreme must be an entity in which the two (knower and known) are one."[103] According to Plotinus, all things exist by virtue of their opposites; for example, "to deny Evil...is necessarily to do away with the Good as well."[104]

Plotinus provides a direct and sustained meditation on the opposites in Tractate 2 of his third *Ennead*. There he argues that the "Reason-Principle" which governs the world is a unity of contrary impulses, things, and ideas. It is "at war with itself" and "has the unity, or harmony, of a drama torn with struggle," not unlike the harmony created by the clash of characters in a play.[105] According to Plotinus, "the Universe is a self-accordant entity, its members everywhere clashing but the total being the manifestation of a Reason-Principle."[106] Plotinus even holds that there can be multiple principles of reason that clash with but ultimately come into harmony with one another. This is because the "one Reason Principle...must be the unification of conflicting Reason-Principles whose very opposition is the support of its coherence."[107] We see here another anticipation of and source for Hegel's dialectical reasoning.

According to Plotinus, the "Reason-Principle" must complete itself in contrariety and multiplicity, a multiplicity that is most evident in the world of sense. Yet, such "partial members" of the One are "urged by a...warmer desire for unification." The Universe is filled with contraries, "white and black, hot and cold, winged and wingless...reasoning and unreasoning—but all these elements are members of one living body...."[108]

Plotinus considers the important question of whether his views on the harmony of opposites result in a reprieve for evil and the wicked. He states:

> Thus, with the good we have the bad; we have the opposed movements of a dancer guided by one artistic plan; we recognize in his steps the good as against the bad, and see that in the opposition lies the merit of the design.[109]

Plotinus then immediately asks, "But, thus, the wicked disappear?"[110] His response is, "No: their wickedness remains; simply, their role [in the harmony of the Universe] is not of their own planning."[111] While evil ultimately plays a role in the "living body" of the world, those who choose to commit wrong have no defense: "the Reason-Principle does not excuse them"[112]

NICHOLAS OF CUSA: TRANSCENDING THE PRINCIPLE OF NON-CONTRADICTION

The notion that a *coincidentia oppositorum* is characteristic of the Jewish or Christian God began to make an appearance in late medieval times. In Chapter 3, I will consider this view as it was manifest in the Jewish Kabbalah. Here, I will discuss its appearance in the philosophy of the Christian theologian, Nicholas of Cusa (d. 1464). "Cusanus," as he provides what is perhaps the best example of a carefully developed understanding of opposition and paradox in Western philosophy prior to Immanuel Kant.

Cusanus argued that rational investigation can only approximate knowledge of the infinite God, who can never be understood in terms of the "relations and comparisons" of philosophy. However, according to Cusanus, there is a similar if less radical limitation of knowledge with regard to all other things; for while "truth" is an absolute, knowledge is always an approximation by degree. Cusanus uses the image of a polygon with an increasing number of sides inscribed in a circle to illustrate how knowledge only approximates its object.[113] Cusanus anticipated Spinoza and the German idealists in holding that each perspective we take upon truth is only partial and relative. However, not even the sum of all perspectives yields truth in an absolute sense.

Nicholas of Cusa argued that the *principle of non-contradiction* invoked by philosophers was simply evidence of the weakness of the human intellect. He criticized the idea that contradictory assertions cannot both simultaneously be true with regard to a given object. For Cusanus, contradictory ideas can each be true regarding both the world and, in particular, God. He held there to be a faculty superior to reason, which he termed the faculty of "knowing" or "intellect," and which transcends the principle of non-contradiction, to comprehend the unity or interdependence of opposites operating in the world and in God.

According to Cusanus, it is in God that all oppositions are reconciled.[114] For example, it is possible to say of the deity that He is both the absolute maximum *and* the absolute minimum. Cusanus again uses geometry to demonstrate how opposites can coincide: for example, he asks his readers to imagine a circle of infinite circumference whose curvature becomes equal to that of an infinitely straight line, yielding a coincidence of opposites between line and circle, straight and curved.

Cusanus explains that God *both* transcends the world and is imminent within it, like a face reflected in a mirror. Echoing a Neoplatonic theme,[115] he extends the mirror analogy to hold that each creature (indeed all things) is mirrored and hence is paradoxically present in each and every other, creating a *coincidentia* between unity and difference. In his work *On the Peace of Faith*, Cusanus made use of the principle of *coincidentia oppositorum* in an effort to reconcile differences among the world's religions.[116] Such reconciliation, he believed, would lead to a universal faith and world peace.

Like nearly all mystics and many philosophers who have considered the question, Nicholas of Cusa held that the principle of *coincidentia oppositorum* ultimately transcends rational comprehension. In

God, both essence and existence, maximum and minimum, and all other opposites fully coincide, but we cannot attain a rational understanding of the synthesis of these oppositions.

THE OPPOSITES IN MODERN THOUGHT

In the modern era, beginning with Immanuel Kant (1724–1804), European philosophy became preoccupied with the oppositions, antinomies, and apparent contradictions that the mind runs up against when it ponders the ultimate nature of the world. While it will not be possible here to survey this entire tradition in detail, it would hardly be imaginable to offer a contemporary analysis of the coincidence of opposites without considering it. In the following sections I will discuss several representatives of the modern and postmodern philosophical tradition— Kant, Schelling, Hegel, Rickert, Dewey, Whitehead, and Derrida—each of whom were concerned with overcoming the polar oppositions of traditional metaphysical thought. I will also provide a description of the views of several more recent thinkers—J. N. Findlay, Morris Lazerowitz, Graham Priest, and Hector Sabelli—who have reflected upon the role of opposition and contradiction in philosophy and logic. In addition, I will briefly discuss the views of the Swiss psychiatrist C. G. Jung and the Danish physicist Niels Bohr, who in the twentieth century imported the notion of the coincidence of opposites into psychological and natural scientific discourse respectively. In Chapter 4, I will examine Hegel's use of the *coincidentia* idea in detail, and in Chapter 5, I will discuss Nietzsche's understanding of the opposites in connection with my detailed analysis of Jung's thought.

IMMANUEL KANT'S DUAL-WORLD SOLUTION

Immanuel Kant (1724–1804) regarded certain contradictions or antinomies[117] generated by common reason to be both the major problems of philosophy and the main impetus to his "transcendental philosophy." Kant argued, for example, that since human reason inevitably regards itself to be *both* determined by nature *and* free,[118] any philosophy failing to do justice to each of these apparently contradictory claims would be woefully one-sided and incomplete. In brief, he held that the postulate of universal causality (determinism) was absolutely necessary for science, while the postulate of human freedom was equally necessary in the realms of morality and the law. Kant's solution to this paradox was to assert that both poles of the antinomy are *valid*, if not "true." However, he endeavored to avoid running afoul of the logical *principle of non-contradiction* by claiming that each postulate is valid in a *distinct realm*. Kant thus felt compelled to posit his now famous distinction between the *phenomenal* and *noumenal* worlds. The former was considered by him to be the arena of knowledge and empirical investigation, while the latter was thought to be an inherently unknowable but necessary postulate for practical action and moral and legal judgments. Kant's solution to the antinomies inherent in philosophy and common sense was to posit two worlds, each of which is completely independent of the other and only one of which (the phenomenal realm) is the proper object of scientific and philosophical knowledge. In his later work, Kant suggested that the unknowable noumenal realm was indeed the realm of religious faith and God, and he thus came close to adopting the quasi-mystical view that there is a realm, unknowable to science and reason, which is nonetheless accessible to a certain ethical or religious intuition.

Kant, in his *Critique of Pure Reason,* had held that an impenetrable barrier to knowledge of the noumenal realm resulted from the structures and categories of the human mind. These categories, or what Kant referred to as "modes of knowledge"[119] (among which are space,[120] time,[121] and causality[122]) make knowledge of phenomenal "appearances" possible but render impossible all knowledge regarding things as they are "in-themselves." Knowledge of the *thing-in-itself* or the noumenal realm is excluded because all knowledge is conditioned by the *a priori* categories and modes of apprehension of the human mind. For Kant, it is because "ultimate reality" is completely unknowable apart from its *appearance* through human modes of apprehension that traditional metaphysics and theology is impossible.

While Kant originally held that the "thing-in-itself" (as well as the noumena, to which it corresponds) is simply a "limiting concept,"[123] by the time of his later works, the *Critique of Practical Reason* and the *Critique of Judgment*, he appeared to have much to say regarding the so-called noumenal world. Kant noted that while the phenomenal world necessarily follows the laws of causal, mechanical necessity, the moral law requires humans to transcend the causal nexus, act on the basis of will, and conform their behavior to the rule of reason. He therefore concluded that the demands of ethics and the individual's capacity to act in accordance with the moral law were windows into a non-phenomenal, noumenal reality (or, according to some of Kant's interpreters, an "aspect" of reality[124]), one that cannot be an object of knowledge per se but which can be accessed through faith and practical reason. For Kant, freedom is a necessary hypothesis for morality, although such freedom lies outside of the phenomenal order and is therefore part of the "unknowable" *noumenal* realm. In his *Critique of Practical Reason,* Kant included God and the immortality of the soul as ideas that, like freedom, are beyond knowledge but which acquire a certain practical necessity as postulates in the world of *noumena.*[125] In *The Critique of Judgment,*[126] he added that the objects of aesthetic and teleological judgment are similarly situated. While Kant continued to hold that there is no metaphysical *knowledge* regarding these noumenal hypotheses, by placing them in a world or "realm" he reopened the door to metaphysics, one which the later German Idealists, Fichte, Schelling, and Hegel were to enter shortly after Kant's death.

Kant's hypothesis of a noumenal order is in many ways characteristic of the religious and particularly mystical consciousness in general. Finding no place in the natural world for the objects of moral and spiritual judgments, and, further, recognizing that these objects often contradict the data of the human senses, the mystically inclined philosopher or theologian is apt to speak of a higher consciousness of a spiritual world, which penetrates but does not completely coincide with material reality, and which is the realm of spirit, God or the "Absolute."

FRIEDRICH SCHELLING: THE "VANISHING POINT" OF ALL DISTINCTIONS

In the philosophy of Friedrich Schelling (1775–1854), we find a post-Kantian reformulation of the views of Nicholas of Cusa. Schelling held that the "Absolute" is the "vanishing point" of all distinction and difference,[127] and, specifically, the *act* through which the distinction between subject and object is overcome. The viewpoints of subject and object are necessary standpoints of all empirical (i.e., human) consciousness, and only God can stand outside of this distinction. If we attempt to grasp the Absolute as it is in itself, we can only conceptualize it as the "point of indifference" or the vanishing point of all distinctions. While rational inquiry cannot apprehend the vanishing of difference, Schelling assures us that all distinctions of thought, including all philosophical controversies (e.g., between subject and object, idealism and realism) have no meaning from the standpoint of the Absolute.

Schelling's question was how the cosmos could make room for the free, "unconditioned" human subject without resorting to the Kantian bifurcation between the phenomenal and noumenal realms. Schelling rejected Fichte's solution, which was to put everything on the side of the subject, in effect absorbing nature into the "I." Schelling sought to make the "I" part of nature by first conceiving nature as having the unconditioned contained within itself prior to the appearance of the human subject. Thus, in Schelling's "Naturphilosophie," man is part of nature, which consists of a whole that unifies subject and object. Nature contains within itself an ascending series of polar oppositions (including subject and object, conscious and unconscious) which, like the poles of a magnet, are inseparable even though they remain contraries. These oppositions contain "potential" within themselves, and it is this potential that both makes nature the absolute creative subject and forms the ground for the unconditioned creativity in man. Within nature, the opposites and, most importantly, the distinction between subject and object, provide the energic tension for creativity and change. For Schelling, these oppositions, like the poles of a magnet, are both different and united.

Hegel considered Schelling's philosophy to be an advance upon Kant and Fichte; for the most part he accepted Schelling's conclusion of the unity between subject and object. However, Hegel held that Schelling's philosophy suffered from the fact that it presupposed this unity rather than demonstrating it through logical argument. Hegel maintains that in this Schelling is akin to the Platonists and Neo-Platonists, who held that knowledge was to be found through an inner intuition of eternal ideas rather than through reason and dialectic. Indeed, Hegel points out that for Schelling the identity of subject and object is achieved through the "imagination."[128] Though Schelling later endeavored to provide a "proof" of the unity of subject and object, Hegel accused him of begging the question by covertly assuming the unity as an axiom.[129]

In Kant—and then in Schelling and the later German Idealists— we have the first clear distinction between *first-person* (subjective) and *third-person* (presumably objective) accounts of experience and the world, and the first systematic efforts to overcome this opposition. It is an opposition that will become critical to our own understanding of *coincidentia oppositorum*. We will have occasion to return to the question of standing outside the subject/object distinction and other polarities of thought later in this work, especially in Chapter 6.

G. W. F. HEGEL'S DIALECTICAL IDEALISM

Georg Wilhelm Friedrich Hegel (1770–1831) recognized the prevalence of antinomies in conceptual thought, but like Schelling he rejected Kant's distinction between phenomena and *noumena*. While Hegel regarded Kant's philosophy as the "starting point"[130] for his own philosophy, he held that Kant's positing of a "thing-in-itself" as the source of freedom, morality, and faith involved an illegitimate extension of the phenomenal category of causality into a realm where on Kant's own theory it could have no legitimate application.[131] Further, Hegel held that any assertion that the noumenal realm exists and provides the foundation for ethics makes it knowable, and thereby undermines Kant's claim that "knowledge" is restricted to phenomena.[132] Hegel concluded that anything whatsoever that can be referred to must, at least in principle, be knowable. Further, since all that can be known is either a presentation to or category of the mind, all knowledge—and, hence, all existence—is essentially "idea." As a result of this equation of knowledge, existence, and idea, the distinction between the mind and its objects collapses, and Kant's reason for speaking about the phenomenal and noumenal realms (and hence about an *essential unknown*) dissolves.

Hegel took a dynamic approach to the antinomies or contradictions that appear in conceptual and philosophical thought, and he proceeded to enlist the Kantian and other antinomies as the fuel for his famous "dialectic," arguing that the mind's taking up a position on one pole of an opposition inevitably leads to a breakdown of that pole, the necessity of entertaining its opposite, and the appearance of a more embracing idea that both deepens the original notion and serves as the ground for the next stage in the dialectical process. Hegel thus attempted to make rational, philosophical sense of the idea that a concept's opposite or contradictory is implicit in itself, and his philosophy is, in effect, a systematic attempt to provide a comprehensive rational basis for the mystical notion of *coincidentia oppositorum*.

Hegel adopts and provides a philosophical basis for the mystical view that all concepts and things have their contraries, as it were, hidden away within themselves,[133] and he holds that there is an important sense in which apparent opposites are identical. For example, he argues that the notion of *being*, which is generally thought to be opposed to and distinct from *knowledge*, contains knowledge as part of its essence. This is because what we mean by saying that something has "being" is that it must at least be potentially known. For Hegel, "being" is precisely what consciousness makes of it, and "knowing" is conversely nothing but the contents (being) of such consciousness. As such, these two apparently contrary ideas exist in a state of *coincidentia oppositorum* and are in an important sense identical.

Hegel makes use of the term "dialectical" to refer to what he considers to be the logical and historical processes through which concepts or things pass into their opposites and the distinctions between opposing terms are broken down.[134] For Hegel, dialectics is the essence of creativity. However, while concepts that are subject to the dialectic are transformed, they are never lost completely; they are "lifted up" in such a manner as to provide insight into their original essence. Hegel's discussion of the relationship between being and knowledge illustrates how apparently opposing or contradictory notions are dialectically understood to be interdependent ideas.

Hegel's views on "dialectic" and the coincidence of opposites will be explored in depth in Chapter 3.

HEINRICH RICKERT'S "HETEROLOGICAL PRINCIPLE"

Heinrich Rickert (1863–1936), a leading German Neo-Kantian philosopher, held that no single model or idea can encompass the world as a whole. While many of his contemporaries argued that an all-encompassing worldview was impossible, Rickert concluded that it could be achieved by invoking what he termed "the heterological principle," a form of thinking that brings together mutually exclusive ideas.[135] According to Rickert, the world is a heterogeneous multiplicity about which each of our concepts and disciplines reveal only a part. However, a comprehension of the whole can be achieved when we take ideas that clearly contradict one another and view them as complementary. As Rickert put it, "We only need ask ourselves whether a part of the whole-world…could not perhaps be completed through the concept of another part of the whole-world."[136] This can occur on the level of both concrete identities and ideas. On the one hand, we can bring together the notions of living things and inert matter, and together these entities encompass everything in the cosmos. On the other hand, we can bring together the notion of nomothetic or generalizing science with the notion of idiographic or individualizing science, and these together enable us to achieve a complete science that circumscribes the entirety of our subject matter. For Rickert, the most basic heterological contrast is not between mind and matter, as many of his contemporaries believed, but rather between empirical reality and value. In his view, these two mutually exclusive concepts provide the broadest and most meaningful account of the world.

Unlike Hegel, Rickert did not rely on a complex dialectical interdependence between opposing categories, but rather on the principle that a concept and its negation must logically cover all possibilities. When we "identify the pairs of concepts that represent world alternatives," this enables us to be "sure that everything in the world falls either under one or the other of the two concepts."[137]

JOHN DEWEY AND THE METAPHYSICS OF ART AND EXPERIENCE

The American pragmatist philosopher and psychologist John Dewey (1859–1952) made interesting use of the coincidence of opposites in formulating his metaphysics of experience. Dewey held that significant philosophical notions are interdependent.[138] In *Experience and Nature*, Dewey writes:

> Qualities have defects as necessary conditions of their excellences; the instrumentalities of truth are the causes of error; change gives meaning to permanence and recurrence makes novelty possible. A world that was wholly risky would be a world in which adventure is impossible, and only a living world can include death. Such facts have been celebrated by thinkers like Heracleitus and Laotze....[139]

As James Garrison points out, "The reference to Heracleitus and

Laotze" signals that Dewey is introducing *"the inherent unity of opposites"* as a significant theme in his metaphysics.[140]

While Dewey's mature philosophy would in many ways seem worlds apart from that of Hegel, Dewey had studied Hegel and the neo-Hegelians in his youth and there remained a significant residue of Hegelianism in his thought.[141] For Dewey, experience involves "an ineradicable union...of the relatively stable and the relatively contingent,[142] and he viewed these two poles of experiences as interdependent. Existence, therefore, involves "an intricate mixture of the stable and the precarious, the fixed and the unpredictably novel, the assured and the uncertain...which sets mankind upon that love of wisdom which forms philosophy." However, he continues,

> too commonly... the result of the search is converted into a metaphysics which denies or conceals from acknowledgment the very characters of existence which initiated it, and which give significance to its conclusions. The form assumed by the denial is, most frequently, that striking division into a superior true realm of being and lower illusory, insignificant or phenomenal realm which characterizes metaphysical systems as unlike as those of Plato and Democritus, St. Thomas and Spinoza, Aristotle and Kant, Descartes and Comte, Haeckel and Mrs. Eddy.[143]

For Dewey, nature as it emerges in history "involves a precarious uncertainty," and our experience of nature is "full of error, conflict, and contradiction."[144]

Dewey was a critic of what came to be known as the spectatorial theory of consciousness, which posits a radical separation between experience and the world. He was highly suspicious of "philosophical theories which detach man from nature, which, in the language of philosophy, oppose subject and object."[145] According to Garrison, for Dewey the earlier philosophical separation of being from becoming evolved into a separation of the object from the subject and the bifurcation of mind and matter, "the consequence of which has been to all but eradicate human purpose from the natural realm."[146]

According to Dewey, the interdependence of opposites has decidedly existential implications:

> We long, amid a troubled world, for perfect being. We forget that what gives meaning to the notion of perfection is the events that create longing, and that, apart from them, a "perfect" world would mean just an unchanging brute existential thing.[147]

Dewey held that art involved a coincidence of opposites, and that an investigation into the nature of art and aesthetics was the key to metaphysics:

> Art is solvent union of the generic, recurrent, ordered, established phase of nature with its phase that is incomplete, going on, and hence still uncertain, contingent, novel, particular...a union of necessity and freedom, a harmony of the many and one, a reconciliation of sensuous and ideal. Of any artistic act and product, it may be said both that it is inevitable in its rightness, that nothing in it can be altered without altering all, and that its occurrence is spontaneous, unexpected, fresh, unpredictable.[148]

It is important to note that for Dewey "art" encompasses all intelligent activity and that "the history of human experience is a history of the development of arts." He goes on to say "knowledge and propositions which are the products of thinking are works of art, as much so as statuary and symphonies."[149] Thus all significant human activity involves a coincidence of the opposing trends of the many and the one, the necessary and free, and the sensuous and ideal.

ALFRED NORTH WHITEHEAD: PROCESS, GOD, AND WORLD

Alfred North Whitehead (1861–1947), developed his speculative "process philosophy" during an era when his contemporaries were highly skeptical of metaphysics, especially of the dialectical variety, which had dominated European and British thought in an earlier generation. Whitehead held that "opposed elements stand to each other in mutual requirement," and he concluded that

> the universe is to be conceived as attaining the active self-expression of its own variety of opposites—of its own freedom and its own necessity, of its own multiplicity and its own unity, of its own imperfection and its own perfection. All the "opposites" are elements in the nature of things, and are incorrigibly there.[150]

Whitehead articulated his understanding of paradox and the interdependence of opposites most pointedly in his account of the relationship between God and the world. "God," according to Whitehead, "is the way we understand this incredible fact—that what cannot be yet is."[151]

More pertinent to our discussion, Whitehead held that "God is dipolar."[152] God's *primordial* nature is conceptual experience but his *consequent* nature is fulfilled in the move toward finitude and physical "experience," and it is only through the latter that God achieves full consciousness. According to Whitehead, the primordial nature of God is to be "the unlimited conceptual realization of the absolute wealth of potentiality."[153] However, in his consequent nature "he is the principal of concretion—the principle whereby there is initiated a definite outcome from a situation otherwise riddled with ambiguity."[154] God is thus "both the beginning and the end." [155] The world is dependent upon God's primordial nature as it is motivated by what Whitehead calls conceptual experience derived from God, but God is himself "consequent upon the creative events of the world."[156] Whitehead writes, "for God the conceptual is prior to the physical, for the world the physical pole is prior to the conceptual pole."[157] Whitehead strikes a Hegelian note when he argues that there is a threefold creative process in the cosmos in which a singular conceptual realization gives way to multiplicity and finitude through physical realization, and that multiplicity ultimately reunites with the singular primordial conceptual act.

For Whitehead, God embodies *permanence* in his primordial nature and the world embodies *fluency*. However, there is a *coincidentia oppositorum* between permanence and fluency. Whitehead states, "There is the double problem: actuality with permanence, requiring fluency as its completion; and actuality with fluency, requiring permanence as its completion." Whitehead believes that "this double problem cannot be separated into two distinct problems. Either side can only be explained in terms of the other." Whitehead, as did Jung, understood that "God is completed by the individual." The temporal occasions which ultimately constitute the individual are only completed through an "everlasting union" with "the eternal order which is the final absolute 'wisdom.'"[158] This insight can only be expressed through a series of antitheses:

> It is as true to say that God is permanent and the World fluent, as that the World is permanent and God is fluent.

> It is as true to say that God is one and the World many, as that the World is one and God many.

> It is as true to say that, in comparison with the World, God is actual eminently, as that, in comparison with God, the World is actual eminently.

> It is as true to say that the World is immanent in God, as that God is immanent in the World.

> It is as true to say that God transcends the World, as that the World transcends God.

It is as true to say that God creates the World, as that
the World creates God.[159]

J. N. FINDLAY'S UNITIVE LOGIC

Among recent philosophers, John Niemeyer Findlay (himself an
expositor of Hegel[160]) held to a conception of the interdependence of
seemingly opposing ideas. In a posthumously published paper, "Philosophy as a Discipline," Findlay wrote:

> There are inconsistencies in the working of all our
> basic concepts…. There are philosophies, for exam-
> ple, Hegelianism, which stress the point that many
> apparently opposed things require one another in or-
> der to be what they are, that which they most resist
> and exclude is thereby most intimately part of their
> essence, and also that they have an inherent tenden-
> cy to develop into, or pass over into other things
> which continue or complete them, and that, when
> all is clearly seen, the antagonisms and antinomies
> of philosophy can be resolved by a more compre-
> hensive vision.[161]

Findlay himself held that our awareness of our own internal psychological states is interdependent with our awareness and understanding of
such interior states in others, and that our experience of material bodies
is fully interdependent with our awareness of the ideas they instantiate:
"Whichever may come first in some outside view, they are mutually dependent…solid things are as much dependent on the one-sided descriptions in terms of which we know them as the latter are on the former."[158]

There is, according to Findlay, a similar interdependence between
"words and things": "Words likewise obviously depend on everything
else, while everything else has its…status set forth in words."[162]

Findlay took a strong interest in the puzzles generated by so-called
"intentional objects," "objects" that appear before, are considered by,
and "intended" by consciousness. He described the "central difficulty"

associated with these objects in the following manner:

> Without really including an object, and without
> merely blindly tending towards it and without being
> at all like it, but in fact differing from it in category,
> and without being close to it in space or in other
> respects, a state of mind can none the less so unam-
> biguously and intimately be of a certain object that
> it is impossible to describe it adequately without
> mentioning the object in question.[163]

Findlay held that intentional objects are ambiguous and even contradictory because they are presumably located within the individual
who intends or considers them, and yet they are identical with the "real"
object that they intend,[164] objects that may be light years away from the
mind intending them.

Only a "unitive logic," according to Findlay, can resolve the paradoxes involved in intentionality. He writes: "Such unitive logic may be
vaguely characterized as directing our thought to an horizon where opposites melt into coincidences, where identity prevails over difference,
and where the 'moment' or aspect replaces the part or element."[165]

For Findlay, the coincidence of opposites points to a higher unity, as
"our endless philosophical puzzles (bear witness)...to our sense of the
surrounding unity which our thought-procedures require although they
often so desperately fight against it."[166] According to Findlay, several
philosophical puzzles, including the problems of intentionality and our
knowledge of other minds, are dissolved once we consider the possibility that *all is essentially one*, and our thoughts about an object and the
object itself are each an *aspect* of a unified existence.

Findlay holds that it is mind that reintroduces the unity that had
been sundered by nature. In Findlay's unitive logic,

> It is not an empirical accident that minds arise in
> the world; minds represent, we may say, the world's
> deep unity asserting itself over the world's attempt-
> ed dispersion, an attempted dispersion as essential

to the deep unity as the latter is essential to the former.[167]

While nature disperses the objects of the universe in space, time,
and category, mind has the capacity to bring them into unity—considering in the same mental act the smallest quantum of energy in the scientist's laboratory and the nuclear furnace of a supernova in a remote
galaxy.

For Findlay, the unitive logic that is an inevitable consequence of
a deep consideration of mind forces us to take seriously not only the
claims of Hegel, but also the quite distinct claims "of various mystical
writers, Neoplatonic, Vedantic, Mahayanist, and Contemplative-Chris-
tian, that there is and must be a whole spectrum of spiritual states varying from those of our normal waking earth-life to a state in which sensuous individuality is attenuated to a vanishing point…"[168]

Findlay writes that these notions were most beautifully expressed
in Plotinus' *Enneads*, where we read, "Each thing holds all within itself,
and again sees all in each other thing, so that everything is everywhere
and all is all, and each all, and the glory infinite."[169]

PARADOX AND CONTRADICTION AS THE HALLMARK OF PHILOSOPHY

In the 1960s, the philosopher Morris Lazerowitz developed the
view that "a paradox or contradiction lies hidden in every metaphysical theory" and that antinomy is in fact the hallmark of philosophy.[170]
Lazerowitz argued that all, or nearly all, metaphysical arguments result
in contradictions, but he acknowledged that "unlike mathematical contradictions, metaphysical contradictions are the kind of contradictions
about which it is possible permanently to disagree as to whether they
are contradictions."[171] Lazerowitz presents as an example the notion of
an *uncaused occurrence* (or uncaused cause), which philosophers from
Empodocles to F. H. Bradley regarded as a self-contradiction but which
other philosophers (notably A. J. Ayer) found perfectly conceivable.
Lazerowitz writes that "this intellectual deadlock, and a great number

of others encountered in philosophy, make inescapable the thought that perhaps every philosophical statement is one side of an antinomy."[172] He points out that philosophers have differed regarding the significance of antinomies in philosophy. For instance, Kant, who developed several such antinomies, held that their existence "points to a transcendent world into which the human mind is not privileged to enter," while Bradley held that the antinomies of experience implied the unreality of sensible phenomena.[173]

Lazerowitz further argues that "in the case of a vast number of… views in philosophy, the paradoxical fact emerges that the arguments adduced for a proposition imply the invalidity of a distinction which the proposition requires." He concludes that "this paradox is a sphinx whose riddle must have an answer, and undoubtedly an answer will someday be forthcoming."[174] Lazerowitz himself developed the Wittgensteinian view that "philosophy has the substance of a verbally contrived intellectual mirage and that it is a subject which only in outward appearance seeks to discover the truths about things."[175] He went on to combine this linguistic analysis with the Freudian view that psychological wishes propel the philosopher to contrive metaphysical positions that are cast in the language of "logical argument" and "truth" but which in fact serve very subjective needs.[176]

Of course, if Lazerowitz is right, then his view that "every philosophical argument is one side of an antinomy" is itself one pole of an antinomy, and thus essentially contestable. Further, we need by no means grant that Lazerowitz (or Wittgenstein) has finally solved the "riddle" of philosophy's tendency to undermine its own propositions. Indeed, Lazerowitz's own psychologization of philosophy seems to back away from his claim that every philosophical proposition generates an antinomy, just when this assertion begins to get interesting. We will have occasion to proffer something of an answer to Lazerowitz's riddle when we consider in Chapter 6 the *philosophical* reasons why arguments adduced for a given philosophical proposition imply the validity of the very position the proposition is meant to exclude. In Chapter

7, I will discuss the Wittgensteinian view that all philosophical positions, including claims regarding the coincidence of opposites, involve a "bewitchment of our intelligence by means of language."[177]

GRAHAM PRIEST AND DIALETHEISM

Recently, the notion that contradictory statements may both be true has been revived by "dialetheistic" logicians, notably Graham Priest, who has argued that it is only Western philosophical prejudice that has held the "law of non-contradiction" (if *P* then *not* not *P*) to be the inviolate condition for rationality. According to Priest, philosophers have long relied on the defense of this "law" in Chapter Four of Aristotle's *Metaphysics*, a defense that in Priest's view is trivial and non-persuasive.[178] Aristotle held that (1) it is impossible for an attribute to both belong and not belong to the same entity at the same time, in the same respect,[179] (2) one cannot simultaneously both believe something and not believe it,[180] and (3) the greatest certainty is that contradictory propositions cannot simultaneously be true.[181] He argued that communication was only possible if each expression has a single meaning. For example, one cannot mean by stating "X is a man" that "X is not a man."[182] Contradiction not only voids communication but belief as well.[183] One who believes that he is on a precipice cannot also believe the opposite—and the proof of this is that he avoids walking over it.

While the law of non-contradiction certainly has a basic common-sense appeal, like all laws of thought it cannot strictly speaking be proved or verified because any purported proof would, of necessity, appeal to the law itself. On the other hand, a major argument against the law and in favor of *dialetheism* (the possibility for true contradictions) stems from such logical anomalies as the *liar's paradox* ("This sentence is not true"), which yield logically sound arguments that result in a contradiction. Graham claims that the only result of numerous attacks against these paradoxes is to relocate the paradoxes elsewhere in a chain of reasoning. Graham believes that apart from the paradoxes, there are a number of other phenomena that can only be adequately handled by a violation of the law of non-contradiction and the adoption of a dialetheistic logic. These include transition states, such as when a person is exiting a room (is he in or out of the room?), paradoxes of motion (as originally described by Zeno), terms (such as "death") that have multiple criteria of application, and the paradoxes of quantum mechanics (in which, for example, a single sub-atomic particle is said to move through two slits at once). To this we might add the paradoxes of time, for example, that the present is both completely distinct from and permeated with the past and the future. In addition, and perhaps more significantly, claims about the ultimate nature of things (such as Kant's claim that it is impossible to assert anything whatsoever about ultimate "noumenal" reality, which he then describes) or the mystical claim that it is impossible to say anything at all about the Absolute (which is also referenced and spoken about) seem to violate the law of non-contradiction. This is because in the very act of making such claims one does precisely what one says cannot be done.[184]

The notion of dialetheistic logic is not without its critics. For example, it has been pointed out that dialetheism has difficulty handling negation and disagreement: If I show an opponent in a debate that his views are false or wrong, he can dialetheistically agree but still assert that his views are also true and correct! Priest has argued that the dialetheist must distinguish between those (presumably few) contradictions that are rationally acceptable and those that are not, but there are difficulties in characterizing the latter within a formal logical system. Efforts to delimit the class of sentences that are dialetheistic have not been wholly successful, and appear to be *ad hoc* in nature.[185] Other critics have held that acceptance of the law of non-contradiction is a pre-requisite for both meaning and rationality. It is thought, for example, that a sentence is meaningful only if it rules something out. Priest counters that the sentence "Everything is true" is meaningful without excluding anything. With respect to rationality, Priest points out that *consistency* is only one criteria that has a bearing on truth; *evidence* is another, *and there is evidence* (even if it is arguably inconclusive) for the truth of certain contradictions such as the liar's paradox.

Priest raises the time-honored question of whether (both Western and Eastern) philosophers' contradictory assertions might be restated in non-contradictory form. While it is his view, for example, that some of Nagarjuna's apparent paradoxes can be re-stated this way, he holds that certain fundamental utterances in philosophy (for example, that it is impossible to speak about ultimate things, or that the nature of ultimates is that they have no ultimate nature) can only be expressed using dialetheistic language.

We will further explore the logical status of the "coincidence of opposites" in later chapters. Here I briefly note that *coincidentia oppositorum* may not be dependent on dialetheism, as opposites that coincide (for example, idealism and materialism) may not necessarily involve formal contradictions. Indeed, in Chapter 7, we will consider the possibility that *coincidentia oppositorum* neither adheres to nor violates the law of non-contradiction because this law may simply be largely inapplicable and irrelevant to fundamental philosophical ideas. Also, it should be noted that even if we hold that the doctrine of *coincidentia oppositorum* can be formalized via dialetheistic logic (as the *truth* of *both* A and *not* A), not all *true contradictions* involve a coincidence of opposites. Indeed, there are true contradictions of the form *neither* A *nor not* A (such as Nagarjuna's view that space is neither an entity nor a non-entity, or the Buddha's purported view that the saint neither survives nor does not survive his physical death) that do not comport well with the *coincidentia opposiotorum* idea. On the other hand, the quantum physics view that photons are *both* particles and *not* particles comports better with *coincidentia oppositorum* because of its *positive* formulation. Among those who accept the possibility of true contradictions, there are some who adopt the point of view of "neither" (for example, "it is *neither* true that God exists nor that God does not exist") and some who adopt the point of view of "both" ("it is *both* true that God exists and does not exist"). Buddhism, for example, is a tradition of "the neither," whereas the Kabbalah (as we will see in Chapter 2) is largely a tradition of "the both." It is, I believe, only within the traditions of "the both" that the doctrine of *coincidentia oppositorum* is easily formulated. For example, one can readily state *positively* that the truth of the world's existence is dependent on its non-existence and vice versa, but it is much more difficult to state *negatively* that the falsity of the world's existence is dependent upon the falsity of its non-existence. With the Buddhist or Wittgensteinian view of "the neither," it would seem that one's entire framework must be overturned and one's concepts discarded rather than synthesized. Of course, both dialetheism and *coincidentia oppositorum* each suggest the possibility of accepting both "both" and "neither," and of holding that the collapse of one's conceptual framework implied by "the neither" is necessary to arrive at "the both" (and the "true" conceptual system) and *vice versa*.[186]

NIELS BOHR: COMPLEMENTARITY IN MODERN PHYSICS

In the twentieth century, the notion of *coincidentia oppositorum* appeared in the sciences, most notably in the theory of wave/particle complementarity as articulated and interpreted by the quantum physicist Niels Bohr. I will explore Bohr's thinking on complementarity in some depth, as I believe it has an important bearing on our own problems in philosophy and psychology. Bohr spoke of two kinds of truths: "common truths," whose opposites are false, and "deep truths," whose opposites are also true.[187]

Citing the fact that the findings of quantum physics support both a particulate and wave theory of light and matter, Bohr concluded: "We are not dealing with contradictory but with complementary pictures of the phenomena, which only together offer a natural generalization of the classical mode of description."[188] In other words, Bohr tells us that it is only by thinking two seemingly opposing theories together that we are afforded an adequate scientific understanding of light and matter. Bohr reminds us that both "radiation in free space as well as isolated material particles are abstractions," but that both are "indispensable for a description of experience in connection with our ordinary space time view."[189]

Bohr notes that modern physics leads to a blurring of certain other distinctions that had earlier been thought to be sharp and clear. Drawing on Heisenberg and others he speaks of the *"impossibility of any sharp separation between the behavior of atomic objects and the interaction with the measuring instruments which serve to define the conditions under which the phenomena appear."*[190] The collapse of a clear distinction between the instruments of knowing the world and the world itself—between the knower and the known, subject and object, epistemology and metaphysics—brings physics close to the insights of both mystical consciousness and German Idealism.

Bohr regarded his "complementarity" to be a philosophical position that stretched well beyond quantum physics, to questions that arise in other sciences—for example, the controversy between mechanism and vitalism.[191] With regard to psychology he wrote:

> As is well known, many of the difficulties in psychology originate in the different placing of the separation lines between object and subject in the analysis of various aspects of psychical experience. Actually, words like "thoughts" and "sentiments," equally indispensable to illustrate the variety and scope of conscious life, are used in a similar complementary way as are space-time and dynamical conservation laws in atomic physics.[192]

Bohr's point is that there is a subjective and an objective use for most "psychological" terms (for example, my inner subjective "thoughts" and the objective "thoughts" or ideas that they are about), and that only by considering both aspects at once can we develop understanding in psychology. Bohr tells us that progress in atomic physics leads us to recall "the ancient wisdom, that when searching for harmony in life one must never forget that in the drama of existence we are both actors and spectators."[193]Bohr was aware that his thought could lead to an impression of mysticism and, while he made use of the metaphor of the simultaneous truth of opposites in describing his and others' work in quantum mechanics, he denied that his thought led to an acceptance of logical contradictions in either the world or our descriptions of it. He held that *apparent contradictions* simply disclose an essential inadequacy in our philosophical viewpoint. Bohr's position on complementarity seems to have been that apparently (though not logically) contrary assertions about reality are (at least on occasion) both true, and that the affirmation of both "truths" is necessary for a complete description of the subject (for example, light, matter, or human psychology) to which they are applied. It is unclear, however, if he ever held that seemingly opposing truths were not only complementary but mutually determinative.

For Bohr, the differences between philosophers and the disagreements between physicists of different schools are rooted "in the preferences for a certain use of language suggesting itself from the different lines of approach."[194] Bohr held that at times the most complete account of the world is given when we use language in ambiguous ways that gives latitude to more than one aspect of the significance of our words. There is, he held, "a mutually exclusive relationship...between the practical use of any word and attempts at its strict definition."[195]

With Bohr's comment on the value and necessity of linguistic ambiguity, we are ready to enter the post-modern, deconstructive philosophy of Jacques Derrida.

JACQUES DERRIDA: THE DECONSTRUCTION OF POLAR OPPOSITIONS

One of the more recent, and perhaps the most radical, of philosophical voices concerned with conceptual opposition involves an anti-metaphysical relativism that rejects any form of unitive mysticism or philosophy.[196] Jacques Derrida (1932–2004), and others in his wake, have argued that the entire history of Western metaphysics is grounded in a wide range of conceptual oppositions (subject-object, inside-outside, good-evil, God-world, etc.) and the *privileging* of one pole of each of these oppositions. Building upon a foundation first laid by Nietzsche, these thinkers have heralded a post-metaphysical consciousness in which traditional philosophical ideas and values become open to their opposites, and in which we come to embrace both poles of these oppositions as well as whatever falls between them.

However, Derrida provides us with what might be spoken of as a *negative inversion* of the *coincidentia* idea, insofar as he uses the idea that philosophical concepts imply their opposites to achieve an anti-metaphysical, "deconstructive" result. As described by Christina Howells, Derrida seeks "to deconstruct the binary oppositions of Western thinking."[197] God-world, subject-object, inside-outside, word-thing, good-evil, reality-illusion, and virtually all other philosophical dichotomies break down in deconstructive and postmodern thought. In some ways then, Derrida is close to the mystics and philosophers we surveyed in this chapter. In Chapter 2, we will see that the distinctions Derrida critiques were also broken down, and in effect "deconstructed" by the Kabbalists, whose symbols can be readily understood as means for overcoming such binary oppositions as being and nothingness, God and world, theism and atheism, concealment and revelation, creation and destruction, reality and illusion, permanence and change, subject and object, and words and things.[198]

However, whereas mysticism generally seeks to overcome metaphysical distinctions in the service of a higher unity, Derrida holds that this effort is a subterfuge, which, while pretending to respect differences in perspectives, theories, cultures, and ideas, ultimately obliterates these differences in favor of a preferred "absolute" point of view. This is the gist of Derrida's long-standing polemic against Hegel, whom Derrida holds to be the first philosopher to genuinely recognize "difference" and the last to make a major effort to eradicate it.

Derrida utilizes the term "the supplement" to indicate that there is always *something additional*, something beyond one's perception, cognition, and language. The supplement disrupts such oppositions as inside/outside, nature/culture, animal/human, child/adult, mad/sane, divine/human, and reality/illusion through its implication that there is always something beyond what one can envision, conceive, or describe using these dichotomous ideas. The supplement undermines the assumptions that things can be fully present to consciousness, that concepts have definite boundaries, and that anything can be fully understood. In using this term, Derrida suggests that what anything is, *is* partly established by what initially appears to be "external" to it—i.e., by what it was initially meant to exclude.[199] As we will see, for Derrida *presence* is conditioned by (and contains) *absence*, the *"now"* is conditioned by (and contains) the *future* and the *past*, and *memory* assumes the possibility and reality of *forgetting*. In effect, he invokes the concept of *coincidentia oppositorum*, the interpenetration of the opposites, but without producing an integrative model of the polarities and subject matters to which it is applied.

Derrida utilizes another concept, this time borrowed from Gödelian mathematics, to further his deconstruction of the hard and fast distinction between the poles of binary opposites. He uses the term "undecidable" to indicate that there are aspects of, and especially terms in, any given text that are ambiguous and *undecidable*, and which thereby disrupt the text that contains them. According to Derrida, these undecidable terms mean *both* X and its opposite, and neither X nor its opposite. Derrida appeals to Plato's dialog, the *Phaedrus*, and points to the term *pharmakon*, which in that dialog is applied to *writing*, and suggests that writing is both a cure and a poison, and both a remedy for and a source of forgetfulness. However, according to Derrida, "undecidables" do not constitute a "third term" that in Hegelian fashion resolves the contradiction between the poles of opposing meaning.[200] Instead, they disturb all efforts to come to a clear one-sided or integrative solution.

Indeed, Derrida's whole interest in opposition is correlative to his critique of "essences," and to his efforts to show the impossibility of arriving at an "essential" perspective or truth about a text, phenomenon, or the world as whole. He is thus highly critical not only of the idea that any particular perspective is absolute, but also of the notion that a sequence of perspectives can (per Hegel or Rickert) be integrated into a comprehensive or "absolute" point of view.

Derrida holds that all categories, all "essences" are subject to accidental variations that cannot be rationalized, explained, or covered via a definition that applies to all cases. He holds that the so-called "accidental features" of a concept or thing are actually necessary and indeed an "essential" possibility for it.[201] What is "outside" of a particular text, concept, or phenomenon is *essential* to the inside. For example, one cannot understand *the human* unless one places it within a wider matrix involving the animate and inanimate, the concrete, the abstract, and the immortal, as well as within the context of the specific physical, emotional, intellectual, and spiritual features that are *accidentally* present in one human being and which illustrate the necessity of accidental features being present in everyone. The essence of being "human" is a function of both features like the inanimate and the immortal that humans do not possess, and those that are not thought to be essential to them and which they possess "accidentally."

Derrida provides additional examples of "essence" being constituted by what is outside, contrary, and accidental to it. One example, which both restates and illustrates this idea, is the notion that an "absence" (i.e., the past and the future) is constitutive of "presence" (the present). For Derrida, it is precisely that which is *not now* (i.e., the past and future) that makes the *now* possible, and it is precisely what is *absent* that serves as the necessary condition for anything being *present*.[202] There are a number of special applications of Derrida's principle.[203] For example, the possibility of *forgetfulness* is essential for there to be *memory* because any so-called memory not subject to forgetfulness would be an "infinite self-presence" and not a *memory;* a memory must be of that which *is no longer present*. Another example, the reciprocal relationship between reality and imagination, appears in the thought of Jean-Paul Sartre, who writes:

The imaginary appears "on the foundation of the world," but reciprocally all apprehension of the real as world implies a hidden surpassing towards the imaginary. All imaginative consciousness uses the world as the negated foundation of the imaginary and reciprocally all consciousness of the world calls and motivates an imaginative consciousness as grasped from the particular *meaning* of the situation.[204]

According to Sartre, while one could not imagine without a perceived "real" world to serve as a starting point that one negates and imaginatively transcends, one could not apprehend "reality" except insofar as one surpasses one's perception and *imagines* it as a whole. This is because what one takes to be "real" is always situated against a background of unperceived objects and relationships that provide it with coherence, continuity, and meaning. We will see that the *coincidentia oppositorum* between reality and imagination is an important principle for Jung, who came to regard the imaginary as a form of reality on par with the perceived world: "The tangible and apparent world is one reality, but fantasy is the other reality."[205]

As we have seen, Derrida holds that Western metaphysics can in virtually all instances be characterized by the setting up of a binary opposition and the privileging of one pole of that opposition over its contrary. In his view, "essence" and "accident" or "identity" and "difference"[206] is the most general of oppositions, which then serves as the foundation for additional oppositions (including being/privation, inside/outside, logical/empirical, meaning/sign, soul/body, good/evil, purity/contamination, and world/language). While, according to Derrida, "metaphysical grammar," following the pattern of *essence* and *accident*, privileges the first pole of each of these oppositions and debases the second, a "deconstructive grammar" allows the debased pole to penetrate and determine its opposite. In the latter case, the debased opposite becomes a positive condition for, and thus an "essential" part of, the privileged "essence."[207]

Derrida does not go so far as to hold that concepts (being, the world, man, goodness, etc.) are overwhelmed and eliminated by their polar opposites and accidental features; he asserts only that they are of necessity penetrated by them.[208] If a concept did not retain at least some measure of identity, it could not be said to be permeable to, contaminated by, or dependent upon its opposite and accidents; it would have no status whatsoever. Concepts cannot be reduced to or held to be equivalent to their opposites. While in the process of deconstructing polar concepts we find that they are dependent upon what they are not, we cannot equate (and should not confuse) essence and accident, being and nothingness, world and language, etc. Derrida is certainly not of the view that concepts have no meaning or value, but simply holds that they do not have the purity and privilege we have given them.

While Derrida is radically opposed to the Hegelian project of realizing "absolute knowledge," his own method has much in common with Hegel's dialectic. Indeed, both philosophers are part of a philosophical tradition (evident in the pre-Socratics and, as we have seen, even at times in Plato himself) which provides a counterpoint to the idealist, "Platonic" view that concepts must have clean boundaries that are impermeable to their opposites.

Several authors have argued that Derrida is linked to mysticism, though in describing this link they typically appeal to his affinity for *apophantics* or negative theology.[209] I believe, however, that Derrida can also be linked to mysticism through his dialectical view that the poles of traditional metaphysical distinctions are penetrated, if not determined by, their opposites. The dialectical overcoming of oppositions links Derrida's deconstruction with the dialectical traditions of ancient China and India, Western Gnosticism, and the theosophical Kabbalah, the last of which will be our subject in the next chapter. And despite differences on many critical points, Derrida's deconstruction also has much in common with the psychology of Jung, which we will examine in Chapter 4. While Derrida differs from both Hegel and Jung in his denial of the possibility of a totality (a metaphysical totality in Hegel, and a psychological totality [the self] in Jung), he shares with each of them a broad acceptance and use of the apparatus of *coincidentia oppositorum.*

We will return to Derrida in Chapter 6 when we consider the demise of the signifier-signified distinction in connection with our efforts to think of and experience the world as an integrated whole. There it will become clear that the deconstruction of the distinction between words and things (and then the deconstruction of this deconstruction!) is critical to a contemporary philosophical application of *coincidentia oppositorum.*

C. G. JUNG: THE NON-RATIONAL UNION OF OPPOSITES

Early in the twentieth century, the interest in opposition and antinomy spread from philosophy to psychology. Psychologists developed theories and therapies that implored individuals to embrace those aspects of their psyches that they had hitherto tended to ignore, reject, or otherwise exclude. Freudian psychoanalysis, for example, sought to expand the psychic field to include conscious and unconscious attitudes, affects, and ideas, and hitherto socially unacceptable emotions and impulses. C. G. Jung went so far as to hold that the fully developed or *individuated* self is a blending of opposites. Drawing upon traditions that had themselves been marginalized in the history of Western thought (Gnosticism, alchemy, and the Kabbalah), and embracing Eastern modes of thought (Taoist and Hindu) as well as Western (Christian) mysticism, Jung's vision of humanity was one that united conflicting aspects of the individual and "collective" psyches.

For Jung, the "coincidence of opposites" is the *key principle* of his psychology. Jung moved beyond Sigmund Freud's basic notion that personality develops through psychological conflict to articulate a conception of the whole "self" that unifies the conscious and the unconscious, the personal and the impersonal, and a host of what he termed archetypal oppositions (for example, between anima [female] and animus

[male], shadow and persona, and chaos and order). As Jung himself put it, "The self is made manifest in the opposites and the conflicts between them; it is a *coincidentia oppositorum.*"[210] For Jung, the union of opposites occurs both in history and within the psyche of the individual.[211] However, in contrast to Hegel, Jung held that the "union of opposites on a higher level of consciousness is not a rational thing, nor is it a matter of will; it is a process of psychic development that expresses itself in symbols."[212] Indeed, Jung himself held that Hegel had erred by intellectualizing intuitive (psychological) insights.[213] One might say that Jung endeavored to achieve in the spheres of the symbolic, mythological, and the psychic what Hegel believed he had achieved in the realm of reason: a dialectical integration of oppositions and antinomies leading to the consummate development of psyche, spirit, or "mind."

From a Jungian perspective, mystical and mythological traditions achieve through symbols an integration of oppositions that would lead to contradiction and absurdity on the level of reason and ideas. For Jung, the coincidence of opposites is not a rational truth, as Hegel supposed, but a symbolic and psychological one to be lived rather than merely thought. According to Jung, the mind becomes preoccupied with antinomies precisely because one pole of a psychic or emotional contrary has seized control of the individual and must be balanced by its opposite. Jung held that repressed unconscious ideas, feelings, and attitudes compensate for those that are acceptable to and therefore dominate consciousness,[214] and that these "compensations" form a "shadow" that expresses itself in images, dreams, and symptoms, and serve as a counterweight to the individual's "persona."

We will examine Jung's symbolic, psychological, and anthropological views of *coincidentia oppositorum* in detail in Chapter 4. There and in Chapter 7, I will evaluate his claim that the coincidence of opposites is a non-rational, symbolic process.

HECTOR SABELLI: THE UNIVERSALITY OF OPPOSITION

In a wide-ranging but overlooked work, *Union of Opposites: A Comprehensive Theory of Natural and Human Processes*, Hector Sabelli (1989) argued that "change and evolution result from the interaction between opposites, which are similar and complementary even though they may appear totally different and even antagonistic."[215] Sabelli draws together two-valued logic, binary-code, Hegelian dialectics, Freudian conflict theory, the DNA double helix, bi-sexuality, and wave-particle dualism in quantum theory (along with other concepts) in making his case for "the universality of opposition" and its character as a foundational philosophical category.[216] Sabelli argues that the ancient Greeks understood sexuality as a "paradigmatic example of the universality, similarity, and creative union of opposites."[217] Building on this observation, modern psychologists have held that the complementarity of opposites is a basic psychological principal. Sabelli cites Freud, Jung, and Jean Piaget in support of his view that the "interpenetration of the opposites" is fundamental to both unconscious and conscious thought. While "either/or thinking" is typically valued by logicians, psychologists have found that such thinking often characterizes immature, disordered, and neurotic personalities.[218]

Sabelli suggests that Hegel epitomized "the 19th century infatuation with conflict as the mainspring of change."[219] He argues that the contributions of Marx, Charles Darwin, and Freud rest upon dialectical ideas,[220] noting, for example, that the conflict between desire and prohibition is the dialectical core of the Oedipus complex and the key to Freud's understanding of the development of both the human personality and society. Sabelli further references "opposition as the mainspring of the legal process,"[221] and points out that, according to Rawls, justice can only occur in a society with conflicting demands.[222]

Dialectics is present in science, Sabelli asserts, where there is "a creative union of opposites between knowing and not knowing," where "false hypotheses are a necessary step toward truth," and "to know requires doubt."[223] Much constructive work in mathematics involves a fusion between a theory and its negation, as where a repudiation of certain assumptions of planar geometry combined with an acceptance of others to produce non-Euclidean geometries.[224]

Sabelli references a series of epistemological dichotomies—including "observable versus non-observable," "hypothetical versus real," "theoretical versus practical," "*a priori* versus empirical," and "understanding versus explanation"—and argues that in each instance both poles are necessary to advance knowledge and practical wisdom.[225] An example, stemming from his experience as a practicing psychiatrist, is the dialectic between empathic understanding and explanatory diagnosis that is involved in psychotherapeutic treatment.[226]

Sabelli held what might be termed a "weak version" of the union of opposites doctrine. In his version, "Nothing can be something and its opposite (e.g., true/false) at the same time and in the same respect…but everything becomes its (partial) opposite at some other time or in some other respect." Sabelli wishes to maintain "the logical principle of no contradiction" but add to it a "dialectic principle of contradiction."[227]

While Sabelli advocated a number of guidelines in philosophy, science, and psychiatry that essentially encourage deep reflection on the opposite of what one thinks, believes, and feels, he held that "we need to protect ourselves from empty misinterpretation of the principle of union of opposites." He explains:

> I do not mean to say that every statement we make must somehow be true. Certainly our imagination is perfectly capable of inventing connections where none exist, as widely illustrated in myths and ideologies, and also in science. Popper criticized dialectic materialists because their ambiguous and all-comprehensive view of the union of opposites allowed any data to fit the theory, and nothing refuted it.[228]

Sabelli was also clear that "we need to protect ourselves from immoral interpretations of the principal such as an absolute moral relativism."[229] He writes, "The opposites are united, not in balance, but in asymmetric struggle."[230]

CHAPTER TWO

THE UNION OF OPPOSITES IN MYSTICISM: KABBALAH AND CHASIDISM

THE OPPOSITES IN WORLD MYSTICISM

As we have seen, the archetype of *coincidentia oppositorum* plays an important role in the history of religion. While expressions of the coincidence of opposites are common in Eastern religion—and are especially prominent in Taoism, Hinduism, and Buddhism—the doctrine has also found its way into the spiritual traditions of the West, where it has mainly operated outside the margins of normative religion. Among Christian thinkers, Nicholas of Cusa (discussed in Chapter 1), St. Bonaventure,[1] and Meister Eckhart made *coincidentia oppositorum* a centerpiece of their theologies. Eckhart, for example, spoke of a *coincidentia* between God and man, writing that "the eye through which I see God is the same eye through which God sees me; my eye and God's eye are one eye, one seeing, one knowing, one love."[2]

While the appeal to a coincidence, interpenetration, or union of opposites is common to many mystical traditions, it is not necessarily the case that each of these traditions is rooted in a single form of "mystical experience." However, my interest in mysticism is not in mystical experience *per se*, but with the claim of some mystics (and mystically oriented philosophers) that there *is an underlying unified reality that is divided by thought and language*, and that the mystic quest involves an effort to transcend this division and return to an encounter with the One.

96

OPPOSITION AS A FUNCTION OF THOUGHT AND LANGUAGE

The thesis that language and thought divides a "unified all" is implicit in several mystical traditions. The Taoist notion of *Yinyang* is one example and as we have seen it reflects the interdependencies of phenomena and ideas that are divided by thinking and language. Indeed, the very first verse of the *Tao Te Ching* indicates that it is language that produces multiplicity:

> The way that can be spoken of
> Is not the constant way;
> The name that can be named
> Is not the constant name.
> The nameless was the beginning of heaven and earth;
> The named was the mother of the myriad creatures.[3]

Further on in the text we learn:

> The way is forever nameless…. Only when it is cut are their names.[4]

The notion that intellect and language produces a "cut" in an otherwise unified totality is also present in Indian thought, where we learn that there is an illusory divide between cosmos and the self, between the infinite and the finite, and between the whole and its parts that is produced by mind and language. In the *Brihadaranyaka Upanishad* we read, "It is name and form that introduce differentiation."[5] In the *Chandogya Upanishad* a master tells his pupil that not only the Vedic scriptures, but also "the funeral rites of the dead, arithmetic, divination, chronometry, logic, politics…archery, astronomy, the art of dealing with snakes, and the fine arts [are all] merely a name…. Everything that you have been studying is no more than a name."[6] Further, "Were it indeed not for speech, there would be no knowledge of right and wrong, truth and falsehood, good and evil, pleasant and unpleasant: for it is speech that makes all this known."[7]

Commenting upon the *Bhagavad-Gita*, Heinrich Zimmer writes:

> The jejune disjunction of the world into matter and
> spirit derives from an abstraction of the intellect and
> should not be projected back upon reality; for it is
> of the nature of the mind to establish differences,
> to make definitions and discriminate. To declare,
> "there are distinctions," is only to state that there is
> an apprehending intellect at work. Perceived pairs
> of opposites reflect the nature not of things but of
> the perceiving mind...the one thing that is the first,
> last, and only reality (this is the basic Brāhman the-
> sis) comprises all the pairs of opposites....[8]

The purpose of the spiritual quest, according to Hinduism, is to
overcome the veil of Maya that conditions the illusion of duality, transcend the distinction between cosmos and self, and return to the unified
One in Brahman.

THE OPPOSITES IN JEWISH MYSTICISM

The sundering of a cosmic unity through language, is explicitly
present in certain strands of Jewish mysticism, particularly in Chabad
Hasidism, whose founder, Schneur Zalman of Lyadi, held that an infinite, singular Absolute is concealed, contracted, and divided through
a *linguistic* process that produces finitude and difference. According to
Schneur Zalman, the light of the Infinite (or *Ein-sof*) is fragmented into
a multitude of finite entities through a concealment (one that is paradoxically also a revelation!) resulting from the language that announces
divine creation in the first chapter of *Genesis*. In short, according to
Schneur Zalman, it is language that produces distinction and difference.
We will see that the writings of Schneur Zalman and his followers clearly anticipate one of the major theses of this work: that a single "world"
or "reality" has been sundered by representation, and that this reality
can be "returned to" via a comprehension of the interdependence of the
divergent perspectives that can be taken upon it.

In this chapter, I will focus upon the doctrine of *coincidentia oppositorum* as it appears in Jewish mysticism—that is, in the symbols of the theosophical Kabbalah and its singular significance for the theology of Chabad (or Lubavitch) Chasidism. My choice of Kabbalah and Chasidism as my paradigm for the mystical understanding of the coincidence of opposites is partly one of expediency, as it is the one tradition that I have a reasonable familiarity with and about which I have written extensively.[9] I am, however, of the view that a deep exploration of other mystical traditions, including those of Hinduism, Buddhism, Christianity, and Islam, would be equally valuable in achieving insight into a mystical understanding of the opposites.

It is the achievement of Elior[10] and other modern scholars of Jewish mysticism to have brought the philosophical use of the *coincidentia* doctrine by the Chabad Chasidim to our attention. In the course of my discussion, I hope to show that Kabbalistic and Chabad formulations provide insights into the relevance of *coincidentia oppositorum* to contemporary philosophical, psychological, and (especially) theological concerns. I will return to the Kabbalistic understanding of the opposites in Chapter 6, where I will consider several of the Kabbalist's symbols in the context of a more comprehensive understanding of "unity in difference" and dialectical thought.

While "Kabbalah" is sometimes defined as the "mystical" tradition in Judaism, this can be doubly misleading: Kabbalah is one of several forms of Jewish mysticism (others include Merkaveh mysticism and the Chasidai Askenaz[11]), and the Kabbalah itself is not fully mystical. While the so-called "ecstatic" Kabbalah stressed mystical experience, other Kabbalistic schools placed a greater emphasis upon myth, magic, and theosophy, the latter consisting of a mythical and, in some respects, conceptual account of the inner workings of the godhead and its relationship to the world and humanity. The "theosophical Kabbalah" takes central stage in the *Zohar*, the most "sacred" and widely known Kabbalistic work. Kabbalistic theosophy reached its fullest development in the sixteenth-century thought of Isaac Luria and his followers. It is in the theosophical Kabbalah that we find both direct and indirect reference to the coincidence of opposites.

THE EARLY KABBALAH: THE SYNTHESIS OF EVERYTHING AND ITS OPPOSITE

A concern with opposition is present in the earliest Jewish mystical writings. For example, in *Sefer Yetzirah*, an important early (third- to sixth-century) work that scholars regard as "proto-Kabbalistic," we encounter the *Sefirot*, the ten archetypal values which, according to later Kabbalistic theosophy, are the elements through which divinity emanates the world. According to *Sefer Yetzirah*, the *Sefirot* are comprised of five pairs of opposites: "A depth of beginning, a depth of end. A depth of good, a depth of evil. A depth of above, a depth of below. A depth of east, a depth of west. A depth of north, a depth of south."[12] Regarding the *Sefirot*, *Sefer Yetzirah* recites, "Their end is imbedded in their beginning and their beginning in their end."[13]

The Catalan Kabbalist Azriel of Gerona (c. 1160–1238) was perhaps the first Jewish mystic to clearly articulate the doctrine of *coincidentia oppositorum* in conceptual terms. Azriel understood *Ein Sof* (the Infinite) in a manner that accords with the Jewish conception of the one God. Accorduing to Azriel, God "is absolutely undifferentiated in a complete and changeless unity…. He is the essence of all that is concealed and revealed."[14] However, Azriel holds that *Ein-sof* unifies within itself being and nothingness, "for the Being is in the Naught after the manner of the Naught, and the Naught is in the Being after the manner [according to the modality] of the Being." In short, "the Naught is the Being and Being is the Naught."[15] Azriel went so far as to hold that *Ein-sof* is "the principle in which everything hidden and visible meet, and as such it is the common root of *both* faith and unbelief."[16] This is an interesting and, I believe, important claim to which I will return in Chapter 6.

According to Azriel, the *Sefirot* are characterized by a union of opposites, one that provides the energy for the creation and activity of the cosmos.

> The nature of *sefirah* is the synthesis of every thing and its opposite. For if they did not possess the power of synthesis, there would be no energy in anything. For that which is light is not dark and that which is darkness is not-light. [17]

For Azriel, the synthesis of opposites is also reflected in the human psyche: "We should liken their (the *Sefirot's*) nature to the will of the soul, for it is the synthesis of all the desires and thoughts stemming from it. Even though they may be multifarious, their source is one, either in thesis or antithesis."[18]

Azriel was not unique among the early Kabbalists in his appeal to the principle of *coincidentia oppositorum*. In the anonymous Kabbalistic text, *Source of Wisdom*, we read that the name of God consists of thirteen pairs of opposites, which are derived from the thirteen traits of God described in the Book of Chronicles. In addition, the *Avir Kadmon*, the "Primordial Ether," is described in this work as the medium through which these oppositions are formed and eventually united.[19]

THE LURIANIC KABBALAH: A SYSTEM RIFE WITH PARADOX

In the Kabbalah, the term *achdut hashvaah* is used to indicate that *Ein-sof* is a "unity of opposites,"[20] one which unites within itself all aspects of the universe, even those that oppose or contradict one another.[21] This idea is prominent in the Lurianic Kabbalah which, beginning in the sixteenth century, came to be the dominant force in Jewish mysticism. Isaac Luria (1534–72) was a mystical visionary who produced a highly complex theosophical system which elaborated upon symbols and ideas of the earlier Kabbalah, in particular those in *The Zohar*, the *locus classicus* of Kabbalistic thought. Luria spent the last two years of his brief life in the Kabbalistic community of Safed on the shores of Lake Tiberias (the Sea of Galilee) in what is now in the northeastern region of modern day Israel. Luria wrote very little, but his disciples, notably Chayyim Vital (1542–1620), recorded Luria's discourses in great detail. The Lurianic system became the foundation for later Kabbalistic thoughts, as well as for the Chasidic movement in the eighteenth century.

The Kabbalists of Safed held the view, common in mysticism but uncommon in normative Judaism, that God is present within and continually sustains every part of the universe. Moses Cordovero (1522–70), who was the leading Safedian Kabbalist prior to Luria's arrival, wrote, "He is found in all things, and all things are found in Him, and He is in everything and beyond everything, and there is nothing beside Him."[22] Luria's chief expositor Chayyim Vital writes:

> Know that before the emanation of the emanated and the creation of all that was created, the simple Upper Light filled all of reality...but everything was one simple light, equal in one *hashvaah*, which is called the Light of the Infinite.[23]

Again, the term *hashvaah*, which can be translated as "equalization," implies a union of opposing principles. While Vital's words are here suggestive of a union of opposites in the godhead only *prior* to creation, when we examine the major Lurianic symbols we find that this union is applicable to God, humanity, and the entirety of creation. Each of these symbols reconciles one or more polar opposition, and each involves a coincidence of opposites between seemingly contradictory ideas.

Luria elaborated upon earlier Kabbalistic symbols in forming a grand, highly intricate view of the relationship between God, humanity, and the world. The major symbols or ideas in this worldview are:

(1) *Ein-sof* (the Infinite God),

(2) *Tzimtzum* (the concealment or contraction of *Ein-sof* that produces a finite world),

(3) *Sefirot* (the ten value archetypes that serve as the elements of creation),

(4) *Adam Kadmon* (the Primordial Human, who both embodies and emanates the value archetypes),

(5) *Shevirat ha-Kelim* (the "Breaking of the Vessels," the displacement and shattering of the *Sefirot*),

(6) *Netzotzim* (divine "sparks" that become trapped in the shards of the shattered *Sefirotic* vessels),

(7) *Kellipot* (the "husks" which hide and encumber the sparks, thereby producing a predominantly evil world),

(8) *Tikkun ha-Olam* (the "Restoration of the World," the liberation of the sparks by humanity, resulting in the redemption of the world and the completion of God), and

(9) *Partzufim* (the personalities or visages of the Primordial Human through which the world is restored and redeemed).

I will now elaborate briefly upon the relationship between these notions.

Luria taught that the light of the Infinite God, which originally filled the entire cosmos, contracts and conceals itself in order to produce the diverse values, ideas, and entities of the finite world. This initial creative act, known as the *Tzimtzum*, results in the differentiation of the divine light into a series of ten archetypes, the *Sefirot*, whose names (including Desire, Wisdom, Understanding, Kindness, Beauty, and Judgment) reflect both the traits (*middot*) of God and essential human values. The *Sefirot*, initially created to be the molecular components of the finite world, are emanated through the orifices of, and are represented by, the Primordial Human (*Adam Kadmon*), who serves as the template for both humanity and the entire cosmos.

Luria understood the *Sefirot* as "vessels" for containing the divine light that was to be emanated into them subsequent to the initial *Tzimtzum* or contraction. However, these vessels were not strong enough to withstand the impact of this light; the three highest vessels were displaced and the lower seven were shattered in a cosmic cataclysm known as the "Breaking of the Vessels" (*Shevirat ha-Kelim*). As a result of this rupture, sparks of light (*Netzozim*) that were originally meant to be contained by the vessels attached themselves to, and were encapsulated by, the shards of the broken vessels. These shards, which enclose and obscure the divine light, fell through the metaphysical void and became the "husks" (*Kellipot*) which are the actual constituents of the empirical world. The divinely appointed task of humanity is to encounter these husks and, through the performance of spiritual and ethical acts codified as the 613 divine commandments, extract (*Birur*) and liberate the sparks in order to unify the *Sefirot* into a series of divine masculine and feminine personas or visages, the *Partzufim*. This process, known as *Tikkun Ha-Olam* (the restoration and emendation of the world) serves to reunite the opposites. This reunification is symbolized in the union between the masculine and feminine *Partzufim*, and is said to perfect not only humanity and the world but also the Infinite God.

As I will discuss in more detail below, the Lurianic system is rife with paradox and the merging of opposites. For example, Luria held that (1) the divine principle of the cosmos is both *Ein-sof* (without end) and *Ayin* (absolute nothingness), (2) creation is both a *hitpashut* (emanation) and a *Tzimtzum* (contraction and concealment), (3) *Ein-sof* (the Infinite Absolute) is both the creator of the world and is itself created and completed through *Tikkun ha-Olam* (the spiritual, ethical, and "world restoring" acts of humanity), and (4) the *Sefirot* are both the original elements of the cosmos and are only themselves realized when the cosmos is displaced, shattered (*Shevirat ha-Kelim*), and reconstructed by humanity (*Tikkun*).

TZIMTZUM: CREATION AS CONCEALMENT AND CONTRACTION

A closer examination of two key elements in the Lurianic system, *Tzimtzum* (concealment/contraction) and *Shevirat ha-kelim* (the Breaking of the Vessels), provides further insight into the Lurianic conception of the coincidence of opposites.

The symbol of *Tzimtzum*—the withdrawal, concealment, and contraction of the infinite God that gives rise to the finite world—involves a coincidence of opposites between creation and contraction, emanation and withdrawal, revelation and concealment, and even being and nothingness. According to Luria, the divine emanation of the finite world paradoxically involves the contraction and concealment of the one infinite divine substance. We can gain clarity regarding this process through an analogy to a photographic slide, which selectively filters and thus conceals portions of the projector's pure white light in order to reveal the details of a world captured on film. Similarly, *Ein-sof* is said to produce and reveal the structural details of the finite world through selectively concealing its own infinite and undifferentiated luminescence. By concealing its infinite unity, *Ein-sof* gives rise to a finite and highly differentiated world. Further, the concealment and contraction of the *Or Ein-sof*, the light of the Infinite God, paradoxically transforms this light—which because of its lack of differentiation is both "all" and "nothing" (*Ayin*)—into something that from at least one perspective is now actual and real. Thus, in the symbol of *Tzimtzum*, we encounter a *coincidentia oppositorum* between the opposites of addition and subtraction, creation and negation, concealment and revelation, and being and nothingness. In order to fully grasp the *idea* behind the *Tzimtzum*, one must think two thoughts simultaneously or in succession: one thought about divine nothingness, limitation, and concealment; and a second thought about divine nothingness, limitation, and concealment as the source of being, creation, and revelation.

Before proceeding, I would like to elaborate on an interpretation of the doctrine of *Tzimtzum* that became current in the eighteenth century among the followers of Schneur Zalman. We will further examine Schneur Zalman's views on the opposites later in this chapter, but here I would like to point out that for him the *Tzimtzum*—the very process through which the infinite plenum contracts and splinters itself into a multitude of finite entities—occurs *via language*.

According to Schneur Zalman, in the act of *Tzimtzum*, God contracts his divine energy into the twenty-two letters of the Hebrew alphabet. These combine to form the so-called "ten utterances of creation,"[24] the biblical phrases by which the world is said to have been created through divine speech (for example, "And God *said* 'Let there be light' and there was light," Genesis 1:3). According to Schneur Zalman, each of the world's entities is created through "combinations of combinations [of letters], by substitutions and transpositions of the letters themselves and their numerical values and equivalents."[25] In his view, the fragmentation of the world into genera, species, and individual entities is the result of a linguistic process, beginning with "the ten utterances." The recombination of words and letters of these utterances, and their "numerical equivalents as revealed through the study of Gematria,"[26] produces the *names* of all things and, by extension, their very existence.

We will later see that the Chabad Hasidim had a very sophisticated, dialectical conception of the relationship between the infinite, all-embracing God and the finite world. Here, we should note that Schneur Zalman (at least initially) expresses a view in which "God is all" and through language "constricts" and divides himself into the entities of the finite world.

SHEVIRAH: CREATION AS DESTRUCTION

There is a second coincidence of opposites in the Lurianic Kabbalah, one between *creation and destruction*, symbolized in the *Shevirat ha-Kelim* (the "Breaking of the Vessels"). According to Luria, *Ein-sof* is only fully actualized and completed with the shattering of the ten value archetypes (the *Sefirot*), and the subsequent redemptive actions of humankind (*Tikkun ha-Olam*). While on the one hand *Ein-sof* is the foundation and "creator"[27] of the cosmos, it only achieves its full essence through humanity's "emendation," "restoration," and "repair" (*Tikkun*) of the rupture in a broken world. According to Luria, humanity is as essential to God's development as God is essential to humankind's; for it is only human beings, in their efforts to repair and perfect a damaged and displaced world, who can actualize the values that constitute the divine essence. In performing the *mitzvoth*, the spiritual, ethical, creative, and intellectual acts enjoined by the Torah, humanity assures that the values and traits which exist only in *potentia* within God become fully actualized in the finite world, the only world where they are meaningful. As the contemporary Kabbalist and sage Rabbi Adin Steinsaltz has put it, "We are living in the worst of all possible worlds in which there is still hope."[28] Paradoxically, for Steinsaltz it is only in an imperfect world on the brink of total disaster that the divine values (the *Sefirot*) can be fully actualized. The possibility of destruction is essential to the very act and meaning of creation. Steinsaltz explains:

> If I want to test a new car, the way that I test it is not on the smoothest of roads, under the best conditions. To have a real road test to prove that a car really works, I have to put it under…*the worst conditions in which there is yet hope*. I cannot test it by driving it off a cliff, but I can test it on the roughest terrain where I must come to the edge of a cliff and have to stop. How is a new plane tested? They put it under nearly impossible conditions, which the plane must withstand. Otherwise the whole experiment doesn't prove anything. The same with Creation. Creation would have been pointless unless it was a Creation under precisely these difficult circumstances. So I am saying, theologically speaking, that the worst possible world in which there is yet hope is the only world in which Creation makes sense.[29]

According to the Lurianists, it is because humankind actualizes the traits and values that are mere abstract potentialities in *Ein-sof* that the *Zohar* can assert "he who 'keeps' the precepts of the Law and 'walks' in God's ways…'makes' Him who is above."[30] The symbols of *Ein-sof*, *Shevirah* (rupture), and *Tikkun* (repair) announce a *coincidentia oppositorum* between the polar opposite notions that God is the creator and foundation of humankind, and humankind is the creator and foundation of God.

The symbol and concept of *Shevirat ha-Kelim*, the "Breaking of the Vessels," is applicable in all times and places, to all things and all ideas, even to the Lurianic Kabbalah itself. It is part of *Ein-sof's* infinite nature that everything is subject to infinite transformation and emendation—that all things (including, as we have seen, the basic manifestations of *Ein-sof* itself) are subject to displacement, destruction, and reconstruction, and all ideas are subject to critique and revision. For this reason, the Lurianic Kabbalah, which purports to be a system of symbols and ideas that provides a full account of the cosmos and humanity's place within it, is a *system under erasure*, a *system that is not a system*, a system that is itself unstable and subject by its very nature to its own sundering and emendation.[31] We might say that it is only by paradoxically maintaining deconstruction and revision at its very core that the Kabbalah emerges as a viable account of humanity in the world. Its truth is fully interdependent with its abrogation.

THE OPPOSITES IN OTHER LURIANIC SYMBOLS

Several other Lurianic symbols overcome distinctions between what are generally thought to be opposing terms and ideas. With the symbol of the ten *Sefirot*, the Kabbalists articulate an interdependence between unity of the Absolute and the multiplicity of both God and the world. In the symbol of *Adam Kadmon* (the Primordial Man, who becomes the divine agent of creation), we have another example of a coincidence of opposites between God and man. In the symbol of the *Kellipot* (the evil husks that envelop the fallen sparks of divine light after the Breaking of the Vessels), there is an explicit *coincidentia* between good and evil, for it is only the capture of divine light by the forces of evil that creates the opportunity for *actual* good.[32]

Each of the Kabbalistic symbols can be understood as a higher order synthesis of an opposition, antinomy, or contradiction that inevitably arises when one thinks deeply about God, humanity, and the world, and each resolves a tension between apparently contradictory philosophical ideas. Further, the whole Lurianic conception of *Ein-sof* is that of a dialectically evolving deity who is understood as logically passing through and embodying a variety of phases and aspects, each of which opposes but also embodies an earlier phase in the overall scheme. As such, the Kabbalistic deity is both nothing (*Ayin*) and everything (*Ein-sof*), perfectly simple and infinitely complex, hidden (*Tzimtzum*) and revealed (*Sefirot*), reality and illusion, broken (*Shevirat ha-Kelim*) and restored (*Tikkun ha-Olam*), creator of humanity and created by humanity, etc. As *Ein-Sof* evolves, it is revealed to be both the totality of its own evolving dialectic and each of the points along the way. For the Kabbalists, this means that *Ein-Sof* must be constantly redefined, as by its very nature it is in a continual process of self-creation that involves a unification of opposing principles, values and ideas.

CHABAD CHASIDISM: THE UNIFICATION OF THE OPPOSITES AND THE MEANING OF THE WORLD

As W. T. Stace has pointed out, various forms of mysticism involve a paradox in which the "Absolute," "universal self," or "truth" of the world is understood as both vacuum and plenum, as both absolutely nothing and the totality of all things.[33] In addition, several other related paradoxes are characteristic of mystical thought, including the simultaneous reality and unreality of space, time, and the self. Such paradoxes are present in the mysticisms of Hinduism, Buddhism, Christianity, and Islam, as well as in the Kabbalah, where, for example, the infinite godhead is regarded simultaneously as both nothingness (*Ayin*) and the infinite (*Ein-sof*). However, these mystical paradoxes, which are a pervasive if not dominant theme in the Kabbalah, achieve what is perhaps their most sophisticated Jewish theological expression in the philosophy of the Chabad Chasidim, where they become the governing principles for both God and the world.

According to the philosophy of the Chabad or Lubavitcher Chasidism, all things infinite and finite can be characterized as a union or coincidence of opposites. Indeed, for Chabad the very goal and purpose of the world is the creation and revelation of the opposites, precisely so that they can be experienced, overcome, and unified. According to Aaron Ha-Lévi Horowitz of Staroselye (1766–1828), a pupil of Schneur Zalmn of Lyadi, the first Lubavitcher rebbe, "The revelation of anything is actually through its opposite."[34] For Ha-Lévi, "All created things in the world are hidden within His essence, be He blessed, in one potential, in *coincidentia oppositorum*...."[35]

Schneur Zalman's son, Rabbi Dov Baer (1773–1827) wrote that "within everything is its opposite and also it is truly revealed as its opposite."[36] According to Dov Baer, the union of opposites in the finite world results in the *shelemut* or completeness of God on high. He writes, "For the principal point of divine completeness is that...in every thing is its opposite, and...that all its power truly comes from the opposing power."[37] For both Ha-Lévi and Dov Baer, it is ultimately within the godhead that all earthly opposites are unified in a single subject. As Ha-Lévi puts it, "He is the perfection of all, for the essence of perfection is that even those opposites which are opposed to one another be made one."[38]

It is worth noting that Chabad philosophy developed contemporaneously with German Idealism. While I am aware of no evidence that the Chasidim were aware of the tenets of German philosophy, it is noteworthy that Chabad thought bears a striking resemblance to the philosophies of Schelling and Hegel. To see this resemblance, one need only compare the dicta of Ha-Lévi and Dov Baer with Hegel's claim that "every actual thing involves a coexistence of opposed elements. Consequently, to know, or, in other words, to comprehend an object is equivalent to being conscious of it as a concrete unity of opposed determinations."[39]

In what follows, I will review the principle of *coincidentia oppositorum* as it appears in three generations of Chabad thinkers.

SCHNEUR ZALMAN OF LYADI: THE INTERDEPENDENCE OF DIVINE AND HUMAN POINTS OF VIEW

According to Schneur Zalman, the *coincidentia oppositorum* that characterizes God, humanity, and the world can be approximately understood by the simultaneous adoption of two points of view:

> (Looking) upwards from below, as it appears to eyes of flesh, the tangible world seems to be *Yesh* (being) and a thing, while spirituality, which is above, is an aspect of *Ayin* (nothingness). (But looking) downwards from above, the world is an aspect of *Ayin*, and everything which is linked downwards and descends lower and lower is more and more *Ayin* and is considered as naught truly as nothing and null.[40]

This startling pronouncement appears in Schneur Zalman's discourse on the *Amidah*, the "Eighteen Benedictions," which is recited by religious Jews during each of the three daily prayer services.[41] In this discourse, Schneur Zalman, affectionately known by his followers as the "Alter Rebbe" (Yiddish for "the Old Rebbe"), discusses *part* of a familiar quotation from *Pirke Avot*, *The Ethics of the Fathers*, an ethical treatise from the period of the *Mishnah*. The portion Schneur Zalman quotes is, "One moment of repentance and good deeds in this world is equal to all eternity in the world to come." However, the full quotation from *Pirke Avot* embodies the same rhetoric of the "truth of opposing perspectives" that the Alter Rebbe will utilize in his dictum regarding the dual earthly and heavenly perspectives that can be taken on being (*Yesh*) and nothingness (*Ayin*). The full quote from *Pirke Avot* is as follows:

> Rabbi Yaakov also used to say, "Better one hour in repentance and good deeds in this world than all the life in the World to Come. And better one hour of tranquility of spirit in the World to Come than all the life of this world."[42]

One senses that Schneur Zalman may well have been inspired to adopt a dual perspective in his dictum regarding being and nothingness (*Yesh* and *Ayin*) by this passage from *Pirke Avot*, which is itself a remarkable early Jewish example of the complementarity of opposing ideas. However, by quoting only the first half of this passage in *Pirke Avot* 4:22, the Alter Rebbe seeks to emphasize the importance of this world—as he puts it, the perspective of "(looking) upwards from below" in which our world seems to be "*Yesh* and a thing." So, despite the divine perspective, from which our world is truly empty and naught, "this world," known in the Kabbalah as *Assiyah* (the world of "action"), has a place within the divine plan. In short, there is a value and reality to the human point of view, the "looking upwards from below." Otherwise, there would be no point to the divine commandments (*mitzvoth*), which are obviously performed in a material realm, the very realm that is "nothing" from the perspective of "looking down from below." Indeed, the rebbe goes so far as to say that the Torah's positive *mitzvoth* correspond both to the 248 *giddim* (sinews) in the human body and to the 248 *evarim di malkha*, the "organs of the King." In saying this Schneur Zalman suggests that the *performance* of divine commandments has a psotivie impact not only on humanity but also upon God himself!

On the other hand, Schneur Zalman holds that it is *also* the case that the material realm is and should be considered as "nothing." This is because the performance of the *mitzvoth* has value not because of their material effects *per se*, but because they either raise matter to the realm of spirit or draw down aspects of spirit into the material world. Indeed, for Chabad, the value of this world is realized only when it is truly *rendered as naught* in favor of the spiritual. Yet, on the other hand, the value of the spiritual world is only insofar as divine traits and values are realized in a material realm ("Better one hour in repentance and good deeds in this world than all the life in the world to come").

Chabad understands the material world in these two opposing ways: as both an illusion resulting from a concealment of the divine essence and as the one true existence set over and against an illusory spiritual realm. In this way, Chabad brings together and, in effect, simultaneously think two ideas that are separated even in other forms of mystical thought. For example, as Heinrich Zimmer points out, in Indian thought, knowledge of the self involves *either* "a systematic disparagement of the whole world as illusion" (as in the Vedanta) or "an equally thoroughgoing realization of the sheer materiality of it all" (as in Sankhya).[43] However, according to Chabad, it is concurrently the case that God is real and lends a measure of his reality to an inherently illusory world, and that the world (in particular humankind) is real and lends its reality to an otherwise empty if not illusory God.[44] While the divine perspective upon the world ("looking downwards from above") is generally spoken of by Chabad as the "inner truth," it is clear that in their view this truth is itself fully dependent upon the human perspective ("looking upwards from below"), which sees humanity as actualizing the reality of an otherwise empty if not illusory God. In suggesting this, the Chabad philosophers followed the early Chasidic leader, the Maggid of Mezrich (1704–1772), who maintained that, although God is the origin and foundation of all ideas, the activation and significance of divine thought depends upon it appearing in the minds of men. According to the Maggid, while God is the source of thought, *actual thinking* can only occur within the human mind.[45] (Two centuries after the Maggid of Mezrich made this claim, Jung, would say that that the Maggid anticipated his entire psychology.[46] Chabad philosophy can be understood as an explication of the *Zohar's* dictum: "Just as the Supernal Wisdom is a starting point of the whole, so is the lower world also a manifestation of Wisdom, and a starting point of the whole."[47] According to Chabad, the most adequate conception of the world and God involves each of the perspectives we have just outlined, one beginning with God and the other beginning with humanity. Indeed, *Ein-sof* is a *coincidentia oppositorum* that encompasses each of these two perspectives at once. It is only by *thinking in both directions simultaneously* that one can achieve wisdom and grasp the mystical insight that divinity is fully present in all things. A God who simply creates the world and humankind (direction one) is less perfect and complete than a God who creates humanity and is created by it (directions one and two). It is only through bi-directional thinking that one can hope to capture what the Kabbalists had referred to as "the Infinite" (*Ein-sof*). In the words of Rachel Elior:

> Hasidic thought is strained to the ultimate stage in a dialectical way; just as there is no separate reality and no discriminative essence in the world without God, so also God has no revealed and discriminate existence without the world, that is, just as one cannot speak of the existence of the world without God, so too one cannot speak of the existence of God without the world.[48]

The notion of "bi-linearity" is, according to Schneur Zalman, applicable not only in the realm of thought but also in the realm of action, specifically in the arena of what the Alter Rebbe refers to as "divine service." There is thus a practical, spiritual, and ethical dimension to the "coincidence of opposites" expressed in Chabad thought. Schneur Zalman implores his followers both to nullify (*bittul*) the self and matter in favor of the Godhead *and* to bring about the infusion of the divine will into the material world through religious worship and the performance of divine *mitzvoth* (commandments). According to Schneur Zalman:

> There are two aspects in the service of the Lord. One seeks to leave its sheath of bodily material. The second is the...aspect of the drawing down of the divinity from above precisely in the various vessels in Torah and the *commandments*.[49]

This declaration comes in the context of the rebbe's discourse on *Parsha Vayishlach*, the passage in the book of Genesis where Jacob wrestles with an emissary of God and as a result of his struggle is renamed "Israel." The rebbe reminds us that in the Kabbalah Jacob represents the *Sefirah* (or archetype) *Tiferet* (Beauty, Compassion), the main function of which is to harmonize the forces of *Chesed* (Kindness, represented by Abraham), and *Gevurah* (Strength, Judgment, represented by Isaac). Schneur Zalman tells us that in much the same way as two ordinary colors are mixed together to make something new and beautiful, Jacob brings together opposing principles of creation in beautiful harmony.

The Alter Rebbe utilizes standard Kabbalistic terminology to inform us that the harmonizing power of *Tiferet* also blends the "outer" light or aspect (*or makif*) of the original chaos (*Tohu*) that existed prior to the world's creation with the "inner" light or aspect (*or pnimi*) that represents the world's restored and restructured destiny (*Tikkun*). Schneur Zalman notes that there is a correspondence between these two opposing metaphysical states and the two levels of divine service that are afforded to mankind. On the one hand, *Tohu* or chaos corresponds to a level of service (*Rotzeh*, "running") in which the adherent experiences such a "great love" (*ahavah rabbah*) and becomes so enraptured with God that his heart is unable to contain his devotion. He seeks to break out of his corporeal shell, like a flame trying to escape the wick of a burning candle. On the other hand, *Tikkun* corresponds to a more "settled" level of service (*shuv*, "sitting") in which the adherent remains firmly established in the corporeal realm, and through the performance of *mitzvoth* seeks to draw divine light down into the world, which comes to serve as a "vessel" (*keli*) for godliness. The Alter Rebbe recalls the Talmudic tale of "Pardes," in which four sages enter the mystical garden but only Rabbi Akiva returns alive and unscathed. The rebbe tells us that this was because Akiva, like Jacob, was able to harmonize these opposing modes of divine service. Unlike Ben Azzai whose service to God was completely other-wordly (*rotzeh*), and who is said to have beheld the mysteries and died, Akiva entered the garden with both *rotzeh* and *shuv* (running and sitting, chaos and order) and returned with his life.[50] We are told further that by harmonizing these aspects of divine service, Rabbi Akiva was able to bring together the feminine waters (*mayim nukvim*) and masculine waters (*mayim dukhrin*) that must be harmonized if the world is to be perfected. (Here we should note that the bringing together of the masculine and the feminine, and the fusion of chaos with order, as prerequisites for entering and surviving the mystical garden, are also aspects of Chabad thought that clearly anticipate Jung's understanding of psychological individuation.)

Later in the same work, Schneur Zalman tells us, "Just as one annihilates oneself from *Yesh* (Existence) to *Ayin* (Nothingness), so too it is drawn down from above from *Ayin* to *Yesh*, so that the light of the infinite may emanate truly below as it does above."[51] Again, there is a coincidence of opposites on the level of spiritual and moral action. One must annihilate one's finite separate existence in favor of the infinite God, and in the process one is paradoxically able to draw down the divine essence into the vessels of the finite world. For Chabad, there is thus an "upper unification" (*Yichud ha-elyon*) in which the world and self are annihilated in favor of their re-inclusion within the godhead, and a "lower unification" (*Yichud ha-tachton*), in which there is an influx of divinity into the world. Further, each of these "unifications" is fully dependent upon the other. It is thus through a doctrine of the coincidence of opposites that Chabad is able to combine the opposing principles of mystical quietism and an active concern with the material world.[52]

Incidentally, I believe that it is through their doctrine of *achdut hashvaah*, the coincidence of the dual aspects of infinite and finite existence, that the Chabad Chasidim are able to avoid the pantheistic implications that might otherwise attach to the view that there is nothing outside of God. Although Schneur Zalman and others in the Chabad tradition make such acosmic declarations as, "Everything is as absolutely nothing and naught in relation to His (God's) being and essence,"[53] "For in truth there is no place devoid of Him...and there is nothing truly beside Him,[54] and "Although the worlds seem like an entity to us, that is an utter lie,"[55] such pronouncements are only from one of two equally valid points of view, the *supernal* one. In Chabad, the traditional Jewish distinction between God and creation is not discarded but is dynamically transformed into the two "starting points" or "points of view" which, though dialectically interdependent, must at the same time remain distinct in order to fulfill the purpose of both God and the universe. Chabad is typically Jewish in its view that God's presence and glory fills the whole world but that humanity must be distinguished from God and granted a measure of freedom, in order that it may return to Him through worship and *mitzvoth*. Metaphysically speaking, Chabad again bids us to think two opposite thoughts simultaneously: (1) God is all and there is nothing beside Him, and (2) God and humanity are separate and distinct, and humanity is implored to *return* to (in effect, constitute God) through divine worship and the performance of the commandments.

DOV BAER OF LUBAVITCH: THE COINCIDENCE OF JOY AND SADNESS

Rabbi Dov Baer, the second Lubavitcher rebbe and the son of Rabbi Schneur Zalman, elaborated upon the tradition of *coincidentia oppositorum* within *Chabad* Chasidism. As we saw earlier, Dov Baer held that all things derive their being, nature, and power from their opposites.[56] Dov Baer sets his discussion of the coincidence of opposites in the very human, psychological context of a blending of the emotions of sadness and joy.[57] His method involves a complex juxtaposition of multiple religious texts and he begins by making brief reference to a passage in his father's *Tanya*, which itself references a passage from the *Zohar*: "Weeping is lodged on one side of my heart, and joy is lodged on the other."[58] In the *Zohar*, this statement comes in the context of a discussion about the destruction of the first temple in Jerusalem (described in 2 Kings 24:13). Toward the end of the discussion, the *Zohar* quotes a verse from the prophet Jeremiah (25:30): "He shall roar mightily from his house." The full verse is as follows:

> And you shall prophesy upon them all these words, and you shall tell them, The Lord roars upon high and gives voice from His holy abode; He shall roar mightily from His house; He will cheer as do they

that tread on grapes, against all the inhabitants of
the earth.

The *Zohar* refers to the fact that on the eve of the first Temple's
destruction, the prophet Jeremiah tries to persuade the Jewish people to
change their ways, as he prophesizes about God's wrath and Babylon's
imminent dominance. The *Zohar* recites that Rabbi Shimon (traditionally held to be the *Zohar's* author) and his son, Rabbi Elazar, have been
studying the relevant verse from the book of Jeremiah, and by extension,
the significance of the destruction of the first Temple and the consequent
Babylonian exile. It is here that the *Zohar* says, "Rabbi Shimon was
weeping and Rabbi Elazar was weeping. Rabbi Elazar said, 'Weeping is
lodged in one side of my heart and joy is in the other side of my heart as
I hear words that I haven't heard until now. How great is my portion.'"[59]
We can surmise that Rabbi Elazar, after much intellectual labor, finally
comes to understand the significance of the destruction of the Temple,
yet as he experiences the great *joy* of understanding, he also, and *as a
result of this understanding*, comes to fully comprehend the *pain* of the
Temple's destruction. Conversely, at the same time that he comes to
comprehend the pain of the destruction, by virtue of his understanding,
he experiences a great intellectual joy. It is for this reason, Dov Baer
suggests, that a given emotion or idea only comes to be realized through
its opposing power. For Dov Baer, this particular example illustrates
and provides us with insight into the more general case. On the view of
the Mittler Rebbe, the level of joy (*tinug*) that one experiences will determine one's level of sadness and vice versa. To take another example
from the rebbe himself, it is only when one becomes fully despondent
regarding the corporeality and the confines of the self that one intuits the
greater joys of godliness.

RABBI YOSEF YITZHAK SCHNEERSON: THE OPPOSITES AS A FUNCTION OF DIVINE SPEECH

More recently, Rabbi Yosef Yitzhak Schneerson, the sixth Lubavitcher rebbe, writes of the complete interdependence of opposites such as kindness (*Chesed*) and severe judgment (*Gevurah*), Sabbath and weekday, joy and suffering, and day and night. In his Shavuot Discourse of 1944,[60] Rabbi Yosef Yitzhak writes that the "oneness" or unity of the day includes *both* day and night, and by analogy the unity of both God and human divine service is a function of a bringing together of opposing ideas and characteristics. The rebbe echoes a common mystical theme when he writes that in the account of creation provided in Genesis, there was no separation and no distinctions prior to God's creative words. Prior to divine speech, heaven was not separate from earth, darkness was not distinct from light, and night was not separate from day. It is only when God *calls* the light day and the darkness night that these opposites emerge as separate and distinct. Yet, these opposites retain a trace of their original unity in the fact of their complete interdependence. Indeed, a full (24-hour) day includes both day (light) and night (darkness). Each of these poles retains a trace of its unity with its opposite because they each exist only by virtue of their contrast with their opposing term.

Similarly, we are told that just as the day is not complete without both day and night, a person is not complete unless he maintains a balance between the traits of *Chesed* and *Gevurah/Din* (Kindness and Strength/Judgment), which are associated with day/light and night/darkness respectively. Rabbi Yosef Yitzhak uses the example of dealing with one's enemies to illustrate the importance of this balance. It is only when one tempers one's judgment with kindness (and vice versa) that the problems with one's enemies—and indeed the problems in all human relationships—can be successfully resolved.

I would like to return for a moment to Yosef Yitzhak's gloss on Genesis in order to explicate a fundamental Kabbalistic idea regarding the nature of the one and the many that is relevant to our concerns. As we have seen, according to Schneur Zalman, prior to divine speech, prior to language, the basic oppositions of creation have no existence whatsoever; the cosmos is in effect a singularity, an eternal indistinguishable One. As we have also seen this is Yosef Yitzhak's view as well. It is only with language that distinctions come into being. Yet language has a way of overcoming the very distinctions that it itself has wrought; this way is articulated in the philosophy of *coincidentia oppositorum*. According to Yosef Yitzhak, one can use language to realize that day and night together form a unity in which each is an interdependent part. To take a more human example, one can also use language to recognize that kindness and judgment together form a unity (the complete human soul) in which these opposites condition and are contained within one another. To illustrate the latter point: On the one hand, no one can exhibit kindness to his children unless he is willing to place limits and exercise judgment and discipline upon them; on the other hand, such judgment and discipline will fail altogether unless it is tempered with mercy and love.

In later chapters, we will provide a more detailed philosophical explication of the notion that a singular, unified world is divided and potentially reunited through language.

DIALECTICS IN CHABAD CHASIDIC THOUGHT

As Elior puts it, in Chabad thought, "divinity is conceived as a dialectical process simultaneously comprising an entity and its opposite."[61] This is because, for Chabad, as we have seen, the Infinite God, *Ein-sof*, integrates within itself a variety of opposites that include being (*Yesh*) and nothingness (*Ayin*), emanation (*shefa ve-atsilut*) and contraction (*Tzimtzum*), ascent (*ratso*) and descent (*vashov*), as well as the oppositions between spirit and matter, structure and chaos, revelation and concealment, annihilation and embodiment, and unity and plurality.[62] In addition, according to Chabad, the infinite nature of *Ein-sof* is such that it integrates and unifies opposing human and divine perspectives on the world, and it incorporates these perspectives within itself. Further, in each case integration and unity is achieved precisely because each pole of the opposition is understood to be necessary and determinative for its opposite. As Elior explains, "The principle emerging from these concepts states that divinity possesses two opposing aspects that condition one another."[63]

According to Schneur Zalman, the truth of both opposing divine and human perspectives is necessary in order for the world and God to actualize their essence. In addition, the Alter Rebbe holds that the meaning and purpose of the cosmos is only realized through a dialectical process that moves from non-being to being and back to nothingness, and which involves the activities of humanity and a movement through the world. He writes, "The purpose of the creation of the worlds from nothingness to being was so that there should be a *Yesh* (Creation), and that the *Yesh* should be *Ayin* (*Nothing*)."[64] According to Chabad thought, in order for *Ein-sof* to fulfill its infinite essence, it must contract and conceal itself (via the *Tzimtzum*) to create a finite world, as it is this world which actualizes all possibilities of existence (*Yesh*). These possibilities, however, must then be understood as dependent upon and united with *Ein-sof*, and this recognition leads to the return to divinity in nothingness (*Ayin*).

While the details of Schneur Zalman's view are not perfectly clear, we can understand him as expressing something like the following: The Infinite God, *Ein-sof*, is *potentially* all things but *actually* nothing (no-thing) until it is differentiated into the innumerable entities, manifestations, points of view, and aspects of the finite world. This differentiation occurs precisely in order that the specific *sefirotic* values (wisdom, understanding, kindness, beauty, compassion, etc.) can be made actual and real through human ethical, spiritual, intellectual, and creative activity, for prior to creation these values are only abstractions within the godhead. It is through such value-making activity that human beings are able to transcend their separate egoistic existence and finite material nature, overcome their distance and alienation from the godhead, and reunite themselves and the world, with the Infinite, *Ein-sof*. It is in this way that there is a movement from the non-being (*Ayin*) of *Ein-sof* to the being (*Yesh*) of humanity in the finite world and back to nothingness (*Ayin*) of *Ein-sof*. According to Schneur Zalman and his followers, a God that passes through a phase of alienation, multiplicity, and finitude but who is then reunited with itself is far superior to a God who had never been alienated, multiplied, and finite (human) at all. The Chabad thinker Rabbi Aaron Ha Lévi explains that it is effectively God's purpose that the world should be differentiated and revealed in all of its finite particulars, but then reunified in its infinite source.[65] According to Rabbi Ha Lévi:

> ...the essence of His intention is that his *coincidentia* be manifested in concrete reality, that is, that all realities and their levels be revealed in actuality, each detail in itself, and that they nevertheless be unified and joined in their value, that is, that they be revealed as separated essences, and that they nevertheless be unified and joined in their value.[66]

There is a double movement in Chabad thought, a movement rooted in a coincidence or interdependence between two opposing perspectives on the reality of God and humanity. From the divine perspective, God is the origin of all and the finite world is an illusory or at best alienated form of fragmented being. From the human perspective, it is precisely this alienated, fragmented being that completes and perfects—if not gives rise to—God. I believe that it is this double movement that highlights the significance of Chabad thought for theology (and by extension for philosophy and psychology as well). Elior writes, "The great intellectual effort invested in Chabad writings is meant to bring one as close as possible to the divine point of view, according to which every creature is considered as nothing and naught with respect to the active power within it."[67] However, I believe that a more comprehensive reading of Chabad thought (as well as Elior's understanding of that thought) reveals a more subtle point—that is, that the goal of Chabad is to bring us to the point of recognizing the truth of both the worldly and divine points of view, thinking them simultaneously, and recognizing their complete interdependence.

As we proceed, we will come to understand that the paradoxes we have been discussing—for example, that God creates humanity and humanity creates the divine, that the world is both an illusion and reality, that *Ein-sof* is and is not identical with the world, that creation is at the same time a negation, that values must be destroyed in order to be actualized, and that an atheistic skepticism (unbelief) is the route to the divine, etc.—are means of expressing within language truths about a whole that is sundered by the very operation of language itself. While each of these paradoxes does not necessarily require the same type of analysis, in general we will see that within the necessary but false (or partial) consciousness of language and concepts, mystical truths can only be expressed as a series of contradictions, which, because of the complete interdependence of opposing terms, dissipate once things are viewed from a "rational mystical" point of view.[68]

It will be my task in later chapters to come as close as possible to articulating this mystical point of view, given the fact that language itself is predicated upon distinctions (between subject and object, and, more fundamentally, between *words* and their *objects*) that prevent this point of view from being completely expressed. But I am getting ahead of myself. Further groundwork in dialectical philosophy, Jungian psychology, and postmodern thought must be laid before we can fully enter this arena.

CHAPTER THREE

THE DIALECTIC OF G. W. F. HEGEL

HEGEL AND THE COINCIDENCE OF OPPOSITES

In Georg Wilhelm Friedrich Hegel (1770–1831), the coincidence of opposites takes an avowedly intellectual turn. Hegel preferred to use "dialectic" to refer to the tendency of ideas, attitudes, entities, and events to pass over into their opposites; he was averse to utilizing the terms "unity" and "coincidence" of opposites on the grounds that these terms stressed unity without a concomitant stress on opposition. However, his philosophy is in many ways the intellectual culmination and radicalization of the *coincidentia* idea.

Chabad Chasidic philosophy, which claims that all things are revealed through their opposites, developed in Poland and Lithuania during the same historical period that German Idealism flowered in Germany. It is remarkable that these two movements, worlds apart in their cultural and religious outlooks, should have arrived at conclusions regarding the nature of opposition that are remarkably alike. While the tracing of historical connections is not my purpose in this work, we should note in passing that the connection between Chabad and Hegel may not be purely coincidental. Each is in certain ways heirs to a medieval and renaissance mystical tradition of *coincidentia oppositorum* that achieved one of its most important expressions in the Kabbalah. Indeed, while Hegel appears to have had only passing familiarity with Jewish Kabbalistic texts, he had a deep interest in the Christian mystic Jakob

Boehme (1575–1624), who held that being arose through the interaction of the opposites, and who was influenced in this view by the Kabbalah. Hegel's thinking on the opposites was, of course, influenced by many other sources—the pre-Socratic philosophers, Meister Eckhart, Immanuel Kant, Johann Gustav Fichte, and Friedrich Schelling, to name a few—sources which the Hasidim likely had no access to or interest in, and it would be misleading to call Hegel a "Kabbalistic philosopher." Nonetheless, his dialectical idealism sprang, in at least some measure, from the same mystical traditions that were passed down to the Chasidim via the Kabbalah. Our transition from Jewish mysticism to German philosophy may not be so abrupt as it might first seem.

Hegel recognized the presence of dialectic in the philosophers who preceded him and even argued that dialectic, in an incomplete form, was the engine that moved philosophers from Socrates to Kant. He further recognized that dialectic is present and even essential to mysticism, and he incorporated mystical notions into his own thought, albeit in a manner that articulated these doctrines in discursive, rational terms. In addition, Hegel was of the view that dialectic had "everyday" psychological implications. In this he clearly anticipated the views of twentieth-century psychologists such as C. G. Jung, who held that the human psyche, indeed the "self" is a *coincidentia oppositorum*.

Hegel's philosophical reputation has swung wildly in the two centuries since he first published his *Phänomenologie des Geistes* (*Phenomenology of Spirit* [or *Mind*])[1]. He has been worshipped by some and reviled by others. His thought is the foundation of later philosophical movements (Neo-Hegelianism, British Idealism, Marxism, existentialism, and even deconstruction) and the foil of others (logical positivism, and [again] both existentialism and deconstruction). During the height of the logical positivist and linguistic analytic movements in British and American philosophy in the mid-twentieth century, Hegel was either disdained or ignored; in more recent decades, there has been a resurgence of interest in his thought.[2] It is fair to say that regardless of whether one holds Hegel in high or low esteem, any serious contemporary discussion of the interplay of opposites in our conception of humanity, the world, or God must take cognizance of Hegel. Whatever else he is (and there are probably more interpretations of Hegel than of any other philosopher), Hegel is the major philosophical representative of the view that contrary if not contradictory ideas are implicit within one another, "pass over" into one another, and are interdependent. While it is debatable whether Hegel discovered or invented a new form of *logic*, it is clear that he articulated a point of view within which (at least apparent) contradiction is essential, not fatal, to thought.

Hegel brings to our awareness that thinking is dependent upon conceptual dichotomies that permit us to express distinctions between things and among our own ideas. Yet he goes beyond the view that thought involves contrasts to argue that there is a class of philosophical oppositions—for example, subject and object, mind and nature, universal and particular, master and slave, God and humanity, freedom and necessity—that when pressed to their extremes and thoroughly understood require their opposites. Kant had argued that human reason falls into antinomy and contradiction whenever it considers abstract ideas and attempts to answer transcendental questions about the world as a whole.[3] Hegel came to regard these contradictions not as a stumbling block to metaphysical inquiry but as an impetus to philosophical insight and development.

"UNDERSTANDING," DIALECTIC," AND "SPECULATION"

To appreciate Hegel's claims about opposition, we must begin with his distinction between three stages in the reasoning process: *Understanding* or "abstract reason," *Dialectic* or "negative reason," and *Speculative Thought* or "positive reason." Understanding, which is the mode of thought involved in much common sense and normal science, "sticks to the fixity of characters and their distinctness from one another,"[4] without ever recognizing their intrinsic dynamic relationship to their own opposites. According to Hegel, Understanding is the form of thought involved in ordinary knowledge; it produces discrete facts, clear ideas, and universal laws.

In Dialectic, the "finite characteristics" of the Understanding are seen to "supersede themselves, and pass into their opposites."[5] Finally, Speculative or "positive reason" is, for Hegel, the natural outcome of Dialectic, as it "apprehends the unity of terms (propositions) in their opposition."[6] In his *Science of Logic* Hegel writes:

> speculative thought...consists solely in grasping the opposed moments in their unity. Inasmuch as each moment shows, as a matter of fact, that it has its opposite in it, and that in this opposite it rejoins itself, the affirmative truth is this internally self-moving unity, the grasping together of both thoughts....[7]

Or, as Hegel states more succinctly, "It is...in grasping opposites in their unity, or the positive in the negative, that *the speculative* consists."[8] Hegel provides his most sustained and accessible discussion of the dialectic and the coincidence of opposites in his *(Encyclopedia) Logic*, especially in the *Zusatze*, the explanatory notes to this work. In the main text of the *Logic*, Hegel points out that dialectic, as it is often conceived and practiced, "is nothing more than a subjective seesaw of arguments pro and con."[9] In the *Zusatze*, he indicates that a significant advance over this pedestrian view of dialectic, an advance introduced by Socrates, involves the dismantling of an idea that initially seemed quite plausible through a demonstration that the idea leads to its opposite or contradiction. Hegel calls this "irony" and sees it as a purely "negative" form of dialectic, one that discredits philosophical propositions without leading to a more positive formulation. Dialectic, when practiced by the *Understanding,* "becomes Skepticism,"[10] as it appears to undermine the validity of all philosophical positions. According to Hegel, Plato, in his more "scientific dialogues" used dialectic to demonstrate the limitations of all "hard and fast" concepts; for example, in the *Par-*

menides, Plato deduces the many from the one and then shows how the many must itself be defined as the one.[11] For Hegel, these earlier uses of dialectic culminated in the Kantian claim that "thought has a natural tendency to issue in contradictions and antinomies, whenever it seeks to apprehend the infinite."[12] Thus the Kantian Antinomies demonstrated "that every abstract proposition of understanding, taken precisely as it is given, naturally veers round into its opposite."[13] Kant, in Hegel's view, was the first to recognize that contradiction is not always the result of accidents or subjective errors of inference, but are inherent to thought itself. Kant's antinomies of pure reason not only loosened the hold of previous systems of dogmatic metaphysics on philosophy but directed philosophical attention to "the dialectical movement of thought" itself.[14] However, according to Hegel, Kant fell short of understanding the positive metaphysical and epistemological implications of the antinomies, which are that "every actual thing involves a coexistence of opposed elements" and that to "comprehend an object is equivalent to being conscious of it as a concrete unity of opposed determinations."[15]

Hegel points out that Kant's antinomies were limited to four basic questions that arose in connection with the metaphysical systems preceding him: questions regarding whether the world is or is not limited in space and time, whether matter is or is not endlessly divisible, whether all things are subject to the laws of causality (to the exclusion of free will), and whether the world in its entirety is caused or uncaused. In Hegel's view, these are just a sample of the many abstract notions that pull thought in opposing directions. Kant's method was to juxtapose the opposing theses that arise from a consideration of his four questions and to demonstrate that each of these opposites inevitably follow from considered philosophical argument and reflection. Thus, one could "prove," for example, the truth of both universal determinism and its contradictory, freedom of the will. However, according to Hegel, neither Kant's "proofs," nor the general thrust of his solution regarding the antinomies were satisfactory. Kant's main achievement was to exhibit the antinomies of reason and to hint that their poles constitute a unity. To hold, as

Kant did, that one pole of an antinomy (for example, universal causality) is true of the "phenomenal" world, and a second pole (freedom of the will) is true of a second, poorly defined, "noumenal" realm avoids the conceptual interdependence of the ideas in question. For Hegel, neither freedom nor necessity, as they are typically understood by philosophers, are independently real; instead, each is simply a "moment" or ideal factor of the "true" interdependent unity of "freedom/necessity," which involves the mind's transcending causal necessity through adherence to reason.[16]

THE DIALECTIC OF PERSPECTIVES AND INTERPRETATIONS

Hegel followed Aristotle in holding that the immediate data of experience cannot be separated from the concepts or mediate structures that are applied to it. In the *Logic*, he tells us "there is nothing, nothing in heaven or in nature or mind or anywhere else which does not equally contain both immediacy and mediation, so that these two determinations reveal themselves to be *unseparated* and inseparable and the opposition between them to be a nullity."[17] Yet, unlike the Platonists, who believed the "Ideas" to be eternal and unchanging, Hegel held that the concepts that mediate experience are dynamic and mind-dependent. He asserted that we cannot clarify the nature of our data and then apply our science to it, because the very process of clarifying, and even experiencing, our data already involves a particular conceptualization of it. We thus arrive at a *coincidentia oppositorum* between "facts" and their "interpretations," as these are apparent contraries, which prove to be interdependent. One might be surprised that this idea, which returned with a vengeance in the second half of the twentieth century in the philosophy of science,[18] was originally Hegel's.

The dialectic of data and theory, of the immediate and mediated, is important for our understanding of the question we raised in the Introduction to this work about the possibility (or impossibility) of intuiting a single, unified "world" that is the subject of our multiple maps and representations. For Hegel, since there is no possibility of unearthing the basic "facts" of the world independent of our perspectives upon them, the only road to knowledge must involve a comprehension of the various perspectives that can be taken upon experience. This is precisely what Hegel proposes to do in his first great work, the *Phenomenology of Mind*,[19] where he argues that knowledge of both the world and the human spirit is not arrived at through an *analysis* of the molecular components of experience but rather through a *dialectical* exploration of the various constructions that the mind places upon it. "The world" is not, as the early Ludwig Wittgenstein was to later affirm, "all that is the case"[20] (i.e., facts), but as Wittgenstein ultimately came to believe, the full panoply of ways in which "world" functions in our theories and language.[21] The same can be said about "the mind." In order to obtain a synoptic understanding of the mind, we cannot reduce it to its component "parts" (whether these be conceived of as sensations, ideas, neurons, information, and so on) but we should rather inquire into the ways in which the mind functions and understands itself.

For Hegel, the panoply of perspectives is arranged in a circle, one that follows the dialectical transformations of each point of view into its opposite. He tells us,

> Philosophy exhibits the appearance of a circle which closes with itself, and has no beginning in the same way that the other sciences have. To speak of a beginning of philosophy has a meaning only in relation to a person who proposes to commence the study, and not in relation to the science as science.[22]

Hegel again invokes the principle of *coincidentia oppositorum* when he says, "The essential requirement for the science of logic is not so much that the beginning be a pure immediacy, but rather that the whole of that science be within itself a circle in which the first is also the last and the last is also the first."[23] He is optimistic that the dialectic of perspectives eventually circles back upon itself, so that no matter where one begins one's investigation one will return to the starting point. Robert Solomon, in his *In the Spirit of Hegel*[24] argues that there is no limit to the perspectives we can take upon the mind or the world, and no reason to believe that we can complete the hermeneutic circle and circumscribe our subject matter, whether it be the world or the human mind. This is also the position adopted by Derrida and other postmodernists who argue that, while Hegel opened thought to a dialectic that yielded multiple perspectives and interpretations, he attempted to achieve premature (and impossible) closure in his efforts to produce a systematic philosophy. The questions of multiple perspectives, realism, and possible closure (and the dialectic between closure and non-closure, system and non-system) are topics that I will consider more deeply in later chapters. However, we should here at least be alert to the possibility that the whole notion of circular closure may bring us dangerously close to the pre-dialectical, linear thinking of the Understanding.

THE DIALECTICS OF KNOWLEDGE AND BEING, BEING AND NOTHING

Hegel held that important philosophical ideas dialectically pass over into notions that are typically thought of as opposed to them. There is, for example, according to Hegel, a *coincidentia oppositorum* between knowledge and being, and between being and nothingness.

Hegel argues that the notion of *being*, which is generally thought to be opposed to and distinct from *knowledge*, contains knowledge as part of its essence. This is because what we mean by saying that something has "being" is that it must at least be *potentially known*. For Hegel "being" is precisely what consciousness makes of it, and "knowing" is conversely nothing but the contents (being) of such consciousness. As such, these two apparently contrary ideas are in *coincidentia oppositorum* and are in an important sense identical. However, to simply affirm that knowledge and being (or subject and object) are identical is to abandon the dialectic altogether. This is because, for many important purposes, knowledge and being are also different![25] There obviously are, for example, many things that exist but about which no human being has any knowledge. Hegel's understanding of *coincidentia oppositorum* is sophisticated enough to include within itself its own opposite, that is, the idea that opposites do not coincide.[26] The failure to recognize this leads to a premature closure of the dialectic and again leaves one mired in the linear thinking of the Understanding.

Hegel argues that Being is also interdependent with another of its presumed contraries, Nothingness. He holds that a plenum of pure, undifferentiated being—the kind that philosophers since Aristotle have imagined to be the source of all creation—is epistemologically indistinguishable from, and therefore identical with, pure nothingness. Again, however, there is a difference as well, as for many purposes the distinction between what does and does not exist is essential.

DIALECTIC IN HEGEL'S *PHENOMENOLOGY OF SPIRIT*

One of Hegel's goals in *The Phenomenology of Spirit* is to demonstrate that particular concepts, theories, and cultural and historical forms are inadequate for the very purposes they are thought to fulfill. Hegel hopes to show that each concept, theory, and perspective, if carried to its logical and historical conclusion, must repeatedly pass over into a more adequate form until such point as an "Absolute," all encompassing, self-reflective position that embraces all perspectives and their contradictions is achieved. There is considerable controversy among Hegelians as to the precise nature, and even the possibility, of ever achieving such an "Absolute" perspective. What is not controversial, however, is Hegel's goal of exhibiting the inadequacy of a point of view which initially appeared to be perfectly adequate. Further, Hegel demonstrates the necessity for each apparently self-sufficient point of view to embrace precisely what it was initially meant to exclude: its contrary or opposite.

This pattern of thought is apparent throughout Hegel's work. However, in the opening arguments of the *Phenomenolgy of Mind*, we find

Hegel's method illustrated with respect to the notion of "sensible certainty," which has profound implications for Hegel's thinking in general. It is here that he articulates what I earlier described as the interdependence between the "immediate" (particulars or facts) and the "mediate" (universals or theory). "Sense certainty" is the view that our awareness of the world is at its fullest, richest, and truest when we simply receive whatever impressions our senses give us prior to any conceptual or categorizing activity of our *mind*. In this view, which is the foundation of a simple empiricism or sensationalism, our knowledge of the world is built upon an incorrigible base of *particular* sense impressions, and it is these sense impressions that lay the foundation for our perception of both everyday objects and our scientific theories about the workings of the world. Thus, from the perspective of sense certainty, our perception of the world at large—of what we call the sky, the sun, rocks, trees, rivers, trains, boats, animals, and people—is constructed on the basis of simple, uncategorized sense impressions. Such a view not only has the imprimatur of positivistic science but also appeals to common sense, as it would seem that the foundation of knowledge is the immediate impression of my senses in the here and now.

Hegel, in the *Phenomenology*, is less concerned with refuting the perspective of sense certainty than he is in showing how this perspective leads to certain absurdities that prompt us to adopt a superior, *contrary* point of view. He asks us precisely what it is that we are able to *know* on the basis of the unmediated, *here* and *now* experience of our senses. He argues that in order for us to answer this question, we must appeal to some *category* or *idea*, whether that be a color, feeling, pain, taste, twinge, light, etc. It does not help for one to simply say that what *I* know is *this sensation here* and *now*, for unless "I," "here," and "now" are further specified, the knowledge claim remains completely empty. Hegel's point is that the perspective of "sense certainty," if it is to make sense in terms of its own criterion as the "guarantor of knowledge," must yield to another view within which it is not bare particular sensations that lie at the foundation of knowledge but the very general ideas and concepts that we utilize in describing them. The perspective of "self-certainty" is itself seen to depend upon its opposite, categorical thinking. It is not the particular but the general, not the sensible but the ideational that lies at the foundation of our knowledge. The *empiricism* of self-certainty is said by Hegel to dialectically pass over into the *idealism* of conceptual, general knowledge. This, of course, is not to say that sensation is irrelevant to knowledge, only that a philosophy that takes it to be foundational is incomplete and in error.

The dialectic in the *Phenomenology* does not end here. The conceptual experience of a categorized object, which Hegel refers to as "perception" (as opposed to "sensation") itself passes over into a dynamic view of the object as a locus of causal force. This notion of force, which manifests itself in a variety of causal, scientific laws, itself breaks down and passes over into the notion of an object as the external manifestation of an inner essence, such inner essence having the characteristic of necessarily positing its own self-expression. Hegel links this "self-expression" to the subjective activity of mind, and arrives at the view that our knowledge of objects is in reality a form of self-knowledge, and that such self-consciousness is the key to understanding absolute knowledge or Absolute Mind.

We need not follow Hegel through the details of the dialectic in the *Phenomenology of Mind* leading to the "Absolute". For our purposes at this point in our discussion, his main arguments are that (1) the very structure and foundation of our knowledge of the world is a reflection of the concepts, ideas, and language of "mind," and (2) any finite perspective we have upon the world, when examined on the basis of its own purposes and criteria, will be shown to require and pass over into its apparent opposite. The first point is the foundation of Hegel's *idealism*; the second lies at the foundation of his *dialectic*.

Hegelian idealism is frequently misunderstood to be the doctrine that the material world does not exist and that everything is a product of subjectivity or the human mind. Such a view, if indeed it was ever held by any idealist philosophers, is certainly not Hegel's. For Hegel, idealism involves a breaking down of the radical distinction between subject and object, between mind and world.[27] Idealism does not result in the swallowing up of the objective by the subjective, but in the recognition of a mind-based conceptual element at the heart of everything whatsoever. The world follows its own course completely independent of our individual will, yet there is a sense in which this very same world is imbued with our own will and subjectivity.

HEGEL'S DEMURRER

While on the one hand Hegel sought to parlay his dialectic into a vehicle that would arrive at absolute knowledge, on the other hand his philosophical outlook precluded the very possibility of achieving such closure, at least in the form of a set of philosophical propositions. This is because philosophical propositions are always one-sided and thus incomplete. He writes,

> A one-sided proposition…can never…give expression to a speculative truth. If we say, for example, that the absolute is the unity of subjective and objective, we are undoubtedly in the right, but so far one-sided, as we enunciate the unity only and lay the accent upon it, forgetting that in reality the subjective and objective are not merely identical but also distinct.[28]

Further:

> It remains to note that such phrases as "Being and Nothing are the same," or "The unity of Being and Nothing,"—like all other such unities…give rise to reasonable objection. They misrepresent the facts, by giving an exclusive prominence to the unity, and leaving the difference which undoubtedly exists in it…without any express mention or notice. It accordingly seems as if the diversity had been unduly put out of court and neglected.[29]

Hegel continues, "The fact is, no speculative principle can be correctly expressed by any such propositional form, for the unity has to be conceived in the diversity, which is all the while present and explicit."[30]

Hegel is, of course, famous for creating a philosophical system, one that is presumably meant to account for all the elements of the spiritual and natural universe. Yet in any endeavor to come to grips with Hegelian philosophy, it is important to recognize the radical open-endedness of his thought, and it is this contrast between Hegel's "system" and his open-endedness that has given rise to the "metaphysical" versus "hermeneutical" schools of Hegel interpretation. The first holds that Hegel regarded his task as a metaphysical ascent to absolute truth, and the second holds that he understood truth as historically conditioned and open to indefinite revision and reinterpretation.[31] Perhaps Hegel's interpreters should heed Hegel's own words: "When our thought never ranges beyond narrow and rigid terms, we are forced to assume that of two opposite assertions...the one must be true and the other false."[32] As we saw in the case of the Lurianic Kabbalah, we may find in the ascent to Hegel's "absolute truth" a deconstruction of its very possibility.

In *The Science of Logic*, Hegel suggests that the dialectic progresses infinitely. In that work, he is adamant that one cannot simply rest with a proposition about the unity of opposites. He writes:

> The claim is made that the finite and the infinite are one unity. This is a false claim that needs correction by its opposite: the two are absolutely different and opposed. This claim is in turn to be corrected by the fact that the two are inseparable; that in the one determination there lies the other by virtue of the claim to unity; and so forth to infinity.[33]

It is indeed this infinite movement between the opposites that, for Hegel, characterizes the dialectic and the very nature of spirit or mind.

Regardless of whether we hold that the value of Hegel's philosophy is in his system or in his having created a philosophy of "infinite reinterpretation," we should note that for Hegel "the battle of reason is the struggle to break up the rigidity to which the Understanding has reduced everything."[34] As we have seen, the Hegelian objection to fixed propositions in philosophy applies to the very notion of *coincidentia oppositorum* itself.

I will now turn to the question of "Hegel's System" and the use he makes of the coincidence of opposites in formulating a comprehensive philosophy that he believed enabled him to advance to the "Absolute Idea."

THE HEGELIAN SYSTEM

As we have seen, Hegel held that, while earlier philosophers made use of and had a rudimentary awareness of the dialectic, they grasped it only in *negative terms*. For example, they understood it as a means of refuting a particular philosophical position by demonstrating that if examined closely it implies the truth of its own contradiction. Hegel, on the other hand, believed that a full understanding of dialectic could (and would inevitably) give rise to a positive philosophy, a view which eventuated in the Hegelian "system." It is this system that propelled Hegel to the center of the philosophical world in the nineteenth century, and which led to his disrepute during the better part of the twentieth. While specific Hegelian ideas are woven into the very fabric of contemporary thought, familiarity with Hegel's *system* of philosophy is often lacking outside (and sometimes even within) university departments of philosophy. As a full comprehension (and critique) of the role of dialectic and the coincidence of opposites in Hegel's thought must involve a basic familiarity with the Hegelian system, I will provide a brief outline of Hegel's metaphysical project.[35] As Hegel is subject to multiple interpretations, my exposition cannot be considered definitive. In explicating Hegel's thinking, I will try to show that his entire system is predicated on the dialectic, and, on his view, follows from the dialectic's *positive implications*.

Hegel thought of philosophy as providing a comprehensive account and explanation for the existence of the word. Hegel's explicit answer to the question, "Why does the world exist?" is that it exists as the vehicle for the fullest possible realization and self-awareness of Mind or Spirit.[36] In a particularly lucid passage in his Introduction to his *Lectures on the History of Philosophy*, Hegel says,

> Everything that from eternity that has happened in heaven and earth, the life of God, and all the deeds of time simply are the struggles for mind to know itself, to make itself objective to itself, to find itself, be for itself, and finally unite with itself. Only in this manner does mind attain its freedom, for that is free which is not referred to or dependent on another. True self-possession and satisfaction are only to be found in this, and in nothing else but thought does mind attain this freedom.[37]

Hegel identifies "mind" or "spirit" with "reason," and he holds that reason is the one independent, self-sufficient, and free principle that can serve as its own foundation. If one asks for an explanation for "reason," one's answer must involve reason itself, as the validity of any explanation depends upon its being rational. Because reason is the one thing in the cosmos that is self-sufficient, independent, and free, Hegel understood it to be both the motive force of the world and the goal of its development. For Hegel, philosophy is in the unique position of being both a rational explanation for and the ultimate manifestation of the "World-Spirit." This set of assumptions was, of course, roundly criticized by the existentialists, and later by Jung, Derrida, and others, but it is important to examine its implications.

According Hegel, it follows from the principle of universal reason and from the notion of philosophy itself that the direction, meaning, and goal of the universe is the full actualization of knowledge, consciousness, and mind. This realization achieves its highest form in the self-realization of mind knowing itself. Like Aristotle, who defined God as "self-thinking thought," Hegel conceived of the Absolute as mind, reason, or the "Idea" coming to think and know itself. The natural world, and its most important manifestation in humankind, exists so that mind or spirit will have a mirror through which it achieves self-awareness. For Hegel, the appearance of nature, the advance of human history, and the development of philosophy are all understood as aspects of the march of "Reason" toward the "Absolute," which is conceived as mind's self-realization.

The "Absolute" progresses through the interrelated stages of "Logic," "Nature," and "Spirit." In the first stage, Logic, ideas are purely abstract; they remain distinct from specific entities and contents. An example of this stage is the abstract number "seven" as opposed to its concrete instantiation as "seven apples" or "seven people." In the second stage, Nature, ideas come to inform the objects of the material, natural world—for example, "seven apples." Finally, in the third stage, Spirit, ideas come to be known and understood: in our example, a consciousness which contemplates the distinction between the abstract number "seven" and its specific *instantiation* as seven apples. In Hegel's manner of speaking, the abstract "Idea" of "Logic" [his translators typically capitalize his technical use of these and other terms] comes to be "alienated" from itself and "negated" in "Nature," as it surrenders its status as a pure concept. However, the Idea "returns" to itself in "Spirit," *where* it is contemplated and known in its abstract purity once more. Upon its return to the realm of Spirit, the Idea has been completed and perfected, for it is in this realm that it becomes conscious of itself. This movement, the transition from Logic to Nature to self-awareness in Spirit, is referred to by Hegel as the "negation of the negation." He utilizes this phrase because, in his view, the Idea negates itself in Nature by becoming a non-ideational "thing," and this negation is in turn negated by consciousness which through its awareness returns the Idea to the realm of Spirit. Hegel equates this "double negation" with the Absolute itself, and he sees it as fulfilling the purpose of the entire cosmos, which is the development of self-conscious Spirit or mind.

The movement of the Idea from Nature to self-conscious Spirit, then, is not an arbitrary or contingent matter. For Hegel, it is the very essence, meaning, and purpose of the Idea that it should alienate itself in Nature and then complete itself in Spirit. We should also note that this process is not essentially a process that occurs in time. While Hegel exerts great effort to show that the Idea does indeed have a temporal dimension in both history and the history of philosophy, its development is essentially conceptual. The triple movement from Logic to Nature to Spirit is, according to Hegel, present in any and every idea, natural event, proposition, and act of mind. The movement of the Idea is essentially the expression of the form of reason he calls "dialectical." A consideration of any idea (for example, the number "three") shows that it is rationally and dialectically part of the idea that it be manifest and instantiated in Nature (for example, as three stones, three coins, or three humans). Further, this idea is potentially and actually known by consciousness or Spirit (for example, as different from the number seven, as figuring in certain calculations). According to Hegel, it is inevitable that the *abstract idea* will dialectically pass over into and inform *concrete instances*, and that it will then come to be known and understood by spirit or mind. The movement of the Idea from Logic to Nature to Spirit is not only present in all mental acts, but also constitutive of the entire world.

Whereas previous philosophers had noted and debated the relationship between universals, particulars, and human knowledge, Hegel had the vision (or temerity!) to put this relationship in "motion." Hegel went so far as to reinterpret this dialectic in theological terms: The movement of a *universal* God in a very *particular* Christian savior and the consequent knowledge of this God in the Christian religion was the highest religious expression of the dynamic relationship of universals, particulars, and mind.[38] In making this claim, however, Hegel set himself apart from normative Christian theology, as he held that knowledge of the incarnation of God in Christ involves an understanding of the necessary movement of "Reason" rather than being the result of divine revelation.

For Hegel, the dialectic of Logic, Nature, and Spirit is not only implicit in all thought but is also manifest in the natural world and human history, as well as in literature, the arts, religion, and philosophy. This is because these seemingly disparate realms are each arenas within which the Absolute in its character as Reason originates and becomes increasingly manifest, conceptually rich, and self-aware. Humanity's consciousness, and its refinement in the history of art, religion, and philosophy, is the self-conscious movement of Reason itself.

Logic, Nature, and Spirit (or Mind) are each "moments" of the Absolute, and each is in an important sense identical with it. Each of these moments implicitly encompasses each of the others and each is part of an integrated whole which, in Hegel's view, is the meaning and purpose of the world. Humanity, particularly in its aspect of Spirit—as it expresses itself in art, religion, politics, society, history, and philosophy— is itself the Absolute as well, as each of these cultural projects is the Idea developing and reaching for self-conscious expression.

Hegel's dynamic understanding of the notions of Logic, Nature, and Spirit (roughly universal, particular, and knowledge) follows from and gives rise to the dialectic, which, as we have seen, is the perspective upon reasoning in which notions are said to "break down" and are then discovered to pass over into other notions, particularly their opposites. *The movement from universal to particular and back again gives rise to creation and knowledge.* This is because creation, according to Hegel, is the particular instantiations of a (universal) idea, and knowledge is the comprehension of a universal idea in a particular object or instance.

In Dialectic, the "passing over" frequently gives rise to a third term, which then serves as a basis for a new logical dialectical movement, and so on. Thus, the transition from nothingness to being and vice versa gives rise to a third notion, *becoming*, which in turn serves as a basic concept in the structure of a new dialectical movement. It is precisely in this manner that Hegel's dialectic proceeds within the realm of Logic: Hegel attempts to show that an entire inventory of ideas and categories, large and rich enough to describe all possible worlds, can thus be derived from what is implicit in the simplest of notions, and is indeed implicit in the notion of (dialectical) thought itself. Though it is no longer fashionable among Hegel commentators to recognize this, there are indications in his writings (e.g., in *The Philosophy of Nature*) that Hegel's project was to achieve in the realm of philosophy something akin to what Bertrand Russell and Alfred North Whitehead were to attempt in the realm of mathematics: to derive all that is known from the simplest of logical principles. Hegel sought to rationally derive the entire ideational universe from any given single notion, holding that it was, in fact, irrelevant where he began because the Idea (all ideas) are implicit in any given one. Hegel endeavored to show that ideas (Logic) must out of rational necessity pass over into Nature and finally into Spirit. In addition, Hegel suggests that the natural world, mankind, and human culture can, at least in a general way, be "deduced" ("dialectically inferred") from such abstract "logical" notions as being, non-being, and becoming, ultimately from the very notion of Reason itself.

The order of *thought* and the order of *things* are effectively the same for Hegel: Thought is both the beginning and end of the cosmos. Thought achieves self-conscious perspicuity in philosophy, and ultimately in Hegel's own philosophy. This last claim left Hegel open to the criticism that on his view, the entire universe, with its countless planets, stars, and galaxies, exists in order that it achieve self-awareness through Hegel himself! Hegel's retort, of course, would be that he is simply the vehicle of a logical progression, the nature of which is open to all.

The Hegelian project in philosophy was to provide a rational explanation of the world through a consideration of the very meaning of being and, especially, thought and reason. Hegel believed that dialectic is the engine of thought and philosophy and, because of the intrinsic relationship between thought and the world, dialectic is the engine of the cosmos. By applying dialectic to virtually any subject matter, one could, in a general way, advance to a comprehensive understanding of the world. The main thrust of Hegel's thinking in this regard is that one can in effect *think the world whole* through an understanding of how presumably contradictory ideas imply one another, and give rise to other ideas that (ultimately) encompass the world as a whole.

After a period of being celebrated among the world's great philosophers, Hegel's project was criticized to such a degree that he had become, by the 1930s, the subject of ridicule among the logical positivists, who saw in his sweeping "dialectical deductions" prime examples of propositions that were meaningless because they were unverifiable. Others accused Hegel of engaging in a series of specious inferences and even word games, of violating his own open-ended dialectical principles by adumbrating a closed philosophical system, or of reifying genuine dialectical insights into the rigid categories of the Understanding. Thus, while Hegel suggested that the dialectic terminates in an "Absolute Idea" (which on Hegel's view closely approximates his own philosophy), others have held that the need to overcome any current form of consciousness is necessarily an interminable process and that the dialectic never arrives at an ultimate "truth."[39]

W. T. Stace had early on written a sympathetic and widely read synopsis of Hegel's system,[40] and later wrote an important book on the philosophy of mysticism.[41] However, he ultimately came to the view that, while Hegel was correct in his observation that the doctrine of the "identity of opposites" abounds in both the history of mysticism and philosophy, "he made the disastrous error of mistaking this for a new kind of logical principle and trying to base his own super logic upon it."[42] Stace came to believe that it is a grave error to hold with Hegel and his followers that mystical experience points us in the direction of a new kind of logic "governed by the principle of the identity of opposites."[43] For Stace, there is only one kind of logic, and Hegel's dialectical logic amounts to a bogus account of the problem posed by mysticism. For Stace, the coincidence of opposites is a venerable and important mystical idea, but it is a "definitely antilogical idea."[44]

Other philosophers accepted or adapted Hegel's dialectical method but completely rejected the notion that it could lead to an ultimate point of view or absolute truth. In later chapters, I will return to the question of whether dialectical *reasoning* can provide the key to thinking of the world as a whole and arriving at the unity that is the presumed object of mystical experience. I will also consider the question of whether the coincidence of opposites provides a vehicle for creating an integrated, multi-perspective account of mind and a unified psychology. In the next section, I will consider how, for Hegel, the reconciliation of the opposites is an expression of the Absolute through the higher activities of humankind: art, religion, and philosophy.

THE OPPOSITES IN HEGEL'S UNDERSTANDING OF THE ABSOLUTE

As we have seen, for Hegel, the Absolute involves the self-realization of mind through the development of the human spirit. The process through which mind comes to know itself is manifest in art, religion, and philosophy. Hegel holds that in art, mind expresses and comes to know itself in the sensuous and material nature of its endeavor, as in art there is both a fusion of subject and object and an interpenetration of thought and meaning with sensuous matter. The artist's subjectivity is fused with its opposite, the object of his or her representation, and a material medium is transformed to express spiritual and ultimately rational themes. Art, in effect, produces a union of opposites between universal and particular, subject and object, and mind and nature.[45] Indeed, mind, which is "alienated" in nature, returns to itself in the artistic depiction of nature, where the sensuous, material realm becomes filled with reason and meaning. Art, like religion and philosophy, also articulates and reconciles the oppositions between inward freedom and natural necessity.[46] These reconciliations are the "truth" and the expression of the Absolute.

According to Hegel, the quest of mind to know itself is also manifest in religion. The process through which the opposites are reconciled serves not only as the basis for human thought but is also the essence of the divine. God can no longer be adequately conceived of as a supreme being or entity, but is rather identified with the very process of thought itself. In this process the infinite appears in the finite, and the finite appears in the infinite. Hegel calls Christianity the "consummate religion,"[47] because the incarnation of the divine in the particularity of Christ gives supreme expression to the dialectic between universal and particular that is essential to thought. This movement from universal to particular is reversed in the ascent of humanity toward the divine, as the very process of rational thought lifts the individual above the particular and finite into a realm of infinite consciousness, where it expresses and articulates the Absolute. The religious significance of humanity is that the human being is the one being who is both finite and infinite and who experiences the conflict between the two.[48] For Hegel, humanity's ascent to God through worship and, moreover through thought—and conversely God's incarnation in man—are the essential moments of religion. The incarnation of God in man is a symbolic expression of mind coming to know itself, which Hegel equates with the Absolute: "The absolute end or goal…is that spirit should know itself, comprehend itself, should become object to itself as it is in itself, [and] arrive at perfect knowledge of itself."[49]

While art and religion is each an expression of the Absolute, the highest expression of the Absolute occurs in philosophy. Hegel makes no distinction between philosophy and its history, and neither is distinguished from the World Spirit, the Absolute, and God. Hegel writes that a superficial reading of the history of philosophy shows it "to be a process in which the most various thoughts arise in numerous philosophies, each of which opposes, contradicts, and refutes the others."[50] However, it is precisely this series of oppositions and contradictions (when understood dialectically) that lead, and are indeed equivalent to philosophical truth. For Hegel, "The diversity and number of philosophies not only does not prejudice philosophy itself (but is) absolutely necessary to the existence of the science of philosophy and…is essential to it."[51] Indeed, it is the dialectic between opposing philosophies and their reconciliation in later philosophies that constitutes the march of Reason and the development of self-consciousness in spirit.

Hegel holds that philosophy reveals a coincidence of opposites both in nature and in mind. In his view, natural objects contain opposition as part of their essence. For example, "It is said that matter must be either continuous or divisible into points, but in reality it has both these qualities."[52] Similarly, mind contains within itself both freedom and necessity. Although these absolutes originally were thought to oppose and exclude one another, the "higher point of view is that mind is free in its necessity, and finds its freedom in it alone, since its necessity rests on its freedom."[53] Hegel's point here is that freedom only exists in that which is completely self-determined—and self-determination involves thinking and acting in accord with the *necessity* imposed by reason. Hegel distinguishes his notion of freedom from the notion that the individual can determine both his will and activity. The latter is the"freedom" that is most often contrasted with determinism, but Hegel describes it as a "false freedom."[54] For Hegel, true freedom involves the capacity to transcend one's will by acting in accord with the dictates of universal reason. The only thing that meets the requirement of self-determination is thought and reason, and it is only when mind is determined by reason alone that it is self-determined and "free." However, because reason is fully determined and is not subject, for example, to opinion or disagreements based on "choice," freedom coincides with (rational) necessity.[55] According to Hegel, mind is typically thought of as being united with nature, and is thus equivalent to will and desire. However, he says, "If the people desire to be free, they will subordinate their desires to universal laws."[56]

Philosophy, according to Hegel, eventually brings oppositions together in the service of a totality. He says that the "general forms of opposition are the universal and the particular, or, in another manner of speaking, thought as such and external feeling, or perception."[56] The reconciliation of the particular and the universal is the essence of philosophy. Stated in another way, the purpose of the world is its reconciliation with mind. Hegel tells us, the "business of the world, taking it as a whole, is to become reconciled with mind, recognizing itself therein."[57]

IS THERE A DIALECTICAL METHOD?

We have seen the dialectic at work in our discussion of Hegel's system and its culmination in an Absolute manifest in art, religion, and philosophy. But is there a specific dialectical method? This question has, since Hegel's own time, spurred considerable commentary and controversy, and I will not attempt to review more than a small portion of it here. At times Hegel speaks about dialectic so as to make it equivalent to change:

> All things, we say—that is the finite world as such—
> are doomed; and in saying so, we have a vision of
> Dialectic as the universal and irresistible power be-
> fore which nothing can stay, however secure and
> stable it may deem itself.[58]

However, in practice Hegel utilizes the dialectic to make transitions between opposites. As Solomon puts it, for Hegel dialectic is "development through various and apparently opposed or contradictory stages."[59] Solomon further suggests that dialectic is "an argument within a form of consciousness in order to show how it is incomplete, inconsistent, or otherwise inadequate *by its own standards*."[60] According to Solomon, for Hegel, dialectic is "not a method to get at the Truth, but rather it is the Truth, that is, the activity of philosophical thinking itself."[61]

J. N. Findlay, initially adamant that Hegel failed to make a case for a "dialectical method,"[62] reversed himself, ultimately holding that dialectical thinking "involves higher-order comment on a thought position previously achieved."[63] According to Findlay, through dialectic "one sees what can be said *about* a certain thought-position that one cannot actually say *in* it."[64] Elsewhere, Findlay describes the dialectic as a kind of reasoning within which ideas develop in the direction of new ideas that they strongly imply but do not strictly entail. It is the kind of reasoning that Descartes made use of when he argued from the premise that he entertained thoughts to the conclusion that he must exist.[65] We might say that dialectic is at work in nearly all philosophical argumentation that is not strictly formal, and that Hegel's use of dialectic is unique only insofar as he saw implicit connections between notions and ideas that had hitherto been thought to be incompatible or mutually exclusive. Indeed, we might summarize the "method" of dialectic with the phrase, "Where at first you see incompatibility suspect interdependence!" Because dialectic typically unveils a coincidence of opposites, any philosopher who follows Hegel in its use must ultimately be "self-subversive."[66]

The question of whether the dialectic is a method is closely tied to but not necessarily identical with the question of whether the dialectic reveals a logic that differs from traditional two-valued Aristotelian logic, the logic grounded in the law of non-contradiction. It is thus important to examine Hegel's views on contradiction, to see if he indeed finds equivalence and interdependence between *formally contradictory* ideas. This is an important question that is critical to the nature of *coincidentia oppositorum* in general. If indeed, formally contradictory ideas can also be equivalent, or at least compatible, we have grounds for asserting the existence of a new logic—or at the very least an exception to logic as it is normally understood.

We will see that in several places Hegel suggests that the world and the "Absolute" are contradictory and that these contradictions cannot be reduced to a simple matter of words or "perspective." Contradiction, in Hegel's view, is not merely apparent or a matter of "linguistic context," although differentiating genuine from apparent contradiction is no simple matter. It is rather the case that, for Hegel, opposition and even contradiction is inherent in the nature of the things themselves and is part of the very essence of reality. Hegel seems to hold that, even after all differences in perspective have been taken into account and all linguistic (and other) contexts clarified, there will remain certain "truths" that can only be adequately expressed using the language of contradiction and paradox. This suggests the necessity of going beyond a two-valued (true or false) logic and abrogating the law of non-contradiction.

HEGEL ON CONTRADICTION

In *The Science of Logic*, Hegel points out that, in the history of Western science and philosophy, it has generally been held that contradiction is to be avoided at all costs.[67] He writes, "Contradiction is ordinarily the first to be kept away from things, away from any existent and from the true; as the saying goes, there is nothing contradictory."[68] Some philosophers have held that contradiction, since it is an impossibility, simply does not exist at all; others have argued that when contradiction does occur, either in actuality or thought, it is an accident, abnormality, or "a momentary fit of sickness."[69]

Regarding the claim that contradictions simply do not exist, Hegel holds that "ordinary experience itself testifies that *there do exist* at least *a great many* contradictory things, contradictory dispositions, etc., of which the contradiction is present not in any external reflection but right in them."[70] Contradiction is hardly an abnormality, which only occurs on occasion but is rather the fundamental "principle of all natural and spiritual life," the moving force in thought, life, and the world.[71] Hegel writes, "It is only in so far as something has a contradiction within it that it moves, is possessed of instinct and activity."[72]

Hegel insists that contradiction is not simply confined to thought and feeling, but is rather a fundamental characteristic of *the world*. We should recall that for Hegel the world both is and is not distinct from mind or spirit—but here in his discussion of contradiction he assumes the validity of this distinction. He tells his readers that it is only "an excessive tenderness for the world to keep contradiction away from it, to transfer it to spirit instead, to reason, and to leave it there unresolved." Hegel[73] writes:

> But nowhere does that so-called world—call it the objective, real world, or, in the manner of transcendental idealism, subjective intuition and sense-con-

tent determined by the category of the Understanding—nowhere, however you call it, does it escape
contradiction.[74]

However, contradiction is a very different thing for the world than
it is for spirit or mind. The world, according the Hegel, is "not capable
of enduring [contradiction] and it is for that reason it is left to the mercy
of the coming and ceasing to be." Spirit, on the other hand, is strong
enough that it can endure contradiction" and "it is spirit…which knows
how to resolve it."[75]

Hegel maintains that contradiction is not the problem for philosophy but its answer, an answer which leads philosophy to the speculative
reason of the dialectic. He makes it clear that the linear thinking of the
Understanding, which is the basis of metaphysical philosophy, fails to
grasp the meaning of contradiction. While it seeks to avoid or resolve
contradictions, and falls under the illusion that it has done so, the Understanding in fact becomes "entangled in unreconciled, unresolved,
absolute contradictions.[76] Contradictions cannot be resolved using the
categories of the Understanding. Only speculative reason, "in grasping
opposites in their unity, or the positive in the negative,[77] can resolve
contradiction by demonstrating that the opposites are implied by and
contained within one another. What earlier skeptical philosophers saw
as the antinomies or stumbling blocks to reason were, for Hegel, the
very essence of reason, spirit and the world itself.[78]

While each position in the history of philosophy can be demonstrated to lead to a contradiction, this does not, for Hegel, mean that
these positions are untrue, only that they are incomplete in their truth.[79]
In the eighteenth century, Kant argued that no truth was discoverable
via dialectic, as philosophy inevitably leads to hopeless contradictions
that cannot be resolved. Hegel agreed with Kant that dialectic produces contradictions but departed from Kant in holding that such contradictions are not "dead ends" but are rather clues to philosophical and
historical "truth." For Hegel, dialectic demonstrates or makes manifest

the contradictions, inadequacies, and limitations in each idea or form of consciousness, and this process leads to the formation of more adequate ideas and modes of understanding, which are in turn subject to the dialectic themselves.

While Hegel held that Kant's antinomies of pure reason were not deserving of great praise, he believed that Kant's idea that the antinomies "are not sophistic artifices but contradictions reason must *run up against*"[80] was an important philosophical discovery. As we have seen, Kant's response to the antinomies or contradictions in philosophy was to invoke "two worlds," the *phenomenal* world that was available to experience and reason, and the *noumenal* world, which was not. It was in this way that Kant was able to keep contradictory things and ideas separated. Hegel rejected Kant's bifurcation of reality, holding that our forms of consciousness provide us with direct access to a single world, and it is for this reason the contradictions that characterize thought reflect contradictions contained in reality. For Hegel, the reality revealed to us in thought is the only "reality" worthy of our consideration.

As we have seen, Hegel claimed, as Solomon puts it, *"The world itself is contradictory*, but philosophy, through reason, is capable of reconciling such contradictions."[81] It is important that we examine Hegel's notion of contradiction in some detail, for our grasp of a Hegelian approach to *coincidentia oppositorum* and its application to philosophy and psychology will be conditioned in some respects by our appraisal of Hegel's claims that the world is contradictory and that a proposition and its contradictory can, indeed, not only both be true, but are "the truth of one another."

Hegel writes that a concept's or thing's opposite or contradictory is *both* revealed in thought and manifest in the world in time. "Dialectic" is both a mode of cognition that can be employed by an individual thinker, and a force that operates in history. Thus, the presence of a notion's opposite or contradictory within itself (the presence of the "slave" in the very heart of the "master," to take one familiar Hegelian example that we will discuss later in this chapter) can be revealed by analysis but will also be borne out in the historical process. Much confusion can be avoided if we understand that Hegel uses "dialectic" in each of these senses, sometimes without carefully distinguishing between them. However, Hegel's failure to separate these two uses of "dialectic" should not necessarily be seen as a deficiency, as on Hegel's view the distinction between thought and history is largely specious: What an individual philosopher thinks today both reflects and serves as an impetus to the historical process, for what is discerned by thought is part and parcel of the very character of "the things themselves."

KINDS OF OPPOSITION

It is important to distinguish between various forms of opposition as they appear in thought and language, and to consider how each of these may or may not be subject to the Hegelian dialectic or the coincidence of opposites. Not all oppositions are contradictions, and it is very difficult (if not impossible) to ascertain with assurance whether oppositions stated in ordinary languages involve formal contradiction.[82] While the distinction between the different types of opposition is not always clear, we can generally distinguish between: (1) factual propositions, the contradictions of which are presumably always false (London is and is not the capital of England); (2) conceptual oppositions involving obvious contradiction (the opposition between true and false); (3) conceptual oppositions that do not obviously involve contradiction (the opposition between good and evil, universal and particular, free will and determinism, anarchy and despotism); (4) general empirical oppositions (hot and cold); and (5) psychological oppositions (love and hate). In addition, there are three special cases of conceptual opposition that are of particular relevance to the Hegelian claim that a proposition and its contradictory can both be true. These are (6) all-encompassing statements regarding the "Infinite" or the "Absolute" (e.g., that it is and is not equivalent to Reason or the "World-Spirit"); (7) predicates that appear both applicable and inapplicable to certain states of affairs (e.g., regarding the "location" of a moving object that while in motion it is both "here" and "not here"); and (8) self-referential contradictions (the liar's paradox, "This statement is a lie" and similar self-contradictory propositions). I will now briefly discuss each of these in turn.

(1) *Factual propositions*: The first of these oppositions, "factual contradictions," correspond to what Niels Bohr once referred to as oppositions between "superficial truths," truths whose contradictions he thought to be clearly false. If the Louvre is in Paris, it is patently false to say that it is (or is also) not in Paris. Factual truths of this specific nature are not candidates[83] for dialectics or *coincidentia oppositorum*. Hegel, as far as I can tell, never claims that they are. The reason for this is that for all practical purposes factual truths (like the location of the Louvre in Paris) are agreed upon by virtually everyone who is knowledgeable and *are not subject to interpretation.*

(2) *Conceptual oppositions*: Oppositions such as between true and not-true (false), yes and no, affirm and deny, are prime examples of the "law of non-contradiction" or the "law of the excluded middle," and involve obvious contradictions. According to traditional, Aristotelian logic, a proposition cannot be both true and false or neither true nor false. By extension, a thing cannot be *truthfully* said to both exist and not exist. Hegel holds that these so-called "laws of thought" lead to contradictions, the poles of which dialectically pass into each other: "The *several propositions* that are set up as absolute laws of thought *are opposed to each other*: They contradict each other and mutually sublate each other."[84]

For example, Hegel argues that the law of the excluded middle, which asserts "nothing is A and -A at the same time," is itself a violation of its own principal. The "A" contained in the principle is "neither +A nor -A and just as much also +A and -A.[85] This is because it is impossible to say, for example, whether the *red Apple* in the statement "nothing is both a *red apple* and not a *red apple* at the same time" is indeed either an apple or red! Hegel refers to this indeterminate "A" as the "indeterminate third" that violates the law of the excluded middle. The principle could not even be stated unless it made reference to an "X" that is suspended between being "Y" and "not Y."

Another so-called "law of thought," the principle of identity, asserts that "everything is what it is and is not another thing." However, Hegel points out that nothing in the world can be identified by simply stating that it is what it is. To say that "a plant is a plant" or that "God is God" says absolutely nothing.[86] In fact, in order to describe anything, one must arrive at a different determination, say something different from simply stating its "identity." For Hegel, the principle of identity, "instead of being in itself the truth and the absolute truth, is thus the opposite; instead of being the unmoved simple, it surpasses itself into the dissolution of itself."[87]

In anticipation of (and later influencing) Derrida and other postmodernists, Hegel held that what is abstractly or concretely wholly positive, which asserts a positive identity, immediately contradicts itself as it requires its opposite (the negative) to achieve its sense. The same is true for the negative, or difference, which in asserting itself carries its own contradiction through the requirement of the positive. What anything is is wholly dependent upon what it is not, just as what anything is not is defined and is dependent upon what it is.[88] The positive is implicit contradiction whereas the negative is positive contradiction. Hegel expends considerable effort in his *Science of Logic* repeating and rephrasing these points, drawing out the subtleties of the relationship between identity and difference. For example, he states that the negative, in order to remain identical with itself, must distinguish itself from identity and in the process paradoxically excludes itself from itself.[89] According to Hegel, the opposites are ceaselessly vanishing into one another.[90]

Hegel suggests that there is indeed a form of logic in which both a proposition (or thing) and its contradictory can be said to both be true, in violation of the "law of contradiction." Indeed, for Hegel, the truth of an abstract proposition is dependent upon its untruth, and the being of anything is interdependent with its non-being. As we have seen, contemporary advocates of "dialetheism" as well as traditional Buddhist logicians allow for the possibility of a proposition being both true and false or neither true nor false. In discussing the limitations of the Understanding, Hegel more than hints at such multi-valued logic when he suggests, "The soul is neither finite only, nor infinite only; it is really the one just as much as the other, and in that way neither the one nor the other."[91] With this, Hegel appears to give his assent to a logic that admits of four values: "true only" and "false only" (the values of the Understanding), and "both true and false" and "neither true nor false" (the values of speculative philosophy).

Yet Hegel goes beyond these forms of non-traditional logic: "Opposites are not resolved through an 'acknowledgment of the equal correctness, and of the equal incorrectness, of both claims.'"[92] This would simply be a reiteration of the abiding contradiction. The resolution only occurs via the notion of *coincidentia oppositorum*, when each member of an opposing pair shows "that it has its opposite in it, and that in this opposite it rejoins itself, the affirmative truth is this internally self moving unity, the grasping together of both thoughts, their infinity...."[93]

(3) Most *conceptual oppositions* do not necessarily involve obvious logical contradiction. For example, "good" and "bad," while opposites, are not necessarily contradictory. Indeed, one can think of many good things that are also bad. For example, one might think of the "goodness" of high calorie desserts and the "badness" of their potential negative impact on health. Here, however, we are speaking about "goodness" and "badness" in different senses. When we take into consideration such variance in perspective or sense, we find that we need not violate so-called logical laws to account for the fact that a given object or event can be good and bad, public and private, mental and physical, and so on. To the extent that dialectic is applicable to such (non-contradictory) oppositions, it need not involve an abrogation of traditional logic but may rather involve the rough and ready dictum: Where at first you see incompatibility suspect equivalence and interdependence! For some, this may well be the extent of the dialectic's acceptance of "contradiction."

Certain *abstract propositions rooted in ordinary life and discourse* are prime targets for misconstrual by the Understanding and are important examples of ideas that are subject to dialectical or speculative investigation. Hegel makes this point with respect to critical ideas in law and morality. He argues, for example, that pushing an abstract right (such as personal liberty) to an extreme results in a wrong, and that "anarchy and extreme despotism naturally lead to each other." In the realm of values, Hegel appeals to such well-worn adages as "Pride comes before a fall" and "Too much wit outwits itself" as illustrations of the dialectical idea that abstract goods pass over into their opposites.[94]

Hegel makes similar points regarding *philosophical oppositions* such as free will and determinism, and universal and particular. We have already seen that, for Hegel, it is a misunderstanding to hold that free will and determinism are simply opposing ideas that could be true independently of one another. Instead, free will passes over into determinism and vice versa. I will have more to say about this particular opposition in Chapter 5 when I consider the fundamental oppositions that underlie different paradigms in psychology. We have also seen how, for Hegel, such oppositions as universal and particular, being and nothingness, and unity and difference are in *coincidentia oppositorum*. Perhaps Hegel's greatest insight can be summed up in the proposition that philosophy is precisely that set of abstract ideas and principles that, when fully analyzed, suggest the truth of other ideas that would at first seem antithetical to the concept under analysis. As we saw in Chapter 1, this was precisely the view of the mid-twentieth century philosopher Morris Lazerowitz, who, while apparently unsympathetic to Hegel's program in philosophy, wrote:

> if we look closely at metaphysical theories we find a surprisingly large number of paradoxes in unexpected places…. The idea which suggests itself is that a paradox or a contradiction lies hidden in every metaphysical theory, that it is the very stuff from which metaphysical theories are woven."[95]

This insight is, of course, simply an expansion of Kant's discovery of philosophical antinomies at the heart of metaphysics. Hegel held this discovery to be just the beginning insight of philosophy.

(4) *General and specific empirical oppositions*: There is a class of oppositions (hot and cold, up and down, large and small, life and death) that can broadly be classified as "empirical," inasmuch as they are dependent upon our experience in order for us to assert them. Hegel avers that "every abstract proposition of understanding, taken precisely as it is given, naturally veers round into its opposite."[96] This leaves open the possibility that "empirical" distinctions, insofar as they are general and abstract, are subject to the dialectic, and indeed Hegel claims that natural phenomena, such as the motions of the heavenly bodies (being now "here" but later "there") are subject to dialectical transformation.[97] In his philosophy of nature, Hegel provides various dialectical deductions. For example, in color we see the dialectical resolution of luminous transparency and opaque darkness, and in chemical interactions we see the dialectical equivalence and transformation between separateness and unity.[98] Hegel's claims regarding such empirical phenomena sound quaint at best to contemporary ears and forced at worst. The main point to consider with regard to empirical distinctions is that they may be considered dependent upon their opposites in general but exclude their opposites in the concrete instance. For example, *high* exists only by virtue of its contrast with *low*, but a building that is 1,280 feet high may be low *in comparison* to Mt. Everest, but it is not both 1,280 *above* and 1,280 feet *below* the ground.

There are certain empirical oppositions that continued to be of major interest to later philosophers. An example of this is the opposition between "life" and "death." Hegel suggests in the *Phenomenology of Spirit* that death is indeed necessary for life, and that negation (and deprivation in general) is necessary for being and truth:

> Death, as we may call that unreality, is the most terrible thing.... But the life of Mind is not one that

> shuns death, and keeps clear of destruction; it en-
> dures death, and in death maintains its being. It only
> wins to its truth when it finds itself utterly torn asun-
> der. It is this mighty power, not by being a positive,
> which turns away from the negative.... Spirit is this
> power only by looking the negative in the face, and
> dwelling with it...the magic power that converts the
> negative into being.[99]

Here, Hegel anticipated the thought of the later existentialists, in particular Heidegger, who understood death as being essential to the very
meaning of human life.

(5) *Psychological oppositions*: Hegel regards a variety of oppositions (for example, love and hate) as being subject to the dialectic. He
reminds his readers that everyone is aware that pain and pleasure pass
into one another, and that joy is often expressed through tears.[100] With
this he anticipates the findings of later depth psychologists who emphasized the role of conflict, compensation, and irony in our mental life.
While Hegel is generally not understood as a progenitor of psychoanalysis, his concern with opposition created an intellectual environment in
Europe that was conducive to dynamic psychology's view that intrapsychic conflict is the determinative factor in mental life.

(6) *Propositions about the "Absolute"*: Hegel holds that mind is both
infinite and finite "and *neither* merely the one *nor* merely the other."[101]
It is important to point out that Hegel's Absolute must not only *contain*
the finite—in the sense that an infinite numerical series "contains" the
numbers "5" and "13"—but it must *be* finite as well; otherwise, there
would be certain essences (those things that *are* finite) which would
transcend the being of the Absolute. A similar line of reasoning is also
at work in the Hindu notion that the Absolute, *Brahman-Atman*, is *this*
spider, *that* very grain of sand, or *this* particular moment in time. An Absolute that was not all things but which, for example, merely contained
them as parts would not be the infinite, unified "All" required by Hegel
or the *Upanishads*. Hegel's Absolute is therefore at once infinite and

finite (non-infinite), unifying this contradiction in its infinite essence.

In a similar fashion, Hegel suggests in *The Phenomenology of Spirit* that the necessity of ascribing finitude (non-infinity) to the infinite is built into the notion of infinity in an even more intimate fashion. It is not only the case that infinitude could not properly be infinite if it were not also finite, but it is also true that the infinite unity, in the very act of positing itself as infinite unity, must bring finitude and plurality into being. Hegel explains this somewhat cryptically: "What becomes identical with itself thereby opposes itself to disruption...in other words it becomes really something sundered."[102]

What Hegel means here is that an absolute notion like the "soul of the world," which conceives itself (or is conceived of) as an absolute, simple unity must, if it is to be conceptualized at all, "oppose" or distinguish itself from "disruption" or difference. It is as if the All must say "I am one, infinite and *non-distinct*." By this very assertion, it brings plurality, finitude, and distinctiveness into the cosmos, which it first must exclude and then re-include within itself if it is to remain the All. The infinite can thus be said to logically or "naturally" exclude (and then include) finitude, plurality, and distinctiveness as part of its very essence. Hegel tells us that such "dialectical diremptions"—through which notions logically exclude then imply and finally include their opposites within themselves—are fundamental to all thought and existence. The Absolute, then, is such that *in being itself* it is also every distinction which arises, as well as the "medium" through which such distinctions are all dialectically resolved.[103]

(7) *The Paradox of Motion*: Hegel regards the so-called "paradox of motion" to be a prime example of the dialectic and the coincidence of opposites. It is both true and false that an object in motion is in a particular place at any particular time. We say, for example that a man traveling from point X to point Z is currently at point Y, but this of course is never more than an approximation; indeed, it is an inaccuracy that is necessary in order to express a practical truth. The man or object that is in continuous motion is never in a particular place but is always just be-

yond any place we attribute to it. Hegel writes, "Something moves, not because now it is here and there at another now but because in one and the same now it is here and not here."[104] For Hegel, ancient paradoxes of motion do not lead to the view that motion is an illusion that does not exist but rather to the conclusion that contradiction is ubiquitous.

(8) *The Liar's Paradox*: "This statement is false," "I am now lying," and other similar self-referential statements yield the paradoxical result that if they are true they are false, and if false they are true. If it is "true" that "this statement is false," then the statement obviously is false; if it is false that "this statement is false," then the statement becomes true. Hegel briefly treats these "liar's paradoxes" in his *Lectures on the History of Philosophy*, holding that they produce "a union of opposites, lying and truth, and their immediate contradiction."[105] As we saw in Chapter 1, certain contemporary logicians regard the liar's paradox as one impetus to a multi-valued logic. Here, we should simply note that for Hegel these paradoxes are a graphic example of the instability of concepts and their tendency to pass into their opposites. It is doubtful, however, if the *coincidentia oppositorum* embodied in this paradox, insofar as it is a very brief circuit that fails even to escape from itself and include any aspect of the world, grants us much insight into any of the pressing questions of philosophy, theology, or psychology.

I will return in Chapter 7 to the question of whether the oppositions involved in the coincidence of opposites reflect formal contradictions. There I will suggest that the answer to this question is itself indeterminable and perhaps indeterminate. However, we will also see that the usefulness of the coincidence of opposites idea is not dependent on a resolution of this issue: All that *coincidentia oppositorum* is required to assert is that if we examine certain presumably mutually exclusive ideas in philosophy, psychology, and theology, we will find not only that they do not exclude one another but that they are, in an important sense, interdependent.

MORE ON THE "WORLD" AS CONTRADICTORY

Slavoj Žižek has argued that while Kant exposed the cracks in our thinking and the irreparable antinomies in every effort to conceive of reality as a whole, Hegel went a step further and located the antinomies or contradictions not in our reason but in *the things themselves*.[106] According to Žižek, the very point of the Hegelian dialectic is to show how everything that occurs is subject to imbalance, sundering, and failure. All things—all phenomena—have their demise and death written into their very core. Kant had demonstrated that all metaphysical systems lead to antinomies and therefore advocated that we abandon metaphysics. Hegel, however, came to the conclusion that metaphysics should not be abandoned but should be understood as involving a progression of logical contradictions, contradictions that are not simply in thought and knowledge but which are located within the world itself.[107]

If we consider Hegel's view that it is the world itself that is contradictory (as opposed to our propositions or sentences about it) in the context of his critique of the Kantian project, we realize that there is an interesting aspect of Hegel's position that is related to Kant's concerns about claims regarding "appearances" versus the "thing-in-itself." A similar problem arises in connection with the contemporary concern with *constructed language*, a concern that parallels Kant's problem of constructed experience. When we use the terms "world" or "reality," we use them in a context that has been determined by linguistic convention, either a pre-existing convention that we adopt or a new one that we establish. And when we speak of "contradictions" within the world, we are again adopting or establishing a linguistic convention through which certain propositions are considered logically incompatible. Because "contradictions" are expressed in language and because language can be used and interpreted in various ways, it becomes difficult (and some would say impossible) to pin down a contradiction in (a pre-linguisticized, pre-conceptualized) world. Wittgenstein once suggested that "the law of non-contradiction" is a convention based on a language game.[108] On such a view, it is not that two things cannot occupy the same space at the same time in some *hard metaphysical sense* but rather that this "impossibility" is a conventionally adopted rule of language and thought. Consider the hypothetical (and "logically" possible) case of an object that looks round but feels square to the touch (certainly not even an empirical impossibility!)—is it *not a rule of language* that would prevent us from saying that in such a case a sphere and a square were both occupying the same place at the same time?

As we have seen, Kant held that claims of knowledge can only be about appearances and never about the "thing-in-itself (*ding an sich*). Hegel argued that by even referencing a "noumenal realm" beyond appearances (as the source of ethical and theological propositions) Kant had made this realm an object of knowledge and thereby undercut his claim that knowledge was limited to appearances. On Hegel's view, since all knowledge of the world is a presentation or abstract category of *mind*, anything that can be referred to is, in principle, an object of knowledge. Given Hegel's idealism, with its equation of "existence" with presentation or "idea," the distinction between phenomena presented to mind and the world collapses and knowledge about appearances becomes knowledge about the world itself. As Žižek suggests, Hegel corrects Kant not through an addition but rather through a subtraction, the subtraction of Kant's metaphysical assumption that there must be an underlying reality beyond our experience and judgments.[109] A similar argument can be made in connection with the Wittgensteinian view that, because "knowledge" and "world" are conventionally defined terms in a "language game," all knowledge is limited to the "world" as it is defined by our conventions, and we thereby have no access to a "pre-linguistic reality."

What happens when Hegel's critique of Kant's psychological constructivism is applied to contemporary linguistic constructivism? The argument might go something like this: Since our language conventions about the *world* provide the only possible sense of "world," our propositions about the world must be about the world itself. However, unlike in the case of Kant's categories and modes of apprehension (for example, space, time, and causality), which he regarded as fixed and essential for any experience and knowledge whatsoever, language can construct a "world" in various ways. If such constructions are regarded as providing direct metaphysical knowledge, then such knowledge is multiple and potentially contradictory. Thus, if we hold that linguistic constructions give us knowledge about the world itself, we are again faced with the question of whether such constructions provide us not only with a varied but also a contradictory world picture. If so, this would be a reason for holding that the world itself is contradictory. Since we cannot describe "the world" without resorting to language, our descriptions within language describe our only meaningful world. If we believe that our descriptions, and even definitions of the "world" are not only multiple but contradict one another, then the world *as it is in itself* is contradictory.

We can illustrate these considerations with an example, one that tackles the very controversy between "linguistic convention" and "the things in themselves" that is at the heart of our present discussion. On the one hand, we can define "reality" by "convention," as that which is generally agreed to be the world or "reality" by members of our linguistic community; but as there are many such communities (religious, secular, scientific, etc.), there are many "realities," many "worlds," that are not entirely consistent with one another. On the other hand, we might understand and define "reality" as that which *breaks through all of our conventions* and is inassimilable to our present schemas[110] (as in the "shock of reality" brought upon by the spectre of trauma and death). This "reality," which we might consider akin to Kant's "thing-in-itself," is currently unknown, and perhaps even "unknowable"; nonetheless, it asserts itself at the boundaries of human experience. However, *when we speak or write about this reality we have created another linguistic convention,* albeit one that is said to be incompatible with the various "realities by convention" that constitute our "worlds." Again, we find that we are unable to move beyond our modes of representation to a "world as it is in-itself" (except as defined by another linguistic convention). Such a "world-as-it-is-in-itself" drops out of the picture—or better, merges with the world as it is described in language. But as we have multiple definitions or accounts of the world (including even, "that which corresponds to linguistic convention" versus "that which breaks through any linguistic convention"), some of which contradict one another, we end up with a contradictory "world."

Again, we might think that "reality" must be something beyond these mere linguistic conventions. But this is precisely the point. If we cannot speak about "reality," *except in the manner in which we speak about it*, then reality as it is described in language is the only reality we can entertain or have, certainly the only "reality" that can be the subject of philosophy. "Reality" includes the language game of a "reality" beyond language, and this is just one more linguistic convention and hence one of a number of contrasting description of the world. As some of these descriptions are logically inconsistent, the world itself is contradictory!

FIRST- VERSUS THIRD-PERSON DESCRIPTIONS

The contrasting world pictures that arise from third-person (objective) versus first-person (subjective) accounts of the cosmos provides another basis for the assertion that the world is contradictory. The philosopher Thomas Nagel, for example, has argued that opposing descriptions of reality arise when one considers certain questions from these two points of view—questions pertaining to the meaning of life, the existence of free will, the nature of the self and personal identity, the relationship between mind and body, and the source of ethics and value. Nagel argues, for example, that the existence of agency or free will is palpable and very real from a first-person perspective, but appears to have no place within the context of a third-person "objective" account of the world. Similarly, from a first-person standpoint the existence of "qualia," the qualitative "feel" of consciousness, is the only thing that is immediately evident and is the source of everything known about both the subjective and objective world. However, from a third-person perspective, the existence of such "qualia" cannot be adequately accounted for, leading some philosophers to hold that conscious experience is an epiphenomenon with no causal function or objective status.[111]

Nagel holds that while each point of view (and the linguistic conventions that describe them) seeks to annex, reduce, or eliminate the other in the service of a "single world" (leading, for example, to philosophies of naturalism and idealism), these two points of view and the contrasting accounts of the world that they engender are irreducible: "The coexistence of conflicting points of view, varying in detachment from the contingent self, are not just a practical necessary illusion, but an irreducible fact of life."[112]

Philosophy, and to a certain degree "common sense," have long labored under the idea that it is possible to provide a single, truthful description of anything whatsoever, including the world as a whole. We seem to have faith in the idea that one "map," if it is sufficiently accurate and detailed, will at least theoretically provide us with a complete account of reality. Hegel wishes to disabuse us of this notion, holding that it is the fundamental error of the Understanding. As in the case of cartography, where no single two-dimensional map can accurately capture the three-dimensional surface of the globe, no single model in philosophy, theology, and psychology can fully account for the world. Perhaps we can say that the world as a whole has properties that transcend our capacity to represent it in a single model.

In Hegel's philosophy, the Absolute can only be described using language that seems paradoxical or contradictory, for the Absolute encompasses a world in which creative acts are "negations," in which events are determined *and* man's actions are free, and in which "things" are both independent of man's consciousness *and* constituted by his mind. It is, in short, a world that answers to all the opposing descriptions of science and philosophy. According to Hegel, the Kantian "thing-in-itself" is a superfluous notion, and to call these contrary descriptions different "worlds," "perspectives," or "languages" does not diminish the inherent "contradictoriness of the object." Indeed, the very fact that incompatible perspectives can be taken upon the world informs us that the world has qualities that lend itself to multiple descriptions. The world is itself is contradictory, because, as Hegel argues, the world is precisely the world that is as known through *our* descriptions.

DIALECTICS IN THE *INTERPRETATION OF HEGEL*

As we have seen, many of the oppositions that are treated both explicitly and implicitly in Hegelian philosophy are not typically logical contradictions, but are poles or dichotomies that are informally understood to be in opposition to, or incompatible with, one another. Often, Hegel's own treatment of these oppositions is not completely clear and this generates seemingly incompatible interpretations among Hegel scholars. For example, throughout his writings, Hegel considers the dichotomy of God and humanity, and it is patent that for Hegel the distinction between these notions is far less rigid than it is in pre-Hegelian thought. However, the question arises as to the precise relationship between God and humanity in Hegel's philosophy. For Solomon, Hegel's God is nothing more "than the human spirit writ large,"[113] while for Charles Taylor, Hegel teaches us that humanity is a vehicle for something larger than itself, i.e., an absolute spirit that posits itself as a matter of rational necessity.[114]

While this is clearly a basic point of disagreement in Hegel scholarship, it can be argued from a Hegelian perspective that each of the opposing interpretations of Hegel's thought regarding the relationship between God and humanity is implicit within the other. For Hegel, humanity transcends itself to fulfill its own nature, and it fulfills its own nature in the process of going beyond that nature. Hegel, it might be argued, perhaps even intentionally, produced a system that can be alternatively understood in immanent and transcendent terms. The notions that mind is something both completely immanent and yet also greater than man himself, and that the mental is identifiable with but at the same time transcends the material, follow from the very core of Hegel's thought. Indeed, he refuses to make any ultimate distinction between spirit and nature, thought and matter, God and the world, while at the same time refusing to see these contraries as equivalents. Hegel's humanism thus dialectically passes over into a religious transcendentalism, and vice versa. Any other position fails to be sufficiently dialectical. The dialectic does not stop at some arbitrary point that, for example, "decides" between humanism and theism, but must swallow up all distinctions in its wake. Like "Brahman-Atman" in Indian thought, which can be compared to Hegel's notion of spirit (*Geist*), there is a series of "equivalences-in-difference" in Hegel's philosophy. Brahman, we are told, is the equivalent of Atman but the former is "all" from the point of view of the entire cosmos, and the latter is "all" from the point of view of the human self or soul. In Chapter 2 we saw nearly the same description of alternate divine and human perspectives in the philosophy of Chabad Chasidism.

A pattern of compatible "alternatives" also emerges when we consider the question of whether Hegel should be regarded as a metaphysician. Solomon completely rejects Stace's early characterization of Hegel as a metaphysician who proceeded into "the citadel of reality itself."[115] Instead, Solomon sees Hegel as the supreme anti-metaphysician, purging philosophy of the Kantian thing-in-itself and rejecting the very idea of a single, correct, world-view. Further, Solomon argues, Hegel rejects the duality of experience and reality, which gives rise to the notion that one can ultimately *know* reality in any absolute way. However, we again have a failure to be fully dialectical. The dialectic must, by its own terms, reject the possibility of choosing between a metaphysical and non-metaphysical view of reality. Indeed, by showing the inadequacy of each successive metaphysical point of view, Hegel, unlike Wittgenstein, does not intend to dissolve them all and escape philosophy altogether; he teaches us a method in which we can, by freeing ourselves successively from each incomplete point of view, obtain a more complete and synoptic view which, in its "limit form," encompasses them all. The purported value of the dialectic is that it achieves its metaphysics by successively moving beyond each successive metaphysical position.

While Hegel himself seemed to suggest that the dialectic ended in his own philosophy, I would suggest that it is consistent with his thinking to hold that there is no final resting point. However, neither is there despair at not achieving one, only the satisfaction of following the route of inquiry and the refusal to be seduced by any single point along the way. As I will argue in Chapter 7, even philosophy or "conceptual thought" has no privileged position, and if one takes the dialectic to heart, one is led out of philosophy and even beyond concepts and language![116] This is *both* non-metaphysical and the most comprehensive of metaphysical views.

THE DIALECTIC OF DESIRE

Thus far, we have considered Hegel's ideas about the opposites in connection with fundamental problems in philosophy and theology. However, he also had much to say about what would now be considered psychology, although writing at time prior to the separation of psychology as a distinct "scientific" discipline (but also consistent with his own all-embracing thought) he felt no need to distinguish between philosophy and psychology. As I am about to explain, Hegel's concern with the opposites, combined with his astute observations about human experience, anticipated major themes in both dynamic, existential, and "self" psychology, and are relevant to the contemporary practice of psychotherapy.

Earlier we saw how, in his *Phenomenology of Mind*, Hegel describes a dialectic of knowledge or "consciousness" in an effort to show how Mind or Spirit moves from a position of self-certainty to an epistemology rooted in the concept. The *Phenomenology* continues with a dialectic of *desire* or "self-consciousness," a dialectic that is supposed to begin where the earlier epistemological dialectic leaves off but which runs parallel to parts of the earlier progression. Hegel's dialectic of desire, particularly his discussion of the master-slave relationship and the desire for recognition, had an enormous impact upon later philosophical and psychological thought, including existentialism and European (particularly French) psychoanalysis. Hegel's master-slave dialectic, in which he develops the idea that the coincidence of opposites between subject and object is the ultimate goal of human consciousness, will also be relevant to our consideration in Chapter 4 of the role of *coincidentia oppositorum* in the thought of Jung. In the course of the master-slave dialectic, the Hegelian notion of the self emerges; it is a dialectic in which a series of more primitive self-notions are described, thought through (and experienced) to their logical conclusions, then found untenable and ultimately abandoned in favor of (logically) later, more adequate notions of the self.

Hegel understood our most fundamental and primitive motives to involve a desire for a state of completeness, self-sufficiency, and non-disturbance. Such a state of total personal integrity—what Freud later identified as the wished-for end-point of the *nirvana* or constancy principle—was identified by Hegel with a type of personal infinity, a condition in which the human subject is not limited by anything beyond itself.[117] The desire for this infinity follows from the dialectic of consciousness or knowledge, as the end point of that dialectic is a condition in which the subject's idea or "mind" merges with the objective particular or "world." This merger of mind and world is written into the very idea of consciousness itself, which involves an interdependence between the subject's idea and the world's objective, immediate presence. Desire, even in its most basic form, necessarily seeks to fulfill this merger of subject and object, thereby striving to achieve a dominance, control, incorporation of, and (finally) reconciliation with, the external world. As we enter into Hegel's dialectic of desire, it will be important to keep in mind that, in his view, the coincidence of opposites between subject and object is the engine driving the various stages he describes.

Consumption, for Hegel, is the first moment or position of desire. Even primitive life forms seek out and consume what they need from the external world, in the process incorporating that part of the world into themselves. The attitude of consumption is, indeed, a means whereby primitive subjectivity can cancel the otherness of an external environment and achieve a form of momentary self-sufficient unity. However, the attitude of consumption is not satisfactory. In consuming an aspect of the environment, the subject destroys it and is left in the same position it was in prior to the consumptive act—needing the environment once more. Thus, the fulfillment of consumption passes over into its opposite, which is emptiness, lack, and need. Further, prior to the consumptive act, the subject finds itself before something that is wholly other; after the consumption, he is before nothing at all. There is no genuine merger of subject and object when the object has been destroyed. The consuming self is therefore a contradiction in terms: Always seeking something new, it is never satisfied.

What the subject next desires is an object whose otherness can be negated or incorporated into the self without being abolished. Hegel informs us that this possibility cannot be realized with an objective, material object, but only through an encounter with another subjectivity. "Self-consciousness," he tells us, "attains its satisfaction only in another self-consciousness."[118] True satisfaction of this kind can only be achieved via a mutual recognition of two or more free subjects. Such mutuality, however, is not the position which subjectivity initially takes up with the demise of the consumptive, incorporative attitude. Rather, the subject enters into a struggle with the other, which conceivably could lead to his death but typically evolves into the dialectic of the master and slave, whereby one subject (the master) attempts to force another (the slave) into recognizing him as dominant. This struggle with the other arises at a point where individual consciousness has not yet understood itself as universal and not yet understood that the recognition and autonomy of one's self requires the recognition and autonomy of all. While the struggle with the other may lead to his death, the death of another subject is as unsatisfactory as the destruction of the consumed object. However, the *dominance* of another subject initially promises something more. The "master" imagines that by subjecting the slave and forcing the slave to recognize him as the master, he is able to achieve a state of continual dominance over the external world (as embodied in an "other") without destroying it. Unlike the consumptive self, which destroys its object in the process of incorporating it, the master believes he can maintain the slave in a state of perpetual recognition of the master's self.

The condition achieved by the master, however, turns out to be unsatisfactory by its own criteria. The master wishes to be recognized as dominant by another subjectivity, by a consciousness that can reflect back to him his status as master. However, precisely because the slave is enslaved he is himself, by definition, not recognized as a subject by the master; because he is viewed by the master as something less than a subject, he cannot give the master the very recognition he desires.

It is, paradoxically, the slave who is able to bring the dialectic of subjectivity and self-hood to the next stage. This is because the slave, whose very life is at the mercy of a force beyond his own control, is shaken from his focus and investment in his individual self by the specter of *death*. Death, for Hegel (as it would be for Heidegger a century later), plays a crucial role in the development of the self, for it is the realization of death that shakes consciousness from its rigid focus upon its individual needs and projects. The prospect of death assures that individual consciousness "has been inwardly dissolved, has trembled to its depths, and everything fixed in it has quaked."[119] The slave, in coming face-to-face with the menace of death, and in having each of his individual projects thwarted, is presented with an opportunity not given to the master: an opportunity to transcend one's self in an identification of that which is beyond the individual ego, the universal man. According to Hegel, the slave, by virtue of the limitations placed upon him, experiences the worthlessness of his individual ego and "this subjugation of the slave's egotism forms the beginning of true human freedom."[120] In this moment of the dialectic, complete subjugation and slavery passes over into an opportunity for freedom. Here, Hegel's view comes close to the great spiritual traditions of the East, in which the recognition of the futility of one's egoistical quest leads to release or *nirvana*.

Hegel tells us, however, that the specter of death and limitation would be insufficient to produce a permanent change in the slave except for the fact that the slave, in his struggle with an environment he is forced to labor upon, realizes a higher unity with that environment in creative work. The master has no struggle of labor and hence falls into a complacency in which he falsely believes himself to be self-sufficient and complete but in which he is really estranged from the world. The slave, on the other hand, by laboring in the world, imprints his own ideas upon the environment and as such comes close to realizing a true coincidence of subject and object, between his self and the world. Thus, the slave points to the possibility of a "laboring self," which is the next stage in the dialectic progression, beyond both the self of consumption and the self of interpersonal dominance.

Several of the ideas we have discussed thus far are familiar themes in post-Hegelian philosophy and psychology. The transformational value of death is, as I have said, a significant theme in modern existentialism, particularly the philosophy of Martin Heidegger, for whom *being-towards-death* is regarded as constitutive of *authentic* human life.[121] In anticipation of the existentialists, Hegel writes:

> We say, for instance, that man is mortal, and seem to think that the ground of his death is in external circumstances only; so that if this way of looking at things were correct, man would have two special properties, vitality—also—mortality. But the true view of the matter is that life, as life, involves the germ of death, and that the finite, being radically self-contradictory, involves its own self-suppression.[122]

This theme has been of profound influence on existential psychology, from the *dasein analyse* of Ludwig Binswanger[123] to the existential psychotherapy of Irwin Yalom.[124] It also anticipated Freud's notion of the "death instinct," and a Hegelian/Heideggerian/Freudian view of death comes to play an important role in the psychoanalysis of Jacques Lacan. The master-slave dialectic and the significance of labor is, of course, at the core of Marxism and plays a critical role in those psychological theories that have been influenced by Marxist thought. This dialectic is also of profound significance for psychology in the twentieth century in France. Sartre, for example, built an entire psychology of interpersonal relations around his refinements of the Hegelian master-slave dialectic.[125] The role of *recognition* is of profound significance in the psychologies of Sartre, Maurice Merleau-Ponty, and Lacan, and a thorough reformulation of the problematic posed by the master-slave struggle for recognition is at work in Martin Buber's *I and Thou*.[126]

For Hegel, the dialectic of the master and slave brings about another definition of the self, one embodied in the philosophy of *stoicism*. The slave, despite his recognition of himself in the world through the imprinting of his ideas on the environment via labor, is still a slave. As such, he is powerless to transform the world; and this powerlessness prompts him to a retreat from that world into a new focus upon his own "I." The stoic maintains his freedom precisely to the extent that he is unaffected by the happenings of the world which are, at any rate, completely beyond his control. The stoic self is indeed the highest stage that can be reached under certain historical circumstances, and it can be recognized as such in, for example, Victor Frankl's account of the freedom attained even by the victims of the Holocaust. Frankl relates how Jews who marched to their deaths in the concentration camps were able to maintain their humanity because, while the Nazis could control and destroy their prisoners' bodies, the guards had no control over the prisoners' minds and faith.[127]

Stoicism, according to Hegel, naturally passes over into *skepticism*, for while the former considers the specific happenings in the world and in one's life as unimportant, the skeptic calls external reality into question altogether. Psychologically speaking, the skeptic is not far from despair: If the basic project of the self is to bring about a harmonious union of subjectivity and the world, this can hardly be achieved if the very existence of the latter is cast into doubt.

Stoicism and skepticism both, Hegel tells us, pass over into the next phase of the self: the unhappy consciousness. This occurs when subjects recognize that the contradiction between their own subjectivity and the world they had attempted to transcend via the stoic self cannot be escaped. The unhappy consciousness appears because the subject recognizes an enormous gap between the ideal and the real. It is the fate of a subject who yearns for unity within the self and with the world but who only experiences chaos, disunity, and alienation. The unhappy consciousness identifies itself with the particularity and chaos of this world, and projects the unified and unchanging into a transcendent realm. But since there is, at this stage, an unbridgeable gap between the alienation, chaos, and mortality of the individual subject and the harmony and unity of a transcendent ideal, the unhappy consciousness is mired in despair. Psychologically speaking, such unhappiness arises when the subject realizes the impotence of each of the prior stages and attitudes: Having failed to achieve the desired unity of subject and object through the attitudes of consumption, master, slave, stoicism, and skepticism, the subject despairs of ever finding an adequate personal solution to his alienation and dividedness.

For Hegel, the unhappy consciousness is both an essential stage in the development of "mind" and the final stage which can be reached by the individual subject *identifying himself as an individual*. Individual consciousness is an inadequate means for the development of mind or spirit.[128] One who defines his fulfillment in terms of his own achievements or pleasure will, in the end, be overcome by his own individuality in death. It is only those who identify themselves with a universal goal beyond the self who can achieve the harmony with the world that is longed for by the subject, for such individuals have identified with something that transcends their own particularity.

There is thus a natural transition in the *Phenomenology* where Hegel moves from a consideration of individual modes of subjectivity to collective ones. The family, state, culture, religion, art, and philosophy become the next stages in the development of spirit, stages which move beyond those possible for the individual self. In making this transition from subjective to "objective" spirit we need not, however, conclude that Hegel has moved beyond that which is of interest to psychology. Rather, Hegel is critical of any psychology that defines the self in purely individualistic terms. Indeed, it is precisely those psychologies which do, he would argue, that result in the unhappy consciousness. It is only when psychology (and the individual) identifies the self with what Hegel calls the rational order of the developing World-Spirit that a true unity and harmony can be achieved. In Jungian terms, we might say that for Hegel, true selfhood is achieved only when the center of one's subjectivity moves from individualistic to collective modes of awareness.

Hegel was later criticized by the existentialists for his emphasis on the family, state, religion, and other aspects of "objective Spirit." The existentialists felt that Hegel had ignored the uniqueness of the individual, what Søren Kierkegaard referred to as the "lonely man of faith." It seemed to these later philosophers that the individual was dispensable for Hegel, and that the only "self" that mattered was the abstract one posited by Hegel as the "World-Spirit" or Absolute. In a sense, the existentialists were right. For Hegel, the individual *is* dispensable, but in order to realize the goals of the individual himself, and not simply in order to achieve the purposes of some supra-individual spirit or mind. For Hegel, the only true transcendence of death, the only true "freedom," and the only lasting meaning and significance result from an identification with values beyond those of the self. Death, for example, is existentially significant, not because it focuses the mind on one's individual goals and pleasures but because it focuses one on that which is genuinely important: the welfare of others, one's principles, and one's contribution to the world.

HEGEL AND PSYCHOLOGY

Hegel's master-slave dialectic understanding of the coincidence of opposites between subject and object and individual and environment is significant for later developments in the field of psychology. We have already briefly discussed several of these in connection with Hegel's views on the nature of interpersonal relationships, and the stages in the development of the self. Hegel was perhaps the first major Western thinker to outline phases of a developing self in its relationship to others and the world. While Hegel conducted this in a philosophical as opposed to a psychological idiom, the notion of successive developmental phases has been taken up by nearly every important psychological theorist of the self, including Freud and Melanie Klein in their theories of emotional development, Piaget and Lawrence Kohlberg in their theories of moral development, and Eric Erikson in his discussion of "life stages." Indeed, the whole notion of psychological development, which has played such an important role in twentieth-century psychology, owes much to Hegel's philosophy.

Hegel's notion of a psychological position, or conception of the self which breaks down in the face of its own purposes and criteria, is of relevance to—and may indeed be said to characterize—the practice of psychotherapy. His dialectic of desire implies that virtually *any* construction of the self, any fixed commitment to emotions, ideas, values, and the like, will ultimately break down by its own criteria and the individual will be forced into adopting a position opposed to himself. The work of psychotherapy is dialectic in precisely this sense: The therapist seeks to uncover the fixed attitudes, beliefs, emotions, and other "complexes" of the individual; then, by challenging them and working to alter their rigid structure, the therapist helps the individual to move forward.

Finally, the specific stages of Hegel's dialectic of desire are particularly relevant to an understanding the development of the self. The transitions from a consumptive, incorporative position, through the need for recognition and the struggle with the other, the encounter with death, the realization of labor, stoicism, skepticism, and despair, and finally the achievement of selfless altruism not only serve as paradigms for much later philosophy and psychology but reflect various "life solutions" that continue to be relevant to individuals in their struggle for "self-actualization." As in Hegel's own time, we frequently encounter individuals who are dominated by each of these positions: the obsessive consumer who believes he can achieve happiness through the acquisition of things; the power hungry boss who seeks to achieve personal fulfillment through the domination of others; the resigned underling who defines his identity by submerging himself in a superior other; the employee who (in spite of his relative impotence) believes he has achieved a measure of fulfillment in the ethic of work; the "stoic," hardened by life's defeats who retreats into himself and (apparently) cares nothing for the events of his life and the world; the "skeptic," who believes that no solution is possible or convinces himself that the problem of life's meaning doesn't even exist; the depressive, who despairs over ever finding personal unity and fulfillment; and the creative artist or altruist, who has achieved a measure of transcendence beyond the self. I believe that Hegel's typology of such life solutions, which is grounded in his notion that consciousness seeks to merge the opposites of mind and world, is as relevant today as it was 160 years ago. It is the work not only of a philosophical giant but of an astute observer of human behavior and self-deception.

DIALECTICS, IRONY, AND DYNAMIC PSYCHOLOGY

Hegel holds that dialectic is closely related to irony, and indeed his views on the complementarity of opposites leads him to posit "irony" as a fundamental principle operating in both reason and the world. For example, according to Hegel, the grand *abstract* notion of "God" is itself (ironically) *empty* without a concrete instantiation of God's expression in *nature*. This idea is but a broad expression of the principle that all abstract notions or ideas (for example, the concept of "apple") are empty without a concrete expression (actual apples). However, it is *ironic* that the very concrete instance of a thing is meaningless, and hence itself quite empty, unless it can be seen under the aegis of a general concept or idea. Indeed, because the concrete instance upon which the abstract notion is dependent is itself dependent upon the abstract notion, the abstract notion's dependence upon the concrete is, ironically, nothing but a dependence upon itself! As Hegel suggests, God (which for Hegel is equivalent to the most abstract Idea) is dependent upon nature (the instantiation of all ideas), but since instantial nature is itself meaningless without the most general Idea, God is ironically dependent upon nothing but himself.

It is interesting to compare Hegel's reflections on irony with the role of "irony" in dynamic psychology. By irony, I refer to a state of affairs in which the reverse of what is expected changes the fortunes of some material, spiritual, intellectual, or other valued enterprise. In this sense, irony can be said to be fundamental to the theories of both Freud and Jung. Indeed, Freud's theories about dreams, the unconscious, slips of the tongue, and the Oedipus complex, are significant not only because these ideas entail the reverse of what had hitherto been believed, but because they claim that the reverse of what we expect, say, and believe is at the heart of our mental life. Freud (and here he is very close to Hegel) raises irony to the level of a supreme interpretive principle. The Oedipus myth, in which Oedipus unknowingly kills his father and marries his mother, is *the* major symbol of psychoanalysis not only because of its content (triumph over the father and desire for the mother) but, perhaps even more fundamentally, because of its form (as an extreme example of irony). It is *ironic* that what we profess to fear turns out to be precisely what we wish, or that the rage we have for others ends up being taken out on ourselves, or that the love we profess so strongly for our parents and spouses turns out to disguise a profound hatred.

As will become clear in Chapter 4, a similar pattern of irony is evident in Jung, who argues through a series of archetypal analyses that what we had hitherto thought to be the province of the gods and heavens is the domain of our (collective) minds, what we had regarded as worthy of our rejection and disdain is instead the key to the perfection of the self, and what we had thought of as purely male or female is in fact dual-gendered.[129]

Hegel was well aware of the relevance of the dialectic to lived experience. He wrote, "Wherever there is movement, wherever there is life, wherever anything is carried into effect in the actual world, there Dialectic is at work."[130] Indeed, he goes so far as to hold that "everything that surrounds us may be viewed as an instance of Dialectic."[131] As we saw earlier in this chapter, long before Freud and Jung, Hegel noted the presence of dualities and compensations in our mental and emotional life.[132] He points to the phenomena of great joy seeking relief in tears and reminds us of how "the deepest melancholy will at times betray its presence in a smile," both in order to illustrate the dialectic at work in human emotions. Of course, Hegel was content to quickly pass over these contingent psychological phenomena; his main interest was in illustrating a basic philosophical principle. However, it can be said that dynamic psychology, if it does not owe anything to Hegel directly, is certainly more consistent with Hegelianism than it is with any linear philosophy of the Understanding. The psychoanalytic view that ideas, feelings, attitudes, and words often signify—and are (ironically) revelatory of and transformed into—their opposites may not have been possible at all except in the intellectual climate of Hegelian thought. Jung once commented that Hegel *misplaced* psychological insights into the philosophical arena.[133] Perhaps it can equally be said that the dynamic psychologists *transposed* philosophical insights into a psychological key.

Hegel's skepticism regarding the "laws of logic" was also transposed into psychology. According to Freud, the personal unconscious is a realm within which the law of non-contradiction simply does not apply.[134] Jung wrote that the reconciliation of opposites is the highest goal of the human psyche and that all mystical and philosophical expressions of this reconciliation (including those of Hegel[135]) were projections of the attempt to contain and integrate the contradictions inherent in human experience. On the other hand, Jung seems to restate Hegelian philosophy in biological terms when he declares that even the most elementary forms of life involve an inner antithesis.[136] Jung tells us, that the "self," which is the goal of the individual's development, can only be achieved through a confrontation with the "abysmal contradictions of human nature."[137] For these reasons the self is a *coincidentia oppositorum*. Jung pursues the theme of the reconciliation of psychic opposites through a study of mystical, Gnostic, and especially alchemical sources. We will see in Chapter 4 how, according to Jung, the alchemists not only conceived their melting pots as vessels for the separation and unification of various metals, but also as vessels for the reunification of spiritual wholes that had been rent apart in the material world.

Irony, as it was first articulated by Hegel, has come to characterize so much of what is regarded as new and creative in modern thought—from Nietzsche through the deconstructionists—and the turning of cherished values and ideas into their opposites has become the favorite past-time of artists as well as intellectuals. Ours, I suppose, is an ironic age, one in which it has become impossible to rely upon any of our expectations; and it is thus no wonder that philosophies and psychologies that capture the prevalent feeling of the surprising, the chaotic, and the unexpected should triumph in our day. Nevertheless, one needs to be careful not to slip into an illusion of profundity through a facile turn to the ironic.

One of the appeals of Hegel is that he offers us a way of embracing irony without being defeated by it. He points to a manner of living with contradiction and paradox and setting them within a context of (and indeed making them a prerequisite for) a synoptic view of the world and the mind. For Hegel, any attempt to understand the mind must comprehend it from the standpoint of contradiction, paradox, and irony; however, the process of doing so does not produce relativism and doubt but is the key to a comprehensive view of ourselves and the world.

In the next Chapter, I continue the discussion of the relevance of the coincidence of opposites to psychology through an examination of the writings of C. G. Jung, for whom an "imaginative" understanding of *coincidentia oppositorum* was as central to his conception of the self as the rational understanding of the coincidence of opposites was to Hegel's conception of the world.

CHAPTER FOUR

C. G. JUNG AND *"COINCIDENTIA OPPOSITORUM"*

THE NON-RATIONAL INTEGRATION OF OPPOSITES

G. W. F. Hegel's view that spirit aims to achieve self-consciousness through a union of opposites provides a natural transition to the psychology of Carl Gustav Jung. Like Hegel, Jung appeals to the coincidence of opposites as a vehicle for understanding the development of the subject or psyche. Unlike Hegel—who understood this development in terms of the mind's *rational* efforts to integrate subject and object, consciousness and world—Jung understood the psyche as endeavoring to *imaginatively* integrate a whole host of oppositions, including masculine and feminine, body and spirit, conscious and unconscious, persona and shadow, and good and evil.

The notion of *coincidentia oppositorum* plays a central role in Jung's thought. Indeed, Paul Bishop has suggested that "for Jung, the aim of psychology was to achieve the union of [the] opposites."[1] Jung proposed that a "non-rational" union of opposites enables the individual to transcend and ultimately overcome his conflicts. Jung held that there is an instinctive imaginative process, the "transcendent function," which mediates and combines opposites through the production of symbols. According to Jung, the transcendent function enables individuals to gain a new perspective upon and a more encompassing and rewarding attitude toward what they formerly regarded to be an insoluble conflict or dilemma. He cites with approbation Friedrich Schiller's claim that the oppositions between intellect and feeling, spirituality and sensual desire can be mediated and reconciled only via symbols.[2] However, Jung writes, "The rational functions are, by their very nature, incapable of creating symbols, since they produce only rationalities whose meaning is determined unilaterally and does not at the same time embrace its opposite."[3] He held that the transcendent function involves a combination of conscious and unconscious elements, and that it goes beyond (and is indeed opaque to) thought and reason.

Jung viewed the problem of the opposites in broad terms that went beyond the conflicts of the individual psyche. As Bishop points out, for Jung this problem traverses a range of widely different categories:

> The epistemological problem of the relation between extended substance and thinking substance; the psychosexual difference between masculine and feminine; Schiller's distinction between the formal drive and the material drive; Nietzsche's opposition between Apollo and Dionysus; [and] the broader categories of rationality/rationalism vs. irrationality/irrationalism, the mind and the body, consciousness and the Unconscious.[4]

Jung held that the coincidence of opposites is constitutive of both the God archetype[5] and the self.[6] He grounded this conclusion in both analytic work with patients and an examination of the treatment of the opposites in the history of ideas, particularly in religious and mystical thought, tracing its appearance in such varied arenas as Hinduism, Gnosticism, Christian mysticism, alchemy, and the Kabbalah.

Jung regarded the problem of the opposites to be as old as civilization itself, and he discussed a variety of symbols in multiple traditions that allude to the unity of opposites within the human psyche. These include the *Tao* of Lao Tse, *Brahman-Atman* in Indian philosophy and religion, a variety of alchemical symbols including the *lapis* or "the philosopher's stone," the "Spirit of Mercurius," the union of "*Sol* and *Luna*," and the hierosgamos (the union between male and female deities), the Kabbalist's "Primordial Man" (*Adam Kadmon*) and the union of God and the *Shekhinah* (the feminine divine principle), and the Christian *quaternity*. In *Symbols of Transformation,* Jung discusses the snake as a symbol of *coincidentia oppositorum*, as it is "both toxic and prophylactic," a symbol of good and evil, Christ and Anti-Christ."[7] Jung held that in the Tibetan religion the mandala serves a similar function, both symbolizing and illustrating the union of yin and yang, and the ultimate unity of all archetypes.[8] Jung believed the mandala to be a unique symbol, because it provides the individual who produces it the very experience of unity that it is meant to symbolize. As such, the "mandala aspires to the most complete union of opposites that is possible."[9]

While Jung did not deny that the opposites can in certain respects be reconciled through art, he was critical of the view, expounded at one point by Friedrich Nietzsche, that such reconciliation occurs on the aesthetic as opposed to the spiritual and religious plane.[10] Jung was, moreover, explicitly critical of the Hegelian effort to arrive at an intellectual resolution of the problem. While early in *Psychological Types* Jung suggested that it "remains an open question whether the opposition between the two standpoints can ever be satisfactorily resolved in intellectual terms,"[11] later in that work he is emphatic that, "opposites are not to be united rationally," and this is "precisely why they are called opposites."[12] According to Jung, "Opposites can be united only in the form of a compromise, or irrationally...only...through living."[13] The latter idea is quite familiar to psychotherapists, who repeatedly learn that their clients often *live* both sides of a conflict that they cannot reconcile intellectually.[14]

Indeed, Jung held that efforts to reconcile the opposites through reason and philosophy were futile. While at times he used metaphysical language (e.g., the Catholic quaternitarian view of God) to describe the coincidence of opposing functions or attitudes, he claimed that he adopted this language in order to express psychological as opposed to philosophical propositions. He held that "psychology cannot advance any argument either for or against the objective validity of any metaphysical view."[15] Jung appears to reject the view that metaphysical assertions can be proven by any means, calling the belief that they are amenable to proof a "somewhat childish assumption."[16] Despite Jung's explicit rejection of the Hegelian rational reconciliation of the opposites, several of his remarks suggest the possibility of a theoretical synthesis. For example, he proposes that we "have the right on purely empirical grounds to treat the contents of the unconscious as just as real as the things of the outside world."[17] This proposal comes very close to an intellectual solution to the problem generated by opposing naturalistic and subjectivist views of reality. Jung's remark that "theosophy and spiritualism are just as violent in their encroachments on other spheres as materialism"[18] seems to invite a theoretical perspective that is inclusive of each. In his discussion of William James, Jung considers the conflict between intellectual and intuitive truths, and he accepts James' pragmatic eclecticism as a necessary part of the solution to the problem of conflicting foundations in philosophy and psychology. However, despite his nods toward a theoretical reconciliation, Jung ultimately concluded that both conceptualism and pragmatism are inadequate to the task of integrating "logically irreconcilable" views, as they inevitably lead to a loss of creativity. Only a "positive act of creation" can "assimilate...the opposites as necessary points of co-ordination."[19]

Jung is critical of past philosophers who attempted to provide a philosophical reading of the coincidence of the opposites. Those, such as Nicholas of Cusa, who accepted the notion of *coincidentia oppositorum* as a principle of rational theology were led, according to Jung, into theological speculation.[20] Jung makes limited reference to Hegel's philosophical efforts to reconcile the opposites. He suggests that although "intuitive ideas"[21] underlie Hegel's system, these remained subordinated to intellect and thus Hegel failed to adequately account for the psychic nature of the opposites. We will later consider Jung's critique of Hegel in detail, but we should here emphasize that for Jung it is not philosophy but the medical or psychological investigation of the opposites that can rescue the coincidence of opposites from its projection into matter and the heavens; it does so by comprehending the opposites in relation to a psychology of the unconscious.[22] In Jung's view, Hegel and those before him, including the alchemists to whom Jung turned as a foundation for his later work, were handicapped because they had no proper understanding of the unconscious. Nevertheless, the alchemists avoided falling prey to the intellect because, while they lacked a sophisticated psychology, they projected the opposites in a manner that reflects "certain fundamental psychological facts."[23] We will consider alchemical notions of *coincidentia oppositorum* later in this chapter.

FRIEDRICH NIETZSCHE: THE APOLLONIAN AND THE DIONYSIAN

Jung's understanding of the coincidence of opposites should be considered against the background of Nietzsche's rejection of Hegelian rationalism in the final decades of the nineteenth century. While Nietzsche, at least initially, accepted the Hegelian problematic of uniting the opposites, he rejected Hegel's view that they could be united through reason. Nietzsche ultimately held that the opposites could only be united creatively, through lived experience, one that involves a fusion of life and art, which, like the music of Richard Wagner, masters "the tremendous abundance of an apparently chaotic wilderness and… brings together in unity that which was formerly thought to be set irreconcilably asunder."[24]

Nietzsche made a distinction between what he termed Apollonian and Dionysian modes of experience. While he believed that the two must be united in production of a whole human, he held the formless, emotional, chaotic Dionysian principle in higher regard than the form-generating, rational, Apollonian principle, a preference that is evident in and motivates Nietzsche's rejection of the Hegelian intellectual synthesis.

In his first book, *The Birth of Tragedy*, published in 1872, Nietzsche held that the union between Dionysian and Apollonian principles is a metaphysical one rooted in nature.[25] However, according to Nietzsche, when this union is expressed in tragedy (the highest form of art), it represents the affirmation and meaning of life. He writes:

> The Greeks, who simultaneously declare and conceal the mystery of their view of the world in their gods, established as the double source of their art two deities, Apollo and Dionysus. In the realm of art these names represent stylistic opposites which exist side by side and in almost perpetual conflict with one another, and which only once, at the moment when the Hellenic "Will" blossomed, appeared fused together in the work of art that is Attic tragedy.[26]

In this model, the Apollonian principle of individuation,[27] form, beauty, and reason merges with and yields to the Dionysian principle of horror, ecstasy, intoxication, self-forgetting,[28] nature, sensuality, and even cruelty.[29] For Nietzsche, the Dionysian principle (which he identifies with music) is irrational, and it is precisely its irrationality that the Apollonian principle (which Nietzsche identifies with the plastic or "image-making" arts) attempts to contain.[30]

Lucy Huskinson has pointed out that, for Nietzsche, the Apollonian principle is necessary to mitigate the horror of the Dionysian, for without such mitigation the individual would suffer dissolution.[31] However, the Apollonian principle cannot fully contain its opposite or eliminate the irrationality and chaos of the world.[32] Indeed, according to Nietzsche, the "Dionysian" principle corresponds to "Mothers of being—the innermost core of things,"[33] "the thing-in-itself,"[34] which Arthur Schopenhauer equated with the Will. Nietzsche goes so far as to assert that the Dionysian principle, through intoxication and ecstasy, can lead the individual to an experience of the "primal unity."[35]

Nietzsche held that the Apollonian and Dionysian principles are interdependent. While Apollonian achievement is fueled and nourished by Dionysian energy, Dionysian experience must be controlled by Apollonian structure lest it shatter the subject.[36] The parallels to Freud's ego and id are apparent, and it is has been argued that, despite his claim to have not read Nietzsche, Freud was profoundly influenced by Nietzsche on this very point.[37] Nietzsche argued that the Apollonian and Dionysian principles are both practically and epistemologically necessary, as reason depends on instinct for its energy and instinct depends upon reason for its articulation. However, it is the Dionysian principle that is ontologically primary, a notion that is later echoed in Freud's claim that the id is primary and that the ego is built upon its foundation.

Nietzsche claims that beginning with Socrates, Western culture has emphasized the Apollonian over the Dionysian, resulting in a "tyranny of reason" which sanctioned a suppression of instinct and the unconscious. Nietzsche held that the development of reason and consciousness, and the surrendering of instinct, resulted in an illness in which man's natural instincts are turned back against himself.[38] However, he eventually abandoned the metaphysical concerns behind the Apollonian-Dionysian distinction and, as Huskinson points out, Nietzsche's later philosophy moves from a metaphysical aestheticism to a psychological existentialism.[39] Art is no longer the means to transcend the meaninglessness and brutality of existence—rather, the individual now relies upon his or her own will to affirm life's meaning in the face of chaos. The Apollonian and Dionysian are no longer ontological principles that describe a reality external to the individual but are understood as subjective experiences or affects. Yet in both his earlier and later models, Nietzsche held that human actualization involves a creative tension between instinct and reason.

Jung, with certain modifications, adopted Nietzsche's *non-rational* understanding of the opposites and their potential reconciliation. For Jung, as for the later Nietzsche, the reconciliation of the opposites is a personal existential task. Jung writes in *The Red Book*:

> You achieve balance…only if you nurture your opposite. But that is hateful to you in your innermost core, because it is not heroic.[40]

> Madness and reason want to be married.... The
> opposites embrace each other, see eye to eye, and
> intermingle. They recognize their oneness in ago-
> nizing pleasure.[41]

In the *Red Book*, for which he began assembling materials in 1913, Jung advances the non-rational union of opposites as his own innovation.[42] He was, however, clearly under Nietzsche's influence. In *Psychological Types*, a work written when Jung was also working on *The Red Book*, he entered into an extended discussion of Nietzsche's views. As Jung understood it, Nietzsche's Apollonian principle "signifies measure, number, limitation, and subjugation of everything wild and untamed."[43] On the other hand, as Jung puts it, the Dionysian principle is "the liberation of unbounded instinct, the breaking loose of the unbridled dynamism of animal and divine nature."[44] Jung was well aware of Nietzsche's rejection of reason as a principle for reconciling the opposites, and Jung adopted Nietzsche's overall distrust of reason in *The Red Book*:

> The ancients called the saving word the Logos, an
> expression of divine reason. So much unreason was
> in man that he needed reason to be saved, [but] in
> the end [the Logos] poisons us all...We spread poi-
> son and paralysis around us in that we want to edu-
> cate all the world around us into reason.[45]

> Whenever I want to learn and understand something
> I leave my so-called reason at home and give what-
> ever it is that I am trying to understand the benefit
> of the doubt. I have learned this gradually, because
> nowadays the world of science is full of scary exam-
> ples of the opposite.[46]

IMAGINATION AS THE PRINCIPLE OF RECONCILIATION

As we have seen, Jung held that the *transcendent function* is the "irrational, instinctive function" that "can unite the opposites"[47] through the creation of symbols. Symbols provide a balance and mutual compensation between the poles of an opposition (for example, spirituality and sensuality[48]) and they can do this because "data from every psychic function have gone into [their] making."[49] Like Claude Lévi-Strauss, who would later hold that mythological thinking serves to unite opposites and reconcile conflicts that cannot be reconciled in either thought or action,[50] Jung held that the transcendent function spontaneously produces symbols that have the potential to redirect the polarizing energies of a conflict into "a common channel."[51] He points out that the founders of religions in both the East and West endured a period of intense conflict prior to their revelations: Christ and Luther struggled with the devil, Buddha struggled with Mara, etc.[52]

While Jung holds that creative fantasy is the "third" that can reconcile such opposites as thinking and feeling, conscious and unconscious,[53] and good and evil, he rejects Friedrich Schiller's notion that beauty is the mediator that will "restore the primal unity of human nature."[54] Jung points out that Schiller held that a high level of aesthetic taste and production typically occurs only in a context of limited political freedom, diminished morals,[55] and "misery, pain, and squalor."[56] If beauty requires its opposite in order to flourish, Jung asks, how can it be the power that reconciles oppositions? Further, he argues that the aesthetic temperament or point of view turns away from anything that is ugly, difficult, and evil, and therefore lacks both completeness and moral force.[57] This position is hard to justify on the facts of art history, as painters, sculptors, dramatists, and other artists have always integrated the morbid, ugly, difficult, and the evil into the creative process and its products. One can almost randomly survey the arts to see this: Picasso's *Guernica*, Dante's *Inferno* (and Carpeaux's wrenching sculpture, "Ugolino and His Sons"), Jean-Paul Sartre's *Nausea*, Dostoevsky's *Crime and Punishment*, and Steven Spielberg's "Schindler's List" come immediately to mind as examples of how artists have not turned away from evil and other "shadow" themes.

We can take the example of painting to see how readily the arts present us with a harmonization of contrasting elements. In painting, there is a blending and harmony of form and color (and contrasting/complementary hues), value and line, surface and depth, and—for the viewer—reality and illusion, subject and object, truth and imagination, the limited and the infinite, time and eternity, the particular and the universal, and so on. We might go so far as to say that painting and other arts, provide a creative solution to the problem of the opposites that is not readily available to thought. When we are moved by a great work of art, we often marvel at how the artist has brought together diverse elements into a unity of form and experience. And it is in art that we thus have what is perhaps the most concrete expression of the coincidence and interdependence of the opposites, and the harmony of the many with the one.[58]

Jung's critique of the aesthetic as a unifying principle provides insight into his view of the opposites in *The Red Book* and explains why he was so adamant that his paintings in it were not "art." In *The Red Book*, Jung saw himself as reconciling the opposites not only within his own psyche but also within the broader psyche of humanity and God,[59] a task that recast on the level of the imagination what Hegel held to be the very purpose and goal of reason. For Jung, the reconciliation was a symbolic and religious function that could not be attained through mere "art" or "aestheticism" but could only be achieved through personal transformation. He later concluded that the compensation by opposites is the source of the "highest principles both of life and philosophy,"[60] that life loses its balance and significance when the coincidence of opposites is ignored,[61] and that both the self[62] and God[63] are symbols of *coincidentia oppositorum*. Jung was already beginning to formulate these conclusions in *The Red Book*, where he declared that Christ had to journey to hell in order for God to integrate opposing principles and encompass the fullness of life.[64] Indeed, Jung wrote that he (and all individuals) must will both good and evil in order for "The God" to develop through the union of these principles in the individual self.[65]

For Jung, "play" (as in Schiller's formulation) is a better candidate for the mediating or unifying principle than art. One advantage of play is that it occurs spontaneously, without desire, compulsion, or even will. For Jung, play occurs via what he calls "inner necessity."[66] He writes, "The creation of something new is not accomplished by the intellect, but by the play instinct acting from inner necessity."[67] Again, we might assert that art itself involves play and spontaneity and, as Hegel well understood, is never merely a construction of the intellect. We will return to this idea later in this chapter.

As we have seen, for Jung it is the symbols of the imagination that unite opposing psychic contents and processes.[68] The imagination, which generates symbols, "is a key that opens the door to the secret of the [alchemical and psychological] opus."[69] A symbol, he says, is a tendency which pursues "a definite but not yet recognizable goal."[70] As such, its meaning cannot be stated definitively, and it is for this reason that a symbol can embrace both poles of an opposition. While it is unclear precisely how symbols reconcile conflicting psychic trends or attitudes, it appears to be this very lack of clarity that enables them to do so. Jung suggests that symbols like the mandala bring about an unconscious experience of reconciliation that is opaque to the rational mind. We might here add that like the *bewusstseinslagene* or "nutshell consciousnesses" of the Wurzburg psychologists,[71] a symbol can condense huge territories of meaning that are not fully present to consciousness and which are not (and perhaps cannot be) fully articulated in words.

Jung held that the source of symbols, and hence the power of the imagination, lay outside the conscious ego. Indeed, he criticized Nietzsche for locating creativity in the "will" and failing to recognize a power beyond the self.[72] Jung approvingly observed that the power to unify the opposites has traditionally been understood as "God," and indeed, as Huskinson puts it, God, for Jung, is the essential "unifying symbol."[73] However, according to Jung, Nietzsche "wiped out his symbol when he declared that God was dead."[74] Nietzsche had tried to substitute "aesthetics," the body, or the individual will for God, but these, according to Jung, are inadequate for reconciling oppositions.[75] Instead, it is the collective unconscious that is the source of all creativity: "The creative process in you is not your own doing.... We are only instrumental in the creative process; it creates in us, through us."[76] In Jung's view, Nietzsche, by inflating the significance of the individual will, made the grave error of believing that with the "death of God" consciousness became the source of all thought, activity, and meaning.[77] Nietzsche, for his part, held that God and religion are merely projections of the individual's own will:

> When a man is suddenly and overwhelmingly suf-fused with the *feeling of power—and* this is what happens with all great affects—it raises in him a doubt about his own person: he does not dare to think himself the cause of this astonishing feeling, and so he posits a stronger person, a divinity, to ac-count for it.[78]

While Jung also believed that humanity had historically projected the archetypal powers onto the heavens, he was, in stark contrast to Nietzsche, adamant that the source of human creativity and power is in the collective unconscious and not in the individual will.

Jung held that the treatment of neurosis also involves a reconciliation of opposing feelings, attitudes, and trends through the *production of symbols*. In neuroses, the resolution of a conflict requires a third thing to mediate between the opposites: the conflicting poles, attitudes, or feelings of the neurotic psyche. Yet this third thing or "solvent" cannot be a rational construct or idea because the intellect knows no third thing that can resolve a logical antithesis. The solvent must be symbolic, and the symbol that services the solvent either comes to one naturally or is induced through meditation upon a fantasy image or dream. One can begin, for example, with an ill mood and see what image is produced by it. The contemplation of this image produces an alteration in it which reflects its unconscious background. In addition, conscious memory material associated with the image will come to mind; in the process, there is the possibility of uniting conscious and unconscious.[79] A person begins to "dream with open eyes," and it is this process of "active imagination" that will ultimately yield compensations for one-sided conscious attitudes. Jung says that it is important to fix this process in writing, as he himself did in *The Red Book*, in order to prevent the psyche from disguising and distorting it.

Jung's notion that a "third thing" must act as a "dynamic factor" to mediate between the opposites distinguished him from Nietzsche, who held that symbols arise from the opposites themselves and are not a "third." The notion of a "third thing" required for opposites to interact with one another was introduced by Aristotle who wrote in his *Physics*:

> It is difficult to see how either density should be of such a nature as to act in any way on rarity or rarity on density. The same is true of any other pair of contraries; for Love does not gather Strife together and make things out of it, nor does Strife make anything out of Love, but both act on a third thing different from both. Some indeed assume more than one such thing from which they construct the world of nature.[80]

In both *The Red Book* and *Psychological Types*, Jung suggests that the role of "third" is played by the *imagination*. He expands on this by indicating that the transcendent function,[81] dreams,[82] and the symbol[83] may function as the mediator between thesis and antithesis.[84] In contrast, Nietzsche held that the will to power is the force that both creates the opposites and reunites them. For Nietzsche, "all driving force is will to power [and] there is no other physical, dynamic or psychic force except this."[85] Interestingly, Jung asserts that "the will to power" must be compensated for by its own opposite, "love."[86]

Nietzsche held that the reunification of opposites does not require a "third" because, as Heraclitus first observed, the opposites were born of each other and naturally tend toward reunification.[87] For Nietzsche, this natural tendency is itself the *will to power*;[88] he suggests that everything that exists both originates in and strives to return to this will, and that life itself "is merely a special case of the will to power."[89]

While Jung held that creativity is channeled through something beyond the ego, via the archetypes of the collective unconscious, Nietzsche rejected all such external or structural views of the creative process, preferring to understand it as arising from within the individual, from formless chaos, and always subject to a multiplicity of interpretations. Nietzsche, Huskinson argues, rejected the Platonism that Jung eventually made the cornerstone for his theory of the archetypes. This is one of the reasons for Jung's deflationary view of Nietzsche in his 1934 seminar. There, Jung concluded that Nietzsche failed to achieve the reconciliation of opposites because he lacked the symbol, which is necessary "to leave one condition and to enter another mental condition."[90]

Bishop provides an insightful contrast between Jung and Nietzsche on the significance of symbols for the psyche:

> In Jung's psychic monism, the archetypes function as categories of the imagination, canalizing the libido, and, by giving it shape and form, endowing life with meaning. Apart from the temporal structuring of the Eternal Recurrence, Nietzsche's 'volitionary monism' by contrast knows no such structures, and the ceaseless flux of Becoming—the perpetual struggle of the Will to Power—resists attempts to exercise conceptual mastery over it.[91]

Bishop and Huskinson, writing before the publication of Jung's *The Red Book*, were not in a position to grasp the radical transformation in Jung's understanding of both Nietzsche and the creative process that had occurred by the time of Jung's 1934 Nietzsche seminars. Indeed, in *The Red Book*, Jung provided a radically deconstructive, existential, view of creativity and self-actualization that was quite close to the one he came to criticize in Nietzsche during the 1930s. In *The Red Book*, Jung writes that the individual (and, by inference, *not* the archetypes of the collective unconscious) is the source of meaning:

> Events signify nothing, they signify only in us. We
> create the meaning of events. The meaning is and
> always was artificial. We make it…. The meaning
> of events comes from the possibility of life in this
> world that you create. It is a mastery of this world
> and the assertion of your soul in this world."[92]

Further, Jung wrote that one must make one's "ordered world horri-ble" in order to enter the "whirl of chaos" and the "wonder world of the soul."[93] Clearly, during this phase of his career Jung was very much un-der the influence of Nietzsche's view that "one must still have chaos in oneself to be able to give birth to a dancing star."[94] However, even in his later, more constructive years, Jung remained open to the Nietzschean "chaos" he celebrated in *The Red Book*. In his *Seminar on Nietzsche's Zarathustra*, Jung writes:

> In certain stages of analysis, particularly in the be-
> ginning, people realize very clearly that they have
> chaos in themselves and they feel lost in it…Now
> Nietzsche's idea is that out of that lack of order a
> dancing star should be born.[95]

Nevertheless, according to Jung, despite its critical importance the embrace of chaos and disorder is not without its dangers, as one "must not underestimate the devastating effect of getting lost in the chaos, even if we know that it is the *sine qua non* of any regeneration of the spirit and the personality."[96]

COMPENSATION AND ENANTIODROMIA

Jung's notion of "compensation" is closely related to his under-standing of the transcendent function and the unification of the oppo-sites, although with compensation it is not clear that the reconciliation necessarily involves a symbol or other "third." Jung held that "uncon-scious processes stand in a compensatory relation to the conscious mind"[97] and that psychic opposites tend to evoke and compensate for each other. In *Psychological Types* Jung writes, "When the individual consistently takes his stand on one side, the unconscious ranges itself on the other and rebels."[98] Jung uses this to explain the phenomenon of "possession" in the Middle Ages, holding that "demons are nothing other than intruders from the unconscious, spontaneous irruptions of unconscious complexes"[99] that *compensate* for the exclusive Christian emphasis upon spirituality and goodness to the exclusion of the material, sensual, evil, and "demonic."

Jung utilizes the term "enantiodromia" to refer to "the emergence of the unconscious opposite in the course of time."[100] He borrows this notion from Heraclitus who used it in connection with his philosophical view that all things eventually transform into their opposites.[101] Nietzsche had provided what amounted to a psychological interpretation of the enantiodromia idea when he wrote, "The more one develops a drive, the more attractive does it become to plunge for once into its opposite."[102] Further, according to Nietzsche, extreme positions are succeeded by their extreme opposites,"[103] and he provides the example of the belief in the total immorality of nature that follows upon the rejection of the belief in God.

Jung later developed similar ideas into a theory of not only individual development but of culture and society: The civilized, rational elements of an individual or society are a façade covering its archaic, power, and barbaric elements, which in each case will eventually emerge. For example, the more an individual or community consciously identifies with a spiritual god of goodness and peace, the greater will be the unconscious tendency to identify with "an archaic god whose nature is sensual and brutal."[104] This idea, which was, again, anticipated by Nietzsche, is illustrated in Jung's *Red Book* description of the God Abraxas as the "cruel contradictoriness of nature.[105] Abraxas is ultimately the union of opposing images of God and self: Abraxas is life and death, "truth and lying, good and evil, and light and darkness."[106] Jung later referred to Abraxas as the Gnostics' "supreme deity."[107] According to Shamdasani, Abraxas is "the uniting of the Christian God with Satan."[108] On a collective level, Jung held that alchemy represented the dark, repressed side of Christianity that emerged as a compensation for Christianity's failure to confront God's shadow side and the reality of evil. Later in this chapter we will see how alchemy served as the major impetus to Jung's understanding of the opposites in the development of personality.

Compensation does not always work to highlight evil or the shadow. For example, Jung discusses a patient's dream in which a "death's head" is gradually transformed into a red ball and then into the luminescent head of a woman. Jung sees this as a case of enantiodromia, in which the ball is the sun and where it and the shining head are each symbols of the self and the potential for wholeness present in the woman's unconscious.[109]

The attitude of the unconscious that serves as a compensation for consciousness can, according to Jung, often be grasped through an interpretation of one's dreams. In contrast to Freud, who held that dreams represent a disguised repressed wish, Jung held that dreams often bring to light a psychological state or attitude that involves a wrong judgment, or which has hitherto been neglected.[110] Although Jung held that it is impossible to create a fully comprehensive theory of dreaming, he believed that dreams frequently compensate for a one-side conscious attitude; at times, however, when one's conscious attitude is adequate, a dream may coincide with and reinforce it.[111]

For Jung, compensation, and thus the balance and integration of opposites plays a critical role in "individuation," the process through which a person becomes nourished by, reconciled to, and distinguished from humanity as a whole. The process of individuation involves a complementarity between the conscious and the unconscious. While the unconscious attitude compensates for the one-sidedness of the conscious mind, the two must ultimately be coordinated. For Jung, "Unconscious compensation is only effective when it co-operates with an integral consciousness; assimilation is never a question of 'this *or* that.' but always of 'this *and* that.'"[112]

While Jung never explicitly outlines the stages of the individuation process, we might observe that in his own case it appears to have involved a series of encounters with archetypal figures, "personifications," and situations, described in *The Red Book*.[113] While cast as a personal odyssey it is easy to infer a more universal pattern. In his *Red Book* journey Jung moves from identifying with his own Will, to assimilating aspects of archetypal figures that include the devil, a simple maiden, and a dying god. In *Reading the Red Book*, I argued that these encounters with archetypal figures set the pattern for a dialectical progression that in a loose way echoes on the level of psychology, the dialectic of human consciousness in Hegel's *Phenomenology of Spirit*.[114] Jung's message seems to be that as one assimilates the significance of symbolic personifications and situations, one-sided conscious attitudes are critiqued and compensated for, and the individual moves closer to assimilating the archetype of the self—an archetype that is a *coincidentia oppositorum*. The process of individuation involves an encounter with, and assimilation of, aspects of both the personal and collective unconscious, specifically the individual's shadow (elements of one's personality that the individual has hitherto ignored, rejected, and detested) and the anima or animus (the aspect of oneself that embodies characteristics opposite to those one and society associates with one's gender). The assimilation of the shadow is illustrated in *The Red Book* as Jung painfully comes to "accept all," including the most repulsive desires and tendencies within humanity and his own psyche.[115] The assimilation of the anima/animus is illustrated in Jung's proclamation that a man must discover his own femininity: "You, man, should not seek the feminine in women, but seek and recognize it in yourself as you possess it from the beginning."[116]

In *Psychological Types*, Jung describes this process as follows:

> The persona, the ideal picture of a man as he should
> be, is inwardly compensated by feminine weakness

> and as the individual outwardly plays the strong
> man, so he becomes inwardly a woman, i.e., the an-
> ima, for it is the anima that reacts to the persona.[117]

Indeed, "the character of the anima can be deduced from that of the persona" by simply noting the opposite of the individual's conscious attitude. For example, the "anima" of a tyrannical individual "contains all those fallible qualities his persona lacks."[118]

Precisely how the compensation process traverses the personal unconscious (which Jung held to represented by the archetype of the shadow) and the collective unconscious (represented by the anima or animus) is unclear—nor is there, in Jung, a very clear distinction between the personal and collective unconscious. What is clear is that the process of individuation involves a confrontation, tension with, and assimilation of attitudes, thoughts, feelings, and behaviors that are initially excluded from one's conscious self-image.

THE TENSION AND CONFLICT OF THE OPPOSITES

A question arises as to the destiny of the opposites subsequent to the process of compensation or enantiodromia. In order to address this, we should distinguish between the "union," "coincidence," "interdependence," and "harmony" of opposites. In "union," ideas, attitudes, feelings, or even entities that appear to exclude one another are united as one and lose their distinct identity. In each of the other cases (coincidence, interdependence, and harmony of opposites), ideas and entities that are opposed to one another retain their distinct character. Thus, in mystical rapture an adept may be said to achieve a *unio mystica* and lose his distinction from the universe or God. On the other hand, a theologian might assert that, while God and humanity are distinct, they are nonetheless interdependent—humanity dependent for its creation upon God and God dependent for his recognition upon humanity. Hot and cold water mixed together become united as one—but the ideas of hot and cold are distinct although interdependent through their relation of contrast. Jung wrote that the "identity of opposites is a characteristic feature of every psychic event in the unconscious state."[119] Yet he also held that "there is no energy unless there is a tension of opposites[120] and that the psyche as an "energetic system" is dependent on this very tension.[121] Clearly, in these latter instances, the opposites remain distinct.

On the whole, Jung falls far short of calling for the complete union of the opposites. While in *The Red Book* he clearly indicates that it is necessary to bring the opposites together in the "quest for one's soul," he also makes it clear that their complete unification is not desirable, as this will eliminate the passion for life. He writes, "After the opposites had been united, quite unexpectedly and incomprehensibly nothing further happened. Everything remained in place, peacefully and yet completely motionless, and life turned into a complete standstill.[122] Also, Satan derogates the union of opposites by stating, "Reconciliation of the opposites! Equal rights for all! Follies!"[123] and Jung suggests that it may indeed be the case that "the conflict of opposites belong(s) to the inescapable conditions of life (and that one) who recognizes and lives the unity of opposites stand(s) still...."[124] Jung's soul queries if he could even live without divisiveness and disunity. This question arises because Jung's soul suggests that one needs to "get worked up about something, represent a party, overcome opposites, if you want to live."[125] Life itself is the oscillation between the tension and overcoming of opposites; when they have been *completely overcome*, a person (for example, the Buddha in his final reincarnation) has no further reason to live on earth.

In *Psychological Types*, Jung writes that all phenomena "consists of pairs of opposites."[126] The idea here is that without the opposites (Jung cites as examples beginning and end, above and below, earlier and later, and cause and effect) nothing could be manifest. Further, he states that his theory of libido (*psychic* energy), which marked his dissension from Freud, also involves the tension between the opposites: "The inseparability of the energy concept from that of polarity also applies to the concept of libido."[127] For Jung, all libido symbols "either present themselves directly as opposites or can be broken down into opposites."[128]

In his essay "On the Psychology of the Unconscious," Jung argued that the development of the human personality involves a tension between opposing mental formations:

> The repressed content [of the psyche] must be made conscious so as to produce a tension of opposites, without which no forward movement is possible. The conscious mind is on top, the shadow underneath, and just as high always longs for low and hot for cold, so all consciousness, perhaps without being aware of it, seeks an unconscious opposite, lacking which it is doomed to stagnation, congestion and ossification. Life is born only of the spark of opposites.[129]

Later, in his essay, "Paracelsus as a Spiritual Phenomenon," Jung wrote, "Great energy springs from a correspondingly great tension of opposites."[130]

As I will discuss in more detail later, Jung held that the tension and compensation between the opposites is also evident in Freud's and Alfred Adler's respective theories of neurosis. He suggests that Freud's theory is grounded in Eros and Adler's in the will to power. These two principles are "psychological" as opposed to semantic opposites: "Where love reigns, there is no will to power; and where the will to power is paramount, love is lacking."[131] Again, the theoretical tension reflects an experienced tension within the individual psyche—and, according to Jung, will is the "compensatory opposite" of love, and vice versa.

The development of personality as Jung explains it can involve *both* a heightening of tension between the opposites[132] and their reconciliation and union. Further, the individuation (or full realization) of the personality means *both* the differentiation of one's unique psyche from that of the collective psyche[133] *and* the compensation of one's individuality by the archetypes of the collective unconscious, which activate dilemmas that face humankind as a whole.[134] The failure to differentiate oneself from the collective results in an absorption in the unconscious, and an over-inflation of the ego (through its identification with the collective unconscious[135]), while the failure to connect with the collective unconscious results in a one-sided and overly narrow ego devoid of creativity and symbolic meaning.

It is because of the need for a continued tension between conscious and unconscious that Jung warns of the dangers associated with a complete immersion in the unconscious mind,[136] within which there is no opposition. We might add that while a complete unification of the opposites appears to be the impetus to certain mystical states (*unio mystica*), it can also lead to a form of psychosis in which the distinctions of everyday life collapse and the individual is unable to distinguish between fantasy and reality.

The *separation* of the opposites is thus as essential to human psychic functioning as is their union, and it is the dialectic between the two processes, what the alchemists spoke of as *solve* et *cogaulum* that serves as the "elixir of life." According to Jung, the opposites must be separated in order to obtain clarity of consciousness, discrimination, and human survival.[137] However, when the separation is carried so far that the complementary opposite is lost sight of, and the blackness of the whiteness, the evil of the good, the depth of the heights, and so on, is no longer seen, the result is one sidedness, which is then compensated from the unconscious without our help.[138]

Such compensation occurs even against the ego's will, and if the will resists this can result in a "catastrophic enantiodromia." As Jung explains, "Wisdom never forgets that all things have two sides."[139]

Jung recognizes that the opposites have a tendency to "flee from one another."[140] However, he believes they must ultimately wear each other out and strive for harmony. This is because conflict, however stimulating, is ultimately "inimical to life."[141] We thus arrive at a further tension, that between maintaining and transcending the conflict between the opposites. This tension both sustains life and permits its transcendence. It is a tension that harnesses our instinctual energies, as evidenced by the fact that the *conflict* of opposites is often symbolized through a battle between dogs, lions, wolves, or dragons,[142] and their synthesis is frequently represented by the erotic union of man and woman.

Jung thus maintained that a tension is necessary even between the meta-psychological notions of the conflict and union of the opposites. He writes that the self is paradoxically both a conflict and unity of opposites.[143] Jung went so far as to hold that the principle of the *coincidentia oppositorum* is applicable to itself and must be complemented by its own opposite, the conflict of opposites.[144] Nevertheless, he embraced the notion of "wholeness." Jung writes:

> Although "wholeness" seems at first sight to be nothing but an abstract idea...it is nevertheless empirical in so far as it is anticipated by the psyche in the form of spontaneous or autonomous symbols. These are the quaternity or mandala symbols, which occur not only in the dreams of modern people who have never heard of them, but are widely disseminated in the historical records of many peoples and many epochs. Their significance as *symbols of unity and totality* is amply confirmed by history as well as by empirical psychology. What at first looks like an abstract idea stands in reality for something that exists and can be experienced, that demonstrates its a priori presence spontaneously.[145]

Huskinson, following Warren Colman, suggests that the self might be better understood in dynamic terms as the mediating process that produces the tension and then union of opposites, as opposed to a static *coincidentia oppositorum* or completed whole.[146] Indeed, Jung himself, drawing upon the Kabbalistic symbol of the Primordial Man, *Adam Kadmon*, suggests that the soul or psychological self is transcended by the "process of transformation."[147]

THE DISCIPLINE OF PSYCHOLOGY AND THE UNION OF
THINKING AND FEELING

While Jung believed that the coincidence of opposites is a natural, non-rational function of the human psyche, he nevertheless made a thoughtful, intellectual application of the *coincidentia* idea to the prevailing controversies in the field of psychology in his own time. In *Psychological Types*, which was published in 1921, he faulted both Freudian and Adlerian psychology for neglecting the viewpoints advocated by each other. He argued that Adler failed to take full cognizance of Freud's notion of "instinct" and that Freud neglected the "aims of the ego" emphasized by Adler. Jung held that each of these psychologies, while apparently complete on its own terms, was incomplete when examined in light of the principle that grounds the other. He also argued that psychological inferences can always be made that accord both with Freudian "infantile wishes" and Adlerian aims of "security and differentiation of the ego."[148] However, Freud and Adler each offer only partial truths that would complement and complete one another but for the fact that their partisans fail to acknowledge and develop the reconciling principle of the imagination.[149] According to Jung, only the imagination, via its production of symbols, and especially religious and spiritual symbols,[150] can produce a reconciliation of the opposing demands of instinct and the aims of the ego.

In *Psychological Types,* Jung proffered a theory of psychology that is rooted in the coincidence of opposites. *Psychological Types* is an extremely wide-ranging work that is loosely structured around Jung's examination of the "type problem" in philosophy, literature, biography and psychology. By "type," Jung refers specifically to personality types that are characterized by the polarities of thinking/feeling and introversion/extraversion. Jung holds that the type problem is not only relevant to the individual personality, but also to our understanding of the discipline of psychology. He argues that a complete understanding of the psyche cannot occur through thinking (science) nor feeling alone:[151] if grounded in the latter it loses its order and claim to validity, if grounded in the former it loses its connection with life.

Jung writes that because the sciences are of necessity grounded in reason, they tend to exclude both feeling and fantasy from their purview and that this is essential for them *as sciences*. Psychology *if it is to be a science* must do the same. However, in doing so it fails to do justice to the human psyche. A scientific standpoint can only consider feeling, sensation and fantasy from an abstract, intellectual standpoint, and because of this it fails to achieve either a vital or practical point of view. For Jung, "when we approach the actual business of living from the side of the intellect and science, we immediately come up against barriers that shut us out from other, equally real provinces of life."[152] However, Jung warns that we should not move to the other extreme and declare with Faust that "feeling is all," because the totality of life can only exist and be comprehended when the psyche unites feeling with intellect. This integration can only occur through creative fantasy, which Jung holds to be the "mother" or origin of both thinking and feeling.[153] Because of this, creative fantasy is the only principle that is capable of uniting the opposites. While creative fantasy also requires restraint, such restraint is not imposed by the intellect or by feeling, but by "the boundaries set by necessity and irrefutable reality."[154]

Jung thus envisions a psychology that is neither reducible to a single perspective nor to a single operation of the mind. Any psychology that proceeds from a particular vantage point can produce truths that are sufficient within its own arena but incomplete when seen from the perspective of another theory or psychological principle. In *Psychological Types,* Jung holds that a psychology that is rooted in creative fantasy is the only possible vehicle for reconciling intellect and feeling and thus the only truly comprehensive psychology.

These considerations help us understand Jung's stance in *The Red Book*, where he eschewed scientific and rational reflection in favor of the creative play of his own imagination. While Jung frequently insisted that he was an "empirical scientist," he seemed to prefer the standpoint of Taoist philosophy to the more conceptualist philosophies of the West.[155] According to Jung, the *"Tao* is the creative process,"[156] an "irrational union of opposites"[157] that transcends both thinking and will.[158] This comes closest to his own view that creative fantasy is the key to progress in psychotherapeutic treatment as well as to progress in the field of psychology.

A primary basis for Jung's rejection of the intellect as a mediating principle is the obvious fact that the intellect itself is one pole of an opposition between intellect and feeling and must be reconciled with its opposite. According to Jung:

> No matter how beautiful and perfect man may believe his reason to be, he can always be certain that it is only one of the possible mental functions, and covers only that one side of the phenomenal world which corresponds to it.[159]

However, Western thought has developed conscious, rational thinking at the expense of other psychological functions, and a correction or compensation on a cultural level is therefore necessary in order to create a proper balance. According to Jung, "Too much of the animal distorts the civilized man, too much civilization makes sick animals."[160] In the end, he suggests that a phenomenology which proceeds only from within one of the four mental functions (thinking, feeling, sensation, intuition) is incomplete, and thus yields only a partial view of reality.

While we might accept Jung's diagnosis of the problem, we are not bound by his solution, as we can just as easily place fantasy or imagination into dialectical opposition with perception or "reality." It seems to me that the main lesson here is that any psychology rooted in a single perspective or mental function is incomplete and requires its own complement as a means of approaching a greater totality. We will have occasion to return to this problem in detail in Chapter 5.

JUNG'S ATTITUDE AND FUNCTION TYPES

In articulating his psychology of "types," Jung adapted Nietzsche's Apollonian-Dionysian distinction, and added several distinctions of his own. In *Psychological Types*, he describes two dichotomous *attitude* types, introversion and extraversion,[161] which he equates with the Dionysian and Apollonian. He also identifies four *function* types, which he divides into two opposing pairs: thinking versus feeling and sensation versus intuition.[162] The introversive type withdraws interest or libido from the object and considers it in removed, abstract terms, while the extroversive type affirms the importance of, and is continuously related to, the object.[163] While one or the other of these attitudes dominates the individual's conscious experience and behavior, the other determines his or her unconscious compensatory position. Thus each individual has both a conscious and unconscious attitude—the latter often appearing in fantasy and dreams. At times the two attitudes intermingle and it becomes difficult to ascertain which is conscious and which is unconscious. Conscious attitudes and functions dominate the individual's experience and behavior unless and until they become over-emphasized, causing a compensatory drive to be set in motion by one's opposing unconscious attitudes and functions. This may manifest in an unexpected, distressing, or impulsive thought or behavior.

While Jung's theory of types has much in common with Nietzsche's, Jung criticizes Nietzsche on the grounds that his over-identification with the Dionysian principle resulted in a failure to realize a balance between the opposites."[164] However, the same criticism can be leveled against Jung, who at various points in his career appeared to celebrate the instinctual or mythological over the rational, a celebration that, most pointedly, led him to an overly optimistic (and terribly misguided) view of National Socialism.[165] For example, in one of a series of lectures he gave in London in 1935, Jung described the hypnotic effect of Nazism:

> Would you have believed that a whole nation of highly intelligent and cultivated people could be seized by the fascinating power of an archetype? I saw it coming, and I can understand it because I know the power of the collective unconscious. But on the surface it looks simply incredible. Even my personal friends are under that fascination, and when I am in Germany, I believe it myself, I understand it all, I know it has to be as it is. One cannot resist it. It gets you below the belt and not in your mind, your brain just counts for nothing, your sympathetic system is gripped. It is a power that fascinates people from within, it is the collective unconscious which is activated…We cannot be children about it, having intellectual and reasonable ideas and saying: this should not be.[166]

With regard to Germans who were caught up in the Third Reich, Jung said, "An incomprehensible fate has seized them, and you cannot say it is right, or it is wrong. It has nothing to do with rational judgment, it is just history."[167] While one may perhaps understand how Jung might have initially experienced Hitler's "archetypal" hold upon the German psyche, one can only fault him for denying that the categories of "right" and "wrong" apply to National Socialism, a denial that was clearly rooted in his derogation of reason.[168] We will return to this question later in this chapter when we consider the limitations and dangers of *coincidentia oppositorum*. Jung not only held that there must be a compensatory relationship between divergent functions and attitude types, he also went to great lengths, in *The Red Book*, to understand how his thinking function must be compensated for with "feeling." For Jung, such compensations are critical for individuation and the process of psychotherapy.

JUNG ON THE PREVIOUS AND PARTIAL SOLUTIONS TO THE PROBLEM OF THE OPPOSITES

Jung recognized that the principle invoked for uniting the opposites varies across religious and philosophical traditions. He commented that for the Christians, this principle was the worship of God; for the Buddhists, the realization and development of the self; and for Goethe and Spitteler (as well as Dante), "the *worship of the soul* symbolized by the *worship* of women."[169]

Jung took a special interest in the Christian mystic and philosopher, Meister Eckhart, who wrote of a *coincidentia oppositorum* between God and man, and who sought to unite the opposites by encountering God within his own soul,[170] a task that occupied Jung himself in *The Red Book*.[171] Jung was also influenced by the coincidence of opposites in the Kabbalah, where it is symbolized by the divine wedding. Jung himself had "Kabbalistic Visions" in which he experienced himself as the union of *Tifereth* and *Malchuth* the masculine and feminine principles in God, and which he regarded as essential for his own individuation process.[172]

Jung turned to the philosophies of India and China for one model for reconciling the opposites.[173] He considered the Brahmanic doctrine that "deliverance from the opposites leads to redemption,"[174] and he cited a series of quotations from the Upanishads and other ancient Hindu texts that imply that Brahman is "the union or dissolution of all opposites,"[175] and that one who is no longer ensnared by the opposites is delivered from "the flux of affects"[176] and reposes in the supreme unity.

Jung points out that the "Tao" of Lao Tzu is divided into but also unifies the fundamental opposites of "yin" and "yang." Whereas yin is associated with cold, darkness, and the feminine, yang is associated with warmth, light, and the masculine. The two fundamental forces are brought together and reconciled in humanity.[177] In this way, Jung observes that the human being "is the equivalent of an irrational symbol that unites the psychological opposites."[178] One must "live in harmony with the *tao*," or else risk falling victim to the conflict of the oppo-sites.[179] Jung held that because in China the opposites in human na-ture were never forced far apart, the Chinese were able to maintain an "all-inclusive consciousness."[180]

In a fascinating chapter in *Psychological Types* Jung reviews the "type problem" as it is discussed by William James in *Pragmatism: A New Name for Some Old Ways of Thinking*.[181] Jung's chapter is im-portant not only for its review of the "pragmatic" solution to the "prob-lem of the opposites," but because it provides the clearest glimpse into Jung's treatment of opposition and antinomy in philosophy. Jung begins by noting that James had distinguished between two philosophical tem-peraments or attitudes, what he referred to as the "tender-minded" and "tough-minded." James claimed that the history of philosophy involves a clash and antagonism between these fundamental temperaments, and that these temperaments each create an unrecognized (and typically sup-pressed) bias in the philosophers that have them. Philosophy becomes less of a quest for truth than an effort to achieve a representation of the universe that suits the philosopher's temperamental predispositions—a view that, as we have seen, was later echoed by the philosopher Mor-ris Lazerowitz.[182] Jung considers the fundamental oppositions between James' tender-minded and tough-minded philosophers: rationalistic ver-sus empiricist, intellectualistic versus sensationalistic, idealistic versus materialistic, optimistic versus pessimistic, religious versus irreligious, free-willist versus fatalistic, monistic versus pluralistic, and dogmatical versus skeptical. Although Jung believes that James' categorization of the "tender-minded" and "tough-minded" philosophers is too rigid, he argues that James' "tender-minded" category generally corresponds to the introversive type and James' "tough-minded" category to the extro-versive type. What is of interest here, however, is that Jung takes issue with James' "pragmatic" effort to resolve the conflict between philo-sophical positions. While for Jung, pragmatism is clearly an advance over any conceptual or intellective effort to resolve philosophical antin-omies and is an important transitional stage on the path to a resolution, it "presupposes too great a resignation and almost unavoidably leads to a drying up of creativeness."[183] According to Jung:

> The solution of the conflict of opposites can come neither from the intellectual compromise of conceptualism nor from a pragmatic assessment of the practical value of logically incompatible views, but only from a positive act of creation which assimilates the opposites as necessary elements of co-ordination, in the same way as a co-ordinated muscular movement depends on the innervation of opposing muscular groups.[184]

In Chapter 5, we will reconsider the question of whether there may indeed be an intellectual or pragmatic reconciliation of the opposites in psychology.

THE OPPOSITES, SELF AND GOD

As we have seen, throughout much of his career, Jung held that both the self[185] and God[186] are a *coincidentia oppositorum*, and that these two symbols of wholeness are inextricably bound to one another. In *Psychology and Alchemy*, Jung makes use of what amounts to a "Hegelian" formulation when he states, "it is absolutely paradoxical in that [the self] represents in every respect thesis and antithesis, and at the same time synthesis."[187] In *The Red Book,* Jung speaks of a "new God" one that has been reborn subsequent to the deity's "death" at the hands of Nietzsche and the scientists and which is a union of opposing principles. Jung may appear to refer to his singular self when he writes that this new God "develops through the union of [such] principles in me,"[188] but we can assume he held that the new God develops through the reconciliation of opposites both within himself and in the mind and souls of other individual men and women. Jung was here developing the notion of the identity of the God and the self archetypes, which figures so prominently in his later psychology, and which later served as part of the foundation for Thomas J. J. Altizer's death of God theology, in which the divine is effectively dispersed in the collective psyche of humanity.[189]

While in *The Red Book*, God is associated with the union of opposites within the human psyche, it is the "serpent" that keeps the opposites apart: "It is always the serpent that causes man to become enslaved now to one, now to the other principle, so that it becomes error."[190] In *The Red Book*, Jung begins to develop the view that one can only surmount evil by accepting it as a part of both God and the self, an idea that was to later become a major theme in his *Answer to Job*. Jung further suggests that there is a great evil or error in the failure to recognize that *both* good and evil are a part of the self. As he writes in *Symbols of Transformation*, the "self, as a symbol of wholeness, as a *coincidentia oppositorum*...contains light and darkness simultaneously."[191] Jung holds that in the Christ figure, the opposites are polarized into the light of the son of God on the one hand and the darkness of the devil on the other. These polar opposites, however, come close to converging "in the figures of Christ and Anti-Christ."[192]

Jung writes that the Buddha and Christ are each highly elaborated symbols of the self. However, the Christ symbol is inadequate or at least incomplete, since Christ represents lightness and good to the exclusion of darkness and evil, which in Christianity is split off and relegated to the devil. However, as we saw in Chapter 3, according to Jung, an exploration of the unconscious can lead to a direct apprehension of the self archetype through a confrontation with "the abysmal contradictions of human nature."[193] In that event, one may glimpse the lightness *and* darkness of both Christ and the devil. Jung holds that very few individuals can have experience and insight into the problem of opposites, but that without such insight "there is no experience of wholeness and hence no inner approach to the sacred figures."[194] He thus suggests that insight into the opposites is necessary for both psychological and spiritual wholeness.

Jung considers the alchemist's "Anthropos," which he describes as the "unitary being who existed before man and at the same time represents man's goal."[195] This is also the "Primordial Man," *Adam Kadmon*, of the Kabbalists, who for Jung is another symbol of a "self"[196] that unifies the opposites of the "One and the Many" and contains "all things."[197] At times, Jung identifies this abstract image of humanity with its animal or primitive attribute,[198] since both the ideal and the debased images of man have in common their great distance from humanity's actual empirical being. This equivalence is another manifestation of the unity between persona and shadow—i.e., between the ideal personal image and the rejected aspects of the self. According to Jung, each aspect of humanity, the godlike and the primitive, is manifest in myths and symbols, and it is in these that the opposites can be mutually compensatory. For Jung, religion is not the antithesis of instinct but is nurtured by it; otherwise it "petrifies into formalism."[199]

In *Mysterium Coniunctionis* Jung describes the self as an "indescribable totality" comprised of both ego consciousness and the shadow,[200] and the latter as a representation of the personal unconscious. Because a collective element intrudes upon the personal sphere, the shadow provides a bridge to the anima and "the impersonal figures of the collective unconscious." As such, the self brings together ego consciousness, the personal unconscious, shadow, anima, and the figures and archetypes of the collective unconscious. Jung enters into a mode of paradoxical or "dialetheistic" logic when he suggests that the self is both "bright and dark and yet neither."[201]

The question arises as to whether such a "unified" self is possible or even desirable—a question that, as we have seen, Jung himself raises in one of his colloquies with the devil in *The Red Book*, where he learns that by reconciling the opposites life comes to "a complete standstill."[202] Indeed, as we saw in Chapter 1, in *Psychology of Alchemy* Jung condenses the conflict between these two views when he writes, "The self is made manifest in the opposites and in the conflict between them; it is a *coincidentia oppositorum*. Hence the way to the self begins with conflict."[203]

For Jung, just as God and the self each involve a union of opposites, the self itself exists in *coincidentia opposotorum* with God. Jung points out that whereas in the East the personal aspect of the ego is merged with the universal soul, as in the Indian conception of *Brahman-Atman*, the West has always pointed to the sinfulness and weakness of the individual psyche. Jung lauds both Eckhart and the alchemists for suspecting that there is a hidden aspect of divinity not only in the one man Jesus Christ but in all human beings. Jung references Meister Eckhart's dictim—"For man is truly God, and God is truly man"[204]—and he quotes the seventeenth-century German mystic, Angelus Silesius: "I am God's child and son, and he is mine...."[205] I will explore Jung's conception of God more fully later in this chapter.

ALCHEMY AND THE PLAY OF OPPOSITES

Jung became fascinated with the series of oppositions that were to be united in the alchemical work. He begins *Mysterium Comiunctionis*, which he subtitled "An Inquiry into the Separation and Synthesis of Psychic Opposites in Alchemy," by enumerating a number of oppositions, among them moist and dry, warm and cold, higher and lower, soul and body, heaven and earth, good and evil, costly and cheap, living and dead, and masculine and feminine (often personified as the King and Queen, the Emperor and the Empress, the Sun and Moon),[206] each of which, according to the alchemists, must be unified as a prerequisite for the distillation of the alchemical "gold." However, according to Jung, the alchemical opus must be understood as a form of psychological and spiritual work disguised as a procedure for the production of precious metals. One reason for this is that in alchemy, "the pairs of opposites constitute the phenomenology of the paradoxical *self*, man's totality."[207] In Jung's view, the psychological significance of the alchemists' expanded catalog of opposites, leads beyond the Freudian dichotomy of conscious and unconscious, into a psychology which endeavors to unify virtually all psychic contrasts. The most important of these oppositions include masculine and feminine, good and evil, chaos and order, reason and unreason, and life and death. Informed by alchemy, the psychologist is in a position to develop a more existentially and phenomenologically rich psychotherapy, one that moves well beyond the goal of undoing repressed thoughts and affects.

While alchemy involved the unification of a host of psychological opposites, and some alchemists believed that the production of gold depended upon the frame of mind of the alchemical adept, the alchemists were not themselves conscious of the fact that they had projected psychological contents onto their metallurgical endeavors. Indeed, according to Jung, classical alchemy "was, in essence, chemical research work into which there entered, by way of projection, an admixture of unconscious psychic material"[208] This, Jung suggests, is what produced the alchemists' interest in the union of the opposites, as "the psychological condition of any unconscious content is one of *potentia*, characterized by the polar opposites 'being' and 'non-being.'"[209]

As we have seen, the alchemists developed a variety of symbols for *coincidentia oppositorum*, including the *lapis* (the philosophical stone), the marriage of *Sol* and *Luna*, fire and water and life and death. Jung points out that the alchemists spoke of "the spirit Mercurius" as both consisting of "all conceivable opposites"[210] and as the agent that unifies the opposites.[211] Mercurius is also the mediator between hostile elements and the spirit of unity. According to Jung, the interpretation of Mercurius as a "peacemaker" is likely derived from the portrayal of Jesus in Ephesians 2:13ff. There, Christ is described as the one who has "broken down the dividing wall of hostility, by abolishing in his flesh the law, commandments and ordinances, that he might create in himself one new man in place of two, so make peace, and might reconcile both to God in one body through the cross, thereby bringing the hostility to an end."[212]

Jung points out that, beginning in the sixteenth century, aspects of the Kabbalah were integrated into alchemy,[213] and he makes reference to several Kabbalistic symbols for the coincidence of opposites that were taken up by the alchemists. He points out that according to the Kabbalists, the world in its current evil state is divided; the *sefirah Tifereth* (the masculine principle of divinity) is separated from the *sefirah Malchuth* (the feminine principle). However, with the coming of the Messiah, the King and Queen will be rejoined, thereby restoring the divine unity.[214] Jung describes how for the Kabbalists the sexual act itself is one that produces unity not only in the spirits of the participants but in the world at large. Referencing Waite's 1929 work *The Holy Kabbalah*, Jung notes that the souls of individual men and women are, for the Kabbalists comprised of the masculine world *above* and the feminine world *below*.[215] While Waite is a somewhat dubious authority on Jewish mysticism, the general point is valid: For the Kabbalists, the rectification of the world and the completion of both God and man involves the unification of the masculine and the feminine. The Kabbalistic unification of *Tifereth* with *Malchuth* is analogous to the alchemical unification of *Sol* and *Luna*. Indeed, the Kabbalists identified the feminine *sefirah, Malchuth*, the "Shekhinah," with the moon.[216] I will examine the union of the masculine and feminine in alchemy more fully later in this chapter.

The alchemists made use of paradoxical language to express their conviction that the unification of opposites is essential to the personal transformation that they understood to be a prerequisite for the transmutation of base metals into gold. Thus, the *lapis* or philosophical stone was on the one hand held to be cheap, base, immature and volatile; on the other hand, it was seen as perfect, precious, solid, and noble.[217] Paradoxical thinking is evident in various alchemical aphorisms such as "in lead is the dead life," "burn in water and wash in fire," and "seek the coldness of the moon and you shall find the heat of the sun."[218] A jarring effect is also achieved in the alchemical juxtaposition of the performative terms "congratulations and condolences."[219] For the alchemists, the philosophical tree paradoxically has its roots in the air, a notion that they may well have derived from the Kabbalistic tree, which represents the cosmic value archetypes, the *Sefirot*.[220]

Jung points out that the alchemists considered the coincidence of opposites an "indispensable condition for the healing of all ills."[221] They sought a substance within which the union of opposites could take place; such a substance would itself have to be dual, even contradictory in nature, exhibiting characteristics that are, for example, both material and spiritual, living and inert, masculine and feminine, and old and young. In addition, it had to be a substance that was created by both God and man.[222] This substance was referred to as the *lapis philosophorum*, the philosophical stone,[223] and the later alchemists regarded it as both a chemical compound and a psychological or spiritual frame of mind.[224] For the *lapis* to be successful, a certain spiritual mindset was necessary, and it was indeed *in the mind* of the alchemical adept that a certain "substance of celestial nature known to very few"[225] could be found. This substance—the "spagyric medicine,"[226] "balsam," "philosophic wine," "quintessence" or "truth"[227] was regarded as an essential ingredient for the alchemical opus. According to Jung, the distillation of this inner yet heavenly substance was necessary for the reconciliation of the opposites. It is the "imago Dei imprinted in man"[228] and yet (again paradoxically) could be distilled from wine and grain.

STAGES IN THE ALCHEMICAL PROCESS

Jung paid considerable attention to the stages in the alchemical opus that were thought to result in the reconciliation of the opposites. These stages are, in Jung's view, roughly parallel to the stages of psychotherapy. The alchemist Gerard Dorn, Jung writes, "recognized the psychological aspect of the chymical marriage (the union of masculine and feminine aspects of nature and the psyche) and clearly understood it in terms of what we today would call the individuation process.[229] Jung points out, however, that Dorn, in accordance with the alchemical principle of "separation prior to unity," held that in order to develop an ultimate union of mind and body, these elements must first be separated from one another. The alchemist must enter into an unnatural state in which his reason is completely isolated from and unaffected by feeling.[230] According to Jung, this preliminary step combines Stoic philosophy with Christian psychology to produce a differentiation of consciousness from its foundation in the unconscious mind. A similar process occurs in psychotherapy when the client is encouraged to take an objective view of his or her affects and instincts.[231] Indeed, we might here note that this position characterizes cognitive methods of psychotherapy which view the goal of treatment as the maintenance of this "objective" stance and the control of affects via reason. However, this "cognitive" approach is only a preliminary stage in the therapeutic/individuation process; for life is crippled when we continue to insist upon the primacy of intellect. According to Jung, reason does not prevent the pious man from sinning or the ego from being "stymied by its own irrationalities."[232] For Jung, the body, instinct, and the irrational must be admitted into the psyche and brought into harmony with the reason of the conscious ego.

It is at this point that a second stage in the alchemical process emerges, the stage in which the body, which had hitherto been separated from the mind, comes to be reunited with it. Indeed, it is only when the body is reintegrated with the psyche that the alchemical work can be actualized.[233] In this stage, the adept has at least "acquired some knowledge of his paradoxical wholeness,"[234] even if this wholeness has yet to be realized within himself. However, full knowledge is impossible, as one has already moved past the cognitive phase of the individuation process. Indeed, in a startlingly candid moment, Jung states that "no one knows how the paradoxical wholeness of man can ever be realized."[235] The idea here is that the production of wholeness cannot arise out of a knowledge or formula of how it is to be produced.

Jung is somewhat inconsistent in his description of the stages of the alchemical work, but his inconsistencies may well reflect the texts and traditions he worked with. For example, Jung tells us that the ego's coming to terms with the shadow corresponds to the first stage of the unifying process in *hermetic* philosophy.[236] Earlier he had described the initial stage in *alchemy* as a separation of the ego from the body.[237] By referencing the hermetic philosophy, Jung emphasizes that reconciliation with the shadow is critical as it provides the tension with one's persona that serves as the impetus to psychic development. The realization of virtue is fully dependent on its tension with its opposite in vice: "Without its counterpart virtue would be pale, ineffective, and unreal."[238] As a result of this conflict, the melancholy and confusion of the earlier phases of the alchemical and psychotherapeutic process gives way to a union of the opposites, symbolized for example in the *ouroboros* (the serpent eating its own tail) of Greek alchemy and in the figure Mercurius of later European alchemy.[239] In addition, as a result of the alchemical opus, one can get to know "the other" in one's psyche, an other who provides a valuable compensatory effect on one's personality.

As we have seen, Jung speaks of the first phase of the *alchemical* process as a separation of consciousness from the body and a consequent freeing up of the rational ego from disturbing bodily influences.[240] He then describes the second stage as the "reuniting of the *unio mentalis* with the body."[241] The third and final phase is a "union of the whole man with the *unus mundus*,"[242] which, according to Dorn, brings the individual back to the first day of creation prior to the division of light and darkness, day and night. This is what many would term a *mystical* union with the ground and origin of all personality and being.[243] Jung describes this third stage of the conjunction as akin to a union with "suprapersonal *atman*" or of "the individual tao with universal tao."[244] In this formulation, personal individuation passes over into a mystical unification with a universal "One." Jung writes, "Time and again the alchemists reiterate that the *opus* proceeds from the one and leads back to the one, that it is a sort of circle like a dragon biting its own tail."[245]

For Jung, the alchemical formula *solve et coagula* (separate and unite) reflects a process in which the individual comes to both distinguish himself from, and unite with his personal and collective unconscious. In the Foreword to *Mysterium Coniunctionis,* he describes how for the alchemists:

There was first of all an initial state in which opposite tendencies or forces were in conflict...[and
then] the great question of a procedure which would
be capable of bringing the hostile elements and
qualities, once they were separated, back to a unity
again.[246]

Drawing an interesting parallel between the alchemical work and
painting, Jung says, "The free ranging psyche of the adept used chemical substances and processes as a painter uses colors to shape out the
images of his fancy."[247] Just as a painter must choose the appropriate complementary colors to achieve his purpose, the alchemist must
choose the appropriate complementary chemicals to achieve his. This
again raises the intriguing possibility that painting, indeed all creative
work, involves a bringing together of opposite or disparate forces into
an encompassing and individuated whole. The alchemist, however,
thought that his mixture must even contain human blood, which he regarded as the seat of the human soul and a "ligament" for binding the
soul to God and uniting the spirit with the body.[248] While today we may
think of this process as "symbolic" of psychological forces, Jung makes
clear that the alchemists did not regard their opus as symbolic in nature.
To suggest to them otherwise would have been tantamount to suggesting to modern scientists that the belief in hormones is a symbol.[249]

The alchemical process, Jung points out, proceeded in stages that
were described in terms of colors. While there was no universal agreement upon the specific colors associated with these stages, the alchemists typically held there to be four that correspond to the essential colors attributed to Heraclitus. These are "*melanosis* (blackening), *leucosis*
(whitening), *xanthosis* (yellowing) and *tosis* (reddening)." Later alchemists, eliminated *xanthosis* (or *citrinitas*), thus reducing the number of
stages to three.[250]

Jung associated colors with moods and feelings,[251] a notion that has
both theoretical and empirical support in the literature on the Rorschach

Inkblot Test. Hermann Rorschach (who was himself influenced by Jung) held, and later research confirmed, that responses involving achromatic color, especially black (which Jung, the alchemists, and countless others have associated with evil and melancholy[252]) are suggestive of constricted, negative affect while chromatic colors (e.g., red, which Jung associated with "emotion and instinct"[253]) are indicative of more healthy and positive emotional expression.[254] For Jung, as the psyche is illuminated by "different lights," it proceeds through "ever-changing moods."[255] These changes proceed from black to yellow or white and finally to red. He writes, "The dawning light corresponds to the *albedo* [whiteness], the moonlight which in the opinion of some alchemists heralds the rising sun, the growing redness (*rubedo*) of which now denotes an increase of warmth and light."[256]

The "constriction" represented by the color black can be understood as a phase in which the ego is sealed off from the unconscious, or "shadow," to be followed by progressive phases of white, yellow and red, in which affects and other contrasting and unconscious elements are progressively integrated into the personality. Jung provides a particularly helpful description of the alchemical process in a difficult passage of his 1937 essay, "Religious Ideas in Alchemy." There, he describes the alchemists' "initial state" as "nigredo or blackness," a condition that is either a "quality of the "prima materia" or "chaos" at the beginning of creation or the result of the product of the alchemist's own "separation (*solutio, separatio, divisio, putrefactio*) of the elements." This separated or deconstructed state can be followed by a union of opposites symbolized by the "coniunctio" or marriage "of male and female." A third stage involves "the death of the product of the union (*mortificatio, calcinatio, putrefactio*)" and a renewed *negredo*. This is succeeded by a baptism or washing (*ablutio*) that leads to a stage of "whitening (*albedo*)." At this point, it is also possible that the "soul (anima)" which had been released in the stage of "death" "is reunited with the dead body and brings about its resurrection, or…the 'many colors' (*omnes colores*) or 'peacock's tail' (*cauda pavonis*)." This leads to the goal of the entire work, the whiteness or *albedo*, which contains within itself all colors. However, there is yet a further stage. The albedo is also silver, the moon and day-break, but it does not become the full "sunrise" until the stage *rubedo* or redness is reached. The white *albedo* now comes together with the red *rubedo*, in the "chymical marriage" of the "King and Queen."[257]

It will be worth our while to devote considerable attention to this color-staged process as it promises to unlock much of Jung's psychological interpretation of the alchemical opus. We should note that in addition to the transformations brought about by changes in color—which as we have seen can be understood in part as changes in feeling or mood states—the process Jung describes involves a series of negative, chaotic and disunified or "death" states (*negredo*) followed by a corrective (*albedo* or whitening) process that results in a *unification of male and female* elements and a consequent "sunrise" or "rebirth." The alternation between chaotic, disunified and dying conditions and their correction through a marriage of male and female cosmic elements reflects a dialectic or *coincidentia oppositorum* between destruction and rebirth, and male and female. This process is highly reminiscent of Kabbalistic dialectics which unify rupture and restoration, and masculine and feminine. I have written elsewhere about how these Kabbalistic unities were a major foundation for the spiritual and psychological aspects of alchemy.[258]

Here I will direct our attention to the psychological significance of the alchemical process as it is described by Jung. The primal *nigredo*, which Jung describes as the "*prima materia*, the *chaos* or *massa confusa*," can be understood to represent the collective psyche, or transcendental subject prior to its division into individual subjects, or prior to the individual subject's division into conscious and unconscious, persona and shadow, animus and anima, rational and irrational, etc. This chaotic condition is conceived either as present from the outset—with the very birth of the subject—or else results from a dissolution of the personality that comes about as a result of an immersion in the unconscious. These possibilities also suggest that human psychological development proceeds through phases of chaos or rupture, which alternate with phases of order, unification, and (re) integration, and that such integration involves both a liberation of unconscious emotion (the transformation from 'black' to 'red') and a unification of disparate, opposing elements of the psyche, the "chymical wedding" of male and female.

Late in his life, Jung wrote that the alchemical opus enabled him to make sense of the experiences that he recorded in *The Red Book*.[259] We can now understand why this was the case—as his *Red Book* visions involve him in a series of ruptures in his manner of thinking and being, followed by his acceptance and integration of aspects of himself (and concomitant affects)—for example, his banality,[260] his femininity,[261] and his "worst"[262]—that he had initially felt to be alien to his ego. For Jung, the process of individuation and self-realization was indeed one of *solve et coagula*: differentiation and unification.

According to Jung, alchemy knows two forms of conjunction, the first involving a descent into darkness and negativity in which incest, murder and death predominate, and the second in which there is an ascent into light, where the conjunction achieves what Jung refers to as a "heavenly" character.[263] Individuation thus becomes a union or coincidence of dissolution and restoration, chaos and order, non-being and being, death and life.

We might ask what it is that alchemy adds to the account of the individuation process that is articulated imaginatively in *The Red Book* and rationally in Jung's more scientific writings. In response, it can be said that alchemy provides a telling metaphor for a process that is only partly under the individual's control, and it proceeds through a combination of nature and mystery to produce a transformation that is anticipated but whose specific character is unforeseen. Alchemy, which lies on the border between science and magic, thereby embodies a *coincidentia oppositorum* between conscious and unconscious, will and fate, rational and irrational, and expectation and surprise; it is thus a perfect metaphor for the individuation process which itself involves an integration of each of these opposites. Jung points out that one of the paradoxes of alchemy is that it is sometimes difficult to distinguish between the alchemists' creativity and their tomfoolery. To the extent that creativity involves play, the distinction between the two may be one of interdependence. As Wittgenstein put it, "If people never did silly things nothing intelligent would ever get done."[264] Alchemy, we might say, is a form of silliness that leads to a greater intelligence and wisdom.

Jung's turn to alchemy suggests that the notion of *coincidentia oppositorum* is applicable to Jung as a thinker and writer. Huskinson points out that insofar as Jung held that the psyche could not be circumscribed in rational-scientific terms, an examination of his difficult and more intuitive works on alchemy "may compensate for the structured exposition of his thought."[265]

SOL AND LUNA: THE UNION OF MASCULINE AND FEMININE

Among the alchemists' symbols of opposition and unity, perhaps the most graphic is the "chymical marriage," the union of male and female, King and Queen, *Sol and Luna*. In *Mysterium Coniunctionis,* Jung describes how the alchemists understood this wedding as the consummation of their own work.[266] This marriage overcomes the "hostility" among the "four elements," and then unites the world's masculine and feminine aspects through the power of love and passion, a passion that overcomes the enmity between the sexes that had been the curse of mankind since the dawn of time. Whereas Christianity had transposed the physical attraction and union between male and female into a sin that perpetuated the primal transgression, alchemy exalted sexuality and the union between the sexes.

According to Jung, the union of (and inevitable conflict between) man and woman "symbolizes every conceivable pair of opposites"[267] In uniting male and female, the marriage of *Sol* and *Luna* brings about a unification between good and evil, as the male principle of the Sun is good, while the feminine is identified with wickedness.[268] However, the feminine contribution of darkness and evil to the "chymical marriage" is to be interpreted positively as a singular contribution of alchemy to the development of the psyche. This is because the masculine aspect of the psyche identifies almost completely with consciousness and as such knows no shadow, coldness, heaviness, nor melancholy. From a masculine perspective, there is no room for black as opposed to white, no room for evil as opposed goodness and no room for "any prestige diminishing weakness."[269] As a result, except in rare moments, symbolized by the *Sol Niger*, the black sun, a conscious awareness of the psyche's potential for evil is completely excluded from male activity and awareness. On the other hand, *Luna*, the feminine aspect of the psyche cannot hide from her own darkness. This is graphically and symbolically illustrated by the lunar phases; the brightness of the full moon yielding to increasing shadow and eventual total darkness. By way of contrast to this regular descent of the feminine into its own darkness, it is only in rare moments of solitary reflection that the presence of the "black sun" is sensed and feared.[270] While the "new" or darkened moon is a monthly occurrence, it is only in the very rare and brief moments of a solar eclipse that we witness a black sun. By analogy, it is only when a man's status or achievements have been eclipsed that he contemplates the dark elements of his personality. Jung asserts that it is because the masculine solar psyche is split off from its shadow, whereas the lunar feminine psyche periodically experiences her darkness, that women are targeted as the source for all the darkness and evil in men.[271] However, men think of themselves as sources of illumination for the women around them and, according to Jung, they would be better off placing their intellectual brilliance in the cauldron of the most profound lunar doubt. Indeed, if a man acknowledges his *Sol Niger* and shadow, women become a source of wisdom for him.[272] Again, it is the union of opposing masculine and feminine principles that brings wholeness to the self.

Jung tells us that *logos* and *eros* are intellectual formulations generally equivalent to the *Sol* and *Luna* archetypes. However, he prefers the latter figures, as they are richer precisely because of their opacity to the intellect. As Jung puts it, "Concepts are coined and negotiable values; images are life."[273] Further, "Myth is the primordial language natural to these psychic processes, and no intellectual formulation comes anywhere near the richness and expressiveness of mythical imagery."[274]

According to Jung, lunar femininity is associated with the unconscious. It is symbolized in the wisdom of salt, and the shapelessness of water, which "in all of its forms—sea, lake, river, spring" symbolize the unconscious." The union of male and female in the "*spagyric* Marriage" symbolizes the union of the conscious and unconscious psyches.[275]

Jung quotes the *Zohar*, the *locus classicus* of the Kabbalah, in support of his view that the human psyche is incomplete without a union of its masculine and feminine elements: "Male and female created he them." From this we learn that every figure that does not comprise male and female elements is not a higher (heavenly) figure.... Observe this: God does not make his abode in any place where male and female are not joined together."[276]

INCEST, TRANSGRESSION, AND THE SHADOW

Jung notes that the union of opposites was often symbolized in alchemy "as a brother and sister incest."[277] The alchemists celebrated this transgression of the law, and it became for them an important symbol of the return of humanity to paradise.[278] Jung tells us that incest represents the supreme union of opposites because it is a bringing together of things that are both related and disparate. Incest was the prerogative of the gods, but Freud's elucidation of the Oedipus complex reveals that incest is also a great temptation for human beings.[279] The fact that incest symbolizes and is indeed a "natural form" of the union of opposites provides insight into why *coincidentia oppositorum* is either not recognized at all or, when recognized, suppressed.[280]

Jung suggests that the symbol of incest may also refer to the union of the masculine psyche with its own forgotten feminine aspect[281] the anima, or the union of the feminine psyche with its masculine *animus*.

Finally, the archetype of incest reflects the union of something that is most exalted—erotic love—with something that is completely dark, detestable, base, and in violation of a strict taboo.[282] This is a radical expression of the union of the persona and shadow.

For the alchemists, incest is the "hierosgamos [holy marriage] of the gods."[283] In elevating incest, the alchemists overcame another opposition, between the law and transgression, suggesting that it is only through transgression that the spirit of the moral law can be fulfilled. This is because the full actualization or individuation of a moral agent can only occur through a transformation that has transgression as its logical and psychological antecedent.[284] Without the possibility of transgression there is no free will, and without free-will humanity does not fulfill its function either as a moral agent or as a partner in the world's creative redemption.[285]

As we have seen, as early as *The Red Book*, Jung engaged in "active imagination" with internal/archetypal figures that resulted in the confrontation and ultimate reconciliation with aspects of himself that his conscious ego had previously found reprehensible. He later described this type of confrontation as an arduous process that initially brings about doubt and paralysis, but which ultimately results in a reconciliation between *persona* and *shadow*. As we have also seen, Jung held that a complete conception and experience of both self and God must include evil or shadow elements. He pointed out that for the alchemists, hell and its fire are internal to God, and that this "must indeed be so if God is held to be *a coincidentia oppositorum*."[286] A God that excluded transgression and evil from itself would, in effect, no longer be infinite, all-encompassing and absolute. Similarly, the self, which in Jung's view is virtually indistinguishable from the God image or archetype,[287] must reconcile good and evil, persona and shadow, law and transgression.

However, beyond reconciling oneself with one's shadow, the individual who engages in reflective active imagination has the potential to bring about a union of the ego with other internal images and archetypes, including those that run counter to one's own gender and even species. Jung claimed that the alchemists independently arrived at an active imagination procedure that resulted in a unification of the individual psyche with the universal soul and liberated the adept from the hold that the opposites have upon his psyche.[288] Jung conceived of this process as analogous to the Indian notion of *Purusha-Atman*, the union of the individual with the universal soul. He points out that in both alchemy and Eastern philosophy the coincidence or union of opposites is associated with freedom. Thus, the union of opposites is a *summa medicina*; it heals both the body and the spirit.[289] The opposites are conceived as a sort of prison, and their union as a liberation.[290]

CHRIST AND CHRISTIANITY

For Jung, the opposites of good and evil are torn asunder in Christianity, and this has led to the "crucifixion and suspension of everything that lives."[291] This crucifixion is tantamount to the moral suffering" that we experience when we fail to recognize the "shadow" side of our own personalities. Jung holds that just as dreams compensate for the one-sidedness of our conscious life, alchemy compensated for Christianity. Indeed, it became an undercurrent to the Christian religion, one that encompassed evil along with good and the feminine along with the masculine.[292] Indeed, the recognition of the shadow in alchemy leads to the *hierosgamos* or "chymical wedding," both with and *within Christianity*, where "the supreme opposites, male and female...are melted into a unity purified of all opposition, and therefore incorruptible."[293]

According to Jung, prior to the advent of Christianity (for example, in classical Chinese philosophy), there was no awareness of the moral problem of the opposites. He argues that it is only with Christianity that the metaphysical opposites begin to enter consciousness in the form of the dualistic contrast between good and evil, an opposition that was expressed forcefully in Manichaeism.[294] In response to the dualism of good and evil the church developed its doctrine of *privatio*, which held that evil, as a "privation" of the good has no true reality and has its origin in man rather than God. As such, evil was removed from the Godhead and placed in the psyche of human beings. On this view, the devil had no recourse but to prey upon the weakness in man. Jung holds, however, that it began to dawn on the alchemists that *both* good and evil were psychic in nature, an idea that they expressed through the symbol of Mercurius. Indeed, for the Alchemists, Mercurius is a "hair's breadth" away from the devil because he embodies the opposites, and as such stands in "compensatory relation" to the all-good Christ.[295]

Jung discusses several early Christian doctrines that anticipated the notion that Christ embodies a coincidence of opposing characteristics. For example, he references an apocryphal saying of Jesus from the Second Epistle to the Corinthians (traditionally attributed to Clement of Rome, d. 99 AD): "The two shall be one, and the outside as the inside, and the male with the female neither male nor female."[296] Jung explains that this saying served as a paradigm for the coincidence of opposites in alchemy, and is a parallel both to the *Tao* of Lao Tse and the union of opposites in Nicholas of Cusa.[297] He also explores the meaning of the Christian doctrine of the Assumption, the taking up of Mary's corporeal body directly into heaven. According to Jung, the Assumption asserts a material/historical event that the alchemists utilized "in describing the glorification of matter in the opus."[298] It suggests that the "darkness of sublunary matter," which is associated with the devil, is a fourth component of the Trinity and essential for redemption.[299] Finally, Jung makes reference to the Peratic (Gnostic) doctrine of the third century Roman Christian theologian, Hippolytus, who believed that the "gods of destruction and the god of salvation are together."[300] According to Jung, this must be understood as a means of describing the destructive and constructive aspects of the unconscious. As for a number of the mystics he references, "light is manifest in the darkness, and out of danger the rescue comes."[301] Finally, in *Aion*, Jung speaks of Christ as a symbol of the self.[302] This is the Christ who descends into Hell and embraces his shadow and the collective unconscious,[303] not the Christ of official Christianity who excludes all evil and darkness from his nature.

LIFE/DEATH, MATTER AND SPIRIT

Jung examined a large variety of oppositions, their treatment in alchemy and other disciplines, and their relevance to the process of individuation. For example, he suggests that in the biblical story of the fall there is a *coincidentia oppositorum* between life and death —as Adam's becoming fully conscious (fully alive) results in human mortality.[304] Jung suggests that a renewal of the life-force often involves a sojourn into the unconscious, which is itself analogous to death. Jung implies this when he argues that in the act of ritual *sacrifice* consciousness surrenders to the unconscious and the one who makes the sacrifice is thereby renewed.[305]

A *coincidentia* also occurs between matter and spirit. In alchemy, the union of these opposites is manifest in the doctrine of the "ascent and descent,"[306] an idea that is also present in the Kabbalah. According to the alchemists, an "arcane substance" rises from earth to heaven unites the opposites and then descends to achieve the transformation that occurs in the alchemists' vessels. The full union of opposites that occurs "in the bath of the tincture"[307] involves a movement from matter to spirit and from spirit back towards corporeality. In astrology, this was represented by the movement from the dark and cold of Saturn to the warmth of the sun[308] (and back again). As we have seen, the Jewish mystics held that there is a *coincidentia oppositorum* between the divine and earthly realm, and certain Chasidim even went so far as to advance the practice of *avodah b'gashmiyut*, or worship through corporeality. Jung himself emphasized that a union of intellect and feeling *within* the spirit or soul is incomplete and must be complemented by "a union with the physical world of the body."[309]

Jung criticized Nietzsche for emphasizing body over spirit and claimed that his own views on the relationship between body and spirit were more balanced. For Jung, "the spirit is the life of the body seen from within and the body the outward manifestation of the life of the spirit—the two being really one."[310]

THE ORIGIN OF OPPOSITION

Jung held that consciousness and reason produce the divide between the psyche's opposing tendencies. This is because consciousness strives for clarity and unambiguity and must therefore free itself from contrary or opposing tendencies, which it either overlooks or suppresses. As a result, consciousness identifies itself with one pole of a divide and seeks to exclude, disparage or ignore its antithesis. Thoughts, feelings and other psychic contents that are incompatible with the determinate thread of awareness are split off from the conscious mind.[311] The result is that a counter position builds up in the unconscious, one that emphasizes the split off contrary and compensates for the one-sidedness of conscious thinking.[312] Jung writes: "Every psychological extreme secretly contains its own opposite or stands in some sort of intimate and essential relation to it."[313] He points out that according to the alchemists' teaching, "every form of life, however elementary, contains its own inner antithesis."[314]

As discrimination is the essence of consciousness, the movement towards unity characterizes the unconscious, where, as in nature, "the opposites seek one another."[315] Freud had held that the distinctions of conscious life and language do not exist within the unconscious, and according to Jung, "so long as consciousness refrains from acting, the opposites will remain dormant in the unconscious."[316] However, once the conscious ego embarks on its quest for clarity, the opposites are activated and pose a problem for the psyche. This occurs with the advent of language. Indeed, according to Jung, it is division into the opposites via thought and language that ultimately gives rise to the division between conscious and unconscious aspects of the personality:

> Yet, serene and tragic at once, it was [the] archaic man who, having started to think, invented the dichotomy which Nietzsche laid at the door of Zarathustra: the discovery of the pairs of opposites,

the division into odd and even, above and below, good and evil.[317]

While thought and language work to keep the opposites distinct, their blending and mutual interdependence is nonetheless evident in certain linguistic ambiguities. Jung points out that in English the word "bad" is related to the old word "bass," which means good.[318] A contemporary manifestation of this is the "urban" use of the term "bad" to mean "amazingly good." Jung relates that in the versions of some fairytales the devil is substituted for by God, and in a footnote, Jung's translator points out that there is an etymological relationship between "devil" and "divinity."[319]

THE OPPOSITES IN PSYCHOTHERAPY

In *The Red Book*, composed in the years immediately after his break from Freud in 1912, Jung began developing the notion that personal development involves an acceptance and bringing together of polar ideas, feelings and attitudes. In it we find the origin of Jung's ideas on the coincidence of opposites, and we see him struggling to make sense of the personal experiences that apparently led him to this notion. In the process, he considers and personally experiences a variety of oppositions: male and female,[320] meaning and nonsense,[321] love and hate,[322] action and thought,[323] madness and reason,[324] the "divine and the devilish,"[325] thinking and pleasure,[326] above and below,[327] etc. Jung echoes Hegel: "Immense fullness and immense emptiness are one and the same."[328] Elsewhere in *The Red Book* he asserts that thinking and feeling "are each other's poison and healing."[329]

Jung says that one only achieves a "presentiment of the whole" and can only "achieve balance" by nurturing one's "opposite."[330] However, this can only be achieved with great difficulty as the cultivation of what is contrary to one's own thoughts, attitudes, and emotions "is hateful to you in your innermost core, because it is not heroic."[331] He held that the drawing together of the psychic opposites was also essential to psychotherapy, and he ultimately came to see it as a natural process, one that occurs gradually unless the ego interferes "with its irritating rationality."[332] For Jung, the fostering of this natural process is essential for effective psychological treatment, which must take its aim at the "whole," "greater," and "future" man and in doing so traverse a winding path that effects a unification.[333]

There are, in Jung's view, obvious analogies between the alchemical process and psychotherapy. The alchemists' confrontation with the opposites is analogous to the psychotherapists' concern with "intrapsychic conflict" and "dissociation of the personality." Typically, consciousness will repress one side of a conflict, resulting in an extension and prolongation of psychological disharmony or neurosis. The aim of psychotherapy is to bring the opposites into consciousness and, as far as possible, integrate or unite them.[334]

Jung claims that any thoroughgoing psychotherapy must confront consciousness with its (unconscious) counter position or "shadow."[335] As we have seen, he holds that the conflict between consciousness and the shadow cannot be abolished through reason but must yield to a process of unification that involves more than the intellect. According to Jung, this was also true for both Freud and Adler. For Freud, the unification involves the making conscious of repressed psychological contents; for Adler, it involves "insight into the fictitious lifestyle."[336] Jung himself held that the union of conscious and unconscious psychic material can only properly be achieved through fantasy, via the symbols of the collective unconscious. While certain conflicts can indeed be resolved through reason,[337] there are others that cannot be so resolved without causing harm to the psyche. The nature of the resolution and union of opposites that occurs in psychotherapy cannot be predicted in advance, as it results in a transformation of both the conscious and the unconscious psyche that is unique to each individual. This transformation typically follows a compensation from the unconscious and often produces a religious or spiritual experience in the subject.[338] In the process, the unconscious produces symbolic formations, similar to or identical to those found in alchemy and the history of mysticism. According to Jung, in psychotherapy, symbols point to tendencies, attitudes, or feelings about which the conscious psyche has paid insufficient attention. Such symbols, which generally occur in dreams, can also be produced in waking fantasies and typically herald a unification of opposites similar to those conceived of by the alchemists. However, Jung holds that both in history and individual development symbols reveal "tendencies whose goal is as yet unknown."[339] It is for this reason that in psychotherapy a symbol from the unconscious does not reveal its meaning immediately and fully.

Jung notes that the psychotherapy patient will often experience a new interest in theological and spiritual matters or even a religious conversion. He explains that patients who undergo such a transformation are relatively rare, and suggests that these are the patients who undergo a "major" as opposed to "minor" psychotherapy." Such patients experience an irrational union of opposites, one that Jung says can be described as "mystical."[340] We here note in passing that if Jung himself was not a mystic,[341] he saw a form of, or at least an analogy to, mystical experience in the psychotherapeutic process. This is an outcome that is impossible to fully describe in words, as it results in paradox and a certain indeterminacy at the limits of knowledge.[342] However, it can be said that in the process of psychotherapy the patient's conscious self moves closer to and forms a union with his or her unconscious psyche.[343]

It is important to remember that for Jung both conscious and unconscious aspects of the psyche remain strong subsequent to a successful psychotherapy. The union of opposites does not lead to complete dissolution of the opposites or the absorption of one pole by the other. If either consciousness or the unconscious comes to dominate the patient's psyche, he will be led to ruin and destruction.[344]

AN IMPOSSIBLE AND UNKNOWABLE UNION

Throughout his career, Jung maintained a great respect and even a reverence for the unknown and unknowable. He came to believe "that all the greatest and most important problems of life are fundamentally insoluble" because "they express the necessary polarity inherent in every self-regulating system."[345] However, Jung concluded that while these problems could not be solved, they could be "outgrown." He suggests that this occurs by way of "action through non-action"—"the art of letting things happen" and "letting go of oneself,"[346] a discipline taught by the German mystic and philosopher Meister Eckhart.

In the Foreword to *Mysterium Coniunctionis*, written in October 1954, Jung tells his readers that the alchemists understood their art as one of "separation and analysis on the one hand and synthesis and consolidation on the other."[347] This process, which is captured in the phrase *solve et coagula* and which I described earlier as a sequence of color stages, begins with chaos or the "prima material" *but actually has no clear and discernible endpoint.* At various points, the alchemists spoke of their unifications as resulting in androgyny, immortality, the prolongation of life, and divinity,[348] but each of these only hint at a process and goal that is essentially unknown and impossible to state in words. This is an extremely important point—for it suggests an openness to unspecified transformation and change that is both frightening and exhilarating to those who engage in the psychological "opus."

Jung is himself quite clear that the nature of the psychic unification is essentially unknown and that indeed no one can say "what a being is like that unites the full range of consciousness with that of the unconscious."[349] For Jung, there is an aspect of the human psyche that is essentially unknown, and it is just this unknowability that is a prerequisite for a sense of meaning and wholeness. He explains that the notion of the unconscious becoming conscious is paradoxical because it is technically inconceivable.[350] Indeed, Jung held that his efforts to understand the unconscious were provisional and subject to error.[351] By definition, one can only know what one is conscious of and thus there is always a vast reservoir of unconscious material that serves as the background for conscious experience. For this reason, the end point, in which consciousness becomes unified with unconsciousness, can itself *never become completely conscious*, and as such can never be explicated in clear, rational terms. This is yet another reason why the union of opposites is "not amenable to scientific explanation."[352] For Jung, all efforts to express the nature of this unity lead one into paradox—for example, the view that the self is both determinate and indeterminate, subject to universal causality and free.

One can reasonably question whether the unity of psychic opposites is actually possible or if it is rather a limit that helps define an ongoing process, one that never reaches a final goal. This notion of a limit may be required to explicate the entire notion of *coincidentia oppositiorum*. While the unconscious can be revealed in consciousness, this can never be achieved *in toto*, and as a result the process is never fully realized.

The question remains whether it is humanly possible to unite the opposites in practice. Indeed, Jung wrote that the nature of the unity of "antagonistic elements eludes our human judgment, for the simple reason that nobody can say what a being is like that unites the full range of [opposites]."[353] Further, "consciousness is too narrow and too one-sided to comprehend the full inventory of the psyche."[354] Wholeness is, then, an ideal that can be approached as a regulative, if unattainable, ideal.[355]

LIMITATIONS AND DANGERS OF THE *COINCIDENTIA* IDEA

Jung understood the coincidence of opposites as a general archetype that has implications for every aspect of our psychological life. Like any other archetype, the coincidence of opposites has its negative as well as its positive side, and despite its pervasiveness it has certain limitations. Indeed, Jung himself held that the concept of the coincidence of opposites itself must be complemented by its own opposite, radical difference if God (or the self) is to avoid canceling itself out. He wrote, "The principle of the coincidence of opposites must therefore be completed by its opposite in order to attain full paradoxicality and hence psychological validity."[356]

Perhaps more significant in this context are the potentially negative ethical and psychological implications of the coincidence of opposites idea. The former becomes apparent the moment we consider the proposition that there is an interdependence between good and evil, a theme that permeates Jung's own writings.

> The grand plan on which the unconscious life of the psyche is constructed is so inaccessible to our understanding that we can never know what evil may not be necessary in order to produce good by enantiodromia, and what good may very possibly lead to evil.[357]

As we have seen, from the time of *The Red Book*, Jung held that one cannot cling to the good within oneself without acknowledging or recognizing one's shadow and potential for evil. He expanded this psychological maxim, however, to include certain very troubling consequences—for example, that certain moments in history, including the rise of National Socialism, could produce a "good" that was heralded by apparent evil and must thus in some sense be embraced. In 1932, as the Nazis began their rise to power, Jung wrote:

> There are times in the world's history—and our own time may be one of them—when good must stand aside, so that anything destined to be better first appears in evil form. This shows how extremely dangerous it is even to touch these problems, for evil can so easily slip in on the plea that it is, potentially, the better.[358]

Jung was not immune from this danger as he not only expressed a certain admitration for Hitler,[359] wrote disparagingly about Jews,[360] and reportedly went so far as to suggest that his disciples cultivate anti-Semitism as a means of getting in touch with their shadow selves.[361] The problem of Jung, anti-Semitism, and National Socialism is controversial and complex, and the reader is referred to works by Aryeh Maidenbaum, Jay Sherry, and my own book on Jung and Jewish mysticism to explore these complexities.[362]

We should here note that Jung was not original in his views on the *coincidentia oppositorum* of good and evil. Indeed, we read in The *Zohar*: "The perfection of all things is attained when good and evil are first of all commingled and then become all good, for there is no good so perfect as that which issues out of evil."[363]

The recognition that contraries imply one another can readily pass over into an overemphasis and even advocacy of the hitherto denigrated poll of certain oppositions. Thus, while according to Jung it is important for consciousness to be compensated and renewed through a sojourn through the unconscious,[364] one runs a risk of falling too deeply into the unconscious. He writes, "If the unconscious rules to the exclusion of all else, everything is liable to end in destruction."[365] As we have just suggested, Jung himself provided an example of this in connection with his own fascination with National Socialism in the 1930s.

In *The Red Book*, Jung evinced what I believe was a tendency to "overcompensate" for the rationality of modern science, by placing a great emphasis upon the irrational and suggesting that reason had poisoned the modern soul. In a passage I quoted more fully earlier, Jung writes: "We spread poison and paralysis around us in that we want to educate all the world around us into reason."[366] He suggests that science is a (perhaps necessary) evil. He says to the ailing God Izdubar:

> We had to swallow the poison of science. Otherwise we would have met the same fate as you have: we'd be completely lamed, if we encountered it unsuspecting and unprepared. This poison is so insurmountably strong that everyone even the strongest,

and even the eternal Gods, perish because of it. If
our life is dear to us, we prefer to sacrifice a piece
of our life force rather than abandon ourselves to
certain death.[367]

As Jung's career moved on, he developed a more considered view
of science and reason, one that recognized the dangers associated with
an overcompensation for its deficiencies. In a 1958 interview with H. L.
Philp, reprinted in Volume 18 of his *Collected Works*, Jung stated:

> Since everybody believes or, at least, tries to be-
> lieve in the unequivocal superiority of rational con-
> sciousness, I have to emphasize the importance of
> the unconscious irrational forces, to establish a sort
> of balance. Thus to superficial readers of my writ-
> ings it looks as if I were giving the unconscious a
> supreme significance, disregarding consciousness.
> As a matter of fact the emphasis lies on conscious-
> ness as the condition *sine qua non* of apperception
> of unconscious contents, and the supreme arbiter in
> the chaos of unconscious possibilities.[368]

There is a potential exclusivist implication to *Jung's* understanding
of the *coincifdentia oppositorum* idea. He is clear that the kind of unification of the opposites of which he speaks is not possible for everyone.
He indicates that it is possible for only a small minority of patients,
those he describes as having "certain spiritual demands."[369] He adds that
the union of conflicting elements in the psyches of these patients can be
described as "mystical."[370] It is, of course, possible and even likely that
Jung prejudged the case by focusing on historical material of a spiritual
nature and on patients who have spiritual interests. One can certainly
imagine an individual for whom the union of opposites or the resolution
of an intrapsychic conflict does not yield a religious or spiritual experience, at least one that is not framed in religious terms. Granted that
it is likely to yield an experience of the self that is deeply meaningful,
but it seems to me that the terms "religious" and "spiritual" involve an

interpretation of an intrapsychic process or experience that can also be understood in different, more secular terms.

The notion that the integration of opposites and the realization of the self (Jung) or *Ubermensch* (Nietzsche) is possible only for certain individuals, those who move beyond the realm of the "mass man,"[371] further raises the question of elitism. A similar question can be raised with regard to Hegel's "Absolute," as Hegel held that the "symbolic" realization of the "Idea" was suitable for the masses but "lower" than the philosophical realization, which required the philosopher to engage in an extraordinarily high level of abstract thinking. It is notable that the "symbolic" level, which for Jung is the *sine qua non* of the whole self, is for Hegel a mere approximation to absolute knowledge. For each of these thinkers, however, the full realization of the coincidence of opposites is reserved for an elite group.

NIETZSCHE: THERE ARE NO OPPOSITES

A criticism of the doctrine of *coincidentia oppositorum*, can be marshalled on the basis of Nietzsche's later view that there are no opposites to begin with. However, as we will see, the view that there are no opposites is difficult to distinguish from the notion that they coincide.

Beginning with *Human, All Too Human* Nietzsche repudiated his earlier philosophical views on the "opposites" as part of his general rejection of metaphysics. In that work, he wrote: "There are no opposites, except in the customary exaggeration of popular or metaphysical interpretations, and...a mistake in reasoning lies at the bottom of this antithesis."[372] In *The Will to Power*, Nietzsche asserts:

> Opposites...do not exist in themselves and...actually express only variations in degree that from a certain perspective appear to be opposites. There are no opposites: only from those of logic do we derive the concept of opposites-and falsely transfer it to things.[373]

Presumed poles of an opposition are in reality a "sublimation" of or different perspective upon their contraries, or are understood simply as differences in the degree of a single quality (as "warm" and "cold"). For example, according to Nietzsche: "Between good and evil actions there is no difference in kind, but at the most one of degree. Good actions are sublimated evil ones; evil actions are coarsened brutalized good ones."[374]

Nietzsche sees great harm deriving from the tendency to think in oppositions. He writes, "An unspeakable amount of painfulness, arrogance, harshness, estrangement, frigidity has entered into human feelings because we think we see opposites instead of transitions."[375] In a gesture that was later taken up by Derrida and other postmodernist thinkers, Nietzsche held that the so-called good poles of oppositions are inundated with or contaminated by their contraries. All things, he said, are subject to dissolution and destruction, and the Platonic effort to shield "ideals" from their destructive contraries is an illusion. Thus Nietzsche, like many mystics (and also Jung) holds it is language that distorts reality by positing clear distinctions. However, he further held, the underlying pre-linguisticized reality is not, as many mystics claim, a unified "one," but rather an inscrutable mass of chaos and change.

Nevertheless, as Derrida has argued, one cannot escape the metaphysics of oppositions in the process of attempting to eliminate it. According to Derrida, once we enter into language "we cannot utter a single destructive proposition which has not already slipped into the form, the logic and the implicit postulations of precisely what it seeks to contest."[376]

We might suggest that the notion of *coincidentia oppositorum* is itself coordinate with the notion that there are no real opposites to begin with. Each, we might say, involves a move towards openness and a rejection of "one-sidedness." Jung praised the Chinese philosophers who recognized the importance of balancing the existential polarities of life; for Jung, the Chinese understanding that opposites always balance each other is "a sign of high culture."[377] One-sidedness, on the other hand, "though it lends momentum, is a sign of barbarism."[378]

JUNG ON THE EXISTENCE OF GOD

Jung was generally quite ambivalent about making pronouncements on theological matters. At various points, he declared that as an empirical scientist he was not in a position to make theological or metaphysical assertions.[379] At times Jung seemed to hold that "God" is as an equivalent of the self archetype;[380] at other times, he resisted the temptation to make this correspondence.[381]

Nevertheless, and in direct contravention of his own stated policy, Jung occasionally made what appear to be theological claims. What is perhaps most interesting about these claims, however, is how they frequently contradict one another. It is as if Jung, like Walt Whitman (who wrote "Do I contradict myself? Very well then…I contradict myself; I am large, I contain multitudes"[382]) had no interest in maintaining consistency in his assertions. For example, on the one hand, Jung held that God is manifest in "all things that cross my path, violently and recklessly upsetting my subjective plans,"[383] while on the other hand he appeared to identify at least the Indian experience of the divine with the sense of serenity that is manifest when one is in repose "with his inner nature."[384] Thus, God is "totally other," beyond the ego," *and* identified with the self. Perhaps we can begin to reconcile these views by saying that God is external to the "ego," but internal to the much wider "self," but a certain contradiction between inner and outer, chaos and serenity remains.

To take another example, Jung initially held that we can have no direct awareness of transcendent things, including God.[385] However, later in his career, in his *Answer to Job*, he came to the view that it is God who is unconscious of himself and only comes to know himself through humanity. In 1959, when Jung is asked in English during a BBC interview whether he believes in God, he responds "I *know*. I don't need to believe I know."[386]

How can we understand these apparently contradictory theological pronouncements about a God who is "totally other" and one who is "totally within," about a God who is unknowable to man and one who can only be known *through* man. Further, how can we even understand the contradiction between Jung's claim that one cannot make theological pronouncements and his making them? Was Jung simply confused, or was there, perhaps, something fruitful to be achieved through his inconsistency?

Here it will be useful to recall two things: the first is Kant's observation that we arrive at antinomies whenever we attempt to speak about transcendent things; the second is the view of many mystics that they must violate the law of non-contradiction in order to express the nature of mystical experience. Perhaps these observations help to shed light on why Jung spoke contradictions when he touched upon theology. And perhaps the object of our theological assertion ("God") is so vast and all-encompassing as to include both "yes" and "no" and all things we may be inclined to say about it—including both that it does and does not exist! I will revisit this question in Chapter 6 when we examine the philosophical foundations and implications of the doctrine of *coincidentia oppositorum* and reexamine the theological insights of the Jewish mystics.

THE OPPOSITES IN JUNG AND HEGEL REVISITED: HEGEL ON THE IMAGINATION

I would like to return to consider the question of Jung's (and Nietzsche's) rejection of reason as a principle for reconciling or uniting the opposites. Earlier, I suggested a comparison between Hegel's dialectic and Jung's transcendent function; I showed how each of these notions was intended to point to a process which reconciles opposites that remain unreconciled within everyday thought and experience. We have seen, however, that while for Hegel this reconciliation occurs in *thought*, for Jung it occurs (and can only occur) unconsciously via the *imagination*, which spontaneously produces a "third" or symbol that unifies oppositions. While the distinction between the reconciling power of thought versus the imagination is an important one that distinguishes Hegel from Jung, we have also seen that Jung's rejection of theory and reason as a means of reconciling the opposites was not as complete as he often suggested. Similarly, Hegel had a far greater interest in the reconciling power of the imagination than Jung appears to have recognized. In fact, Hegel held that the imagination was an important historical stage in the reconciliation of the opposites, one that was manifest in the history of art and religion. Indeed, in his lectures on aesthetics and religion,[387] Hegel adopted a view that comes closer than is often realized to Jung's understanding of the value of myths and symbols.

Hegel holds that *art expresses ideas in sensuous, material form* and that both art and religion are imaginative and symbolic in their expression. He argues that art, religion, and philosophy each express the *Absolute Idea*, which involves *Geist* (mind/spirit) alienating itself in nature (matter and sensuous form), then returning to itself self-consciously as spirit. In this way, the opposites of mind and nature, particular and universal, subject and object, finite and infinite are reconciled. In art, religion, and philosophy, mind comes to recognize itself. However, while art and religion express this "self-recognition" in sensuous, imaginative form, philosophy does so in the arena of pure thought.

According to Hegel, art and religion do not result from a conscious, "thinking" process. He compares the artistic act to the pronouncements of a man who has great life experience and an immense understanding of human psychology, one who is able to convey this understanding in particular cases but is unable to explain to others the process that leads to his reflections.[388] Hegel goes so far as to call this "a kind of imagination."[389] He writes:

> the productive imagination of the artist is the imagination of a great mind and heart, the apprehension and creation of ideas and of shapes, and, indeed, the exhibition of the profoundest and most universal

interests in the definite sensuous mode of pictorial representation.[390]

Further, he asserts that:

> it would be possible in poetical creation to try and proceed by first apprehending the theme to be treated as a prosaic thought, and then by putting it into pictorial ideas, and into rhyme, and so forth; so that the pictorial element would simply be hung upon the abstract reflections as an ornament or decoration. Such a process could only produce bad poetry, for in it there would be operative as two separate activities that which in artistic production has its right place only as undivided unity.[391]

For Hegel, in "artistic *imagination*...the rational element...extrudes itself into consciousness, but yet does not array before it what it bears within itself till it does so in sensuous form."[392] Religion, like art, involves an imaginative turn of Geist. Both art and religion involve a form of "thought which comprehends through the organ of imagination alone."[393] However, both art and religion, while imaginative in form, point to rational truths. For example, Hegel claims that "the main part of mythology is the work of the imaginative reason."[394] Mythology, then, is the product of reason, "though not of thinking reason." On Hegel's view, mythology, like genuine art, contains rational truths implicit in its core.[395]

While Hegel is careful not to disparage religion, Christianity in particular (which he calls the "consummate religion"), he is less cautious with regard to art, holding that "only a certain and grade of truth is capable of being represented in the medium of art."[396] Like Jung, Hegel diminishes the significance of art, but for reasons which involve a critique of the entire mode of imaginative reconciliation. He argues that:

> the peculiar modes to which artistic production and works of art belong no longer satisfies our supreme

need. We are above the level at which works of art can be venerated as divine, and actually worshipped.... Thought and reflection have taken their fight above fine art.[397]

For Hegel:

Art no longer affords that satisfaction of spiritual wants which earlier epochs and peoples have sought therein, and have found therein only; a satisfaction which, at all events on the religious side, was most intimately and profoundly connected with art. The beautiful days of Greek art and the golden time of the later Middle Ages are gone by.... Our present and its universal condition is not favorable to art.[398]

Hegel considers and rejects the notion, later endorsed by Jung, that the life of the mind is "disfigured and slain" by thought and comprehension and that by using thought "as the means of grasping what has life, man rather cut himself off from...his purpose." According to Hegel, "Thought – to think – is precisely that in which the mind has its innermost and essential nature. In gaining this thinking consciousness concerning itself and its products, the mind is behaving according to its essential nature...."[399]

Jung suggested that Hegel was a "psychologist *manqué*,"[400] a "misfired psychologist"[401] who expressed psychological (i.e., unconscious and imaginative) truths in a manner that disguised them as rational philosophy. According to Jung, Hegel failed to grasp that his thinking resulted from an "invasion by the unconscious,"[402] and while (likely for this reason) "intuitive ideas" underlie the Hegelian system,[403] his use of "high-flown language" is "reminiscent of...schizophrenics"[404] and thus presumably without value in its original form. Jung essentially held that Hegel failed to appreciate the role of the imagination in psychic development and used rational categories as a means of disguising psychic processes. However, it is clear in Hegel's texts that he understood the role of imagination in art and religion but held that in the modern era it had been largely superseded by philosophy, by thought in its "purest" form.

Conversely, a careful reading of Jung's language suggests that despite his rejection of the intellect as a basis for *coincidentia oppositorum*, he at times adhered to a form of "logic" similar to Hegel's. Jung's interest in the coincidence of opposites led him to what logicians would describe as a rejection of the law of non-contradiction, and the embrace of alternative, more inclusive, logical principles. In *The Red Book* he writes, "The magical is good and evil and neither good nor evil."[405] This is an assertion that accords well with Buddhist and other multi-valued logics, which hold that in addition to "true" and "false" there are the additional logical possibilities "both true and false" and "neither true nor false." Jung later claimed that "the symbol is neither abstract nor concrete, neither rational nor irrational, neither real nor unreal. It is always both...."[406] Such multi-valued or dialetheistic logic[407] has rarely been advocated in the West, which (with the exception of the several decades when Hegelian logic rose to prominence) has been largely dominated by Aristotelian, either/or, linear thinking. We can see that despite Jung's demurrers, there is evidence that his *thinking* was in greater accord with Hegel's than he allowed.

I will return to the question of "logic" and the coincidence of opposites in Chapter 7.

GIEGERICH ON JUNG AND HEGEL

Wolfgang Giegerich has criticized Jung for "betraying" the truth of the psyche—which in Giegerich's view is *thought*—by returning to an historical earlier and less developed mode of reconciliation—myth and imagination.[408] He holds that Jung failed to keep pace with the historical development of the psyche, failed to face the challenge of the modern world, and thus failed to make the very transition from myth and imagination to thought that Hegel characterized as the world spirit's most recent and highest form. According to Giegerich, Jung's "basic stance was an anti-enlightenment one."[409]

> By insisting on *"dreaming* the *myth* onwards" [Jung] showed that he precisely held onto the old *form* characteristic of the primitive and ancient, in part also medieval and early-modern, worlds, namely the form of content, images, narratives in their immediacy.[410]

For example, Jung's introduction of the "reality of evil" as a "fourth" to expand the Christian trinity remained within the "basic thinking form of traditional religious thinking, namely pictorial thinking."[411] According to Giegerich, Jung's notion that contemporary man, having fallen into a virtual cult of reason, and having banished the Gods from his awareness, required man to be "re-ensouled" through an encounter with the intrapsychic manifestation of those Gods—i.e., the archetypes of the collective unconscious. Giegerich saw this as just another means for Jung to cling to, or reinstate, the pre-modern forms of religious and mythic imagination. Jung (in his failure to come to terms with Hegel's philosophy) did not recognize that the soul is characterized by *thinking*, and hence "pure negativity" and doubt; he thus clung to a mythical positivity that simply recast mythology and religion in psychological garb.

Giegerich suggests that a similar, regressive, attitude informs Jung's understanding of the "transcendent function," and leaves it mired in a pre-logical, pre-enlightenment perspective, one that is particularly troubling when applied to the contemporary psyche. Giegerich uses an alchemical metaphor to explain dialectical thinking. In dialectic, he says, one takes "an initial thesis, thought, or phenomenon," places it metaphorically in a "retort," and listens intently upon "what it precisely states."[412] In the process, one "becomes aware of its self-movement," which causes it to go "over into its opposite."[413] The self-movement is "logical," an effect of the thesis, idea or phenomenon itself, and is in no ways dependent upon the conscious (or unconscious) thinking of the "observer." By way of contrast, "active imagination," a process through which the "transcendent function" can presumably be set in motion, does not involve logic or thought at all; instead, according to Giegerich, it produces "an unpredictable emergence of a reconciling third."[414] While Giegerich allows that "the imagination may also follow laws," he suggests that, when "active imagination" is employed, it is typically "contaminated by fortuitous subjective factors."[415] For Giegerich, Jung's historically regressive error involves the mere "entertaining of thoughts" (as if they are objects presented to consciousness) and a failure to actually think. Jung, without rational justification, holds that thoughts and images result in the production of a reconciling "third," and thus fails to be truly dialectical. According to Giegerich, Jung disparages thinking, as he "unthinkingly takes it simply for granted that thought is 'ego' and not 'soul.'"[416]

Giegerich, however, has an odd conception of thinking. On the one hand, it is modeled upon logic and mathematics, but on the other hand it is mired in a kind of regressive mysticism that eschews argumentation and debate. His analysis of the Hegelian dialectic as involving a form of logical necessity and his use of phrases like "Not a subject that thinks, but objectively ongoing thinking" reveals each of these tendencies. When Giegerich speaks about "thinking," he does not refer to a process through which an individual human subject (you or I) entertains an idea and consciously attempt to discern its entailments or implications (which he disparages as "ego stuff"); rather, he refers to an "objective thinking" that transcends any individual subject and involves (in Hegel's phrase) "the cold march of necessity."[417]

The problem with this is that while such necessity may readily apply to traditional (Aristotelean) logic and much of mathematics, it is by no means clear that it applies to the kinds of "deductions" that characterize Hegelian philosophy. Indeed, there is nary a proposition in Hegelian philosophy (and for that matter, in any philosophy) that does not generate controversy and debate. While Giegerich justly accuses Jung of failing to read and *think* about Hegel's philosophy (which Jung dismisses as an intrusion from the unconscious decorated with philosophical "power words"[418]), he neglects to note that this same critique of Hegel appeared (and continues to appear) in the writings of philosophers who considered Hegel deeply. Even W. T. Stace—a philosopher who began his career as a sympathetic expositor of the Hegelian system[419]—ultimately concluded that this system depended upon illogicalities, chicanery, and word play.[420] It is noteworthy that in explaining *his* understanding of the Hegelian dialectic, Giegerich draws on the notion of placing thought in an "alchemical retort."[421] It is through this alchemical analogy that he advances the thesis that the Hegelian dialectic operates via hard necessity This analogy, which is used to demonstrate that "thought" proceeds objectively without conscious "ego" involvement, argument and debate, itself has the mark of a regressive, pre-scientific, irrational procedure. What we should learn from the Hegelian dialectic is not that it produces deductions that are "analytic" and which we are logically obliged to follow—but a more interesting and nuanced lesson: Where we see what appears to be a positive truth, we should suspect the relevance (and truth) of its opposite or contradictory; and where we find opposition we should consider the likelihood of interdependence. In each of these cases, we are obligated to think and debate (in the usual sense of these words) in order to ascertain the validity of our conclusions.

In a moment, I will consider the validity of the claim that modern consciousness has moved beyond the imagination. However, even if we agree that this is the case, it is unclear why a post-enlightenment "thinking" *must* end up in anything like a Hegelian philosophy and, in particular a Hegelian view of the psyche. A contemporary appraisal of the state of "modern thinking" would identify it with the methods and achievements of natural science or perhaps with the skepticism and relativism manifest in deconstructive or postmodern philosophy. Given the quaint, anachronistic claims, for example, in Hegel's philosophy of nature, one might be justified in regarding a return to Hegel as regressive.

Let us consider the claim that the imagination, along with its narratives, myths, symbols, and artistic products, is passé. As we have seen, Hegel recognized the role of the imaginative products of art and religion in the development of *Geist*, and as vehicles for the realization and recognition of the Absolute. He also held these routes to be imperfect and outmoded approximations, and their goals to be more effectively articulated in philosophy—more specifically, his own dialectical or speculative philosophy. One may ask, however, if in insisting upon a general distinction between the imagination and thought Hegel (and by extension Giegerich) was sufficiently dialectical. While Hegel recognized that thinking is implicit in the imagination (as Ricouer puts it "symbols invite thought"[422]), he failed to adequately recognize the role that symbols and the imagination have in thinking. Thought (and this, of course, includes philosophical thought) is expressed in and advances through the medium of language—language that is always subject to *imaginative* interpretation. Indeed, Hegel himself can be said to engage in such imaginative interpretation in each of his dialectical inversions: for example, when he argues that Absolute being, because it is completely nondescript, passes over into nothing. Hegel's opponents simply refuse to enter into such imaginative understanding of equivalence and "passing over" when they accuse him of resting his dialectic on "wordplay."

Let us examine this Hegelian notion that Absolute being passes over into nothing a bit more closely. One must imagine an infinite expanse of undifferentiated being in order to see (think) how being "passes over" into nothing. In addition, in imagining this "infinite expanse," one must focus upon its lack of differentiation rather than, for example, its utter fullness. If one focuses upon or imagines the latter (being's fullness), thought might "naturally" pass over into the infinitely detailed and differentiated cosmos that such fullness can engender! Thus, at least in this case, the march or force of the dialectic is dependent on how one "imagines" its initial thesis or component.

Jean Paul Sartre, in his study of the imagination,[423] argued that the very process of negation (the very negation that serves as the engine of the dialectic) is itself *wholly dependent upon the imagination*—as one must enter into an imaginative process in order to negate the immediate contents of consciousness, enter into doubt, consider alternatives, etc. Indeed, we might observe that the very development of thought typically results from an imaginative process, one that not only "negates presence," but which draws upon unconscious shifts of perspective and interpretation that can be described as thought's "incubation." Giegerich's alchemical retort analogy (designed to distinguish Jung's regressive imaginative transcendent function from Hegel's progressive dialectics) is, ironically, a valid account of the imaginative (and not wholly logical or rational) process that leads to new discoveries and inventions in the arts, sciences and philosophy. Imagination, far from being excluded or transcended by thinking is at thinking's very core!

This point of view is explicit in the philosophies of Ernst Cassirer (1874–1945) and Suzanne Langer (1895–1985). According to Cassirer, humanity's capacity for symbolic thought and expression is foundational for our understanding of the universe.[424] Humans, for Cassirer, are essentially symbol-making beings; the development of not only the arts and the humanities but also the natural sciences and philosophy is embedded within language, symbols, and culture. The objectivity of both the natural sciences and humanities is conditioned by the symbolisms within which they are framed. Langer, expanding on Cassirer, held that symbols are the central concern of philosophy and that art and music have a claim to the production of meaning on par with science and the humanities.[425] As we have seen, the "symbol" becomes the starting point for psychology for Jung, who held that it is only through the formation of imaginative symbols that the psyche is able to reconcile the conflicts that produce neurotic symptoms.

Giegerich, we remember, accuses Jung of attempting to escape the negative and skeptical implications of actual thinking by evading doubt and reclaiming positivity through his reframing of the old myths as the archetypes of the collective unconscious. Jung, according to Giegerich, fails to comprehend the "Absolute negativity" of the psyche. We may, however, ask whether Jung evaded doubt—or rather entered into it and worked through it to something new and positive. Certainly, a fair reading of Jung's *Red Book* is that he entered into and even embraced chaos and radical doubt as a prelude to his more positive and constructive later work.[426] On this reading, *The Red Book* falls in the tradition of many great works of autobiography and literature wherein the author recounts his or her "night of the soul," a voyage into Hades, chaos, depression and spiritual doubt, and his or her emergence into a renewed faith and positive world-view. Jung was (at least implicitly) aware of the dialectic between the negative and the positive, a dialectic that is so clearly present in Hegel. And even if Giegerich is correct in his assessment that the narrative of *The Red Book* is steeped in learning and not a spontaneous production of the unconscious (as Jung suggests),[427] this does not undermine its message. The principle of the positive emerging from the negative, of faith and a renewal of the spirit developing out of chaos and doubt, is present in too many great thinkers—St. Augustine, Pascal, Kierkegaard, Hegel himself!—to be so readily dismissed.[428]

Indeed, Giegerich is correct in his assertion that Hegel "embraced doubt and integrated it into his own thinking by making it the *spiritus rector* of his very method."[429] Giegerich (like some other contemporary Hegel scholars) fails to adequately consider that Hegel utilized his doubt in the service of a "positivity," of a philosophy and theology of the Absolute—one that hardly remains with doubt but instead embraces a positive view of the nature of reality as the development of spirit or mind. The very idea that human consciousness has *developed* from an imaginative to a thinking form is itself a positive thesis. Indeed, Giegerich himself is positive in his claim that the key to the "soul" is its "interiority" or "logical life."

MODES OF THE PSYCHE/SOUL

As I see it, the issue between Jung and Hegel (and Jung and Giegerich) is whether the psyche or "soul" is best identified with one of the "aspects" of consciousness or subjectivity, or with a wider range of aspects (what Jung called "functions"). Hegel, and moreover Giegerich, holds that "thought" is the aspect of consciousness that, at least for the modern psyche, embodies "soul." Giegerich argues that had Jung remained within the sphere of psychotherapy

> the way it was, for example, conceived by Freud or Adler, as a project that has its true horizon in the consulting room, so long Jung could have done quite well without ever entering the sphere of thought. However, the moment that he instead conceived of a psychology that wants to apply itself to *the Seelenproblem des modernen Menschen*...and to the objective psyche, the moment that he says, "I see the suffering of mankind in the individual's predicament and vice versa": at that very moment the fact became *a betrayal of his self-set task* that he radically refused to let himself in for the problem of form and that he immunized the stuff of psychological experience against the intrusion of modernity's native principle and foundation, the thinking form.[430]

What is the "thinking form"? Presumably, if thought, including the Hegelian dialectic, proceeds (as Giegerich claims) via "cold necessity," and if such necessity is the defining characteristic of modern consciousness, the psyche can be programmed into and perhaps even be better operated within the matrix of a digital computer, which itself embodies the notion of logical necessity. Of course, Giegerich would immediately protest: He does not identify *any* sort of thinking with the "objective psyche" or "soul" but only the sort of "interiorizing" speculative thinking that characterizes the Hegelian dialectic, the sort of reflective thinking in which the thinker is in "the same alchemical vessel as the thoughts" he thinks.[431] He sees this as the opposite of any "abstract" point of view—presumably the thinker fully comprehends that his thoughts apply to himself in the concrete instance. I am at a loss to account for what is "added" to such thought that differentiates it from the "cold rational necessity" of a computer operation—unless one adds other aspects or functions of consciousness—for example, qualitative experience, desire, imagination, or reflectivity, which are not themselves reducible to thinking.

In fact, it can be argued that it is not only the actual, empirical, human psyche but any psyche—any consciousness or sentience whatsoever—that must include aspects, functions, characteristics, or vicissitudes not wholly cognitive in nature if it is to think at all. It is for this reason that consciousness cannot be adequately characterized by today's digital computers. These various vicissitudes or "modes of mind" can be characterized in a number of ways. Jung spoke of thinking, feeling, sensation, and intuition. We might provide an expanded catalog that would include such aspects or functions as experience (qualia), desire, action, relatedness, symbolization, personal identity, sociality, temporality, reflection and transcendence, in addition to "cognition."[432] As I am about to explain, these "modes of mind," each alone and together, give rise to a matrix of meanings and values, without which the psyche (and the world) would be woefully incomplete.

Briefly put, we can utilize the sort of quasi- or implicative logic present in Hegel to discern that each of a variety of psychological functions gives rise to specific values and conceptions of the good life. In addition, each of a variety of psychological functions has given rise to entire schools of both psychology and, significantly in the current context, philosophy. This, of course, follows Hegel's own observation that certain key ideas in philosophy become foundational for a period of time before being sublated—that is, incorporated within, superseded by, and historically replaced by new, more complete, foundational notions. The interesting point, however, is that philosophy has in the last 200 years moved beyond Hegel to consider notions that supplant the claim that thought is central and foundational.

Emmanuel Lévinas (1906–1995) provides a good example of a philosopher who held that a psychic function other than "thinking" is foundational for what Giegerich refers to as "soul." Lévinas held that philosophy, and thus our understanding of the world, is grounded in the "face to face" encounter between two subjects. According to Lévinas, the call to address the other's suffering is prior to and the foundation for both thinking and the experience of a subject or self.[433] This "asymmetrical" call of the other leads both to the ethical ground of subjectivity and an intuition of transcendence and thus infinity. Lévinas' thought is sometimes compared to that of Martin Buber (1878–1965), who held that a more "symmetrical" or reciprocal "I-thou" encounter between human subjects, or between such subjects and the natural world, is revelatory of an infinite "Other" or "Eternal thou."[434] The notion that relationality is foundational for the construction of subjectivity becomes the basis for "relational psychoanalysis" and other forms of interpersonal psychology—which understand the psyche to be constituted by its relationships. Philosophies (and psychologies) grounded in relationality naturally emphasize such values as love, empathy, intimacy, kindness, friendship, and compassion, as opposed to the "cognitive" values of knowledge and truth, and hold that it is these "relational" values that are keys to the "good life."

One can readily discern a number of other perspectives on "psyche" and, by implication, on philosophy and psychology that are grounded in psychic functions other than "thought." One need only turn to phenomenology of Edmund Husserl, grounded in "lived experience"; the philosophies of Arthur Schopenhauer and Nietzsche, grounded in "will"; the philosophy of Wittgenstein, grounded in symbolization and language; or the personalism of such thinkers as Edgar Sheffield Brightman and Max Scheler, grounded in an ethics of "the person," to see that the philosophical conception of the psyche since Hegel has moved beyond what can be encompassed by the single function of "thinking." Indeed, for many philosophers and psychologists, "thinking" is a superstructure that appears only on the foundation of a more basic psychic function: for Lévinas, "the "other"; for Wittgenstein, language; for Nietzsche, "instinct" and later the will to power, etc. In *The Birth of*

Tragedy, Nietzsche proclaims, "Whereas in the case of all productive people instinct is precisely the creative-affirmative force and consciousness [i.e., reason] makes critical and warning gestures, in the case of Socrates, by contrast, instinct becomes the critic and consciousness the creator—a true monstrosity...."[435]

Without in any way denigrating the importance of "thinking" and "reason" to the nature and function of psyche or "mind," we can observe that it is only a colossal prejudice, fostered by the partiality of "thinkers" in preference to (and blind to) the relativity of their own endeavor, that seeks to reduce the "psyche" or "soul" to its thinking function. Jung is to be credited for recognizing this, even if in certain cases he was led astray by an immersion in the "irrational." Our efforts in later chapters to engage "thought" in order to explicate the coincidence of opposites between opposing psychological perspectives (Chapter 5) and philosophical theories (Chapter 6) must remain cognizant of, and ultimately return to the role of other psychic functions—especially *the imagination*—in the thinking and dialectical process (Chapter 7).

CHAPTER FIVE

THE COINCIDENCE OF OPPOSITES IN CONTEMPORARY PSYCHOLOGY

WILLIAM JAMES AND THE "OPPOSITES OF THE WORLD"

In *The Varieties of Religious Experience*, William James writes that reflecting upon his life experiences, they all seem to converge into a reconciliation in which "the opposites of the world, whose contradictoriness and conflict make all our difficulties and troubles, were melted into unity." James suggests that, despite its apparent illogicality, this notion "must mean something, something like what the Hegelian philosophy means, if one could only lay hold of it more clearly.[1]

In this chapter, I will take up James' charge to clearly articulate the meaning of the reconciliation of the opposites as it applies to psychology. It is only now—after our historical survey and the more detailed examination of the coincidence of opposites as understood by the Jewish mystics, G. W. F. Hegel, and C. G. Jung—that we are in a position to consider the broad philosophical and psychological significance of the *coincidentia* idea. To achieve this, I will expand upon the *cartographic analogy* I described in the Introduction and articulate a *conceptual model* that will aid our understanding of the implications of the coincidence of opposites for contemporary thought. In this chapter, I will apply this model to the problem of conflicting paradigms in psychology and to certain problems in the philosophy of mind. In Chapter 6, I will extend the model's application to issues in epistemology and the philosophy of language, and I will argue that *coincidentia oppositirum* is a vehicle for resolving a wide range of philosophical controversies and for providing a rational analog to (and understanding of) the "mystical ascent" to the Absolute or "Unified One." The application of *coincidentia opposito-rum* in this chapter to conflicts in the field of psychology will provide an important foundation for understanding the more abstract philosophical and theological questions that I will address in Chapter 6.

FRAGMENTATION IN PSYCHOLOGY

A growing literature addressing the problem of psychology's frag-mentation has emerged over the past thirty years.[2] However, even a cur-sory review of this literature reveals there to be nearly as much division among those who propose solutions to psychology's disunity as there is within the field itself. Proposals to unify psychology range from those that reaffirm positivism[3] to those that would have theoretical debate in psychology settled on evolutionary,[4] hermeneutic,[5] or even moral grounds.[6] Others have argued that disunity in psychology is healthy for the discipline[7] or that the question of unity/disunity will be decided by social, political and other non-intellective factors.[8]

Nowhere is the fragmented state of psychology more evident than in the clinical field. As we have seen, nearly 100 years ago, Jung not-ed that the interpretations based in Freudian and Adlerian psychology, while valid *in their own terms*, were grounded in opposing psychologi-cal principles.[9] We saw how Jung observed that while clinical phenom-ena can always be interpreted in accord with the principles of each theo-ry, for example, in accord with Freudian "wish-fulfillment" or Adlerian "ego superiority"[10]—there is no neutral theoretical perspective from which one can adjudicate between them. Further, while Jung held that psychologies could be developed from the points of view correlative to each of what he termed the main psychological functions (thinking, feeling, intuition, and sensation), neither thinking nor any of the other functions can produce an integrated account of the psyche as a whole. According to Jung, if such an integrative perspective is indeed possible, it must arise through creative imagination.[11]

Today, the fragmented state of psychology—clinical psychology in particular—is even more pronounced than it was in Jung's time. Psychotherapies are not only grounded in the various schools originally associated with the psychoanalytic tradition (Freudian, Jungian, Adlerian, ego-psychological, object-relational, Lacanian, etc.), but there are numerous therapeutic approaches that have their foundation in neurobiological, behavioral, cognitive, existential, and systems perspectives in psychology. In this chapter, I will examine the conceptual, and particularly the philosophical, assumptions that underlie six different perspectives and modes of treatment in psychology. Further, I will show how the notion of the coincidence of opposites provides a vehicle for comprehending these perspectives' complementarity and ultimate unity, thus enabling us to approach an intuition of the psyche as a whole. The application of *coincidentia oppositorum* to the relatively tangible (but still abstract) question of reconciling paradigms in psychology will serve as a model for its use in the reconciliation of opposing views on fundamental philosophical and theological questions. To achieve this, it will be necessary to lay some groundwork via a description of six psychological paradigms that I will later show to be complementary.

The six psychologies I will discuss hardly exhaust the possibilities for psychological paradigms. Later in this chapter, I will introduce a model for understanding the philosophical foundations of psychology that has the potential to generate many other psychological paradigms, some of which (for example, archetypal and sociobiological psychology) currently exist but others of which have yet to be formulated. It will, however, become clear that whether we analyze six or sixty paradigms in psychology, the model has the potential to reconcile them via the principle of *coincidentia oppositorum*.

SIX PSYCHOLOGICAL PARADIGMS[12]

There is something arbitrary in making sharp divisions between "schools" of clinical psychology; in actual practice, the work of any practicing psychologist, psychiatrist, or other mental health professional is almost always a function of a variety of greater and lesser influences. The behaviorist, for example, is often influenced by concepts derived from cognitive psychology (hence the term "cognitive behaviorism"); the family-systems therapist may be influenced by psychodynamic thinking. Nevertheless, for our purposes it will be useful to examine six relatively discrete schools of thought: the biological, behavioral, cognitive, systems, psychodynamic, and existential. I have, for reasons discussed below, divided the psychodynamic school into two sub-classifications. Table 5 . 1 and the discussion that follows summarizes these schools of thought by (1) noting their views of the presumed underlying nature or "deep structure" of psychopathological phenomena, (2) describing their theoretical conceptions of a common psychiatric disturbance (depression), (3) providing examples of their prescribed treatments, (4) indicating each of their value orientations or treatment goals, (5) tracing some of their historical antecedents, and (6) linking them to a philosophical perspective that serves as their conceptual foundation.

Table 5.1: Contemporary Schools of Psychiatry

School of Psychiatry/ Psychology	Presumed Underlying Nature of Psychological Phenomena	Conception of Depression	Treatment for Depression	Value Orientation/ Goal of Treatment	Historical Antecedents	Philosophical Foundations
I. Biological Psychiatry	Events and processes in the brain and nervous system	Neurotransmitter abnormalities	Antidepressant Medication	Cure of mental illness	Pre- and Post-Socratic Materialistic philosophy; Hippocrates and Humoral Theory	Scientific Materialism
II. Behavioral Psychology	Behavioral dispositions resulting from an organism's interaction with the environment	Lack of reinforcement Learned-helplessness	Behavior Therapy	Behavioral change, removal of symptoms	Age-old common sense; the *Book of Job*. Behavioral notions in Aristotle's *De Anima*, Cartesian "Mechanism," British Associationism, Modern Positivism, Darwin's Theory of Evolution	Philosophical Behaviorism
III. Cognitive Theories	Beliefs, judgments, and other cognitive processes	Distorted, negative cognitions	Cognitive or Rational Therapy	Rational living	Greek Stoicism; European 17th c. rationalism, e.g., Spinoza's *Ethics*, cognitive psychology, cybernetics	Rationalism
IV. Family Systems Approaches	Disturbed patterns of interaction and equilibrium that transpire in a network of individuals	Boundary issues, scapegoating, conflict of roles	Family Therapy	Family equilibrium	Plato's *Republic*; Marx and dialectical materialism; Sociological point of view, e.g. Durkheim	Collectivist philosophies General systems theory.
V. Psycho-dynamic Approaches a. Metapsychology	Mechanisms of abstract mental structures: e.g. intrapsychic conflict	Overdevelopment of the superego, prohibiting release and expression of libidinal energy	Psychoanalytic after-education of the super-ego	Psychic equilibrium	Pre-Socratic philosophies of conflict and strife; Pythagorean ideal of the soul's harmony' Plato's tripartite division of the soul; Helmholtzian physiology; Darwinian genetics	Structuralism
b. Clinical Theory	Meanings and intentions	Pathological mourning response; anger turned inwards; radical disappointment in the self	Psychoanalytic interpretation leading to insight	Self-knowledge leading to self-liberation	Judeo-Christian hermeneutics, e.g. Talmudic interpretation of scripture; 19th-c. philosophy of the social sciences: Dilthey, Rickert, Weber on "interpretive understanding"	Hermeneutics
VI. Existential Psychology	Basic choices that individuals make in their modes of relating to themselves and others	Depression as a "call" to the self and a communication to others	"Here and now" existential or humanistic therapy	Fulfillment, freedom and self-actualization	Socrates dictum "know thyself"; St. Augustine, 19th century existential philosophy: Kierkegaard, Nietzsche	Phenomenology and Existentialism

Biological psychology is committed to the view that the most fundamental explanations for psychological phenomena derive from the discoveries of human biology, particularly the biology of the nervous systems and the brain. Biological psychology therefore seeks a physical deep structure to psychopathological phenomena and is inclined to view psychological disorders as akin to organic disease—for example, resulting from functional abnormalities in neurotransmitters in the brain. For a time, a commonly held biological theory of depression stated that depression involves a functional deficit of one of more brain neurotransmitter amines (serotonin or norepinephrine) at specific central synapses. The treatments, which follow from the biological point of view, are somatic in nature and generally pharmacological. Thus, for depression, medications (antidepressants) that inhibit the reuptake of brain amines into the presynaptic neurons are prescribed. While the specific details of any given biological hypothesis may prove incorrect (and indeed, the amine theory itself has been modified if not abandoned[13]) and the specific mechanisms by which antidepressant medications are effective may for a time remain unknown, biological psychology is committed to the idea that the best way to both understand and treat depression is to view it as a disorder of the brain and nervous system. In this view, the ultimate somatic treatment for depression and other psychiatric disorders will not simply alleviate symptoms but will correct the underlying biological causes of a disease. Biological psychology/psychiatry ultimately aims to cure mental illness in the same way that general medicine aims to cure cancer.

While the biological perspective on the mind dates back at least to Hippocrates, today's biological psychology has its philosophical foundations in *scientific materialism*. This doctrine, which has been advocated in various guises since the pre-Socratic philosophers Democritus and Leucippus, holds in its contemporary form that the world consists of material things (the ultimate entities of physics), their states, and their relations.[14] All phenomena, including conscious states, are understood as a casual function of material events. While the empirical findings of biological psychology do not stand or fall upon the defense of a particular philosophical doctrine, one impetus to the view that biological explanations in psychology are *fundamental* is an *a priori* commitment to scientific or reductive materialism. This generally remains the case even as biological psychology and psychiatry become increasingly interdisciplinary, turning to the interaction between biochemical, neurophysiological, and genetic factors with social and environmental processes to formulate more integrative models of psychological functioning.[15]

Behavioral psychology, like biological psychology, understands psychological and psychopathological phenomena to be a function of material events, but the material events with which it concerns itself are macroscopic as opposed to microscopic in nature. Behavioral psychologists are committed to the view that psychological concepts are best understood as referring to behavioral dispositions, generally thought to result from an organism's interaction with the environment.[16] Behavioral psychology rejects the notion that psychological symptoms have a "deep structure" within either the mind or brain of the individual who suffers from them. Rather, it seeks to discover the environmental conditions that maintain these symptoms though various contingencies of reinforcement, postulating, for example, that depression is the result of a lack of reinforcement or the result of environmental events that make an individual incapable of achieving or controlling outcomes (learned helplessness[17]).

Behavioral psychology can trace its historical roots to influences as diverse as age-old common sense, the biblical book of Job, Aristotle, Charles Darwin, and the various objectivist and positivist tendencies in modern philosophy. It has its current philosophical foundation in a broad doctrine known as philosophical behaviorism.[18] From this point of view, consciousness and introspective states are either an illusion, or methodologically irrelevant for psychology, and consequently for clinical practice. While philosophical behaviorists recognize the role of the brain and nervous system in human conduct, they argue that because psychological language is grounded in observations of molar units of behavior, it is this level that provides the key to the proper understanding of human psychology.

Cognitive theories: Broadly speaking, psychologists with a cognitive orientation are committed to the view that psychopathological phenomena are best understood as a function of beliefs, judgments, and a variety of other cognitive states and processes. While often recognizing that cognitive states are themselves dependent upon biological processes, cognitive psychologists argue that the most useful way to conceptualize psychological and psychiatric phenomena is in terms of functional relations between cognitions rather than through descriptions of concrete events on the neurophysiological o r behavioral level.[19] Using a cybernetic analogy, they argue that the mind is better understood though an explanation of its "software" (the concepts and information that characterizes it) than through a detailed consideration of the hardware (or neuroanatomical circuitry) through which the information is processed. It is this reasoning that permits cognitive psychologists to produce computer-generated "mind models" that serve as analogs of human thinking, feeling, and other experiences.[20]

Cognitively oriented clinicians see psychopathology as a disorder or distortion of normal cognitive processes. For example, depression is understood as resulting from a series of negative a n d irrational judgments and generalizations, about the self, the future, and the environment.[21] The prescribed treatment is a form of verbal therapy in which the client is encouraged, conditioned, and "educated" to produce more optimistic, rational, and less depressogenic cognitions. The aim of cognitive therapy is the treatment of psychological symptoms by altering the disordered cognitions that are presumed to serve as their foundation. The ultimate goal of this treatment has been described as the promotion and production of rational living.[22]

Cognitive psychology has its historical roots in the Stoic doctrine that all of life's virtues are based upon knowledge and in the various rationalist trends in Western thought. It has its philosophical moorings in rationalism that has seen a revival in recent years, both as a result of the revolution in cognitive science[23] and because of important developments in psycholinguistics.[24]

Systems approaches: Grouped under this heading are clinicians and theorists who can be characterized by their rejection of an assumption that behavior and symptoms are to be understood as resulting from processes within the bodies or minds of *individuals*. Instead, systems theorists understand individual psychology as a function of the patterns of interaction and equilibrium that occur in a network of individuals. The source of what appears to be individual psychopathology (such as depression or schizophrenia) is a disordered interaction between individuals or disequilibrium within a wider group.[25] The family, for example, forms such a system and it is often taken by systems theorists to be the basis for both psychological explanation and psychiatric treatment. However, wider systems, including those that characterize social, political, and even national collectives have been posited as the locus for understanding individual, including intrapsychic, psychological states and processes.[26]

From the systems point of view, depressive symptoms exhibited by an individual are an expression of a dysfunction of, or imbalance within a system of two or more persons. For example, depression can result when individuals are forced into a family or social role that conflicts with their desires and values or with the role they are expected to take in a wider social system. Depression can also occur when an individual is *scapegoated* for difficulties in a relationship between two or more other persons,[27] if there are serious family boundary issues,[28] or if an individual is prevented from attaining a sense of self-esteem or personal control by political, social, and/or cultural restrictions or repression.[29]

Systems theory is radical in its rejection of the individualism (both methodological and substantive) that has been the hallmark of Western philosophy and psychology. Nevertheless, one can find its historical antecedents in the various collectivist ideologies in Western thought. Plato's views in the *Republic,* Karl Marx's collectivism, and the sociological viewpoint exemplified by Durkheim are all important antecedents. Still, systems psychology has no ready-made philosophical foundation. Some theorists attempt to integrate their findings through concepts derived from general systems theory,[30] a conceptual system originally formulated to account for the interaction of biological processes on microscopic and macroscopic levels.

Psychodynamic approaches: For many years, psychodynamic concepts dominated psychiatry and psychotherapy, and they continue to be quite influential with many clinicians and a new generation of empirically oriented theorists.[31] It is nonetheless difficult to define precisely what psychodynamic psychology is. This is in part due to the fact that a wide variety of important contributions to psychology have been broadly classified as "psychodynamic" and "psychoanalytic," and in part to a tension that many believe exists within psychodynamic thought itself: a tension between a scientific, naturalistic, and deterministic view of the individual and a humanistic, libertarian approach.[32] This tension has a variety of sources. One is the dichotomous nature of Sigmund Freud's own professional development—his background in medicine and particularly neurology on the one hand, and his interests in the humanities and literature on the other. The ultimate expression of this tension within psychoanalysis is in the distinction between Freud's metapsychology (his abstract theoretical formulations) and his clinical observations and practice.[33]

Freud operated as an "interpreter" in all of his clinical work. But when it came to formulating theories to account for his findings, he adopted a mechanistic or structuralist rubric, which reflected the influences of late nineteenth-century neurology. Thus, Freudian metapsychology came to reflect a philosophical commitment to *structuralism*, the view that concrete psychological phenomena are understood as a mechanical or hydraulic function of abstract mental structures (for example, id, ego, and superego). By way of contrast, Freud's clinical theory reflects a commitment to *hermeneutics*, the view that concrete psychological and behavioral phenomena are to be understood in terms of the meanings they have for the individual who exhibits them. The tension between structuralism and hermeneutics, and in a wider sense between natural science and what was referred to as "the human sciences,"[34] is at the core of psychodynamic psychology and accounts for some of its theoretical difficulties and perhaps much of its popular appeal.

The distinction between structuralism and hermeneutics is reflected in the specific techniques and value-orientations of psychoanalytic psychotherapy. In general, the structuralist viewpoint emphasizes psychic equilibrium as the goal of treatment, whereas the hermeneutic point of view is far more humanistic and libertarian in spirit.

The historical antecedents of "structural psychoanalysis" include the pre-Socratic philosophies of conflict and strife,[35] Plato's tripartite division of the human soul,[36] and the neurological theories of the late 1800s.[37] The antecedents of hermeneutics or "interpretive" psychoanalysis are to be found in the exegetical traditions of Judaism and Christianity and the incorporation of hermeneutics into the social sciences in the late nineteenth century.[38] As we have seen, the philosophies of G. W. F. Hegel and Friedrich Nietzsche were also important antecedents and, at least in the case of Nietzsche, very likely a direct influence on Freud's theory and therapy.

Because of the dichotomous nature and origins of psychoanalytic thought and because Freud and his followers attempted to bridge the gulf between the "two cultures" of the sciences and the humanities, there can be no simple explanation of philosophical foundations of psychoanalysis. How natural scientific and humanistic approaches to experience and behavior can be integrated into a single paradigm is seen by some to be the challenge not only for psychoanalysis[39] but for psychology and psychiatry in general.[40] This is an issue that will be addressed later in this chapter via the application of the principle of *coincidentia oppositorum.*

Existential-humanistic psychology: This heading groups those psychotherapeutic approaches that Abraham Maslow referred to as the "third alternative" or "third force" in psychology, which on his view included not only existentialists and humanists but also Otto Rank, Jung, and various Ego-psychologists, Neo-Freudians, Gestalt psychologists, and a host of others.[41] Maslow contrasted the libertarianism and humanism of the third force with the determinism and mechanism implicit within behaviorism and the metapsychological reading of psychoanalysis. Psychotherapists broadly sharing Maslow's point of view hold that psychological symptoms reflect basic choices that individuals make in their modes of relating to themselves and others in the here and now and are not relics of the forgotten past. While there is a great deal of diversity within the existential-humanistic school, the school is unified in its emphasis on current experiences and relationships, and the potential for individual choice and freedom. The aim of existential-humanistic psychology is to bring about the fulfillment, freedom, and self-actualization of individuals involved in treatment.

For existentialist and humanistic psychologists, depression and other so-called psychopathological states are not diseases or disorders that simply "happen" to an individual. Rather they are understood as ways of calling ourselves, our values, our relationships and the paths of our lives into question, and their potential aftermath is a burst of productivity and creativity.

The existential/humanistic school has its contemporary philosophical foundations in phenomenology[42] and existentialism.[43] The former can be understood as the "descriptive" and the latter as the "normative" science of "lived experience." Phenomenologists such as Edmund Husserl,[44] Maurice Merleau-Ponty,[45] and Immanuel Lévinas,[46] as well as existentialists such as Martin Heidegger,[47] Martin Buber,[48] and Jean Paul Sartre[49] have exercised enormous direct and indirect influence upon contemporary existential and humanistic psychology.

SIX POTENTIAL SOLUTIONS

Contemporary psychology is faced with a crucial dilemma, a dilemma that in some ways parallels on a large scale the problems of psychotherapy clients who are faced with a bewildering array of theories and potential treatments for their psychological difficulties. Psychology is confronted with the questions of how it is to deal with its current factionalization. Does either science or logic dictate that a single paradigm, a unified science and clinical understanding will ultimately emerge? If such a unified paradigm does emerge, will it include the theories and findings of only one of the current schools, or will it result in an integration of several or all of them? Or perhaps the subject matter of psychology is such that a multiplicity of perspectives and continued fragmentation is theoretically and practically inevitable.

There are, of course, considerations other than logical, scientific, and clinical ones that condition the current divisions of psychology and will contribute to its future.[50] Nevertheless, it will be worthwhile to exclude factors such as economics and politics from consideration and focus on the purely conceptual issues involved in the future unity or diversity of psychology. Later in this chapter, I will return to the coincidence of opposite archetypes as a potential means of establishing integration in psychology. Before doing so, I will examine several commonly discussed options for understanding psychology's theoretical diversity and fragmentation.

Philosophically minded psychologists have at least six options in their efforts to come to grips with the multiplicity of psychological schools.[51] They can (1) opt for some form of *reductionism,* (2) hold that psychological theories are in open scientific competition or are *commensurable,* (3) hold that they are relative to one's point of view or *incommensurable,* (4) opt for some form of *eclecticism,* (5) hold that theories in psychology are *referentially distinct,* or (6) hope for an *ultimate synthesis* that will encompass the findings and theories of each of the contemporary schools. Each of these options will be examined briefly in turn.

1) *Reductionism* is a philosophical theory, which, broadly speaking, holds that the propositions of one or several theories in an area of inquiry can be translated or "reduced" to propositions in another, more fundamental, theory without any loss of meaning. Freud, for example, was reductionistic in his proclaimed hope that someday the psychological concepts of his metapsychology (e.g., id, ego, and superego) would be understood as neuroanatomic structures and physiological

processes.[52]

It is theoretically possible to be a reductionist in the direction of any of the psychological paradigms I have discussed. For example, there have been noteworthy behavioral reductionists, who attempted to translate psychodynamic concepts into the language of reinforcement theory or who argued that the effectiveness of all forms of psychiatric treatment, including psychopharmacology, can be explained using the principles of learning theory and behavior modification.[53] However, in point of fact, most reductionists in psychology are biologically oriented. The appeal of biological reductionism is that, if successful, its program would unify psychology with biology and biochemistry and the natural sciences in general.

The problem with any reductionist program is that it encounters the seemingly insurmountable task of translating and ultimately reducing propositions about consciousness, thoughts, behavior, will, feelings, relationships, images, and neurophysiology into a language that acknowledges only one of these human dimensions as real.

2) *Commensurability* theorists hold that the propositions in one of more of the various theories in psychology are not reducible to propositions in any of the other theories, but that one theory may prove to be "better" or more valid with respect to some criterion of truth. Thus, those who hold that psychological theories are commensurable typically argue that an experiment or series of experiments could decide between them. The problem with commensurability theory is that it is exceedingly difficult to arrive at criteria for validity that are acceptable to the advocates of each of the competing psychological schools and that do not simply reflect the value orientation of o n l y one of them. The criteria that had early appeal to scientifically minded psychologists involved the notions of "operationalism"[54] (which holds that theories in science must define their terms through observable and replicable operations) and falsificationism (which insists that theories make "risky" falsifiable predictions).[55]

However, several psychological theories (including but not limited to those that have their foundations in existentialism and hermeneutics) hold that psychological variables cannot be reduced to the operations that purport to measure them, and, further, that while human behavior is (to a degree) understandable, it is essentially non-predictable[56] and extremely difficult to study using experimental or correlational methods. These factors have led to the introduction of other criteria for the evaluation of psychological theories, such as the phenomenologists' notion that the value of a psychological theory is a function of its coherence with "lived experience." The criteria that are used in evaluating theoretical predictions and treatment outcomes in clinical psychology and psychiatry are more often than not colored by the theoretical stance of the evaluator, and the results of attempts to place psychological theories in direct competition have generally not proven persuasive to the advocates of each theory.

3) *Relativism or Incommensurability Theory* is the view that no criteria for making effective decisions regarding the validity of various theories in the social sciences will or should ever be acceptable to the advocates of all theories.[57] This is particularly true for psychology because each psychological theory is dependent upon initial assumptions about the nature of man, assumptions that are not open to empirical testing. The relativist would argue, for example, that one cannot test the philosophical assumptions of materialism or universal determinism underlying biological psychiatry; these assumptions are accepted as a matter of conviction or faith. The fundamental assumptions of psychology are, according to relativists, essentially contestable, and the various psychological theories are, therefore, incomparable or incommensurable. The emergence of a single dominant paradigm for psychology, if it occurs at all, will be determined by historical, economic, sociological, and other nonscientific factors.[58] More likely, the various psychological schools will continue to coexist like a plurality of different religions or cultures.

One might accept the notion that the value of religious or cultural ideas and institutions is relative but nonetheless hold that relativism is unacceptable for science. For example, primitive cultural institutions may be incommensurable with our own, but the outcomes of their medical practices are commensurable and decidedly inferior. While the notion of a simple experimental test deciding the validity of two of more theories has been recognized as philosophically naïve, attempts can be made to formulate more sophisticated rational bases for attaining commensurability between scientific ideas. Thomas Kuhn, for example, held that one theory is superior to another if it manages to *solve puzzles* better than its competitor.[59] It might be further held that a theory that can *fulfill the goals of its competitor* better that the competitor itself has a rational claim to being a better theory. This certainly does not resolve the problem of multiple and contested criteria, but it does point to how a solution to the problem of fragmentation in psychology might ultimately be achieved. If, in formulating their theories, psychologists can at the very least *address* (if not satisfy) the puzzles, goals and truth-criteria of theories perceived as competitors, then grounds for commensurability of theories and genuine exchange between theoretical camps can be established.

4) *Pragmatic Eclecticism* is the view that while theoretical unity in psychology is unlikely or impossible, an approach in which the best features of each point of view are combined can overcome the fragmentation of psychological *practice*. Many patients are treated eclectically today, either by a single eclectically minded therapist or by a therapeutic team comprising professionals who are advocates of and have expertise in different treatment modalities. For example, it is common for inpatients in many public facilities to receive a complement of biological (psychopharmacological), behavioral (milieu), and cognitive or dynamic treatments. Those who object to eclecticism argue that unless a psychological treatment is applied in rather pure form, its effectiveness is undermined. For example, certain anti-therapeutic consequences can result when humanistically oriented psychiatrists ask their clients to accept responsibility for their depression and also comply with a prescription for antidepressant medication. The

drug therapy, it might be said, tends to undermine the psychotherapy; as such psychiatrists, by prescribing medication, contradict their own verbal message that patients can and should be responsible for their own emotional states. Eclectic practice is much more difficult than is generally supposed, for it requires a sensitivity to the effects that a variety of implicit messages can have on patients and a skill in steering clear or "reframing" potentially confusing or aversive combinations. However, even if acceptable in practice, eclecticism does little to resolve the differences in theory between advocates of the various psychological perspectives.

5) The idea that various theories in psychology are *referentially distinct* follows from the notion that different theories result from research on different subject populations. From a clinical perspective, this view suggests that careful differential diagnosis will determine the appropriate explanation and treatment for an individual's psychological difficulties. The notion that some depressions are "reactive" and are to be treated with verbal psychotherapy while others are "endogenous" and are to be treated pharmacologically is illustrative of this view. Theories in psychology, on this view, do not compete with one another, not because of their different philosophical assumptions but because they describe different phenomena.

While it may be true that existential theories of depression are generated through a consideration of a different population from the one that gives rise to biological or behavioral theories, it is difficult to maintain the position that adequate diagnosis would bring universal agreement regarding the understanding of, and treatment of choice for, each individual. Perhaps as important as careful diagnosis in determining the appropriate treatment modality for a given patient, is a careful assessment of the client's own world-view and psychological presuppositions. Some patients, for example, resist behavior therapy because of its failure to deal with existential problems and "meaning"; others are attracted to it because it is practical and measurable. Patient-therapist match is often seen to be an important variable determining success in psychotherapy. Patient-modality match may be an important variable as well.

6) Psychologists who hope for an *ultimate theoretical synthesis* may hold that the various schools or points of view in their field are each a level of analysis or perspectives upon complex psychological phenomena. According to this view, diverse theories in psychology will ultimately be joined in a unified science that will incorporate the significant insights of the various schools without either reducing one point of view to that of another or combining various points of view in a purely pragmatic-eclectic manner. At various times, psychoanalysis and phenomenology have been proposed as the foundation for such a synthesis. Psychoanalysis, as has been indicated, has the advantage of incorporating within its conceptual structure one of the major tensions in contemporary psychology: that between natural scientific and humanistic viewpoints. Phenomenology, as it was conceived by its founder Edmund Husserl, sought to establish even naturalistic perspectives on psychology upon an experiential and thus humanistic epistemological foundation. More recently, general systems theory, via the biopsychological model[60] of psychology has provided a framework for understanding the various levels of analysis in psychology as distinct and yet built upon and interacting with one another. Whether the psycho-social model or any other theory will ultimately provide either a practical or theoretical synthesis of contemporary psychological theories is an important and open question.

COMPLEMENTARITY IN PSYCHOLOGY[61]

Joseph F. Rychlak proposed a "principle of complementarity" adapted from quantum physics that sees physical, biological, social, and psychological perspectives as independent but complementary bases for a positivistic psychological science.[62] In the remainder of this chapter, I will develop a non-positivistic theoretical foundation for complementarity in psychology, one based upon a *dialectical* understanding of the mutual interdependence of psychology's apparently conflicting paradigms and points of view. I agree with those who hold that a unique theoretical solution *within psychology* to the field's fragmentation is impossible. However, I do not hold that a multi-perspectivist position inevitably leads to a radical social constructivism and relativism. Rather, I believe that a dialectical approach to the various paradigms in psychology will enable us to maintain a multi-perspectival but realist position regarding the nature of the mind, one that provides room for natural scientific, structuralist, humanistic, and even spiritual points of view.

As we saw in Chapter 3, the term "dialectic" has a long and equivocal history. Over the centuries, it has been used variously to refer to "analysis by division," "refutation by examining consequences," formal logic in general, and even "sophistical" reasoning. Socrates' dialectic involved a prolonged examination of an original thesis that resulted in the drawing of a consequence that refuted that thesis. It is this Socratic procedure, which is the starting point of Hegel's dialectic, where concepts are shown to imply their contraries *in the service of a higher unity*. The Hegelian sense of dialectic will be of service in my own argument here. I will attempt to show that when pressed to their logical conclusions, the very concepts that underlie diverse paradigms in psychology imply contrary ideas that support paradigms that the original concepts were thought to exclude. Further, I will argue that only by maintaining the truth of *both* notions in certain pairs of presumably contrasting ideas about the mind will we be able to attain a coherent and comprehensive account of our subject matter. In this way, I will approach, if not be in full accord with, the ideas of Buddhist and "dialetheistic" logicians, who hold that a proposition and its apparent negation can both be true.

However, before presenting my formal argument, I will show, by way of a series of analogies, how my dialectical argument is going to work. I will then highlight certain features of my proposed solution by describing a similar solution to a problem that is much simpler than that of providing a theory of the mind—the problem of producing a two-dimensional map of a three-dimensional world. As we saw in the

Introduction to this volume, the "cartographic analogy" enables us to conceptualize how a single *underlying reality* can give rise to radically different, even apparently contradictory descriptions that are equally valid and true.

A MATTER OF "PERSPECTIVE"

A typical response to the fragmentation within contemporary psychology is to hold that each school views the mind from a particular "perspective" or "point of view." Biological psychology, for example, is said to view human behavior, cognition, and affect from the *perspective* of genetics and the neurophysiology of the brain, whereas systems theory is said to view the same phenomena from the perspective of its place and function within a social structure. It is very important to realize, however, that the word "perspective" has a very different sense when it is used with reference to an object whose ultimate nature is a mystery as compared to its more common use, for example in painting or photography where the object is completely known and understood but simply painted or photographed from one or another "side" or "point of view." It is by no means clear what "the mind" is *in and of itself.*[63] Indeed, by adopting different solutions to the nature of the "deep structure" of the mind, it is sometimes said that the various psychological schools define their object of inquiry in different ways as opposed to taking a different perspective upon it.

A solution to the problem of "perspectives" in psychology would be forthcoming if it could be shown that our inability to understand the "ultimate object" results from a failure to generate the appropriate meta-theory of the mind. Indeed, there are certain situations outside psychology in which apparently incompatible descriptions of a single object turn out to be compatible when we shift to a superior point of view or "meta-perspective." An example of this is what might be called the "New York-Buenos Aires moon paradox." Two observers, one in New York and the other in Buenos Aires, observing the moon simultaneously on any given evening will realize, if they compare their observations, that while they are both seeing the same portion of the moon illuminated, that portion is inverted left to right and upside down in Buenos Aires as compared to New York. Further, the moon appears in the Northern sky when viewed from Buenos Aires and in the Southern sky when viewed from New York. This last fact provides us with a clue to the resolution of the paradox: When we move from New York to Buenos Aires, the observed position of the moon has effectively traversed 80 degrees of arc in the sky and in so doing has, in effect, rotated itself relative to the viewer so that it appears upside down and inverted right to left. The apparent paradox of these "contradictory perspectives" is resolved once we recognize the spherical nature of the geometry that controls the positions of objects on the "celestial sphere." The paradox only exists when we continue to view the earth naively as a flat plane. Further, the resolution of the paradox forces us to comprehend that when we travel from New York to Buenos Aires, it is not the moon but we ourselves who have been turned upside down!

Another example of an apparent paradox, discussed in the Introduction to this book and which also depends upon the distinction between planar and spherical geometry, can be called the "Mercator-Polar Map Paradox." As children, we have all likely seen and been puzzled by maps that represent the entire world alternatively as a rectangle or as two circles on a flat, two-dimensional, plane. Perhaps we wondered how both of these seemingly incompatible representations could each depict the world in its entirety. The clue to the paradox, of course, is that each is an attempt to do something that is virtually impossible: to represent on a two-dimensional surface (a map) what is, by nature, a three-dimensional phenomenon (the globe). Once we compare the maps to the globe, we can see how and from what perspective the maps were constructed; in this way, we can comprehend the advantages and the limitations of each.

Our two paradoxes are instructive inasmuch as they each provide us with an example of the resolution of an apparent contradiction in our experience or representation of reality through a process of gaining a meta-perspective, which explains the appearance of the phenomena from the original and apparently incompatible points of view. With the moon paradox, a contradiction in our immediate experience is clarified once we reframe that experience in terms of the geometry of the earthly globe within the celestial sphere. Similarly, regarding the map paradox, a contradiction in *two* dimensions is resolved once we view the world depicted in three dimensions via a globe. As we will see in Chapter 6, the cartographic paradox has the important advantage of suggesting that it is our *methods of representation* (and not the "things themselves") that produce what appear to be contradictions in our understanding.

Perhaps a line of reasoning similar to those used in resolving the moon and map paradoxes can be applied in psychology and the philosophy of mind. Is there a meta-perspective we can take that will resolve the apparent incompatibilities among the various psychological schools? Is there some philosophical theory or perspective that will enable us to grasp the various descriptions of human behavior, from psychoanalytic, behavioral, existential, biological, cognitive and systems perspectives as variations upon or distortions of a superior point of view? In other words, can we lay hold of the *globe* for which each of these perspectives in psychology and psychiatry is merely a distorted two-dimensional *map*?

SEEING THE WORLD IN "2D"

A certain advantage is gained with respect to our dilemma if, instead of attempting to confront it head on in all its complexity, we constrict our point of view and first attempt to understand how we might resolve a similar, more concrete dilemma if we were limited in our experience and powers of observation. In order to do this, we can return to the cartographic paradox and attempt to resolve it *without* the aid of a three-dimensional globe.

Consider for the moment a hypothetical situation, one that I briefly discussed in this work's Introduction, in which individuals only experience the world in two dimensions. Indeed, this is the very "world" Edwin Abbott described in his 1884 book, *Flatland*.[64] Let us assume that the denizens of Flatland were provided with Mercator (rectangular) and Polar (dual circular) maps of our three-dimensional world. With no experience of three-dimensional "globes," such individuals would be forced to construct a model of the 3D world on the basis of their two-dimensional experiences. They might construct various maps and regard them as "theories" or "models" of the earth. Seeing that within their two-dimensional experience these maps were apparently mutually exclusive, they might believe that their various models are contradictory or completely incommensurable. For them, the true nature of the "globe" would be as much a mystery as the true nature of the mind is for us.

Given that "2D" individuals have no opportunity to reconcile their models via an experience of the world in three dimensions, we might inquire as to their best course of action with respect to their maps or models. Would it be best for them to decide upon criteria that might help to determine that one map is correct and the other wrong (open competition)? Or would it be better for them to attempt to show how one map could be reduced (mapped on) to the other without loss of meaning (reductionism)? Perhaps they might hold that the two maps were incommensurable, each being true for the cartographer who created it, but false or irrelevant to cartographers who created or "believed" in the other maps (relativism). Another option would be for them to use one map on some occasions and the other map on other occasions, choosing in each instance the map that seemed to "work" best under the circumstances (pragmatic eclecticism). Finally, they might spend their energies in an ultimately futile effort to create a new perfect map, one that synthesized the best features of the Mercator, Polar, and other global projections (Ultimate Theoretical Synthesis) without having any of their drawbacks. We might ask ourselves, however, if any of these options would bring the 2D people any closer to the "truth," or whether, in their efforts to eliminate (or ignore) the apparent incompatibilities between their maps or models they sought a premature or misleading theoretical closure.

What if the 2D people took a dialectical approach to their carto-graphic dilemma? They might, in a Socratic manner, convince the ad-vocates of the Mercator projection to acknowledge that two individuals on the opposite east and west extremes of their map are actually in the same place instead of being at opposite ends of the world. They could then argue that this very contradiction in the Mercator map can only be resolved by adopting the dual polar projections in which the continuous "circular" nature of east and west is represented. A similar argument could be made by advocates of the Mercator map to elicit contradictions in the dual polar map (for example, that this map seems to imply "two worlds"), which could only be resolved by adopting something like the (single) rectangular projection. The results of such critical examinations of "competing cartographic theories" would reveal that each map, each theory, is incomplete without the other, and that the adoption of both perspectives is a necessary step in providing an adequate description of the world. Further analysis would also show that these two projections hardly exhausted the number of fruitful cartographic possibilities, and that an indefinite number of perspectives (or maps) could be generated, each contributing some new insight into the three-dimensional world that had not been provided by any of the others.

In the absence of a concept or experience of a three-dimensional world, it would then appear that the best, "truest," alternative would be for the 2D people to hold that both maps (as well as various other pro-jections they may possess), as different as they are, are valid and true. Such a dual or "multi-perspectivist" conclusion would come closer to describing a three-dimensional space than any of the other theoretical resolution procedures (reductionism, relativism, eclecticism, etc.).

It seems that our 2D people would best characterize the earth as an entity that can be described both with a rectangular model and a dual circular model, as well as via an indefinite number of other two-dimensional models. Such a position would have several distinct advantages. It would, for example, enable the 2D people to navigate the world much more accurately and efficiently, utilizing the Polar projection near the poles and the Mercator projection closer to the equator (but then using the Polar projection again to show how the two opposite ends of the Mercator projection actually meet). The two projections would allow them to arrive at the valid conclusion (within the confines of their own possible experience) that the earth was a plane that is nevertheless circular, inasmuch as it ultimately returns to itself, its end being the same as its beginning. In this way, they would achieve a more intellectually satisfying result than they would, for example, via a pragmatic eclecticism. In short, the denizens of a two-dimensional world would fare better in maintaining the truth and complementarity or interdependence of each of their world models than they would if they were to adopt any of the other procedures (e.g., reductionism, relativism, or theoretical synthesis) that have often been adopted with respect to psychological models and paradigms. Further, this solution, in some ways similar to pragmatic eclecticism, would have the advantage of providing something in the way of an explanation of why such eclecticism is necessary.

Some of the 2D people who held that both maps were "true" might in fact be accused of speaking a mystical, paradoxical language, or of violating the "law of non-contradiction." Some of the more venturesome among them might infer that there is indeed a "true" 3D world, of which their own two-dimensional experience is but an imperfect reflection.[65] Such a "true" world would likely be posited by them as reconciling the antinomies of their own, and explaining why each of their apparently contradictory maps were "true." Some might accuse these thinkers of metaphysical speculation. However, the accusation would hardly be apt: The view only appears metaphysical because it attempts to describe a reality that lies outside the bounds of the 2D people's experience. From our 3D point of view, we can understand why their multi-perspectivist account is precisely the one that is demanded by their reality.

A SYNOPTIC VIEW OF THE MIND?

Consider the possibility that with respect to the human mind we are in the identical, or at least analogous, position to that of our hypothetical 2D people with the earthly globe.

Like the 2D people who have perspectives on a three-dimensional earth but no experience of the globe with which to compare and adjudicate their perspectives, we have perspectives on the "mind" without having a synoptic view of the mind itself. Since we do not have a view of the mind as a whole, we must attempt to construct a theory that approaches synopsis from within the structure of our own epistemological limitations. However, to make full use of this analogy, we must first assume that each of our maps, each of our constructions—the biological, behavioral, cognitive, psychoanalytic, existential and systems—purport to, and in some sense do, provide a complete view of the human mind, much as each of the cartographic projections of the globe provide a "complete" map of the earth *from a given point of view*. Like the cartographic projections, each of the major theories of the mind will end up distorting certain of the phenomena under its purview. Thus, while it may be possible to provide a neuro-biological theory of, for example, "normal mourning" or a psychoanalytic theory of "learning," such theories are likely to create more distortion than illumination, much like an equatorial Mercator projections or dual polar projections are respectively likely to cause more distortion than illumination with respect to the poles and equator of the earth.

In general, it is my view that the various schools or paradigms within psychology—like the various planar projections of the human globe—while appearing to be mutually exclusive are actually complementary and interdependent. Each paradigm can only be adequately understood by assuming the truth of what we normally regard to be its contrary. This interdependence can only be demonstrated through an examination of the *deep philosophical structure* of the various theories: by examining the philosophical assumptions that underlie biological, behavioral, cognitive, psychoanalytic, and the other paradigms in psychology. It is these underlying assumptions that a dialectical analysis shows to be complementary and interdependent, and it is only through a multiplicity of paradigms and perspectives that we can ever hope to arrive at a "full dimensional" synoptic view of the mind.

ANTINOMIES OF THE MIND

For us to appreciate how the different paradigms within psychology complement one another like different cartographic projections of the globe, it is necessary for us to gain additional clarity with respect to the philosophical differences that underlie the various psychological schools. Just as cartographers construct their world-maps based on cartographic principles, psychologists construct their models of the mind on the basis of certain philosophical and psychological ideas. These ideas are often implicit and require some investigation. However, if we reflect upon the problem, we will readily see that underlying the fragmentation within contemporary psychology are a series of polarities, philosophical antinomies, or apparent contradictions regarding the nature of the mind.[66] Several of these antinomies have been known to philosophers at least since the time of Kant; others have emerged in more recent times. Once these antinomies have been articulated we can examine how the position that a theorist takes on each of them underlies the formation of the various psychological paradigms.

Let us then, in somewhat Kantian fashion, articulate several of the antinomies relevant to theory formation in psychology in some detail. My list is by no means meant to be exhaustive. As W. Smythe and S. McKenzie have suggested, the specific polarities that are thought to characterize debates regarding psychological theory are not static but vary over time.[67] The polarities I have selected to discuss below are particularly useful in understanding the distinctions between the schools of psychology considered in this chapter. My description of each of these polarities condenses a considerable body of philosophical reflection and psychological research into apparently contradictory (or at least contrary) statements about human experience and behavior.

(1) *Free will versus determinism*:[68] It would seem from the perspective of our own subjectivity (and from the demands of morals and ethics) that many human actions are freely chosen and thus the responsibility of the actor. However, a scientific view of the world suggests that all human behavior is subject to the same causal laws which govern the physical world. Hence, human behavior is both free and not free.

(2) *Objectivism versus constructivism*: Common and scientific sense dictates that we live in a world of objects and things, which in their existence and nature are completely independent of the human mind. However, reflection prompts us to realize that we cannot name, describe, nor even experience any of these presumed objects except under the aegis of a category, kind, language, or idea, the natures of which are themselves apparently dependent upon the human mind. Thus, the world is both completely independent of and completely dependent upon the mind.

(3) *Elementism versus holism*: Natural science seems to dictate that the properties of the molar phenomena of mind are completely dependent upon and explicable on the basis of molecular units. However, the phenomenology of such "mental objects" as thought, consciousness, and will, as well as the complexities of human behavior, leads to the conclusion that the mind is *sui generis*; its peculiar properties cannot be explained on the basis of underlying material elements of biology or physics or mental elements (e.g., sensations). Thus, the nature of the mind seems to be simultaneously dependent upon both its molecular and molar properties.

(4) *Public versus private criteria*: Experience suggests that we each have privileged, introspective access to our own thoughts, states of mind, moods, and other mental states. However, observation and reflection upon the way in which we learn and utilize so-called "mental terms" suggests that we do so on the basis of publicly observable situations and behaviors. Hence, the subject matter of psychology is and is

not the inner experience of the human mind.

(5) *Individualism versus collectivism*: It would seem almost by definition that such mental entities as thought, perception, anxiety, depression, or schizophrenia (indeed, the entire subject matter of psychological research and inquiry) are wholly contained within the individuals to which these terms are applied. However, an analysis of how these and other terms are used suggests that they invariably involve a relationship between two or more persons and a society or sub-society of "speakers" who have not only tacitly agreed to use this language in a certain, specified way, but who, in effect, have constructed the "mental entity" as part of their language and culture. Hence, mental attributes are both within an individual mind and the society within which the individual dwells (in the system).

(6) *Factualism versus hermeneutics*: Common and scientific sense dictates that the events that determine human behavior are "facts" that reflect efficient causes that presumably operate in the natural world. However, both research and reflection suggest that the "facts" of human experience are only "facts," and the causes of human behavior are only "causes," insofar as they are conceived and interpreted by a human subject. Hence, psychology does and does not deal with the factual basis of human behavior.

(7) *Knowledge versus the unknown*: It would seem that the entire cosmos, including the human mind, is a rationally ordered system that will be progressively subject to the conquest of human theory and knowledge. However, the existence, nature, and ultimate value and significance of the world and humanity present themselves as insuperable mysteries essentially impenetrable to human reason. Thus, the subject matter of psychology is both (potentially) completely knowable and essentially unknown.

Each of these antinomies operate tacitly within contemporary psychology and one might, in fact, characterize various psychological "schools" by noting the position that they take on each of these seven philosophical questions.

"POSSIBLE" AND "ACTUAL" PSYCHOLOGICAL SCHOOLS

By enumerating our seven antinomies and articulating the philosophical views that are derived through the adoption of one or the other of the two "poles" within each of them we are in a position to map out a system of potential psychologies, based upon the combination of positions taken on these critical questions. We can then locate the actual schools of psychology and psychiatry within our map or system. The seven basic antinomies and the philosophical positions they engender are summarized in Table 1. I have included in parentheses abbreviations for each of the various philosophical positions, as they will be useful in the discussion to follow.

Table 5.2.

1) Determinism versus Free Will	(Det1 vs. Fr2)
2) Objectivism versus Constructivism	(Ob1 vs. Con2)
3) Elementism versus Holism	(El1 vs. Ho2)
4) Public versus Private mental criteria	(Pu1 vs. Pr2)
5) Individualism versus Collectivism	(Ind1 vs. Col2)
6) Factualism versus Hermeneutics	(Fac1 vs. Her2)
7) (Complete) Knowability versus (an essential) Unknown	(Kn1 vs. Un2)

We can readily imagine psychological theories that hold as axiomatic several of these philosophical points of view. While, unlike Gregory Kimble,[69] I have not put these propositions to empirical survey or tests, we can infer, for example, that neuro-biologically oriented psychologists, who hold that all mental events are ultimately neuro-physiological events that transpire in the brain, are likely to be *deterministic, objectivistic*, and *elementistic*. They are also likely to hold that such mental events as thought or depression are, at least potentially *publicly observable*; that the locus of psychological phenomena is in the *individual*;

that *facts*, irrespective of the interpretations the mind places upon them, are of ultimate importance in psychology; and that the nature of the human mind is, at least in principle, completely *knowable*. Conversely, existential psychologists (who hold many philosophical positions that are diametrically opposed to those above) are likely to affirm *free will*; the *constructive* nature of reality; the existence of *emergent properties*; the ultimate *privacy* of human experience; the importance of *hermeneutics* (interpretation); and the ultimate *unknowability* of basic issues regarding the psyche.

I have divided the philosophical positions discussed above into two basic groups, according to what many would regard as their most natural affinities or coherences. These groups roughly correspond to what William James referred to as the "tough" and "tender-minded" approaches to philosophy and psychology.[70] The positions whose abbreviations I have characterized with the numeral "1" (determinism, materialism, reductionism, public criteria, individualism, factualism, and knowability) cohere together in what one might call a natural scientific or "tough-minded" view of the mind. On the other hand, the positions whose abbreviations I have labeled with the numeral "2" (freedom of the will, idealism, "private criteria," collectivism, hermeneutics, and "unknowability") exhibit a certain coherence in constituting a "tender-minded" or humanistic point of view. Between the extremes of the psychologies that adopt each of the philosophical positions of one or the other of the two groupings are a wide variety of intermediate psychologies that adopt some of the philosophical axioms of each of the two most polarized perspectives. Table 5.3 provides a summary analysis of various psychological theories according to the scheme I have just described. (The table is meant to be heuristic as opposed to authoritative—several of the perspectives straddle both sides of at least one of the oppositions; for example, family systems and cognitive psychology straddle both sides of the binary objectivism/constructivism).

Table 5.3

Biological Psychology	Det1	Ob1	El1	Pu1	Ind1	Fac1	Kn1
Socio-biological	Det1	Ob1	El1	Pu1	Col2	Fac1	Kn1
Behaviorism	Det1	Ob1	Ho2	Pu1	Ind1	Fac1	Kn1
Family Systems	Det1	Ob1	Ho2	Pu1	Col2	Fac1	Kn1
Cognitive Psychology	Det1	Con2	Ho2	Pr2	Ind1	Her2	Kn1
Psychoanalytic I *	Det1	Ob1	Ho2	Pr2	Ind1	Her2	Kn1
Psychoanalytic II	Det1	Con2	Ho2	Pr2	Ind1	Her2	Uk2
Existential	Fr2	Con2	Ho2	Pr2	Ind1	Her2	Uk2
Analytical/Archetypal	Fr2	Con2	Ho2	Pr2	Col2	Her2	Uk2

I have highlighted the six (or seven) psychological schools I have discussed earlier in this chapter and have included two more schools (socio-biological and archetypal) that have generated interest both within and beyond the field of psychology. One will, for example, notice that socio-biological psychology differs from a more traditional biological approach only by virtue of its collectivist assumptions. Behaviorism adopts many "hard scientific" assumptions but differs from a brain-based biological psychology because it is more holistic," as it focuses upon molar units of behavior rather than biological elements. Cognitive psychology represents a position that is in many ways midway between the natural scientific and humanistic perspectives. The last of the psychologies on our list, Analytical/Archetypal or Jungian, psychology is noteworthy for its embodiment of a philosophy that is, in every respect, antithetical to the "scientism" that is manifest most clearly in the neuro-biological theories of mind. While Jung insisted that his approach was purely descriptive, and in that sense scientific,[71] a close examination of his writings and practice suggests that his psychology, by virtue of its philosophical assumptions, is far closer to other more "humanistic" and even spiritual points of view. This should not be surprising to those familiar with Jung's writings (for example, his *The Red Book*) where he expresses deep suspicions regarding the value of natural science.[72] However, as we have seen in Chapter 4, Jung also adopted a point of view that opposite viewpoints within (and about) the psyche do not exclude one another, a position that will become critical to our resolution of psychology's dilemma.

It should be apparent both on logical and historical grounds that there are many more possible psychological theories than those I have enumerated in Table 5.3. Our seven antinomies yield the potential for numerous combinations of philosophical positions, many of which are not represented among contemporary psychological theories.

As is evident from our discussion, psychology has generally attempted to resolve the question of multiple maps or perspectives by assuming or adopting specific solutions to the questions raised by the apparent contradictoriness of the human mind. I have questioned, however, whether there might not be a solution, on the analogy to the solution of the cartographic dilemma, which, instead of advocating one map or another of the human psyche, utilizes them all in a dialectical effort to gain a synoptic understanding of the psyche.

THE DIALECTICAL INTEGRATION OF PERSPECTIVES IN PSYCHOLOGY

In this section, I conduct a dialectical analysis of the polarities that serve as the foundation for the variety of paradigms in psychology. I plan to show in a programmatic way that each of the philosophical antinomies I have described consist of complementary/interdependent ideas. In addition, because the schools of psychology are conditioned by and are in effect built upon, various combinations of these ideas, they are themselves complementary and interdependent. Each paradigm provides seemingly complete but ultimately inadequate maps of the psyche. They each break down and ultimately require the other models in order to provide anything like a synoptic view of the human mind.

Before discussing the dialectical integration of the perspectives in psychology, it is important to point out that although I am in sympathy with the philosophically critical, interdisciplinary, and pluralistic approach to the psyche that was perhaps first proffered by James,[73] I agree with Rychlak that the expedient of adopting one or another position with respect to the various philosophical antinomies is essential for there to be cumulative progress in the psychological *sciences*.[74] In constructing a map, one must, at least initially, take a definite perspective and stick to it; otherwise, one runs the risk of ending up with disorder and confusion.[75] We might argue that because of the radically different assumptions at the core of the various psychological schools, several or a number of different psychological sciences have developed, each with its own body of knowledge, research criteria, professional organs, and methods of psychological treatment. This indeed is nothing more than a restatement of our problem. Psychology is not a single science; it is several. However, the fact that we have several relatively distinct psychological sciences does not entail that we have several distinct subject matters to which they are applied. The psychologies may be many, yet the mind may remain one.

If we analyze the various antinomies that underlie the divisions between distinct psychological schools, we will realize that the poles of each of these antinomies blend into one another in such a manner as to reveal their mutual interdependence. In this I am following the lead not only of James and Jung but also of Sigmund Koch who held that there is a class of important propositions of radical significance for psychology, which suggest their contradictions (or contraries) as strongly as they suggest their own affirmation.[76] Let us then reexamine each of the seven antinomies I have outlined with this dialectical view in mind.

(1) *Determinism versus Free Will*: A recognition of the mutual interdependence of determinism and free will begins with Hume's observation that one cannot *act* freely unless one can assume the regularity of causal effects, i.e., that one's actions will generally bring about one's desired ends. Included in this assumption are all the causal mechanisms that obviously operate within the human body, sustaining life and supporting and *causing* the very behaviors that we produce *volitionally*.

However, even if "free will" is conceived of as the ability to somehow transcend the causal nexus of the body, it must embody an element of determinacy (causality) in bringing about the ends it desires, because otherwise both free actions and their effects would be chaotic and ineffectual. The very concept of free will is thus dependent upon the concept of determinate causality. However, the reverse is true as well. In order for us to arrive at the cause of a given phenomenon in particular, and the concept of determinate causality in general, we must be able to reason freely about the objects of our experience in a manner that is completely non-prejudicial and ultimately beyond the frame of material causality. For example, the conclusion that a certain belief X was caused by another event Y cannot be justified on the grounds that there were certain causally determined events involving neurons in *my* brain. The existence of brain events does not provide a justification for any scientific or philosophical proposition. The only possible justification for a mathematical, scientific, or philosophical proposition (this includes all conclusions about "causality") is that it was arrived at in the light of observation, experimentation, and reason, a justification that, as Hegel insisted, implies independence from material necessity.[77] A similar line of reasoning is applicable to causal statements regarding a person's beliefs and actions. As Stuart Hampshire wrote in 1971:

> No matter what experimental knowledge of the previously unknown causes that determine a man's beliefs is accumulated, that which a man believes, and also that which he aims at and sets himself to achieve, will remain up to him to decide in the light of argument.[77]

Thus, the very concept of material causality is itself dependent upon a certain freedom from such causality. The argument can be formulated as follows:

> a) If my reasoning about X is reducible and hence completely equivalent to certain events transpiring

in my brain, and

b) if my reasoning justifies my conclusion that X, then

c) certain events Y transpiring in my brain justify the conclusion X.

d) However, to know that X is rationally justified one cannot examine brain events,

e) but one must conduct experiments, formulate arguments, and evaluate them freely in the light of reason.

f) Therefore, my reasoning about X is not completely reducible to events transpiring in my brain.

g) The reasoning that produces the claim that brain processes are equal to or involved in reasoning is itself not justified by examining brain processes, but only through free experimentation (involving the intentional, reasoned manipulation of variables) and rational inquiry.[78]

Freedom of the will (to the extent that it exists) is dependent upon a causally determined chain of physical events. However, our capacity to achieve knowledge of such a chain, and thus the doctrine of determinism is dependent upon our freedom from any purely causal nexus—as it requires our capacity to freely manipulate variables in experiments and freely evaluate the results in the light of reason.

(2) *Objectivism versus Constructivism*: The interdependence of these contrasting perspectives becomes evident when we note that the very things (trees, animals, rocks, and so on), which common sense regards as examples of the objective, material world, cannot be comprehended *unless they are subsumed under a category or idea*. As Hegel understood, even the pointing to a material object or a mere reference to

"this" involves us in categorical thinking, and such thinking inevitably leads to an element of "mind" in all things. On the other hand, the very categories or ideas through which we divide up and cognize the world are themselves dependent upon the existence of concrete examples that subsist independently from the mind. The very concept of the objective or physical implies the constructed or mental and vice versa.

(3) *Elementism versus Holism*: The holistic "molar" properties of the mind—such as thought, volition, and consciousness—are in ways that are not fully understood dependent upon more elementary neuro-biological and cognitive or perceptual processes, including brain processes, sensations, perceptions, images, and the elements of language. However, such molecular units are themselves dependent upon the molar properties they explain. The claim that molecular units, whether conceived in biological or psychological terms, explain the mind is dependent upon the molar acts, thoughts, and experiences needed to articulate and verify the reductionist point of view. More basically, any attempt to analyze the mind into its component sensations, cognitions, etc., will reveal that the "particles" of the psyche can only be identified as a part of more global perceptions, thoughts, and acts of consciousness. What enables me to call something a sensation, for example, is that it is a part of my ongoing molar experience of, say, "this red table." The notion of an isolated sensation element is itself an abstraction that is dependent upon a more holistic point of view. A further illustration of the interdependency of molar and molecular properties is seen in the fact that it would be impossible to identify the neurobiological components of, for example, memory without the more "molar" notion of memory itself.

While science accepts that the mind is completely dependent upon its molecular parts and in no way contains any "substance" that is over and above its biological, psychological, and behavioral units, these "elemental particles" of mind are dependent upon holistic "emergent properties," without which they would have no identity or function. The very notion of molecular properties of mind is dependent upon there being molar properties and vice versa.

(4) *Public versus Private mental criteria*: The idea that our private, introspective knowledge of our own mental states, moods, and feelings is secondary to these states' public or behavioral display originates with such twentieth-century philosophers as Ludwig Wittgenstein[79] and Gilbert Ryle[80] and was explicitly or implicitly adopted by the school of psychological behaviorism. Wittgenstein, for example, argued that the very possibility of our having introspective knowledge of our thoughts and feelings is itself dependent upon a process in which we learn to label the thoughts and feelings of ourselves and others based on publicly observable behavior. Depression, for example, is not primarily when I *feel* a certain way but is more fundamentally a way in which I and others *act* which the community of speakers calls "depression." Only after learning the concept behaviorally, based upon public criteria, do we apply mental terms to our own case through introspection. The same is true for such common mental terms as "thinking," "believing," "intending," and "expecting": their use and application are all rooted in publicly observable thinking, believing, intending, and expecting behaviors. The very notion of an inner mental state is thus necessarily dependent upon a public, behavioral display and a shared language based upon publicly observable behavior. The reverse, however, is true as well: My awareness of the existence of certain behavior is itself dependent upon my own (private) experience that this behavior is the *same* as other behavior that the community labels with a certain mental term. Furthermore, regardless of how a word like "memory" or "depression" is learned or used, it makes little or no sense to speak of a memory or depression that could not be introspectively experienced. Thus, behaviorism and introspection, public and private criteria, which are usually thought to be mutually exclusive notions, are seen to be interdependent ideas.

(5) *Individualism versus Collectivism*: The interdependence of individual and collective perspectives in psychology follows naturally from the dialectic implicit in the previous antinomy between introspection and behaviorism. There we saw that the very language that we utilize to describe our individual, interior life is dependent upon a commu-

nity of speakers. (As Wittgenstein put it, "There cannot be a private language.") To be an individual self means to be distinguished from and yet to be a part of a community. The "other" is essentially implicit in the individual via language, culture, and the laws of a society. I am who I am by virtue of a series of identifications with, distinctions from, recognitions by, and judgments of, others. As both Hegel and Freud recognized, it is a series of struggles, conflicts, and identifications with others that weave the tapestry of the "individual" self. Yet, the opposite is obviously true as well: The community or "system" is nothing without its component individual parts, and, indeed, the community is a mere abstraction apart from its representation (and actualization) in the lives of individuals. Again, individualism and collectivism are seen to be interdependent ideas.

(6) *Factualism versus Hermeneutics:* As philosophers from Nietzsche[81] to Sellars[82] and Kuhn[83] argued, there are no "facts" of human experience that are independent of the cognitive schemas, theories, and interpretations of human subjects. As behavioral psychology slowly came to recognize, there are no "causes" in the life of the mind until they are apprehended and hence interpreted by a human subject. Indeed, the "cognitive revolution" in psychology rested on the very discovery that the "stimuli" of the behaviorists often did not achieve their character and causal effect until and unless they were cognized and interpreted in a particular way.

Yet the very notion of interpretation implies a primary datum that must be interpreted, an observation that prompts philosophers to posit a hard "factual" reality behind the categories and appearances of the phenomenal world. The antinomy of "facts" versus "interpretations" has for many years been hotly debated in the philosophy of science.[84] It is also silently at work in the debate around "repressed memories."[85] One question raised by these debates is whether there are indeed memories independent of subsequent re-signification and interpretation. What these debates have prompted us to realize, however, is that facts and their interpretations are mutually supportive and interdependent ideas.

(7) *(Complete) Knowability versus (an essential) Unknown*: The mutual interdependence of knowledge and the unknown is evident from a number of considerations. One of these is the observation that all knowledge, all science, proceeds out of mystery. With each advance, however, there is an acknowledgment of a further "unknown," which itself then becomes the subject of new investigation, and an awareness that what was once known to be "fact" is, at least in part, error. Psychologists are all too familiar with the notion that truth itself is a species of "error" which only approximates an ideal. Most so-called scientific "truths" of the past and present have been, or will be, revealed to be *errors* of one form or another.

Further, since the very structure of human awareness limits it to some specific "presence" or content, all knowledge is dependent upon its emergence from a background of what is (and remains in part) unknown. There is always something, some potential knowledge or mental content that exists beyond our reach; such content is notable for its "absence," salient for the fact that it is unknown. While the content of consciousness changes from one moment to the next, the general dialectic between "presence" and "absence," between known and unknown, always remains. It is thus part of the concept of consciousness or mind that there is something not yet specified that is absent, beyond awareness, or unconscious. Hence, it is part of the very concept of the known that there is yet something unknown or undiscovered. However, the reverse is true as well: What is unknown can only be articulated against a background of what (is believed) to be known.

Further insight into the interdependence of the known and the unknown can be obtained via an analogy from mathematics. An infinite mind, we might surmise, would have no need for mathematical knowledge, for example the infinite number of mathematical expressions equal to the number seven. This is because such a mind would comprehend instantaneously the equivalence of all such operations. It is only for a finite intellect that such equivalences (for example, 4+3, 91/13, and 100-93) must be spelled out. Indeed, it is only because of our failure to have perfect mathematical knowledge that the detailed system of mathematical knowledge is necessary at all, such system being a tool for the finite mind. By analogy, it can be argued that what we call *knowledge* is itself predicated upon a *failure to know*; one who understood the world *sub species aeternae* would comprehend the totality instantaneously and therefore have no need whatsoever for individual facts, theories, or knowledge in the human sense of these terms. What we call *knowledge* is fully dependent upon some things being opaque or *unknown*—yet the "unknown" makes no sense at all without the backdrop of the known to serve as its boundary.

THE OPPOSITE IS THE COMPLETION

Though tentative and schematic, the above discussion suggests that in their deep, philosophical structure, the various models of contemporary psychology are actually interdependent. This is because the philosophical principles that each model or theory regards as axiomatic are dependent upon the very opposing principles that each theory rejects. Like the Mercator and Polar two-dimensional maps of the globe, the principles of free will and determinism, private and public criteria, knowledge and the unknown, etc., can be regarded as complementary rather than contradictory or contrary ideas. Put another way, our dialectical analysis of the seven psychological antinomies suggests that apparently contrary truths need not be mutually exclusive. As the physicist Niels Bohr held, it is only superficial truths whose opposites are false; the opposites or contraries of "deep" truths are also true themselves.[86]

But how can this "complementarity of opposites" be understood on the level of psychological theory? How, for example, can one integrate existential with biological psychology? I want to suggest that the solution to the problem is not so much one of integrating the split between existentialism and biology. Rather, it is in the facilitation of our own ability to move dialectically between them, and to retain within our understanding the possibility that what appear to be contrary points of view are in fact, complementary, interdependent, and mutually correcting perspectives. Indeed, clinicians do this on a daily basis. The biological psychiatrist medicating a patient is dependent upon the patient's own phenomenological self-report to assess a medication response, and the psychoanalyst treating a depression is dependent upon the patient's publicly observable behavior as an indication of his resistance or transference.

In psychology, we must take seriously the notion of an object (that is, the human mind) that maintains its identity and coherence in spite of being subject to apparently contrary descriptions. This is what clinicians frequently ask of their patients in psychotherapy. Patients are, in effect, asked to expand their notions of themselves so that they can tolerate feeling both love and hate toward the same person, acknowledge being conditioned by their past but at the same time feel free to decide their future, tolerate a relationship that simultaneously feels both untrustworthy and secure and a life that is experienced as both infinitely meaningful and absurd, and accept within themselves certain characteristics that they normally regard as reprehensible. Indeed, the prescription I have made for psychology as a discipline is in accord with Jung's understanding of and prescription for the individual psyche: the recognition and incorporation into the self of those hitherto rejected "shadow elements" that are necessary for wholeness.

The problem of the multiplicity of psychological theories is analogous to the problem of the multiple self. The "treatment" for each of these multiplicities is effectively the same: that is, a dialectical expansion of consciousness to tolerate and include opposition and apparent contradiction. Such "treatment," which I have offered with respect to the various psychological schools, is the opposite of "dogmatics," or the adoption of one point of view to the exclusion of all others. It is my hope that the analogies and arguments set forth in this chapter have provided a certain justification for an integrative pluralism and multi-perspectivism in psychology. Psychology unified under a single, dogmatic paradigm is an impossible and unlaudable ideal, but this need not lead to the conclusion that the psyche itself is not one—only that grasping its oneness requires us to take multiple points of view upon ourselves.

CHAPTER SIX

UNDERSTANDING THE MYSTICAL PARADOX

THE IDEA OF AN ABSOLUTE

The past 250 years have seen both an exponential increase in human knowledge and a progressive retreat from all claims that such knowledge is complete or absolute. During this period, there has been a rejection of religious authority and dogma, the advent of scientific reason and experimentation, an understanding (with Immanuel Kant) of the contributions of the mind to knowledge and experience, the radical and cumulative critique of earlier traditions and points of view, and an increasing awareness of the unconscious determinants of human experience. At the same time, philosophy, particularly in the West, has become increasingly *anti-foundational*. While science has made great strides in providing a coherent account of the physical universe, European and Anglo-American philosophy has come to view knowledge as historically and culturally relative and has largely come to reject the possibility of a single "master narrative" that can account for the universe and humanity's place within it. The idea of an absolute—whether it be of the mystical, theological, philosophical, or scientific variety—is seen by many as a relic of the past. Even the notion of a single world that is the object of scientific and philosophical investigation has been disparaged and all but abandoned. Indeed, G. W. F. Hegel, perhaps the last major philosopher to take the notion of an absolute, is regarded as a major impetus to the "Absolute's" demise, as the very form of critical, dialectical thinking he advocated evolved into the relativistic thought of existentialism, deconstruction, and postmodernism.

It is both within and against these modernist and postmodernist trends that my exploration of the coincidence of opposites as an "archetype of the Absolute" is situated. In this chapter, I will return to the paradoxes of philosophy and mysticism. Building upon the arguments outlined in previous chapters, I will develop a model for reconciling philosophical conflicts that parallels the model I introduced for reconciling diverse paradigms in psychology in Chapter 5. I will argue that the coincidence of opposites can be marshalled to resolve the conflicts or antinomies of philosophy and theology, including the conflicts between idealism and materialism, constructivism and objectivism, first-person and third-person descriptions of mental states, free will and determinism, and theism and atheism My working hypothesis for this exploration is that language and representation, by virtue of its intrinsic need to establish distinctions and dichotomies, sunders a singular pre-linguistic unity, and that philosophical antinomies and tensions are a byproduct of this representational rupture. My project in this chapter is to find *a path back through language to the original unity* and my argument is that the *coincidence of opposites is the vehicle that will take us along this path.* It is in this sense that I call the coincidence of opposites the *archetype of the Absolute.* By coming to understand the interdependence of such seemingly opposing notions as subject and object, words and things, and identity and difference, we can work our way back to a *trace* or *echo* of the pre-linguistic unity that stands behind our philosophical representations of the world.

Throughout this work, I have appealed to a cartographic analogy to provide a graphic illustration of how representation sunders and divides a unified world. I have argued that the problem of creating a "flat" two-dimensional map or "projection" of a three-dimensional globe provides an analogy to the more abstract problem of providing a linguistic, philosophical representation of the cosmos. In both cases, the cartographic and metaphysical—the effort at representation—distorts and ultimately divides its object. It is only through a thorough under-standing of how the various representations complement, and are in fact interdependent with, one another that their object can be properly and completely understood. However, while in the case of cartography we have ready access to the underlying reality that we are representing (in the form of a three-dimensional globe), in the case of philosophy we have no such access and we are in the difficult position of having to construct that underlying reality on the basis of our complementary rep-resentations.

We have seen how religious traditions, including Taoism, Hindu-ism, and Chabad Chasidism, hold that a singular unified world is divid-ed by language and that an awareness of the coincidence of opposites is said to lead one to a restoration of that sundered unity. In addition, var-ious expressions of mysticism and mystically inspired philosophy (for example, Neo-Platonism) reference a "Unity" (that is, a unified world, reality, God, or Absolute) that can be experienced in states of ecstasy or *unio mystica*, but which cannot properly be described in language. As Walter T. Stace has pointed out, in an effort to describe their experience, mystics often resort to paradoxical language that asserts, for example: that God is both identical and non-identical with the world; that the world is both "many" and "one"; that God or the Absolute is both the fullness of being and complete emptiness; and that the enlightened in-dividual both retains and surrenders his individuality. These paradoxes are thought by Stace to be expressions in language of an intuition of the unity that language by its very nature divides. However, when both poles of each opposition *are asserted together*, these antinomies can be understood as ways of referring to a unity that cannot adequately be put into words. This is precisely *because* language and representation by its very nature, categorizes, sunders, and divides. Philosophers, therefore, are caught in the cycle of defending philosophical positions because they fail to see that their preferred philosophical perspective is but one pole of a unity, a unity that can be intuited through an application of the *coincidentia oppositorum* idea.

In this chapter, I discuss several instances of *coincidentia opposito-rum* that lie at the foundation of language, experience, and knowledge and consider their implications for philosophy and mysticism and our *efforts to think of the world as a unified whole.*

CAN THE COINCIDENCE OF OPPOSITES BE UNDERSTOOD IN RATIONAL TERMS?

The philosopher of mysticism, W. T. Stace (1886–1867), argued that logic does not apply to so-called mystical "truths" because mystics speak about a "unity" whereas logic applies to, and indeed defines the nature of, multiplicity.[1] It is for this reason that mystical insights, regardless of their perceived value, cannot be expressed in rational terms. While mystics of various traditions have suggested that paradoxes are approximate means of expressing insights within language about a whole that is fragmented by language itself, efforts to analyze these paradoxes and provide them with a philosophical or rational sense are doomed precisely because philosophy and analysis is rooted in logic and language. According to Stace, "The many is the sphere of logic, the One not so. For this reason, there is no clash between mysticism and logic."[2]

However, as we have seen, the idea of providing mystical paradoxes with a discursive, logical sense through the acceptance of both poles of a philosophical or theological dichotomy has been explicitly or implicitly advocated in several religious traditions, including Buddhism, Gnosticism and both Jewish and Christian mysticism. As we saw in Chapter 1, Buddhism even developed a "logic" that permits both a proposition and its contradiction to have the same truth value, i.e., both true or both false. In Chapter 2, we elaborated upon the Jewish mystical view that various oppositions—including revelation and concealment, creation and negation, values and their abrogation, truth and error, God and humanity, good and evil, language and the world—are interdependent ideas.

Hegel is the philosopher in the West most strongly identified with the doctrine of the coincidence and interpenetration of the opposites.[3] We have, in Chapter 3, considered Hegel's efforts to provide a philosophical interpretation of this idea. However, Hegel's notion that *coincidentia oppositorum* produces a *logical principle* was rejected and even ridiculed by later philosophers. For example, Stace, who was originally an expositor of Hegel and who had a sympathetic view of mysticism, ultimately concluded that in his efforts to produce a logical principle from the coincidence of opposites, Hegel fell "into a species of chicanery." Indeed, Stace concluded, "Every one of [Hegel's] supposed logical deductions was performed by the systematic misuse of language, by palpable fallacies, and sometimes...by simply punning on words."[4] Stace held that we should abandon the idea that *coincidentia oppositorum* can be understood logically, and he resolved that "the identity of opposites is not a logical, but definitely an alogical idea."[5]

In his book, *Mysticism and Philosophy*, Stace, during his post-Hegelian phase, examined the problem of "mystical contradiction" from a logical point of view. According to Stace, the various paradoxes described by mystical adepts—such as the idea that the Absolute is both the fullness of being and complete emptiness—are in fact "flat contradictions" that violate the laws of logic. He argues that efforts to avoid logical contradiction by understanding these paradoxes as rhetorical, metaphorical, or mistaken descriptions of experience—or by viewing them as referring to different aspects of experience, proceeding from different perspectives, or making equivocal use of essential terms—all fail. According to Stace, despite their claims that their experience is "ineffable," mystics must use contradictory language if they are to describe their mystical experiences at all. Yet Stace does not draw the conclusion that the mystic thereby speaks nonsense, or that he undermines his own assertions in the very process of making them. Rather, he holds that the mystic, in recalling his experience of complete singularity but speaking from a (later) perspective of multiplicity, uses the best language available to describe the experience from which he has emerged. Since this experience is of a completely unified "world" and must be expressed using the language of distinctions, the mystic is faced with a logically impossible task. For Stace, "the laws of logic have no application to mystical experience."[6] This is because these laws assume multiplicity, apply only to multiplicity, and in fact *define the very nature of multiplicity*: "When there are no separate items to be kept distinct," there is no application or violation of the law of non-contradiction. In a gesture reminiscent of the Kantian distinction between phenomenal and noumenal worlds, Stace argues that logic has no application and significance for the "realm" that the mystic describes, and it is only by the standards of our very different world—the world within which the mystics' words are in fact uttered and heard—that logic is violated. Stace concludes that it is logic rather than mystical experience that suffers from this state of affairs. He argues that the mystical experience of a singular, undifferentiated world shows that there are indeed "possible worlds" (or at least one such world, the world of complete unity and non-differentiation) in which the laws of logic do not apply.

Stace believes, however, that it is a grave error to hold with Hegel and his followers that mystical experience points us in the direction of a new kind of logic grounded in the identity of opposites.[7] Stace held that, while Hegel was correct in his observation that the doctrine of the "identity of opposites" abounds in both the history of mysticism and philosophy, "he made the disastrous error of mistaking this for a new kind of logical principle and trying to find his own super logic upon it."[8] For Stace, there is only one kind of logic, and Hegel's dialectical logic amounts to a bogus account of the problem posed by mysticism.

In spite of Stace's demurrer, I believe that we can attain philosophical insight into the nature of the mystics' unified world by ascertaining whether and how this world impacts upon, or has implications for, our own realm of multiplicity. On the one hand, it seems obvious that if indeed there is such a unified realm, it has impacted our world in the proclamations and texts of the mystics themselves. But what I have in mind is an impact that is far more widespread. Such an impact might be thought of figuratively as a logical or linguistic echo of the non-differentiated state that pre-exists logic, language, and representation, an echo that is metaphorically akin to the "echo" of the "Big Bang," which astronomers say is faintly discernible through radio telescopes "listening in" to the earliest moments of our universe. This echo I have in mind is manifest in the archetype of *coincidentia oppositorum*.

It is indeed with the thought of listening in on this echo that I have offered two strategies or models for comprehending in discursive terms how overcoming polar oppositions—via the simultaneous affirmation of opposing, seemingly contradictory ideas—leads to an intuition and account of the "world as a whole." The first model, which I described in Chapter 5, is "cartographic." The second model, which I will elaborate upon in this chapter, is "linguistic." Each model is grounded in the view that *representation* fragments a unified metaphysical whole. The cartographic model appeals to the sundering effect that efforts to create two-dimensional maps have on the unified globe, and the linguistic model appeals to the sundering effect of philosophical ideas on the mystical Absolute or Neoplatonic "One."

MODEL 1: A TWO-DIMENSIONAL WORLD

The first model, which I introduced briefly at the start of this book and discussed in detail in Chapter 5, involves adopting a viewpoint on our world that is *less complete* than the one we normally assume. In doing this, we take on the role of beings—like those in Edwin Abbot's novel, *Flatland*—who are unable to perceive or conceptualize the world in three dimensions, and who therefore have maps but no globes. We saw that the process such beings would go through in working out the relationship between apparently contradictory maps of the world without recourse to a globe, can shed considerable light on certain philosophical antinomies that are difficult for us to resolve from within our actual world. I believe that this "constricting" procedure, where we limit our epistemological capacities, may assist us in overcoming the problem, posed by Stace, of making a *rational* transition from the un-differentiated realm of the mystic to our world of differentiated things and relations.

The cartographic analogy suggests that, in order to represent things as a whole, we must describe them using two (or more) seemingly contrary representations or descriptions. As we saw in Chapter 5, just as a "Mercator" map, which represents the world as a single rectangle, is complemented, and in a sense "completed," by dual polar projections, which represent the world as two circular projections, our understanding of the human psyche must involve such apparently opposing but actually complementary and interdependent ideas as objectivism and constructivism, free will and determinism, factualism and hermeneutics, and public and private criteria for mental terms. It is not only mystics who feel compelled to express truths that "move in opposite directions," but this tendency is apparent in the field of psychology as well. As we will see, a similar tendency is present in philosophy and theology. The history of these disciplines, as both Kant and Hegel recognized, is filled with philosophers who hold opposing views on virtually all topics of significance: The world is both completely independent of and yet completely conditioned by thought and language; God is both the creator and essence of the universe and completely non-existent; values are both the constituents of reality and a purely subjective and ephemeral coloring of it; human actions are both fully determined by a chain of causality, and essentially free; human existence is both deeply meaningful and totally meaningless, etc. Kant was the first modern philosopher to explicitly assert the validity (albeit in different "realms") of both poles of several philosophical oppositions. However, even a casual examination of the history of ideas will show that this history, if it were to be personified as "the world-spirit," is very much like a mystic who makes contradictory declarations about "truth." As we saw in Chapter 5, such "contradictory" ideas underlie opposing paradigms in the discipline of psychology, and a unified understanding of psychology and its object (the mind) is possible only when we recognize that ideas that seem to be opposed to one another are on a deeper level complementary and interdependent. In this chapter, I argue that the principle of *coincidentia oppositorum* that we applied to psychology in Chapter 5 is applicable to philosophy and theology as well.

FROM ANALOGY TO ANALYSIS: THREE FUNDAMENTAL DISTINCTIONS

The cartographic model provides an *analogy* that moves us in the direction of comprehending the mystics' understanding of multiplicity and unity. It suggests that we must abandon dichotomous either/or thinking and accept the validity of two or more apparently contradictory thoughts at once. I have provided an *analysis* of how this can be achieved with regard to contrasting points of view on the human mind in *psychology*. We will see how a similar analysis is possible with respect to three foundational *epistemological and metaphysical* polarities, which underlie the philosophical controversies discussed in Chapter 5. These polarities are the distinctions between (1) subject and object, (2) signifier and signified, and (3) identity and difference.

These three polarities are highly abstract, as each of them are applicable to virtually all experience and all things. The first of these distinctions, between subject and object, involves the fundamental disjunction between consciousness and the world, between things and our experiences of them. The second distinction, between sign and signified, reflects the very sundering of the "One" by language and representation. It is, in effect, the primary representational or linguistic distinction, as it sets up (or rests upon) a difference between *what is* and *what is pictured or said.* The third distinction, between identity and difference is, as Stace suggested and Jacques Derrida later argued,[9] perhaps even more basic than the other two. Without difference, and hence the distinction between identity and difference, there could be no distinctions whatsoever, and certainly no distinctions between sign and signified, and subject and object.

I will argue that an analysis of the complementarity and interdependence of the poles of each of the three oppositions follows from *the very nature of representation, both linguistic and "mental."* I will also suggest that a range of philosophical controversies rests upon these three distinctions, and the dissolution of these distinctions results in the resolution of philosophical controversies.

Our task is complicated by the fact that the three distinctions we will consider are themselves interrelated and interdependent, and it is impossible to treat them each completely separately. The distinction between words and things cannot be made without the distinction between consciousness and its objects (and vice versa), and neither of the first two distinctions would make any sense without the notions of identity and difference. Our discussion will at times range over, and move back and forth among them, but the reader will do well to keep them each in mind as we proceed. We will see that the first of these polarities, the subject-object distinction (as Thomas Nagel's work suggests) has the most concrete relevance to specific philosophical problems. This is followed by the distinction between sign and signified. By the time we get to the point of overcoming the distinction between identity and difference, we are at a place where we have overcome all distinctions, and all philosophical and other questions will have vanished.

AN "UNDECIDABLE" PHILOSOPHICAL VOCABULARY

Before proceeding, I want to underscore the importance of developing a philosophical vocabulary that subverts, transcends, and is in effect "undecidable" between the classical distinctions of Western metaphysics, a task that Jacques Derrida recommended in the course of developing his method of deconstruction.[10] As we have seen, Hegel spoke of "freedom/necessity," a term he used to bridge the gap and assert the interdependence of what others regarded as distinct, contrary notions. We have also seen how the category of *Yin Yang* in Taoism, *Brahman-Atman* in Buddhism, and the major symbols of both the Kabbalah and Chasidism traverse and are "undecidable" with respect to one or more basic philosophical polarities; each expresses the idea that these polarities are a *coincidentia oppositorum*. For example, in Chapter 2 I detailed how the Kabbalistic term *Ein-sof* (the Infinite), which is used to designate the metaphysical ground of God and the world, both undermines and reconciles the concepts of being and nothingness, universal and particular, origin and end, divine and human, personal and impersonal, and faith and disbelief. We might say that the Kabbalists invoke *Ein-sof* to indicate the "metaphysical whole" that we cannot intuit directly, just as the hypothetical "3D blind" inhabitants of "Flatland" cannot directly intuit the three-dimensional earth. And like the three-dimensional globe which is a *physical whole* "prior" to its being fragmented into an indefinite array of imperfect cartographic projections (maps), *Ein-sof* is a *metaphysical whole* prior to its being fragmented into an array of conceptual dichotomies that imperfectly represent God and the world. In both instances, a primal, non-representable whole[11] is ruptured *by the very system of representation* that attempts to describe it; the three-dimensional globe is ruptured by a system of two-dimensional maps, and *Ein-sof* (the unified Infinite) is sundered by a system of dichotomies and distinctions that are the necessary conditions for linguistic representation. By drawing an analogy with the unified "globe," we can perhaps overcome Stace's objection to the idea that we can ever "know" anything about the unity that the mystic claims lies at the foundation of our experience and world. Just as the 2D people of Abbott's novel can have some knowledge about the (to them unknowable) 3D globe through the interconnections among their apparently contradictory maps, we can perhaps gain *knowledge* about the unified Absolute (*Ein-sof*) through the interconnections among the apparently contradictory philosophical perspectives we have about our life and world.

SUBJECT AND OBJECT

The metaphysical point of view that dominates contemporary philosophy, at least in Great Britain and the United States, is a form of naturalism, physicalism, or *objectivism*. This view holds that a complete account of the universe, including the phenomenon of consciousness, can be fashioned on the basis of an "objective" world that is independent of the mind and which is thus understood from a "third person," scientific point of view. Objectivism seeks to overcome the gap between subject and object by explaining everything, including first-person subjective experience, from an objective, and typically naturalistic or material point of view. On this view, consciousness is caused by, and is in effect identical with, brain processes, and language is a natural human function that enables individuals to *represent* their immediate environment and the wider world.

There are two main philosophical challenges to the hegemony of the objectivist view of the world, the *idealist* and the *linguistic-constructive* critiques. Each of these suggests that objectivism, despite its significance for progress in the natural sciences, fails to provide an adequate account of our knowledge of either consciousness or the world. The *idealist* challenge, which is the older of the two, holds that all knowledge is grounded in experience or mind, i.e., in sensations, perceptions, and ideas—and that for this reason, mind rather than its so-called objects is the ground of knowledge and being. The *linguistic-constructivist* challenge emerges from the view that all knowledge, including scientific knowledge, is a function of language, and that "signifieds" (the so-called objects of our linguistic descriptions) are themselves constructed by signifiers. In this view, it is language rather than nature that is the primordial ground of knowledge and being.

I will now take up the idealist and linguistic challenges to objectivism and representationalism. In each instance, my goal is to render these challenges plausible. This is followed by a discussion of considerations that lead to the conclusion that both poles of each of these (related) subject-object oppositions are required for a full account of "the world" and, further, that these poles are interdependent with one another. It is precisely our understanding of this interdependence that provides us with an "echo" of, or initial glimpse into, a unified world.

THE IDEALIST CHALLENGE TO OBJECTIVISM

Advocates of philosophical idealism hold that the objective, material world is a construction based upon conscious experience. Philosophical idealism has a long lineage in Western thought, having been advocated in various forms by philosophers as varied as Bishop Berkeley, Kant, Hegel, and Edmund Husserl. Jung made a strong and concise case for the philosophical view that the psyche, while it is thought to originate in the brain, is itself the origin of all existence:

> The vast majority (of thinkers in the West) consider the psyche to be a result of biochemical processes in the brain cells.... It is indeed paradoxical that *the* category of existence, the *sine qua non* of all existence, namely the psyche, should be treated as if it were only semi-existent. Psychic existence is the only category of existence of which we have *immediate* knowledge, since nothing can be known unless it first appears as a psychic image.... To the extent that the world does not assume the form of a psychic image, it is virtually non-existent."[12]

A recent reaffirmation of the idealist position by Piet Hut and Roger Shepard, argues that:

> the standard approach [in natural science] builds upon an epistemologically weak foundation: what it takes for granted is a physical world containing physical brains composed of atoms, molecules, ions, electric fields and so on. But what are directly given to any scientist are only the consciously experienced appearances (filled with 'qualia' and their relationships) that (on the basis of certain regularities and correlations) are interpreted as independently existing physical objects.[13]

According to Hut and Shepard, the hypothesized elemental constituents of matter are referred to with words, equations, and diagrams—which themselves must relate either to "constellations of qualia in the scientist's own conscious experience" or to ideas that scientists interpret and understand.[14] They acknowledge that each model or perspective, the one beginning with "mind" and the other with "matter" has its advantages, but each results in seemingly insuperable difficulties. From the third-person, materialistic perspective, we have two problems: How is it that conscious experiences can be generated from physical processes, and how can the mental in turn have a causal effect upon the physical? From the first-person, phenomenological perspective, we are faced with the dual problems of how experience can guarantee that we are in contact with an objective world, and how we know of the existence of minds other than our own.

However, Hut and Shepard argue that the attempt to ground our conception of the world in the unobservable particles of physics—which have no definite reality until they are observed and measured—is far more precarious than a phenomenological effort to ground reality in the qualia of lived experience, for it is the physical world and not experience that must be *inferred*. On this view, consciousness, far from requiring an explanation, is itself the foundation for any explanation whatsoever. This is a restatement of the classical argument for idealism.

Nagel has been one of the most eloquent defenders of the irreducibility of the subjective (or the "psychic") in our account of the world. His work in the 1970s set the stage for contemporary debates about the status of "qualia," the qualitative "feel" of conscious experience. Nagel's work has fueled questions regarding the capacity of brain and computer science to fully explain consciousness and reduce subjectivity to material, functional, or computational processes and states. He argues that an adequate resolution of several important philosophical questions require that we take a subjective perspective on ourselves and the world, and, for this reason, the subjective is an irreducible part of our account of reality.[15] These questions include the problems of the meaning of life, the existence of free will, the nature of personal identity, and the relationship between mind and body. Nagel argues that in each of these cases, there is a tendency, based upon the success of modern science, to attempt to view the problem from a detached objective perspective. However, in each case the meaning and significance of the phenomena in question can only be adequately accounted for from a subjective, internal point of view.

Nagel argues that looked at objectively, from a third-person point of view, no individual's life has any particular significance or meaning, but looked at subjectively, from a first-person point of view, every life is of ultimate significance. When viewed from the "outside," an individual's actions are causally produced behaviors, whereas from the "inside" they are freely chosen products of a person's will. Concerning the problem of personal identity, Nagel points out that no objective criteria (couched, for example, in terms of physical continuity, memory, or similarity of character), can account for the persistence of the *person* over time, yet internally we are each aware of the persistence of self-identity as an obvious fact. Regarding the mind-body problem, Nagel argues that it seems "impossible to include in a physical conception of the world the facts about what mental states are like for the creature having them."[16] While biologically or computationally oriented psychologists look for ways to dismiss or ignore qualia, the internal, subjective element of "mind" always remains.

The insuperable difficulties of "reconciling subjective and objective points of view" are, according to Nagel, present in other philosophical problems as well—for example, in connection with the nature of space and time, death, and the theory of knowledge. He holds that our only viable option in the face of these difficulties is to accept that "reality" contains both objective and subjective points of view, and to resist the idea that we can have an integrated understanding of our world. While Nagel suggests that this realization prompts us to "deny that there is a single world,"[17] we may be justified in holding that there is one world that can be understood from (at least) two interdependent points of view.

The view I have developed in this book is that there is a single world that must be understood from opposing yet interdependent perspectives. In philosophy, the *explanans* (the thing explained) is at any moment ready to trade places with the *explanandum* (that which does the explaining). For example, while consciousness is necessary for the experience and construction of an objective, material reality, it inevitably posits the independent existence of material objects it intuits and constructs. Certain of these objects, i.e., those constituting the human body, particularly the nervous system and brain—are in turn the conditions for the existence of consciousness itself.

The view that the world only appears in and through consciousness (idealism) is thus complemented by and interdependent with the view that consciousness is itself a product of the material world (materialism). Jung held that one pole of these oppositions was associated with introversion and the East, while the second pole was associated with extraversion and the West. He concluded "that the two standpoints, however contradictory, each have their psychological justification" and that "both are one-sided in that they fail to see and take account of those factors which do not fit in with their typical attitude.... The result is that, in their extremism, both lose half the universe."[18]

The validation of both terms of an opposition is characteristic of much Eastern thought. For example, Jung writes in his commentary to "The Tibetan Book of the Dead" (The *Bardo Thodol*) that the "unspoken assumption" of this work "is the antinomian character of all metaphysical assertions."[19] The *Bardo Thodol* holds that consciousness is both completely void[20] and the condition (and even "being" of) all metaphysical reality,[21] including God.[22]

THE ARGUMENT FROM THE SIMULATED UNIVERSE

Those who defend idealism in philosophy and those who hold that consciousness is an irreducible property of the universe are typically unreceptive to the view that mind is produced by and reducible to material properties and processes. However, when taken to its logical conclusion, a materialist, reductionist view of consciousness ultimately dissolves and becomes indistinguishable from the idealism that it opposes. Indeed, a "coincidence of opposites" between materialist and idealist views of reality follows from one of the consequences that many philosophers draw *from the materialist view* of the mind—the idea that consciousness, even human consciousness, can be produced in a computer.

In a paper entitled "Are You Living in a Computer Simulation?" Oxford philosopher Nick Bostrom has put forth a rather startling argument. He suggests that we may not be the biological, material beings we think we are, but are instead computer simulated minds, existing in a digital matrix.

Many works of science fiction as well as some forecasts by serious technologists and futurologists predict that enormous amounts of computing power will be available in the future. Let us suppose for a moment that these predictions are correct. One thing that later generations might do with their super-powerful computers is run detailed simulations of their forebears or of people like their forebears. Because their computers would be so powerful, they could run a great many such simulations. Suppose that these simulated people are conscious (as they would be if the simulations were sufficiently fine-grained and if a certain quite widely accepted position in the philosophy of mind is correct). Then it could be the case that the vast majority of minds like ours do not belong to the original race but rather to people simulated by the advanced descendants of an original race. It is then possible to argue that, if

this were the case, we would be rational to think that
we are likely among the simulated minds rather than
among the original biological ones.[23]

The idea that we may be living in a "simulation" clearly emerges from a materialist view of the mind, which taken to its extreme suggests that conscious experience can be produced in an ultra-sophisticated computer. However, an interesting implication of the notion that consciousness can be digitally replicated and that we may be living in a "simulation" is the paradox that idealism, as opposed to (or in addition to) materialism, may well be the correct philosophical perspective. Indeed, the simulation argument unwittingly provides us with a vehicle for this conclusion.

Let us consider this in detail. Advocates of simulation theory argue that if it will indeed one day be possible to produce a simulation of a community of conscious minds, and if future civilizations reach the point where they do so, then it is possible that the majority of conscious entities in the universe and the majority of "living worlds" are simulated, digitally constructed rather than natural and biological. Bostrom argues that if we believe "it may one day be possible to construct such a simulation," then we have no reason to believe that this has not already occurred and that we are not ourselves living in a simulated world. Further, on the materialist/digital view of mind, it would be possible and perhaps even likely that *simulations could be constructed within simulations*. For example, on the assumption that *we are a simulation*, we may soon reach a point in our own technology where we become capable of channeling information in such a manner as to create a simulation ourselves. There may be *n* orders of such simulations: simulations within simulations within simulations and so on, limited only by the potential for computing power within the original supposedly "natural" universe—a power that, given the possibility of creating quantum computer systems, would be quite vast indeed.

An interesting aspect of these hypothesized simulations within simulations is that they would be so remote from their purported material foundation as to mimic the character of spiritual "worlds within worlds" spoken of in the Kabbalah and other mystical and theosophical traditions. Indeed, it would be virtually impossible for anyone within any of these worlds to test or verify the hypothesis that there is a material ground to their being. Philosophers who (are convinced that they) live in a simulated world might *speculate* that there is such a material ground, in the same way that philosophers who believe that they live in a material world speculate that there is a spiritual or ideational ground to their universe. However, there would be no way of proving the issue one way or another. The simulated world, which may be our own world, becomes the mirror or inverse of the one in which previous generations believed themselves to be living. While they believed themselves to be residing in a material world and in some cases speculated about a spiritual or ideational foundation for that world, we ("simulations") would be living in an ideational world and speculating about a material foundation for it.

However, on the assumption that we are living in a simulation within in a simulation many times removed from its "natural" origin, the idea of a material foundation may drop out altogether, as from any epistemological or even scientific point of view *all we would have is information*. This is another way of saying that one way of looking at our own world is that it is based upon sense data and phenomenological experience. The interesting thing here, however, is that the opposite assumption— that we are living in a material universe, in which mind is simply the function of material events and processes—ultimately leads to the view that we may indeed be living in a simulated world in which matter has no immediate (and perhaps no genuine) place but is simply a speculative foundation for an ideational reality.

What is entailed by the assertion that we cannot know whether or not we are living in a computer simulation? This assertion entails that what we can know are the experiences and ideas of our conscious minds—anything beyond that, including the presumed underlying foundation of that experience, is speculative. The same doubt that leads us to consider the possibility that we are living in a simulation can lead us, as René Descartes long ago understood, to doubt whether there is anything at all beyond our consciousness and experience. The radical materialistic philosophy that leads to our postulating the possibility of a digital simulation begins to dissolve in the face of its own assumptions. If we are living in a digital stimulation, all of our ideas about matter, the laws of physics, black holes, the Big Bang, etc., have been programmed into that simulation and do not necessarily reflect the reality that underlies it. All of our science is simply an organized awareness of the manner in which information is presented to our experience. While a materialist philosophy begins with the assumption that there is a material substrate to our conscious experience, it ends with the conclusion that information channeled through our conscious experience lies at the foundation of all that we can know. It leads to a recognition of a circularity and interdependence of subject and object, and mind and matter; through this, we can recognize that a simple linear understanding of our world and experience is inadequate. Rather, a bilinear or even circular understanding is required, one that encompasses both poles of the subject-object and mind matter distinctions. It is only in this way that we can achieve a full measure of philosophical understanding.

Our discussion suggests that the distinction between subject and object is philosophically untenable. And yet, as Marc Taylor reminds us,[24] we could neither experience any *thing* nor reference a world without this distinction. Perhaps this should not surprise us: the distinctions we are "overcoming" are, as we have intimated, necessary foundations of the representational process and in philosophy we use words in an effort *to represent*. We are left with the uneasy feeling that each time we overcome a critical philosophical distinction it re-emerges, creating a new opposition between the view that the distinction must be overcome and the view that it is necessary and inviolable. We will later explore the implications of this second-order "re-emergence" in connection with our discussion of language and the world.

SIGN AND SIGNIFIED: OVERCOMING THE DISTINCTION BETWEEN LANGUAGE AND THE WORLD

The second of our challenges to an objectivist account of the world (and the second of what I earlier described as the three foundational *epistemological and metaphysical* polarities) is the distinction between signifier and signified. The objectivist holds that, just as the world is completely independent of our subjective awareness of it, it is independent of the language we use to describe it. However, if language plays a major role in the construction (as opposed to description) of the world, we have another reason to doubt objectivism, materialism, and naturalism.

To address this challenge to objectivism, we must focus our attention on the fundamental vehicle of linguistic representation the relationship between sign and signified, i.e., the relationship of words to things, of language to the world.

With the advent of the "linguistic turn" in twentieth-century British, American, and European philosophy, the traditional view that words are distinct from the things they refer to has been placed in considerable doubt. Philosophers from Wittgenstein to Derrida have questioned the viability of the signifier/signified distinction; they have suggested that what we regard as the "world" is something that exists within among, rather than beyond, our words and texts. This view, which we can call "linguistic constructivism," is in apparent stark contrast to the traditional (common sense) view that there is a genuine and obvious distinction between words and things, and that language *represents* rather than *constructs* reality. As we proceed, we will see that, just as there were regarding idealism, there are good grounds for adopting a linguistic-constructivist view, despite the fact that such a view initially appears to violate both science and common sense. We will see that not only is there a "first order" interdependence between words and things, but there is also a "second order" *coincidentia oppositorum* between the constructivist and the representational perspectives that can be taken on the relationship of language to the world.

THE INTERDEPENDENCE OF WORDS AND THINGS

If words could not be distinguished from the things they refer to or represent, the foundation for the distinction between the world and our representation of it would be dissolved. For this reason, the word/thing or signifier/signified distinction is a foundational "test case" for our application of the coincidence of opposites to philosophy and theology. If this distinction can be dissolved, if a coincidence of opposites between word and thing can be demonstrated, we will arrive at the foundation for a rational (and not merely an intuitive) vehicle for comprehending the underlying unity of the world that was sundered by creation.

Derrida has suggested that despite the fundamental role of the distinction between sign and signified in language and thought, this distinction is ultimately untenable on the grounds that words point to other words rather than to an extra-linguistic object. The signified, in this view, is just another signified; the thing represented just another sign. It will be worthwhile to review the chain of reasoning that leads to the dissolution of the signifier/signified distinction in some detail. We will then see that there is a *coincidentia oppositorum* not only between words and things (signifier and signified) but also between the *view* that the signifier/signified distinction is spurious and the *view* that this distinction is absolutely essential.

What is meant by the claim that the signified is just another signifier and that the "thing in itself" is itself a sign?

To answer this question, we can begin with a simple example. When I hold up a pencil and say, "This is a pencil," the word "pencil" is presumably the *signifier* and the pencil itself the *signified*. However, even in this apparently simple case we can ask "What is the reference?" when I say the word "pencil"? This is because, *depending on the context,* I could hold up a pencil to illustrate or refer to "wood," "yellow," "writing implement," or any of a number of objects or ideas. When I point to something and utter a word, this is not an unambiguous act of reference; my word "pencil" refers, but it does so only within a context and ultimately via a series of other explicit or implicit words that disambiguate my reference, and these words require other words to disambiguate *them,* and so on, potentially *ad infinitum.* While we typically do not need long explanations to discern the reference when someone points and speaks, this is in large measure because as members of a common culture we already share a language and a whole host of standard interpretations. (This, by the way, is not the case when it comes to communications between a small child and an adult; and when a child points to something it is often completely unclear what the child *means*—and this is because the child does not have words to disambiguate its gesture). A signified, like "pencil," only has significance within the context of a social practice and language that expresses the routes of interest of a certain culture; a pencil is what it is only in the context of a *form of life* in which writing is a significant act, in which there is a difference between erasable and non-erasable writing. To an individual from a completely different culture, a pencil may not have the meaning we assign to it, and any efforts we make to get that individual to attach the word "pencil" to what we refer to with this term will be fruitless. This is because a pencil does not have a *place* in that person's form of life and system of representation. Hence, when I use the word "pencil" (even within my own culture), I am not pointing immediately to an object or "transcendental signified." Rather, I am (implicitly) invoking a series of other signifiers that disambiguate and explain my use of this term and which situate "pencil" within a cultural practice and language. The same is true for *any* word, including words that designate so-called "natural" objects. It is only within a culturally conditioned "language-game" or "form of life" that we regard "copper" or "tuberculosis," to take two somewhat arbitrary examples, as meaningful terms," "ideas," "objects," or "natural kinds." My meaningfully asserting that

"X is copper" invokes a linguistic setting and series of disambiguating signifiers—in this case about elements and metals, and their differences, uses, and value. Whether the object of our attention is "cultural" or "natural," the meaning of the so-called *signified* is dependent upon a series of signifiers. Pointing to or referring to anything involves an indefinite regress of words that disambiguate what one is saying.

It is for this reason that what we regard as the *signifier* as opposed to the *signified* is arbitrary. Since our words never directly seize hold of *the thing itself*, all language involves a reversible chain of signification. "Pencil" does not directly attach itself to an object in the world; it only does so through its place in a language and culture within which a "long, wooden, and graphite instrument for writing" is given sense. It thus becomes arbitrary whether we regard "pencil" as the sign and the pencil as the signified, or vice versa. Indeed, we might say that the concrete object, rather than being the signified, is actually a signifier that itself points to an intricate pattern of language and cultural practice.

It is important to see how on this view there is an arbitrariness or reversibility of signifier and signified. Since "words" and "things" are both signifiers, what plays the role of the *signified* is also dependent upon context. I can write a treatise about man, the world, or God, and establish any of these three as my ultimate signifieds, but it can also be that my treatise is the signified and these "ultimates" are mere signs. A Kabbalistic treatise is about the transcendental object *Ein-sof*, but we can just as easily say that *Ein-sof* is the role played by the word "Ein-sof" in that treatise. Or, to take a more mundane case, if I write a text on American history, it is presumably about the nation "America"; however, "America" can just as easily be understood as the role played by the word "America" within my treatise or text (for example, "Drob's America"). In this way, it refers to a series of other words. (And indeed, someone visiting America could experience it largely as a signifier of the ideas in my treatise!) This relates to the problem of the philosopher's so-called imprisonment within language.[25] I want to write about God himself, or freedom, or the world, but in the end I am simply setting up these terms within a certain discourse; this is something akin to setting up a game with rules (like chess) and using "God," "the world," or "freedom" as one of the pieces. The playwright Samuel Beckett once said in reference to Joyce's *Finnegan's Wake*: "Writing is not *about* something; *it is that something itself.*"[26]

The notion that words refer only to other words and sentences is particularly evident in psychology. Wittgenstein suggests that words naming so-called mental states and processes do not achieve their meanings by attaching themselves to things but by the position they occupy within a language and form of life. Consider, for example, the question of how many *mental acts and processes* are required for you to read and comprehend this paragraph. *Attention, concentration?* Surely one must attend to and concentrate upon the meaning of the words. *Memory?* Certainly, one must remember the sounds of the letters and the meanings of the words, as well as recall the beginning of the paragraph to understand its end. *Intention?* Clearly one must intend to read and understand. *Recognition?* In reading we are constantly recognizing words, meanings, and ideas with which we are familiar. *Thought?* One can read without thinking, but in that event, one would not understand what one has read. What of other mental terms? *Interpretation, expectation, perception?* Nearly any cognitive term we can think of names a process that is necessary for one to read. However, should we then conclude that there is a process in the mind or brain corresponding to each of these terms when you read this paragraph? Wittgenstein suggests that the necessity of attention, concentration, memory, recognition, thought, expectation, intention, interpretation, and understanding is a "requirement of the language" rather than a reference to or description of actual, concrete mental acts or brain processes. We have a whole host of mental terms that have meaning by virtue of their distinctiveness from (and entailments *vis a vis*) one another but whose application to the "world" is quite tenuous and indirect. The idea that the signified is in reality another signifier or series of signifiers might be said to generalize from these examples to most, if not all, of language.

If we thoroughly follow this line of reasoning, we soon realize that the very distinction between words and things is not what we originally held it to be, and this distinction is itself dependent upon a use of language that overcomes or obliterates this distinction. My ability to use the word "pencil" to refer to pencils does not proceed via a direct attachment of the word "pencil" to the "pencil thing." It *must operate through a chain of other signifiers* involving marking, written language, drawing, erasing, and so on. This disambiguates my pointing to the pencil as a "pencil" as opposed to pointing to "it" as an instance of wood, graphite, cylinder, stick, pointy thing, weapon, lettering on a pencil, or any other "it." If words and things were completely distinct, and words attached themselves directly to their objects unmediated by other words, we would paradoxically not be able to speak or write meaningfully at all because objects would then lie completely beyond the matrix of signification. In such a case, one would make a noise or a mark and point to a presumed object, but one would not be able to unambiguously communicate one's meaning. This is because without using additional words one would not be able to indicate what aspect of the thing one was pointing to, what class of things it belongs to, and how it differs from all other things. In fact, when we point to an object and speak or write meaningfully about it, we are able to do this only because our pointing and reference carries with it an entire language.

LINGUISTIC CONSTRUCTIVISM / IDEALISM

In collapsing the distinctions between words and things, we have already taken an initial step on the ladder to thinking of the world as a unified whole. We begin to recognize that an integrated web of nature, culture, and language is implicit in each and every utterance we make and any meaningful experience we have. In addition, we have a certain understanding of how opposing ideas in philosophy can both be true—for example, if meaning is completely contained within language, then "God's existence" is a proposition that has meaning and truth within a language game or linguistic practice that associates God with existence. However, it is false within an atheistic linguistic practice within which God is separated from the domain of existence. As I have argued elsewhere, the "God" of Judaism can be understood as the place that "God" plays in Jewish religious discourse and the Jewish way of life, just as the "king" (in chess) is what it is by virtue of the rules and practice of the game of chess.[27] On this view, to try to determine whether God "truly" exists (outside of linguistic and cultural practice) is akin to picking up the plastic "king" figurine and asking, "But is this truly a king?" We will return to this idea and develop (as well as critique) it later in this chapter.

As we have seen, the view that there is no distinction between signifier and signified, word and thing, leads to linguistic constructivism. It can also lead to a philosophical position sometimes referred to as "linguistic idealism." Linguistic idealism involves the radical proposal that there is literally nothing outside the text, nothing beyond language. On this view, held or at least attributed to thinkers as varied as Derrida, Wittgenstein, Jacques Lacan, and Wilfred Sellars, the world is limited to our linguistic representations.[28] While there are certain compelling considerations that lead to this view, it is on its face absurd; our senses repeatedly present us with a world beyond language. We will come to see that linguistic constructivism, which overcomes the signifier-signified distinction, must be complemented by the view that the signifier-signified distinction is not only important but inviolable. Nonetheless, I have shown that linguistic constructivism and even linguistic idealism cannot be dismissed out of hand. Like their theoretical cousin ordinary idealism (which identifies the world with phenomenal experience) they offer a compelling map of what we ordinarily regard to be a world of experience, matter, and things.

EXCURSUS: LINGUISTIC CONSTRUCTIVISM IN JEWISH MYSTICISM

The theory of linguistic constructivism, which holds that the signified is itself a signifier and that language is effectively coterminous with the world, is not new. These ideas were put forth centuries ago by the Jewish mystics, who effectively "deconstructed" the distinction between language, the world, and God. Moshe Idel has suggested that Derrida's now famous aphorism, "There is nothing outside the text," through which he proclaimed the collapse of the signifier-signified distinction in 1967, may have actually been derived from the Kabbalist R. Menaham Recanti's maxim that there is *nothing outside the Torah*. Recanti, writing in the early fourteenth century, held that "All the sciences altogether are hinted at in the Torah, because there is nothing that is outside of Her.... Therefore, the Holy One, blessed be He, is nothing that is outside the Torah, and the Torah is nothing that is outside Him, and this is the reason why the sages of the Kabbalah said that the Holy One, blessed be He, is the Torah." Idel points out that the French translation of this passage would have been available to Derrida in the 1950s.[29]

Elliot Wolfson has argued that there is a clouding of the difference between narrative and event in both *Sefer ha-Bahir* and *Sefer ha-Zohar*, one that leads to a breakdown of the distinction between *mashal* and *nimshal*, signifier and signified:

> In the Kabbalistic mind-set, there is no gap between signifier and signified, for every *nimshal* becomes a *mashal* vis-à-vis another *nimshal*, which quickly turns into another *mashal*, and so on *ad infinitum* in an endless string of signifiers that winds its way finally (as a hypothetical construct rather than a chronological occurrence) to the in/significant, which may be viewed either as the signified to which no signifier can be affixed or the signifier to which no signified can be assigned.[30]

Later, in the eighteenth century, the Chabad Chasidim held that the *Tzimtzum*, the act of contraction and concealment (which according to the Lurianic Kabbalah wrought all distinctions and brought the world into being) was a *linguistic* act. As we saw in Chapter 2, Schneur Zalman, the founder of the Chabad movement, taught that the *Tzimtzum* is a revelation and concealment in which the infinite (*Ein-sof*) contracts itself *into language*, specifically into the combinations of letters that comprise the so-called "ten utterances of creation."[31] Such contraction into language is both a concealment and revelation of the divine essence.[32] The *Tzimtzum* inaugurates what amounts to an illusory distinction between language and the world, one that conceals the unity of *Ein-sof* but reveals an infinite multitude of finite objects and ideas. These notions suggest that by undoing the *Tzimtzum*, we can overcome the distinction between language and the world, and thereby return to the primal unity of the infinite God.

SIGN AND SIGNIFIED: RECLAIMING THE DISTINCTION

Linguistic constructivism is but one moment, in our analysis of representation, and we must proceed in the opposite direction from the one we have just taken. The point of view in which the signifier-signified distinction is overcome is itself dependent upon another point of view, the "traditional" one, *linguistic representationalism*, which holds the word-thing distinction to be inviolable and absolute.

Indeed, Derrida himself suggested that one could not use language at all without adopting the very word-thing distinction that he himself was at pains to deconstruct. One could not speak *about* anything unless one assumed a distinction between one's words and their subject matter. While it is true that when we refer to purported objects, referents, or signifieds we are only using language to refer to something that is constructed by consciousness and language. Consciousness, as Marc Taylor has observed, *consistently regards itself to be using language to refer to things outside of itself*, and in almost all cases it *obscures from itself the role it has in constructing such objects.*[33]

We can thus see that, while a clear distinction between the signifier and the signified is philosophically unsustainable, *we could neither speak nor function without assuming its validity.* To say anything at all we must set up a distinction between what we are saying and what we are speaking about, at least temporarily. For example, we must speak *about* copper, pencils, and tuberculosis; we must speak *about* language or *about* consciousness *constructing* objects and assume their independence from our words. The advocates of constructivism often speak about an organism's construction of its environment, or the interaction between two individuals' constructions of reality. However, the very process of articulating their position requires constructivists to make reference to objects or persons in a shared world, and this reveals their hidden assumption of an objective reality. Thus, the equivalence of signifier and signified is an idea that can be written or spoken about, but which can never become a working, active assumption in writing or speech. This is because the word/thing distinction is a necessary assumption of language, without which we would *literally* not be writing (or talking) *about* anything. Our everyday distinctions between truth and error, reality and illusion, and sense and nonsense—and indeed all of our fundamental arenas of discourse, including those of daily life, science, history, psychology, and so on)—ultimately depend upon the signifier-signified distinction. If we abandoned this distinction completely, we could neither speak nor think at all.

We therefore arrive at the paradoxical conclusion that for language to function at all, we must accept the validity of the two apparently contradictory propositions, "the signified is another signifier" and "the signified and signifier are distinct." *Linguistic constructivism turns out to be interdependent with linguistic representationalism.* On the one hand, the very distinction between words and things is itself dependent upon a use of language that overcomes or obliterates this distinction by permitting an indefinite chain of signifiers to locate, disambiguate, and construct a reference or "object"; on the other hand, in order to use language, in order to even think, we must assume the very distinction between words and things that our analysis has overcome.

These considerations lead to the conclusion that there is not only a *coincidentia oppositorum* or interdependence between words and things, but that there is also a second order *coincidentia oppositorum* between the *view* that words and things are absolutely distinct and the *view* that there is actually no distinction between them. As we have seen, the dissolution of the word-thing distinction is necessary for expressing the distinction itself, *as it is necessary that there be* an indefinite chain of signifiers to pinpoint the meaning of any word, phrase, or "thing." On the other hand, the word-thing distinction is necessary even for expressing its own transcendence, dissolution, or collapse. In grasping the interdependence of these seemingly contradictory points of view, we have moved one step closer to having a glimpse into the world as an undivided whole. On the view described here, the conceptual distinctions through which we view the world are a function of two opposing but necessary forms of consciousness. Our efforts to articulate a point of view or philosophy that explains the relationship of language to the world inevitably leads us to formulate two contrasting, even contradictory, propositions (i.e., that words are distinct from and constitutive of the things they signify) that turn out to be true and interdependent.

In recognizing this, we have an intellectual apprehension of a unified whole—a whole that unites the distinctions between language and world, subject and object, and which is very much akin to the union of opposites spoken of in various forms of mysticism and which is referred to as *Ein-sof* in the Kabbalah. By comprehending the *coincidentia oppositorum* between subject and object and between words and things, and further, through our understanding of the second order or meta-coincidence between the *views* that subject *can and cannot* be distinguished from object and that words *can and cannot* be distinguished from things, we gain rational insight into these mystically inspired propositions. We grasp how an integrated web of subject and object, language and world is implicit in each and every experience, linguistic utterance, proposition, and object. We also gain insight into how each experience and utterance rends that unity apart and helps create the multiplicity of things and ideas that constitute our finite world.

Earlier we saw how the deconstruction of the signifier-signified distinction can provide us with a hint of a unitary whole that antedates language or, alternatively, restores the unity between words and things, subject and object, that had been sundered by language. However, we can now see that since the very process of thought is predicated on the distinction between signifier and signified, our initial conception of unity is fleeting. This is because our deconstruction involves thoughts which necessarily again sunder the world into a multitude of entities and ideas distinct from and presumably represented by words. However, after grasping *the coincidence of opposites* between the demise of the signifier-signified distinction and its reclamation, we can now see that the world we apprehend is simultaneously both unity and difference, *and* this unity and difference is again united in a greater unity in *coincidentia oppositorum*. There is, in effect, an oscillation between the world's unity and its falling apart. It is with this that *coincidentia oppositorum* begins to take on its character as the "archetype of the Absolute."

THE DISSOLUTION OF THE DISTINCTION BETWEEN IDENTITY AND DIFFERENCE

The third foundational philosophical polarity is the distinction between *identity* and *difference*. Dennis McCort, in his book *Going Beyond the Pairs*, writes that "identity and difference" is the fundamental opposition or antinomy:

> If identity and difference are each themselves somehow also one, then all the other eternally warring pairs of opposites (truth/falsity, good/evil, beauty/ugliness, etc.) subsumed as it were under this template, come into ineffable harmony even as they *appear* to carry on the ancient struggle.[34]

McCort writes that Chandrakirti, an Indian commentator on the Buddhist philosophy of Nagarjuna, shows "clearly that the identity/difference issue is one intrinsic to language, in other words to the very means by which the issue itself is conceived and formulated and that therefore language can never suffice to resolve it."[35] I agree that the issue is grounded in representation. However, in contrast to McCort, I believe that we can get a handle upon the *coincidentia oppositorum* between identity and difference through an examination of how this distinction operates within our discourse.

As McCort suggests, if we can show that there is a coincidence of opposites between *identity* and *difference,* then we are *en route* to understanding why there should be a coincidence of opposites between *any* two opposing ideas or things. This is because if I assert that A has such and such an "identity," I am asserting that it does not have an identity different from A (that is, not A) and vice versa. Indeed, this is the general form of all propositions in classical logic: "If A, then not *not A*," or as Bishop Butler put it, "Everything is what it is and not another thing." If it turns out, on the contrary, that being something means that in addition to being itself it must also be what is different from itself, we have in effect overcome the classical assumption about the relationship between "A" and "not A" and again entered into a "logic" of *coincidentia oppositorum.*

Let us revisit the problem of identity and difference that we first raised in connection with Hegel in Chapter 3. (I am here returning to an argument that I detailed in my earlier book, *Kabbalah and Postmodernism.*[36]) Following Hegel's lead, we can begin by noting that the identity of anything exists only in virtue of its *difference* from all other things, and *moreover* from the position that it has in an entire system of distinctions. The knight figure in chess, for example, attains its identity by virtue of its position and role in the game of chess, which is defined in relation to the rules of the game and the positions and roles of the other pieces. Thus, the knight obtains its identity only through *what is different from it*. Identity is, in the case of the knight, determined by difference, not through a simple contrast (in the way "cold" is defined in contrast to "hot" or "near" in contrast to "far") but through a complex and systematic set of defining others. We can make the same argument regarding *location*. "Location" is meaningless in and of itself. A thing cannot be located at point X unless it is placed within the context of a host of other points that differ from and are coordinated with it. Derrida makes a similar argument with respect to a "present" experience, as he points out that "the present" has no identity apart from its relationship with a future and a past.[37] Just as "things" can only be identified through a regress of contextualizing words, a thing's "identity" can only be articulated via its position in a coordinated series of differences or "others" that are thus "internal" to the "identity" itself. What gives something its identity is its difference from all other things and its participation in a system of signification in which all things are inseparably related to and interdependent with one another. Something cannot be itself (identity) until it is part of a system or community of things that is *different* from itself. We can thus conclude that our reference to any one specific thing implicitly requires a reference to an entire world. Like the Kabbalists' *sefirot* and Gottfried Leibniz's monads, each "thing" in this world is conditioned by and reflected in each and every other thing.

The objects of our world—for example, silver, soap, wristwatches, and the Nile River—are what they are only because they are positioned within the complex system of language and meaning which constitutes our "world." In order to make sense of any of these randomly named "identities," one would need to be familiar with very significant portions of the world. Here we should note that for the *Zohar*, the dependence of identity on difference goes beyond the world and is even applicable to God. This is because when the Infinite (*Ein-sof*) is separated from creation: "He has no name of his own at all."[38] We might go so far as to assert that *identity* is not only constituted by *difference*, it is virtually "identical" with it.

However, upon further reflection, we soon realize that the reverse is true as well. While identity is dependent upon difference, difference is itself dependent upon identity. This is because *difference* is wholly reliant upon the fact that things hold their *identities* long enough for a distinction to obtain. We are left with a conceptual circle. A thing's identity can only be established through implicitly noting its difference from all other things, but such differences cannot obtain unless things already have identities through which such differences can be noted!

There is a second reason why difference is dependent on identity. Like identity, difference is enmeshed within a matrix of signification, and this matrix is itself a unified system of things and relations comprising a language, thus constituting a superordinate "identity" or "thing." A unified, integrated linguistic or "world" matrix is required in order for specific differences in quantity, location, quality, etc., to be articulated as actual. In the West, the systematic relations found in mathematics, cartography, measurement, color theory, etc., are all subsets of this "unified world." While the "world" may be systematized differently by various cultures, in each case it is systematized as an identity—a "world." Thus, the very notion of difference has as its necessary background an "identity," a unified system of signification.

We thus come to see that identity and difference are completely interdependent ideas. There is an historical irony in this conclusion, as difference was originally welcomed by deconstructionists as the means of undermining all systematic absolutes and identities. The irony we have uncovered is that difference, the great adversary of absolute identity and system, is itself wholly dependent upon "identity" for its status as difference. In short, difference only exists in contrast with individual identities but also only within a complex system of relations which itself constitutes a superordinate identity or "whole."

Commenting on the dissolution of the notion of "identity" in Hegel and William Blake, the Christian theologian Thomas Altizer writes:

> By moving through an actual death of its original form, every opposite will dialectically pass into its other: this self-annihilation will wholly dissolve the original identity of each opposite, and this process of the negation of the negation will draw all the estranged contraries of a fallen Totality into a final coincidence of the opposites.[39]

But here we must be careful to assert that our claim that the distinction between identity and difference is specious must be balanced by the opposite claim that without this very distinction there would be no language, no experience, and no world. This is obvious and requires no argument, since experience, language, and world are all dependent upon making identifications and distinctions. Indeed, without making such identifications and distinctions we could hardly make the argument that identity and difference are interdependent. However, without this very interdependence, the possibility of making such identifications and distinctions would be impossible. There is thus (as there was in connection with our deconstruction of the subject-object and signifier-signified distinctions) a "second order" *coincidentia oppositorum* between the deconstruction of the viability of the distinction between identity and difference and the necessity of maintaining it.

It is through an understanding of the necessary relationships that exist between and among all things—and especially the interdependence of opposing notions, specifically the *coincidentia oppositorum* between the basic polarities of subject and object, signifier and signified, identity and difference (as well as the second-order theses about the viability of these distinctions!)—that we are able *within language and reason to intuit an echo of the pre-linguistic unity* (which the Kabbalists spoke of as the distinctionless unity of opposites, the Infinite or *Ein-sof*). The question remains, however, whether, as Altizer suggests, the coincidence of opposites reaches a final endpoint or continues infinitely, approaching but never reaching a limit. I will return to this question in Chapter 7.

THE DISSOLUTION OF PHILOSOPHICAL PROBLEMS AND THE UNIFIED WORLD

How can these considerations about the nature of subject and object, representation and language, and identity and difference be applied to problems raised by philosophy, theology, and mysticism? Earlier I suggested that it is the very process of language and representation that produces distinctions within an original unity or whole, distinctions between kinds of entities in the world, between those entities and the minds that experience them, and distinctions between language and the things that it is said to represent. I have argued that evidence of the interdependence between apparently contradictory philosophical ideas provides us with an echo or trace of the original unity that was sundered by language—one that, in contrast to the claims of Stace, can be expressed discursively.

Philosophical controversies are stated in language, and for this reason opposing philosophical positions are colored by, if not rooted in, deeper formulations regarding the nature of language and representation. However, as these fundamental theses about language turn out to be interdependent ideas, the supervening philosophical positions are therefore also interdependent and complementary.

In this chapter, I have outlined two views regarding the nature of three foundational philosophical polarities. On one view, the traditional divide between subject and object, language and the world, and identity and difference, is untenable. The subject constructs the world, language is in effect "autonomous," and differences between and among ideas and entities merge together in an overarching systemic identity and unity.

On the other hand, we have also developed a viewpoint from which the reverse is true as well. On this second view, our subjective experiences are a function of the objects in the external world and the very purpose of a representational system is to differentiate among objects, and, moreover, to differentiate between subject and object, sign and signified, thinker and thing. Consciousness, if it is to be *aware of anything*, and language, if it is to function as language, must assume that the distinctions it makes "exist" in a world beyond representation. In short, it must assume the validity of difference.

I will focus for a moment on the distinction between language and the world. In utilizing language, we must, despite the potential indefinite reinterpretability of our signs, assume the existence of an "external" reality. Our consciousness, and moreover our language, operates on the assumption *that our experience is of, and language refers to, objects outside of itself.* As we have seen (following Taylor), consciousness and language even *obscures from itself its own role in constructing such objects.* Indeed, the assumptions that things exist outside of conscious awareness, beyond the language we use to refer to them, and that they have a distinct identity clearly distinguishing them from what they are not, is a bedrock common-sense assumption that enables us to function in an objective and intersubjective reality.

We have seen how the two views on the relationship between subject and object, language and the world, and identity and difference are interdependent. There is a *coincidentia oppositorum* between the views that there is no distinction between signifier and signified, subject and object, consciousness and the world, and the view that these distinctions are extra-linguistic and real. The two views are opposing, but interdependent ideas. Let us consider their philosophical implications:

(1) The first of these views (the unity of subject and object, sign and signified, and identity and difference) points to a reality suffused with mind, will, and meaning; the second (the separation of sign and signified, subject and object, identity and difference) points to an objective, likely material reality, one comprised of an infinite series of separate, intrinsically meaningless finite entities.

(2) The first of these views suggests that the world is an experiential (idealist) and linguistic/symbolic construction (constructivism); the second holds that the world is objective and completely independent of our experience and the language we use to describe it (objectivism).

(3) The first of these views leads to an objectivism in axiology and ethics, where meanings and values are infused in and thought to part of the very fabric of the cosmos; the second view, while it supports scientific objectivism and naturalism, leads to an ethical and axiological subjectivism or emotivism, where values are said to merely reflect the attitudes of individual minds that "color" but do not inhere within, an

objective reality.

(4) The first of these views leads to an assumption of human agency, and the capacity for independent rational inquiry, meaning-making and free will; the second view leads to philosophical determinism. The doctrine of "free will" is understandable within a constructivist/idealist framework where the world-forming linguistic or ideational acts of a human subject are regarded as foundational.[40] The human subject is then understood to freely (within certain limits) construct and act within and upon the world.

It is thus clear that the two views on the nature of the relationship between subject and object, words and things, and identity and difference tend to lead to opposing philosophical conclusions. However, when we understand that constructivist and objectivist views of the relationship between experience/language and the world are interdependent, the philosophical and theological positions and attitudes that follow from them are seen to be complementary and interdependent as well. On a deep level, language (within which the various philosophical positions are expressed) has two interdependent aspects, two aspects to its relationship with the world. It is the assumption that only one of these aspects is true that leads philosophers, theologians, and psychologists to adopt philosophical theses that exclude their contraries. When we grasp the interdependence of the two views—that is, when we understand that the unity of subject and object, sign and signified, and identity and difference is interdependent with these notions' radical separateness—we enter into the bilinear, dialectical thinking that enables us to embrace both idealism *and* materialism, constructivism *and* objectivism, free will *and* determinism, meaning *and* absurdity, etc.

Let us briefly review the last of these conclusions. From the point of view that it is the subject and the unified system of linguistic signifiers that constructs the world, the world is inherently and essentially meaningful. Indeed, on this view, there is no "world" apart from the meanings imparted by the system of signs. However, from the point of view of representationalism or objectivism, the world is a collection of external elements and events with no essential meaning. At the same time, because of the *coincidentia oppositorum* between our two perspectives, there is one world that is both meaningful and non-meaningful (or absurd), a conclusion which happens to coincide with human experience. Perhaps this way of thinking is behind Jung's claim in *The Red Book* that the "Supreme Meaning" involves a merging of sense and nonsense, meaning and absurdity.[41]

We have discussed how the dissolution of the hard and fast distinction between identity and difference has a concomitant deconstructive impact upon various philosophical controversies—each of which are predicated on the assumption that one can articulate a philosophical thesis or idea and insulate it from its converse or contradiction. Indeed, if matter cannot be adequately distinguished from mind, signified from sign, unity from difference, then the grounds for holding fast to one or another of the poles of any philosophical conflict are undermined. The dissolution of the distinction between identity and difference is the general case of which the various *coincidentia oppositorum* are instances. This is why McCort can claim that this dissolution leads to truce between all the pairs of opposites.

Let us take for an example the problem on the "Many and the One," an age-old philosophical dilemma of central concern to this book. Is the world essentially one of difference and multiplicity, or does it ultimately cohere into a unity within which all of its parts are integrally related and absorbed? We earlier concluded that on the one hand what is one and identical to itself is dependent for its identity on that from which it is different—and that this would be true even for an identity that is considered infinite and all-inclusive, as it too would be defined by its difference from the finite and not all-inclusive. Identity is thus dependent upon difference. However, difference is itself dependent upon a vast integrated system of relationships and representation, which itself constitutes an infinite identity. Thus, the world cannot be characterized as either the One or the Many, but rather as One/Many, Identity/Difference.

Similar analyses can be conducted with respect to a variety of philosophical polarities, including each of those considered in Chapter 5 in relation to the foundations of the conflicting paradigms in psychology. Generally speaking, the interdependence of philosophical polarities can be grasped by considering the fundamental dichotomies discussed in this chapter, the dichotomies between subject and object (idealism and objectivism), sign and signified (linguistic constructivism and represen-tationalism) and identity and difference. While the *coincidentia opposi-torum* between specific philosophical polarities, such as elementism and holism, facts and interpretations, introspection and public observability, etc., can be articulated without specific reference to these more general dichotomies, they ultimately rest upon them.

THEISM AND ATHEISM

What of the opposition between theism and atheism? Can this too be resolved or overcome via the notion of *coincidentia oppositorum*? As we have seen, certain Gnostics held that "God created men, and men created God,"[42] and the thirteenth-century Kabbalist Azriel of Gerona held that *Ein-sof* involves a union of faith and unbelief, suggesting the possibility of an interdependence between the views about the existence and non-existence of God. I will now provide a preliminary philosoph-ical analysis of this idea.

We begin by noting that if we adopt linguistic constructivism, one of our two perspectives on language, "God's existence" is rooted and guaranteed by the religious language within which it appears—for ex-ample, in the language of Scripture. This is because phrases like "God exists" or "there is but One God" are in this view "true" by virtue of their place in a series of signifiers that constitute a language game or form of life. While the term "God" appears in a wide variety of "language games," the "truth" of any positive theological assertion—within, for example, any of the world's religions—is established by the connec-tion between "God," "existence," and "truth" within the language game within which "God" appears. Individuals who *fully* participate in such language games, and the "form of life" concomitant to them, "know" God's existence like they know any other fact (for example, about the ultimate particle of physics) about which they may or may not have a direct acquaintance.

However, if we step outside the language-game within which God's existence is assured and take a strictly representational view of language, then it becomes highly questionable whether there is a thing in the world that answers to the word "God." Further, if we take a representionalist viewpoint on constructivism itself, we see that the language game within which God exists was itself created by human beings. From the point of view of linguistic constructivism or idealism, God exists by virtue of the place "God" has in a system of signifiers; but from the point of view of objectivism/linguistic reprentationalism, it is highly doubtful that anything in the cosmos answers to the name and scriptural description of God. Therefore, since the two points of view on language are interdependent and both true, *God both does and does not exist*. This amounts to a contemporary, if perhaps unsatisfying, gloss on the Gnostic paradox that God creates man and man creates God. It is unsatisfying precisely because the existence of God on this view is guaranteed by the very constructivist premise that leads us to deny that he *actually* exists beyond language. Further, taking a broad constructivist view, God appears to "exist" in some language games but not others—a rather humbling position for a god to find itself! He *exists* withn the linguistic and cultural complex of a religious discourse but cannot be shown to exist within *all* discourse, particularly within a scientific-objectivist language game and form of life. Because the linguistic-constructivist view denies the possibility of either producing a "master narrative" or getting beyond particular linguistic constructions, God cannot be coherently described as the "Absolute." Thus far, however, we do not have a very satisfactory solution to our theological problem.

Let us explore these ideas further by elaborating on the notion that belief in God is linked to a constructivist and idealist view of language and truth. Once "God" is established within a religious language game and form of life, philosophers and theologians often have the impulse to relocate "God" in another, broader philosophical language game, one presumably more comprehensive than the language-game of a particular scriptural tradition, and one that moves beyond linguistic constructivism to a form of objectivism. The attempt is made to identify the deity with notions that are either derived from other language games (for example, those of philosophy) or which *purport* to transcend all language games and all particular forms of life. "God" then becomes a signifier that presumably represents or at least points to something like "the origin of all being," "the source of all signification," "the process through which meaning is generated," and the like. From the point of view of traditional religion, this attempt to provide a philosophical sense to God fails not only because it is quite removed from the "personal God" of traditional religion but because it takes "God" out of the language game that is its original home, as if one were to attempt to define the king in chess from a perspective that stands outside the game of chess. Further, it identifies God with an abstract principle, as opposed to the "personal being" represented in Scripture. Yet, here we should note that it is just this abstract God, one that purports to lie outside the language-game, that was its original home (i.e., Scripture), that is indeed the God of many philosophers and mystics, some of whom suggest that he/she/it is a god above the God of Scripture.

Therefore, from the point of view of objectivist philosophy, and even from the perspective of alternative linguistic constructions, the God defined by Scripture and the language game/form of life of normative religion is a construction that cannot be sustained by anything beyond the community within which it has its origins. On this view, God is seen to be a "creation of man" and (for certain objectivists) a figment of human imagination. This is because the atheists and representationalists claim that they can find no object in the universe that corresponds to the religious term "God," and they refuse to participate in the religious language game and form of life within which this God is "real."

But what happens when we adopt the increasingly broad perspective that prompts the atheist to reject the language-games within which God is said to exist? At first, this broad perspective leads to the atheist's realism and objectivism; however, if we push it further, it leads to an acknowledgement that in *matters regarding ultimate origins one has no knowledge at all.* Broad-minded atheists, if they are to remain true to their broad thinking and open-economy of thought, are forced to acknowledge that they are neither the creator nor the foundation of their existence; if they remain true to an infinitely open mind, they must become open to the (philosophical or mystical) theist's efforts to contemplate an indescribable, unknowable "foundation of all," "origin of all significance," or "oigin beyond the ego."

One way of stating the *coincidentia oppositorum* between atheism and theism is as follows: Theism, because of its tendency to establish a specific and thus limited conception of God, leads to an atheism, which unmasks and rejects all specified, parochial, and limited conceptions of the world. Atheism, precisely because of its openness to infinite inquiry, thought, and experience leads to an open, indeterminate, and "infinite" understanding of the cosmos and its foundations, which comes very close to a mystical or philosophical conception of an infinite "God." The very "openness to all" that undermines the particularist claims of religion converges on a "mystical openness" to an unknown and perhaps unknowable origin and undefinable Absolute.

My thinking here is influenced by John Caputo's interpretation of Derrida's views on messianism.[43] Caputo understands Derrida as holding that a conception of the messiah within which it is possible that the he will arrive and be recognized in historical time is decidedly inferior to a conception within which the messiah symbolizes an ideal, a good and a form of justice for which we continually hope and wait. This is because any "messiah" who will arrive and be recognized in real time will participate in the finite, authoritarian, and closed economy of a faith which claims to distinguish truth from error and believers from infidels. By extension, any God who reveals "truth" in historical time to a select part of humanity, whose will is said to be known in some unqualified way, and whose acceptance is said to be the condition for personal and world salvation, is a God who restricts possibilities of thought, faith, feeling, and action, and who will in the process lead us into dogmatism and idolatry.

It is an exclusive, parochial, dogmatic view of God and truth that produces the Crusades, pogroms, and al Qaedas of this world. It is precisely such a view of God that leads free, open-minded, scientifically minded minds into atheism. We might therefore say in Hegelian fashion that when interrogated historically and conceptually, the God of normative religion passes over into atheism. Yet the very open-minded process of thought and experience that produces skepticism toward the God of theism and results in atheism produces an open-ended, continually revisable conception of "origins" and "foundations" that is the necessary ground for what can be regarded as a more adequate conception of the divine. Thus atheism returns to a theism in which God is conceived of in totally infinite, open-ended terms—the God of the mystics and negative theology (the god that can only be understood through "negative attributes" that define what it is not), the Pleroma of the Gnostics as opposed to their demiurge, the God *Ein-sof* of the Kabbalists as opposed to Yahweh, the God of Israel. Indeed, various mystics have affirmed that the God they experience in states of mystical union and ecstasy is so vast, so all-inclusive as to be undefinable and subject to no attributes whatsoever, an "Absolute" that one might well arrive at through an infinitely open rational inquiry. Thus "negative theology" has been closely linked to various mystical traditions. It is also a potential end-product of the open economy of thought and experience that produces atheism.[44]

ON THINKING THE WORLD WHOLE: THE APPLICATION OF THE PRINCIPLE OF *COINCIDENTIA OPPOSITORUM* TO ITSELF

In this chapter I have suggested that the process of grasping the interdependence of opposing philosophical positions, like the process of understanding the interdependence of opposing cartographic projections of the globe, enables us to form a rational intuition of a unified "whole" that was originally sundered by logic and language.

The view I have offered leads to the dissolution of fundamental philosophical controversies involving the oppositions between idealism and realism, constructivism and representationalism, and free will and determinism, as it entails that both poles of each of these oppositions are necessary and true. We must recognize, however, that the view that each pole of a philosophical opposition is valid and that such poles are interdependent forces us to conclude that the coincidence of opposites itself must be interdependent with its own opposite. Thus, the view I have developed in this chapter must be in *coincidentia oppositorum* with its opposite. This yields an even broader view that includes both the dissolution and continuance of philosophical controversies, as well as both an intuition of absolute unity and absolute difference, and so forth.[45] We thus find ourselves on the threshold of an infinite regress of interdependent philosophical claims.

There may indeed be an infinite regress of philosophical interdependencies, but this does not undermine the basic principle or vitiate the interdependencies that are "earlier" in the chain. In addition, it does not undermine the possibility that we can arrive at "regional interdependencies" that shed important light on the complementarities among theories in a relatively circumscribed arena—like the one we examined with respect to the field of psychology in Chapter 5. It does, however, suggest that there are no limits to the dialectic and that the resultant "whole" must be conceptualized as a limit that (again like Derrida's "messiah") can never actually be reached.

We can nonetheless continue to apply the principle of *coincidentia oppositorum* to what we might speak of as the infinite Absolute, an absolute that, as Hegel opined, must include both infinite unity and infinite difference if it is to be truly infinite. Whereas in the case of cartography we have a finite globe approximated by cartographic projections of a whole that we can fully circumscribe, in the case of philosophy we have an infinite "whole" that cannot be intuited and can only be approximated in language through a regress of *coincidentia*. While this may not leave us with a sense of complete intellectual satisfaction, it does have significant implications, including the need to maintain an open-economy of thought and experience with respect to foundational intuitions and ideas—and (perhaps) the need to adopt a logic in which "both true and false" and/or "neither true nor false" are accepted.[46]

Again, it is important to remember that we have not here arrived (nor will we ever arrive) at an ultimate viewpoint. Indeed, each time one arrives at a seemingly conclusive dichotomy, new dichotomies appear, and each is a pair of incomplete halves necessary to complete a whole, which is in turn incomplete, and so forth. According to Derrida, the demand for a single "truth" is the demand for an objectivity that would transcend actual discourse, obliterate otherness, and deny death.[47] He describes how the demand for objectivity and unity "dispenses with passage through the world,"[48] a world that creates fragmentation and otherness.[49] Howard Coward, in his book *Derrida and Indian Philosophy*, holds that for Derrida "the tension of the opposites...is the hallmark of the real." Coward argues that according to Derrida, "Identifying oneself with either of the terms that make up these oppositions...is the trap of language that must be overcome."[50] Derrida holds, however, that one must not leave language to avoid this trap but must stay equipoised between the opposites, continually deconstructing our own and language's tendency to identify the real with one and then the other pole of an opposition.[51] Only in this way can the real be experienced as the middle point. Coward sees Derrida adopting a perspective that is quite close to Hegel's: Hegel explicitly stated that we cannot emphasize unity at the expense of difference and that we must continually think both poles of each.

While they may cut against the grain of common sense and language, the ideas I have articulated in this chapter can be grasped *within language*. In grasping them we have entered into what might be spoken of as "rational mysticism," a parallel, within reason and language, to the "overcoming of distinctions" that is the hallmark of non-logical, non-representational mystical experience.

TRUTH AND REALITY

What happens to such ultimate concepts as "truth" and "reality" when we understand them from our "rational mystical" perspective? Philosophers have long understood that the terms "truth" and "reality" are "essentially contestable" concepts, notions of such singular value and significance that their very meaning varies according to one's worldview. We have seen that from a materialist perspective, reality is identified with the natural world, whereas ideas, concepts, and values are understood as approximations to or subjective responses to nature. Idealist thought, on the other hand, identifies "reality" with concepts and (in some cases) values and sees the material world as a mere instantiation of ideas, a derivative product of spirit or a formless and empty substance awaiting the stamp of mind. We have seen how these two points of view are complementary and interdependent—each, as Jung suggested, "half" a world.[52]

There is, however, another dialectic involving the "real" that should command our attention, one that is suggested by certain trends in recent European philosophy.[53] In this dialectic, a "real" that accords with what is articulated, conceptualized, and known is contrasted with a "real" that breaks open all discourse and theory and intrudes upon our awareness in a manner that is completely unanticipated. According to the latter pole of this opposition, the "real" that is a function of conventional thought and discourse—and accords with both "common sense" and our best scientific theories—*provides us with an illusory belief that we have grasped reality, when in fact all we have done is replaced reality with our conventional discourse about it.* On this view, all of our theoretical constructions (idealism, materialism, etc.) are on the near side of a chasm between the *constructed* and the *real.* From this perspective, the "real" (Lacan) is a pre-linguistic, pre-conceptualized, undigested "monstrous" (Derrida), a "traumatic" *reality* that renders all of our theory and discourse inoperative. This "real," for example, is the reality of trauma, suffering, and death, in the face of which all our theories and discourse (whether philosophical, theological, or scientific) are wholly inadequate. This is the "real" of the unknown divine energy that, as we saw in our discussion of the Lurianic Kabbalah in Chapter 2, produces the "Breaking of the Vessels," shatters the *Sefirotic archetypes*, and with them, all our concepts and values. On this view, the real, rather than being the "known," is precisely what is "unknown," breaking apart what we believe to be our knowledge at any given point of time. This dialectic of the real supplements the idealism-materialism dichotomy described above and thus provides a second axis through which we can understand "truth" and "reality."[54] This latter "real" is irrational and deconstructive, and essentially unknown.

The two "reals"—what I have termed the "conventional" and the "deconstructive"—are depicted schematically in Figure 6.1.

Figure 6.1: Conventional and Deconstructive "Reality"

The Conventional "Real"	Real	Illusion
Known (Rational)	The "Real" is that which accords with our best understanding and theory	Our concepts are constructions that provide us with the illusion that we have grasped reality
Unknown (Irrational)	The "Real" is that which intrudes, traumatizes, and breaks through conventional discourse	"Illusion" is that which does not accord with conventional discourse
The Deconstructive "Real		

Just as form and instance are related to one another as a *coinciden-tia oppositorum*, there is a coincidence of opposites between "reals" that respectively attach to knowledge and the unknown. As we saw in Chapter 5, knowledge and the unknown are reciprocally determinative in several ways. One of these is the observation that all knowledge, all science, proceeds, as it were, out of mystery. As Hegel argued, the history of human endeavor is one in which the forest of mystery is continuously pushed back in favor of the clearing of knowledge. With each advance, however, there is an acknowledgment of a further "unknown," which itself then becomes the subject of new investigation and an awareness that what was once known to be fact, was at least in part, error. Natural scientists are all too familiar with the notion that truth itself is a species of "error" that only approximates an ideal. All so-called scientific "truths" of the past and present have been, or will be, revealed to be *errors* of one form or another.

Further, since the very structure of human awareness limits it to some specific "presence" or content, there is always something, some potential content, that exists beyond its reach; such content being notable for its "absence," the fact that it is unknown. On a more psychological level, while the content of consciousness changes from one moment to the next, the general dialectic between "presence" and "absence," between known and unknown, always remains. It is thus part of the concept of consciousness or mind that there is something not yet specified that is absent, beyond awareness or unconscious. Hence, it is part of the very concept of the known (consciousness) that there is yet something unknown (unconscious) or undiscovered.

However, the reverse is true as well. What is unknown can only be articulated against a background of what (is believed) to be known. The "real" in the postmodern sense only exists as an intrusion from beyond the "symbolic order." It is, by definition, that which has not (yet) been assimilated by our categories and schemas. The "ruling discourse," in effect defines the boundaries, which through relief, give rise to *an unassimilated reality.* Kabbalistically, it is only because we have vessels that can be broken by the divine light, that this light has its *real* impact upon the world.

DIALECTICAL ONTOLOGY

In all of what has been said thus far, I am attempting to provide a window into the dialectical logic of *coincidentia oppositorum*. Figures 6.1 and 6.2 graphically illustrate this logic and provide a means for working out aspects of the *coincindentia oppositorum* archetype or idea. The figures can be utilized to illustrate some general features of the coincidence of opposites. Figure 6.2 presents the interdependence of idealism and materialism, a form of "objectivism" discussed earlier in this chapter.

Figure 6.2: Idealism and Materialism

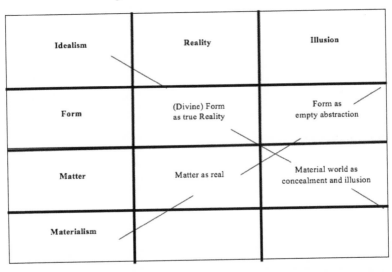

As is evident in both Figures 6.1 and 6.2, opposing metaphysical or epistemological notions are placed on the vertical axis (in Figure 6.2 "Form" and "Matter"); two other opposing metaphysical or epistemological notions are placed on the horizontal axis ("Reality" and "Illusion"). The resulting four cells contain descriptions of how each of the opposing notions on one axis are instantiated in terms of each of the opposing notions on the other axis, yielding four cells. For example, "Form" as the "true Reality" occupies the upper left cell, and "Matter" as "illusion" occupies the lower right cell. The diagonals yield two opposing philosophical or metaphysical points of view (in Figure 6.2, Idealism versus Materialism). The intersection of the diagonal axes graphically expresses the notion that these general points of view exist in *coincidentia oppositorum*, precisely because the polar concepts (form and matter, reality and illusion) that generate them are not mutually exclusive but are interdependent ideas. (The same general pattern holds for Figure 6.1.)

We are now in a position to further advance our understanding of the whole or "Absolute" that follows from what I have called the "archetype of *coincidentia oppositorum*." We might suggest that this Absolute is the point of dialectical intersection or transformation, where concepts swing into their apparent contraries or opposites. This point of view on the Absolute was, as we saw in Chapter 1, anticipated by Schelling, who understood the "Absolute" as the place of "indifference" or "vanishing point" of all distinctions and difference.[55]

In presenting these *coincidentia oppositorum* in diagrammatic form, I am suggesting that the "world," instead of being comprised of "realities," "truths," and "entities" understood through the lens of a particular ontology or metaphysics, is better understood as composed of the dialectical inter-dependencies represented in these figures. I am proposing what might be referred to as a "metaphysics" of *coincidentia oppositorum*, a metaphysics that enables us to intuit the sort of whole that mystics have described as the union of all contradictions, and which, for example, the Kabbalists designated with the term *Ein-sof.* These diagrams, however, are *static representations of an infinite dynamic*, as each term within each diagram enters into another dialectic and so on, *ad infinitum*. The process can be multiplied indefinitely, revealing the dialectical potential in all of our concepts—and I would propose the dialectical nature of the broadest possible concept, the Absolute.

RETURN TO MYSTICISM: "FORMAL INDICATORS," UNITY, AND DIFFERENCE IN RELATION TO THE ABSOLUTE

Strictly speaking, terms like *"Ein-sof," "*the Pleroma," and *"Brahman-Atman,"* which presumably refer to the Absolute, cannot be used as a signifier or thought of as referring to a signified, as one who does so enters into the very bifurcating, sundering process which these terms are meant to transcend. To use *"Ein-sof"* as a word with the intention of referring to an infinite, sublime, or exalted object is to have it take its place as one term among others in a system of differences. As a result, *Ein-sof* is effectively reduced to the role that the term *"Ein-sof"* plays in the language of Jewish mysticism or in the conceptual scheme described in this book. For this reason, *"Ein-sof"* can only be used as what Martin Heidegger termed a "formal indicator" of what is whole and unsundered, and which therefore cannot be directly pointed to, referred to, or spoken about. However, even using *"Ein-sof"* with this qualification assumes the risk of it becoming just another word or thing. Perhaps it is for this very reason that the Kabbalists insisted that *Ein-sof* is *Ayin*—that is, no-thing—and why they held that it cannot be represented but can only be hinted at through forgetting or silence. As the proto Kabbalistic work *Sefer Yetzirah* had counseled, "Restrain your mouth from speaking and your heart from thinking, and if your heart runs let it return to its place."[56]

Similarly, in describing the path to enlightenment that is offered in Vedanta Hinduism, Heinrich Zimmer suggests that, properly speaking, to talk about Brahman as the "Eternal Essence" is misleading. He writes,

> This great idea was only meant to inspire the beginner and guide the advanced pupil on the road to the true, concept-shattering experience. In itself, in the end, it proves to be an impediment. Where it stands, the initiate stands and is thus kept within the realm of contradictory pairs of opposite; for the notion of Eternity demands its opposite, that of the transient,

the phenomenal, the illusory world. And so the initiate who has found "Eternity" still is entangled in the devious net of myā.[57]

Even accepting the dichotomy of "bondage and release" leads one into error. In the *Avadhūta Gītā,* we read, "I am the all-pure divine essence (*brahman*), devoid of all differentiating, limiting, and mutually conflicting qualities (*guna*). Then how should there be any anything like bondage or release?"[58] As Zimmer puts it,

> Positing Brahman involves the positing of the experience of liberation; positing liberation involves automatically the positing of bondage; and when this pair-of-opposites is posited all the other pairs-of-opposites are posited too. Illusion, ignorance, the world of birth and death become thus reestablished and nothing has been gained. The speculating mind has again snared itself in its own web of thought.[59]

A similar notion is expressed in the philosophy of Mahayana Buddhism where, according to Zimmer,

> there is an unremitting insistence that so long as one can see a distinction between nirvana and the sphere of birth and death, one is still in a state where distinctions are made, and not a Bodhisattva, not yet a being "whose nature is enlightenment."[60]

Hegel tells us that the Absolute *can never be articulated in a proposition.* Based on this we might say that it is the very *process of the dialectic*, one that ultimately merges with an open economy of thought and experience, that we can identify with "the whole." (I will examine this view more closely in Chapter 7.) In his *Tractatus*, Wittgenstein proposed that there are things *that can be shown and not said.* Like Heidegger, he suggests that language can point to things that cannot be stated propositionally. Such is the "archetype of the Absolute" that emerges from our consideration of the opposites. *Coincidentia oppositorum* is an archetype that points to an open economy of thought and experience, one that traverses reason and unreason, reality and the imagination, science and art, philosophy and poetry, and all other conceptual polarities.

In referring to *coincidentia oppositorum* as the "archetype of the Absolute," I am suggesting that the interdependence of opposites is a *logical echo of the a-logical primal unity*, which has been dichotomized and fragmented by language and logic. For example, the recognition that words are both (1) fully interdependent with, and (2) distinct from things, and that these two propositions are themselves fully interdependent, provides a trace or echo within language and thought of the unity that had been sundered by language and thought to begin with. A philosophical inquiry into and understanding of these *coincidentia oppositorum* is a vehicle through which one can temporarily undo the bifurcating tendencies of language and intellect and in doing so effectively move backwards towards an intuition of the original unity.

Here I would like to return for a moment to how the "ascent to the mystical One" was understood in the Kabbalah. For the Kabbalists, the return to an intuition of the primal unity is all the more exalted after one has passed through the dichotomies and multiplicities of the temporal world. This is because consciousness of the restored unity is not merely an awareness the original divine oneness but is actually among the acts that complete and perfect this oneness (*Ein-sof*) itself. This, of course, accords with Hegel's recognition that the Infinite must pass through and include the finite, and that an absolute unity must be inclusive of difference.

The Jewish mystics believed that it is the task of humankind to recognize and even facilitate the distinctions within the finite world, while at the same time to comprehend the unity of all things through an appreciation of the coincidence of opposites. As we saw in Chapter 2, the Chabad Chasidic thinker, Rabbi Aaron ha-Lévi held that the divine purpose is only achieved when reality is revealed in all its multiplicity, "as separated essences, and that they nevertheless be unified and joined in their value."[61] An important implication of this general view is that in disciplines as diverse as philosophy, psychology, and theology, we must (1) investigate our subject matters in all their detail, (2) develop specific ideas and perspectives, (3) but nonetheless guard against fragmented, dichotomous "either/or" thinking that forestalls the possibility of integration by permanently excluding ideas that are opposed to our own. Indeed, it is my view that we must seek integration in our thinking by being open to the possibility that contrasting and even opposing ideas and points of view are complementary. As we have seen, among the candidates for such complementarity in philosophy and theology are theism/atheism, being/nothingness, freedom/necessity, and (as will be discussed in greater detail in Chapter 7), reason/unreason. One should also be open to such complementarity and integration in more "mundane" arenas such as human interpersonal, social, and political relationships. From a Kabbalistic perspective, in seeking to comprehend the whole we must fully articulate oppositions while simultaneously grasping how they are permeable to and interdependent with one another. In doing this, we not only comprehend but actually participate in producing the "unity of opposites" that according to the Jewish mystics perfects *Ein-sof*, the Infinite God.

Kabbalistic thinking is bilinear. As *Sefer Yetzirah* says regarding the *Sefirot*, a Kabbalistic idea is one whose end is wedged in its beginning and its beginning in its end. This is well illustrated in the Kabbalist's own understanding of *Ein-sof*, which is both the origin of everything and only realized once it is manifest in a world—a world which, from *Ein-sof's* initial perspective, is totally illusory and unreal. For the Kabbalists, the supreme reality is defined and completed by its end, an end that from the point of view of the beginning is an illusion. Just as there is a starting point from the supernal heights, there is also a starting point from the worldly (and even infernal) depths. Kabbalistic thinking can be understood through a musical analogy. We might say that in the Kabbalah there is a theistic melody line that exists in counterpoint with an atheistic one. There is a melody line that asserts that God creates man, which is in counterpoint with a melody line where man is said to create God; there is a melody which announces that the past generates all that is present and future, in harmony with one which declares that the future constructs both the present and the past. For the Kabbalah, *a true view of the world must involve listening to two melody lines at once, or thinking two or perhaps more seemingly opposing thoughts as harmonious rather than discordant*. Indeed, it is such harmony, symbolized in the Kabbalah by the *sefirah Tiferet/Rachamim* (Beauty/Compassion), that is identified with "The Holy One."

As we have seen, the antinomous yet harmonious nature of philosophical ideas, a cardinal principle in much Eastern thought, is accepted by mystics of various traditions and was acknowledged by a handful of Western philosophers from Heraclitus to Hegel. These philosophers paved the way for the insight that the oppositions between words and things, consciousness and its objects, self and other, as well as the oppositions between a host of opposing philosophical ideas are ephemeral and collapse under close scrutiny.

While in this work I have endeavored to give sense to the notion of "The Absolute" that is indicated by such terms as *"Ein-sof," "Brahman-Atman,"* and "The Pleroma," this Absolute can never be fully defined or circumscribed. The ideas that we are discussing thus imply that there is no single, objective truth outside of the fallible notion of a "single objective truth" that exists in some "language games" and enters into the dialectics we are discussing. These ideas suggest that we are always simultaneously in truth and in error, reality and illusion, and so forth. Further, they suggest that error and illusion are not only necessary for truth but that they are each to be valued as well as disvalued. Our concepts are always in flux, and it is only for certain limited purposes that we can *freeze* things and provide our conceptual matrix with a (relatively) fixed sense. The error of traditional metaphysics is to mistake a single "frozen" take on the cosmos for the cosmos itself. In this book, I have attempted to *unfreeze* things and to introduce a form of thinking that does not rest in any particular, reified, or static point of view. While the initial results of such an enterprise may be confusing and even dizzying, this is the price that one must pay to be freed from more conventional (and limiting) modes of thought. A certain ungroundedness is a necessary consequence of any attempt to think of the world as a whole.

CHAPTER SEVEN

INTIMATIONS OR FABRICATIONS
OF AN ABSOLUTE?

CHALLENGES TO THE DOCTRINE OF *COINCIDENTIA OPPOSITORUM*

In the previous chapter, I argued that the coincidence of opposites between significant polarities in philosophy, in particular the polarities of
subject and object, words and things, and identity and difference, provides an echo or trace of the singular "one" that mystics of various eras
and cultures have held to be the reality underlying the world of appearances. In this final chapter, I take up a series of questions and challenges
related to this thesis and the coincidence of opposites in general. Among
these challenges, one I referred to earlier, is that the dialectical process
informing the *coincidentia oppositorum* archetype must be applied to
the coincidence of opposites itself. In this chapter I will consider several
additional challenges to the philosophical perspective I have outlined
in this work: (1) the charge that coincidence of opposites yields a purely linguistic, and hence illusory, resolution of philosophical problems,
(2) doubts about the coherence of the notions of "hard reality" and a
unified world or "One," (3) concerns regarding the misuse of dialectics to achieve a "content" (as opposed to "process") understanding of
the "Absolute," (4) concerns that *coincidentia oppositorum* violates the
laws of reason and logic, (5) issues pertaining to the nature of the God
concept that arises from the *coincidentia* archetype, and (6) questions
regarding the consequences of the coincidence of opposites for ethics
and the problem of evil. My responses to each of these questions will

be provisional since, as should by now be abundantly clear, the coincidence of opposites itself is inimical to final philosophical resolutions. Indeed, the very notion of *coincidentia oppositorum* implies that there will and should be challenges to both its significance and application, and, further, that such challenges have validity and are indeed necessary for a fuller understanding of *coincidentia oppositorum* itself.

A LINGUISTIC ILLUSION?

I have argued that a close examination of fundamental oppositions in philosophy, theology, and psychology reveals these oppositions to be expressions of interdependent as opposed to contradictory ideas. I have explored this interdependence with respect to such fundamental dichotomies as idealism and realism, language and the world, unity and difference, constructivism and objectivism, and free will and determinism; I have also argued that there are interdependencies between such higher level philosophical propositions such as (1) there is and (2) there is not, an inviolable distinction between language and the objects it presumably represents. I have suggested that many abstract philosophical and meta-theoretical controversies in philosophy and psychology result in a *coincidentia oppositorum* whereby each pole of the controversy is understood to be true and dependent on its contrary. I have also argued that realizing this provides insight into the higher order unity that stands behind the world of difference. Finally, I have attempted to demonstrate that it is language and representation which generates theoretical dichotomies, that the coincidence of opposites reverses the sundering effect of language and in this way enables one to intuit the "echo" of an original unity, prior to its being fragmented by representation. This "echo of the Absolute," I have said, is evident in the collapse of the subject-object, signifier-signified, and identity-difference distinctions.

However, a very different take on the implications of the coincidence of opposites is possible—one which suggests that our so-called "resolution" of philosophical controversies through the *coincidentia* principle is an illusion—one created by the malleability of language and our capacity to arbitrarily define terms and, in effect, "say what we like" regarding philosophical ideas.

Such a "Wittgensteinian" approach, instead of crediting the coincidence of opposites with a passage to a synoptic view of the world or the "Absolute," suggests that philosophical propositions and theses say nothing of significance at all and that their lack of meaning is evident in the very observation that they are both "true and false" and imply the very propositions that they are intended to exclude. It can be argued that while both materialism and idealism, for example, might be regarded by some to make claims about the deep structure of reality, they actually say nothing of genuine significance at all. One might argue, along the lines of Ludwig Wittgenstein, that in matters of such great generality and abstraction we can "say what we like," simply by virtue of a subtle (and perhaps covert) redefinition of our key terms. In the case of materialism, we associate "reality" with the *object* of perception and knowledge, whereas in the case of idealism we redefine "reality" by associating it with perception, experience, or the epistemological process. Since both perception and its objects are necessary for one to make assertions about concrete, "real" things, the two forms of "reality" become "interdependent." However, this seemingly profound solution to a presumably "deep" philosophical problem is actually a pseudo-solution to a pseudo-problem, resulting from our subtly shifting the meaning of a key term, "reality." On this view, the very notion of contrasting philosophical views being in *coincidentia oppositorum* is itself a product of our covert linguistic manipulations. Further, the very idea that there is a "single reality" that all our representations are "about" (as will be discussed in more detail below) is itself the product of a particular and arbitrary definition of "reality," one that in turn differs from the definitions we utilized with respect to materialism and idealism.

On this deflationary view, *the cartographic analogy*, which has played a critical role in the argument made in this book, provides us with a misleading picture: It assumes that, just as there is a globe that serves as a foundation for each cartographic projection, there is an underlying mind or world that is the subject of each of our philosophical representations, an assumption that is without warrant except perhaps within the context of our "say what you like" understanding of the "real." The coincidence of opposites, rather than being a pathway to an intuition of the Absolute, is thus itself reduced to a *reductio ad absurdum* argument against the very controversies in philosophy that it purports to resolve.

This is certainly a line of thought that might be said to follow from the idea that philosophical ideas are a function of our forms of representation. If philosophical theses are products of language, and philosophical language has no direct access to anything beyond itself, then the assumption of an underlying world becomes just one more "language game," one more piece of representation that is not grounded in anything but itself.

A response to this critique can be found in the observation that philosophical propositions actually have practical, "real-world" significance and that their unity via the coincidence of opposites resolves critical problems that reach beyond philosophy. To see how this is the case, we can return to our consideration of the philosophical assumptions underlying various psychological paradigms that were outlined in Chapter 5. There we saw that philosophical assumptions make a *crucial difference* for the psychologies that are constructed on their bases, and that psychologies constructed on the foundations of various combinations of philosophical points of view each provide a foundation for programs of research and practice—programs that yield positive and indeed practical and clinically significant findings that are far from meaningless or trivial. We saw, for example, that taken together the working assumptions of materialism, individualism, factualism, determinism, and elementism serve as the foundation for a potent biological psychology that not only provides us with scientific data regarding the nature of human behavior, thought, and emotion, but also has major implications for psychiatric practice. On the other hand, the assumption of free will, holism, hermeneutics, etc., yields an "existential" or humanistic psychology, one that has produced understanding and "practical wisdom" regarding human action, relationships, and meaning. While we may "say what we like" regarding the basic philosophical issues that underlie the different paradigms in psychology, such "orienting decisions" have major empirical and practical implications for the psychologies we develop on their basis and are hardly, to borrow another Wittgensteinian metaphor, "wheels that spin but which are not part of the mechanism." Philosophical assumptions in psychology are frequently tacit rather than expressed. However, they are not only important gears in the "mechanism" of psychological theory but are arguably the very engines that drive the enterprise of psychological description, research, theory, and practice. That the assumptions underlying different psychological paradigms are interdependent hardly suggests that these assumptions are meaningless or, more radically, that psychology itself is meaningless and should be dissolved. Rather, it suggests (as I have argued in Chapters 5 and 6) that there is indeed a unified whole (*the psyche*) that each perspective in psychology—like each of the varying flat projections of the earthly globe in cartography—represents in a fruitful but incomplete way. The same, I believe, holds for the opposing yet interdependent theses of philosophy in general—theses that apply not only to the psyche but to reality as a whole.

I believe the philosophical view that the truth of opposing philosophical theses demonstrates that they are devoid of meaning suggests, without intending to do so, something of philosophical and spiritual importance. What this view suggests is that as we approach the "apex" of the "One" (where we grasp the interdependence of the most abstract philosophical ideas) difference fades and meaning diminishes, in effect merging with nonsense. This is a broad implication of the *coincidentia* idea, one that as we have seen was suggested by C. G. Jung in *The Red Book*, when he said that "The Supreme Meaning" is the "melting together of sense and nonsense."[1] We might further propose that the doctrine of *coincidentia oppositorum* reveals that philosophical significance is to be found (as J. N. Findlay suggested[2]) in the middle regions of our dialectical "ascent"—where connections are plentiful but distinctions are still evident—rather than in the lower regions where there are few or no connections between ideas, or at the apex where everything becomes so connected as to merge into an all-encompassing but in effect "meaning-less" "One."

"HARD REALITY" AND THE UNDIFFERENTIATED "ONE"

I have argued throughout this book that an "original" or "primal" unity is sundered by representation, and that an "echo" or "trace" of this "One" can be rationally intuited through a comprehension of the *coincidentia oppositorum* that can be discerned with respect to polar oppositions in philosophy. In doing so, I place myself in direct opposition to much recent, especially European, philosophy, which (as did Wittgenstein) holds that any intuition of an "Absolute," "foundation," or "One," rational or otherwise, is impossible. Jacques Derrida, for example, in proffering his notion that "*differánce* is older than being"[3] staked out a claim that philosophy is deluded when it seeks a foundation in an original being or undifferentiated singularity. More recently, Slavoj Žižek, in part through a radical reading of G. W. F. Hegel, has argued that multiple philosophical (as well as political, aesthetic, and historical) perspectives are incommensurable, and their reconciliation or synthesis impossible. According to Žižek, it is this very impossibility or unbridgeable "parallax gap" between points of view that provides us with the closest thing to an intuition of what Immanuel Kant spoke of as the "transcendental object" or "thing-in-itself."[4] In Žižek's view, the world is riddled with contradiction, and it is this "negative" appraisal, as opposed to any metaphysical positivity or synthesis, that is both the chief legacy of Hegel and the closest approximation to "truth." Further, for Žižek, it is precisely (and only) this negative conclusion that opens the space for spontaneity, creativity, freedom, and political and societal transformation.

In two major works, *The Parallax Gap* and *Less Than Nothing,*[5]

Žižek argues that there is no "hard reality" beyond the world of appearances, and that the notion of a singularity, unity, or One is a mirage created by language. Indeed, Žižek interprets Hegel (in almost Wittgensteinian terms) as holding that "reality" is nothing more or less than what we might put into it and say about it, and that the metaphysical foundations we believe ourselves to discover in philosophy are in fact retroactive, creative fictions.

Žižek further argues that there cannot be a "One," as "one" is a creation of reflection and language, and language already assumes a bifurcation or "two," presumably between words and what these words are about (signifier and signified). He writes:

> Whenever we read a description of how an original unity becomes corrupted and splits, we should remember that we are dealing with a retroactive ideological fantasy which obfuscates the fact that such an original unity never existed, that it is a retroactive projection generated by the process of splitting....[6]

While Žižek makes this point in reference to original unities within the social and cultural sphere, his point applies equally well to his understanding of unities in metaphysics—which, in his view, are an "ideological fantasy."[7]

The question of whether there is a "One" or any reality underlying appearances is obviously critical to the entire enterprise of reconciling the opposites with the goal of attaining "syntheses" in order to approach a mystical or philosophical "Absolute." Žižek, following Kojin Karatani, argues that the project of pursuing reconciliations between philosophical polarities is deeply misguided and that the antinomies and contradictions one encounters in philosophy should be regarded as irreducible facts about the world as opposed to problems to be resolved through philosophical synthesis.[8] Indeed, Žižek holds that if there is any sense to be given to the "real," it is to be understood as the very gaps that prevent us from attaining coherent understanding. While at times Žižek gives his assent to the postmodern (and on his view, Hegelian) notion that the opposition between appearance and reality must be abandoned because reality is itself an appearance,[9] at other times he holds that reality is neither appearance nor some inaccessible "thing-in-itself"; it is, rather, the split or "gap which prevents our access to it"[10] For Žižek, "there is no final reality"[11] or underlying world upon which we take perspectives. Truth or reality is "the very gap or passage which separates one perspective from another" and which makes these perspectives incommensurable.[12] While things are not all relative, the "truth" is "perspectival distortion" as opposed to some neutral entity that we take perspectives upon.[13] Indeed, for Žižek, the dynamic of Hegel's dialectic describes such a series of "vacillating semblances."[14]

According to Žižek, when we are confronted with an antinomy we should neither attempt to reduce one side of the antinomy to the other nor enact some sort of dialectical synthesis. Rather, we should simply "assert antinomy as irreducible, and conceive the point of radical critique not as a certain determinate position as opposed to another position, but as the irreducible gap between the positions itself, the purely structural interstices between them."[15] Žižek again follows Karatani in holding that this is how we should read Kant's thing-in-itself—i.e., as a reality or truth that is encountered in parallax or difference. The gap, Žižek suggests, is itself the "transcendental" dimension in Kant's philosophy, yet it is one completely lacking in substantial being. Žižek further describes the parallax of the "Lacanian real," which he says has "no positive substantial consistency, [as] it is just the gap between the multitude of perspectives on it.[16]

Žižek describes the parallax gap as that which "separates the one from itself."[17] This, of course, suggests that the one is indeed two. He holds that the parallax gap is evident in the wave particle duality of quantum physics as well as in the gap between a first-person sense of self-awareness and the third-person "emptiness" of what is inside the human skull.[18] With his notion of the parallax gap, Žižek appears to be creating a philosophical category out of what Jacques Derrida spoke of as *differánce*. In all of this, Žižek holds a philosophical position that is in many ways the inverse of the philosophical mysticism that I have set forth in this book.

How are we to respond? With regard to Žižek's philosophy of *gaps as opposed to syntheses*, it should be pointed out that throughout his work, Žižek himself actually makes use of numerous cases of the coincidence of opposites in arriving at his philosophical conclusions. For example, he discusses what amounts to a *coincidentia oppositorum* between contingency and necessity in the philosophy of Hegel. Žižek explains this by first arguing that, for Hegel, the very process of reflection, which is the return of mind or spirit to its hidden foundation in nature, actually "produces what it returns to.[19] He points out that, in the *Phenomenology of Spirit*, Hegel makes it clear that our path toward truth is part of the truth itself. As a result, the *contingent* processes of human thought and reflection actually produce the *necessary* "essences" that reflection "discovers." At the same time, our contingent thought processes are grounded in these very essences. This, we might observe, is the same sort of circular interdependence that, as we have seen, characterizes the relationship between subject and object, and words and things. *In fact, it is the very same interdependence.* By appealing to this interdependence, this *coincidentia oppositurum*, Žižek is able to conclude that the Hegelian dialectic is both a logical and creative process, another coincidence of opposites. As Žižek puts it, "This is what it means to reproduce a process through its dialectical analysis: to reintroduce possibility and ontological openness into what retroactively appears as closed succession determined by its immanent necessity."[20] There is, according to Žižek, an interdependence between the logic and imagination, and this interdependence is brought out in the Hegelian dialectic.

Hegel's critics, Žižek points out, typically understand him as holding that contingency is a function of necessary essences, as if Hegel could infer the specifics of our concrete contingent world from necessary principles. However, Žižek claims that what Hegel's critics fail to grasp is that there is a *relationship in the opposite direction as well*, in which necessity or essence is nothing more than an elevated or generalized form of contingency. Žižek makes the connection with Martin Heidegger, who holds that essence is something that is historically dependent and appears only via certain epochal disclosures through language, which Heidegger refers to as the "house of being." Žižek writes that according to Heidegger, it is again language that constructs or produces essence.[21]

While Žižek claims that he wants to replace "new age" notions of the polarity/unity of the opposites (such as *ying/yang*) with a conception of their inherent "tension," he himself explicitly appeals to the principle of *coincidentia oppositorum*. He states, for example, that the Lacanian *"objet a"* (object a) is "the name for the ultimate unity of opposites in Plato."[22] Žižek also describes the interdependence between reality and fiction, writing that in order to conceal its emptiness "reality has to be supplemented by fiction."[23]

With regard to the impossibility of "unity," Žižek has no problem providing a sense to the notion of the subject's union with its objects or with being. He suggests that for Holderlin the only possible union or reconciliation between subject and object or being and reflection "is a *narrative* one, that is the subject telling the story of his endless oscillation between the two poles."[24] However, according to Žižek, Hegel transposes Holderlin by claiming that the problem of the split between subject and object *is its own solution*. This is because this split is inherent in being itself, and it is thus "our very division from Absolute Being which unites us with it."[25]

Žižek appeals to the figure of the Moebius strip to illustrate his understanding of the parallax gap. He describes this gap as "the confrontation of two closely linked perspectives between which no neutral common ground is possible."[26] The Moebius strip, he says, provides a graphic representation of this gap.[27] However, the interesting thing about the Moebius strip is that the opposing "sides" of the strip imperceptibly but inexorably pass into one another and are ultimately indistinguishable. In fact, the Moebius strip is a continuous "One" that gives the illusion of being a "Two." Žižek at times conveniently ignores this aspect of his own metaphor, and in the process he fails to incorporate the most significant part of the parallax gap into his thinking: *that opposites are not at all incommensurable but are rather interdependent and pass into one another.* At other times, however, he appears to recognize this, as when he states, "The minimal ontology of parallax is...that of the Moebius strip, of the curved space that is bent onto itself."[28] Further, he uses the Moebius strip analogy to argue that subject and object "designate one and the same X, conceived either in the mode of 'being' (object) or 'becoming' (subject)."[29] Here Žižek acknowledges a unity of opposites, between two "perspectives" that appear to be incommensurable, but which are actually interdependent and united. Yet, his overall philosophical stance is to deny the unity of opposites and the existence of a primal "One."

Let us return for a moment to Žižek's claim that there is no substantial reality underlying appearances—that the thesis of a singular, underlying reality is an "ideological fantasy." If we examine Žižek's own words, we find that he often does and must make reference to the very underlying reality, the existence of which he adamantly denies.

Recall that for Žižek "there is no 'neutral' reality within which gaps occur, within which frames isolate domains of appearances...."[30] He says that the parallaxes are,

> not symmetrical, composed of two incompatible perspectives on the same X: there is an irreducible asymmetry between the two perspectives.... We do not have two perspectives, we have a perspective and what eludes it, and the other perspective fills in this void of what we could not see from the first perspective.[31]

Further, according to Žižek, "there are no Qualia."[32] This means that there is no direct contact with reality, no direct experience, which is then, on a second occasion, elaborated by our mind—what we experience as "reality" is already the result of this elaboration.[33]

However, by writing about an "elaboration," Žižek assumes the very thing he denies: a reality behind the appearances that is elaborated upon! The very notion of elaboration or interpretation, as we saw in Chapter 5, necessitates the assumption of a factual core upon which the elaboration or interpretation is superimposed. The question of whether such elaboration occurs contemporaneously with perception or is something that is secondary is beside the point. The very argument that there is no such thing as non-mediated experience must assume the theoretical existence of something unmediated upon which this experience is elaborated.

As we saw in Chapter 6, we could not speak or write at all, could not even assert the thesis that "there is no underlying reality" or the "all is appearance" without assuming the very existence of a distinction between words and what they signify. Our deconstruction of the signifier-signified distinction is dependent upon assuming the distinction itself! And with the assumption of a "signified," we are required to assume the existence of something beyond language—in other words, a reality that we are referring to and endeavoring to describe.

In Žižek's view, the world that we perceive and discover is, in effect, created through our process of active perception and discovery. Whereas cartographers have a concrete foundation upon which to draw their maps, philosophers *produce their globe or world in the process of mapping it*. Yet the very process of producing such a world is itself dependent upon our *assumption that there is an actual world to be discovered and mapped*. This, as we have seen, is an unavoidable assumption of meaningful language and representation. It is evident, for example, in the distinction between strings of words that refer and make sense and those that have no conceivable reference; it is graphically evident in the distinction between abstract art that has no reference beyond itself and representational art that does. The question raised here is whether philosophy is more akin to abstract or representational art. Žižek seems to hold that it is in the very process of non-representational language that "representation" arises!

Žižek here engages in the same bilinear (that is, coincidence of opposites) thinking that we saw was necessary in understanding the relationship between language and the world: language *both does and does not* represent a signified beyond itself, and he himself states that "language provides the ultimate example of this dialectical unity of opposites."[34] Žižek's own analogy, which he utilizes to explain the parallax gap, unavoidably posits an "underlying reality" upon which he elaborates. He cites Claude Lévi-Strauss, who describes two subgroups of the Winnebago Indians, each of which has an understanding of the layout of their village. Each of their understandings is incommensurable with the understanding of the other:

> Both perceive the village as a circle; but for one subgroup there is within the circle another circle of central houses, so that we have two concentric circles, while for the other subgroup the circle is split in two by a clear dividing line."[35]

Žižek points out that for the latter "revolutionary-antagonistic" group the village is perceived "as two distinct heaps of houses separated by an invisible frontier...."[36]

Our understanding of this example of "parallax gap," however, is completely dependent on our assumption of the existence of an objective village. Žižek suggests that the "real" is not the social arrangement described by the tribes but rather "the traumatic core of some social antagonism which distorts the tribe's members' view of the actual arrangement of the houses in the village."[37] What he ignores is the other "real"—the objective arrangement of the houses,[38] the real that makes the example interesting and which is absolutely necessary for Žižek to even articulate his point about "distortion" and "the actual arrangement."

There is indeed a strong tendency in contemporary philosophy to deny the existence of the "underlying realities" that everyone assumes exist, and an equally strong tendency to assume the existence of what is denied in the process of the denial. Nowhere is this more evident than in the denial of the existence of the "self." Žižek, following Thomas Metzinger, holds that the "self" is a model or representation and that the existence of a "core" or underlying self is an illusion resulting from our lack of transparency regarding the neuronal basis of our phenomenal experience. Yet, as Žižek himself points out, Metzinger concludes that an understanding that there is actually "no one whose illusion the conscious self could be" frees one to "grow up, define one's own goals, and become autonomous."[39] In the very paragraph that Metzinger calls the self an illusion, he argues that recognition of the illusion effectively liberates the very self that he has just dismissed! Indeed, a conscious aware self is necessary in order to perform the scientific and philosophical procedures necessary to call the self an illusion. After all, it is persons (in the sense of individuals who have a history, biography, and salaries) and selves (simply put, experiencing subjects with cohesive identities) who make scientific discoveries and philosophical claims. The upshot of this is that the underlying reality that one seeks to deny returns in both the process and conclusion of one's denial.

We will see in the next section that Žižek's critique of foundationalism results in a reading of Hegel that emphasizes the negative or deconstructive moment of the dialectic at the expense of its positive and integrative aspect. As we have seen, Žižek holds that the oppositions, antinomies, and contradictions that we encounter should be accepted as an irreducible part of reality itself. Reality, for Žižek, is the "irreducible gap" between oppositions—which, again, is precisely the inverse of our thesis that an underlying unified reality is to be intuited through an understanding of the interdependence between opposing perspectives. Might not these two views themselves be in *coincidentia oppositorum*?

NEGATIVE AND POSITIVE PHILOSOPHY

It would not be an exaggeration to say that since the time of Kant, there has been a progressive questioning of the possibility of not only metaphysics but of what might generally be spoken of as "positive" philosophy. The origins of "negative philosophy" can be traced at least as far back as the Greek skeptics who, within a century after Plato's death, developed a viewpoint that eschewed Platonic metaphysics in favor of doubt regarding the human capacity to attain knowledge about the world, and who turned the Platonic tendency to argue both sides of a proposition into the foundation of such doubt. For centuries, if not millennia, negative philosophy remained on the periphery of Western philosophy. But, with the advent of modernity and its attendant skepticism toward the claims of religion, the doubts explicit in the philosophies of René Descartes and David Hume, and Kant's criticism of metaphysics, negative philosophy became a dominant force in Western thought. Later, philosophers as diverse as Friedrich Nietzsche, the logical positivists, Ludwig Wittgenstein, and Jacques Derrida adopted a primarily negative philosophical stance, one that is skeptical regarding the possibility of arriving at philosophical truth. "Negative philosophy" is also present, albeit in a more productive manner, in philosophers such as Friedrich W. J. Schelling, Jean Paul Sartre, and Martin Heidegger, who understood "negation," "nothingness," finitude, and death as central to philosophical understanding. Within religious thought, negative philosophy can be traced to the negative theologians and mystics who held that God can only be described as possessing "negative attributes" and who held that nothing positive or substantive can be said about the Absolute.

Much recent negative philosophy is rooted in Hegel, whose dialectic—at least on one interpretation—involves a negative or deconstructive maneuver that uncovers the gap, flaw, demise, or "death" inherent in all historical forms and ideas. We have seen how this "Hegelian" emphasis on negation in philosophy is present in Žižek and Wolfgang Giegerich, each of whom, in their own manner, rejects the possibility of any synoptic, positive, or content-oriented philosophy or psychology, and who understand their respective disciplines as more properly grounded in a negation—for Žižek the "parallax gap," and for Giegerich "negative interiority."

Žižek, in a work aptly entitled *Less Than Nothing*, places a "negative philosophical" interpretation on both Kant and Hegel. With respect to the former, he points out that there are two justifications for the noumenal realm in Kant. The first, which is generally more explicit in Kant's writings, is that this realm is required as the underlying substrata or cause of the phenomenal world. This justification, despite Kant's skepticism regarding the possibility of *noumenal knowledge*, leaves the door open to positive philosophy—in which the noumenal realm is understood not only as the cause of appearances but also as the seat of God and freedom. However, the second justification for the noumenal is totally negative. On this view, a noumenon is simply a "limiting concept," one that curbs our intellectual pretensions and in this case is "therefore only of negative employment."[40]

The Hegelian philosophy, on Žižek's "negative" view, does not, as is often supposed, create a "super totalization" but rather describes the gap between each successive worldview:

> Hegel's dialectic is the science of the gap between the Old and the New, of accounting for this gap; more precisely, its true topic is not directly the gap between the Old and the New, but its self-reflective doubling—when it describes the cut between the Old and the New, it simultaneously describes the gap, within the Old itself, between the Old "in-itself" (as it was before the New) and the Old retroactively posited by the New. It is because of this redoubled gap that every new form arises as a *creation ex nihilo*.[41]

In Chapter 6, we spoke of the infinite regress of *coincidentia oppositorum*—that is, the continual passing of each successive philosophical thesis into its opposite. This regress is understood by Žižek in purely negative terms—the dialectic does not create larger and larger integrations, but rather deeper and deeper fragmentations, resulting in a situation in which everything is essentially self-created and independent of (as opposed to interdependent with) all previous forms and ideas. Žižek quotes with approbation, Alain Badiou's claim that "the real is not what brings together, but what separates."[42] As we have seen, for Žižek it is a fantasy to think that we can either arrive at an origin that precedes our presuppositions, prejudices, and myths, or an integration that comprehends philosophy, history, and the world as a unified totality.

Nonetheless, and despite his negativity, Žižek refuses to go along with those who interpret Hegel in purely epistemological terms. For Žižek, it is "too modest" to reduce "Hegel's logic to a system of global epistemology, of all possible epistemological stances." He continues:

> what gets lost is the intersection between the episte-
> mological and ontological aspects, the way 'reality'
> itself is caught in the movement of our knowing it
> (or, vice versa, how our knowing of reality is em-
> bedded in reality itself...).[43]

It is here that Žižek comes closest to proffering a positive philosophical statement, one that again appeals to a coincidence of opposing points of view, that of knowledge and being. He argues that epistemology is intrinsically linked with ontology and vice versa. Only the ontology that Žižek describes is purely negative—the parallax gap is linked to doubt, contradiction, and fragmentation.

I fully agree with Žižek's characterization of the link between epistemology and ontology (or metaphysics). My difference with Žižek is on how to interpret (or move beyond) Hegel. Is the Hegelian project essentially a "negative" one that understands reality in terms of sunderings and negations, or is it a "positive" one that understands reality in terms of the interdependent relationships between the negated/sundered perspectives?

Hegel's own words belie the notion that philosophy is entirely negative. As we saw in Chapter 3, Hegel distinguished between *Dialectic* or "negative reason" and *Speculative thought* or "positive reason." He describes the latter as consisting "solely in grasping the opposed moments in their unity." According to Hegel, "Inasmuch as each moment shows, as a matter of fact, that it has its opposite in it, and that in this opposite it rejoins itself, the affirmative truth is this internally self-moving unity, the grasping together of both thoughts...."[44]

We have seen how Hegel was critical of what he described as a purely "negative" form of dialectic, which questions philosophical propositions without leading to positive results and which thus leads to Skepticism.[45] The skeptical use of negative dialectic eventually led to Kant's antinomies of reason. However, Kant, on Hegel's view, failed to grasp the *positive* philosophical implication of the antinomies, that is, that "every actual thing involves a coexistence of opposed elements" and that to "comprehend an object is equivalent to being conscious of it as a concrete unity of opposed determinations."[46]

Žižek focuses upon the negative moment of dialectic and fails to give due weight to the positive moment, to what Hegel refers to as "speculative, positive reason." However, what is at stake here is not so much the correct interpretation of Hegel but the relationship between the two points of view on the antinomies—the negative one, resulting in an identification of reality with the sunderings of the "parallax gap" and the positive one, which identifies the Absolute with the integrating movement of *coincidentia oppositorum*. I have, in this chapter and throughout this work, attempted to show why *both* the negative and positive poles of the dialectic are intellectually productive and unavoidable. I have argued, for example, that there is both a radical distinction between identity and difference and an inextricable unity between them, and that these two points of view are themselves completely interdependent. I believe that Hegel understood the world to be replete with difference, but ultimately understood philosophy in positive terms, as Jonathan Red has put it, "as a single unified masterpiece composed by the one living spirit."[47]

Perhaps the divide between positive and negative philosophy involves a question of preference or even mood. Recall here the Chasidic parable of the "two pockets"—only in this case we might place "negative dialectics" in one pocket and "positive dialectics" in the other, in the hope that we will have the wisdom to reach into the right pocket on the right occasion!

PROCESS OR CONTENT?

Our discussion of "negative" and "positive" philosophy brings us to a related discussion of whether "reality," the Absolute, and even philosophy itself—even if positively conceived—should be understood in *process* or *content* terms. We might ask, for example, if the "Absolute" is to be identified with the *process* of thinking or with the *thoughts* that thinking thinks? What I am calling a "content" view holds that reality and the Absolute can be identified with specific thoughts and descriptions. The content view holds that our deepest level of understanding arrives at an all-encompassing underlying reality that serves as the basis for all of our experience and ideas, and that such an underlying reality, if not completely specifiable and identifiable, can in some sense be intuited or indicated. Examples of "content" Absolutes are apparent in views that hold that reality to be the sum total of all ideas, experiences, phenomena, facts, matter, energy, and information.

On the other hand, a "process" view identifies reality and the Absolute with *a form of thinking or experience.* It holds that our deepest level of understanding can never assume or arrive at a specifiable content. On this view, because contents are relative to processes of perception, cognition, theory, and "culture" and are in constant flux, they cannot serve as "the all" or as a philosophical foundation. Further, because contents are always present to a mind that perceives them, there is always something that is not encompassed by them. By way of contrast, a process view might identify the Absolute with an experiential, cognitive, or other process such as reason, dialectic, Badiou's "event" (to be discussed below), or (the process of) experience itself. Hegel himself appreciated this problem and concluded that the Absolute was both abstract and concrete, thought and thinker.

The cartographic analogy I have appealed to throughout this work is suggestive of a *content* view of the Absolute, a view that might be termed "perspectival realism." Perspectival realism recognizes the diversity of perspectives and theories that are brought to experience and which condition our thoughts about the world. It nevertheless holds that these perspectives are *perspectives upon* a single underlying world. Taken together, these perspectives are complementary and afford us an approximation of the whole. For perspectival realism, while there is an objective basis for our perception and representation of the mind and the world, our actual perceptions and representations are always colored by our point of view, language, and the questions we ask. While our points of view and descriptions can never fully depict how the world is *in itself*, our descriptions and representations are constrained by an "actual nature." This actual nature serves as a *limit* upon our representations, in two senses of the term "limit." First, actual nature limits the range of our representations, which must accord with an underlying reality. Second, actual nature serves as a "limiting notion," which each of our representations singly (and all of them together) strive toward but can never reach. In the view outlined in this book, we come closest to the "limit" of actual reality through the integration of multiple perspectives that is achieved when we understand that our perspectives are interdependent and complementary rather than mutually exclusive or incommensurable.

An instructive comparison can be made between the perspectival realism I have just described and the philosophy of Badiou.[48] Stated briefly, Badiou holds that there are four independent truth procedures—

science, art, love, and politics—that are on equal footing with regard to accessing truth. Philosophy becomes problematic when it ties or "sutures" itself to one of these procedures to the neglect of the others. For Badiou, truth is invariant, though not singular. However, in contrast to the perspectival realist view I have described above, he held that truth is not accessible through normal experience but only reveals itself when there is a rupture in that experience, what Badiou refers to as an "event." During such ruptures, truth can be momentarily discerned by one who happens to witness or experience it. However, an event lies outside the scope of "reality" as it is conventionally constituted and therefore cannot be named or otherwise circumscribed.

In Chapter 6, I described the relationship between two views of reality: the "conventional" view in which "reality" is said to be discerned and constituted by language and society, and the "deconstructive" view in which "reality" is said to be that which creates a rupture in discourse, theory, and convention. I broadly identified this second anti-conventional view of reality with the rupture symbolized in the Kabbalist's "Breaking of the Vessels" and the Lacanian "real" (as a rupture in the symbolic order). The "perspectival realist" view is "conventional" and contrasts with Badiou's "realism," which is "deconstructive," as Badiou holds that truth and the "real" always involve *rupture*. However, as we saw in Chapter 6, there is a coincidence of opposites between the conventional and deconstructive views on the real, and as such there is a higher order *coincidentia oppositorum* between the truths that are entailed by these opposing ways of understanding reality.

Badiou's understanding of "truth" contains elements of both a content and process view. A certain disruption results in an event that produces insight into an invariant truth (content). A fully "process" understanding of the Absolute rejects (or bypasses) the idea that there is an underlying truth or reality that can potentially be described or intuited, either through conventional representations or ruptures in those representations.

A process view suggests that the Absolute, if it can be provided with a coherent sense at all, has no specifiable content but must be understood in terms of a process, procedure, or practice. Hegel, who was an advocate of something akin to a "Reason" process interpretation of truth and reality, famously held that the Absolute was to be identified with the efforts of mind to know itself. As we saw earlier, in his *Lectures on the History of Philosophy*, he stated:

> Everything that from eternity has happened in heaven and earth, the life of God, and all the deeds of time simply are the struggles for mind to know itself, to make itself objective to itself, to find itself, be for itself, and finally unite with itself. Only in this manner does mind attain its freedom, for that is free which is not referred to or dependent on another.[49]

For Hegel, at least in this passage, it is the "struggle of mind to know itself" (which he identified with the dialectical process in both philosophy and history) that explains the phenomena of the universe and is hence to be identified with the Absolute.

In this view, the Absolute cannot be anything that we can think; it cannot be anything presented to our consciousness but must be identical with the process of thinking itself, not the ordinary thinking of the Understanding but the dialectical thinking that thinks both the truth of a thought and the truth of its opposite. As we have seen in Chapter 3, Robert Solomon argued that dialectic does not arrive at the truth but is the truth itself, a truth that can be, according to Hegel, traced through the history of religion, art, philosophy, and history. This truth is the successor of Aristotle's "thought thinking itself" and it has an element of reflexivity or self-consciousness at its core. After all, the dialectic is precisely a reflection upon one's own (prior or current) thinking.

While Hegel at times suggests that the Absolute is to be identified with the *process* or development of "mind," a process view of dialectic can be dissociated completely from any conception of an Absolute or totality. Terry Pinkard, who provides a "hermeneutic" interpretation of Hegel, holds that the Hegelian dialectic essentially involves principles through which one can criticize assertions about experience and the world, and is also a means through which one can criticize one's principles, including the so-called laws of logic or reason. On this view, nature imposes no structure or limits on our mental activity and the norms that had heretofore been imposed upon us by society (or which we had created and imposed upon ourselves) are always subject to criticism, change, and modification. We might thus understand the Hegelian dialectic as moving toward a complete *open economy of thought*. We will return to the question of such an open economy later in this chapter.

While the dialectic may not be perceived as yielding a definitive content, it nonetheless, at any given point of its application, does arrive at certain contents. For example, such contents are arrived at through the application of dialectic to the subject matters of psychology, theology, and philosophy. Nevertheless, all such contents (for example, "the union of subject and object" or the "interdependence between language and the world) should only be regarded as temporary insights or expedients, as all "contents" or conclusions (including all of those arrived at in this book) must be subject to a renewed dialectical critique. Hegel is clear about this when he says that it is misleading to understand the dialectic as ultimately arriving at the conclusion that there is, for example, a unity of subject and object.[50] This is also Wolfgang Giegerich's point about the nature of "soul," that it has no definite empirical or even conceptual characteristics but is identified with pure reflectivity, or what he refers to as "interiority." Soul, for Giegerich, is the process of mind critiquing its own contents and hence reflectively coming to know itself. It is in this way that the process view of the Absolute, which is at times present in Hegel, readily passes over into a critical, deconstructive view, in which there is no Absolute at all but simply a series of perspectives that are subject to indefinite criticism and modification.

A process view of the Absolute is evident in the Lurianic Kabbalah's understanding of *Ein-sof*, the Infinite, which the Lurianist's believed to be inherently subject to criticism, modification, and reform.

As discussed in Chapter 2, Isaac Luria held that *Ein-sof* only realizes itself through creation—moreover, a creation that is initially incomplete and broken, and which must be completed, emended, and restored through the ethical, spiritual, and meaning-making activities of humankind. Because the "shattering" of creation (the "Breaking of the Vessels") impacts upon and is an inherent property of all things, the entire world—including all events, thoughts, and theories—is in a perpetual state of rupture and continually requires emendation and repair. *Ein-sof*, the Kabbalist's Absolute *becomes the limit of this revisionary process.*

We have also seen how certain Kabbalists regarded *Ein-sof* to be the union of all contradictions and how the Lurianic Kabbalah, which understands the Absolute to traverse the oppositions of God and humanity, infinite and finite, beginning and end, creation and destruction, etc., fulfills this understanding of the Absolute as a *coincidentia oppositorum.* However, for the Lurianists, it would seem that the Absolute does not take a final form but embodies the principle of criticism, emendation, and opposition that characterizes the dialectical process.

We can see how the principle of *coincidentia oppositorum* entails that a content view of the Absolute, in which perspectives converge upon a single world, passes over into a radical constructivist (and even deconstructivist) view in which "perspectives" may complement one another but converge on nothing at all. However, the reverse is true as well: Radical constructivism passes over into and is indeed dependent upon the view that there must be *something* that perspectives or constructions are *about.* We have already encountered this double-movement in our consideration of the views that language is both completely autonomous and must refer to extra-linguistic entities and ideas. The dialectic, whether it is applied to experience, mind, history, or the world, cannot even get started unless it makes the assumption that it is considering, referring to, or critiquing *something.* As we have seen throughout this work, a "perspective" must assume a substratum that the perspective is about, and an "interpretation" must assume the existence of an underlying event or phenomena that is interpreted.

The notion that dialectic is simply a critical apparatus that prevents closure regarding our conception of ourselves and the cosmos *appears* to be in complete opposition to the idea that dialectic leads to a comprehensive view of reality and, in effect, brings one to the "doorstep" of the Absolute. Yet, it can be argued that these contrasting "hermeneutic" and "metaphysical" interpretations of the dialectic are in themselves interdependent, in *coincidentia oppositorum*. This is because we can understand the *dialectic that prevents closure* as the very vehicle that enables us to intuit the possibility of an epistemological and metaphysical infinite, and it is this very "infinite" (a vague but nonetheless "content" idea) that provides for the possibility of the *dialectic that prevents closure*.[51] We have already seen this in connection with our discussion of God and atheism in Chapter Six. If God is indeed infinite, it is only by opening our minds and hearts to a (potentially) infinite thought, experience, doubt, and critique that we can fathom such a God. But it is also just such an opening to the Infinite that leads to the possibility of doubt and atheism—and this, in effect, leads to a coincidence of opposites between atheism and (a mystical form of) theism. If, as Hegel suggests, we are the finite vehicle through which Spirit's infinite consciousness recognizes itself,[52] then it must be that there is an unbounded infinity that conditions this capacity. Further, the very notion of a "remainder" that exceeds all our efforts to circumscribe ourselves and "the world" does not, as the deconstructionists claim, undermine the possibility of a totality. Instead, it ensures that such a totality is *truly infinite*, always "plus one," and that any consciousness of such an infinite totality is a consciousness of a *limit upon* rather than a full intuition of an actual whole. When one identifies the "Absolute" with the open economy of thought and experience, hermeneutics and metaphysics coincide.

The results of our own inquiry are compatible with *both* a "one-world" and "no-world" interpretation of experience, and with both a content and process view of the Absolute. On the one hand, we have posited an underlying reality, an actual nature that our various perspectives approach as a limit, and we understand these perspectives to be in *coincidentia oppositorum*. On the other hand, we recognize that the "perspectival realist" representation of the world at any given time will be limited by both the state of our knowledge within the perspectives we have at hand and by the limitations inherent to these perspectives themselves—limitations that can and will be superseded by new discoveries and future dialectical critique. It is our participation in the process of discovery and critique, while at the same time intuiting "actual nature" through a series of interdependent perspectives, that provides us with our closest intuition of what is broadest, deepest, and foundational in our world. The coincidence of opposites plays a critical role in both the content and process understanding of the Absolute. With respect to the former, it is the "glue" that ties together divergent and seemingly incompatible points of view; with respect to the latter, it is the engine of "the process" that provides an impetus to move on to new perspectives that differ radically from (and are indeed opposed to) our own. One reason that I call the coincidence of opposites an "archetype of the Absolute" is because it is the one thing that survives each dialectical inversion.

THE HISTORICIST CRITIQUE

One potential criticism of any philosophy, theology, or psychology that purports to be foundational is that *it is, and of necessity must be, limited by its author's time and culture.* While historicism makes the now almost obvious point that all knowledge is historically and contextually conditioned, the annals of both Western and Eastern philosophy are filled with thinkers who have claimed to transcend their time and place and who have produced ideas that purport to be trans-historical.

The cartographic model that I have developed throughout this book is trans-historical in that it posits a unified, eternal truth or whole that gives rise to historically conditioned thought and experience. This view, at least at first, is mystical and Neoplatonic rather than Hegelian. This is because Hegel's philosophy, even when it is understood metaphysically, does not point backward toward an origin but forward to an evolving truth that develops logically and in time, with the advance of the dialectic in philosophy and history. In short, Hegel's Absolute progressively realizes itself through the rational and creative development of the "World-Spirit."

Can the trans-historical and historicist points of view be reconciled? We have seen how Slavoj Žižek, even as he endeavors to reject the reconciliation of opposites, argues that for Hegel the very process of contingent creative thought produces the very foundations that it presumably discovers, thus forming a link between necessity and contingency,[53] and between the present and past. As I have argued above, this link is itself an instance of the *coincidentia oppositorum* between subject and object, signifier and signified. Further, as I suggested in Chapter 6, the subject, through its culturally and historically conditioned experience and language, constructs a reality that it *must* take to be objective, real, and foundational, if it is to be constructed at all. The subject creatively forges what it then posits as its own origins, but these origins (for example, in the physical world) are in fact the origin of its subjectivity.

A *coincidentia oppositorum* between eternity and history is present in the Lurianic Kabbalah, which holds that the Absolute, *Ein-sof*, is both the origin of the world and only realized as the endpoint of human historical development—in the words of the proto-Kabbalistic work, *Sefer Yetzirah*, "Its beginning is wedged in its end and its end wedged in its beginning."[54] Whereas mystics typically assert that the Absolute is timeless, eternal, and unchanging, the Kabbalists held that the eternal is intimately intertwined with the ruptures, emendations, and transformations that characterize human history. Like Žižek--who interprets Hegel to suggest that Spirit actually "produces what it returns to"[55] and holds that the past only becomes what it is via the (re)signification of the present—the Lurianists believed that *Ein-sof* (the Infinite) achieves its identity only through the meaning-making and value-making acts of humankind. This suggests that the historicist and mystical-Plotinian points of view converge and complement one another. There is no history without being, yet being is always cognized, signified, transformed, and in effect created through a historically conditioned process.

BEYOND REASON, LANGUAGE, AND REPRESENTATION

As we have seen, one way to conceptualize the Absolute is to identify it with the open economy of thought and experience. Indeed, if "Absolute" is conceived of as "The Infinite," as is *Ein-sof* in the Kabbalah or *Brahman-Atman* in Hinduism, then any effort to think or represent it must be infinite as well. Since the human mind is not itself infinite and cannot encompass the entirety of the universe, the closest it can come to "representing" an "infinite Absolute" is through its participation in a form of thinking that is completely open and indefinitely revisable. As we have seen, such an open economy follows from the principle of *coincidentia oppositorum*, which holds that all conclusions are subject to critique, and that thought and experience must consider and embrace that which opposes any current idea, position, or state of affairs.

Indeed, when we examine the history of Western thought, beginning with the Enlightenment, we see that it has involved an expansion of the mind's range well beyond the categories that were available during previous eras. With Descartes, Gottfried Leibniz, and Baruch Spinoza, there was an expansion of thought beyond (and in a manner which *opposed*) the authority of religious texts and a movement toward a fully independent reason; with the advent of natural science, observation, unfettered by (and *opposed* to) dogma, became a source of ideas about the world; with Kant, thought was expanded (in *opposition* to purely objective points of view) to include the contributions of an experiencing subject; with Hegel, a critical apparatus was put in place that would question and invert all seemingly fixed perspectives and points of view; and with Sigmund Freud and his successors, it became possible to recognize the impact of unconscious (as *opposed* to conscious) psychological processes and activities on our understanding of ourselves and the world. Each of these, and many other developments in modern (and postmodern) thought, have expanded the open economy of thought through an embrace of that which *opposed* the received view. In this way, each brought humanity closer to a fuller, richer, and "more infinite" representation of mind and world.

Still, we may ask whether even an infinitely open economy of thought is itself adequate to the task of approaching the "All." Is not thought itself subject to limitations? Here I am no longer referring to the limitations of any particular thinker or line of thought, but the limitations of thought itself.

Why think? Why should thought, particularly rational thought, be our vehicle for comprehending the world? A Hegelian might respond that the question "Why think?" asks for a *reason*, and ultimately the stopping point of any such inquiry is *reason itself.* But we may then ask, *Why think one thought as opposed to another?* And here we inevitably arrive at motive, intent, and desire. Indeed, desire conditions and places a limit on thought; we see that our dialectic, which initially seems to be a tool of thinking, ultimately brings us beyond thought to a realm that involves desire and motivation. Further, desire inevitably leads to the imagination of possibilities to fulfill desire, as well as to a matrix of values (including many that are non-cognitive such as love, compassion, pleasure, beauty, and justice) that reflect and guide desire. These values are, again, often expressed in imaginative form, and they ultimately impact upon thought. The point here is that the open economy of thought is not sufficiently broad to encompass the Absolute. In order to sufficiently expand our approach to the "All," we need something like an open economy of experience, consciousness, or mind.

Philosophy, theology, and even psychology are typically conducted and presented in propositional language, and such language has a strong tendency to emphasize thought over other modes of experience and representation. Indeed, to the extent that we remain *philosophers* we cannot stray far from thinking. While this offers many advantages, it is, from an important perspective, a trap and a prison. Certain philosophers of the last century (Sartre and Albert Camus come to mind) found that they could best advance philosophical ideas through the medium of imaginative literature. We might question whether in some instances the objects of philosophical inquiry, if not the process of philosophizing itself, might not best be represented or expressed through such mediums as painting, music, or for that matter, the conduct of living.

If we consider the various modes of our conscious life, we find that few of them are confined to thinking and reason. Jung spoke of the "four functions" of thinking, emotion, sensation, and intuition. We might perhaps go beyond Jung and recognize an even wider series of psychological functions, each of which have modes of interest and values that are attendant to them. While this is a subject that warrants separate study, an ensemble of conscious modes or functions—including feeling, desire, cognition, action, symbolization, personal identity, temporality, relationality, and reflection—characterize experience and give rise to core values. While certain philosophers, notably the European rationalists (Descartes, Leibniz, and Spinoza), developed philosophies grounded in cognition (and its value correlates knowledge and understanding), others have sought to base philosophy in non-cognitive modes of mind: relationality (Martin Buber, Emmanuel Lévinas); personality (Max Scheler, Edgar S. Brightman); desire/will (Arthur Schopenhauer, Friedrich Nietzsche); symbolization (Ernst Cassirer); temporality (Bergson, Heidegger); and action (Sartre). These philosophers have thereby emphasized various non-cognitive values, including love, compassion, meaning, and freedom.

If we are to equate the Absolute with the dialectic or an open economy, this economy cannot be limited to thought but must include such "modes of mind" as desire, symbolization, action, feeling, relationality, personality, and imagination. Further, an open economic approach to the Absolute must include *values other than knowledge and truth.* We might thereby identify the Absolute with an infinitely open economy of *thought, experience, and value.* As we have seen, Jungian thought expands the compass of the coincidence of opposites into the realm of feeling and the imagination. Unlike Hegel, who identified the Absolute with *reason,* Jung identified God with the self, an archetype that incorporates both the rational and non-rational elements of the psyche. As we saw in Chapter 4, the elements of the Jungian "self" exist in *coincidentia oppositorum*, and this suggests that the coincidence of opposites is itself an archetype that encompasses both rational and non-rational modes of experience.

CONTRADICTION REVISITED

As we have seen, a criticism that has been levied against the coincidence of opposites is that it gainsays contradiction and thus results in confusion rather than insight. We have also seen, in our discussion of both Buddhist and dialetheistic logic, that there are those (and Hegel was apparently among them) who hold that formal contradiction is essential rather than fatal to thought. Nevertheless, I believe that the entire question of whether oppositions that are expressed in *non-formal* (i.e., ordinary) language involve formal contradictions is itself indeterminate and undecidable. This is because words are always subject to multiple interpretations. If I say it is a contradiction to hold that an act X (such as eating ice cream) is both good and bad, it can be said that this is not a contradiction because I am speaking about good and bad in two different senses (for example, taste and health). Even if we endeavor to constrict the field by specifying "good and bad for one's health," it is always possible to suggest that there are different aspects of one's health and to thus specify situations that would enable us to say "both good and bad" without formal contradiction. If we say "good" and "bad" in "precisely the same sense," anyone who holds that "X is both good and bad" will nonetheless be subject to the suspicion that he is *surreptitiously invoking different senses* of these evaluative terms. The old philosophical maxim, "When confronted with a contradiction, make a distinction," continues to have significant appeal. It is only when we meet the "liar's paradox" and perhaps a few other direct contradictions that we cannot maintain a proposition and avoid violating the law of non-contradiction. However, the Kantian antinomies and Hegel's dialectical oppositions can all be interpreted so as to avoid formal contradiction. When we therefore come to the question of whether the coincidence of opposites violates Aristotelian logic, our answer must be that in some instances it may, but the question is not clearly answerable with respect to most of the *coincidentia opposotorum* I have considered in this book.

I say, "God exists and does not exist." Does this express a contradiction? Might it not simply signify that God has characteristics that I as a speaker believe can only be expressed metaphorically, using these words? Perhaps God has certain of the characteristics that I associate with existence and others that I associate with nonexistence. Now one may say, "I don't mean it in this way; I mean to express a flat contradiction with my words," but does this additional qualification about my intention somehow place a binding constraint on the meaning or your understanding of the original claim? I may say I mean a "flat contradiction," but it is open for others to say, "I don't think that's what you really mean" or to hold that my words simply *could not have that meaning*. In fact, this is what the dialectical process uncovers, hidden ambiguities or characteristics of an idea that enable one to infer things that were not intended by a speaker or writer. Thus, as Hegel argued, full being is also total nonbeing, because anything so total as to be completely full would be without difference and distinctions and would thus be empty. No "flat contradiction" here. Indeed, this could be the one sense of the phrase or claim discussed above—that is, that "God both exists and does not exist" (He is the "fullness of being" and therefore "nothing at all"). Whether a sentence in *ordinary language* constitutes a contradiction in the form of "both P and not P" is thus never possible to determine with any certainty. This is because virtually all sentences in ordinary language are potentially ambiguous and subject to multiple interpretations. Indeed, Willard Quine's "indeterminacy of translation"[54] thesis states just this: When it comes to translating words and sentences from one language to another, or even understanding and paraphrasing words and sentences from one's own language, it is impossible to uniquely specify meaning. Everything is subject to (re)interpretation.

When we subject a philosophical proposition to dialectic, we do so by exploiting the ambiguities inherent in it. As I noted earlier in this chapter, one might be tempted to argue that this exposes the emptiness and "word play" of the whole coincidence of opposites idea, but this would not be a fatal criticism; no philosophical pronouncements, including those that "expose" philosophical disputations as "word play," are immune from word play—that is, immune from the ambiguities that are inherent to the process of representation. Philosophy, and in particular dialectical philosophy, produces insight precisely because it uncovers ambiguities and heretofore unrecognized implications of words. Therefore, criteria other than pure "logical consistency" must be utilized to determine the value of philosophical ideas—and this is certainly the case when assessing the value of dialectic and *coincidentia oppositorum*. Because language is essentially ambiguous, a procedure like dialectic that recognizes and plays off this ambiguity is essential in philosophy. In Chapter 4, we saw that, according to Jung, a *symbol* can embrace both poles of an opposition. It is for this reason that its meaning cannot be stated definitively. What Jung says about symbols is true for virtually all language, and for this reason Jung's "imaginative" understanding of reconciling the opposites is closer to Hegel's "rational" dialectic than one might initially suppose. Reason, in Hegel's sense of the term, requires something on the order of imagination to uncover the ambiguities that are latent in the concepts to which it is applied.

The ambiguity of concepts and language (what is "real," what is "truth," what is "right," what is "valued") is not only the source of philosophy but is also a source of our sundered world, a world within which there are not only multiple things and ideas but multiple representations and interpretations of these representations. Further, as Hegel recognized, it is virtually impossible in many instances to distinguish a thing or idea from our understanding and interpretation of it. Once we begin to speak or write, we enter into interpretive possibilities. Dialectic utilizes these interpretive ambiguities, effectively holding that the principle of non-contradiction is simply inapplicable and non-efficacious outside of a rigidly formalized system, and thus it is ultimately not applicable to philosophical and theological ideas. *We neither adhere to nor abrogate this principle but are liberated from the burden of strictly maintaining it.* This enables us to elaborate multiple perspectives on mind and the universe and to draw various connections between them. It is in this way that dialectical philosophy exploits the very fragmenting tendencies of representation, and works within language to restore or at least approach the limit of a pre-linguistic unity.

The notion of quasi-logicality is perhaps more useful and interesting in philosophy and theology than strict formal entailment. It is "quasi-logical," for example, that one who has a desire seeks to satisfy that desire, but it is not a logical contradiction to have a desire that one does not try (or even want) to satisfy—indeed many if not most individuals curtail fulfillment of their desire for extramarital sex or to wreak havoc out of revenge. Indeed, it is not even a logical contradiction (for a Buddhist monk, for example) to not to want to satisfy any of his desires. We can even imagine the view that in order to satisfy one's desires—for example, for riches, fame, or success—one must first truly not want to satisfy these desires at all. We might call all of this paradoxical, but none of it involves a formal contradiction. This is because auxiliary hypotheses or interpretations can be brought in to logically explicate each of these paradoxes. For example, normally, we might define a desire as a want and think of it as a contradiction to say, "I don't want what I desire." However, the "contradiction" vanishes when we introduce the notion of a "second-order desire," a desire about a desire.

Similarly, it appears to be a logical contradiction to hold (1) that the world is composed of material objects and (2) that material objects are themselves constructions of the mind, but we can provide interpretations of these propositions that render them logically compatible. For example, it might be said that minds evolve through material nature, but it is only when mind turns to consider that nature that nature actually takes the form of, and comes to be understood as, "matter." (A similar idea is expressed in the quantum physics understanding of the instrumental role of measurement in the actual position of subatomic particles). Or we might say more generally that the world is a unified entity with certain characteristics of both matter and mind, best expressed by the aforementioned propositions. (Again, a similar idea is expressed in the quantum theory of "wave-particle dualism"). However, in these cases we have an interpretation that removes the need to posit a flat contradiction. Nevertheless, from the point of view of our ordinary way of thinking, both the case of "desire and want" and "nature and knowledge" produce a paradox that calls forth an analysis resulting in a *coincidentia oppositorum*.

Walter T. Stace held that logic does not apply to the utterances of the mystics because logic always involves multiplicity, relations posited between two or more entities—and mystics generally speak about a singular "One." I am arguing something different: The logic of contradiction, the logic of "if P then *not* not P," does not apply to many philosophical, psychological, and theological propositions because these propositions are ambiguous and subject to interpretation. Aristotle held that logic requires non-ambiguity.[57] The point is that philosophy does not meet this requirement. Language, as J. N. Findlay used to say in his lectures at Boston University, is "iridescent,"[58] and this is a virtue rather than a fault.

The ambiguity of language, however, must lead to the conclusion that philosophical problems are not permanently resolved by the doctrine of *coincidentia oppositorum*. Our acknowledgement that language—and in particular abstract, philosophical language—is always subject to multiple interpretations ensures that no final solution to philosophical problems will be forthcoming. The coincidence of opposites, however, precisely by relying upon the possibilities of interpretation, is a powerful tool that can help us move beyond theoretical impasses. It allows us to acknowledge and incorporate the multiplicity of perspectives that are intrinsic to philosophical, theological, and meta-psychological inquiry. What the coincidence of opposites shows is that it is possible to frame a meta-perspective within which the underlying assumptions of opposing psychological, philosophical, and theological ideas are understood to be both compatible and interdependent. As we have seen in Chapter 5, in the case of psychology, this way of thinking provides critical support for a multi-perspectival view of the mind. It also provides support for a philosophical meta-perspective within which each of a variety of apparently incompatible philosophical ideas are validated. Finally, the coincidence of opposites idea provides us with a vehicle for understanding multiple perspectives upon a cosmos while continuing to regard it as a unified whole. In short, it provides us with the opportunity to maintain difference and an open economy of thought and experience without surrendering the notion of a single world. As we have seen, according to Hegel, "the diversity and number of philosophies [is] absolutely necessary to the existence of the science of philosophy and... is essential to it."[59] This, we might say, is one important philosophical yield from the *coincidentia oppositorum* idea.

It is an open question as to whether it is possible to fully move beyond the dichotomous thinking that has dominated Western philosophy and science. If that occurs, the archetype of *coincidentia oppositorum* will have dissolved into thought itself and will no longer be needed as a means of widening our consciousness to embrace hitherto excluded points of view. However, as long as our thinking remains within the traditional dichotomies of subject and object, word and world, identity and difference, the coincidence of opposites must be invoked as a means of setting limits on our assumptions and achieving a wider range of thought and experience.

THE NATURE OF GOD

From a theological point of view, the coincidence of opposites can be criticized as leading to an overly abstract theology. Certainly, our inquiry into *coincidentia oppositorum* does not readily yield support for a traditional view of God. For the most part, Western religions, at least in their normative expressions, have understood God as if he, she, or it were an *all-powerful, personal being*—a being who preexists the world as we know it, creates and directs through his own will, has a personal relationship with individual human beings, issues commandments, and makes demands upon his/her subjects. While our discussion may not preclude the existence of such a being, the picture of the Absolute that emerges through a consideration of the coincidence of opposites is one that is far more abstract and inclusive. The Absolute that emerges from our study is closer to the infinite open economy of thought and experience or the full realization of mind and value than it is to an all-powerful "king" who has a lordly, parental or personal relationship with his subjects. Indeed, as we have seen, the coincidence of opposites results in a viewpoint that must embody atheism as well as theism, doubt as well as faith, and skepticism as well as belief. One is here inclined to think of this God in terms that are commensurate with the Gnostics' Pleroma, the Hindus' *Brahman-Atman*, or the Kabbalists' *Ein-sof*, as a "God above the God," the God of the mystics and philosophers rather than the God of normative religion. We are here confronting the same problem that preoccupied Hegel when he spoke of the Absolute manifesting itself both in philosophical and symbolic or mythological terms.

How and whether to reconcile this Absolute with the God of the historical religions is a significant theological problem, one that is intimately related to our discussion of mind as including non-rational as well as rational modes and aspects. I have suggested in this chapter that there are a series of psychic modes or functions beyond cognition and that these include experience, desire, action, symbolization, relationality, reflection, and *personal identity*. If, like cognition, each of these modes stand in *coincidentia oppositorum* with their objects (in the manner that subject is interdependent with object and epistemology is interdependent with metaphysics), then an objective correlate of "personal identity" may be said to be constitutive of the cosmos as a whole—in the manner, for example as Hegel argued "mind" is constitutive of the world. While this is a topic that requires further development, such an objective cosmic correlate to personality leaves room for a "personal" aspect of the Absolute that is identified, for example, with *Brahman* or *Ein-sof.*

THE ROLE OF THE IMAGINATION IN THE DIALECTIC AND THE OPEN ECONOMY OF THOUGHT

Let us look at the problem of reason and imagination in the dialectic from another angle. The motivation to keep the dialectic and hence the coincidence of opposites *free of the imagination* and completely on the plane of logic is understandable, as it appears that only this can serve as the guarantor of objective truth. If all philosophical oppositions could be *rationally* shown to pass into their opposites, one would presumably have means for dissolving or resolving all philosophical controversies—and as I have suggested throughout this book, a vehicle for thinking about and even describing the world as a whole. By overcoming the fragmentation that was brought about by dualistic thought and language, one could presumably return to the initial, all-encompassing One that lies behind all phenomena and ideas, and which is their ultimate endpoint. As attractive as such a move may seem, at least in its rational "thought only" form, it is one-sided, as it leaves out whole regions of the psyche and the world as it fails to consider the all-important notion that reason itself is in *coincidentia oppositorum* with non-reason, or what Jung referred to as the creative imagination. If the coincidence of opposites is to serve as an archetype of the Absolute, it must traverse this opposition as well.

Some would, of course, argue that the dialectic is vitiated completely if imagination is part of the engine that makes it run. Certainly, any claim that the dialectic reflects an objective psyche, the universe as a whole, etc., would seem to be undermined by introducing the vagaries associated with non-reason and the imagination, as these seem to contain, as Giegerich has suggested, a "subjective" element.[60] But this is precisely the point: As we proceed along the path of the dialectic, we inevitably must enter the imagination and even the personal, and we find that the universe itself is incomplete without imaginative, personal, and other seemingly non-rational elements. The "objective psyche" may be far more complex and "vague" than we wish it to be, but we must follow it where it leads and accept its full character.

THE PROBLEM OF EVIL

The notion that all ideas pass over into and are interdependent with their opposites runs up against a serious problem: *the opposition between good and evil*. As we have seen, mystics (e.g., the Kabbalists) and psychologists (e.g., Jung) who have subscribed to the *coincidentia* idea have not hesitated to extend it into the sphere of ethics and values. The *Zohar*, the *locus classicus* of the Kabbalah, declares that "there is no good so perfect as that which issues out of evil."[61] Jung held that the effort to purge oneself of evil and adhere only to the good paradoxically prevents one from achieving the good at all. As we saw in Chapter 4, Jung's view is that one must come to recognize and even affirm one's "shadow" in order to become a fully individuated person who actualizes positive values.

I believe that there is indeed a strong sense in which the good is interdependent with evil and values are conditioned by their abrogation. The idea is expressed metaphorically by the Kabbalists in the image of the "Breaking of the Vessels," which symbolizes the notion that the *Sefirot* (the archetypes of value such as kindness, judgment, and compassion) must shatter as a condition for their actualization. Adin Steinsaltz's gloss on this symbol—that it suggests that "we live in the worst of all possible worlds in which there is yet hope and that this is the best of all possible worlds"—provides an essential insight into the coincidence of opposites between good and evil. Steinsaltz points out that it is only in a world on the brink of disaster, one where the potential for evil, suffering, and ignorance is always at hand, that such values as kindness, compassion, courage, and wisdom can be actualized. A "Garden of Eden" world would afford little or no opportunity for the exercise of values and for the development of character. Conversely, without values—for example, the values of life, pleasure, tranquility, and justice—the evils of the world, which all involve a measure of deprivation and suffering, would have no foothold. In short, the value archetypes of the good are fully interdependent with the existence of evil.

And yet there is something deeply unsettling, indeed even perverse, in the notion that there is no good that does not pass through the gates of evil. In contrast to the polarities involved in epistemology and metaphysics (for example, between idealism and materialism), there is a clear and obvious *asymmetry* in the relationship between good and evil and between values and their abrogation. To say, as we read in George Orwell's book *1984*, that "freedom is slavery" or "war is peace" is troubling in a way that saying "matter is idea" is not.

Indeed, Orwell's "Big Brother aphorisms," which are said to be characteristic of "doublethink," have a striking resemblance to the "bilinear thinking" that I have described in connection with the doctrine of *coincidentia oppositorum*. This resemblance underscores the dangers of the coincidence of opposites idea and constitutes what I believe to be a powerful challenge to the notion that the coincidence of opposites is the "archetype of the Absolute." The asymmetry of value, it would seem, is the "remainder," left over after the full application of the coincidence of opposites to the problems of philosophy. This was already evident in Chapter 4, where we considered Jung's early positive assessment of National Socialism and his claim that sometimes in history the good first appears as an inherent evil.[62] Without gainsaying this possibility, the question remains as to how to assess the particular case, and the coincidence of opposites by itself does not appear to provide us with a basis for doing so.

Here I can only provide the beginnings of a response to this challenge. I will begin with a question: Does the open economy of thought and experience provide a basis for ethics, morality, and value? My response is a tentative "yes." Assuming that such an open economy (which follows from the endless criticism and reversals of the coincidence of opposites) is applicable to all experience, all objects, and all sentient creatures, it follows that *the basic ethical and axiological imperative is to do that which permits this open economy to flourish*. Minimally, this would amount to doing all that is possible to prolong the existence and widest possible expression of life and mind. Since mind manifests itself—as we have seen, in a variety of modes that involve not only reason and imagination, but also desire, relationality, action, symbolization, imagination, reflection, and personal identity—it becomes an axiological imperative to promote the fulfillment of these modes of mind and the values attendant to them. Evil, in effect, is that which thwarts the fulfillment of these modes of mind and destroys or impedes the open economy of thought and experience. When the coincidence of opposites is employed as a justification for evil it undermines the possibility of its own further employment and implodes in on itself.

ARCHETYPE OF THE ABSOLUTE? "STRONG" VERSUS "WEAK" *COINCIDENTIA OPPOSITORUM*

It is important to distinguish between a "strong" and "weak" reading of *coincidentia oppositorum*. The strong version holds that many and perhaps all abstract propositions and "theses" in philosophy, theology, and meta-psychology, are poles of a theoretical opposition, and that each pole of these oppositions is completely conditioned by and fully interdependent with its opposite. An inference I have made from this strong reading is that an original unity—underlying the poles of subject and object, language and world, identity and difference, and other philosophical distinctions—is ruptured by language and representation. Further, a recognition and understanding of the coincidence between the opposites produces an intuition of this original unity.

In one version of the strong thesis, the interdependence of opposites and hence the intuition of the primal unity is a purely rational process, achieved through dialectical "logic." In a second version, one that I have explained in this work, the interdependence of the opposites is only fully realized through a form of "reason" that is itself advanced by and interdependent with imagination. In this view, all rational thinking, if it is not to remain fixed, linear, and repetitive, must partake in the imagination. While the imagination must always be subject to rational examination and critique, this is simply an expression of the very dialectic of reason and imagination that leads to progress in virtually any field of endeavor.

The "weak version" of the coincidence of opposites, which as we saw in Chapter 2, was advocated by Hector Sabelli.[63] Sabelli regards all rational, psychological, and natural phenomena to be conditioned by opposition, in some cases polar opposition and in other cases multiple contrasting ideas or phenomena. In this view, no idea, concept, or natural process is complete or can be adequately understood outside of its relationship to that which it initially appears to oppose or exclude. Further, creativity in a wide range of disciplines and human endeavors, including the conduct of life itself, must always take into account that which opposes and which at least appears to contradict one's ideas, attitudes, preferences, and experiences. Oppositions condition one another through union, complementarity, and conflict, but it is an error to simply regard both polls of an opposition as equals in theoretical, experiential, and especially ethical terms. While one must always "deeply consider the opposites," not all oppositions are necessarily united into a complementary inter-dependent whole.

How do these two versions of *coincidentia oppositorum* interface with the notion that the coincidence of opposites is "the archetype of the Absolute"? Each of them, I would argue, yields a vision of the Absolute, which is potentially complementary, however different they initially may seem.

The strong version, as we have seen, is compatible with the mystical and Neoplatonic notion that there is a *primal unity*, sundered by life, experience, and language, which can be "returned to" and intuited through an understanding of the interdependence of the very experiences and ideas that were sundered and polarized by the representational process. Alternatively, while such a unified Absolute does not preexist human ideational, imaginative, and historical endeavor, this Absolute is the omega or end-point of art, religion, philosophy, and history. While never fully achieved or even achievable, this "Hegelian Absolute" is a limit to which all human endeavor can and ought to aspire.

On first glance, the "weak version" of the coincidence of opposites idea runs counter to, and indeed opposes all conceptions of, an Absolute, as it holds (1) that no cognitive, attitudinal, or experiential position is stable, and that each is necessarily subject to critique by its opposite; and (2) that such critique does not in all cases lead to integration, complementarity, and unity. All things are conditioned by their opposites (by what they are not and by what they appear to exclude), but this does not, cannot, and should not lead to an obliteration of difference. Indeed, this weak version of the coincidence of opposites doctrine is in many ways a restatement of the deconstructionist critique of Hegelian and other philosophical absolutes. Opposites, it is said, interpenetrate and contaminate one another but always in a way that preserves difference and open dialogue.

Yet this very version of *coincidentia oppositorum*, despite itself, leads to a conception of something so wide, so general, and so uncompromising that it can arguably fall under the category of an Absolute—an Absolute that is indeed equated with an infinitely open economy of thought and experience—thought and experience that is never closed off or circumscribed, and which never ends. One might even equate such an infinite economy with certain views of the divine, for example, the Infinite (*Ein-sof*) of Jewish mysticism, the *Tao* of Lao Tse, or *Brahman Atman* in Indian philosophy. Even in the Old Testament, we read God described in such open-ended, infinite terms: *Ehye asher ehye*, "I will be that which I will be." Such an Absolute might also be likened to the creative process that informs the theology of Alfred North Whitehead and Pierre Teilhard de Jardin. Understood in this way, the "Absolute" becomes completely open-ended and convergent with its own opposite, the repudiation of all absolutes: *Whatever you believe and experience*

*refuse to be at rest, and deeply consider what your thoughts and experi-
ence is inclined to oppose and exclude.*

A PHILOSOPHICAL PYRAMID

The philosophical route we have traveled in this book suggests
that the world has a structure analogous to a pyramid. At the base of
the pyramid are the diverse phenomena, differences, genera, species,
individuals, and linguistic distinctions of the everyday world. Above
this are the various philosophical, scientific, and theological efforts to
comprehend the world of difference in its totality. These efforts are, as I
have repeatedly emphasized, akin to various maps of the world, each of
which is grounded in philosophical assumptions which provide important theoretical and practical insights, but which also distort the world of
difference in various ways.

Moving up the pyramid, we have efforts to integrate various competing worldviews and to reconcile the polls of significant philosophical, theological, and psychological oppositions (for example, the oppositions between subject and object, idealism and materialism, language
and the world, identity and difference, and free will and determinism).
In this work, I have described one such effort, one that appeals to the notion or archetype of the coincidence of opposites, and which asserts that
apparently opposing philosophical theories, worldviews, and modes of
apprehension (including reason and imagination) are interdependent. It
has been my thesis throughout this work that it is an intuition and recognition of the coincidence of opposites between seemingly contradictory
points of view, paradigms, theories, and modes of consciousness brings
us as close as possible to a synoptic view of a single mind and world.

Yet, by its own standard, even the coincidence of opposites is subject to dialectic critique, a critique that suggests it too is interdependent with its own opposite, the assertion and recognition of radical difference. It is this recognition that is in accord with and has led to the
post-modern and deconstructive skepticism of all "master narratives."

However, the dialectic of opposites continues beyond postmodernism, beyond deconstruction, beyond any conceivable resting place. The coincidence of opposites then becomes a process that increasingly opens us to that which we had hitherto rejected or excluded. This leads to a higher point on the pyramid, one that I have described as the *open economy of thought and experience*. However, even here we are not yet at the apex of the pyramid. This is because, as we have seen, the very dialectical process that has led us to the open economy prompts us to consider a series of values that support and sustain it—values such as open-mindedness, respect for knowledge, and freedom of thought—but also values related to reflection, compassion, transcendence, and person. Without these values, the open economy becomes an empty unsupported abstraction. Indeed, what is the open economy of thought and experience without the values of knowledge, wisdom, truth, and freedom of thought and expression, and without the compassion that supports such an open economy for others?

Metaphysics thus naturally passes over into ethics and axiology, which at least in this view is at the apex of our philosophical, psychological, and theological pyramid. Interestingly, as mystics (notably the Kabbalists) have asserted, this apex reverses itself and also becomes the base—as it is only in the world of finitude and difference that life and mind can actualize the values that are, in effect, our highest ideals. However, the elucidation of this *axiological dialectic* must await another day.

NOTES

Foreword

[1] Plato. *The Republic of Plato*, trans. Allan Bloom (New York, NY: Basic Books, 1968), 115. For further discussion, see Hendrik Lorenz, "Plato on the Soul," in *The Oxford Handbook of Plato*, edited by Gail Fine (Oxford, England: Oxford University Press, 2011), 243-266, §4.1, and "The Principle of Opposites," 254-258.

[2] Proclus, *Commentary on Plato's "Parmenides,"* trans. Glenn R. Morrow and John M. Dillon (Princeton, NJ: Princeton University Press, 1987).

[3] Bloom, trans., *The Republic of Plato*, p. 278.

[4] Aristotle, Metaphysics, Book 1, 990b13; and Book 13, 1079a9. In *The Complete Works of Aristotle*, ed. Jonathan Barnes, 2 vols. (Princeton, NJ: Princeton University Press, 1984), vol. 2, 1565-66 and 1706.

[5] See Paul Vincent Spade, ed. and trans., *Five Texts on the Mediaeval Problem of Universals: Porphyry, Boethius, Abelard, Duns Scotus, Ockham.* (Indianapolis, IN: Hackett, 1994).

[6] C. G. Jung, *Psychological Types*, trans. R. F. C. Hull. Vol. 3 of *The Collected Works of C. F. Jung.* (Princeton, NJ: Princeton University Press, 1974), §1-§100.

[7] See Jung, "Psychological Typology," in *Psychological Types*, §960-§987.

[8] Jung, *Psychological Types*, 543-4 §962.

[9] Ibid., 544, §962.

[10] Ibid.

[11] Ibid., 544, §963. For a more detailed presentation of Jung's notion of the archaic, see "Archaic Man," [1931] in *Civilization in Transition* [*Collected Works*, vol. 10], trans. R. F. C. Hull (London, England: Routledge, 1970), §104-§147. For further discussion, see Paul Bishop, ed., *The Archaic: The Past in the Present* (London, England: Routledge, 2012), especially the contributions by Susan Rowland, Robert Segal, and Paul Bishop.

¹² Jung, *Psychological Types*, 544, §963.

¹³ Ibid.

¹⁴ Friedrich Nietzsche, *Ecce Homo: How One becomes What One Is*, trans. R. J. Hollingdale (Harmondsworth, UK: Penguin, 1979), 127.

¹⁵ Nietzsche, *Ecce Homo*, 128.

¹⁶ For further discussion, see Michael B. Cosmopoulos, ed., *Greek Mysteries: The Archaeology and Ritual of Ancient Greek Secret Cults* (London, England: Routledge, 2003); Jennifer Larson, *Ancient Greek Cults: A Guide* (New York, NY: Routledge, 2007); Daniel Ogden, ed., *A Companion to Greek Religion* (Oxford, England: Blackwell, 2007); Hugh Bowden, *Mystery Cults in the Ancient World* (London, England: Thames & Hudson, 2010); and Esther Eidinow and Julia Kindt, ed., *The Oxford Handbook of Ancient Greek Religion* (Oxford, England: Oxford University Press, 2015).

¹⁷ Jung, *Psychological Types*, 544-5, §963. Ever alert to the continuities of cultural and spiritual tradition, Jung notes that the ideas underlying the Mysteries "never died out," but underwent something of a "philosophical renaissance" in the second century CE. In the Alexandrian world of thought, as Jung puts it, they fused with Old Testament prophecy and hence gave rise to Christianity as a world religion.

¹⁸ Plato, *Collected Dialogues*, ed. Edith Hamilton and Huntington Cairns (Princeton, NJ: Princeton University Press, 1989), 493 & 499-500.

¹⁹ For discussions of this parable elsewhere, see "Archetypes of the Collective Unconscious" (1934; 1954). "In Plato's parable [the black horse] stands for the unruliness of the passions" (C. G. Jung, *The Archetypes of the Collective Unconscious*, trans. R. F. C. Hull, *The Collected Works of C. G. Jung*, 2nd ed., Vol. 9, Part I (Princeton, NJ: Princeton University Press, 1968), 34-5, §72); and "A Psychological View of Conscience" (1958): "There is scarcely any other psychic phenomenon that shows the polarity of the psyche in a clearer light than conscience.... We are faced logically with a metaphysical dilemma: either there is a dualism, and God's omnipotence is halved, or the opposites are contained in the monotheistic God-image, as for instance in the Old Testament image of Yahweh, which shows us morally contradictory opposites side by side. This figure corresponds to *a unitary image of the psyche dynamically based on opposites*, like Plato's charioteer driving the white and the black horses" (C. G. Jung, *Civilization in Transition*, trans. R. F. C. Hull. *The Collected Works of C. G. Jung*, Vol.

10, 2nd Edition (Princeton, NJ: Princeton University Press, 1970), 448, §844; my emphasis). In his Visions seminar, Jung suggested that there could be a parallel between the black horse in Plato's parable and the animus in women: "You remember the horses in Plato, the charioteer driving the black horse and the white horse, the black horse being always unruly. It is what they call in China the Yin side, which is connected with the idea of evil; it is not necessarily evil but it often appears as such. It is the feminine side...." (C. G. Jung, *Visions: Notes of the Seminar given in 1930–1934*, ed. Claire Douglas (Princeton, NJ: Princeton University Press, 1997), 114-116; cf. p. 436). For further discussion, see Barbara Hannah, *The Archetypal Symbolism of Animals: Lectures given at the C. G. Jung Institute, Zurich, 1954–1958*, ed. David Eldred, Wilmette, IL: Chiron, 2006, 96-7). In his seminar on Nietzsche's *Zarathustra*, Jung at one point remarked, "To handle the good is no art but to handle evil is difficult. Plato expresses this in his parable of the man in a chariot driving two horses; one is good-tempered and white, the other black and evil-tempered, and the charioteer has all the trouble in the world to manage it" (C. G. Jung, *Nietzsche's "Zarathustra": Notes of the Seminar given in 1934–1939*, ed. James L. Jarrett, 2 vols. (London, England: Routledge, 1989), vol. 2, 846).

[20] Jung, *Psychological Types*, 544, §963.

[21] Plato, *Collected Dialogues*, 500.

[22] See Plotinus, *Enneads*, III.8, "On Nature and Contemplation and the One," §5-§8, where Plotinus interprets the ambrosia and nectar with which the charioteer feeds the horses as the share which lower parts of the soul can receive of the divine vision of the higher (Plotinus, *Ennead III*, trans. A. H. Armstrong (Cambridge, MA: Harvard University Press, 1967), 377). For further discussion, see Kevin Corrigan, *Reading Plotinus: A Practical Introduction to Neoplatonism* (West Lafayette, IN: Purdue University Press, 2005), 136. In another *Ennead*, I.6, "On Beauty," Plotinus alludes to the parable in the *Phaedrus* when he writes (§6): "Go back into yourself and look; and if you do not see yourself beautiful, then...you too must cut away excess and straighten the crooked and clear the dark and make it bright, and never stop 'working on your statue' [cf. *Phaedrus*, 254d] till the divine glory of virtue shines out on you, till you see 'self-mastery enthroned upon its holy seat' [cf. *Phaedrus*, 254b]" (Plotinus, *Porphyry on Plotinus; Ennead I*, trans. A. H. Armstrong (Cambridge, MA; London:

Harvard University Press, 1966), 259).

[23] C. G. Jung, *Liber Novus: The Red Book*, ed. Sonu Shamdasani, trans. Mark Kyburz, John Peck, and Sonu Shamdasani (New York, NY: Norton, 2009). For further discussion, see Sanford L. Drob, *Reading the Red Book: An Interpretive Guide to C. G. Jung's "Liber Novus,"* New Orleans, LA: Spring Journal Books, 2012.

[24] Aniela Jaffé (ed.), *Memories, Dreams, Reflections of C. G. Jung*, trans. Richard and Clara Winston (London, England: Collins, Routledge & Kegan Paul, 1963), 210.

[25] For further discussion, see David Pugh, *Dialectic of Love: Platonism in Schiller's Aesthetics* (Montreal, QC: McGill-Queen's University Press, 1996); Nicholas Martin, *Nietzsche and Schiller: Untimely Aesthetics* (Oxford, England: Clarendon Press, 1996); and Paul Bishop and R. H. Stephenson, *Friedrich Nietzsche and Weimar Classicism* (Rochester, NY: Camden House, 2004).

[26] See Dilthey's masterful essay on Schiller in *Von deutscher Dichung und Musik: Aus den Studien zur Geschichte des deutschen Geistes* (Leipzig: Teubner, 1933), 325-427.

[27] Friedrich Schiller, *On the Aesthetic Education of Humankind in a Series of Letters*, ed. and trans. Elizabeth M. Wilkinson and L. A. Willoughby (Oxford, England: Clarendon Press, 1982), 57.

[28] Schiller, *On the Aesthetic Education*, 57.

[29] Jung, *Psychological Types*, 84, §126.

[30] Schiller, *On the Aesthetic Education*, 84.

[31] Wilkinson and Willoughby, "Commentary," in Schiller, *On the Aesthetic Education*, 239.

[32] See Peter Kingsley, *Ancient Philosophy, Mystery, and Magic: Empedocles and Pythagorean Tradition* (Oxford, England: Clarendon Press, 1995), 15-35.

[33] Cf. Kingsley, *Ancient Philosophy, Mystery, and Magic*, 13; cf. "Hear first the four roots of all things: bright Zeus, life-bringing Hera, Aidoneus, and Nestis, who waters with her tears the mortal fountains" (fragment 6), in *Early Greek Philosophy*, trans. Jonathan Barnes, (Harmondsworth, England: Penguin, 1987) 173-174.

[34] For an overview of the notion of the daimonic in classical times and in relation to German literature, see Angus Nicholls, *Goethe's Concept of the*

Daemonic: After the Ancients (Rochester, NY: Camden House, 2006); and Andrei Timotin, *La démonologie platonicienne: Histoire de la notion de 'daimōn' de Platon aus derniers néoplatoniciens* (Leiden and Boston: Brill, 2012).

[35] Jung, *Psychological Types*, 84, §126.

[36] Ibid.

[37] Schiller, *On the Aesthetic Education*, 67.

[38] Jung, *Psychological Types*, 84, §127.

[39] Ibid., 85, §126.

[40] As Frank Fowler has pointed out in relation to Schiller's poem "The Ideal and Life" (1795; 1800; 1804), it is vital to realize that Schiller "does not advocate an ivory-tower escapism or a permanent withdrawal from the unpleasant realities of life"; rather, "in order that we may make full use of our human potential Schiller reminds us that, although we are seldom if ever capable of achieving absolute perfection, we should not underestimate the value of our ability to entertain in our minds the notion of perfection." Schiller shows "how in the midst of our struggles and conflicts this thought may strengthen and sustain us" (see Schiller, *Selected Poems*, ed. Frank M. Fowler (London, England: St. Martin's Press, 1969), 158).

[41] Jung, *Psychological Types*, 84-5, §126.

[42] Ibid., 128, §208.

[43] Ibid., 190-91, §322.

[44] Ibid., §706 and 481, §829.

[45] R. H. Stephenson, ed. and trans., *Goethe's "Maximen und Reflexionen"* (Glasgow, Scotland: Scottish Papers in Germanic Studies, 1986), 83.

Introduction

[1] William James, *The Varieties of Religious Experience: A Study in Human Nature* (New York, NY: Mentor, 1958/1902), 233.

[2] Niels Bohr, "Discussion with Einstein on Epistemological Problems in Atomic Physics," in *Great Books of the Western World*, vol. 56, ed. Mortimer J. Adler (Chicago, IL: Encyclopedia Britannica, Inc., 1990) 354.

[3] C. G. Jung, *Psychology and Alchemy*, trans. R. F. C. Hull. *The Collected Works of C.G. Jung*, Vol. 12 (Princeton, NJ: Princeton University Press, 1968), 186.

[4] Ibid., 19, §22.

[5] C. G. Jung, "The Spirit Mercurius," In *Alchemical Studies, Collected Works of C. G. Jung*, Vol. 13, trans. R. F. C. Hull (Princeton, NJ: Princeton University Press, 1967), 210, §256.

[6] In this sense, the application of the *coincidentia* idea to itself differs, for example, from the application of the logical positivist's "verifiability principle" (the idea that only empirically verifiable propositions are meaningful) to itself. Whereas some have argued that the inability to empirically verify the verifiability principle is fatal to the principle itself—the interdependence of *coincidentia oppositorum* with its negation is both required by and an example of the *coincidentia* principle at work and therefore not fatal to it.

[7] See, for example, C. G. Jung, *Psychological Types*, trans. H. G. Baynes and R. F. C. Hull. *The Collected Works of C. G. Jung*, Vol. 6 (Princeton, NJ: Princeton University Press, 1971), 478-9, §824-5.

[8] Mircea Eliade, *Patterns in Comparative Religion*, trans. R. Sheed. See "Coincidentia Oppositorum—the Mythical Pattern" (Lincoln, NE: Bison Books, 1996), 419 ff.; Cf. M. Eliade, *Myths, Rites, Symbols: A Mircea Eliade Reader*, Vol. 2, ed. W. C. Beane and W. G. Doty (New York, NY: Harper Colophon, 1976), where he writes that many myths, "present us with a twofold revelation: they express on the one hand the diametrical opposition of two divine figures sprung from one and the same principle and destined, in many versions, to be reconciled at some *illud tempus* of eschatology, and on the other, the *coincidentia oppositorum* in the very nature of the divinity, which shows itself, by turns or even simultaneously, benevolent and terrible, creative and destructive, solar and serpentine, and so on (in other words, actual and potential)," 449).

[9] For example, Claude Lévi-Strauss writes, *"Mythical thought always progresses from the awareness of oppositions toward their resolution."* Claude Lévi-Strauss, *Structural Anthropology*, trans. Claire Jacobson and Brooke Grundfest Schoepf (New York, NY: Doubleday Anchor Books, 1963), 224.

[10] Edwin Abbott, *Flatland: A Romance of Many Dimensions* (New York, NY: Classic Books International, 2009).

[11] Slavoj Žižek, *The Parallax View* (Cambridge, MA: MIT Press, 2006), 29.

[12] C. G. Jung, *Mysterium Coniunctionis: An Inquiry into the Separation and Synthesis of Psychic Opposites in Alchemy*, trans. R. F. C. Hull, Vol. 14 of *The Collected Works of C. G. Jung* (Princeton, NJ: Princeton University Press, 1970), 364.

[13] Robert C. Solomon, *In the Spirit of Hegel: A Study of G. W. F. Hegel's Phenomenology of Spirit* (New York, NY: Oxford University Press, 1983), 277.

[14] For example, McCort points out that Chandrakirtim, an Indian commentator on the Buddhist philosophy of Nagarjuna holds "that the identity/difference issue is one intrinsic to language, in other words to the very means by which the issue itself is conceived and formulated, and that therefore language can never suffice to resolve it" (Dennis McCort, *Going Beyond the Pairs* (Albany, NY: State University of New York Press, 2001), 99.

Chapter One

[1] See "A Note on Terminology" at the close of the Introduction.

[2] See W. T. Stace, *Mysticism and Philosophy* (London, England: MacMillan Press, 1960), especially "Mysticism and Logic," Chapter 5.

[3] Niels Bohr, "Discussion with Einstein on Epistemological Problems in Atomic Physics," in *Great Books of the Western World*, vol. 56, ed. Mortimer J. Adler (Chicago, IL: Encyclopedia Britannica, Inc., 1990), 337-55.

[4] For example, Jung, in *Psychology and Alchemy* writes, "The self is made manifest in the opposites and the conflicts between them; it is a copincidentia oppositorum." C. G. Jung, "Psychology and Alchemy," in *The Collected Works of C. G. Jung*, vol. 12, trans. R. F. C. Hull (Princeton, NJ: Princeton University Press, 1944/1968). Jung writes, "The self is made manifest in the opposites and the conflicts between them; it is a *coincidentia oppositorum*," 186.

[5] Mercea Eliade, *Patterns in Comparative Religion*, trans. Rosemary Shee (Lincoln, NE: University of Nebraska Press, 1958/1996). "Coincidentia Oppositorum—the Mythical Pattern," 419 ff.: "*Mythical thought always progresses from the awareness of oppositions toward their resolution.*" Cf. Claude Lévi-Strauss, *Structural Anthropology*, trans. Claire Jacobson and Brook Grundfest Schoepf (New York, NY: Basic Books, 1974).

[6] Among the oppositions to have come under the deconstructive gaze are word and thing, knowledge and ignorance, meaning and nonsense, permanence and change, identity and difference, public and private, freedom and necessity, God and humanity, good and evil, spirit and nature, mind and matter, inside and outside, plus and minus, and accident and essence. See, for example, Jacques Derrida, *Positions*, trans. Alan Bass (Chicago, IL: University of Chicago Press, 1981), 42-3.

[7] Georges Ohsawa, *The Unique Principle* (Chico, CA: Georges Oshawa Macrobiotic Foundation, 1976). Original French edition published in 1930 by J. Vrin Philosophical Library, Paris, France.

[8] Robin Wang, "Yinyang (yin-yang)," Internet Encyclopedia of Philosophy, accessed July 25, 2016, http://www.iep.utm.edu/yinyang/.

[9] Lao Tzu, *Tao Te Ching*, D. C. Lau, trans. (London, England: Penguin Books, 1963), Verse 4, 58.

[10] Ibid., Verse 186, 140.

[11] Ibid., Verse 81, 96, cf., Verse 108, 109.

[12] Ibid., Verse 79-79a, 95.

[13] Ibid., Verse 165, 129.

[14] Ibid., Verse 82, 99.

[15] Ibid., Verse 83, 99.

[16] Sarvelli Radhakrishnan and Charles Moore, ed., *A Sourcebook in Indian Philosophy* (Princeton, NJ: Princeton University Press, 1957), 55, 65, 77.

[17] Ibid., 65.

[18] Ibid., 40.   [19] Ibid.

[20] Ibid., 42.

[21] R. C. Zaehner, ed. and trans. *Bhagavad Gita* iix, 16-9, *Hindu Scriptures* (Rutland, VT: Charles E. Tuttle, 1966), 320.

[22] Radhakrishnan and Moore, *A Sourcebook*, 109.

[23] Jay L. Garfield and Graham Priest: "Nagarjuna and the Limits of Thought," *Philosophy East and West*, *43*(Jan 2003): 1-21.

[24] Graham Priest, "Dialetheism," *The Stanford Encyclopedia of Philosophy (Summer 2004 Ed.)*, ed. Edward N. Zalta. Accessed from http://plato.stanford.edu/archives/sum2004/entries/dialetheism .

[25] Ibid.

[26] Lazerowitz, "Garfield and Priest," 8, 13. A similar view is attributed to Jacques Derrida. See John D. Caputo, *The Prayers and Tears of*

Jacques Derrida: Religion Without Religion (Bloomington, IN: Indiana University Press, 1997), 311.

[27] Dennis McCort, *Going Beyond the Pairs: The Coincidence of Opposites in German Romanticism, Zen, and Deconstruction* (Albany, NY: State University of New York Press, 2001), 129. McCort asks, "Is the West finally yielding to the East's age-old insistence that the intellect has no significant role to play in leading us to ultimate Truth or Reality?" He then trots out a long list of academic, psychoanalytic, and pop-culture masters who warn of "reason's utter impotence in the face of the Mystery." However, McCort tells us that an exception to this trend is the philosopher Franklin Merrell-Wolff (1887–1985), whom he describes as a "spiritual teacher whose mission in life it was to show how intellect, and its objective correlative, language, could, when used in a certain way by a certain type of person, be a most dependable and efficient raft to that 'other shore' of the land beyond the pairs of opposites" (135).

[28] Aristotle, *Physics*, A4 187a20, in G. S. Kirk and J. E. Raven, eds., *The Presocratic Philosophers* (Cambridge, MA: Cambridge University Press, 1957), 129.

[29] G. S. Kirk and Raven, J. E., *The Presocratic Philosophers*, 189. (Heraclitus, Fr. 111, Stobaeus).

[30] Ibid. (Heraclitus, Fr. 61, Hyppolytus, *Refutation of all heresies*, IX, 10, 5).

[31] Ibid., 191 (Heraclitus, Fr. 10, Aristotle, *de mundo* 5, 396b20).

[32] Ibid. (Heraclitus, Fr. 67, Hippolytus, *Refutation of all heresies* IX 10, 9).

[33] Ibid., 189 (Heraclitus, Fr. 60 Hippolytus, *Refutation of all heresies* IX, 10, 4).

[34] Ibid., 194-5 (Heraclitus, Fr. 18 Clement *Strom* II, 17, 4).

[35] Aristotle, *Metaphysics*, IV, 7, 23., trans. W. D. Ross. In ed. M. Adler, *Great Books of the Western World*, vol. 7 (Chicago, IL: Encyclopedia Britannica, Inc., 1991), 532. Hegel, in his *Lectures on the History of Philosophy*, translates this as "Being and non-being are the same; everything is and yet is not" (G. W. F. Hegel, *Lectures on the History of Philosophy*, vol. I, trans. E. S. Haldane and F. H. Simon (London, England: Routledge, 1974), 282.

[36] Sextus Empiricus (adv. Math. IX 337), as quoted by Hegel, *Lectures on the History of Philosophy*, vol. 1, 284.

[37] Kirk and Raven, *The Presocratic Philosophers*, 209 (Heraclitus, Fr. 51).

[38] Hegel, *Lectures on the History of Philosophy*, vol. I, 284-5.

[39] Daniel Graham, "Heraclitus," in the *Stanford Encyclopedia of Philosophy*

(Stanford: The Metaphysics Research Lab, 2011). Accessed November 15, 2015, http://plato.stanford.edu/archives/sum2011/entries/heraclitus.

[40] Ibid., 6.

[41] "Heraclitus, Fragment 12, Arius Didymus in Eusebius," *Preparation for the Gospel*, XV, 20, 2. J. Burnet, *Early Greek Philosophy*. (London), 1912, 1920. Accessed July 27, 2016, http://en.wikisource.org/wiki/Fragments_ of_Heraclitus.

[42] Ibid., "Heraclitus, Fragment 49a,"

[43] Ibid., "Heraclitus, Fragment 91,"

[44] Plato, *Cratylus* 402, *The Dialogues of Plato*, ed. Mortimer J. Adler, trans. B. Jowett, *Great Books of the Western World*, vol. 6 (Chicago, IL: Encyclopedia Britannica, Inc. 1990), 94.

[45] Graham, "Heraclitus," 10.

[46] Ibid., 11.

[47] "Heraclitus, Fragment 88, Ps. Plutarch," *Consolation to Apollonius*, 106 E. Accessed November 18, 2016. http://en.wikisource.org/wiki/Fragments_ of_Heraclitus.

[48] Aristotle, *Metaphysics*, IV, 3b, 17-25, Ross, 524.

[49] Ibid., IV, 7, 23, 282.

[50] Ibid., V, 6, 36ff., 536.

[51] "Heraclitus, Fragment 88, Ps. Plutarch."

[52] C. J. Emlyn-Jones, "Heraclitus and the Identity of Opposites," *Phronesis* 21 (1976): 89-114, 95-5.

[53] Kirk and Raven, *The Presocratic Philosophers*, 187.

[54] Ibid., 188, 9.

[55] "Heraclitus, Fragment 48," *Etymologicum magnum*, Article: βιός. Accessed November 18, 2016, http://en.wikisource.org/wiki/Fragments_of_Heraclitus.

[56] Emlyn-Jones, "Heraclitus," 99.

[57] Ibid., 101.

[58] Matthew Colvin, "Heraclitean Flux and Unity of Opposites in Plato's "Thaetetus" and Cratylus," *The Classical Quarterly, New Series* 57 (Dec. 2007): 759-69.

[59] Ibid., 760.

[60] Ibid.

[61] Plato, *Thaetetus* 183a. Jowett, *The Dialogues of Plato*, 534.

[62] Colvin, "Heraclitean Flux," 763.

[63] Ibid., 767.

[64] Hegel, *Lectures on the History of Philosophy*, vol. I, 284-5. Jowett renders this as, "The One is united by disunion, like the harmony of the bow and the lyre." Plato, Symposium 187a. Jowett, *The Dialogues of Plato*, 156.

[65] "Heraclitus, Fragment 67." Hippolytus, *Refutation of all heresies*, IX, 10, 8. Accessed November 18, 2016, http://en.wikisource.org/wiki/Fragments_of_Heraclitus.

[66] Emlyn-Jones, "Heraclitus," 107.

[67] Kirk and Raven, *The Presocratic Philosophers*, 192.

[68] "Heraclitus, Fragment 10." Aristotle, *On the World*, 5. 396 b, 20. Accessed November 18, 2016, http://en.wikisource.org/wiki/Fragments_of_Heraclitus.

[69] "Heraclitus, Fragment 51" Hippolytus, *Refutation of all heresies*, IX, 9, 2. Accessed November 18, 2016, http://en.wikisource.org/wiki/Fragments_of_Heraclitus.

[70] Hegel, *Lectures on the History of Philosophy*, vol. I, 279.

[71] Kirk and Raven, *The Presocratic Philosophers*, 195 (Heraclitus, Fragment 80).

[72] Ibid., 196 (Aristotle Ethics Eudem. H1, 1235a).

[73] "Heraclitus, Fragment 126." *Scholis ad Exegesin in Iliadem* (Tzetzes, *Commentary on the Iliad*). Accessed November 18, 2016, http://en.wikisource.org/wiki/Fragments_of_Heraclitus.

[74] Kirk and Raven, *The Presocratic Philosophers*, 196.

[75] Ibid., 194-5. (Heraclitus, Fragment 80). Clement of Alexandria, *Stromata*, II, 17, 4.

[76] Kirk and Raven, *The Presocratic Philosophers*, 193. (Heraclitus, Fragment 51).

[77] Plato, *Symposium*, 186-7. Jowett, *The Dialogues of Plato*, 156.

[78] Ibid., 372-3. (Plato, *Republic* VI, 479).

[79] Ibid., 273. (Plato, *Republic* VI, 479).

[80] Ibid, 351. (Plato, *Republic* IV, 436-7).

[81] Ibid., 226. (Plato, *Phaedo,* 70).

[82] Ibid., 227. (Plato, *Phaedo,* 71).

[83] J. N. Findlay, *Plato: The Written and Unwritten Doctrines* (London: Routledge & Kegan Paul, 1974), 133.

[84] Plato, *Phaedo*, 102, Jowett, *The Dialogues of Plato*, 244.

[85] Ibid., 244. (Plato, *Phaedo*, 103).

[86] Ibid., 504. Plato, *Parmenides*, 155.

[87] Ibid.

[88] Ibid., 505. (Plato, *Parmenides* 157).

[89] Findlay, *Plato: The Written and the Unwritten Doctrines*, 246.

[90] Plato, *Parmenides* 157, Jowett, *The Dialogues of Plato*, 511.

[91] Findlay, *Plato: The Written and Unwritten Doctrines*, 247.

[92] Plato, *Sophist* 238, Jowett, *The Dialogues of Plato*, 562.

[93] Ibid., 564. (Plato, *Sophist* 241).

[94] Ibid., 564. (Plato, *Sophist* 241).

[95] G. Filoramo, *A History of Gnosticism*, trans. Anthony Alcock (Cambridge: Basil Blackwell, 1990), 42.

[96] K. Rudolph, *Gnosis: The Nature and History of Gnosticism,* ed. and trans. R. M Wilson (San Francisco: Harper & Row, 1987), 93. (Quoting the *Nag Hammadi Codex* II 3, 71 (119), 35-72 (120), 4.)

[97] Ibid., 81.

[98] J. M. Robinson, ed., *The Nag Hammadi Library*, 3rd ed. (San Francisco: Harper & Row, 1988). "Thunder: The Perfect Mind," 295-303. Compare to *Bhagavad Gita* iix, 16-19 where the "blessed lord" describes himself as father and mother, origin and dissolution, death and deathlessness (R. C. Zaehner, ed., *Hindu Scriptures* (London, England: J. M. Dent & Sons, Ltd., 1966).

[99] Rudolph, *Gnosis*, 81. Quoting the Nag Hammadi Codex II, 3, 75 (123), 2-9.

[100] Plotinus, *The Six Enneads,* trans. Stephen Makenna. In *The Great Books of the Western World*, vol. 11 (Chicago, IL: Encyclopedia Britannica, 1952). *Enneads* 1:8:7.

[101] Plotinus, *Enneads* 3:9:3, Ibid., 444.

[102] Plotinus, *Enneads*. 3:8:8, Ibid., 449.

[103] Plotinus, *Enneads* 3:8:8, Ibid.

[104] Plotinus, *Enneads* 1:8:12, Ibid., 336.

[105] Plotinus, *Enneads* 3:2:16, Ibid. 395.

[106] Plotinus, *Enneads* 3:2:16, Ibid., 396.

[107] Ibid.

[108] Ibid.

[109] Ibid.

[110] Ibid.

[111] Plotinus, *Enneads* 3:2:16, Ibid., 396.   [112] Ibid.

[113] Nicholas of Cusa, *De Docta Ignorantia* I, 3–4: 10. Cusanus writes, "Whatever is not truth cannot measure truth precisely. (By comparison, a noncircle [cannot measure] a circle, whose being is something indivisible.) Hence, the intellect, which is not truth, never comprehends truth so precisely that truth cannot be comprehended infinitely more precisely. For the intellect is to truth as [an inscribed] polygon is to [the inscribing] circle". The more angles the inscribed polygon has the more similar it is to the circle. However, even if the number of its angles is increased *ad infinitum*, the polygon never becomes equal [to the circle] unless it is resolved into an identity with the circle. Hence, regarding truth, it is evident that we do not know anything other than the following: that we know truth not to be precisely comprehensible as it is." Nicholas of Cusa, "On Learned Ignorance," *De Docta Ignorantia* (Minneapolis, MN: The Arthur J. Banning Press), 1981. Translation of Book I from *De docta ignorantia. Die belehrte Unwissenheit, Book I* (2nd ed.), ed. Paul Wilpert, revised by Hans G. Senger (Hamburg, Germany: Felix Meiner, 1970). Accessed November 15, 2016, http://www.jasper-hopkins.info/DI-I-12-2000.pdf.

[114] Clyde Lee Miller, "Cusanus, Nicolaus [Nicolas of Cusa]," *The Stanford Encyclopedia of Philosophy* (Fall 2015 Edition), ed. Edward N. Zalta. Accessed July 26, 2016, http://plato.stanford.edu/archives/fall2015/entries/cusanus.

[115] See, e.g., Plotinus, *Enneads* 5:8:4, 552.

[116] Nicholas of Cusa, *On the Peace of Faith* (*De Pace Fide*): *A Dialogue on World Religious Peace*, trans. Lawrence Bond, last modified 2000. Accessed August 4, 2016, http://www.appstate.edu/~bondhl/bondpeac.htm.

[117] Immanuel Kant, *Critique of Pure Reason*, trans. Norman Kemp Smith (London, England: MacMillan, 1929), 396ff.

[118] Ibid., 409ff.

[119] Ibid., 42.

[120] Ibid., 27, 45, 67 ff.

[121] Ibid., 27, 74 ff.

[122] Ibid., 50 ff.

[123] Ibid., 272.

[124] Michael Rohlf, "Immanuel Kant," in *The Stanford Encyclopedia of Philoso-*

phy (Spring 2016 Edition), ed. Edward N. Zalta. Accessed August 6, 2016. http://plato.stanford.edu/archives/spr2016/entries/kant

[125] Immanuel Kant, *The Critique of Practical Reason*, trans. Lewis W. Beck. (Indiana, IN: Bobbs-Merrill, 1956).

[126] Immanuel Kant, *Critique of Judgment*, trans. James Creed Meredith. (Oxford, England: Oxford University Press, 2007).

[127] According to Hedley and Ryan, in Schelling's early system "the absolute is the identity or indifference point in which subject and object, spirit and nature, the ideal and the real, are unified." Douglas Hedley and Chris Ryan, "Nineteenth Century Philosophy of Religion: An Introduction," in Graham Oppy and N. N. Trakakis, *Nineteenth Century Philosophy of Religion* (London, England: Routledge, 2014), 9.

[128] Hegel, *Lectures on the History of Philosophy*, Vol. III, 524.

[129] Ibid., 535 ff.

[130] G. W. F. Hegel, *Science of Logic*, trans. George di Giovanni (Cambridge, MA: Cambridge University Press, 2010), 40, note e.

[131] Hegel discusses his differences with Kant in Ibid., 36ff.

[132] W. T. Stace, *The Philosophy of Hegel: A Systematic Exposition* (New York, NY: Dover Publications, 1955), 44 ff.

[133] Ibid., 90.

[134] Ibid., 104.

[135] My account here follows Andrea Staiti's in Andrea Staiti, "Heinrich Rickert," in *The Stanford Encyclopedia of Philosophy* (Winter 2013 Edition), ed. Edward N. Zalta. Accessed February 15, 2016, http://plato.stanford. edu/archives/win2013/entries/heinrich-rickert .

[136] Andrea Staiti, "The Neo-Kantians on the Meaning and Status of Philosophy," in *New Approaches to Neo-Kantianism*, ed. N. De Warren and Andrea Staiti (Cambridge, MA: Cambridge University Press, 2015), 19-38, 27, citing: H. Rickert, *Grundprobleme der Philosophie, Methodologie, Ontologie, Anthropologie* (Tübingen, Germany: Mohr Siebeck, 1934), 41.

[137] Staiti, "The Neo-Kantians," 27, citing Rickert, *Grundprobleme,* 41.

[138] I am indebted to a paper by James Garrison for pointing out the places in Dewey's *Experience and Nature* where the coincidence of opposites appears. J. W. Garrison, "Dewey and the Empirical Unity of Opposites," *Transactions of the Charles S. Peirce Society* 21 (Fall 1985): 549-561.

[139] John Dewey, *Experience and Nature* (London, England: George Allen &

Unwin, 1929), 47-8.

[140] Garrison, "Dewey and the Empirical Unity of Opposites," 550.

[141] James Good, *A Search for Unity in Diversity: The "Permanent Hegelian Deposit" in the Philosophy of John Dewey* (Oxford, England: Lexington Books, 2006).

[142] Dewey, *Experience and Nature*, 59.

[143] Ibid.   [144] Ibid.

[145] Ibid.

[146] Garrison, "Dewey and the Empirical Unity of Opposites," 552.

[147] Dewey, *Experience and Nature*, 63.

[148] Ibid., 359.

[149] Dewey, *Experience and Nature*, 378.

[150] Alfred North Whitehead, Process and Reality (Corrected Edition). (New York: The Free Press, 1978). Originally the Gifford Lectures, 1927-8.

[151] Ibid.   [152] Ibid., 145.

[153] Ibid., 343.   [154] Ibid., 345,

[155] Ibid.   [156] Ibid.

[157] Ibid., 348.   [158] Ibid., 347.

[159] Ibid., 348

[160] J. N. Findlay, *Hegel: A Re-examination (New York, NY: Oxford University Press*, 1058).

[161] J. N. Findlay, "Philosophy as a Discipline," *The Philosophical Forum* XXX-VI (Summer 2005): 147.

[162] Findlay, *The Discipline of the Cave*, (London, England: George Allen Unwin, 1966), 33.

[163] Findlay, "Intentional Inexistence," in *Ascent to the Absolute,* ed. J. N. Findlay. (London, England: George Allen Unwin, 1970), 244.

[164] Ibid., 243.   [165] Ibid., 245.

[166] Ibid.   [167] Ibid., 246.

[168] Ibid., 247.

[169] As quoted in Ibid., 247.

[170] Morris Lazerowitz, *Philosophy and Illusion* (London, England: George Allen & Unwin, 1968), 1.

[171] Ibid., 47.

[172] Ibid.

[173] Ibid., 48.

[174] Ibid., 46.

[175] Ibid., 99.

[176] Ibid., 99, ff.

[177] Ludwig Wittgenstein, *Philosophical Investigations*, 3rd edition, trans. G. E. M. Anscombe (New York, NY: MacMillan), 47e, par. 109.

[178] Graham Priest, "Dialetheism," in the *Stanford Encyclopedia of Philosophy*. Accessed from https://plato.stanford.edu/entries/dialetheism/.

[179] Aristotle, *Metaphysics*, Book IV, Ch. 3, 1005b, 19-20, in *Great Books of the Western World* vol. 7, ed. M. Adler, trans. W. D. Ross (Chicago, IL: Encyclopedia Britannica, Inc., 1991), 524.

[180] Ibid.

[181] Ibid., Book IV, Ch. VI, 1011b, 13-14, 531.

[182] Ibid., Book IV, Ch. 4, 1006b 35, 527.

[183] Ibid., 1011b, 13-4, 531.

[184] For a discussion of this problem see Jay L. Garfield, and Graham Priest, "Nagarjuna and the Limits of Thought." Accessed from https://pdfs.semanticscholar.org/7b8d/3ca63f676e2306ba33dc4350a9d659c3ec6b.pdf.

[185] See J. C. Beal, "Dialetheism and the Probability of Contradictions," *Australasian Journal of Philosophy* 79 (March 2001): 114-18.

[186] An *interchangability* between the "neither" and the "both" is suggested by Jacques Derrida in *Positions*, where in describing his "logic" of "undecidables" he says the *pharmakon* is "neither remedy nor poison, neither good nor evil, neither the inside nor the outside, neither speech nor writing; the *supplement* is neither a plus nor a minus, neither an outside nor the complement of an inside, neither accident nor essence, etc.; the *hymen* is neither confusion nor distinction, neither identity nor difference, neither consummation nor virginity, neither the veil nor the unveiling, neither the inside nor the outside, etc.... Neither/nor, that is *simultaneously* either/or..." (J. Derrida, *Positions*, trans. Alan Bass (Chicago, IL: University of Chicago Press, 1981), 42-43.

[187] Niels Bohr, "Discussion with Einstein on Epistemological Problems in Atomic Physics," 354. I have quoted Bohr's full statement on the two kinds of opposites in the Introduction.

[188] Niels Bohr, "Selections from Atomic Theory and the Description of Nature," in *Great Books of the Western World*, ed. Mortimer J. Adler (Chicago, IL: Encyclopedia Britannica, Inc. 1990), vol. 56, 305-337, 315.

189 Ibid., 316.

190 Bohr, "Discussion with Einstein," 341.

191 Ibid., 353.

192 Ibid., 347.

193 Ibid., 353.

194 Ibid., 354.

195 Ibid., 347.

196 It is my view that deconstruction's very opposition to mysticism and meta-physics may well leave it open to its being determined by them.

197 Christian Howells, *Derrida: Deconstruction from Phenomenology to Ethics* (Cambridge, MA: Polity Press, 1999), 82.

198 For example, the Kabbalistic symbol *Ein-sof* overcomes the distinctions between being and nothingness, God and the world, and theism and atheism. *Tzimtzum* overcomes the distinctions between concealment and revelation, and reality and illusion. The *Sefirot* overcome the distinctions between unity and diversity, permanence and change, and subject and object. The *Otiyot Yesod* (Foundational Letters) overcome the distinction between language and the world, and words and things. The *Shevirat ha-Kelim* overcomes the distinctions between creation and destruction, life and death, and so on.

199 An interesting effect of the supplement is that, because one cannot circumscribe the world with one's speech or perception, the supplement makes possible (and necessary) desire; for desire is precisely a reaching toward that which one does not—yet—have.

200 Jacques Derrida links these undecidables to the Freudian unconscious.

201 Harry Staten, *Wittgenstein and Derrida*, (Lincoln, NE: University of Nebraska Press, 1986), 16ff.

202 One who was, in effect, "glued" to the "present," would have nothing present to mind as there would be no context, category, or existent in one's awareness. This is, in effect, the goal of certain forms of meditation, the most radical of which involves meditation on "nothingness," which dissolves all temporal and other distinctions. Such meditation may bring one into a pre-temporal, pre-linguistic state in which even the distinction between being and nothing is dissolved.

203 Howells, *Derrida*, 17.

204 Jean-Paul Sartre, *Psychology of the Imagination*, trans. Hazel Barnes (Lon-

don, England: Routledge, 2001), 218. Original French edition published in 1940.

[205] C. G. Jung, *The Red Book, Liber Novus*, ed. Sonu Shamdasani, trans. Mark Kyburz, John Peck, and Sonu Shamdasani (New York, NY: W.W. Norton & Company, 2009), 283a.

[206] I discuss the deconstruction of the distinction between identity and difference in Chapter 6.

[207] Staten, *Wittgenstein and Derrida*, 18.

[208] Ibid.

[209] See Howard Coward & Toby Foshay, *Derrida and Negative Theology* (Albany, NY: State University of New York Press, 1992).

[210] Jung, *Psychology and Alchemy*, 186.

[211] C. G. Jung, "Commentary on 'The Secret of the Golden Flower,'" in *Alchemical Studies, Collected Works of C. G. Jung*, vol. 13, trans. R. F. C. Hull (Princeton, NJ: Princeton University Press, 1967), par. 31, 21.

[212] Ibid. We should here note that the structural anthropologist, Claude Lévi-Strauss later held that the very purpose of myth and symbols is to reconcile conflicts and contradictions that cannot be reconciled via other forms of thought or behavior. Because all cultures organize thought and knowledge into binary oppositions, all cultures require myth and symbols to reconcile the contradictions that are engendered.

[213] See, for example, C. G. Jung, *Psychological Types*, 321, par. 540; C. G. Jung, *Letters, Volumes I and II,* ed. Gerhard Adler, Aniela Jaffe, and R. F. C. Hull (Princeton, NJ: Princeton University Press, 1973), vol. I, 194. Letter to Friedrich Siefert, 31 July 1935. I will discuss Jung's views on Hegel in Chapter 4.

[214] C. G. Jung, "The Relations Between the Ego and the Unconscious" in *Two Essays on Analytical Psychology. In The Collected Works of C. G. Jung,* 2nd ed., vol. 7, trans. R. F. C. Hull, (Princeton, NJ: Princeton University Press, 1966), 177, par. 274.

[215] Hector Sabelli, *Union of Opposites: A Comprehensive Theory of Natural and Human Processes* (Lawrenceville, VA: Brunswick Publishing Corporation, 1989), xv.

[216] Ibid., xvii.

[217] Ibid., 2.

[218] Ibid.

[219] Ibid, 150.

[220] Ibid.

[221] Ibid., 141.

[222] Ibid.

[223] Ibid., 206.

[224] Ibid., 214.

[225] Ibid., 216ff.

[226] Ibid., 219.

[227] Ibid., 296.

[228] Ibid., 297

[229] Ibid.

[230] Ibid.

Chapter Two

[1] See Ewert H. Cousins, *Bonaventure and the Coincidence of Opposites* (Chicago, IL: Franciscan Herald Press, 1978).

[2] Meister Eckhart, "True Hearing," Sermon on Ecclesiasticus xxiv, 30—"Whoso heareth Me shall not be confounded." *Meister Eckhardt's Sermons*, trans. Claud Field (London, England: H. R. Allenson, Ltd., 2005), 14. Accessed August 8, 2016, http://www.catholicprimer.org/eckhart/eckhart_sermons.pdf.

[3] Lao Tzu, *Tao Te Ching*, D. C. Lau, trans. (London, England: Penguin Books, 1963).

[4] Ibid., Verse 72, 91.

[5] R. C. Zaehner, ed., *Hindu Scriptures* (London, England: J. M. Dent & Sons, Ltd., 1966), 41.

[6] Ibid., 126.

[7] Ibid., 127.

[8] Heinrich Zimmer, *Philosophies of India*, ed. Joseph Campbell (Princeton, NJ.: Princeton University Press, 1951), 380.

[9] Sanford Drob, *Symbols of the Kabbalah: Philosophical and Psychological Perspectives.* (Northvale, NJ: Jason Aronson, 2000); Sanford Drob, *Kabbalistic Metaphors: Mystical Themes in Ancient and Modern Thought* (Northvale, NJ: Jason Aronson, 2000); Sanford Drob, *Kabbalah and Postmodernism: A Dialogue* (New York, NY: Peter Lang, 2009); Sanford Drob, *Kabbalistic Visions: C. G. Jung and Jewish Mysticism* (New Orleans, LA:

Spring Journal Books, 2010).

[10] Rachel Elior, *The Paradoxical Ascent to God: The Kabbalistic Theosophy of Habad Hasidism,* trans. J. M. Green (Albany, NY: State University of New York Press, 1993); Rachel Elior, "Chabad: The Contemplative Ascent to God," in *Jewish Spirituality: From the Sixteenth Century Revival to the Present,* ed. Arthur Green (New York, NY: Crossroads, 1987), 157-205.

[11] See Gershom Scholem, *Major Trends in Jewish Mysticism* (New York, NY: Schocken, 1941).

[12] Ibid., 44 (*Sefer Yetzirah* 1:5).

[13] *Sefer Yetzirah* 1:7. Aryeh Kaplan, *Sefer Yetzirah: The Book of Creation,* revised ed. (York Beach, NE: Samuel Weiser, 1997), 57.

[14] Azriel of Gerona, "The Explanation of the Ten *Sefirot,*" in Joseph Dan, *The Early Kabbalah,* trans. Ronald C. Kieber (New York, NY: Paulist Press, 1966).

[15] Gershom Scholem, *Origins of the Kabbalah,* trans. R. J. Zwi Werblowski (Princeton, NJ: Princeton University Press, 1962/1987), 423.

[16] Ibid., 441-2.

[17] Azriel, "The Explanation of the Ten Sefirot," 94.

[18] Ibid.

[19] Scholem, *Origins of the Kabbalah,* 332-3.

[20] Scholem translates *achdut hasvaah* as a "complete indistinguishability of opposites," Gershom Scholem, *Kabbalah.* (Jerusalem, Israel: Keter, 1974), 88.

[21] See Scholem. *Origins of the Kabbalah.* According to Elior, the term *achdut hashvaah* connotes "two contradictions within a single entity." It is "the divine element that encompasses contradictions and reconciles their existence," Elior, 3, 69.

[22] Moses Cordovero, Elima Rabati, fol. 25a, as quoted in Elior, *The Paradoxical Ascent to God,* 50.

[23] R. Chayyim Vital, Sefer Etz Chayyim (Warsaw, 1891), "Sha'are ha-Hakdamot." Quoted in Elior, *The Paradoxical Ascent to God,* 68.

[24] Schneur Zalman, *Likutei-Amarim-Tanya,* bilingual ed. (Brooklyn, NY: Kehot Publication Society, 1981), 319. (*Shaar ha Yichud VehaEmunah* 7).

[25] Ibid.

[26] In Hebrew, each letter is assigned a numerical equivalent. Gematria is an

interpretive procedure whereby the meaning of a word or passage is transformed through a calculation of its "numerical value," and then other words or expressions that have the same numerical value as the original are substituted.

[27] *Zohar* III, 113a. Harry Sperling, Maurice Simon, and Paul Levertoff, ed., *The Zohar, Vols. I–V* (London, England: Soncino Press, 1931-34), vol. 5, 153.

[28] "The Mystic as Philosopher: An Interview with Rabbi Adin Steinsaltz," *Jewish Review*, 3(4) (March 1990/Adar 5570). Accessed August 8, 2016, http://thejewishreview.org/articles/?id=180.

[29] Ibid.

[30] *Zohar* III, 113a. Harry Sperling and Maurice Simon, *The Zohar*, vol. 5, 153. Moshe Idel translates this passage as follows: "Whoever performs the commandments of the Torah and walks in its ways is regarded as if he made the one above." Moshe Idel, *Kabbalah: New Perspectives* (New Haven, CT: Yale University Press, 1988), 187.

[31] See Sanford L. Drob, "A-Systematic Theology" in *Kabbalah and Postmodernism: A Dialogue* (New York, NY: Peter Lang, 2009), Ch. 5, esp. 123-4.

[32] According to the *Zohar*: "Each and every one [of the people of Israel] ought to write a scroll of Torah for himself, and the occult secret [of this matter] is that he made God Himself." Quoted in Idel, *Kabbalah*, 188.

[33] W. T. Stace, *Mysticism and Philosophy*, 161 ff.

[34] Quoted in Elior, *The Paradoxical Ascent to God*, 64.

[35] Quoted in Rachel Elior, "Chabad: The Contemplative Ascent to God," in *Jewish Spirituality: From the Sixteenth Century Revival to the Present*, ed. Arthur Green (New York, NY: Crossroads, 1987), 157-205, 163.

[36] Rabbi Dov Baer, Ner Mitzvah ve-Torah Or, II, fol. 6a. Quoted in Elior, *The Paradoxical Asccent to God*, 64.

[37] Ibid.

[38] Quoted in Elior, "Chabad," 166.

[39] *Hegel's Logic,* William Wallace, trans., (Oxford, England: Clarendon Press, 1975), par. 48, Zusatz 1, 78.

[40] Schneur Zalman *Likutei Torah, Devarim*, fol. 83a. Quoted in Elior, *The Paradoxical Ascent to God*, op. cit., 137-8.

[41] Here and in what follows I am indebted to Rabbi Zalman Abramowitz for his explanation of relevant passages in Schneur Zalman's, Rabbi Dov Baer's, and Rabbi Yosef Yitzhak3 Schneersohn writings.

[42] Aryeh Kaplan, ed., *Ethics of the Talmud: Pirke Avot, MeAm Lo'ez* by *Rabbi Yitzchak (ben Moshe) Magrino* (New York, NY: Maznaim, 1979), 208.

[43] Zimmer, *Philosophies of India,* 13.

[44] The Chabad view is implicitly present in Azriel's *coincidentia oppositorum* between faith and unbelief, and the *Zohar's* precept that "He who 'keeps' the precepts of the Law and 'walks' in God's ways…'makes' Him who is above," and finally, in the Lurianic notion that *Ein-sof* both creates, and is itself completed by, humankind.

[45] Rifka Schatz Uffenheimer, *Hasidism as Mysticism: Quietistic Elements in Eighteenth Century Hasidic Thought* (Jerusalem, Israel: Hebrew University, 1993), 207.

[46] C. G. Jung, "An Eightieth Birthday Interview," in *C. G. Jung Speaking,* ed. W. McGuire & R. F. C. Hull (Princeton, N.J.: Princeton University Press, 1977), 268-72. Jung, like the Maggid, held that the godhead has a hidden life within the minds of human beings.

[47] *Zohar* 1:153a. Harry Sperling, Maurice Simon, and Paul Levertoff, ed., *The Zohar,* vol. 2, 89-90.

[48] Elior, *The Paradoxical Ascent to God,* 62.

[49] Schneur Zalman, Torah Or, p. 49, quoted in Elior, *The Paradoxical Ascent to God,* 134.

[50] Talmud Tractate Chagigah 14b. Accessed August 8, 2016, http://halakhah. com/pdf/moed/Chagigah.pdf.

[51] Schneur Zalman, *Torah Or,* 58, quoted in Elior, *The Paradoxical Ascent to God,* 150.   [52] Ibid., 31.

[53] Schneur Zalman. Igeret Ha Kodesh, Ch. 6, *Likutei-Amarim-Tanya,* op. cit., 421.

[54] Schneur Zalman, *Likutei-Amarim-Tanya,* Ibid., Chapter 35, 159.

[55] Elior, "Chabad," 80.

[56] Rabbi Dov Baer, *Ner Mitzvah ve-Torah Or* (Brooklyn, NY: Kehot, 1820/1974), 225 ff. Quoted in Elior, *The Paradoxical Ascent to God,* 64.

[57] Rabbi Dov Baer, *Ner Mitzvah ve-Torah Or.* I am indebted to Rabbi Zalman Abramowitz for the translation and interpretation of this passage.

[58] Zalman, *Likutei-Amarim-Tanya,* Ch. 34, 155, referencing *Zohar* II, 255a and esp., III, 75a.

[59] Quoted in Rabbi Dov Baer333, *Ner Mitzvah ve-Torah Or,* 225. Translated from the Hebrew by Rabbi Zalman Abramowitz.

[60] Yosef Yitzhak Schneersohn, *Sefer Hamamerim* (Brooklyn, NY: Publisher unknown, 1944), 223 ff. I am again indebted to Rabbi Zalman Abramowitz for the translation and interpretation of this passage.

[61] Ibid., 25.

[62] Ibid. According to Elior, these *coincidentia* appear in the Lurianic Kabbalah but presumably apply only to the heavenly realms. In Chabad, they apply to the earthly and human realms as well (Ibid., 25-6).

[63] Ibid.

[64] Zalman, *Likkutei Torah*, Léviticus, 83, quoted in Ibid., 137.

[65] Elior, "Chabad," op. cit., 165.

[66] Ibid, 167.

[67] Elior, *The Paradoxical Ascent to God*, op. cit., 56.

[68] I am not alone in holding that the Kabbalistic doctrine of *coincidentia oppositorum* is crucial both for understanding mystical consciousness and significant questions in philosophy. A similar point of view is adopted by Elliot Wolfson in his recent *Alef, Mem, Tau: Kabbalistic Musings on Time, Truth, and Death*, where he holds that "in death…the truth of the world of unity is disclosed—a truth predicated on discerning the coincidence of opposites, that is the mystical insight that in ultimate reality opposites are no longer distinguishable, for they are identical in virtue of being opposite." Elliot Wolfson, *Alef, Mem, Tau: Kabbalistic Musings on Time, Truth, and Death* (Berkeley, CA: University of California Press, 2006), xiv.

Chapter Three

[1] Hegel's *Phänomenologie des Geistes*, was originally published in 1807. The two major English translations are G. W. F. Hegel, *Phenomenology of Mind*, trans. J. B. Baillie (London, England: Harper & Row, 1967) and G. W. F. Hegel. *Phenomenology of Spirit*, trans. A. V. Miller with analysis of the text and foreword by J. N. Findlay (Oxford, England: Clarendon Press, 1977).

[2] The English language resurgence of interest in Hegel can be traced to J. N. Findlay, *Hegel: A Re-Examination* (New York, NY: Oxford University Press, 1958). Since that time, the English literature on Hegel has exploded. Works that cover the full scope of his philosophy include: Charles Taylor, *Hegel* (Cambridge, MA: Cambridge University Press, 1975); Frederick C. Beiser, *The Cambridge Companion to Hegel* (Cambridge, MA: Cambridge

University Press, 1993); Terry Pinkard, *Hegel: A Biography* (Cambridge, MA: Cambridge University Press, 2000); Allegra DeLaurentis and Jeffrey Edwards, ed., *The Bloomsbury Companion to Hegel* (London, England: Continuum Press, 2013). A general account and bibliography can be found online: Paul Redding, "Georg Wilhelm Friedrich Hegel" in *The Stanford Encyclopedia of Philosophy* (Spring 2016 Edition), ed. Edward N. Zalta. Accessed from http://plato.stanford.edu/archives/spr2016/entries/hegel/.

[3] Immanuel Kant, *Critique of Pure Reason*, trans. Norman Kemp Smith (London, England: MacMillan, 1929), Preface to the First Edition, 7.

[4] *Hegel's Logic,* William Wallace, trans., (Oxford, England: Clarendon Press, 1975), sec. 80, 113. Being Part I of the *Encyclopedia of the Philosophical Sciences.*

[5] Ibid., sec. 81, 115.

[6] Ibid., sec. 82, 119.

[7] G. W. F. Hegel, *Science of Logic*, trans. George di Giovanni (Cambridge, MA: Cambridge University Press, 2010), 122.

[8] Ibid., 35.

[9] Wallace, *Hegel's Logic*, sec. 81, 115.

[10] Ibid.

[11] Ibid., sec. 81, *Zusatz* 1, 117.

[12] Ibid., sec. 48, *Zusatz*, 78.

[13] Ibid., sec. 81, *Zusatz* 1 , 117.

[14] Ibid., sec. 48, *Zusatz*, 78.

[15] Ibid.

[16] Ibid., sec. 48, *Zusatz*, 79.

[17] Hegel, *Hegel's Science of Logic*, 68.

[18] See Thomas Kuhn, *The Structure of Scientific Revolutions* (Chicago, IL: University of Chicago Press, 1996).

[19] G. W. F. Hegel. *The Phenomenology of Mind*, 2nd ed., trans. J. B. Baillie, (New York, NY: Macmillan, 1931).

[20] Ludwig Wittgenstein, *The Tractatus Logico Philosophicus*, trans. D. F. Pears and B. F. McGuinness (London, England: Routledge, 1961), Prop. I, 5.

[21] Ludwig Wittgenstein, *Philosophical Investigations*, trans. G. E. M. Anscombe (New York, NY: MacMillan, 1958).

[22] Wallace, *Hegel's Logic,* sec. 17, *Zusatz* 1, 23.

[23] Hegel, *Science of Logic*, 70 ff.

[24] Robert C. Solomon, *In the Spirit of Hegel: A Study of G. W. F. Hegel's Phenomenology of Spirit* (New York, NY: Oxford University Press, 1983).

[25] Wallace, *Hegel's Logic*, sec. 88, 131, and sec. 82, *Zusatz* 1, 120-1.

[26] This is a view later endorsed by Jung. He wrote, "The principle of the coincidence of opposites must...be completed by that of absolute opposition in order to attain full paradoxicality and hence psychological validity." C. G. Jung, "The Spirit of Mercurius" in *Alchemical Studies, Collected Works of C. G. Jung*, vol. 13, trans. R. F. C. Hull (Princeton, NJ: Princeton University Press, 1967), 210, par. 256).

[27] G. W. F. Hegel, *Philosophy of Right*, trans. T. M. Knox (London, England: Clarendon Press, 1952), Sec. 26, 32.

[28] Wallace, *Hegel's Logic*, sec. 82, *Zusatz* 1, 120-1.

[29] Ibid., sec. 88, 131.

[30] Ibid.

[31] Metaphysical interpretations of Hegel's system can be found in W. T. Stace, *The Philosophy of Hegel: A Systematic Exposition.* (New York, NY: Dover Publications, 1924/1955); Charles Taylor, *Hegel* (Cambridge, MA: Cambridge University Press, 1975); and J. N. Findlay, *Hegel: A Re-Examination* (New York, NY: Oxford University Press, 1958). The last two also engage Hegel from the perspective of analytic and phenomenological philosophy. Non-metaphysical interpretations can be found in Solomon, *In the Spirit of Hegel*, op. cit.; T. Pinkard, *Hegel: A Biography* (Cambridge, MA: Cambridge University Press, 2000); and Paul Redding, *Hegel's Hermeneutics* (Ithaca, NY: Cornell University Press, 1996).

[32] Wallace, *Hegel's Logic*, sec. 32, 52.

[33] Hegel, *The Science of Logic*, 121.

[34] Wallace, *Hegel's Logic*, sec. 32, *Zusatz*, 53.

[35] For full expositions of Hegel's metaphysics, see citations in note 31.

[36] The following is an expanded version of the brief account of the Hegelian system that appears in Chapter 6 of my book, *Kabbalistic Metaphors* (Northvale, NJ: Jason Aaronson, 2000).

[37] G. W. F. Hegel, *On Art, Religion, Philosophy: Introductory Lectures to the Realm of Absolute Spirit,* ed. J. Glenn Gray (New York, NY: Harper & Row, 1970), 230. Note: "On Art" is J. Glenn Gray's slightly modified version of Bernard Bosanquet's translation of Hegel's *Lectures on Aesthetics*, vol. I (London, England: Routledge, 1905). "On Religion" is a translation

of Hegel's "Lectures on the Philosophy of Religion" trans. E. B. Speirs and I. Burdon Sanderson (London, England: Routledge & Kegan Paul, Ltd., 1895, 37-211). "On Philosophy" is a translation of Hegel's *Lectures on the History of Philosophy*, vol. I. by trans. E. S. Haldane (London, England: Routledge, 1892), 1-116.

[38] See, for example, G. W. F. Hegel, *Lectures on the Philosophy of Religion*, vol. II, trans. E. B. Speirs and J. B. Sanderson (London, England: Routledge, 1974), 330. Here Hegel writes, "It is the Christian religion which is the perfect religion, the religion which represents the Being of Spirit in a realized form...." See also G. W. F. Hegel, *Hegel's Philosophy of Mind* (Oxford, England: Clarendon Press, 1971), par. 482, 239: "It was through Christianity that the Idea came into the world."

[39] Solomon, in *In the Spirit of Hegel*, writes, "The dialectic for [Hegel] is not a method to get at the Truth, but rather it is the Truth, that is, the activity of philosophical thinking itself" (277).

[40] Stace, *The Philosophy of Hegel.*

[41] W. T. Stace, *Mysticism and Philosophy* (London, England: Macmillan, 1960).

[42] Ibid., 269, cf. 213.

[43] Ibid., 268.

[44] Ibid., 213.

[45] G. W. F. Hegel, *On Art, Religion, Philosophy*, 30.

[46] Ibid., 85.

[47] G. W. F. Hegel, *Lectures on the Philosophy of Religion, Vol. III: The Consummate Religion*, ed. Peter Hodgson (Oakland, CA.: University of California Press, 1998).

[48] G. W. F. Hegel, *On Art, Religion, Philosophy*, 186-7.

[49] Ibid., 197.

[50] Ibid., 224.

[51] Ibid., 226.

[52] Ibid., 233.

[53] Ibid.

[54] I will return, in Chapters 4 and 7, to the question of whether reason always follows the path of necessity. I will argue that, while this may be true of reason as it is conceived of in Aristotelean logic and in mathematics, it is not true of dialectical reason, which involves a measure of (and is in *coin*

cidentia oppositorum with) creative fantasy.

[55] Hegel, *On Art, Religion, Philosophy*, 299.

[56] Ibid., 305.

[57] Ibid. 308.

[58] *Hegel's Logic*, Wallace, sec. 81, *Zusatz* 2, 118.

[59] Solomon, *In the Spirit of Hegel*, 277.

[60] Ibid., 230.

[61] Ibid., 277.

[62] Findlay, *Hegel: A Re-Examination*, 354.

[63] J. N. Findlay, *Language, Mind and Value* (London, England: George Allen & Unwin, 1962), 219.

[64] Ibid., 220.

[65] J. N. Findlay, personal communication, 1981. Findlay also writes: "Whatever one may think of the detailed application of his Dialectic, (Hegel) has certainly made plain that our notions do carry with them a certain natural shading into other notions, a natural implication of such notions, and a natural favourableness and unfavourableness to other notions, which is not in our power to create or alter, but which may be said to rest solely on their affinity of content" (Findlay, *Hegel: A Re-examination*, 79).

[66] Findlay, *Language, Mind and Value*, 218.

[67] Hegel, *The Science of Logic*, 382.

[68] Ibid.

[69] Ibid.

[70] Ibid.

[71] Ibid.

[72] Ibid.

[73] Ibid., 201.

[74] Ibid.

[75] Ibid.

[76] Ibid., 111.

[77] Ibid., 35.

[78] Ibid.

[79] Hegel, *On Art, Religion, Philosophy*, 243-4.

[80] Ibid., 158.

[81] Solomon, *In the Spirit of Hegel*, 192.

[82] This is a topic I will discuss more fully in Chapter 7.

[83] Except perhaps in philosophical hypotheticals where the Louvre is somehow duplicated molecule for molecule, the resulting two Louvres are confused and one remains in Paris and the second brought elsewhere.

[84] Hegel, *The Science of Logic*, 356.

[85] Ibid., 381.

[86] Ibid., 359.

[87] Ibid., 360.

[88] Hegel, *The Science of Logic*, 375.

[89] Ibid., 375-6.

[90] Ibid., 376.

[91] Wallace, *Hegel's Logic*, sec. 32, *Zusatz*, 52.

[92] Hegel, *The Science of Logic*, 122.

[93] Ibid.

[94] Wallace, *Hegel's Logic*, Sec. 82, Zuzatz 1, 118.

[95] Morris Lazerowitz, "Paradoxes" in *Philosophy and Illusion* (London, England: George Allen & Unwin, 1968), 19.

[96] Wallace, *Hegel's Logic*, Wallace, sec. 81, *Zusatz* 2, 117.

[97] Ibid., sec. 81, *Zusatz* 2, 118.

[98] G. W. F. Hegel, *The Philosophy of Nature*, cited in Findlay, *Hegel: A Re-Examination*, 281-3.

[99] Hegel, *Phenomenology of Mind*, 93.

[100] Wallace, *Hegel's Logic*, sec. 81, *Zusatz* 1, 118.

[101] Wallace, *Hegel's Philosophy of Mind*, par 386, Zusatz, 24.

[102] Hegel, *Phenomenology of Mind*, 209.

[103] Ibid., 208.

[104] Hegel, *Science of Logic*, 382.

[105] G. W. F. Hegel. *Lectures on the History of Philosophy*, vol. I, trans. E. S. Haldane and F. H. Simon (London, England: Routledge, 1968). Part 1, Ch. 2, C. 1.b, 459 ff.

[106] Slavoj Žižek, *Less than Nothing: Hegel and the Shadow of Dialectical Materialism* (London, England: Verso, 2012), 8.

[107] Ibid., 268.

[108] Ludwig Wittgenstein, *Remarks on the Foundations of Mathematics*, 3rd ed., ed. G. H. von Wright, R. Rhees, and G. E. M. Anscombe, trans. G. E. M. Anscombe (Oxford, England: Basil Blackwell, 1978). Wittgenstein writes, "But you can't allow a contradiction to stand!—Why not? We do some-

times use this form in our talk, of course not often—but one could imagine a technique of language in which it was a regular instrument."

[109] Žižek, *Less Than Nothing*, 269.

[110] This is the understanding of "the real" proffered by the psychoanalyst Jacques Lacan. See Jacques Lacan, *The Seminar of Jacques Lacan, Book VII: The Ethics of Psychoanalysis, 1959–1960*, ed. J. A. Miller, trans. D. Porter (New York, NY: W.W. Norton and Company, 1992).

[111] See William Robinson, "Epiphenomenalism," *The Stanford Encyclopedia of Philosophy* (Fall 2015 Edition), ed. Edward N. Zalta. Accessed November 19, 2016, http://plato.stanford.edu/archives/fall2015/entries/epiphenomenalism.

[112] Thomas Nagel, "Subjective and Objective," in *Post-Analytic Philosophy,* ed. J. Rajchman and C. West (New York, NY: Columbia University Press, 1985).

[113] Solomon, *In the Spirit of Hegel*, 6.

[114] Charles Taylor, *Hegel*, 138.

[115] Stace, *The Philosophy of Hegel*, 43.

[116] I discuss this question in Sanford Drob, "James Hillman On Language, Escape from the Linguistic Prison," in *Archetypal Psychology: Reflections in Honor of James Hillman*, ed. S. Marlan (New Orleans, LA: Spring Journal Books, 2008).

[117] Charles Taylor, *Hegel*, 148.

[118] Hegel, *Phenomenology of Mind*, 226.

[119] Ibid., 148; cf. Taylor, *Hegel*, 155.

[120] G. W. F. Hegel. *Hegel's Philosophy of Mind*. Being Part III of the *Encyclopedia of the Philosophical Sciences,* trans William Wallace. Together with Zusatz in Bouman's edition (1845), trans. A. V. Miller, Foreword by J. N. Findlay (Oxford, England: Clarendon Press, 1971), par 435; Zusatz, 175.

[121] Martin Heidegger, *Being and Time*, trans. J. Macquarrie and E. Robinson (Oxford, England: Basil Blackwell, 1927/1962), 279-311.

[122] Wallace, *Hegel's Logic*, sec. 81, *Zusatz* 1, 116-117.

[123] Ludwig Binswanger, *Being in the World: Selected papers of Ludwig Binswanger*, trans. Jacob Needleman (New York, NY: Basic Books, 1963).

[124] Irwin Yalom, *Existential Pychotherapy* (New York, NY: Basic Books, 1980).

[125] Jean-Paul Sartre, *Being and Nothingness*, trans. Hazel E. Barnes (New York, NY: Washington Square Press, 1966).

[126] Martin Buber, *I and Thou*, trans. Walter Kaufmann (New York, NY: Touchstone, 1970).

[127] Victor E. Frankl, *Man's Search for Meaning*. Part I, trans. Ilse Lasch (Boston, MA: Beacon Press, 2006).

[128] Hegel, *Phenomenology of Mind*, 415-53; cf. Taylor, *Hegel*, 161.

[129] C. G. Jung, *The Red Book, Liber Novus*, ed. Sonu Shamdasani, trans. Mark Kyburz, John Peck, and Sonu Shamdasani (New York, NY: W. W. Norton & Company, 2009).

[130] Wallace, *Hegel's Logic*, sec. 81, *Zusatz* 1, 116.

[131] Ibid., sec. 81, *Zusatz* 1, 118.

[132] Wallace, *Hegel's Logic*, sec. 81, *Zusatz* 1, 118.

[133] C. G. Jung, "On the Nature of Dreams" in *The Structure and Dynamics of the Psyche,* trans. R. F. C. Hull, *The Collected Works of C. G. Jung*, 2nd ed., vol. 8 (Princeton, NJ: Princeton University Press, 1969), where, Jung writes: "A philosophy like Hegel's is a self-revelation of the psychic background," 170, par. 360. See also C. G. Jung, *Psychological Types*, trans. H. G. Baynes and R. F. C. Hull, *The Collected Works of C.G. Jung*, vol. 6 (Princeton, NY: Princeton University Press, 1971), where Jung writes that "intuitive ideas" underlie Hegel's whole system, 321. par. 540. Also see C. G. Jung, *Letters*, Volumes I and II, ed. Gerhard Adler, Aniela Jaffe, and R. F. C. Hull (Princeton, NJ: Princeton University Press, 1973) where, in a letter to Frederich Seifert, 31 July 1935, Jung refers to Hegel as a "psychologist *manqué*," vol. I, 194. In a letter to Joseph F. Rychlak, 27 April 1959, Jung calls Hegel a "misfired psychologist," vol. 2, 501. The connection (and disconnect) between Hegel and Jung will be discussed in greater detail in Chapter 4.

[134] Sigmund Freud, *Collected Papers*, vol. 3, ed. James Strachey, trans. Joan Riviere (New York, NY: Basic Books, 1959), 559.

[135] See note 133.

[136] C.G. Jung, *Psychology and Alchemy*, trans. R. F. C. Hull. *The Collected Works of C. G. Jung,* Vol. 12 (Princeton: Princeton University Press, 1968). Originally published, 1944, 280, par. 397.

[137] Ibid., 20, par. 23.

Chapter Four

[1] Paul Bishop, "Introduction," in *Jung in Context: A Reader*, ed. Paul Bishop and Anthony Storr (London, England: Routledge, 2000), 1.

[2] C. G. Jung, *Psychological Types* in *The Collected Works of C. G. Jung*, Vol. 6, trans. H. G. Baynes and R. F. C. Hull (Princeton, NJ: Princeton University Press, 1971), 111, par. 178.

[3] Jung, *Psychological Types*, 111, par. 179.

[4] Bishop, "Introduction," 2.

[5] C. G. Jung, "Answer to Job" in *The Collected Works of C.G. Jung*, vol. 11, trans. R. F. C. Hull (Princeton, NJ: Princeton University Press, 1968), 419, par. 664.

[6] C. G. Jung, *Symbols of Transformation* in *The Collected Works of C.G. Jung*, vol. 5, trans. R. F. C. Hull (Princeton, NJ: Princeton University Press, 1967), 419, par. 664; 368, par. 576. See also C.G. Jung, *Psychology and Alchemy* in *The Collected Works of C. G. Jung*, vol. 12, trans. R. F. C. Hull (Princeton, NJ: Princeton University Press, 1968), 19, par. 22.

[7] Jung, *Symbols of Transformation*, 374, par. 580.

[8] C. G. Jung, *Mysterium Coniunctionis: An Inquiry into the Seperation and Synthesis of Psychic Opposites in Alchemy* in *The Collected Works of C. G. Jung*, vol. 14, trans. R. F. C. Hull, (Princeton, NJ: Princeton University Press, 1970), 463-4, par. 681-2; cf. Jung, *Symbols of Transformation*, 375, n. 154.

[9] C. G. Jung, *Psychology and Alchemy* in *The Collected Works of C.G. Jung*, vol. 12, trans. R. F. C. Hull (Princeton, NJ: Princeton University Press, 2nd ed. 1968), 205, par. 311.

[10] C. G. Jung, *Psychological Types*, 141, par. 231 and n. 14.

[11] Ibid., p. 57, par. 84.

[12] Ibid., 105, par. 169.

[13] Ibid.

[14] An example of this is the frequent conflict observed between a religious individual's behavior and the demands of religious orthodoxy.

[15] C. G. Jung, *Mysterium Coniunctionis,* 468, par. 667.

[16] Ibid., 477, par. 680.

[17] C. G. Jung, *Psychological Types*, 168, par. 279.

[18] Ibid.

[19] Jung, *Psychological Types*, 321, par. 541. With respect to the fragmentation

in philosophy and psychology and the reconciliation of the two types of truth, one wonders if Jung's "creative fantasy" promises more than it delivers. Perhaps a "positive act of creation" can produce a reconciliation that is acceptable on both a theoretical and intuitive (experiential) level.

[20] Jung, *Mysterium Coniunctionis*, 194-5, par. 124-5.

[21] Jung, *Psychological Types*, 321, par. 540.

[22] Jung, *Mysterium Coniunctionis,* 105, par. 125.

[23] Ibid., 106, par. 127.

[24] Friedrich Nietzsche, *Untimely Meditations*, ed. Daniel Breazeale, trans. R. J. Hollingdale (Cambridge, MA: Cambridge University Press, 1997), IV, Sec. 5, 214.

[25] Friedrich Nietzsche, "The Dionysiac World-View, Sec. 1," in *The Birth of Tragedy and Other Writings*, ed. Raymond Gess and Ronald Spiers, trans. Ronald Speirs (Cambridge, MA: Cambridge University Press, 1999), 19.

[26] Friedrich Nietzsche, *The Birth of Tragedy* (Cambridge, MA: Cambridge University Press, 1999) 119.

[27] Ibid., 26.

[28] Ibid., 17.

[29] Ibid., 20.

[30] Ibid., 122.

[31] Lucy Huskinson, *Nietzsche and Jung: The Whole Self in the Union of Opposites* (New York, NY: Brunner-Routledge, 2004), 15.

[32] Ibid., 15.

[33] Nietzsche, *The Birth of Tragedy*, 76.

[34] Ibid., 77.

[35] Ibid., 44.

[36] Huskinson, *Nietzsche and Jung*, 16. As Huskinson points out, while Nietzsche attributes *reason* exclusively to the Apollonian principle and *instinct* exclusively to the Dionysian, this is a distinction that cannot be sustained on the basis of the nature of the Greek Gods and notions on which these principles are named and based. For example, Nietzsche failed to recognize that for the Greeks, Apollo (as the God of music) embodies ecstatic experience, and Nietzsche instead attributes these characteristics to Dionysus.

[37] A. H. Chapman and M. Chapman-Santana, "The Influence of Nietzsche on Freud's Ideas," *British Journal of Psychiatry*, *166*(2) (2009): 251-53.

[38] Friedrich Nietzsche, *On the Genealogy of Morality,* ed. Keith Ansell-Pearson, trans. Carol Dieth (Cambridge. MA: Cambridge University Press, 2006), Second Essay, Sec. 16, 56-7.

[39] Huskinson, *Nietzsche and Freud*, 20ff.

[40] C. G. Jung, *The Red Book, Liber Novus*, ed. Sonu Shamdasani, trans. Mark Kyburz, John Peck, and Sonu Shamdasani (New YorkNY: W.W. Norton & Company, 2009), 263a.

[41] Ibid., 317b.

[42] Ibid., 319a.

[43] Jung, *Psychological Types*, 138, par. 226.

[44] Ibid., 138, par. 227.

[45] Jung, *The Red Book*, 280b.

[46] Ibid., 313a.

[47] Ibid., 115:184. Interestingly, Jung here compares the transcendent function to a mathematical function that unites real and imaginary quantities.

[48] Ibid., 479, par. 825.

[49] Ibid., 478, par. 823.

[50] Claude Lévi-Strauss, "The Structure of Myth," in *Structural Anthropology*, trans. Claire Jacobson and Brooke Grundfest (New York, NY: Allen Lane, 1963). Originally published in the *Journal of American Folklore*, LXVII (1955): 428-44.

[51] Jung, *Psychological Types*, 480, par. 827.

[52] We might add Moses, who struggled with the contradictions in his own identity as a Hebrew and an Egyptian, and between the polarities in his own character, which resulted in both his love for and his intense anger at the people whom he led to freedom.

[53] Jung, *Psychological Types*, 117, par. 187.

[54] Ibid., 85, par. 127.

[55] Ibid., 84, par. 126.

[56] Ibid., 84, par. 127.

[57] Ibid., 121, par. 194.

[58] I am indebted to Paul Bishop for his critique of Jung's perspective on beauty in the writings of Schiller.

[59] Jung, *The Red Book*, 254b.

[60] C. G. Jung, "On the Psychology of the Unconscious" in *Two Essays on Analytical Psychology*. In *The Collected Works of C. G. Jung*, 2nd ed., vol.

7, trans. R. F. C. Hull (Princeton, NJ: Princeton University Press, 1966), 54, par. 80.

[61] Jung, *Mysterium Coniunctionis*, 167, par. 201.

[62] Jung, *Psychology and Alchemy*, 186, par. 259.

[63] Jung, "Answer to Job," 419, par. 664.

[64] Jung, *The Red Book*, 243b.

[65] Ibid., 254b.

[66] Jung, *Psychological Types*, 123, par. 197.

[67] Ibid.

[68] Ibid., 478-9, par. 824-5.

[69] Jung, *Psychology and Alchemy*, 282-3, par. 400.

[70] Jung, *Mysterium Coniunctionis*, 468, par. 667.

[71] J. N. Findlay, "The Logic of 'Bewusstseinslagen'" in *Language, Mind and Value,* ed. J. N. Findlay (London, England: George Allen & Unwin, 1963), 182-96.

[72] C. G. Jung, *Nietzsche's Zarathustra: Notes on the Seminar Given in 1934-9,* Vol. I., ed. James L. Jarrett (London, England: Routledge, 1981), 60-61 (23 May 1934).

[73] Huskinson, *Nietzsche and Jung*, 112.

[74] C. G. Jung, *Nietzsche's Zarathustra: Notes on the Seminar Given in 1934-9,* vol. II, ed. James L. Jarrett (London, England: Routledge, 1981), 1249 (18 May 1938).

[75] Jung, *Psychological Types*, 141 n14.

[76] Jung, *Nietzsche's Zarathustra* Vol I, 61.

[77] Ibid., 113.

[78] Friedrich Nietzsche, *The Will to Power*, trans. Walter Kaufman (New York, NY: Random House, 1967), 86, sec. 135 (March–June, 1888).

[79] Jung, *Mysterium Coniunctionis*, 495-6, par. 706.

[80] Aristotle, *Physics* I, vi, 189a in *The Complete Works of Aristotle*, vol. I, ed. Jonathan Barnes (Princeton, NJ: Princeton University Press, 1984), 323. See Jung's comments on Empedocles in C. G. Jung, *Memories, Dreams, Reflections*, ed. Aniela Jaffe (New York, NY: Random House, 1961), 87.

[81] C. G. Jung, *Psychological Types*, 480, par. 848.

[82] C. G. Jung, "On the Nature of Dreams" in *The Structure and Dynamics of the Psyche* in *The Collected Works of C. G. Jung*, 2nd ed., vol. 8, trans. R. F. C. Hull (Princeton, NJ: Princeton University Press, 1969), 288, par 546.

[83] C. G. Jung, "The Psychology of the Child Archetype" in *The Archetypes of the Collective Unconscious*. In *The Collected Works of C.G. Jung*, 2nd ed., vol. 9, Part I, trans. R. F. C. Hull (Princeton, NJ: Princeton University Press, 1968), 164, par. 278.

[84] Recently, Wolfgang Giegerich criticized Jung's requirement of a "third" to reconcile the opposites—arguing that because of this the opposites always remain distinct for Jung, and that in contrast to Hegel, Jung does not appreciate their true interdependence. Wolfgang Giegerich, "'Jung and Hegel' Revisited" in *Wolfgang Giegerich, Collected English Papers, Vol. VI; "Dreaming the Myth Onwards": C. G. Jung on Christianity and Hegel," Part 2 of the Flight into the Unconscious* (New Orleans, LA: Spring Journal Books, 2013).

[85] Nietzsche, *The Will to Power*, 366, sec. 688 (Marc–June, 1888).

[86] Jung, "On the Psychology of the Unconscious," 53, par. 78.

[87] Friedrich Nietzsche, *Philosophy in the Tragic Age of the Greeks*, trans. Marianne Cowan (Washington, D.C.: Regnery Publishing, 1962), 54, sec 5. Here, Nietzsche writes (with assent) that Heraclitus observed that "the actual process of all coming-to-be and passing away [involves] the diverging of a force into two qualitatively different opposed activities that seek to re-unite" Cf. C. G. Jung, "On the Psychology of the Unconscious," 53, par. 78. At times, Jung also seems to suggest that compensation by the opposites is a natural operation of the psyche.

[88] Here I am indebted to Huskinson, *Nietzsche and Jung*, 151-2.

[89] Nietzsche, *The Will to Power*, 369, sec. 692 (March–June 1888).

[90] C. G. Jung, *Nietzsche's Zarathustra: Notes on the Seminar Given in 1934-9*, vol. II, 1250 (Princeton, NJ: Princeton University Press, 1988) (18 May, 1938), cf. Huskinson, *Nietzsche and Jung*, 89.

[91] Paul Bishop, *The Dionysian Self: C. G. Jung's Reception of Friedrich Nietzsche* (New York, NY: Walter de Gruyter, 1995), 207.

[92] Jung, *The Red Book*, 239a. Interestingly, in this same passage Jung echoes Nietzsche's notion of the Eternal Recurrence when he writes, "Everything that happens outside has already been." However, "Whoever considers the event from outside sees only that it already was, and that it is always the same. But whoever looks from inside, knows that everything is new." A Kantian influence is also evident here.

[93] Jung, *The Red Book*, 264a.

[94] Friedrich Nietzsche, *Thus Spake Zarathustra* Part I in *The Portable Nietzsche*, ed. and trans. Walter Kaufmann (New York, NY: Viking Press, 1968), 129.

[95] Jung, *Nietzsche's Zarathustra: Notes on the Seminar Given in 1934-9*, 106.

[96] Jung, *Psychology and Alchemy*, 74, par. 96.

[97] C. G. Jung, "The Relations Between the Ego and the Unconscious" in *Two Essays on Analytical Psychology*. In *The Collected Works of C. G. Jung*, 2nd ed., vol. 7 (Princeton, NJ: Princeton University Press, 1966), 177, par. 274. Cf. Jung, *Psychology and Alchemy*, 44, par. 48.

[98] Jung, *Psychological Types*, 109, par. 175.

[99] Ibid.

[100] Ibid., 426, par. 709.

[101] Ibid., 425, par. 708.

[102] Nietzsche, *The Will to Power*, 57, sec. 92.

[103] Ibid., 35, sec. 55.

[104] Jung, *Psychological Types*, 96, par. 150.

[105] Jung, *The Red Book*, 350b.

[106] Ibid., 350a.

[107] Sonu Shamdasani, Editorial Note in C. G. Jung, *The Red Book*, 349 n 93— citing Jung's *Visions Seminar,* June 7, 1933, vol. 2, 1041-2.

[108] Sonu Shamdasani, Introduction in C. G. Jung, *The Red Book*, 206.

[109] Jung, *Psychology and Alchemy*, 83, par. 107-8.

[110] C. G. Jung, "The Tavistock Lectures" in *The Symbolic Life* CW 18, 2nd ed. in *The Collected Works of C. G. Jung*, 2nd ed., vol. 18, trans. R. F. C. Hull (Princeton, NJ: Princeton University Press, 1980), 110, par. 248. The contrast with Freud may not be as sharp as it might first seem, as a disguised wish must frequently, if not always, run counter to a conscious thought, attitude, belief, or societal sanction.

[111] Jung "On the Nature of Dreams" in *The Structure and Dynamics of the Psyche*, 288, par. 546.

[112] C. G. Jung, "The Practical Use of Dream Analysis" in C. G. Jung, *The Practice of Psychotherapy*. In *The Collected Works of C. G. Jung*, 2nd ed., vol. 16, trans. R. F. C. Hull (Princeton, NJ: Princeton University Press, 1966), 156, par. 338.

[113] Sanford Drob, *Reading the Red Book: An Interpretive Guide to C. G. Jung's Liber Novus* (New Orleans, LA: Spring Journal Books, 2012), 115-6.

[114] Jung, *Psychology and Alchemy*, 19, par. 22.

[115] Jung, *The Red Book*, 305b.

[116] Ibid., 263b.

[117] Jung, "The Relations Between the Ego and the Unconscious," 309-10, par 309.

[118] Jung, *Psychological Types*, 468, par. 804.

[119] Jung, *Psychology and Alchemy*, 282, par. 398.

[120] Jung, "On the Psychology of the Unconscious," 53, par. 78.

[121] C. G. Jung, "The Phenomenology of the Spirit in Fairy Tales" in *The Acrchetypes of the Collective Unconscious*. In *The Collected Works of C. G. Jung*, 2nd ed., vol. 9, Part I, trans. R. F. C. Hull (Princeton, NJ: Princeton University Press, 1968), 269, par. 483.

[122] Jung, *The Red Book*, 319a.

[123] Ibid., 326b.

[124] Ibid, 318b.

[125] Ibid., 319b.

[126] Jung, *Psychological Types*, 202, par. 337.

[127] Ibid.

[128] Ibid.

[129] Jung, "On the Psychology of the Unconscious," 53, par 78.

[130] C. G. Jung, "Paracelsus as a Spiritual Phenomenon" in *Alchemical Studies, The Collected Works of C. G. Jung*, vol. 13, trans. R. F. C. Hull (Princeton, NJ: Princeton University Press, 1967), 118, par. 154.

[131] Jung, "On the Psychology of the Unconscious," 53 par. 78.

[132] Jung, "Paracelsus as a Spiritual Phenomenon," 118, par. 154.

[133] Jung, "The Relations Between the Ego and the Unconscious," 173, par 266.

[134] Ibid., 177, par. 275.

[135] Ibid., 169, par 260.

[136] Jung, *Psychology and Alchemy*, 74, para. 96.

[137] C. G. Jung, "The Spirit Mercurius" in *Alchemical Studies* in *The Collected Works of C. G. Jung*, vol. 13, trans. R. F. C. Hull (Princeton, NJ: Princeton University Press, 1967), 243, par. 291; cf. Jung, *Mysterium Coniunctionis*, 333, par. 470.

[138] Ibid.

[139] Ibid.

[140] Jung, *Mysterium Coniunctionis*, 230, par. 307.

[141] Ibid.

142 Ibid., 360 note 389. Here as in so many other places, Jung follows and expands upon Nietzsche. As Huskinson puts it, Nietzsche spoke of a "dynamic interplay" between the opposites in which life and experience is energized by a conflict between a thesis and antithesis that are in equilibrium and are fully complementary. In *The Birth of Tragedy,* Nietzsche claimed that the greatest human achievements, most notably in the dramatic arts, arise out of strife between the opposites, for example, between the chaos and horror of life and its joyful affirmation, a strife that produces both tragedy and art. Tragedy induces a hybrid of fear and pleasure in the viewer, but the aesthetic experience that ensues enables one to affirm life in the face of its horror and meaninglessness. Huskinson, *Nietzsche and Jung,* 11-13.

143 Jung, *Psychology and Alchemy*, 19, par. 22.

144 Jung, "The Spirit Mercurius," 210, par, 256.

145 C. G. Jung, *Aion: Researches into the Phenomenology of the Self* in *The Collected Works of C. G. Jung*, 2nd ed., vol. 9, Part II, trans. R. F. C. Hull (Princeton, NJ: Princeton University Press, 1968), 31, par 59.

146 Huskinson, *Nietzsche and Freud,* 62.

147 Jung, *Mysterium Coniunctionis*, 429, par 619.

148 Jung, *Psychological Types*, 61, par. 89.

149 Ibid., 63, par. 93.

150 Ibid., 478-9, 824-5.

151 Ibid., 58-9, par. 85.

152 Ibid., 58, par. 85.

153 Ibid., 59, par. 85.

154 Ibid., 59, par. 86.

155 Ibid., 64, par. 95, 214-18, par. 358-70.

156 Ibid., 215, par. 363.

157 Ibid., 215, par. 362.

158 Ibid., 217, par. 369.

159 Jung, "On the Psychology of the Unconscious," 71, par. 110.

160 Ibid., 28, par. 32.

161 Jung, *Psychological Types*, 505, par. 872-3.

162 Ibid., 436-7, par. 731. According to Jung, "The essential function of sensation is to establish that something exists, thinking tells us what it means, feeling what its value is, and intuition surmises whence it comes and whith-

er it goes," Ibid., 553, par. 983. Thinking and feeling are, in Jung's view, both "rational" functions as they involve judgments, the former judging what is true versus false, and the latter what is pleasant versus unpleasant. Sensation and intuition are "irrational" inasmuch as they involve perception as opposed to evaluation; sensation involves a direct perception of things as they are while intuition involves an "inner perception" of direction and change. Just as each individual has a dominant attitude of either introversion or extraversion, each also has a dominant function and partly unconscious auxiliary function, which serves the dominant one. If one's dominant function is one of the rational pair (thinking, feeling), his or her inferior function must be one of the irrational pair (sensation, intuition), and vice versa. According to Jung, the unconscious is determined by one's "inferior" function, which is the opposite of the function that dominates consciousness. Thus, if one's superior function is thinking, one's unconscious (inferior) function will be feeling. One's inferior function also has an auxiliary function, which consists of the remaining function of the pair that opposes one's dominant/superior function.

[163] Ibid., 330, par. 557.

[164] This problem is discussed in Huskinson, *Nietzsche and Jung*, 106.

[165] James Kirsch wrote in 1982 that in 1933 Jung had expressed that "he had some hopes there would be a positive outcome of [the] Nazi movement," and he could not accept Kirsch's "decision to leave Germany as soon as possible." James Kirsch, "Carl Gustav Jung and the Jews: The Real Story," reprinted in *Lingering Shadows: Jungians, Freudians, and Anti-Semitism*, ed. Aryeh Maidenbaum and Stephen A. Martin (Boston, MA: Shambhala, 1982), 51-87.

[166] C. G. Jung, "The Tavistock Lectures: On the Theory and Practice of Analytical Psychology," Lecture V, in, *The Symbolic Life*, trans. R. F. C. Hull, *Collected Works of C. G. Jung*, Vol. 18 (Princeton, NJ: Princeton University Press, 1954), 135-82, 164, par. 372.

[167] Ibid.

[168] See my discussion of "Carl Jung, Anti-Semitism, and National Socialism" in Chapter 10 of Sanford Drob, *Kabbalistic Visions: C. G. Jung and Jewish Mysticism* (New Orleans, LA: Spring Journal Books, 2010), 161-206.

See also Aryeh Maidenabaum and Martin, *Lingering Shadows*, and Aryeh Maidenbaum, ed., *Jung and the Shadow of Anti-Semitism* (Berwick, ME: Nicolas-Hays, 2002). Also, a very comprehensive and insightful discussion of these matters can be found in Jay Sherry, *Carl Gustav Jung: Avant-Garde Conservative* (New York, NY: Palgrave MacMillan, 2010).

[169] C. G. Jung, *Psychological Types*, 221, par. 375.

[170] Ibid., 245, par. 416. See the extended discussion of Jung and Eckhart in John P. Dourley, *Jung and His Mystics: In the End It All Comes Down to Nothing* (New York, NY: Routledge, 2014).

[171] Jung, *The Red Book*, 338b. Jung writes, "Through uniting with the self we reach God." See my discussion of the relationship between self and God in *The Red Book* in Sanford Drob, *The Red Book of C. G Jung*, "Jung on Self and God" http://theredbookofcgjung.blogspot.com/2009/12/jung-on-self-and-god-i-and-thou-part-i.html; and Sanford Drob, *Reading the Red Book* (New Orleans, LA: Spring Journal Books, 2012), 208-14.

[172] C. G. Jung, *Memories, Dreams, Reflections*, ed. Aniela Jaffe (New York, NY: Random House, 1961), 293-5. See my discussion in Sanford Drob, "Jung's Kabbalistic Visions," *Journal of Jungian Theory and Practice*, 7(1) (2005): 33-54; and Sanford Drob, *"Kabbalistic Visions,"* Ch. 11, 207-28.

[173] Jung, *Psychological Types*, 118, par. 188.

[174] Ibid., 195, par. 327.

[175] Ibid., 198, par. 330

[176] Ibid., 199, par. 331.

[177] Ibid., 216-17, par. 366.

[178] Ibid., 217, par. 367.

[179] Ibid., 217, par. 369.

[180] C. G. Jung, "Commentary on 'The Secret of the Golden Flower.'" In C. G. Jung, *Alchemical Studies* (Princeton, NJ: Princeton University Press, 1967), 14, par. 15.

[181] Jung, *Psychological Types*, 300-21, par. 505-41. See William James, *Pragmatism: A New Name for Some Old Ways of Thinking* (Cambridge, MA: Harvard University Press, 1907/1975).

[182] Morris Lazerowitz, *Philosophy and Illusion* (London, England: George Allen & Unwin, 1968).

[183] Jung, *Psychological Types*, 321, par. 541.

[184] Ibid.

[185] Jung, *Symbols of Transformation*, 368, par. 576. See also *Psychology and Alchemy*, where Jung writes, "The self is a union of opposites *par excellence*," 19, par. 22.

[186] Jung, "Answer to Job," 419, par. 664.

[187] Jung, *Psychology and Alchemy*, 19, par. 22.

[188] Jung, *The Red Book*, 254b.

[189] Thomas J. J. Altizer, *The Gospel of Christian Atheism* (Philadelphia, PA: Westminster Press, 1966).

[190] Jung, *The Red Book*, 247b.

[191] Jung, *Symbols of Transformation*, 368, par. 576.

[192] Ibid.

[193] Jung, *Psychology and Alchemy*, 20, par. 23.

[194] Ibid., 20, par. 24.

[195] Ibid., 162, par. 210.

[196] C. G. Jung *Mysterium Coninunctionis*, 429, par. 619.

[197] Ibid., 414, par. 594, 429, par. 619.

[198] Ibid., 417, par. 602.

[199] Ibid., 418, par. 603.

[200] Ibid., 107, fn 66.

[201] Ibid., 108, fn 67.

[202] Jung, *The Red Book*, 319b.

[203] Jung, *Psychology and Alchemy*, 186, par. 259.

[204] Jung, *Psychological Types*, 245, par. 416.

[205] Jung, *Mysterium Coniunctionis*, 110, fn 71.

[206] Ibid., 3, par. 1.

[207] Ibid., 6, par. 4.

[208] Jung, *Psychology and Alchemy*, 476, par. 557.

[209] Ibid. Again, Jung utilizes what appears to be a Hegelian formulation to argue that the union of opposites must play a decisive role in the alchemical process. The idea here is that any sojourn into the unconscious must reveal the opposites of being and non-being, and the necessity of their reconciliation.

[210] Jung, "The Spirit Mercurius," 237, par. 284.

[211] Ibid., 216, par. 266.

[212] Jung, *Mysterium Coniunctionis*, 13-14, par. 10.

[213] Ibid., 24, par, 19, cf. 384-5, par. 551.

[214] Ibid., 23, par. 18.

[215] Ibid.

[216] *Zohar* I 199. Isaiah Tishby and Fischel Lachower, ed. *The Wisdom of the Zohar: An Anthology of Texts*, 3 vols., trans. David Goldstein (Oxford: Oxford University Press, 1989), 402-3, as discussed metaphorically in *Zohar* I:249b, 250a, *The Zohar,* vol. 2, ed. Harry Sperling and Maurice Simon (London, England: Soncino Press, 1931-4), Vol. 2, 389-90.

[217] Jung, *Mysterium Coniunctionis*, 42, par 36.

[218] Ibid., 43, par. 37.

[219] Ibid.

[220] Ibid.

[221] Ibid., 475, par. 676.

[222] Ibid.

[223] Ibid., 42, par. 36: 473, par. 674. 396, par 568.

[224] Ibid., 475, par. 677.

[225] Ibid.

[226] Ibid.

[227] Ibid., 477-8, par. 681.

[228] Ibid., 478, par. 681.

[229] Ibid., 469, par. 869.

[230] Ibid., 471, par. 671.

[231] Ibid., 471-72, par. 672.

[232] Ibid., 472, par. 672.

[233] Ibid., 476, par. 679.

[234] Ibid.

[235] Ibid. 476, par. 680.

[236] Ibid., 497, par. 707.

[237] Ibid., 471, par. 671.

[238] Ibid. 497, par. 707.

[239] Ibid., 504, par. 718.

[240] Ibid., 471, par. 671.

[241] Ibid., 476, par. 679.

[242] Ibid., 534, par. 760.

[243] Ibid.

[244] Ibid. 535, par. 762.

[245] Jung, *Psychology and Alchemy*, 293, par. 404.

[246] Jung, *Mysterium Coniunctionis*, xiv.

[247] Ibid., 48, par. 687.

[248] Ibid., 485, par. 690.

[249] Ibid., 477, par. 680.

[250] Jung, *Psychology and Alchemy*, 229, par. 333.

[251] C. G. Jung "On the Nature of the Psyche" in *The Structure and Dynamics of the Psyche* (Princeton, NJ: Princeton University Press, 1969), 187, par. 384; 211, par. 414; Jung, *Mysterium Coniunctionis*, 248, par. 333; 286, par 388.

[252] Jung, *Mysterium Coniunctionis*, 229, par. 306; 320, par. 446.

[253] Jung, "On the Nature of the Psyche," 187, par. 384.

[254] On color in the Rorschach see John Exner, *The Rorschach: A Comprehensive System*, Vol. 2: Interpretation, 2nd ed. (Hoboken, NJ: John Wiley & Sons, 1991).

[255] Jung, *Mysterium Coniunctionis*, 311, par. 430.

[256] Ibid., 229, par. 307.

[257] Jung, *Psychology and Alchemy*, 230-1, par. 334.

[258] Sanford Drob, *Kabbalistic Visions: C. G. Jung and Jewish Mysticism* (New Orleans, LA: Spring Journal Books, 2010); Sanford Drob, "Jung and the Kabbalah," *History of Psychology*, 2(2) (1999): 102-18.

[259] Jung, *The Red Book*, "Epilogue," 360.

[260] Ibid., 262b.

[261] Ibid., 263b.

[262] Ibid., 249b, 250a

[263] Jung, *Mysterium Coniunctionis*, 371, note 402.

[264] Ludwig Wittgenstein, *Culture and Value,* trans. Peter Winch (Chicago, IL: University of Chicago Press, 1980), 50e.

[265] Huskinson, *Nietzsche and Freud*, 47.

[266] Jung, *Mysterium Coniunctionis*, 89, par. 104.

[267] Jung, *Psychology and Alchemy*, 152, par. 192. Jung also cites an alchemical text in which the union of male and female principles, symbolized by the sun and the moon, results in the birth of a third being, "a son who resolves the antagonisms of the parents and himself..." (Jung, *Mysterium Coniunctionis*, 29, par. 22).

[268] Jung, *Mysterium Coniunctionis*, 31-2, par. 24.

[269] Ibid., 247, par. 330.

270 Ibid.

271 Ibid., 248, par. 332.

272 Ibid.

273 Ibid., 180, par. 226.

274 Jung, *Psychology and Alchemy*, 25, par. 28.

275 Jung, *Mysterium Coniunctionis*, 272, par. 364. Jung also describes the androgyne as an important symbol of *complexio oppositorum*. He quotes a fragment from an apocryphal Gospel cited by Clement of Alexandria, which states: "When ye have trampled on the garment of shame, and when the two become one and the male with the female is neither male nor female" (Jung, *Mysterium Coniunctionis*, 374, par. 528).

276 Jung, *Mysterium Coniunctionis*, 440 note 277, quoting from *Zohar*, I 55b, see Harry Sperling and Maurice Simon, *The Zohar*, 177.

277 Jung, *Psychology and Alchemy*, 153, note 69.

278 Jung, *Mysterium Coniunctionis*, 91, par. 107.

279 Ibid., 9, par. 107.

280 Ibid., 92, par. 108.

281 Ibid., 360, par. 506.

282 Ibid., 150, par. 178.

283 Ibid., 91, par. 107.

284 See my "Transgression and Transformation: Is Psychoanalysis a Dangerous Method?" *Talking Cures* (Newsletter of the Alonso Center for Psychodynamic Studies in the School of Psychology at Fielding Graduate University), *10*(1) (June 2012): 1.

285 Jung discusses the notion of humanity as a partner with God in creation in a letter to Eraster Evans in February 1954. See C. G. Jung, *Letters*, Volumes I and II, ed. Gerhard Adler, Aniela Jaffe, and R. F. C. Hull (Princeton, NJ: Princeton University Press, 1973), 157.

286 Jung, "The Spirit Mercurius," 209, par. 256.

287 Jung, *Aion*, 40, par. 73; Jung, *Psychology and Alchemy*, 241, par. 289. However, Jung, in his lectures on Nietzsche's Zarathustra, says that he would not identify the self with God. C. G. Jung, *Nietzsche's Zarathustra:*

Notes on the Seminar Given in 1934-9, 977 (3 June 1936).

[288] Jung, *Mysterium Coniunctionis*, 499, par. 711.

[289] Ibid., 65, par. 66.

[290] Ibid.

[291] Jung, *Psychology and Alchemy*, 21, par. 24.

[292] Ibid., 23, par. 25.

[293] Ibid., 37, par. 43.

[294] Jung, *Mysterium Coniunctionis*, 79, par. 86.

[295] Jung, "The Spirit Mercurius," 245, par. 295.

[296] Jung, *Mysterium Coniunctionis*, 166, par. 200.

[297] Ibid.

[298] Ibid., 187, par. 238.

[299] Ibid., 187, par. 238.

[300] Ibid., 200, par. 258.

[301] Ibid., 201, par. 259.

[302] Jung, *Aion*, 37, par. 70.

[303] Ibid., 39, par.72.

[304] Jung, *Symbols of Transformation*, 271, par. 415: "Thus through Adam's sin, which lay precisely in his becoming conscious, death came into the world."

[305] Ibid., 432, par. 671.

[306] Jung, *Mysterium Coniunctionis*, 217, par. 287.

[307] Ibid., 220, par. 292.

[308] Ibid., 230, par. 308.

[309] Ibid., 466, par. 664.

[310] C. G. Jung, "The Spiritual Problem of Modern Man" in *Civilization in Transition. In The Collected Works of C. G. Jung*, vol. 10, 2nd ed., trans. R. F. C. Hull (Princeton, NJ: Princeton University Press, 1970).

[311] Jung, *Mysterium Coniunctionis*, xvii.

[312] Ibid.

[313] Jung, *Symbols of Transformation*, 375, par. 581.

[314] Jung, *Psychology and Alchemy*, 280, par. 397.

[315] Jung, *Psychology and Alchemy*, 25, par. 30.

[316] Ibid., 338, par. 440.

[317] Jung, *Psychological Types*, 544, par. 963.

[318] Jung, *Symbols of Transformation*, 376, par. 581.

[319] Ibid., 376, note 155.

[320] Jung, *The Red Book*, 263a.

[321] Ibid., 230a. He writes, "Nonsense is the inseparable and undying brother of the supreme meaning." And again, "I lived into the depths, and the depths began to speak. The depths taught me the other truth. It thus united sense and nonsense in me," 234a.

[322] Ibid., 343b.

[323] Ibid., 293b.

[324] Ibid., 317b.

[325] Ibid., 247a.

[326] Ibid. Jung writes, "Forethinking needs pleasure to be able to come to form. Pleasure needs forethinking to come to form, which it requires." And on page 247b, he writes, "Pleasure is not older than forethinking, and fore-thinking is not older than pleasure. Both are equally old and in nature intimately one."

[327] Ibid., 315a.

[328] Ibid., 273b.

[329] Ibid., 248a.

[330] Ibid., 248a.

[331] Ibid., 263a.

[332] Jung, *Mysterium Coniunctionis*, 360, par. 506.

[333] Jung, *Psychology and Alchemy*, 6, par. 6 12 6/6.

[334] Jung, *Mysterium Coniunctionis*, xv: "The repression of one of the opposites leads only to…neurosis. The therapist therefore confronts the opposites with one another and aims at uniting them permanently."

[335] Ibid., 365, par. 514.

[336] Ibid., 365, note 396.

[337] Ibid., 365, note 397.

[338] Ibid., 366, 514.

[339] Ibid., 468, par. 668.

[340] Ibid., 366, par. 515.

[341] For a discussion of Jung and mysticism, see John P. Dourley, *Jung and His Mystics: In the End It All Comes to Nothing* (New York, NY: Routledge, 2014).

[342] Jung, *Mysterium Coniunctionis*, 368, par. 518.

[343] Ibid., 369, par. 520.

[344] Ibid., 367, par. 517.

[345] Jung, "Commentary on 'The Secret of the Golden Flower,'" 15, par. 18.

[346] Jung, *Mysterium Coniunctionis*, 16, par. 20.

[347] Ibid., xiv.

[348] Ibid.

[349] Ibid., 368, par. 518.

[350] Ibid., 381, par. 542.

[351] Jung, *Aion*, 269, par 429.

[352] Jung, *Mysterium Coniunctionis*, 381, par. 542.

[353] Ibid., 368, par. 518.

[354] Ibid., 533, par. 759.

[355] Lucy Huskinson suggests that the opposites are in a continual state of tension and reunion, and as such the coincidence of opposites and the formation of the self is never complete. Huskinson, *Nietzsche and Jung*, 168.

[356] Jung, "The Spirit Mercurius," 215, par, 256. This is an interesting logical point which suggests that the dialectic encompassed by *coincidentia oppositorum* is involved in an infinite regress (or progression), a topic that we will return to in Chapter 6.

[357] Jung, "The Phenomenology of the Spirit in Fairy Tales," par. 397.

[358] C. G. Jung, "The Development of Personality" in *The Development of Personality*. In *The Collected Works of C. G. Jung*, vol. 17, trans. R. F. C. Hull (Princeton, NJ: Princeton University Press, 1954), 185-6, par. 321.

[359] In a 1938 interview, Jung stated: "Hitler's secret is twofold: first, that his unconscious has exceptional access to his consciousness; and second, that he allows himself to be moved by it. He is like a man who listens intently to a stream of suggestions from a whispered source and then *acts upon them*. In our case, even if occasionally our unconscious does reach us through dreams, we have too much rationality, too much cerebrum to obey it. This is doubtless the case with Chamberlain, but Hitler listens and obeys.... The true leader is always *led*. Because of his "*unconscious perception...* [Hitler] makes political judgments which turn out to be right against the opinions of all his advisers and against the opinions of all foreign observers." C. G. Jung, "Diagnosing the Dictators," in *C. G. Jung Speaking,* ed. William McGuire and R. F. C. Hull (Princeton, NJ: Princeton University Press, 1977), 119-20.

[360] This is a broad topic that I have treated in Chapter Ten of my book, *Kabbal-*

istic Visions: C. G. Jung and Jewish Mysticism (New Orleans, LA: Spring Journal Books, 2008). To take just one example, in a letter written February 9, 1934, to his former assistant W. M. Kranefeldt, Jung had this to say: "As is known, one cannot do anything against stupidity; but in this instance, the Arian (*sic*) people can point out that with Freud and Adler specifically Jewish points of view were publicly preached, and, as can be proven likewise, points of view that have an essentially corrosive (*zersetzend*) character. If the proclamation of this Jewish gospel is agreeable to the government, then so be it. Otherwise, there is also the possibility that this would not be agreeable to the government." (Cited by M. Vannoy Adams and Jay Sherry, "Significant Words and Events." In Ayreh Maidenbaum & S. Martin, *Lingering Shadows*, 349-396; a portion of a letter originally published by I. A. Stargard Auction House, Marburg, Germany, Catalog No. 608. Originally reprinted in *International Review of Psycho-Analysis 4* (1977): 377.)

[361] C. G. Jung Biographical Archives. Irene Champernowne Interview. December 19, 1969. Cited in Richard Noll, *The Aryan Christ: The Secret Life of Carl Jung* (New York, NY: Random House, 1997), 274.

[362] Maidenabaum and Martin, *Lingering Shadows*; Maidenbaum, *Jung and the Shadow of Anti-Semitism*; Sherry, *Carl Gustav Jung: Avant-Garde Conservative*; Sanford Drob, "Carl Jung, Anti-Semitism and National Socialism," 161-206.

[363] *Zohar* II: 184a, Sperling and Simon, *The Zohar*, Vol. IV, 125.

[364] Jung, *Mysterium Coniunctionis*, 369, par. 520.

[365] Ibid., 367, par. 517.

[366] Jung, *The Red Book*, 280b.

[367] Ibid., 279a.

[368] Jung, "Jung and Religious Belief," 704, par. 1585.

[369] Jung, *Mysterium Coniunctionis*, 366, par. 514.

[370] Ibid., 366, par. 515.

[371] C. G. Jung, "The Psychology of the Transference" in *The Practice of Psychotherapy*. In *The Collected Works of C. G. Jung*, 2nd ed., vol. 16, trans. R. F. C. Hull (Princeton, NJ: Princeton University Press, 1966), 323, par 539.

[372] Friedrich Nietzsche, *Human, All Too Human, A Book for free Spirits*, trans. R. J. Hollingdale (Cambridge, MA: Cambridge University Press, 1986),

12, sec. 1. For a discussion of Nietzsche's views on the metaphysical opposites, see Huskinson, *Nietzsche and Jung*, Ch. 3.

[373] Friedrich Nietzsche, *The Will to Power: A New Translation.* ed. Walter Kauffmann, trans. Walter Kaufmann and R. J. Hollingdale (New York, NY: Vintage Books, 1968), 297, sec. 552.

[374] Nietzsche, *Human, All Too Human*, 48, sec. 107.

[375] Ibid., 326, sec 67.

[376] Jacques Derrida, *Writing and Difference*, trans. Alan Bass (Chicago, IL: University of Chicago Press, 1978), 280.

[377] Jung, "Commentary on 'The Secret of the Golden Flower,'" 9, par. 7.

[378] Ibid.

[379] In *Mysterium Coniunctionis,* Jung writes: "I do not go in for either metaphysics or theology, but am concerned with psychological facts on the borderline of the knowable. So if I make use of certain expressions that are reminiscent of the language of theology, this is due solely to the poverty of language, and not because I am of the opinion that the subject-matter of theology is the same as that of psychology. Psychology is very definitely not a theology; it is a natural science that seeks to describe experiencable psychic phenomena.... But as empirical science it has neither the capacity nor the competence to decide on questions of truth and value, this being the prerogative of theology," vii.

[380] "Strictly speaking, the God image does not coincide with the unconscious as such, but with a special content of it, namely the archetype of the self" (C. G. Jung, "Answer to Job," *Psychology and Religion: West and East,* 2nd ed. (Princeton, NJ: Princeton University Press, 1958/1969), 469. par 757. Cf. C. G. Jung, *The Red Book*, 245b: "...your self is the mother of the God."

[381] Jung, *Nietzsche's Zarathustra*, 997-8.

[382] Walt Whitman, "Song of Myself, Part 51. In *Leaves of Grass*, The Original 1885 Edition (Mineola, NY: Dover Press, 2007), 67.

[383] Jung, "Letter to *The Listener*," January 21, 1960. In *Letters*, Volume 3, 525.

[384] C. G. Jung, "The Psychology of Eastern Meditation," in *Psychology and Religion: West and East, The Collected Works of C. G. Jung*, 2nd ed., vol. 11 (Princeton, NJ: Princeton University Press, 1958, 1969), 675, par. 949.

[385] Jung, "Jung and Religious Belief," 706, par. 1589.

[386] C. G. Jung, "The 'Face to Face' Interview in C. G. Jung Speaking: Inter-

Views and Encounters (Princeton, NJ: Bollingen Paperbacks, 1977), 424-39. Jung regretted, however, that this statement would be misunderstood by those unfamiliar with the full scope of his thinking (See Steve Myers, "Jung's Regret Over 'I Don't Need to Believe I Know'" http://steve.my-ers.co/jungs-regret-over-i-dont-need-to-believe-i-know/).

387 G. W. F. Hegel, *On Art, Religion, Philosophy: Introductory Lectures to the Realm of Absolute Spirit*, ed. J. Glenn Gray (New York, NY: Harper & Row, 1970). "On Art" is J. Glenn Gray's slightly modified version of Bernard Bosanquet's translation of Hegel's *Lectures on Aesthetics*, Vol. I (London, England: Routledge, 1905). "On Religion" is a translation of Hegel's "Lectures on the Philosophy of Religion" Vol. I, in The Introduction to Hegel's Philosophy of Fine Art, trans. E. B. Speirs (London, England: Routledge, 1905, 37-211), "On Philosophy" is a translation of Hegel's Lectures on the History of Philosophy, Vol. I. by. E. S. Haldane (London, England: Routledge, 1892), 1-116.

388 Hegel, *On Art, Religion, Philosophy*, 68-9.

389 Ibid., 69.

390 Ibid., 69.

391 Ibid., 68.

392 Ibid.

393 Ibid., 274.

394 Ibid., 285.

395 Ibid., 286.

396 Ibid., 32.

397 Ibid.

398 Ibid., 33.

399 Ibid., 35.

400 Jung, *Letters*, volume I, 194. To Friedrich Siefert, 31 July 1935.

401 Jung, *Letters*, volume II, 501. To Joseph Rychlak, 27 April 1959.

402 Jung, "On the Nature of the Psyche," 170, par. 360.

403 Jung, *Psychological Types*, 321, par. 540.

404 Jung, "On the Nature of the Psyche," 170, par. 360.

405 Jung, *The Red Book*, 314a, cf. "Thinking and feeling are each other's poison and healing," 248.

406 Jung, *Psychology and Alchemy*, 283, par. 400.

407 "Dialetheism," *Stanford Encyclopedia of Philosophy*. Accessed May 2011, http://plato.stanford.edu/entries/dialetheism/; Graham Priest, *In Contradiction.*, 2nd ed. (Oxford, England: Oxford University Press, 2006.)

408 Wolfgang Giegerich, "The End of Meaning and the Birth of Man: An Essay about the State Reached in the History of Consciousness and an Analysis of C. G. Jung's Psychology Project." *Journal of Jungian Theory and Practice*, 6(1) (2004).

409 Wolfgang Giegerich, "'Jung and Hegel' Revisited" in Wolfgang Giegerich, Collected English Papers, *Vol. VI; "Dreaming the Myth Onwards": C. G. Jung on Christianity and Hegel, Part 2 of the Flight into the Unconscious* (New Orleans, LA: Spring Journal Books, 2013), 352.

410 Ibid., 353.

411 Ibid.

412 Ibid. 335.

413 Ibid.

414 Ibid., 337.

415 Ibid., 335.

416 Ibid., 341.

417 Ibid., 335.

418 Jung, "On the Nature of the Psyche," 171, par. 360.

419 W. T. Stace, *The Philosophy of Hegel* (New York, NY: Dover, 1924/1955).

420 W. T. Stace, *Mysticism and Philosophy* (London, England: MacMillan, 1960), 212, 268-9.

421 Giegerich, "'Jung and Hegel' Revisited," 335.

422 Paul Ricouer, *The Conflict of Interpretations*, ed. Don Ihde, (Chicago, IL: Northwestern University Press, 1974), 332.

423 Jean-Paul Sartre, *The Imaginary*, trans. Jonathan Webber (London, England: Routledge, 1940/2005).

424 Ernst Cassirer, *The Philosophy of Symbolic Forms. Volume One: Language* (New Haven, CT: Yale University Press, 1923/1955); Ernst Cassirer, *The Philosophy of Symbolic Forms. Volume Two: Mythical Thought.* (New Haven, CT: Yale University Press, 1925/1955).

425 Susan Langer, *Philosophy in a New Key: A Study in the Symbolism of Reason, Rite, and Art*, 3rd ed. (Cambridge, MA: Harvard University Press, 1957).

426 A point of view suggested by Nathan Schwartz-Salant, in "The Mark of One

Who Has Seen Chaos: A Review of C. G. Jung's *Red Book*," *Quadrant: The Journal of the C. G. Jung Foundation*, *40*(2) (Summer 2010): 11-40.

[427] Giegerich, "Liber Novus," 337.

[428] I am indebted to Clarina Bezzola for this observation.

[429] Giegerich, "'Jung and Hegel' Revisited," 396.

[430] Ibid., 365.

[431] Ibid., 313.

[432] Sanford Drob (2016), "An Axiological Model of the Relationship between Consciousness and Value." *New Ideas in Psychology*, 43, 57-63.

[433] Emmanuel Lévinas, *Totality and Infinity: An Essay on Exteriority*, trans. A. Lingis (Pittsburgh, PA: Duquesne University Press, 1961/1969).

[434] Martin Buber, *I and thou*, trans. R. G. Smith (New York, NY: Scribners, 1923/2000). On Lévinas and Buber, see Peter Atterton, Matthew Calarco, and Maurice S. Friedman, ed., *Lévinas and Buber: Dialogue and Difference* (Pittsburgh, PA: Duquesne University Press, 2004).

[435] Nietzsche, *The Birth of Tragedy*, sec. 13, 66.

Chapter Five

[1] William James, *The Varieties of Religious Experience: A Study in Human Nature* (New York, NY: Mentor, 1958/1902), 233.

[2] See the following for more discussion: B. J. Baars, "The Logic of Unification," *Contemporary Psychology* 30 (1985): 340; G. H. Bower, "The Fragmentation of Psychology?" *American Psychologist* 48 (1993): 905-907; R. A. Dixon, "Theoretical Proliferation in Psychology: A Plea for Sustained Disunity," *The Psychological Record* 33 (1983): 337-40; Sanford Drob, "The Dilemma of Contemporary Psychiatry," *American Journal of Psychotherapy* 43 (1987): 54-67; Sandford Drob, "Fragmentation in Contemporary Psychology: A Dialectical Solution. *Journal of Humanistic Psychology* 43 (2003): 102-23; A. Giorgi, "Theoretical Plurality and Unity in Psychology," *The Psychological Record*, *35*(1985): 177-81; J. R. Goertzen, "Dialectical Pluralism: A Theoretical Conceptualization of Pluralism in Psychology," *New Ideas in Psychology*, *28*(2010): 201-9; R. McNally, "Disunity in Psychology: Chaos or Specialization? *American Psychologist*, *47*: 399-413; B. D. Slife, "Are Discourse Communities Incommensurable in a Fragmented Psychology? The Possibility of Disciplinary Coherence," *The Journal of Mind and Behavior*, *21*(2000): 261-272.

[3] A. W. Staats, "Unified Positivism: A Philosophy for Psychology and the Disunified Sciences," *Theoretical and Philosophical Psychology* 6 (1986): 77-90.; A. W. Staats, "Unified Positivism and Unification Psychology: Fad or New Field?" *American Psychologist, 46*(1991): 899-912.

[4] S. J. C. Gaulin and D. H. McBurney, *Psychology: An Evolutionary Approach* (Upper Saddle River, NJ: Prentice Hall, 2001).

[5] J. Martin, "Fragmentation, Hermeneutics, Scholarship, and Liberal Education in Psychology," *The Journal of Mind and Behavior, 21*(2000): 305-314.

[6] K. Kristensen, B. D. Slife, and S. Yanchar, "On What Basis Are Evaluations Possible in a Fragmented Psychology? An Alternative to Objectivism and Relativism." *The Journal of Mind and Behavior, 21*(2000): 273-88.

[7] R. Dixon, "Theoretical Proliferation in Psychology: A Plea for Sustained Disunity," *The Psychological Record, 33*(1983): 337-40.

[8] R. Walsh-Bowers, "Some Social-Historical Issues Underlying Psychology's Fragmentation," *New Ideas in Psychology, 28*(2010): 244-252.

[9] Jung, *Psychological Types*, par. 89.

[10] Ibid., par. 90.

[11] Ibid., par. 85.

[12] The following discussion has been modified from my article "The Dilemma of Contemporary Psychiatry," *American Journal of Psychotherapy, 43*(1989): 54-67.

[13] G. Heninger, P. Delgado, and D. Charney, "The Revised Monoamine Theory of Depression: A Modulatory Role for Monoamines, Based on New Findings from Monoamine Depletion Experiments in Humans," *Pharmacopsychiatry, 29*(1996): 2-11.

[14] D. Armstrong, *A Materialist Theory of the Mind*, 2nd ed. (London, England: Routledge, 1993); D. Lewis "Reduction of Mind" in *A Companion to the Philosophy of Mind, ed.* S. Guttenplan (Oxford, England: Blackwell, 1994). For overviews regarding the debates on scientific materialism, see J. J. C. Smart, "The Mind/Brain Identity Theory," *The Stanford Encyclopedia of Philosophy* (Winter 2014 Edition), ed. Edward N. Zalta, http://plato.stanford.edu/archives/win2014/entries/mind-identity/; W. Ramsey, "Eliminative Materialism," *The Stanford Encyclopedia of Philosophy* (Summer 2013 Edition), ed. Edward N. Zalta, http://plato.stanford.edu/archives/sum2013/entries/materialism-eliminative.

[15] R. Belmaker and G. Agam, "Major Depressive Disorder," *New England*

Journal of Medicine, 358(2008): 55-68.

[16] Christine *Matthews, "Review of Behavioral Theories of Depression and a Self-Regulation Model for Depression," Psychotherapy: Theory, Research, and Practice, 14*(1977): 79-86; P. Lewinsohn, "Behavioral Theory and Treatment of Depression" in *Handbook of Depression* (2nd ed.), ed. E. Beckham and William R. Leber (New York, NY: Guilford Press, 1995), 352-375, xii, 628.

[17] M. Seligman. *Helplessness: On Depression, Development, and Death* (San Francisco, CA: W. H. Freeman, 1975).

[18] G. Zuriff, *Behaviorism: A Conceptual Reconstruction* (New York, NY: Columbia University Press, 1985). See also George Graham, "Behaviorism," in *The Stanford Encyclopedia of Philosophy* (Spring 2015 Edition), ed. Edward N. Zalta, http://plato.stanford.edu/archives/spr2015/entries/behaviorism.

[19] J. R. Anderson, *Cognitive Psychology and Its Implications* (New York, NY: Worth Publishers, 2010).

[20] M. Boden, *Computer Models of Mind* (Cambridge, MA: Cambridge University Press, 1988).

[21] Aaron Beck, A. Rush, B.Shaw, and G. Emery, *Cognitive Therapy of Depression* (New York, NY: The Guilford Press, 1979).

[22] Albert Ellis and R. Harper, *A Guide to Rational Living*, 3rd rev. ed. (Chatsworth, CA: Wilshire Book Company, 1997).

[23] G. A. *Miller, "The Cognitive Revolution: A Historical Perspective," Trends in Cognitive Sciences, 7*(2003): 141-144.

[24] Noam *Chomsky, "A Review of B. F. Skinner's Verbal Behavior," Language. Linguistic Society of America, 35*(1959): 26–58; See also Noam Chomsky, *Language and Problems of Knowledge* (Cambridge, MA: MIT Press, 1988).

[25] I. Goldenberg and H. Goldenberg, *Family Therapy: An Overview* (Belmont, CA: Thomson Brooks/Cole, 2008).

[26] A. Etiony, ed., *Advancing Social Justice Through Clinical Practice* (New York, NY: Routledge Taylor & Francis, 2007).

[27] M. McCouat, "Family Scapegoating Patterns and the Management of Depression." *Australian Journal of Social Work, 23*(1970): 17-23.

[28] D. Jacobvitz, N. Hazen, M. Curran, and K. Hitchens, "Observations of Early Triadic Family Interactions: Boundary Disturbances in the Family Pre-

dict Symptoms of Depression, Anxiety, and Attention-Deficit/Hyperactivity Disorder in Middle Childhood." *Development and Psychopathology,* 3(2004): 577-92.

[29] W. Dressler, *Stress and Adaptation in the Context of Culture: Depression in a Black Southern Community.* (Albany, NY: State University of NewYork Press, 1991).

[30] L. von Bertalanffy, *Organismic Psychology and System Theory* (Worcester, MA: Clark University Press, 1968).

[31] For example, D. Westen, "The Scientific Legacy of Sigmund Freud: Toward a Psychodynamically Informed Psychological Science," *Psychological Bulletin, 124*(1998): 333-71; L. Aron and K. Starr, *A Psychotherapy for the People: Toward a Progressive Psychoanalysis* (New York, NY: Routledge, 2013); J. Shedler "The Efficacy of Psychodynamic Psychotherapy," *The American Psychologist, 65*(2010): 98-109.

[32] Paul Ricoeur, *Freud and Philosophy: An Essay in Interpretation,* trans. D. Savage (New Haven, CT: Yale University Press, 1970); R. Schafer, *A New Language for Psychoanalysis* (New Haven, CT: Yale University Press, 1976).

[33] G. S. Klein, *Psychoanalytic Theory: An Exploration of Essentials* (New York, NY: International Universities Press, 1976).

[34] See D. Polkinghorne, *Narrative Knowing and the Human Sciences* (Albany, NY: State University of New York Press, 1988).

[35] Heraclitus, fragment 80: "All things happen by strife and necessity" in *The Presocratic Philosophers,* ed. G. S. Kirk and J. E. Raven (Cambridge, UK: Cambridge University Press, 1957), 195. Empedocles held that love and strife are the motive forces which set the elements of earth, water, air, and fire in dynamic motion. For Empedocles, our world exists as a phase in between the successive triumphs of love and strife.

[36] In Book IV of *The Republic,* Plato states that the soul is composed of three parts: the *logistikon* (logical, represented by "the charioteer"), the *thymoeides* (high-spirited, associated with anger), and the *epithymetikon* (appetitive, associated with carnal love, hunger, thirst, and the pursuit of monetary gain).

[37] Freud's early work "The Project for a Scientific Psychology" (1895) reflects the influence of then contemporary neurology on his emerging psychology.

38 See D. Polkinghorne, *Methodology for the Human Sciences: Systems of Inquiry* (Albany, NY: State University of New York Press, 1983); and D. Polkinghorne, *Narrative Knowing and the Human Sciences* (Albany, NY: State University of New York Press, 1988).

39 J. Lichtenberg, "Humanism and the Science of Psychoanalysis," *Psychoanalytic Inquiry*, 5(1985): 343-67; W. Meissner, "Psychoanalysis: The Dilemma of Science and Humanism," *Psychoanalytic Inquiry*, 5(1985): 471-98.

40 R. Sperry, "Psychology's Mentalist Paradigm and the Religion/Science Tension," *American Psychologist*, 43(1998): 607-13. See also D. Brendel and T. Luhrmann, *Healing Psychiatry: Bridging the Science/Humanism Divide* (Boston, MA: MIT Press, 2006).

41 Abraham Maslow, *Toward a Psychology of Being* (Floyd, VA: Sublime Books, 1962/2014), 8. Cf. F. Goble, *The Third Force: The Psychology of Abraham Maslow* (Richmond, CA: Maurice Bassett Publishing, 1970).

42 See H. Spiegelberg, *Phenomenology in Psychiatry and Psychology: A Historical Introduction* (Evanston, IL: Northwestern University Press, 1972). On phenomenological research in psychology, see A. Giorgi, *The Descriptive Phenomenological Method in Psychology: A Modified Husserlian Approach* (Pittsburgh, PA: Duquesne University Press, 2009).

43 The impact of existential thought on psychotherapy has been sustained over many decades. Three important examples, from three generations of psychologists are Rollo May, *Man's Search for Himself* (New York, NY: Norton, 1953); Irwin Yalom, *Existential Psychotherapy* (New York, NY: Basic Books, 1980); and K. Schneider, *Existential-Integrative Psychotherapy: Guideposts to the Core of Practice* (New York, NY: Routledege, 2007).

44 An accessible selection of Husserl's writings can be found in: D. Welton, ed., *The Essential Husserl: Basic Writings in Transcendental Phenomenology* (Bloomington, IN: Indiana University Press, 1999). See also J. Kockelman, *Edmund Husserl's Phenomenological Psychology* (New York, NY: Humanities Press, 1978).

45 Maurice Merleau-Ponty, *The Phenomenology of Perception*, trans. D. Landes (New York, NY: Routledge, 1945/2012); D. Kennedy, *Healing Perception: An Application of the Philosophy of Merleau-Ponty to the Theoretical Structures of Dialogic Psychotherapy* (Queensland: Ravenwood Press, 2013). Originally published in French, 1945.

46 E. Gantt, "Lévinas, Psychotherapy and the Ethics of Suffering," *Journal*

of Humanistic Psychology, 40(2000): 9-28; K. Krycka, G. Kuns, and G. Sayre, ed., *Psychotherapy for the Other: Lévinas and the Face-to-Face Relationship* (Pittsburgh, PA: Dusquesne University Press, 2015).

[47] Martin Heidegger, *Being and Time,* trans. J. Stanbaugh (Albany, NY: State University of New York Press, 2010). Originally published in German in 1927. Cf. H. Cohn, *Heidegger and the Roots of Existential Therapy* (New York, NY: Bloomsbury Academic, 2002).

[48] Martin Buber, *I and Thou,* trans. W. Kaufmann (New York, NY: Simon & Schuster, 1923/1970). Cf. J. Agassi, *Martin Buber on Psychology and Psychotherapy: Essays, Letters, and Dialogue* (Syracuse, NY: Syracuse University Press, 1999).

[49] Jean Paul Sartre, *Being and Nothingness,* trans. H. E. Barnes (New York, NY: Washington Square Press, 1956); B. Cannon, *Sartre and Psychoanalysis: An Existentialist Challenge to Clinical Metatheory* (Lawrence, KS: University Press of Kansas, 1996); J. Iucalano and K. Burkum, "The Humanism of Sartre: Toward a Psychology of Dignity," *Journal of Theoretical and Philosophical Psychology,* 16 (1996).false

[50] R. Walsh-Bowers, "Some Social-Historical Issues Underlying Psychology's Fragmentation," *New Ideas in Psychology, 28*(2010): 244-52.

[51] J. Goetzen has argued that the options for unity/disunity in psychology exist on a continuum, ranging from unity to fragmentation, with various degrees of convergent and divergent pluralism in between these extremes. J. Goertzen, "Dialectical Pluralism: A Theoretical Conceptualization of Pluralism in Psychology," *New Ideas in Psychology, 28*(2010): 201-9.

[52] Sigmund Freud, "On Narcissism," *Collected Papers of Sigmund Freud,* vol. 4 (New York, NY: Basic Books, 1914/1959).

[53] J. Dollard and N. E. Miller, *Personality and Psychotherapy* (New York, NY: McGraw-Hill, 1950).

[54] P. Bridgman, *The Logic of Modern Physics.* (Delhi, India: Facsimile Publisher, 1927/2015).

[55] K. Popper, *The Logic of Scientific Discovery* (London, England: Routledge, 1934/2001).

[56] As Alasdair MacIntyre points out, there are several sources of systematic unpredictability in human affairs. First, there is the fact that we cannot in advance predict future creative acts and inventions that may change the contingencies of our and others' future behavior. Second, one cannot

predict one's own future decisions, and such decisions can and will have an impact upon self, others, and potentially the world. Third, we are all involved in multiple game-like interactions with others in which we attempt to predict what move the other will make, but this is dependent upon the other's appraisal of what move we think he will make, which is in turn dependent upon our appraisal of what move he will make, and so on ad infinitum. This is compounded by the innumerable games we enter into and the innumerable players involved (no such reflective game-theoretic situations apparently exist, for example, in physics or chemistry). Fourth, pure contingency has an impact in human affairs that it does not appear to have in the physical world. Pascal, for example, once observed that the Roman Empire fell because of the length of Cleopatra's nose—had it been different, Marc Antony would not have fallen in love with her and allied himself with Egypt and so on. See Alasdair MacIntyre, *After Virtue* (Indianapolis, IN: University of Notre Dame Press, 1984).

[57] P. Feyerabend, *Against Method* (London, England: NLB, 1975).

[58] R. Walsh-Bowers, "Some Social-Historical Issues Underlying Psychology's Fragmentation," *New Ideas in Psychology* 28 (2010): 244-252.

[59] T. Kuhn, *The Structure of Scientific Revolutions*, 2nd ed., with postscript, (Chicago, IL: University of Chicago, 1962/1970), 206.

[60] L. von Bertalanffy, "General Systems Theory and Psychiatry: An Overview" in *General Systems Theory and Psychiatry*, ed. W. Gray et. al. (Boston: Little, Brown & Company, 1969), 33-50; G. L. Engel, "The Clinical Application of the Biopsychosocial Model," *American Journal of Psychiatry*, *137*(1980): 535-44.

[61] The following discussion, through the end of this chapter, has been modified from my article, "Fragmentation in Psychology: A Dialectical Solution," *Journal of Humanistic Psychology*, *43*(4) (2003), 102-23.

[62] J. F. Rychlak, "A suggested principle of complementarity for psychology," *American Psychologist*, *48*(1993): 933-42.

[63] Slavoj Žižek has argued that "multiple perspectives" does not necessarily entail a single reality upon which each perspective is directed. Slavoj Žižek, *The Parallax View* (Cambridge, MA: MIT Press, 2009). We will discuss the coherence of his argument in Chapter 7.

[64] E. Abbott, *Flatland: A Romance of Many Dimensions* (Princeton, NJ: Princeton University Press, 1884/1991).

[65] Some might endeavor to create a mathematical model of the world in three dimensions—as we endeavor to model dimensions greater than three.

[66] Gregory A. Kimble, "Psychology's Two Cultures," *American Psychologist*, *39*(1984): 833-9.

[67] W. Smythe and S. McKenzie, "A Vision of Dialogical Pluralism in Psychology," *New Ideas in Psychology*, *28*(2010): 227-34.

[68] Kant stated the third of his "antinomies of pure reason" as follows: "Thesis: Causality in accordance with laws of nature is not the only causality from which the appearances of the world can one and all be derived. To explain these appearances, it is necessary to assume that there is also another causality, that of freedom" and "Antithesis: There is no freedom; everything in the world takes place solely in accordance with laws of nature." Immanuel Kant, *Critique of Pure Reason*, trans. Norman Kemp Smith (London, England: MacMillan, 1929), 398.

[69] Kimble, "Psychology's Two Cultures," 833-9.

[70] William James, *Pragmatism, Lecture I: The Present Dilemma in Philosophy* (Mineola, NY: Dover Publications, 1907/1995).

[71] Late in his career, Jung wrote: "Psychology is very definitely not a theology; it is a natural science that seeks to describe experienceable psychic phenomena.... But as empirical science it has neither the capacity nor the competence to decide on questions of truth and value, this being the prerogative of theology" (C. G. Jung, *Mysterium Coniunctionis* in *The Collected Works of C. G. Jung*, vol. 14 (Princeton, NJ: Princeton University Press, 1955/1956), vii.

[72] C. G. Jung, *The Red Book, Liber Novus*, ed. S. Shamdasanui, trans. M. Kyburz, J. Peck, and S. Shamdasani (New York, NY: W. W. Norton & Company, 2009). In *The Red Book*, Jung proclaims to a dying God, "We had to swallow the poison of science. Otherwise we would have met the same fate as you have: we'd be completely lamed, if we encountered it unsuspecting and unprepared. This poison is so insurmountably strong that everyone, even the strongest, and even the eternal Gods, perish because of it. If our life is dear to us, we prefer to sacrifice a piece of our life force rather than abandon ourselves to certain death," (279). Later in that work Jung's "soul" tells him: "You should become serious and hence take your leave from science. There is too much childishness in it. Your way goes toward the depths. Science is too superficial, mere language, mere tools.

But you must set to work," (36). In 1929, in his "Commentary on 'the Secret of the Golden Flower,'" soon after Jung abandoned work on the *Red Book*, he writes: "Science is not, indeed, a perfect instrument, but it is a superior and indispensable one that works harm only when taken as an end in itself.... Science is the tool of the Western mind and with it, more doors can be opened than with bare hands. It is part and parcel of our knowledge and obscures insight only when it holds that the understanding given by it is the only kind there is."

[73] W. James, *A Pluralistic Universe* (Cambridge, MA: Harvard University Press, 1909/1977). Cf. C. Tolman, "Pluralistic Monism: William James as Closet-Heraclitean," *The Psychological Record, 39*: 177-94. A Freudian pluralistic perspective is described in P. Kitcher, *Freud's Dream: A Complete Interdisciplinary Science of Mind* (Cambridge, MA: Harvard University Press, 1992).

[74] J. Rychlak, "A Suggested Principle of Complementarity for Psychology," *American Psychologist, 48*(1993): 933-42.

[75] This problem is beautifully illustrated in cubist art which, despite (and because of) its confusion of perspectives, has had an enduring appeal. One might consider both the negative and positive implications of a "cubist psychology."

[76] S. Koch, "The Nature and Limits of Psychological Knowledge: Lessons of a Quarter Century Qua Science," *American Psychologist, 36*(1993): 257-69.

[77] S. Hampshire, *Freedom of Mind* (Princeton, NJ: Princeton University Press, 1971), 3.

[78] While there is indeed experimental evidence that we are often unaware of our own ideas, emotions, motives, and attitudes (as Freud long ago understood), the evaluation of this evidence (and all other scientific evidence) is dependent upon the first-person observations of experimenters and our first-person reasoning about what these observations imply. While there are certainly times when we infer that we have thoughts that we were unaware of, science is grounded in the assumption that when it comes to experimental evidence and rational truths, *we learn about other's thoughts but think our own*. If I "discover" my rational and scientific conclusions rather than "think" them, I have no more basis for accepting these conclusions than I have for uncritically accepting on authority what has been handed down from the past.

[79] Ludwig Wittgenstein, *Philosophical Investigations*, trans. G. E. M. Anscombe (Oxford, England: Basil Blackwell, 1953/1968).

[80] Gilbert Ryle, *The Concept of Mind* (London, England: Hutchinson, 1949).

[81] Nietzsche famously wrote in his notebooks in the 1880s, "There are no facts, only interpretations."

[82] W. Sellars spoke of "the myth of the given." W. Sellars, *Empiricism and the Philosophy of Mind*, with an introduction by Richard Rorty and a study guide by Robert Brandom (Cambridge, MA: Harvard University Press, 1997). Sellars delivered his original paper on this topic in 1955.

[83] Thomas Kuhn held that observations change according to the theory of the scientific observer. Thomas Kuhn, *The Structure of Scientific Revolutions*, 2nd ed., with postscript (Chicago, IL: University of Chicago Press, 1962/1970).

[84] J. Bogen, "Theory and Observation in Science," *The Stanford Encyclopedia of Philosophy* (Summer 2014 Edition), ed. Edward N. Zalta. Accessed from http://plato.stanford.edu/archives/sum2014/entries/science-theory-observation/.

[85] L. Patihis, L. Ho, I. Tingen, S. Lilienfeld, and Elizabeth Loftus, "Are the 'Memory Wars' Over? A Scientist-Practitioner Gap in Beliefs About Repressed Memory." *Psychological Science*, 25(2013): 519-30.

[86] Niels Bohr, "Discussion with Einstein on Epistemological Problems in Atomic Physics" in *Great Books of the Western World*, vol. 56, ed. Mortimer J. Adler (Chicago, IL: Encyclopedia Britannica, Inc, 1990), 337-355.

Chapter Six

[1] Walter T. Stace, *Mysticism and Philosophy* (London, England: MacMillan, 1960).

[2] Ibid., 271.

[3] Hegel was, as we saw in Chapter 1, inspired by a host of previous thinkers from Heraclitus to Jacob Boehme and Hegel's own contemporary F. W. J. Schelling. The thirteenth-century German-Christian Meister Eckhart appears to have anticipated the notion of "rational mysticism." According to Eckhart, "The whole scattered world of lower things is gathered up to oneness when the soul climbs up to that life in which there are no opposites. Entering the life of reason, opposites are forgotten, but where this light does not fall, things fall away to death and destruction" (Meister Eckhart, *Meister Eckhart. A Modern Translation*, trans. Raymond Bernard Blakney

(New York, NY: Harper, 1941), 173). Dennis McCort suggests that we read Eckhart's reference to "reason" as insight or enlightenment, arguing that Eckhart himself held the idea "that any pair of opposites, if known intimately enough, will resolve itself into unity." Dennis McCort, *Going Beyond the Pairs: The Coincidence of Opposites in German Romanticism, Zen, and Deconstruction* (Albany, NY: State University of New York Press, 2001), 21.

[4] Stace, *Mysticism and Philosophy*, 213.

[5] Ibid.

[6] Ibid., 270.

[7] Ibid,. 213, 268.

[8] Ibid., 269.

[9] Jacques Derrida, "Différance" in *Margins of Philosophy*, trans. Alan Bass. (Chicago, IL: Chicago University Press, 1982), 11. Original French edition, 1967. Derrida is famous for his claim that *différance* is "older than being."

[10] Derrida did this by using such terms as "différance," "trace," "pharmakon," and so on. Jacques Derrida, "Plato's Pharmacy," *Dissemination*, trans. Barbara Johnson (London, England: The Athlone Press, 1981), 61-71.

[11] Postmodern philosophers, like the Kabbalists, typically hold that concepts are "permeable" and conditioned by their opposites and that the world is subject to indefinite (re)interpretations. They do not follow the Kabbalists in holding that there is one world, the manifestation of a single, unitary God.

[12] C. G. Jung, "On the "Tibetan Book of the Great Liberation" in *Psychology and Religion: West and East*, 2nd ed. (Princeton, NJ: Princeton University Press, 1958, 1969), 480, par 769.

[13] Piet Hut and Roger N. Shepard, "Turning 'The Hard Problem' Upside Down and Sideways" in *Explaining Consciousness: The Hard Problem*, ed. Jonathan Shear (Cambridge, MA: MIT Press, 1999), 307.

[14] Ibid., 308.

[15] Thomas Nagel, "Subjective and Objective" in *Post-Analytic Philosophy*, ed. J. Rajchman and C. West (New York, NY: Columbia University Press, 1985), 31-47.

[16] Ibid., 35.   [17] Ibid., 45.

[18] Jung, "On the 'Tibetan Book of the Great Liberation,'" 493, par. 786.

[19] Ibid., 511, par 833.

[20] Ibid.

[21] Ibid., 512, par. 836.

[22] Ibid., 513, par. 840.

[23] Nick Bostrom, "Are You Living in a Computer Simulation?" *Philosophical Quarterly*, *53*(211) (2003): 243-55. Accessed July 23, 2016 from http://www.simulation-argument.com/simulation.html.

[24] Mark C. Taylor, *Erring: A Postmodern A/Theology* (Chicago, IL: University of Chicago Press, 1984).

[25] See Sanford Drob, "James Hillman On Language, Escape from the Linguistic Prison" in *Archetypal Psychology: Reflections in Honor of James Hillman*, ed. S. Marlan (New Orleans, LA.: Spring Journal Books, 2008).

[26] Quoted in Andrew Gallix, "In Theory: The Unread and the Unreadable," *The Guardian*. Last modified February 18, 2013. Accessed from https://www.theguardian.com/books/booksblog/2013/feb/18/unread-unreadable-books.

[27] Sanford Drob, "Judaism as a Form of Life," *Tradition: A Journal of Orthodox Jewish Thought*, *23*(4) (1988): 78-89.

[28] Wilfred Sellars, for example, wrote, "All awareness of sorts, resemblances, facts, etc., in short, all awareness of abstract entities—indeed, all awareness even of particulars—is a linguistic affair." Wilfred Sellars, "Empiricism and the Philosophy of Mind." *Science, Perception, and Reality* (London, England: Routledge, 1963), 160.

[29] Moshe Idel, *Absorbing Perfections* (New Haven, CT: Yale University Press, 2002), 122. Idel indicates that this passage had not been translated and was largely unknown to Western scholars prior to Gershom Scholem's discussion of it at the Eranos Conference in Ascona in 1954. Scholem's comments and a translation of the passage into English and French were subsequently published in the journal, *Diogenes* (*Diogene*). The 1955-6 French translation by the Judaic scholar Georges Vajda, reads, "There is nothing outside her (i.e., the Torah)." Idel suggests that "the fact that this statement about the identity between the Torah and God was available in French in 1957 may account for the emergence of one of the most postmodern statements in literary criticism: "There is nothing outside the text." Idel speculates that Derrida, who had a general interest in the Kabbalah, in his 1967 book *Grammatologie*, "substituted the term and concept of Torah

with that of text" (Idel, *Absorbing Perfections*, 123).

[30] Elliot Wolfson, *Alef, Mem, Tau: Kabbalistic Musings on Time, Truth, and Death* (Berkeley, CA: University of California Press, 2006), xii.

[31] Schneur Zalman, *Likutei Amarim-Tanya* (Brooklyn, NY: Kehot, 1983), 319.

[32] See Sanford Drob, *Symbols of the Kabbalah* (Northvale, NJ: Jason Aaronson, 2000), Chapter 3 "Contraction into Language."

[33] This is an interesting parallel to the Kabbalistic notion of *Tzimtzum*—the divine self-concealment that is necessary for the creation of the world. The idea here is that in order for God to create a world He must conceal from the world that it is simply a diminished aspect of Himself. See my *Kabbalah and Postmodernism: A Dialogue* (New York, NY: Peter Lang, 2009), Chapter 3: "Tzimtzum and Différance."

[34] McCort, *Going Beyond the Pairs*, 96.

[35] Ibid., 99.

[36] Drob, *Kabbalah and Postmodernism*, 202ff.

[37] Jacques Derrida, *Speech and Phenomena and Other Essays on Husserl's Theory of Signs* (Chicago, IL: Northwestern University Press, 1979).

[38] Isaiah Tishby and Fischel Lachower, ed. *The Wisdom of the Zohar*, vols. I–III, trans. D. Goldstein, (Oxford, England: Oxford University Press, 1989), 259. Translation of *Zohar* III 225a, Raya Mehemna.

[39] Thomas J. J. Altizer, *The New Apocalypse: The Radical Christian Vision of William Blake*. (East Lansing, MI: Michigan State University Press, 1967), 218.

[40] It is possible to be a linguistic constructivist without holding that human beings exercise free will and action. One might, for example, hold that the human subject is the product of a linguistic matrix that is beyond his or her control. The point I am making is that within linguistic constructivism and idealism, free will is conceptually coherent.

[41] C. G. Jung, *The Red Book, Liber Novus*, ed. Sonu Shamdasani, trans. Mark Kyburz, John Peck, and Sonu Shamdasani (New York, NY: W. W. Norton & Company, 2009), 229b-230a.

[42] Kurt Rudolph, *Gnosis: The Nature and History of Gnosticism,* ed. and trans. R. M. Wilson. (San Francisco, CA: Harper & Row, 1987), 93.

[43] John Caputo, *The Prayers and Tears of Jacques Derrida: Religion without Religion* (Bloomington, IN: Indiana University Press, 1997); cf. Jacques Derrida, *Specters of Marx: The State of the Debt, the Work of Mourning,*

and the New International, trans. Peggy Kaman (New York, NY: Routledge, 1994).

[44] See my "The Only God Who Can Save Us from Ourselves." Accessed July 23, 2016 from http://www.newkabbalah.com/dogma.pdf.

[45] Jung, as we have seen, recognized that the principle of *coincidentia oppositorum* must be applied to itself, yielding a principle of absolute difference.

[46] In his discussion of the thought of August Wilhelm Schlegel, Dennis McCort speaks of the "radically nondiscriminatory spirit of the *coincidentia oppositorum*, which is, in effect a "commitment to everything." According to Schlegel, one "cannot be a connoisseur (in art) without universality of spirit, that is, without that flexibility that puts us in a position, even as we disavow personal preferences and blind habituation, to ensconce ourselves amidst the peculiarities of other peoples and times, to sense these directly from within their own center." This moves beyond the enlightenment humanistic commitment to tolerance to a vision of the Absolute that is constructed by openness and the multiplicity of points of view. McCort, *Going Beyond the Pairs*, 23-4, quoting from Schlegel's 1808 *Vienna Lectures*.

[47] Henry Staten, *Wittgenstein and Derrida* (Lincoln, NE: University of Nebraska Press, 1984), 148.

[48] As discussed by Staten, ibid. Jacques Derrida, *Of Grammatology*, trans. G. C. Spivak. (Baltimore, MD: Johns Hopkins Press, 1974), 154.

[49] Staten, *Wittgenstein and Derrida*, 148, referencing Derrida, *Of Grammatology*, 165-6.

[50] Howard Coward, *Derrida and Indian Philosophy* (Albany, NY: State University of New York Press, 1990), 88.

[51] Ibid., 87-9.

[52] C. G. Jung, "On the 'Tibetan Book of the Great Liberation,'" 493, par. 786.

[53] Here I am referring to Jacques Lacan's conception of "the real" and Jacques Derrida's notion of "the monstrous." Jacques Derrida, *Points... Interviews, 1974-94*, ed. Elizabeth Weber, trans. Peggy Kamuf et. al. (Stanford, CA: Stanford University Press, 1995), 386-7. See also, Jacques Derrida, *Deconstruction and the Other*, in *Dialogues with Contemporary Continental Thinkers*, ed. R. Kearney (Manchester, England: Manchester University Press, 1984), 123.

[54] There are, indeed, many more such axes. For example, we could consider the "objective" versus the "subjective," the "factual" versus the "hermeneu-

tic," the "molar" versus the "molecular" and so on. Although it is impossible to go into each of these here, each can be understood as a *coincidentia oppositorum* between seemingly opposing conceptions of "truth" and "reality."

55 See Douglas Hedley and Chris Ryan, "Nineteenth Century Philosophy of Religion: An Introduction." In *Nineteenth Century Philosophy of Religion,* ed. Graham Oppy and N. N. Trakakis (London, England: Routledge, 2014), 9.

56 *Sefer Yetzirah.* I. 8. As translated in Isaiah Tishby and Fischel Lachower, ed. *The Wisdom of the Zohar,* 234. See also, Aryeh Kaplan, *Sefer Yetzirah: The Book of Creation,* rev. ed. (York Beach, ME: Samuel Weiser, 1997), 66. Ludwig Wittgenstein, in the *Tractatus,* holds that we must remain silent regarding the nature of the link between language and the world, precisely because this link cannot be said.

57 Heinrich Zimmer, *Philosophies of India,* ed. Joseph Campbell (Princeton, NJ: Princeton University Press, 1951), 451.

58 Quoted in Ibid., 448 (Avadhūta Gītā 1. 59).

59 Ibid., 457.

60 Ibid., 448.

61 Rachel Elior, "Chabad: The Contemplative Ascent to God" in *Jewish Spirituality: From the Sixteenth Century Revival to the Present,* ed. Arthur Green. (New York, NY: Crossroads, 1987), 157-205, 167.

Chapter Seven

1 Jung, *The Red Book,* 234a.

2 J. N. Findlay, *The Transcendence of the Cave* (London, England: George Allen & Unwin Ltd., 1967), 123-4.

3 Jacques Derrida, "Différance" in *Margins of Philosophy,* trans. Alan Bass. (Chicago, IL: Chicago University Press, 1982), 22.

4 Slavoj Žižek, *The Parallax View* (Cambridge, MA.: MIT Press, 2009), 21.

5 Slavoj Žižek, *Less Than Nothing: Hegel and the Shadow of Dialectical Materialism* (London, England: Verso, 2012).

6 Ibid., 475.

7 Ibid.

8 Žižek, *The Parallax Gap,* 20 ff.

[9] Žižek, *Less Than Nothing*, 47.

[10] Ibid., 48.

[11] Ibid., 47.

[12] Ibid., 48.

[13] Ibid.

[14] Ibid.

[15] Žižek, *The Parallax View*, 20.

[16] Ibid., 7.

[17] Ibid.

[18] Ibid.

[19] Žižek, *Less Than Nothing*, 467.

[20] Ibid., 468.

[21] Ibid., 472.

[22] Ibid., 40.

[23] Ibid., 4.

[24] Ibid., 14.

[25] Ibid., 15.

[26] Žižek, *The Parallax View*, 4.

[27] Žižek suggests that at first such gaps appear to be a kind of Kantian "revenge over Hegel" as they describe a fundamental antinomy that produces "an irreducible obstacle to dialectics" (Ibid., 4). However, according to Žižek, the parallax gap actually reveals the "subversive core" of dialectical thinking.

[28] Ibid., 29.

[29] Ibid., 213.

[30] Ibid., 29.

[31] Ibid.

[32] Qualia can be defined as raw, uninterpreted "felt" qualitative experiences.

[33] Žižek, *The Parallax View*, 233.

[34] Žižek, *Less Than Nothing*, 469.

[35] Žižek, *The Parallax View*, 25.

[36] Ibid. Žižek is here quoting from Claude Lévi-Strauss, *Structural Anthropology* (New York, NY: Basic Books, 1963).

[37] Ibid., 26.

[38] Ibid. 25.

39 Quoted by Žižek, Ibid., 221. Thomas Metzinger, *Being No One: The Self-Model Theory of Subjectivity* (Cambridge, MA: MIT Press, 2004), 634.

40 Žižek, *Less Than Nothing*, 281. Žižek references first pages 269-70 and then page 272 of the Norman Kemp Smith translation of the *Critique of Pure Reason*. For Žižek, both the Kantian "transcendental object" and the "transcendental subject" appear as a void (Žižek, *The Parallax View*, 21). However, according to Žižek, the new dimension that emerges in the parallax gap is the spontaneity of the transcendental "I," which he regards as the subject's freedom. Žižek links the parallax gap to the Lacanian "real," which involves the negativity of desire and has "no positive-substantial consistency" (Ibid., 7). It is in this way that he forges a link between philosophy and psychoanalysis.

41 Žižek, *Less Than Nothing*, 273.

42 Ibid., 474.

43 Žižek, *The Parallax View*, 28.

44 G. W. F. Hegel. *Science of Logic*, trans. G. Giovanni (Cambridge, MA: Cambridge University Press, 2010), 122.

45 G. W. F. Hegel. *Hegel's Logic*. Being Part I of the *Encyclopedia of the Philosophical Sciences,* trans. William Wallace. Foreword by J. N. Findlay (Oxford, England: Oxford University Press, 1975), sec. 81, 115.

46 Hegel, *Hegel's Logic*, Wallace, sec. 48, *Zusatz*, p. 78.

47 Jonathan Rée, "*Less Than Nothing* by Slavoj Žižek—review." *The Guardian.* Last modified June 27, 2012. Accesssed July 24, 2016 from https://www.theguardian.com/books/2012/jun/27/less-than-nothing-slavoj-Žižek-review.

48 Alain Badiou, *Being and Event*, trans. Oliver Feltham (New York, NY: Continuum, 2005).

49 G. W. F. Hegel, *On Art, Religion, Philosophy*: *Introductory Lectures to the Realm of Absolute Spirit,* ed. J. Glenn Gray (New York, NY: Harper & Row, 1970), 230.

50 Hegel, *Hegel's* Logic, sec. 82, *Zusatz* 1, 120-1.

51 We might be able to imagine a world, perhaps one akin to that described in some of Ludwig Wittgenstein's language games, within which thought is finite, resulting in a "closed loop" akin to the "moves" in a game of checkers. Yet, as far as we can see, this is not the case in our own world.

Our hermeneutics, our thought, is indeed potentially infinite, and for this reason, our "Absolute" (our "whole") is infinite as well. This "whole" is the unending limit of all thought and experience, the "plus one" beyond any endeavor at closure. See Ch. 5, n. 56.

[52] Hegel, *On Art, Religion, Philosophy*, 30.

[53] Žižek, *Less Than Nothing*, 467.

[54] *Sefer Yetzirah* I:7. Aryeh Kaplan, *Sefer Yetzirah: The Book of Creation*, rev. ed. (York Beach, ME: Samuel Weiser, 1997), 57.

[55] Žižek, *Less Than Nothing*, 467.

[56] Willard Quine, *Word and Object* (Cambridge, MA.: MIT Press, 2013), Chapter 2, "Translation and Meaning," 23-72.

[57] Aristotle, *On Sophistical Refutations*, in *The Complete Works of Aristotle: The Revised Oxford Translation*, ed. J. Barnes, trans Pickard-Cambridge (Princeton, NJ: Princeton University Press, 1984), Book 4.

[58] J. N. Findlay's term for concepts that show more than one face.

[59] Hegel, *On Art, Religion, Philosophy*, 226.

[60] Wolfgang Giegerich, "'Jung and Hegel' Revisited" in Wolfgang Giegerich, *Collected English Papers, Vol. VI; "Dreaming the Myth Onwards": C. G. Jung on Christianity and Hegel, Part 2 of the Flight into the Unconscious* (New Orleans, LA: Spring Journal Books, 2013), 335.

[61] *Zohar* II: 184a, Harry Simon and Maurice Sperling, *The Zohar*, vol. IV, 125.

[62] C. G. Jung, "The Development of Personality" in *The Development of Personality*. In *The Collected Works of C. G. Jung*, vol. 17, trans. R. F. C. Hull (Princeton, NJ: Princeton University Press, 1954), 185-6, par. 321.

[63] Hector Sabelli, *Union of Opposites: A Comprehensive Theory of Natural and Human Processes* (Lawrenceville, VA: Brunswick Publishing Corporation, 1989).

BIBLIOGRAPHY

Adler, Mortimer, ed. *Great Books of the Western World*, vol. 7. Chicago, IL: Encyclopedia Britannica, Inc., 1991.

Altizer, Thomas J. J. *The Gospel of Christian Atheism*. Philadelphia, PA: Westminster Press, 1966.

_____. *The New Apocalypse: The Radical Christian Vision of William Blake*. East Lansing, MI: Michigan State University Press, 1967.

Aristotle. *Metaphysics*, in *Great Books of the Western World*, vol. 7. Edited by Mortimer Adler, translated by W. D. Ross. Chicago, IL: Encyclopedia Britannica, Inc., 1991.

_____. *Physics*, in *Great Books of the Western World*, vol. 7. Edited by Mortimer Adler, translated by W. D. Ross. Chicago, IL: Encyclopedia Britannica, Inc., 1991.

Atterton, Peter, Matthew Calarco, and Maurice Friedman, ed. *Lévinas and Buber: Dialogue and Difference*. Pittsburgh, PA: Duquesne University Press, 2004.

Azriel. "The Explanation of the Ten *Sefirot*." In Joseph Dan, *The Early Kabbalah*. Edited by Joseph Dan, translated by Ronald C. Kieber. New York, NY: Paulist Press, 1966.

Badiou, Alain. *Being and Event*. Translated by Oliver Feltham. New York, NY: Continuum, 2005.

Barnes, Jonathan, ed. *The Complete Works of Aristotle*, vol. I. Princeton, NJ: Princeton University Press, 1984.

Beal, J. C. "Dialetheism and the Probability of Contradictions." *Australasian Journal of Philosophy*, *79*(March 2001): 114-8.

Beiser, Frederick C. *The Cambridge Companion to Hegel*. Cambridge, MA: Cambridge University Press, 1993.

Binswanger, Ludwig. *Being in the World: Selected Papers of Ludwig Binswanger.* Translated by Jacob Needleman. New York: Basic Books, 1963.

Bishop, Paul. "Introduction." In *Jung in Context: A Reader.* Edited by Paul Bishop and Anthony Storr. London, England: Routledge, 2000.

_____. *The Dionysian Self: C. G. Jung's Reception of Friedrich Nietzsche.* New York, NY: Walter de Gruyter, 1995.

Bohr, Niels. "Discussion with Einstein on Epistemological Problems in Atomic Physics." In *Great Books of the Western World,* vol. 56. Edited by Mortimer J. Adler Chicago, IL: Encyclopedia Britannica, Inc., 1990.

_____. "Selections from Atomic Theory and the Description of Nature." In *Great Books of the Western World,* vol. 56. Edited by Mortimer J. Adler. Chicago, IL: Encyclopedia Britannica, Inc. 1990.

Bostrom, Nick. "Are You Living in a Computer Simulation?" *Philosophical Quarterly, 53*(211) (2003): 243-55. Retrieved July 23, 2016 from http://www.simulation-argument.com/simulation.html.

Buber, Martin. *I and Thou.* Translated by Walter Kaufmann. New York, NY: Touchstone, 1970.

_____. *I and Thou.* Translated by R. G. Smith. New York, NY: Scribners, 2000.

Caputo, John D. *The Prayers and Tears of Jacques Derrida: Religion Without Religion.* Bloomington, IN: Indiana University Press, 1997.

Cassirer, Ernst. *The Philosophy of Symbolic Forms. Volume One: Language.* New Haven, CT: Yale University Press.

_____. *The Philosophy of Symbolic Forms. Volume Two: Mythical Thought.* New Haven, CT: Yale University Press, 1955.

Chapman, A. H., and M. Chapman-Santana. "The Influence of Nietzsche on Freud's Ideas," *British Journal of Psychiatry, 166*(2) (2009): 251-53.

Colvin, Matthew. "Heraclitean Flux and Unity of Opposites in Plato's Thaetetus and Cratylus." *The Classical Quarterly, New Series, 57*(December 2007): 759-69.

Cousins, Ewert H. *Bonaventure and the Coincidence of Opposites*. Chicago, IL: Franciscan Herald Press, 1978.

Coward, Harold. *Derrida and Indian Philosophy*. Albany, NY: State University of New York Press, 1990.

DeLaurentis, Allegra, and Jeffrey Edwards, ed. *The Bloomsbury Companion to Hegel*. London, England: Continuum Press, 2013.

Derrida, Jacques. *Points...Interviews, 1974-94*. Edited by Elizabeth Weber, translated by Peggy Kamuf, et al. Stanford, CA: Stanford University Press, 1995.

_____. *Specters of Marx: The State of the Debt, the Work of Mourning, and the New International*, translated by Peggy Kaman. New York, NY: Routledge, 1994.

_____. "Deconstruction and the Other." In *Dialogues with Contemporary Continental Thinkers*. Edited by Richard Kearney. Manchester, England: Manchester University Press, 1984.

_____. "Différance." In *Margins of Philosophy*. Translated by Alan Bass. Chicago, IL: Chicago University Press, 1982.

_____. "Plato's Pharmacy." In *Dissemination*. Translated by Barbara Johnson. London, England: The Athlone Press, 1981.

_____. *Positions*. Translated by Alan Bass. Chicago, IL: University of Chicago Press, 1981.

_____. *Speech and Phenomena and Other Essays on Husserl's Theory of Signs*. Chicago, IL: Northwestern University Press, 1979.

_____. *Writing and Difference*, translated by Alan Bass. Chicago, IL: University of Chicago Press, 1978.

_____. *Of Grammatology*. Translated by Gayatri Chakravorty Spivak. Baltimore, MD: Johns Hopkins Press, 1974.

Dewey, John. *Experience and Nature*. London, England: George Allen & Unwin, 1929.

Dourley, John P. *Jung and His Mystics: In the End It All Comes Down to Nothing*. New York, NY: Routledge, 2014.

Drob, Sanford. "An Axiological Model of the Relationship between Consciousness and Value." *New Ideas in Psychology*, 43,57-63,

2016.

_____. *Reading the Red Book: An Interpretive Guide to C. G. Jung's Liber Novus*. New Orleans, LA: Spring Journal Books, 2012.

_____. *Kabbalistic Visions: C. G. Jung and Jewish Mysticism*. New Orleans, LA: Spring Journal Books, 2010.

_____. *Kabbalah and Postmodernism: A Dialogue*. New York, NY: Peter Lang, 2009.

_____. "James Hillman on Language, Escape from the Linguistic Prison." In *Archetypal Psychology: Reflections in Honor of James Hillman*. Edited by Stanton Marlan. New Orleans, LA: Spring Journal Books, 2008.

_____. *Kabbalistic Metaphors: Mystical Themes in Ancient and Modern Thought*. Northvale, NJ: Jason Aronson, 2000.

_____. *Symbols of the Kabbalah: Philosophical and Psychological Perspectives*. Northvale, NJ: Jason Aronson, 2000.

_____. "Jung and the Kabbalah." *History of Psychology*, 2(2) (1999): 102-18.

_____. "Judaism as a Form of Life." *Tradition: A Journal of Orthodox Jewish Thought*, 23(4) (1988): 78-89.

_____. "The Red Book of C. G Jung, 'Jung on Self and God.'" Retrieved December 12, 2016 from http://theredbookofcgjung.blogspot.com/2009/12/jung-on-self-and-god-i-and-thou-part-i.html

_____. "The Only God Who Can Save Us from Ourselves." Retrieved July 23, 2016 from http://www.newkabbalah.com/dogma.pdf.

Eckhart, Meister. *Meister Eckhart. A Modern Translation*. Translated by Raymond Bernard Blakney. New York, NY: Harper, 1941.

_____. "True Hearing" Sermon on Ecclesiasticus xxiv, 30, "Whoso Heareth Me Shall Not Be Confounded." In *Meister Eckhart's Sermons*. Translated by Claud Field. London, England: H. R. Allenson, Ltd., 2005. Retrieved August 8, 2016 from http://www.catholicprimer.org/eckhart/eckhart_sermons.pdf.

Elior, Rachel. "Chabad: The Contemplative Ascent to God." *Jewish Spirituality: From the Sixteenth Century Revival to the Present*. Edited by Arthur Green. New York, NY: Crossroads, 1987.

_____. *The Paradoxical Ascent to God: The Kabbalistic Theosophy of Habad Hasidism*. Translated by Jeffrey M. Green. Albany, NY: State University of New York, 1993.

Emlyn-Jones, C. J. "Heraclitus and the Identity of Opposites." *Phronesis* 21 (1976): 89-114.

Exner, John. *The Rorschach: A Comprehensive System, Vol. 2: Interpretation*, 2nd ed. Hoboken, NJ: John Wiley & Sons, 1991.

Filoramo, Giovanni. *A History of Gnosticism*. Translated by Anthony Alcock. Cambridge, MA: Basil Blackwell, 1990.

Findlay, J. N. "Philosophy as a Discipline." *The Philosophical Forum* XXXVI (Summer 2005): 147.

_____. *Plato: The Written and Unwritten Doctrines*. London, England: Routledge, 1974.

_____. "Intentional Inexistence." In *Ascent to the Absolute*. London, England: George Allen & Unwin Ltd., 1970.

_____. *The Transcendence of the Cave*. London, England: George Allen & Unwin Ltd., 1967.

_____. *Language, Mind, and Value*. London, England: George Allen & Unwin, 1962.

_____. *Hegel: A Re-Examination*. New York, NY: Oxford University Press, 1958.

Frankl, Victor E. *Man's Search for Meaning*. Translated by Ilse Lasch. Boston, MA: Beacon Press, 2006.

Freud, Sigmund. *Collected Papers*, vol. 3. Edited by James Strachey, translated by Joan Riviere. New York, NY: Basic Books, 1959.

Gallix, Andrew. "In Theory: The Unread and the Unreadable." *The Guardian*. Last modified February 18, 2013. Retrieved July 23, 2016 from https://www.theguardian.com/books/booksblog/2013/feb/18/unread-unreadable-books.

Garfield, Jay and Graham Priest: Nagarjuna and the Limits of Thought." *Philosophy East and West*, 43(Jan 2003): 1-21.

Garrison, James W. "Dewey and the Empirical Unity of Opposites."

Transactions of the Charles S. Peirce Society, 21 (Fall 1985): 549-61.

Giegerich, Wolfgang. "'Jung and Hegel Revisted." In *Wolfgang Giegerich, Collected English Papers, Vol. VI; "Dreaming the Myth Onwards"*: C. G. Jung on Christianity and Hegel, Part 2 of the Flight into the Unconscious*. New Orleans, LA: Spring Journal Books, 2013.

_____. "The End of Meaning and the Birth of Man: An Essay About the State Reached in the History of Consciousness and an Analysis of C. G. Jung's Psychology Project." *Journal of Jungian Theory and Practice*, 6(1) (2004).

Good, James. *A Search for Unity in Diversity: The "Permanent Hegelian Deposit" in the Philosophy of John Dewey*. Oxford, UK: Lexington Books, 2006.

Graham, Daniel. "Heraclitus." *Stanford Encyclopedia of Philosophy*. Accessed November 15, 2015 from http://plato.stanford.edu/archives/sum2011/entries/heraclitus.

Hedley, Douglas, and Chris Ryan, "Nineteenth Century Philosophy of Religion: An Introduction." In Graham Oppy and N. N. Trakakis, *Nineteenth Century Philosophy of Religion*. London, England: Routledge, 2014.

Hegel, G. W. F. *Science of Logic*. Translated by George D. Giovanni. Cambridge, MA: Cambridge University Press, 2010.

_____. *Lectures on the Philosophy of Religion, Vol. III: The Consummate Religion*. Edited by Peter Hodgson. Oakland, CA: University of California Press, 1998.

_____. *Phenomenology of Spirit*. Translated by A. V. Miller with analysis of the text and foreword by J. N. Findlay. Oxford, UK: Clarendon Press, 1977.

_____. *Hegel's Logic*. Being Part I of the *Encyclopedia of the Philosophical Sciences*. Translated by William Wallace. Oxford, UK: Oxford University Press, 1975.

_____. *Lectures on the History of Philosophy*, vol. I. Translated by

E. S. Haldan and Francis H. Simon. London, England: Routledge, 1974.

_____. *Hegel's Philosophy of Mind.* Being Part III of the *Encyclopedia of the Philosophical Sciences.* Translated by William Wallace. Together with Zusatze in Bouman's edition (1845). Translated by A. V. Miller. Oxford, UK: Clarendon Press, 1971.

_____. *On Art, Religion, Philosophy: Introductory Lectures to the Realm of Absolute Spirit.* Edited by J. Glenn Gray. New York, NY: Harper & Row, 1970.

_____. *The Phenomenology of Mind.* Translated by J. B. Baillie. London, England: Harper & Row, 1967.

_____. *Philosophy of Right.* Translated by T. M. Knox. London, England: Clarendon Press, 1952.

_____. *Lectures on Aesthetics*, vol. I. London, England: Routledge, 1905.

_____. "Lectures on the Philosophy of Religion," vol. I. In *The Introduction to Hegel's Philosophy of Fine Art.* Translated by E. B. Speirs and I. Burdon Sanderson. London, England: Routledge, 1905.

Heidegger, Martin. *Being and Time.* Translated by John Macquarrie and Edward Robinson. Oxford, UK: Basil Blackwell, 1962.

Heraclitus. *The Fragments of Hercalitus.* Accessed October 1, 2015 from http://en.wikisource.org/wiki/Fragments_of_Heraclitus.

Howells, Christian. *Derrida: Deconstruction from Phenomenology to Ethics.* Cambridge, MA: Polity Press, 1999.

Huskinson, Lucy. *Nietzsche and Jung: The Whole Self in the Union of Opposites.* New York, NY: Brunner-Routledge, 2004.

Hut, Piet, and Roger N. Shepard. "Turning 'The Hard Problem,' Upside Down and Sideways." In *Explaining Consciousness: The Hard Problem.* Edited by Jonathan Shear. Cambridge, MA: MIT Press, 1999.

Idel, Moshe. *Absorbing Perfections.* New Haven, CT: Yale University Press, 2002.

_____. *Kabbalah: New Perspectives*. New Haven, CT: Yale University Press, 1988.

James, William. *Pragmatism: A New Name for Some Old Ways of Thinking*. Cambridge, MA: Harvard University Press, 1975.

Jung, C. G. *The Red Book, Liber Novus*. Edited by Sonu Shamdasani, translated by Mark Kyburz, John Peck, and Sonu Shamdasani. New York, NY: W. W. Norton & Company, 2009.

_____. *Nietzsche's Zarathustra: Notes on the Seminar Given in 1934-9*, vol. I. Edited by James L. Jarrett. London, England: Routledge, 1981.

_____. "An Eightieth Birthday Interview." In *C. G. Jung Speaking: Interviews and Encounters*. Edited by William McGuire & R. F. C. Hull. Princeton, NJ: Princeton University Press, 1977.

_____. "Diagnosing the Dictators." In *C. G. Jung Speaking: Interviews and Encounters*. Edited by William McGuire and R. F. C. Hull. Princeton, NJ: Princeton University Press, 1977.

_____. "The 'Face to Face' Interview." In *C. G. Jung Speaking: Interviews and Encounters*. Princeton, NJ: Bollingen Paperbacks, 1977.

_____. *Letters*, vol. I and II. Edited by Gerhard Adler, Aniela Jaffe, and R. F. C. Hull. Princeton, NJ: Princeton University Press, 1973.

_____. *Psychological Types*. Translated by H. G. Baynes and R. F. C. Hull. *The Collected Works of C. G. Jung*, vol. 6. Princeton, NJ: Princeton University Press, 1971.

_____. *Mysterium Coniunctionis: An Inquiry into the Separation and Synthesis of Psychic Opposites in Alchemy*. In *The Collected Works of C. G. Jung*, vol. 14. Translated by R. F. C. Hull. Princeton, NJ: Princeton University Press, 1970.

_____. "The Spiritual Problem of Modern Man." In *Civilization in Transition*. Translated by R. F. C. Hull. Vol. 10 of *The Collected Works of C. G. Jung*, 2nd ed. Princeton, NJ: Princeton University Press, 1970.

_____. "On the Nature of Dreams." In *The Structure and Dynamics of the Psyche*. Translated by R. F. C. Hull. Vol. 8 of *The Collected*

Works of C. G. Jung, 2nd ed. Princeton, NJ: Princeton University Press, 1969.

_____. "On the Nature of the Psyche." In *The Structure and Dynamics of the Psyche*. Princeton, NJ: Princeton University Press, 1969.

_____. "The Psychology of Eastern Meditation." In *Psychology and Religion: West and East*. Translated by R. F. C. Hull. Vol. 11 of *The Collected Works of C. G. Jung*, 2nd ed. Princeton, NJ: Princeton University Press, 1958.

_____. *Aion: Researches into the Phenomenology of the Self*. Translated by R. F. C. Hull. Vol. 9., Part II of *The Collected Works of C. G. Jung*, 2nd ed. Princeton, NJ: Princeton University Press, 1968.

_____. "Answer to Job." Translated by R. F. C. Hull. Vol. 11 of *The Collected Works of C. G. Jung*, 2nd ed. Princeton, NJ: Princeton University Press, 1968.

_____. "The Phenomenology of the Spirit in Fairy Tales." In *The Acrchetypes of the Collective Unconscious*. Translated by R. F. C. Hull. Vol. 9, Part I, of *The Collected Works of C. G. Jung*, 2nd ed. Princeton, NJ: Princeton University Press, 1968.

_____. *Psychology and Alchemy*. Translated by R. F. C. Hull. Vol. 12 of *The Collected Works of C. G. Jung*, 2nd ed. Princeton, NJ: Princeton University Press, 1968.

_____. "The Psychology of the Child Archetype." In *The Archetypes of the Collective Unconscious*. Translated by R. F. C. Hull. Vol. 9., Part I of *The Collected Works of C. G. Jung*, 2nd ed. Princeton, NJ: Princeton University Press, 1968.

_____. "Commentary on 'The Secret of the Golden Flower.'" In *Alchemical Studies*. Translated by R. F. C. Hull. Vol. 13 of *The Collected Works of C. G. Jung*, 2nd ed. Princeton, NJ: Princeton University Press, 1968.

_____. "Paracelsus as a Spiritual Phenomenon." In *Alchemical Studies*. Translated by R. F. C. Hull. Vol. 13 of *The Collected Works of C. G. Jung*, 2nd ed. Princeton, NJ: Princeton University Press, 1967.

_____. "The Spirit of Mercurius." In *Alchemical Studies*. Translated by R. F. C. Hull. Vol. 13 of *The Collected Works of C. G. Jung*, 2nd ed. Princeton, NJ: Princeton University Press, 1967.

_____. *Symbols of Transformation*. Translated by R. F. C. Hull. Vol. 5 of *The Collected Works of C. G. Jung*, 2nd ed. Princeton, NJ: Princeton University Press, 1967.

_____. "On the Psychology of the Unconscious." In *Two Essays on Analytical Psychology*. Translated by R. F. C. Hull. Vol 7 of *The Collected Works of C. G. Jung*, 2nd ed. Princeton, NJ: Princeton University Press, 1966.

_____. "The Practical Use of Dream Analysis." In *The Practice of Psychotherapy*. Translated by R. F. C. Hull, Vol. 16 of *The Collected Works of C. G. Jung*, 2nd ed. Princeton, NJ: Princeton University Press, 1966.

_____. "The Relations Between the Ego and the Unconscious." In *Two Essays on Analytical Psychology*. Translated by R. F. C. Hull. Vol. 7 of *The Collected Works of C. G. Jung*, 2nd ed. Princeton, NJ: Princeton University Press, 1966.

_____. "The Psychology of the Transference." In *The Practice of Psychotherapy*. Translated by R. F. C. Hull. Vol. 16 of *The Collected Works of C. G. Jung*, 2nd ed. Princeton, NJ: Princeton University Press, 1966.

_____. *Memories, Dreams, Reflections*. Edited by Aniela Jaffe. New York, NY: Random House, 1961.

_____. "Answer to Job." In *Psychology and Religion: West and East*, 2nd ed. Princeton, NJ: Princeton University Press, 1958.

_____. "On the "Tibetan Book of the Great Liberation." In *Psychology and Religion: West and East*, 2nd ed. Princeton, NJ: Princeton University Press, 1958.

_____. "The Development of Personality." In *The Development of Personality*. Translated by R. F. C. Hull. Vol. 1 of *The Collected Works of C. G. Jung*, 2nd ed. Princeton, NJ: Princeton University Press, 1954.

_____. "The Tavistock Lectures: On the Theory and Practice of Analytical Psychology." Lecture V. In *The Symbolic Life*. Translated by R. F. C. Hull. Vol. 18 of *The Collected Works of C. G. Jung*, 2nd ed. Princeton, NJ: Princeton University Press, 1954.

Kant, Immanuel. *Critique of Judgment*. Translated by James Creed Meredith. Oxford, UK: Oxford University Press, 2007.

_____. *Critique of Practical Reason*. Translated by Lewis W. Beck. Bloomington, IN: Bobbs-Merrill, 1956.

_____. *Critique of Pure Reason*. Translated by Norman Kemp Smith. London, England: MacMillan, 1929.

Kaplan, Aryeh, ed. *Ethics of the Talmud: Pirke Avot, MeAm Lo'ez by Rabbi Yitzchak (ben Moshe) Magrino*. New York, NY: Maznaim, 1979.

_____. *Sefer Yetzirah: The Book of Creation*, rev. ed. York Beach, ME: Samuel Weiser, 1997.

Kirk, G. S. and J. E. Raven. *The Presocratic Philosophers*. Cambridge, MA: Cambridge University Press, 1957.

Kirsch, James. "C. G. Jung and the Jews: The Real Story," reprinted in *Lingering Shadows: Jungians, Freudians, and Anti-Semitism*. Edited by Aryeh Maidenbaum and Stephen A. Martin. Boston, MA: Shambhala, 1982.

Kuhn, Thomas. *The Structure of Scientific Revolutions*. Chicago, IL: University of Chicago Press, 1996.

Lacan, Jacques. *The Seminar of Jacques Lacan, Book VII: The Ethics of Psychoanalysis, 1959–1960*. Edited by Jacques Alain Miller, translated by Dennis Porter. New York, NY: W. W. Norton and Company, 1992.

Langer, Susan. *Philosophy in a New Key: A Study in the Symbolism of Reason, Rite, and Art*, 3rd ed. Cambridge, MA: Harvard University Press, 1957.

Lazerowitz, Morris. *Philosophy and Illusion*. London, England: George Allen & Unwin, 1968.

Lévinas, Emmanuel. *Totality and Infinity: An Essay on Exteriority*.

Translated by Alphonso Lingis. Pittsburgh, PA: Duquesne University Press, 1969.

Lévi-Strauss, Claude. *Structural Anthropology*. New York, NY: Basic Books, 1963.

_____. "The Structure of Myth." In *Structural Anthropology*. Translated by Claire Jacobson and Brooke Grundfest. New York, NY: Allen Lane, 1963.

Maidenbaum, Aryeh, ed. *Jung and the Shadow of Anti-Semitism*. Berwick, ME: Nicolas-Hays, 2002.

Maidenabaum, Aryeh, and Stephen A. Martin. *Lingering Shadows*. Boston, MA: Shambhala, 1982.

McCort, Dennis. *Going Beyond the Pairs: The Coincidence of Opposites in German Romanticism, Zen, and Deconstruction*. Albany, NY: State University of New York Press, 2001.

Miller, Clyde Lee. "Cusanus, Nicolaus [Nicolas of Cusa]." *The Stanford Encyclopedia of Philosophy*. Fall 2015 edition. Edited by Edward N. Zalta. Accessed July 26, 2016 from http://plato.stanford.edu/archives/fall2015/entries/cusanus.

Myers, Steve. "Jung's Regret Over 'I Don't Need to Believe I Know.'" Retrieved from http://steve.myers.co/jungs-regret-over-i-dont-need-to-believe-i-know/.

Nagel, Thomas. "Subjective and Objective." In *Post-Analytic Philosophy*. Edited by John Rajchman and Cornel West. New York, NY: Columbia University Press, 1985.

Nicholas of Cusa. *On the Peace of Faith* (*De Pace Fide*): *A Dialogue on World Religious Peace*. Translated by Lawrence Bond. Last modified 2000. Accessed August 4, 2016 from http://www.appstate.edu.

_____. *On Learned Ignorance* (*De Docta Ignorantia*). Minneapolis, MN: The Arthur J. Banning Press, 1981. Translation of Book I from *De docta ignorantia. Die belehrte Unwissenheit*, Book I, 2nd ed. Text edited by Paul Wilpert, revised by Hans G. Senger. Hamburg, Germany: Felix Meiner, 1970. Accessed November 15, 2016 from http://www.jasper-hopkins.info/DI-I-12-2000.pdf.

Nietzsche, Friedrich. *On the Genealogy of Morality*. Edited by Keith Ansell-Pearson, translated by Carol Dieth. Cambridge, MA: Cambridge University Press, 2006.

_____. "The Dionysiac World-View, Sec. 1." In *The Birth of Tragedy and Other Writings*. Edited by Raymond Gess and Ronald Spiers, translated by Ronald Speirs. Cambridge, MA: Cambridge University Press, 1999.

_____. *Untimely Meditations*. Edited by Daniel Breazeale, translated by R. J. Hollingdale. Cambridge, MA: Cambridge University Press, 1997.

_____. *Human, All Too Human: A Book for Free Spirits*. Translated by R. J. Hollingdale. Cambridge, MA: Cambridge University Press, 1986.

_____. *The Will to Power: A New Translation*. Edited by Walter Kauffmann, translated by Walter Kaufmann and R. J. Hollingdale. New York, NY: Vintage Books, 1968.

_____. *The Will to Power*. Translated by Walter Kaufman. New York, NY: Random House, 1967.

_____. *Philosophy in the Tragic Age of the Greeks*. Translated by Marianne Cowan. Washington, D.C.: Regnery Publishing, 1962.

Noll, Richard. *The Aryan Christ: The Secret Life of Carl Jung*. New York, NY: Random House, 1997.

Ohsawa, Georges. *The Unique Principle*. Chico, CA: Georges Oshawa Macrobiotic Foundation, 1976.

Pinkard, Terry. *Hegel: A Biography*. Cambridge, MA: Cambridge University Press, 2000.

Plato. *The Dialogues of Plato*. Edited by Mortimer J. Adler, translated by B. Jowett. Vol. 6 of *Great Books of the Western World*. Chicago, IL: Encyclopedia Britannica, Inc. 1990.

Plotinus. *The Six Enneads*. Translated by Stephen Makenna. Vol. 11 of *The Great Books of the Western World*. Chicago, IL: Encyclopedia Britannica, 1952.

Priest, Graham. "Dialetheism." In *The Stanford Encyclopedia of Phi-

losophy (Summer 2004 Edition). Edited by Edward N. Zalta. http://plato.stanford.edu/archives/sum2004/entries/dialetheism.

_____. *In Contradiction*, 2nd ed. Oxford, UK: Oxford University Press, 2006.

Quine, Willard. *Word and Object*. Cambridge, MA: MIT Press, 2013.

Radhakrishnan, Sarvelli and Charles Moore, ed. *A Sourcebook in Indian Philosophy*. Princeton, NJ: Princeton University Press, 1957.

Redding, Paul. "Georg Wilhelm Friedrich Hegel." *The Stanford Encyclopedia of Philosophy* (Spring 2016 edition). Edited by Edward N. Zalta. Accessed from http://plato.stanford.edu/archives/spr2016/entries/hegel/.

_____. *Hegel's Hermeneutics*. Ithaca, NY: Cornell University Press, 1996.

Rée, Jonathan. "*Less Than Nothing* by Slavoj Žižek—review." *The Guardian*. Last modified June 27, 2012. Accessed July 24, 2016 from https://www.theguardian.com/books/2012/jun/27/less-than-nothing-slavoj-zizek-review.

Rickert, Heinrich. *Grundprobleme der Philosophie. Methodologie, Ontologie, Anthropologie*. Tübingen, Germany: Mohr Siebeck, 1934.

Ricouer, Paul. *The Conflict of Interpretations*. Edited by Don Ihde. Chicago, IL: Northwestern University Press, 1974.

Robinson, James M., ed. *The Nag Hammadi Library*, 3rd ed. San Francisco, CA: Harper & Row, 1988.

Robinson, William. "Epiphenomenalism." *The Stanford Encyclopedia of Philosophy* (Fall 2015 Edition). Edited Edward N. Zalta. Accessed January 15, 2016 from http://plato.stanford.edu/archives/fall2015/entries/epiphenomenalism.

Rohlf, Michael. "Immanuel Kant." *The Stanford Encyclopedia of Philosophy* (Spring 2016 edition). Edited by Edward N. Zalta. Accessed August 6, 2016 from http://plato.stanford.edu/archives/spr2016/entries/kant.

Rudolph, Kurt. *Gnosis: The Nature and History of Gnosticism*. Edited and translated by Robert McLachlan Wilson. San Francisco, CA:

Harper & Row, 1987.

Sabelli, Hector. *Union of Opposites: A Comprehensive Theory of Natural and Human Processes*. Lawrenceville, VA: Brunswick Publishing Corporation, 1989.

Sartre, Jean-Paul. *The Imaginary*. Translated by Jonathan Webber. London, England: Routledge, 1940/2005.

_____. *Psychology of the Imagination*. Translated by Hazel Barnes. London, England: Routledge, 2001.

_____. *Being and Nothingness*. Translated by Hazel E. Barnes. New York, NY: Washington Square Press, 1966.

Scholem, Gershom. *Origins of the Kabbalah*. Translated by R. J. Z. Werblowski. Princeton, NJ: Princeton University Press, 1987.

_____. *Kabbalah*. Jerusalem: Keter, 1974.

_____. *Major Trends in Jewish Mysticism*. New York, NY: Schocken, 1941.

Schwartz-Salant, Nathan. "The Mark of One Who Has Seen Chaos: A Review of C. G. Jung's *Red Book*." *Quadrant: The Journal of the C. G. Jung Foundation, 40*(2) (Summer 2010): 11-40.

Sellars, Wilfrid. "Empiricism and the Philosophy of Mind." In *Science, Perception, and Reality*. London, England: Routledge, 1963.

Sherry, Jay. *Carl Gustav Jung: Avant-Garde Conservative*. New York, NY: Palgrave MacMillan, 2010.

Solomon, Robert C. *In the Spirit of Hegel: A Study of G. W. F. Hegel's Phenomenology of Spirit*. New York, NY: Oxford University Press, 1983.

Sperling, Harry, Maurice Simon, and Paul Levertoff, ed. *The Zohar Vols. I–V*. London, England: Soncino Press, 1931-4.

Stace, Walter T. *Mysticism and Philosophy*. London, England: MacMillan Press, 1960.

_____. *The Philosophy of Hegel: A Systematic Exposition*. New York, NY: Dover Publications, 1955.

Staiti, Andrea. "Heinrich Rickert." *The Stanford Encyclopedia of Philosophy* (Winter 2013 edition). Edited by Edward N. Zalta. Ac-

cessed February 15, 2016 from http://plato.stanford.edu/archives/
win2013/entries/heinrich-rickert.

_____. "The Neo-Kantians on the Meaning and Status of Philoso-
phy." In *New Approaches to Neo-Kantianism*. Edited by Nicolas de
Warren and Andrea Staiti. Cambridge, MA: Cambridge University
Press, 2015.

Staten, Harry. *Wittgenstein and Derrida*. Lincoln, NE: University of
Nebraska Press, 1986.

Jewish Review. "Steinsaltz, Adin: "The Mystic as Philosopher: An Interview with Rabbi Adin Steinsaltz." *Jewish Review*, 3(4) (March
1990/Adar 5570). Accessed August 8, 2016 from http://thejewish-
review.org/articles/?id=180.

Taylor, Charles. *Hegel*. Cambridge, MA: Cambridge University Press,
1975.

Taylor, Mark C. *Erring: A Postmodern A/Theology*. Chicago, IL: University of Chicago Press, 1984.

Tishby, Isaiah and Fischel Lachower. *The Wisdom of the Zohar*, vols.
I–III. Translated by D. Goldstein. Oxford: Oxford University Press,
1989.

Lao Tzu, *Tao Te Ching*, D. C. Lau, trans. London, England: Penguin
Books, 1963.

Uffenheimer, Rifka S. *Hasidism As Mysticism: Quietistic Elements in
Eighteenth Century Hasidic Thought*. Jerusalem, Israel: Hebrew
University, 1993.

"Yinyang (Yin-Yang)." *Internet Encyclopedia of Philosophy*. Accessed
July 25, 2016 from http://www.iep.utm.edu/yinyang/.

Whitman, Walt. "Song of Myself, Part 51." In *Leaves of Grass*. The
original 1885 edition. Mineola, NY: Dover Press, 2007.

Wittgenstein, Ludwig. *Culture and Value*. Translated by Peter Winch.
Chicago, IL: University of Chicago Press, 1980.

_____. *Remarks on the Foundations of Mathematics*, 3rd ed. Edited
by G. H. von Wright, R. Rhees and G. E. M. Anscombe, translated
by G. E. M. Anscombe. Oxford, UK: Basil Blackwell, 1978.

_____. *The Tractatus Logico Philosophicus*. Translated by D. F. Pears and B. F. McGuinness. London, England: Routledge, 1961.

_____. *Philosophical Investigations*. Translated by G. E. M. Anscombe. New York, NY: MacMillan, 1958.

Wolfson, Elliot. *Alef, Mem, Tau: Kabbalistic Musings on Time, Truth, and Death*. Berkeley, CA: University of California Press, 2006.

Yalom, Irwin. *Existential Pychotherapy*. New York, NY: Basic Books, 1980.

Zaehner, Robert. C., ed. and trans. *Hindu Scriptures*. London, England: J. M. Dent & Sons, Ltd., 1966.

Zalman, Schneur. *Likutei Amarim-Tanya*. Bilingual ed. Brooklyn, NY: Kehot, 1981.

Zimmer, Heinrich. *Philosophies of India*. Edited by Joseph Campbell. Princeton, NJ: Princeton University Press, 1951.

Žižek, Slavoj. *Less Than Nothing: Hegel and the Shadow of Dialectical Materialism*. London, England: Verso, 2012.

_____. *The Parallax View*. Cambridge, MA: MIT Press, 2009.

Index

A

Abbott, Edwin, 9, 29 35, 308, 410
Abraxas, 197–98
absence, 87–88, 282, 298, 351
Abramowitz, Rabbi Zalman, 10
Absolute 9, 25, 25, 37–9, 40, 46,
    53–4, 108–9, 138–9, 141,
    152, 158–59, 165, 252, 302–
    4, 308, 353–58, 360 ff., 374,
    377–89, 396–97, 401–2
    archetype of, 25, 54, 303,
        333, 356, 385, 399
    in thought and language, 38
Absolute Being, 253, 369
Absolute Idea (Hegel), 137, 143,
    245
absurdity, 26, 92, 133, 340–41
active imagination (Jung), 194,
    228-29, 250
Adam Kadmon, 103, 108, 183,
    204, 214, cf. Primordial
    Human
Adler, Alfred 202, 205, 234, 255,
    411, 413–14, 420, 452, 465,
    474–75, 487
Adlerian psychology, 205, 260
Advata Vedanta, 46
Aion (work by C. G. Jung), 230,
    442, 448–49, 451, 482
albedo, 222–23
alchemical opus, 215, 218, 219–
    21, 223–24
Alchemical Studies (work by C. G.
    Jung) 410, 429, 441, 444,
    483
alchemists, 180, 186, 203, 213,
    215–18, 220–22, 225, 227–
    32, 234–36
alchemy, 6, 91, 183, 198, 212,
    215–17, 219, 222–27, 229–
    31, 235, 409, 411, 422, 434–
    35, 438, 440–42, 445–50,
    454, 481–82
alienation, 121–22, 174

Altizer, Thomas J. J., 10, 213,
    336–7, 445, 468, 474
analogy, cartographic, 9, 32, 35–
    36, 259, 278, 303, 309, 362,
    379
analytical psychology, 13, 20–21,
    422, 437, 440, 443, 483–84
Anaximander (pre–Socratic
    philosopher), 48
Anscombe, Elizabeth M., 420,
    428, 432, 465, 490
Answer to Job (work by C. G.
    Jung), 435, 438, 445, 453,
    482–83
antinomies, 7, 64–65, 68–69, 76,
    78–79, 91–92, 108, 126,
    128–29, 150–51, 161, 283,
    285, 287–88, 291–92, 296–
    97, 303–4, 366–67, 373, 377
    psychological, 299
Anti–Semitism, 239, 443–44, 452,
    484–85
Apollonian and Dionysian
    principles, 186–88, 208
appearances, world of, 25, 360,
    366
archaic, 13, 197, 232, 405
archetype, archetypal. 6–8, 102–4,
    114, 184, 194–96, 198–200,
    202, 208–10, 214, 228, 236–
    38, 248–50, 252–54, 261,
    290, 303–4, 388–90, 396–
    98, 402–4, 406, 438–40,
    452–54
    figure, archetypal, 199, 228
Aristotelian, two valued logic, 148
Aristotle, 12, 37, 48, 51, 54, 72,
    80, 132, 138, 194, 265, 381,
    394, 405, 413–15, 420, 438,
    473–74
Armstrong, D. 457
art, artists, 16–17, 19–20, 71, 73,
    97, 141, 144, 147, 180, 184,
    186–88, 190–92, 236, 245–

491

47, 253, 380–81, 429–31,
442, 454–55, 469, 472–73
art and religion, 145, 245–46, 248,
252
atheism, atheists, 7, 25–26, 43, 86,
303, 342, 344–46, 357, 384,
396, 421
Atman, 46, 167
Avadhūta Gitā, 355, 470
axiological, 400
Ayin (Kabbalah, nothingness),
104–5, 109, 111–12, 116,
120–22, 354
Azriel of Gerona, 100–101, 424,
474

B

Badiou, Alain, 376, 379–80, 472,
474
Bardo Thodol, 317
beauty, 15–16, 19–20, 56, 103,
114, 121, 187, 190, 333,
358, 388, 437
Beck, Aaron, 458
Beck, Lewis W., 418, 484
Beckett, Samuel, 326
behavioral psychology, 265, 297
behaviorism, 269, 290, 296, 458
being, 69–70, 72, 88–90, 110–11,
116–17, 120–23, 131, 138,
141–43, 145–46, 154, 157–
59, 219–20, 252–53, 281–
83, 308, 312–13, 357, 361–
63, 369–70
Bewusstseinslagen, 192, 438
Bhagavad Gita, 47, 98, 412, 416,
490
"Big Bang," 308, 321
Bilinear thinking, 27, 114, 321,
340, 357, 372
Binswanger, Ludwig, 475
biological psychology, 263–65,
278, 299, 363
biopsychosocial model, 462
Bishop, Paul, 5, 10–11, 182, 405,
408, 435, 437, 439, 475

Bohr, Niels, 23, 43, 64, 83–85,
153, 409, 411, 420–21, 465,
475
Bonaventure, Saint, 96, 476
Bostrom, Nick, 318, 318, 467
Bradley, F. H., 78–79
brahman, 46, 98, 167, 210, 354–
55, 397
Brahman–Atman, 46, 158, 167,
183, 215, 311, 354, 358, 387
Brahmanic doctrine, 210
brain, 209, 263–65, 278, 288,
293–94, 314–15, 317, 326
Brain process, 294–95, 313, 326
Breaking of the Vessels, 103, 106,
108, 350, 380, 383, 398, cf.
Shevirat ha–kelim
Brightman, Edgar S., 389
Brihadaranyaka Upanishad, 97
Buber, Martin, 257, 270, 389, 434,
456, 461, 474–75
Buddha, 47, 82, 190, 201, 213
Buddhism, Buddhist, 46–48, 82–
83, 96, 99, 109, 219, 248,
277, 305, 311 cf. Nagarjuna
Buddhist monk, 393
Buenos Aires moon paradox, 278–
79

C

Campbell, Joseph, 423, 470, 490
cartography, cartographic analogy,
31, 32, 34, 36, 37, 165, 281–
82, 284–85, 371, 303–4,
308, 336, 347, 363–4
Cassirer, Ernst, 253, 389, 455
Chabad Hasidim, 99, 106, 109–10,
112–14, 116–117, 120–124,
356, 424–27, 470, 477
Chandogya Upanishad, 97
chaos, chaotic, 36, 92, 115–16,
120, 174, 180, 187–88, 196,
216, 222–24, 236, 240, 242–
43, 254, 293, 442, 456, 488
formless, 195
original, 115

492

Chasidism, Hasidim, 5, 96–97, 99,
101, 103, 105, 107, 109–
111, 113, 115, 117, 119,
121, 123, 125, 231
Chesed (Kindness), 114, 119
Child Archetype, 439, 482
Chinese Philosophy, 5, 44
Chomsky, Noam, 458
Christ, Jesus, 6, 140, 145, 184,
190–91, 213, 216, 229–30
Christianity, 99, 109, 144, 198,
213, 225, 229–30, 246, 269,
406, 430
coincidentia oppositorum (cf.
opposites, coincidence of),
23–25, 39–40, 82–83, 91–
92, 100, 131–32, 180–83,
185–87, 203–5, 209–17,
223–25, 227–29, 231, 241–
45, 332–34, 341–42, 351–
53, 360–62, 383–86, 394–
97, 410–11
application of, 29, 260–61
archetype of, 96, 308, 353, 360,
395
doctrine of, 7, 24, 82–83, 99,
241, 244, 360, 364, 394, 399
challenges to, 27, 40, 360ff.
instances of, 37, 305
in German Romanticism, 413,
466
limitations and dangers, 209,
237–41
principle of, 27, 63, 101, 110,
130, 261, 269, 310, 346–47,
369, 383, 387, 469
radical, 60
second order, 323, 332, 337
collective unconscious, 406, 439,
441, 482
collectivism, 287, 289, 296–97
commandments, 114, 117, 216,
396, 425, cf. *mitzvoth*.
commensurability, 274
compensation, 6, 57, 158, 179,
191, 194, 196, 198, 200,
202–3, 207, 209, 234, 439

complementarity, 7, 9, 24–6, 32,
34, 37, 44–46, 83–85, 93,
112, 177, 198, 203, 261,
276, 283–85, 291, 299–300,
309–10, 338, 340, 347, 349,
357, 379, 401–2, 462, 464
in psychology, 276–8
complexio oppositorum, 448
consciousness, 13–14, 66–67, 70,
92, 138–40, 165, 168–69,
171, 232, 234–37, 239–40,
255–56, 258, 295, 310–11,
313, 315, 317–19, 330–32,
338–39
unhappy, 174–75
constructivism, constructivist, 162,
277, 286, 289, 294, 303,
309, 322–23, 327–8, 330–
31, 339–40, 342–43, 347,
361, 383, 468
contraction, 5, 102–5, 120, 329–
30, See *Tzimtzum*
contradiction, 5–6, 26–27, 47, 64,
78, 80–82, 92, 94, 126–28,
148–56, 159–61, 180, 243–
44, 280, 282, 365–66, 390–
91, 393–94, 422, 424
flat, 306, 391, 394
formal, 47, 82, 152, 160, 390–
91, 393
law of, 49, 51, 154
logical, 41, 85, 155, 161, 166,
306, 393
philosophical, 26, 338
true, 80, 82
contraries, 38, 47, 61, 67, 69, 167,
194, 239, 242, 277, 292,
299, 340
Copenhagen interpretation of
quantum physics, 23, See
Neils Bohr
Cordovero, Moses, 102, 424
corporeality, 118, 231
Coward, Howard, 348, 422, 469,
476
Cratylus (Platonic dialog), 50, 52,
414, 475

creation, 5, 101–2, 104–8, 110,
115–16, 119–21, 123, 141,
190, 192, 200, 220, 222,
383, 421, 424, 448, 468,
470, 473
creativity, 18, 68, 70, 93, 185, 193,
195, 203, 225, 270, 365, 401
criteria, private, 31, 286, 289, 296,
309, cf. public criteria

D

Dan, Joseph, 424, 474
Darwin, Charles, 93, 265
death, 30, 37, 60, 71, 81-2, 157,
158, 161, 170-75, 177, 197,
216, 222, 231-32, 350, 374,
416, 421, 427, 449
instinct, 173
specter of, 171–72
deconstruction, 5, 85, 87, 89, 91,
108, 125, 136, 180, 303,
311, 333, 336–37, 371, 374,
383, 404, 412–13, 421–22,
466, 469, 480, 485
Democritus, 72, 264
depression, 254, 262–67, 270,
274–75, 287–88, 296, 300,
457–59
Derrida, Jacques, 44, 64, 85–91,
131, 138, 154, 242, 310–11,
322–23, 328–30, 335, 345,
347–49, 365, 368, 374, 412–
13, 420–22, 453, 466–70,
475–76, 480, 489
critique of essence, 87-90
Indian Philosophy, 348, 469,
476
mysticism, 90
Descartes, Rene, 72, 147, 387, 389
desire, 12, 29, 61, 101, 103, 178,
183, 256, 388–9, 393–4,
396, 400, 421, , 472
dialectic of, 93, 140,
168–75, 176
determinism, 25, 43, 65, 146, 152,
156, 269, 286, 289, 292,

294, 299, 303, 309, 340,
347, 361, 363, 403
devil, 190, 199, 213–14, 230, 233
Dewey, John, 71–73, 418–19, 476,
478–79
dialectic, dialectical, 24, 29, 37–
40, 58, 68–70, 90, 124–37,
139–43, 145, 147–53, 155–
59, 165–73, 175–77, 179,
250, 252–54, 292, 349–50,
353, 373–74, 376–77, 381–
84, 388–89, 392, 397, 400
imaginative aspect, 29, 397-8
logic, 43, 352
Logic, Nature, and Spirit,
140-1
master–slave, 169, 173
method, 6, 147
of perspectives, 129–30
negative, 377–78
philosophy, 54, 123, 393
process, 27, 69, 120–21, 258,
360, 381, 383, 391, 404
thinking, 25, 147, 249, 303,
340, 381, 471
dialetheism, dialetheistic logic, 41,
47, 80–83, 155, 214, 248,
390. 412, 420, 455, 474,
486–87
différance (Derrida), 466, 470, 476
difference, 7, 67, 85–86, 89–90,
98, 154, 156, 242, 310–11,
324–25, 333–42, 353–54,
356, 360–61, 363, 376–78,
395, 400, 402–4, 418
absolute, 347, 469
psychosexual, 183
radical, 238, 403
unity in, 99
the world of, 361, 403
differentiation, 97, 103, 105, 121,
202, 205, 219, 224, 252
Dilthey, Wilhelm, 17, 408
dimensions, 35, 280–81, 308, 410,
462–63
Diogenes, 467
Dionysian (principle), 6, 14, 186–
89, 208, 436, 486

Dionysian Self, 439, 475
Dionysus, 183, 187, 436
divine, 6, 87, 103, 111, 114, 123,
    144–45, 167, 213, 231, 243,
    247, 312, 346, 402
  light, 103–4, 108, 115, 352
  nothingness, 105
  perspective, 112–13, 121–22
  speech, 106, 119–20
divinity, 100, 113–14, 116, 120–
    21, 193, 215, 217, 233, 236,
    410
dogma, 300, 302, 346, 387
Dov Baer of Lubavitch, 110, 117–
    120, 425
dreams, 16, 92, 178, 193–94, 198,
    204, 208, 229, 235, 408,
    434, 438, 440, 444, 451,
    482–83
Drob, Sanford, 10, 11–12, 21, 408,
    423, 425, 433, 440, 443–44,
    447, 452, 456, 467–68, 470

E

Ecce Homo (Nietzsche), 14, 406
eclecticism, 185, 271, 274–75,
    281–83
ecstasy, 187, 304, 346
ego, 188, 195, 203, 205, 215, 219,
    222, 224, 228, 234, 243,
    250–51, 268, 271, 422, 440–
    41, 483
ego consciousness, 214
Ein–sof (The Infinite, Kabbalah),
    98, 100–102, 104–9, 113–
    14, 120–23, 312, 325, 330,
    332, 335, 337, 342, 354,
    356–58, 382–83, 386–87,
    397, 402, 426
  transcendental object, 325
Einstein, Albert, 409, 411, 420,
    465, 475
elementism, 286, 288, 295, 342,
    363
Eliade, Mercea, 29, 44, 411
eliminative materialism, 457

Elior, Rachel, 114, 120–22, 424–
    27, 470, 477
emanation, 102, 104–5, 120
Emlyn–Jones, C. J., 51–52, 54,
    414–15, 478
emotions, 24, 29, 31, 36, 41, 117–
    18, 176, 233, 363, 389, 464
Empedocles, 18, 408, 438, 459
enantiodromia, 6, 55, 196–98, 200,
    238
Enneads (Plotinus), 407, 416–17,
    487
Ephesians, 216
epiphenomenalism, 433, 487–88
epistemological problems, 183,
    409, 411, 420, 465, 475
equal areas projection, 34–35
Erikson, Eric, 176
error, 14, 27, 30, 71–72, 134, 213,
    237, 298, 305, 331, 345,
    351, 355, 358, 401
Eryximachus, 55–56
essence, 57–58, 64, 69–70, 76,
    87–90, 100, 106, 110, 116,
    121–22, 131, 140, 144, 146,
    148, 150, 158–59, 368–69,
    412, 420
Eternal Recurrence, 195, 439
ethics, 66, 69, 111, 164, 177, 257,
    286, 339, 360, 398–99, 404,
    421, 426, 433, 460, 480, 484
Evans, Eraster 448
evil, 14, 16, 27, 30, 60–62, 97,
    100, 108, 182, 184, 190–91,
    197, 213, 215–16, 225–26,
    228–30, 238–39, 248, 398–
    400, 407
  actions, 242
  reality of, 198, 249
  world, 103
existence, 19–20, 69, 72, 114, 116,
    120–21, 145, 162, 164–65,
    286–87, 289, 293, 295–96,
    314–17, 327–28, 342–43,
    345, 370–73, 395–96, 399–
    400

existentialism, existentialists, 125,
138, 158, 169, 172, 269–70,
273, 299, 303
Exner, John, 447, 478
experience
lived, 179, 186, 257, 270, 273,
315
two–dimensional, 281, 283

F

factualism (vs. hermeneutics),
287, 289, 297, 309, 363
fairytales, 233
fantasy, 89, 203, 206–8, 234–35,
376
creative, 190, 206–7, 431
fate, 174, 224, 239, 463
feminine, 6, 44, 116, 182–83, 199,
210, 215–18, 223, 225–26,
229
Feyerabend, P.K., 462
Fichte, Johann, 38 66, 67, 68, 125
Filoramo, Giovanni, 416, 478
Findlay, J.N. 9, 57, 64, 76–78,
147, 364, 394, 415–16, 419,
427, 429, 431–33, 438, 470,
472, 478–79
on "unitive logic," 5, 76–77
Flatland (novel by Edwin Abott),
9, 35, 281, 308, 312, 410,
462
formal indicator (Heidegger), 354
form of life (Wittgenstein), 232,
324, 326, 342-44, 467
fragmentation (in psychology and
philosophy), 7, 24, 28, 106,
260, 271, 274, 278, 285,
348, 376, 397, 435, 456–57,
461–62
Frankl, Victor E., 173, 434, 478
freedom, 28, 30, 66, 69, 73–74,
126, 128–29, 138, 146, 172–
73, 175, 270, 289, 293–94,
325–26, 357, 365, 375, 381,
463
free will, 25, 128, 152, 156, 164,
228, 286, 289, 292–93, 299,

303, 309, 316, 340, 347,
361, 363, 403, 468
Freud, Sigmund, 91, 93, 169, 176,
178–79, 188, 198, 201–2,
205, 232–34, 255, 268–69,
271, 297, 387, 434, 437,
440, 442, 447, 452, 459,
461, 464
Freudian, 79, 173, 205, 260–61,
421, 443, 484
Friedman, Maurice S., 456, 474
function
inferior, 443
mental, 207
function types, 6, 208

G

Garfield, Jay L., 420
Geist, 167, 245–46, 252 See Spirit
Gematria, 106, 424
General Systems Theory, 267,
276, 462
German Idealists, 63, 66, 68
German Romanticism, 413, 466,
485
Gevurah (Strength, Kabbalah)115,
119
Giegerich, Wolfgang, 248–51,
253–55, 257, 375, 382, 397,
439, 455–56, 473, 478
globe, 32, 36, 165, 279–81, 284–
85, 299, 308, 312, 347, 362,
371
three–dimensionality of, 9, 32,
34–35, 280, 303–4, 312
Gnosis, 416, 468, 488
Gnosticism, 5, 59, 91, 183, 305,
416, 468, 478, 488
Gnostics, 12, 59–60, 180, 197,
230, 342, 346
goal, universal, 174, 343
God, 5–7, 53–54, 59–60, 63–67,
74–76, 96, 100–103, 106–
19, 121–23, 144–45, 177–
79, 191–93, 212–13, 215–
18, 227–28, 243–44, 325–
29, 342–46, 395–96, 424–27

archetype, 183
  and humanity, 117, 122, 126,
    166, 200, 305, 383, 412
  death of, 10, 193, 213
  nature of, 395-97
  new, 212
  personal, 344
godhead, 99, 102, 110, 114, 116,
  121, 230, 426
God image, 228, 453
Goethe, Johann Wolfgang von, 21,
  210, 409
Golden Flower, 422, 444, 451,
  453, 482
Gottfried Leibniz, 335, 387
Graham, Daniel W., 50–1, 413
Gray, Glenn, 429, 454, 472, 480
Greek Gods, 436

H

Ha–Lévi, Judah, 110
heavens, 18, 45, 97, 119, 129, 138,
  179, 185, 193, 215, 230, 381
Hegel, Georg Wilhelm Friedrich,
  37–40, 53–54, 68–72, 90–
  93, 124–182, 182, 244–48,
  251–57, 306–7, 368–69,
  373–79, 381–82, 389–92,
  413, 418–19, 427–34, 454–
  56, 472–74, 487–90
  dialectic, 93, 152, 161, 250–
    51, 255, 368, 382
  Absolute, 158, 386
  dialectic, 90, 141, 169, 176,
    277, 367, 375
  idealism, 68, 134, 162
  interpretation of, 166-88
  on contradiction, 149-166
  Phenomenology of Spirit
    (*Mind*), 130, 132–136, 168,
    199, 411, 427–29, 432–34
  philosophy, 23, 28, 136, 165–
    7, 176, 249–51, 259,
    375,385
  philosophical reputation, 125
  psychology, 176-79

Science of Logic, 127, 130,
  136, 149, 154, 418, 428–29,
  431–32, 472, 479
Skepticism, 173-4, 177
Speculative thought, 126-7,
  135, 150
Stoicism, 173–74, 177
system, 6, 137–144, 147,
  185, 247, 251, 429
understanding of *coincidentia*
  oppositorum, 132
Hegelianism, 72, 76, 179
Heidegger, Martin, 158, 171–3,
  270, 354, 355, 369, 389,
  461, 480
hell, 14, 191, 228, 230
Heraclitus, 5, 48–56, 71, 194, 197,
  221, 358, 413–15, 439, 459,
  465, 478–80
Flux, 42–3
hermeneutics, 52, 260, 268–69,
  273, 287, 289, 297, 309,
  363, 384, 457, 473
heterological principle (Rickert),
  70
Hillman, James, 433, 477
Hinduism, 96, 98–99, 109, 183,
  304, 354, 387
Howells, Christina, 86, 421
humanistic psychology, 270, 363
human subject, 29, 67, 169, 257,
  287, 297, 340, 468
Huskinson, Lucy, 187, 188, 192,
  195, 204, 225, 436–39, 442–
  43, 447, 451, 453, 480
Husks (*Kellipot*, Kabbalah), 103–4
Husserl, Edmund, 257, 270, 314,
  460, 468, 476
Hut, Piet, 314, 466

I

idealism, 7, 25–26, 43, 67, 82,
  134–35, 165, 289, 303, 315,
  317–19, 327, 340, 342–43,
  347, 349, 352–53, 361–62,
  399, 403
linguistic, 328

497

transcendental, 149
ideas, interdependent, 336, 338–
39, 353
Idel, Moshe, 329, 425, 467–68,
480
identity, 7, 30, 51–53, 68, 77, 89–
90, 154, 177, 212, 295, 300,
333–36, 341, 386, 411, 417–
18, 420, 422, 437, 467
personal, 164, 256, 316, 389,
396, 400
principle of, 154
identity and difference, 7, 21, 38,
154, 303, 310–11, 333–34,
336–42, 360, 377, 395, 400,
403, 412
identity of opposites, 51–52, 143,
201, 306–7, 414, 478
ignorance, 60, 355, 398, 412
Ihde, Don, 455, 487
Iliad, 415
images, 29, 40, 59, 62, 92, 193,
221, 227, 249, 272, 295, 398
imaginary, 89
quantities (numbers), 437
imagination, 6–7, 21, 26, 29, 38,
88–89, 94, 189, 191–92,
194–95, 205–7, 244–48,
250–53, 256, 258, 388–89,
392, 397, 400–401, 403
as principle of reconciliation,
39, 68, 189-96, 244, 246
imaginative process, 253
incest, 6, 224, 227–28
Indian Philosophy, 348, 402, 412,
469, 476
Individuation (Jung), 187, 198–
200, 202, 218–19, 224, 209,
224, 228, 231
Individualism (vs. Collectivism),
267, 287, 289, 296–97, 363
Infinite God (see Ein–sof), 62,
102–5, 116, 120–21, 330,
357
integration of opposites, 49, 198,
241
intellect, 29, 48, 63, 97–98, 182,
185–86, 192–93, 206–7,

219, 227, 231, 234, 248,
356, 413, 417
interdependence, complete, 119,
123
intuition, 28, 37, 207–8, 256–57,
260–61, 304, 308, 347, 356,
363, 365, 384, 389, 400,
403, 443
irrational union of opposites, 207,
235
irony, 177-78
Isa Upanishad, 46
Isaac, 115
Isaiah, 489
Islam, 99, 109

J

Jacobson, Claire, 410–11, 437,
485
James, William, 23, 185, 211, 259,
289, 292, 409
Jeremiah, 117–18
Jesus (see Christ)
Jewish Mysticism, 5, 7, 10, 21, 28,
98–99, 101, 125, 217, 239,
328, 354, 402, 423–24, 443,
447, 452, 477, 488
Jewish mystics, 231, 244, 259,
329, 356, 466
Jewish theology, 60
Jews, 173, 239, 443, 484
Joyce, James, 326
Judaism, 99, 102, 269, 328
Jung, C. G., 5–6, 10–21, 23–24,
26–27, 29, 36, 89–93, 178–
251, 253–58, 260–61, 290–
92, 389, 397–99, 405–11,
422–23, 426, 429, 434–57,
463–64, 473, 475–85, 488
conception of God, 215
distrust of beauty, 20
Hitler, 209, 239, 451
Meister Eckhart, 215
treatment of opposition and
antinomy in philosophy, 211
understanding of coincidentia
oppositorum, 13

individuation, 116
justice, 65, 93, 206, 345, 388, 399

K

Kabbalah, Kabbalistic, 21, 25, 96,
99, 101, 108–9, 112, 124–
25, 227, 231, 329, 332, 334,
356–58, 423–25, 467–68,
474, 477, 480, 488
theosophical Kabbalah, 90, 99–
100, 424, 478
Kabbalah and Chasidism, 5, 97,
99, 101, 103, 105, 107, 109,
111, 113, 115, 117, 119,
121, 123
Kabbalists, 60, 86, 102, 108–9,
114, 183, 214, 217, 312,
329, 337, 346, 353–54, 356–
57, 380, 383, 386, 398, 404,
466
Kant, Immanuel, 62, 64–66, 68–
69, 72, 79, 125–26, 128–29,
150–51, 161–63, 302, 309,
314, 365, 367, 374–75, 377,
387, 417–18, 428, 463, 484,
488
"Dual–World Solution," 64
antinomies, 128, 151, 377,
390
Kaplan, Aryeh 424, 426, 470, 473
Kellipot (Husks, Kabbalah), 103–
4, 108
Kenny, Rabbi Joel, 10
Kimble, Gregory A., 288, 463
Kindness (see Chesed), kindness
103, 114, 119–21, 257, 398
Kirk, G. S., 51, 54–55, 413–15,
459, 484
Klages, Ludwig, 13
Knowability/ unknowability, 236,
289, 298
knowledge, 46–47, 53, 55, 59–60,
62–63, 65–66, 68–70, 130–
34, 138, 140–41, 161–63,
168–69, 219, 287, 298–99,
302, 312–13, 350–51, 385,
389

absolute, 90, 134–35, 241
Koan, Zen, 41
Koch, Sigmund, 292, 464
Kuhn, Thomas, 274, 428, 465

L

Lacan, Jacques, Lacanian, 173,
261, 328, 349, 367, 410,
433, 484
Lachower, Fischel, 446, 468, 470,
489
language
contraction into, 468
paradoxical, 41, 48, 52, 217,
283, 304
language and representation, 37,
303–4, 310, 338, 361, 371,
400
language and thought, 21, 38, 97,
162, 323, 356
language–game(s) (Wittgenstein),
162, 164, 324, 328, 342–45,
358, 363
religious, 343–44
Laotze, Lao Tzu, 71–72, 183, 210,
230, 402
Lapis (philosopher's stone,
alchemy), 183, 216–18
law of non–contradiction, 80, 153,
283
Lazerowitz, Morris, 78–79, 211,
412, 485
Morris, 64, 79, 419, 432, 444
Leucippus, 264
Lévinas, Emmanuel, 256–7, 389,
456, 460–61, 474, 485
Lévi–Strauss, Claude, 39, 44, 190,
372, 410–11, 422, 437, 471,
489
Lévy–Bruhl, Lucien, 13
liar's paradox, 80, 82, 153, 160,
390
liberation, 103, 189, 224, 229, 355
Liber Novus (Jung, See Red Book)
libido, 195, 201, 208
life and death, 52, 57, 157, 197,
216, 231, 421

Likutei–Amarim–Tanya (Schneur Zalman), 424, 426, 490
linguistic constructivism, 7, 322, 327–28, 330–31, 342–44, 468
linguistic idealism, 327-28
linguistic representationalism, 330–31
logic, laws of, 179, 306–7, 382
Logos, 51, 52, 54, 89, 236
Ludwig Wittgenstein, 28, 296, 362, 374, 420, 428, 432, 447, 465, 470, 472
Luna, 6, 216–17, 225–26
Luna archetypes, 226
Luria, Isaac, 99, 101–6, 383
Lurianic Kabbalah, 101–6, 108, 136, 329, 350, 383, 386, 427
Lurianic symbols, 6, 102, 108
Lurianic system, 101–110
Lurianists, 107, 382–83, 386

M

MacIntyre, Alasdair, 461–62
Maggid of Mezrich, 113, 426
Maidenbaum, Aryeh, 443–44, 484
Malchuth (Kabbalah), 210, 217
Maps (cf. cartography), 34, 37, 165, 279, 281–84, 288, 291–92, 308, 312, 328, 371, 403
contradictory, 283, 308, 312
Martin, Stephen A., 443, 484–85
Marx, Karl, 38, 43, 93, 125, 173, 267, 468, 476
masculine, 44, 104, 116, 210, 217–18, 225, 227, 229
masculine and feminine, 182–83, 215–18, 223
Maslow, Abraham, 269, 460
master–slave, 97, 126, 169, 170–76,
master narrative, 302
material objects, 170, 294, 317, 393
material world, 112, 114, 116, 134, 180, 294, 314, 317, 320, 349

mathematics, 94, 142, 250, 298, 336, 430, 432, 490
matter, 6–7, 71, 73, 83, 85, 112, 114, 127–28, 131, 146, 148, 166–67, 172, 230–31, 315, 320–21, 352–53, 377–78, 389, 393–94
McCort, Dennis 333–34, 341, 411, 413, 466, 468–69, 485, 9
meaning, 38, 40, 256, 268, 275, 315–16, 324–27, 332, 335, 339–41, 344, 349, 362, 364, 389, 391–92, 412, 425
Meister Eckhart, 43, 45, 96, 125, 210, 215, 423, 444, 465–66, 477
memory, 87–88, 295–97, 316, 326
Mercator–Polar Map Paradox, 279
Mercator projection, 32–34, 281–83, 299, 309
Mercurius, 216, 220, 230, 429, 483
Merleau–Ponty, Maurice, 173, 270, 460
messiah, 217, 345, 347
metaphysical opposites, 229, 453
metaphysical theories, 78, 156
metaphysics, 14, 66, 71–73, 84, 157, 161, 168, 241–42, 353, 366, 374, 376, 384, 396, 399, 404–5, 413–14, 420–21, 453, 474
Metzinger, Thomas, 373, 472
Middle Ages, 197, 247
Mishnah, 111
mitzvoth, 107, 112, 115, 117, cf. commandments
modes of mind, 256, 389
Moebius strip, 369–70
Mysterium Coniunctionis (Jung), 220, 225, 236, 411, 435–36, 438, 441–42, 445–53, 463, 481
mystical experience, 96, 144, 235, 244, 307
mystical paradox, 109, 283, 302, 305

mystical traditions, 25, 96–97, 99, 125, 346
mysticism, 5, 7, 27, 39, 85–86, 90–91, 96, 102, 109, 143, 303–7, 332, 337, 411, 421, 425–26, 430, 450, 455, 465–66
mystics, 38, 41, 43, 96, 230, 235, 242, 244, 304–7, 309–10, 344, 346, 353, 358, 360, 394, 396, 398, 477, 481
mythical thought, 410, 411
mythology, 39, 246, 249
myths, 15, 18, 29, 44, 94, 99, 214, 227, 245, 248, 252–53, 376, 410, 422, 437, 439, 485
myths and symbols, 214, 245, 422

N

Nagarjuna, 47–48, 82, 333, 411–12, 420, 485
Nagel, Thomas, 164–65, 315–16, 485
National Socialism, 39, 208–9, 238–39, 399, 443, 452
Needleman, Jacob, 433, 475
negation, 71, 94, 105, 123, 139, 157, 165, 252, 305, 336, 374–76, 410
negative theology, 90, 346, 422
Neo–Hegelianism, 125
Neo–Kantianism, 418, 489
Neoplatonism (Cf. Plotinus), 9, 60, 63, 68, 78, 304, 308, 385, 401, 407
nervous system, 263–65, 317
Netzotzim (Kabbalah, cf. Sparks) 103
Nicholas of Cusa (Cusanus), 5, 43, 62–63, 67, 96, 185, 230, 417, 485
    God as absolute maximum and minimum, 63
Nietzsche, Friedrich, 10, 14, 17, 20, 44, 184, 186–89, 192–97, 208, 212, 231–32, 241–42, 244, 257–58, 269, 374,

389, 406–8, 436–40, 442, 447, 452–53, 456
    and Jung, 436, 438–39, 442–43, 451, 453, 480
    Zarathustra, 196, 407, 438–40, 448, 453, 481
nirvana, 47, 169, 172, 355
nonbeing, 56, 59
non–rational union of opposites, 5, 91, 189
nonsense, 233, 306, 331, 341, 412, 450
    merging with sense, 364
nothing, 45, 94, 109, 111–12, 116–17, 121–22, 129, 131, 153–54, 178, 196–97, 201, 209, 252, 328–29, 362, 365–66, 374–75, 467, 470–73, Also see Ayin.
nothingness, 30, 86, 90, 100, 105, 109, 111–12, 116, 120–22, 131–32, 141, 156, 312, 357, 374, 421, 433, 461, 488
noumena, noumenal (Kant), 65– 9, 81, 129, 16, 375

O

objective truth, 358, 397
objectivism, 7, 286, 294, 303, 309, 313–14, 322, 339–40, 342–45, 352, 361, 457
objects
    intentional, 76–77
    transcendental, 365, 472
Oedipus, 93, 178, 227
Ohsawa, Georges, 412, 486
Old Testament, 402, 406
One, the, 50, 54, 58, 60, 61, 96, 367, 407, 415
One and the Many, the, 11–12, 20, 73, 120, 128, 305, 341
open economy (of thought.
    experience), 25, 27, 346, 355–56, 382, 384, 387–89, 395–397, 399–400, 402, 404
    infinite, 382, 389, 396, 404

opposites
  coincidence of, 5–7, 24–29, 39–
    41, 43, 54–55, 63–64, 70–71,
    82, 91–92, 116–17, 159–60,
    181–83, 237–38, 258–59,
    303–6, 333–34, 360–63, 384–
    85, 389–92, 394–404, cf.
    coincidentia oppositorm
  conflict of, 201, 204, 212
  interdependence of, 26, 44, 63,
    73–74, 356, 400
  pairs of, 14, 48, 54, 98, 100–101,
    215, 232, 341, 413, 466
  psychic, 180, 197, 233, 237
  strong vs. weak version, 400–
    401
  union, unity of, 23, 40, 43, 45,
    49, 51, 53–54, 92–94, 96,
    101–2, 110,136, 182–83,
    201, 204, 213, 215, 217–18,
    222, 227, 229–31, 234–35,
    237, 240, 357, 370, 414,
    445, 473, 475 480, 488
    empirical union, 418–19,
    478
    through "living," 184
oppositions
  binary, 26, 36, 44, 86, 89, 422
  conceptual, 28, 30, 85, 152–53,
    155
  psychological, 152, 158, 403
original unity, 9, 24, 119, 303,
    338, 356, 361, 366, 400
Orphic, 14
Orwell, George, 399
Oshawa, Georges, 486

P

pain, 19, 47, 118, 133, 158, 190,
    330
painting, 190–91, 221, 278, 389
paradigms, 26, 28, 99, 156, 177,
    230, 259, 277, 283–85, 291,
    303, 342, 364, 403
  psychological, 7, 24, 261–62,
    272, 285, 363–64

paradoxes, 5, 46–47, 62, 65, 74,
    77–81, 101, 104, 109, 123,
    148, 156, 160, 180, 224,
    235, 237, 278–79, 303–6,
    393–94
paradoxical, 51, 55, 165, 212, 214,
    236, 314, 393
parallax, 36, 367, 370
parallax gap (, 365, 367, 369–70,
    372, 375–77, 470–72
Parallax View (Žižek), 410, 462,
    470–72, 490
Parmenides (Plato), 12, 57–59,
    405, 416
Peck, John, 408, 422, 434, 437,
    468, 481
persona, 29, 92, 199–200, 220
persona and shadow, 36, 182, 214,
    223, 228
personality, 13, 91, 103, 196, 199,
    202, 220, 222–23, 226, 229,
    232, 389, 396, 451, 461,
    473, 484
perspectival realism, 35, 379–80,
    385
perspectives, 6–7, 26–27, 35–36,
    63, 111–13, 129–34, 261,
    278–80, 282, 284–86, 291,
    306, 341–42, 344–45, 348–
    49, 364–65, 367, 370, 379,
    382–85
  contradictory, 279
  contrasting, 294
  detached objective, 316
  humanistic, 290
  incompatible, 37, 166, 370
  interdependent, 317, 385
  multiplicity of, 36, 271, 394
  new, 182, 385, 425, 480
  phenomenological, 315
  subjective, 315
  systems, 261, 280
Phaedo (Plato) 15, 16, 56–8, 415–
    16
Phaedrus, 87, 407
pharmakon, 420, 466
philosophical antinomies, 157,
    211, 285, 291–92, 303, 308

philosophical argument, 79, 128
philosophical behaviorism, 265
philosophical controversies, 28,
  67, 260, 310–11, 338, 341,
  347, 361, 397
philosophical, philosopher's stone,
  183. 216–18
philosophy, 24–25, 27–29, 78–79,
  136–47, 149–51, 167–68,
  252–54, 256–57, 302–7,
  363–66, 374–82, 392–95,
  contemporary, 28, 312, 372
  negative, 374, 378
  objectivist, 344
  phenomenological, 429
  post–Hegelian, 172
  postmodern, 25, 35, 251
  rational, 39, 247
  speculative, 155, 252
  transcendental, 64
physics, 84, 194, 264, 286, 315,
  321, 343, 413, 438, 462, 474
  quantum, 21, 82, 84, 276, 367
Piaget, Jean, 93
Picasso's *Guernica*, 190
Pinkard, Terry, 381, 428
Pirke Avot, 111–12, 426, 484
Plato, Platonic, 5, 11–12, 15–17,
  50, 52–53, 55–59, 72, 90,
  127–28, 267, 369, 375, 405–
  7, 412, 414–16, 459, 475,
  478, 487
Platonism, Platonists, 68, 129,
  195, 408
Plotinus, 5, 16, 60–62, 407, 416–
  17, 487
  Enneads, 60, 78, 407, 416
pluralism, pluralistic 211, 292,
  456, 461
Pluralistic Monism, 464
Plus one, 384, 473
poetry, 17, 356
polar projection, 33–34, 283
Polkinghorne, D., 459–60
polygon, 417
postmodernism, 36, 64, 131, 154,
  303, 334, 367, 387, 404,
  423, 425, 467, 468, 477, 489

pragmatism, 185, 211, 444, 463,
  481
pre–linguistic unity, 303, 337, 393
pre–Socratics, 55, 90
Priest, Graham, 47, 64, 80–82,
  412, 420, 455, 458, 485, 487
primal unity, 26, 187, 330, 356,
  365, 400–401
prima materia (alchemy), 222–23
Primordial Human, 103, cf. *Adam
  Kadmon*
process philosophy (Whitehead),
  74
psyche, 36–37, 91–92, 191, 194–
  95, 201–2, 218–20, 224–26,
  229–30, 232, 234–35, 237–
  38, 248, 253–58, 261, 291–
  92, 314, 438–40, 447, 454–
  55, 482
  collective, 91, 202, 213, 223
  objective, 255, 397–98
  unconscious, 227, 234–35
psychiatry, 94, 263–64, 269, 273,
  280, 288, 436, 460, 462, 475
psychic functions, 190, 256–58
psychoanalysis, psychoanalytic,
  26, 36. 158, 169, 173, 178–
  9, 268–70, 276, 280, 284–5,
  300, 413, 433, 448, 459–61,
  472, 484
psychological research, 28, 286–
  87
psychological schools, 271, 273,
  278, 280, 285, 288, 290,
  292, 300
psychological symptoms, 265–66,
  270
psychological theories, 173, 271–
  73, 288–89, 291, 299–300,
  364
Psychological Types (Jung), 11–
  12, 17, 20, 184, 197, 189,
  194, 199, 201, 205–6, 208,
  211, 405–10, 422, 434–38,
  440–42, 444–45, 449, 454,
  457, 481
psychological typology, 12–13,
  15, 405

psychology, 6–7, 27–29, 168,
172–73, 175–77, 179–82,
184–86, 205–8, 255–57,
259–61, 267–78, 284–92,
300, 309–10, 363–64, 441–
42, 452–53, 456–57, 460–
63, 482–83
cognitive, 262, 266, 289–90, 458
complementarity in, 7, 276
dynamic, 6, 158, 177–79
Psychology and Alchemy (Jung),
212, 409, 411, 422, 434–35,
438, 440–42, 445–50, 454,
482
psychotherapy, 6, 44, 168, 176,
216, 218–19, 233–35, 255,
268, 275–76, 300, 456–61
public vs. private criteria, 31, 289,
296, 299, cf. private criteria

Q

qualia, 165, 256, 314–16, 471
quasi–logicality (implicative
logic), 256, 293

R

Rabbi Akiva, 115
Rabbi Elazar, 118
Rabbi Shimon, 118
Rachamim, 358
Radhakrishnan, 412, 487
rationality, 80–81, 183, 239, 451
Raven, 51, 54–55, 413–15, 459,
484
Real (Lacan), 349
realism, 12, 25–26, 67, 131, 361,
380
perspectival, 35, 379
reality, 25, 27, 87–89, 98, 112–14,
122–23, 151, 161, 163–65,
167, 203–4, 315–16, 349–
50, 352–53, 362, 366–67,
369–71, 373, 376–78, 380–
81

hard, 7, 40, 360, 365–66
objective, 331, 340
reality and illusion, 86, 109, 191,
331, 353, 358, 421
reason, 38–40, 65–66, 128–29,
138–42, 144–46, 148–53,
183–84, 188–89, 191–92,
206–7, 215–16, 218–19,
232–35, 237, 239–40, 244–
47, 258, 322–23, 387–89,
400–401
positive, 126–27, 377
Reason–Principle, 61–62
reconciliation of opposites, 179,
195, 212, 386
Red Book (Jung), 16, 188–89, 191,
194–96, 199, 201, 209–10,
212–14, 224, 233, 238–39,
254, 408, 437–41, 444–45,
447, 450, 452–54, 463–64,
476–77
regress, infinite, 347, 376, 451
relativism, 26, 35, 180, 273, 277,
281–83, 457
relativists, 273
religion, 44, 46, 63, 86, 144, 146-
47, 175, 190, 193, 214, 245-
46, 248-49, 252, 273, 342,
344-46, 374, 381, 395, 402
remainder, 384, 399
representationalism, 313, 340,
342, 347
Repressed Memory, 465
Republic (Plato), 405
Rickert, 70–71, 88, 418, 487
Ricouer, Paul, 252, 455, 487
Rifka Schatz Uffenheimer, 426
Rorschach, 447, 478
Rychlak, Joseph F., 276, 292, 434,
462, 464
Ryle, Gilbert, 465

S

Sabbath, 119
Sabelli, Hector, 93–95, 401, 422,
488
Hector, 5, 93, 401, 422, 473

Safed, 101–2
Sartre, Jean Paul, 88–9, 173, 190,
    252, 270, 374, 388–89, 421,
    461, 488
"say what we like" (Wittgenstein),
    25, 362, 364
Scheler, Max, 257, 389
Schelling, Friedrich, 64, 66–68,
    110, 125, 353, 374, 418, 465
Schiller, Friedrich, 17–20, 190,
    408–9, 437
Schindler's List, 190
schizophrenia, 247, 267, 287
Schneerson, Rabbi Yosef Yitzhak
    119–20, 427
Schneur Zalman of Lyadi (Alter
    Rebbe), 98, 105–6, 110–12,
    114–16, 120–22, 330, 424–
    26, 468.
Scholem, Gershom, 39, 424, 467,
    488
Schopenhauer, Arthur, 187, 257,
    389
Schwartz–Salant, Nathan, 455,
    488
Seelenproblem, 255
Sefer Etz Chayyim (Vital), 424
Sefer ha–Bahir (Kabbalistic
    work), 329
Sefer Yetzirah (proto–Kabbalistic
    work), 100, 354, 357, 386,
    424, 470, 473, 484
Sefirot (Kabbalah), 100–104, 106–
    9, 217, 357, 398, 421, 424,
    474
self, 23–24, 36, 46, 91–92, 97–98,
    113–14, 168–77, 179–81,
    191–92, 197–99, 204, 212–
    15, 228, 237–38, 240–41,
    243, 373, 389–90, 444–45,
    453
    individual, 171, 175, 191, 297
    stoic, 173–74
self–actualization, 177, 195, 270
self and God, 6, 228, 444
self archetype, 212–13, 243
self–awareness, 138–39, 142, 367

self–consciousness, 134, 145, 168,
    170, 182, 381
self–realization, 138, 144, 224
Sellars, Wilfred, 297, 328, 465,
    467, 488
    sense certainty, perspective of,
    133
shadow (Jung), 6, 20, 29, 36, 92,
    182, 198–200, 202, 214,
    219–20, 222–23, 226–30,
    234, 238, 398, cf. persona
    and shadow
Shamdasani, Sonu,198, 408, 422,
    434, 437, 440, 463, 468, 481
Shekhinah, 184, 217
Shevirat ha–Kelim, 103–4, 106,
    108–9, 421, c.f. Breaking of
    the Vessels
signifier, 313, 322–27, 329, 331,
    342–44, 354
signifier and signified, 21, 37–38,
    91, 310–11, 322–23, 325,
    328–331, 333, 337, 338–40,
    342, 366, 371, 386
simulated reality, 318–21
slave, 126, 151, 170–74, cf.
    master–slave
Socrates, 11–12, 57, 125, 127,
    188, 258
Sol, 6, 216–17, 225–26
Sol Niger, 226
solar eclipse, 226
Solomon, Robert, C., 131, 147,
    151, 166–67, 381, 411, 429–
    31, 433, 488
soul, 6, 12–13, 15–16, 57, 66, 196,
    204, 210, 212, 215, 217,
    221, 231, 249–50, 254–55,
    257–58, 382, 459, 463, 465
    universal, 215, 229
sparks, 103–4, 202, cf. Netzotzim
Spielberg, Steven, 190
spirit, 6, 111–12, 132, 136, 138–
    42, 145, 149–50, 157–59,
    167–68, 196, 199, 228–29,
    231–32, 245, 368, 384, 386,
    411–12, 427, 429–30
    objective, 175

realm of, 67, 112, 139
self-conscious, 139
Stace, Walter T., 109, 143, 167,
251, 304–7, 309–10, 338,
394, 411, 418, 425, 429–30,
433, 455, 465–6, 489
Staten, Harry, 422, 469, 489
Steinsaltz, Adin, 107, 398
strife, 54–55, 194, 269, 442, 459
subject and object, 67–68, 72, 84,
86, 123, 126, 144, 169, 172,
310, 313, 321, 332–33, 337–
40, 342, 368–70, 400, 403,
418, 421
merger of, 169–70
unity of, 68, 174, 339–40, 382
subjectivity, 134–35, 170–71,
174–75, 255, 257, 286, 315,
386, 472
subject–object, 85–86, 311, 321,
337, 361
sun, 16, 133, 198, 215, 217, 225,
231, 447
superego, 268, 271
superficial vs. deep truths, 43, 153,
299
supplement (Derrida), 87, 420–21
supreme meaning, 341, 364, 450
symbolization, 256–57, 389, 396,
400
symbols, 92, 99, 101–2, 107–8,
178, 183–84, 190–96, 198,
212–14, 216, 221, 225, 227,
230, 234–35, 245, 248, 252–
53, 392, 422–23
Symbols of Transformation (Jung),
184, 213, 435, 445, 449, 483
Symposium (Plato), 50, 53, 55, 415

T

Taoism, 25, 44, 91, 96–97, 304,
311, cf. Laotze
Taoist philosophy, 207
Taylor, Charles, 166, 427, 429,
433, 489
Taylor, Marc, 321, 330, 339, 467,
489

tension of opposites, 54, 201–2
Thaetetus (Plato), 52–53, 414, 475
theism (and atheism), 7, 25–6, 43,
86, 167, 303, 342, 345–46,
357, 384, 396, 421, cf.
atheism
theology, 21, 24–25, 28–29, 96,
99, 160, 165, 168, 309–10,
357, 361, 382, 385, 388,
393, 400, 402, 453, 463, 467
thing–in–itself (ding an sich,
Kant), 65–66, 68, 161–63,
365, 367
thinking, linear, 131–32, 150, 248
"third" (reconciling opposites), 87,
190, 194, 196, 245, 250, 439
"thinking the world whole," 25–
26, 346–8
thought and language, 24–26, 38,
96, 152, 232–33, 309
"thought thinking itself+
(Aristotle), 37, 381
Tiferet (Kabbalah), 114–15
Tikkun Ha–Olam (Kabbalah),
103–4, 106–7, 109, 115
Tishby, Isaiah, 446, 468, 470
Tohu (formless chaos), 115
Torah, 107, 112, 114, 329, 425–
26, 467
totality, 25, 36, 91, 109, 146, 204,
206–7, 215, 299, 381, 384,
403, 456, 485
trace, 39, 119, 265, 303, 338, 356,
360, 365, 466
transcendence, 27, 177, 203, 256–
57, 332, 404, 470, 478
transcendent function (Jung), 182–
83, 189–90, 194, 196, 249–
50, 437
transgression, 6, 60, 227–28, 448
truth, 23–24, 26–27, 30, 62–63,
79, 81–83, 147–48, 150,
153–54, 156–60, 246–48,
283–84, 298–99, 342–43,
345–46, 348–51, 367–68,
380–81, 417, 427
absolute, 26, 136, 143, 154
deep, 23–24, 43, 48, 83

philosophical, 145, 374
rational, 92, 246, 464
ultimate, 47, 413
truth and reality, 7, 381
Tzimtzum, 5, 102–5, 109, 120–21,
329–30, 421, 468. Cf.
contraction.
symbol of, 104–5

U

Undecidables (Derrida), 87, 311,
420–21
underlying reality, 162, 304, 370,
372–73, 378–79, 384
unified world, 7, 37, 40, 120, 303–
4, 307, 313, 336–37, 360
unio mystica, 200, 203, 304
union of opposites, See: opposites,
union of,
universe, 46, 50, 54, 57, 61–62,
74, 78, 101–2, 117, 138,
142, 200, 302, 308–9, 313,
317–20, 381, 387, 393, 397–
98
Upanishads, 46–47, 97, 158, 210

V

value archetypes, 100, 102–3, 106,
399
cosmic, 217
values, 85–86, 106–7, 109, 112,
121–23, 155–56, 175–76,
245, 247, 256–57, 273, 339,
349–50, 388–89, 392, 396,
398–99, 404, 431, 476
transformational, 172
vanishing point (Schelling), 67,
353
verifiability principle, 410

W

Wagner, Richard, 186
Werblowski, Zwi, 424

Western philosophy, 25, 38, 59,
62, 267, 374
Whitehead, Alfred N., 5, 59, 74–
75, 142, 402, 419
Whitman, Walt, 243, 453
wholeness, 198, 204, 219, 226,
236–37, 300
symbols of, 212–13
wisdom, 60, 72, 75, 94, 101, 103,
113, 121, 203, 225–27, 378,
398, 404, 446, 468, 470, 489
Wittgenstein, Ludwig, 40, 79, 130,
161, 167, 225, 257, 296–97,
322, 326, 328, 355, 365,
421–22, 432, 469, 489–90
Philosophical Investigations,
302, 420, 428, 465, 490
*Tractatus Logico
Philosophicus*, 355, 428,
470. 490
cf. "language games, "saw
what you like"
Wolfson, Elliot, 329, 427, 468
words and thing (cf. signifier and
signified), 35, 37, 76, 86,
91, 303, 311, 322, 323-27,
331-33, 340, 358, 368, 421
World
as contradictory, 151, 161, 164
external, 169–71, 338
noumenal, 65–66, 151, 307, cf.
noumena
objective, 165, 313, 315
opposites of the (William
James), 23, 259
phenomenal, 66, 129, 151, 207,
297, 375
physical, 231, 286, 314–15, 386,
462
simulated, 319–20
single, 34, 151, 165, 302, 316–
17, 383, 395
spiritual, 66, 112
whole, 25–26
World Spirit, 138, 145, 248, 386
worldviews, 102, 349, 403

Y

Yahweh, 346, 406
Yalom, Irwin, 173, 433, 460, 490
Yesh (Positivity, Kabbalah), 111–12, 116, 120–22
yin–yang,5, 44–46, 97, 184, 210, 311, 369. 412, 489

Z

Zaehner, Richard 412, 416, 423, 490
Zimmer, Heinrich, 98, 113, 354, 423, 470
Žižek, Slavoj, 35–6, 161–62, 365–73, 375–77, 386, 432–3, 470–73, 487, 490

Zohar (*Sefer ha–Zohar*, Kabbalistic work), 99, 101, 107, 117–18, 227, 239, 329, 335, 398, 425–26, 446, 448, 452, 468, 470, 473, 489

Biography, Sanford L. Drob

Sanford L. Drob is a Core Faculty Member in the doctoral program in Clinical Psychology at Fielding Graduate University and is on the faculty of the C. G. Jung Institute in New York. He holds doctorates in both philosophy and clinical psychology, is a prolific artist, and has made contributions in the fields of philosophy, theology and clinical/forensic psychology. For many years, he served as the Senior Forensic Psychologist and Director of Psychological Assessment at Bellevue Hospital Center in New York. Dr. Drob is well known for his writings on the psychology of C. G. Jung and for his efforts to develop a universalist rational-mystical theology through a synthesis of Jewish mysticism and contemporary thought.

In a series of books (*Symbols of the Kabbalah*, 2000, *Kabbalistic Metaphors*, 2000, *Kabbalah and Postmodernism*, 2009,) as well as on his website, **www.newkabbalah.com,** Drob shows how the symbols of the Lurianic Kabbalah articulate a "basic metaphor" that is reprised in a philosophical idiom in the writings of such later thinkers as Hegel, Freud, Jung and Derrida, and which serves as a compelling model for understanding the world and the place of humanity within it. Drob is also known for his writings on the psychologist C. G. Jung. His books, *Kabbalistic Visions: C. G. Jung and Jewish Mysticism* (2010), and *Reading the Red Book: An Interpretive Guide to C. G. Jung's Liber Novus* (2012) approach Jung from a philosophical, theological and psychological point of view. Dr. Drob maintains an active practice in forensic psychology and psychological assessment in New York City. As a painter, he works in a traditional representational idiom in order update and resignify theological, mystical and archetypal themes, and addresses basic philosophical and theological questions through the medium of narrative painting.

His paintings can be seen at www.sanforddrobart.com.